Celluloid Dragons: Asian Films A History and Guide to Asian and Asian-American Cinema

by
John Daemin
johndmin@gmail.com

Hundreds of Films on:
Kung-Fu Action: Bruce Lee - Jackie Chan - Jet Li
Triad and Yakuza Gangsters
Japanese Animation: Japanime
Chinese Epics and Dramas
Samurai Shogun Classics
Ninjas and Demons
Godzilla, Gamera, and Kaiju Monsters
*   And Much More*

Dedicated to Edward T. and Theresa C., my parents, who sparked my love for Asian films and encouraged me to write about them.

Contents

TABLE OF CONTENTS

Acknowledgments

I wish to thank my sister, Catherine, for supporting my passion to write.

I wish to also thank the following people:

Ben Dungee, Chris Mattos, David Wasserman, Jon McCary, and Alexis Williams, friends who supported me, watched films with me, and listened to my literary rants and raves.

To my friend and mentor, Bob Campbell of Newhouse News Service, who encouraged me to critique films on a professional level and shared with me his insights.

My former agent, Frank Weimann, and associates from The Literary Group International.

To Valerio Rossi and associates at Central Park Media Corporation for their support and access to materials which were indispensable.

To Frank Dajeng and associates at Tai Seng Video Marketing, Inc.

To Steve Wilson and associates at McFarland & Company, Inc. for supporting my first major book project.

To the professors, staff, and students of New York University's film department.

And a special thanks to all the people I've conversed with in video stores and on the internet who shared my enthusiasm for Asian films.

INTRODUCTION

IN THE BEGINNING (Before 2000)

As a boy growing up in Salt Lake City, Utah, I remember other children asking me if I was related to Bruce Lee or if I knew flying crane Kung-Fu or how to use a samurai sword. How cool if I could have answered yes to all those inquiries. This was probably my first realization that prominent Asian stories and actors existed on the big screen, and I quickly cultivated a passion for Asian films. In the beginning, I don't know what initially captured my fascination with cinema, but I never missed an opportunity to watch a movie on television or to follow my father to the local theater. I watched stories unfold and fell in love with screen heroes/heroines, regardless of race, nationality, or belief. After watching so many films about Italians, Irish, Germans, Russians, and Jewish families, I wondered if there were any stories about Asian people like myself. Why didn't anyone on screen share similarities with my own family, I wondered? Why aren't there any actors eating Asian foods, wearing Asian clothes, or singing Asian songs? Who was Bruce Lee? This lack of cultural identification made me become aware of how few American films were dedicated to Asian subjects, and more so Korean cinema was non-existent compared to Chinese and Japanese films. Sure there were token Asian characters sprinkled into mainstream movies and television. You could always find someone working at a laundry, a Chinese restaurant, or as a cook named Hop Sing on the Ponderosa in Bonanza. Even worse were supposed Asian films played by obviously non-Asian actors like those in the Good Earth, Breakfast at Tiffany's and the Charlie Chan films. Asian actresses, exotic and beautiful, were true to birth but often portrayed as demure, dependent characters in love with western male suitors. My only redemption and early favorite Asian would be Lieutenant Hikaru Sulu (George Takei) from Star Trek (1966-1969), he broke racial stereotypes and became helmsman aboard the Starship Enterprise. And of course, there were the war films: World War II in the Pacific, the Korean War, the Vietnam War which offered plenty of memorable enemy soldiers, communist killers or diabolic leaders who wanted to take over the world, like Fu Manchu. No wonder the kids called me Ho Chi Minh, General Tojo, or Chairman Mao when we flooded onto the playground. None of them are even Korean. It seemed obvious that Hollywood wouldn't spend any efforts to portray positive Asians, so my only other choice was to find films directly from Asia.

Luckily, my parents introduced and guided me to many Asian films, including those of Bruce Lee, at an early age. My parents, though big fans of American movies, were very close to their heritage and would watch films from their native country of Korea. My father would go one step further and watch Chinese and Japanese films with an equal passion, gifting me the benefits of a broad cultural background. One of my first film memories as a child, probably at three, was entering a theater to see my first Hong Kong kung-fu movie. I was frightened since the dark theater was enormous and our seats were high up on the balcony level. I was with my father, hand in hand, as we found seats and sat down. Then bright lights flashed and giants appeared before me on the large screen. The Asian heroes yelled and kicked, brandishing weapons and vowing for vengeance. Some may disagree with the choice of film for a child, but I loved the kung-fu movie I saw on that day (the title eludes me) and would so for the rest of my life. So from that moment on, I was hooked on Asian martial arts films though more for reasons of entertainment than cultural enlightenment.

Though I had not officially studied film until college, I saw myself as an amateur film critic from an early age. As a growing student of film, I seriously became culturally aware of the small number of Asians portrayed in American films. Then I took disturbed notice that Asians were sometimes portrayed by Caucasians made to look Asian, similar to the black-face painted actors who portrayed African-Americans in early films. As I grew older, I caught anything on television or video that featured Asian culture, settings, and characters, even a minor glance. Thanks to the Bruce Lee phenomenon which occurred around the same time I started watching films, I could easily find martial arts movies at theaters or on television and eventually video. Due to the censors in America, martial arts movies were originally deemed too violent and a bad influence on children. Nothing was wrong with the westerns or crime dramas of American cinema, but kung-fu movies were always criticized and frowned upon. My father and I would trek to Chinatown or seedier parts of the city to see a good kung-fu film. Gradually as moral tastes gained broader acceptance, martial arts films started to make their appearance on television. The golden era of the 1970s and 1980's saw an abundance of action films very unique to the East. Hordes of kung-fu movies, ninja films, and samurai epics ignited the screen on a weekly basis. Every now and then, my father and I would venture to Times Square, NYC or Plainfield, New Jersey to catch up on the latest kung-fu movie from Hong Kong. My love for kung-fu films was so great that I actually started learning martial arts at age nine.

Everything seemed perfect, but suddenly the popularity of Asian films, in particular kung-fu films, slowed and died in the American market. In the early eighties, I remember turning on the television and seeing half a dozen kung-fu movies a week. Black Belt Theater, Kung-Fu Theater, Saturday Matinee, and Action Theater would show martial arts movies on a regular weekly basis. Then one by one, the stations stopped airing martial arts films from Hong Kong. The same happened with the monster genre-crazed Godzilla and Gamera films I loved as a child; I assumed they had stopped making them overseas but the monster movies are still alive and kicking in Japan. Japanese animation (long before I even realized it was from Japan) was a keen interest of mine, but at the time I was watching, video copies were difficult to acquire. And if you could find them, legal copies were extremely expensive. I had to resort to going to conventions where Japanese sampler video tapes cost $20 or more, sometimes without subtitles. Even then you took a chance and didn't know exactly what you were getting, since there were no books on the subject and Japanese animation fans weren't too common in New Jersey. Sadly I became jaded and my interest in Asian films died for awhile. The eighties saw the growth of the video market and the boom of rental stores. This didn't help me much since most stores carried a limited selection of Asian films, and usually the titles were old films (every video store in the world has a Bruce Lee movie) or horrible exploitation films picked up by distributors because of their low cost. Contrary to popular beliefs, not all kung-fu movies are the same caliber and long-time viewers can attest to the difference in quality, but for some reason video stores didn't care..

So I pretty much stopped looking for Asian films, and at the time, it didn't bother me. After all, I loved Hollywood films and there were plenty of new titles to occupy my time. I even delved into European films for awhile. My next big step came in college where I discovered people who had a similar passion for films from the East. Ironically, most of them were non-Asians who grew up in America and discovered Asian films through similar venues. Japanese animation clubs, Asian Societies, Martial Arts Clubs, and other organizations helped introduce me to new Asian films, though reading subtitles was a must for viewing. I enrolled in East Asian history, language, and literature courses, hoping to broaden my own cultural awareness. I never limited myself to one culture, but saw myself as a representative of all Asian nations and would pursue topics and films from all over Asia. Since I had stopped watching Asian films for so long, I was amazed at how many new titles had appeared and at the improvement in quality and budget. Bigger and better Godzilla movies, gorgeous Japanime, dramatic kung-fu epics, John Woo action films, historical dramas from China, the list was endless and I felt lost in the wave of new titles that were upon me.

ASIAN FILMS

Hoping to inspect the new wave of Asian films that entered the market, I decided to purchase a popular film guide with 10,000 movie entries. Then came my complete shock and disappointment. Many of the Asian films were not mentioned or rated, only a few famous Asia films that had won awards were graciously listed. I then bought another guide with over 20,000 film entries. To my surprise, it did include many Asian films, but the ratings appeared biased and unfair. Rather than judging the films on their individual merit, I noticed every kung-fu film was given the same rating across the board. Most of the films were given 1 star out of 4 and the descriptions were very modest and incorrect at times. Trust me, a level of quality does exist between Street Gangs of Hong Kong and Master Killer (36th Chamber), but not in the eyes of this particular film reviewer. For anyone who has seen Master Killer, imagine my anger at seeing only one star and the film chided for its violence, juvenile plot, and lack of originality. This was one of my favorite films of all time, a masterpiece of martial arts cinema. Eventually I had to find speciality books or magazines, just to read up on films I had seen over a decade ago.

I was annoyed and disheartened in my futile search for research materials. Here I was in the greatest film country in the world and there was a negative attitude toward Asian films. In recent years, critics have praised the new wave of Chinese dramas starring Gong Li, but the vast majority of new Asian films were ridiculed by so-called respected critics and industry experts. My resentment toward this narrow-minded and prejudiced view, invoked me to search for books written solely on Asian films. One day critics would discover the beauty of all Asian films, and even martial arts epics will receive accolade and praise from American critics.

There were a handful of books dedicated to specific topics: kung-fu movies, samurai movies, ninja movies, which offered a welcome breath of fresh air, but they presented the genre from a historical viewpoint, stressing the filmmakers, actors, and studios rather than reviewing the films on an individual basis. I was trapped between two extremes. The films should speak for themselves and to the casual American viewer, the list of names and studios would be completely meaningless without a frame of reference. Even long-time fans of Hong Kong movies are often oblivious to the studios who produced their favorite films and the names of the stars and filmmakers. These books were more appropriate for someone already familiar with the genre or someone doing research on the subject like myself, but not user friendly for beginning viewers. Sometimes I found a reverse bias, instead of all the kung-fu movies getting one star, they all got four stars and were touted as the best action films in the world. Trust me, the range of martial arts films is as vast as Chinese restaurants in the world. This was before the internet took off which also provided an expansive source of information. Therefore, I was resolved to spend time and money, exploring Asian films at my own risk. I rummaged through dozens of stores and hundreds of titles, always asking people's opinions along the way. I went to Chinatown, Little Tokyo, Koreatown, and Asian film conventions in my search for Asian films. Sometimes the missions were successful, often times they were not. Frustrated, I decided there should be a better way to search for good titles and dedicated my own efforts to compiling a book on Asian films available in the American market.

Often Asian films are stereotyped by the popularity of their specific genre such as kung-fu/Godzilla/anime films which gives the illusion that Asian filmmakers are not as serious-minded and respected as American/European filmmakers. Thankfully, a variety of new Asian films have started to reinvent themselves in the American market and even Hollywood is looking to the East for inspiration. A sudden boost in popularity has again captured the average American viewer: Japanese animation is booming and easily available with English dubbing, a new Godzilla film hit the big screens, Chinese dramas win international awards, and re-released Jackie Chan movies are visiting your local theaters. On top of that, a wave of Hong Kong-based action films from John Woo, Ringo Lam, and Tsui Hark have captured millions of overseas fans. And wait for the Korean cinema explosion to rock the film fans. So forget about your past experiences with Bruce Lee 'chop socky' films, a rubber-suited Godzilla, and the black & white dramas from Ozu and Kurosawa. That's only the tip of an ancient iceberg.

Asian filmmaking has come a long way since the 1960's and 1970's. Now a slew of Asian filmmakers abroad and in the United States are making their names known, delving into all genres and gaining the respect of western critics and filmmakers. Instead of imitating western filmmakers, Asian filmmakers are now being imitated and praised for their ingenuity and style. Hollywood is taking even more Asian films and giving them the western makeover, previous examples included Magnificent Seven (1960) inspired by Kurosawa's Seven Samurais (1954). Superstars like Jackie Chan and Jet Li have taken over for Toshiro Mifune and Bruce Lee. Directors such as John Woo, Ang Lee, and Tsui Hark usher in a new wave of modern films, replacing Kurosawa, Chang, and Ozu. If awards are a representation of success, numerous American and European nominations and prizes have been garnered by Asian films and filmmakers. Even the popular MTV Movie Awards have recognized two of Asia's biggest superstars with lifetime achievement awards: Jackie Chan (1995) and Godzilla (1996). The trend looks to gain more steam as American producers rush to dub and re-market Asia films for a hungry western audience. Chan's multipicture deal with New Line Cinema guarantees a steady stream of action films for American theatrical release and Quentin Tarantino's Rolling Thunder joint-production company promises to bring more of the director's favorite Asian films, such as "Chungking Express" and "The Street Fighter".

A decade ago, an entire book dedicated to Asian and Asian-American films would have seemed premature and limited. Now a host of talented Asian and Asian-American filmmakers, writers, actors, and industry workers have helped shape a new image of Asian culture and identity. It is fortunate that the new popularity of Asian films has coincided with the video boom which offers an alternative life for films not theatrically released or shown on television. Asian Films on Video captures a portion of the thousands of films that have poured into the country and are available for rent or purchase. The Asian influence of streaming, the internet, and on demand will be discussed fully in the second book volume. The most obvious criteria is that the film should involve Asian characters and deal with their story. I do not include films about non-Asian characters that were made by Asian filmmakers, but I do include Asian films which were made by non-Asian filmmakers such as Bernardo Bertolucci's "The Last Emperor", due to its high involvement of Asian people and their portrayal of Asian culture. Some films fall on the fringe, but since Asians are such an ignored race in Hollywood, I've included many American-made films with strong Asian characters in the lead role, such as "Dragon: The Bruce Lee Story", or sharing the lead role with a Caucasian ally, "Mortal Kombat" and "Best of the Best". You'll also find a number of films dealing with Americans who are placed in an Asian environment and how they react with their eastern counterparts, such as "Shogun", "Black Rain", and "Karate Kid 2". Known as the Westerner in a strange Eastern-land plot, the concept is very popular in Hollywood. The main character (American/Westerner) is the viewer's anchor, a common reference point of entry, to help introduce the exotic land and people through the eyes of someone familiar with the audience, almost acting like a tour guide for the film. I do not fault this overused premise, but encourage it because many American viewers may feel uncomfortable and intimidated in watching an all-Asian film with no points of reference. For example, sushi may be a common food in Japan, but it is always humorous (and helpful) for the American character to go, "Yuck, what the hell is this?" then have the dish explained to him (and the audience) by a native Japanese who educates and encourages the American to try some more and say, "Not too bad...I like raw fish!" I've always found these films interesting, especially in their portrayal of East versus West mentality since I am a product of both cultures myself.

So finally after compiling my data, I started to organize my book. Luckily, I've been watching Asian films for four decades, so most of the films were easy to track down. Some films have difficult subtitles and horrendous dubbing, so keep in mind that my information is based on those sources. What you see is what you get. In general, I recommend subtitles over dubs, but for fast-paced action films short on plot go for the dubbed version and avoid the lag spent on reading. Some of the movies on this list will be available at your online video store or available for sale. However, many titles are only available on DVD or boot-legged video. I do not condone piracy in any manor, but some Hong Kong films from Chinatown are copied from digital format. Then again, this may be your only source, so be careful of the quality of these films and ask to view a segment. Not all films will have subtitles and those that do can be extremely small and blurry. I've actually seen white subtitles on white background. Often grammar, meaning, and spelling can be erroneous as well. The popularity of the widescreen format may make the film look quite narrow on smaller televisions which also increases the difficulty of reading subtitles. Some films may only be available in Cantonese, Mandarin, or Japanese, so always check your copies for English subtitles.

Because Asian languages are written in a unique alphabet of their own, the names of characters and performers are phonetically spelled in English and may be pronounced differently depending on which dialect they represent. Depending on the translator, subtitles and credits can be very confusing, and sometimes spelling changes occur within the film itself. The legendary character Wong Fei Hung who has appeared in hundreds of films and shows, may be spelled as Wung Fay Hung, Wong Fay Hong, or even Huang Fey Kong. Be warned that subtitles are often written from a British point of view and may also contain different syntax and spelling than their American counterparts. And of course, the biggest hurdle is trying to pronounce Asian names (languages are unique and different among the Asian nations). Titles are translated loosely into English or altered to accommodate American tastes, so when speaking to someone form Asia, the same film may have two completely different titles. American filmmakers do the same thing when releasing Hollywood movies overseas. In Asia, Bruce Lee's Chinese Connection is called Fists of Fury while in America The Big Boss is called Fists of Fury. Even Chinese fans who know actor Jet Li as Li Lian Jie may not understand who you are talking about, because of phonetic pronunciation and dialect. Some Asian actors westernized their names in some form or manner to aid American viewers. Actor Liu Chia Hui called himself Gordon Lau in England and Gordon Liu in the United States for awhile, but he is also known as Lau Kar Fai (Cantonese pronunciation) and then again he might be called Liu Chia Hui (Mandarin) or Gordon Liu Chia Hui. Asian names always include the family/last name first which is the opposite of western name placement. As for example, my western name, John Daemin would be written in the Asian manner, Daemin John while my Korean name would be Min Daehgeun, notice the position of the family name. When both the Asian name and western name are combined, it becomes one long name which is written John Min Daehgeun. Confusing...I know, and there are even more problems of note. To make matters worse, Japanese names are written both ways (western and eastern placement), depending on the source of information. For those who are not familiar with Asian films, it's a fifty-fifty guess which part's the family name and which is the surname. Another name problem occurs in translation, since many Asian names are derived from Chinese characters which represent objects. The characters are used only for sound, but instead of the name, the literal translation is used. For example, my name Daehgeun should appear the same in subtitles, but if translated directly, my film character would be called Big Root. Not quite appealing and incorrect to use, since the word big root in Korean would have a different pronunciation. This would be the same as using an American name and finding the Greek/Latin root and then translating the direct meaning of the name rather than the sound. I apologize for the confusion and any mistakes I may have produced in spelling names or titles.

If an alternative film title exists, look for it in ( ) next to the main title. In many instances the title is changed depending on the country of release. Below the title, you will find additional information, including the year of release which may also change since films are released at different times in Asia and the United States. The genre subject which is fairly simple, but keep in mind that all kung-fu/samurai/ninja movies could be considered action films. The running time which is a big headache, since re-editing films is a common practice and a multitude of versions may be available on the market. My reviews are based on the version I've seen and in some instances, I've seen more than one version so don't be too surprised if you notice something different in the review. The rest of the information contains detailed production listings (when available), a rating, and the review. Background information is presented when available and I have tried to seek out the most reliable sources. Unfortunately in any transfer of one culture to another culture something is always lost from the original language. Don't let this deter you, since many films are being remastered with better English subtitles, and action is always a universal medium. Try to enjoy the films and keep an open mind to the different nuances and styles of Asian filmmakers.

Author's note, the original version of the book was written twenty years ago and some publication material may have changed since then. I have done my best to keep accurate while maintaining the original integrity of the reviews and content. Since hundreds of Asian films are released each year, I have decided to keep this version of Celluloid Dragons as volume one before the year 2000. A second volume will cover newer films and the historical and cultural changes of Asian cinema with the advancement of digital and social media technology. Thank you for your support and understanding.

JAPANESE CINEMA

Japan has played a major part in the growth and development of Asia, garnering praise and curses from its fellow neighbors while shaping the West's perception of Eastern culture. It comes as no surprise then that Japan has been a consistent force and leader in Asian cinema. Asia's pride and joy, Japan has also been her most infamous symbol of conquest and arrogance. Starting from simple rural beginnings, Japan was influenced greatly by China and Korea but gradually became isolated and distinctive. Her failed attempts to conquer and occupy Korea and China during the Imjin War (1592-1598) led to stalemate and withdrawal from the continent. In 1853, the Tokugawa Era came to a close when American warships "Black Ships" under Commodore Matthew Perry demanded Japan open her ports to foreign trade and assistance. The Japanese were amazed by the West's advancements and humiliated by their own lack of industrial development which prompted a major shift in Japanese policy, the Meiji Restoration (1868). In less than one generation, Japan developed into the most modern nation in Asia and one of the most sophisticated nation's in the world. European dress was adopted, the train introduced, modern warfare and political doctrines instituted, electrical power, the telegraph, the steam engine, metal warships, and of course the film projector.

In the beginning, film seemed a magical medium and was eagerly grasped by Japanese politicians to document historical events and propaganda rallies. Traditional Kabuki and Noh plays were filmed as were other stories, but artistic filmmaking gave way to military tendencies as Japan expanded to subjugate Asia and create the Greater East Asia Co-Prosperity Sphere. Japan annexed Korea in 1910, successfully fought against the Chinese and Russians, and participated in World War I, allying herself with the United States and Great Britain. Not content with her aggressive gains and chided by inferiority complexes, Japan decided to expand her empire. On December 7, 1941, Japan launched a surprise attack against American forces at Pearl Harbor, Hawaii and entered World War II. Four years later and nearly three million dead, Japan was totally decimated and became the first and only nation to experience the catastrophic effects of an atomic bomb on civilians in Hiroshima and Nagasaki. The post-war era would breed a new wave of Japanese filmmakers who were revered throughout the world. Cinematic themes such as anti-war, mass destruction and reconstruction, nuclear contamination, social conformity, and economic growth would become common themes among Japanese filmmakers.

Even till recently, Japan has been the vanguard of Asian films in the international market.

Ironically, the Asian country (China/Hong Kong) who initially resisted western influences would gradually adopt them and become a leader in the film industry, surpassing Japan's cinematic dominance. The popularity of Japanese films dwindled and were replaced by Hong Kong action/martial arts films led by pioneers like director John Woo, Tsui Hark, and Ringo Lam. In mainland China, the grand historical drama has prospered under "Fifth Generation" filmmakers like Zhang Yimou and Chen Kaige. As techniques and profits grow throughout Asia, Japan has seen her dominance in the film industry diminish, though Japanese films are still regarded in high esteem.

The three main types of Japanese films that have been successful in American society are the chanbara films, "sword fighting" period samurai (sword action in a historical setting) films, the monster/scifi films, and the animated films, known as Japanime or simply "anime" (Japanese animation) which still maintains a strong underground cult status. Numerous other genres did enter the American market including yakuza "modern crime" gangster films, the satirical comedies of Juzo Itami and the beautiful dramas of Yasujiro Ozu and others, and though their cinematic weight in history are assured, they did not garner much attention among the American public as a whole, but are better known among critics and connoisseurs of foreign films.

SAMURAI FILMS - AKIRA KUROSAWA

Without denying or debating, the most famous director in Japan and one of the most influential directors in the world is Akira Kurosawa. When it comes to chanbara/samurai films, only two names come to mind: Akira Kurosawa and Toshiro Mifune, director and actor, respectively. This duo worked in close conjunction to create a number of classic samurai films. Their collaborations are akin to the Martin Scorsese-Robert DeNiro and John Ford-John Wayne collaborations which respectively popularized the American crime genre and the western genre. Samurais were feudal warriors who served a lord of a Japanese province, those not in service were known as ronins, masterless samurais. Set primarily in the Tokugawa era between the 1500's to the 1800's, the key ingredient to a samurai film is the warrior and his sword which carries mythical status in Japanese folklore and legend. Kurosawa reinvented the samurai epic, placing his own influences from American westerns and Shakespearean themes into a Japanese genre. Casting Toshiro Mifune as his lead actor, the two collaborated on a string of films that have reached worldwide fame. During the early post-war era, films like Yojimbo, Sanjuro, The Seven Samurai, Hidden Fortress, Red Beard, and Kagemusha guaranteed Kurosawa legendary status with few peers. The samurai genre is most common in theme to the American western or older swashbuckling pirate or period pieces. Samurais were incredibly loyal and dedicated, they lived to defend the honor of their master and followed a code known as bushido, "way of the warrior." Following the warrior's code of Bushido, the samurai were master swordsmen, carrying a long single-bladed katana for battle and a waikazashi for ceremonial suicide when they failed. The sword became their symbol of authority and power, as the gun did in the old west...have sword will travel. Numerous reincarnations exist in television, novels, comics, and animation. The samurai genre is still around in Japan, but has lost much ground in the United States due to the swirling sword and blazing gun films from Hong Kong.

"KAIJU" MONSTER/SCIFI MOVIES

Ask your average American if he's seen Ozu's "Tokyo Story", then ask if he/she has ever seen a Godzilla film. The second category known as the Kaiju monster/scifi films were popularized by the incredible success of Godzilla, a radioactive fire-breathing dinosaur who destroyed Tokyo on numerous occasions. To a lesser extent of popularity was Gamera, the giant flying, fire-breathing turtle who loved children and hated alien monsters. Incorporating giant rubber suits and detailed miniatures, the Godzilla/Gamera phenomenon enjoyed immense success with children and viewers looking for something more light-hearted and action-packed than traditional horror films. Godzilla appeared in a number of forms, as a morning cartoon, a celebrity spokesmonster, comic book hero, but its appearance is best loved and known in the dozen of import films shown in theaters, on video, and on television. A slew of imitators also followed from Japan, China, and Korea, but Godzilla remains in a class of its own and is still breathing success in Japan. It might not be too long when the prehistoric lizard makes a return to the limelight in America. The films available incorporate a common theme of mass destruction, while adding a ton of camp, science fiction, and action in one package. Human subplots may follow, but are usually not critical to the main action which is Godzilla fighting the Japanese army or battling a rival monster. Hollywood has experimented with their versions of Godzilla and similar Kaiju films like Pacific Rim and Cloverfield. Take warning that the earlier monster films are extremely dated, the dubbing is laughable, effects rudimentary, and the plots barely surface above standard B-rated scifi fare. If you can get beyond those points, you'll have a wonderful time.

JAPANESE ANIMATION "JAPANIME" – STUDIO GHIBLI

The last major category "anime" is the newest and fastest growing import from Japan, but also the most misunderstood by viewers unfamiliar with the genre. Misconceptions of big-eyes, multi-colored hair girls in tight bikinis blowing up cities while splattering blood and gore over spaceships is exaggerated and represents a specific segment of the market. Though I do warn that with the exception of Kiki's Delivery Service, My Neighbor Totoro, and a few others, Japanime should be viewed by older children and adults only. Most Americans expect animation to fall into the constraints of traditional Disney fashion, light-hearted family entertainment with rich colors, cheery tunes, and life-like fluidity. Though Disney/Pixar may corner this market, Japanese animation surpasses the best American animated films through sheer diversity, maturity, and technical style. In Japan, animation is a serious art form covering all genres and ratings from hardcore violence and sex with X ratings to light Disney-esque films for G-rated lovers. The animation is unique and beautiful while the theme and mood reach a maturity level beyond any Disney film, rivaling live-action mainstream Hollywood films in sheer horror, excitement, comedy, and drama. Heavy Metal, Watership Down, and Lords of the Rings are examples of mature American films that share similarities to Japanese-style animation. No matter your specific tastes, most likely there will be an animated film garnered toward your interest. The first step is to see them as individual films that happen to be animated and not to treat them merely as kiddy cartoons. Though childish slapstick and irreverent satire are popular themes among Japanese animators, they are only one branch from a larger tree. In many ways, animators use Japanime as a release from the strict traditional norms of society. Wild themes, graphic violence, perversion, scantily-clad females, and moral messages appear in various incarnations. Big-eyed characters are extremely popular as is the use of robots in animation. Eyes are the so-called "windows of the soul" and the facial feature best used to express emotions while animating. The large eyes are a representation (or criticism) of the western image of classic beauty, and the larger than life heroes popular among Japanese. Hair color is also exaggerated and colorful to distinguish the difference between homogeneous characters. American animators prefer drawing animals, since more leeway is given in shape and color than drawing humans. Japanese animators don't limit themselves to animals and use all shapes and colors to animate human characters. Robots represent the fascination with technological growth and can symbolize the average Japanese worker who conforms and functions in society like a mindless machine. Japan is the leading user of robotics technology and a nation known for its amazing scientific advancements.

Japanese animation first received recognition as imported titles like Astroboy, Speed Racer, Symba the Lion, Star Blazers, Battle Beyond the Planets, Galaxy Express 999, and Cyborg 009 appeared on American television. Gradually gaining popularity in colleges and among comic book collectors, an underground video market developed with college students passing out copies among themselves. The fascination grew and so did the legion of fans who demanded more titles and better quality copies. Mainstream distributors started to carry Japanese animated titles and rental stores created a section dedicated to the topic. The most common anime genre is science fiction, but action, horror, comedy, historical, sex, and fantasy have popped up in various forms. Now in full force, the industry has seen a skyrocket in growth and promises to be Japan's most popular film export. What parent or child has not heard of Pokemon? In Japan, anime enjoys extreme popularity with a variety of market segments on television, in theaters, and video. A few years back, the only source for animation would be anime clubs or conventions, but now major video retailers carry sections wholly dedicated to the subject ranging in price from $10 to $30 with English dubbed or subtitled versions readily available.

HONG KONG AND CHINA

Though both countries have developed their own distinct cultural identities, prospering economically from opposite streams of idealogy: mainland China is the largest communist nation in the world, while Hong Kong is small and capitalist, both nations share a distinct past with a rich Chinese heritage. The year 1997 marked a momentous period in China and Hong Kong's long history when the countries were remerged into one. Hong Kong was officially given control over to mainland China by the ruling British government. Currently, Mandarin is the official language of China while Cantonese and English are the most common in Hong Kong. Hong Kong had developed an independent, capitalist government over the century it was separated from China and created one of the world's most popular film industries. Before Shaw Brothers Studios disbanded its film division in the mid-80's, it was the largest film studio in the world, producing hundreds of films a year. Due to the influx of escaping refugees during World War II and the communist takeover of mainland China, many talented artisans helped Hong Kong's film industry grow.

Hong Kong is especially renowned for wuxia and kung-fu martial arts films and high-paced modern action films with stars and directors like Chang Cheh, Lau Kar Leung, Bruce Lee, Jackie Chan, Jet Li, Donnie Yen, John Woo, Chow Yun Fat, Ringo Lam, Yuen Woo Ping, and Tsui

Hark. Every genre is produced in Hong Kong and stars regularly appear in a variety of films and different roles. Also the crossing of genres is a popular theme within Hong Kong cinema where romantic comedies can have a good dose of martial arts and action. American examples include Alien (horror and science fiction), Ghostbusters (fantasy, action, and comedy) and Back to the Future (science fiction, comedy, and romance). Some political experts worry that Hong Kong will suffer radical changes with China's takeover as the ruling government may adversely effect the film industry. A large group of talented stars like Chow Yun Fat, Jet Li, and Jackie Chan are shaping their films to a more Western audience while many Hong Kong directors have left to do Hollywood films: John Woo (Hard Target, Broken Arrow, Face Off, MI2), Ringo Lam (Maximum Risk) and Tsui Hark (Double Team). Recently in mainland China, a new generation of filmmakers known as the "Fifth Generation" have enjoyed the support and additional relaxation of control over the filmmaking process. At times their films have been banned within their native country due to political ideology, but still enjoy a healthy overseas audience. Mainland China has emerged as a leader in dramatic and historical films, and one can only speculate how the film industry will grow with the introduction of Hong Kong's additional talent and market capital.

KUNG-FU FILMS

It may seem to you that a large portion of films from Asia are martial arts related, especially Chinese Kung-fu films starring Jackie Chan, Jet Li, Donnie Yen, or Bruce Lee. In fact, many of the films in this book are martial arts related which tend to be the best recognized and most popular import from Asian filmmakers. Most of the thanks is due to a lithe actor named Bruce Lee and a studio giant called Shaw Brothers. In general, action films have a tendency to translate better from one culture to another since action sequences do not suffer from translation loss in language structure and meaning. The most successful American films in Asian also tend to be action films with Stallone, Willis, Cruise, and Schwarzenegger or comic book heroes with superpowers and amazing martial arts abilities. Due to language and cultural barriers, comedies, musicals and romances are not as successful as action films that popularize the martial arts theme.

Let me take a few moments to explain the importance of martial arts culture. Martial arts was created in China many centuries ago, and a proud tradition of styles and techniques have developed all over Asia into firmly established schools of martial arts. Practitioners dedicate their life and live by a traditional code of martial arts ethics and beliefs. Styles like Tai Chi Chuan, Wing Chun, Hung Gar, and Shaolin are quite famous in China with branches around the world. It is not unusual for a Chinese character to know some kung-fu and most times the practitioner specializes in a certain technique: drunken monkey, tiger, iron body, crane, or wing chun. The word kung-fu means ability and can refer to any discipline or skill achieved through hard work, practice, or determination, so any person can achieve kung-fu.

The importance of kung-fu talents is similar to the western reliance on gun abilities or sword fighting in films. Guns played a huge part of American (Western World) exploration, development, and maturity. In American films, all types of characters used guns: the hero, the villain, the bartender, the gambler, kids, women, Indians, and even the elderly. Think of all the different types of guns and the level of skills. The same goes for kung-fu which becomes a tool for a character. Remember the popularity of westerns in earlier decades where every major actor was in a Hollywood western from Clark Gable to Jimmy Stewart. Western TV shows, radio programs, and movies dominated America pop culture and everyone owned a Davy Crockett coonskin cap. Now imagine that any film in Hollywood with a gun was mislabeled a Western. Imagine that every time you saw a gun on screen, you'd swear you were watching a Western. By that definition, the movie Godfather would be a Western, so would Gone With the Wind, Casablanca, Dr. Zhivago, Forrest Gump, Raiders of the Lost Ark, The Patriot, and thousands of others. But we realize the guns are just an implement and not the reflection of the entire film. Martial arts plays such an important and all encompassing cinematic tool in Asian culture. Whether you're watching action, horror, comedy, or risqué adult, don't be too surprised if the characters know martial arts. I always enjoyed Indian Bollywood films where all the characters can sing and dance in perfect unison.

Since the introduction of filmmaking in 1896 by the British, martial arts has played a key ingredient in Chinese filmmaking. Early silent films captured the beauty of Chinese Opera/martial arts, and even the popular Wong Fei Hung films can be traced back to the early era of black and white films. Kung-fu films can be broken into a number of popular categories: Comedy Kung-fu, a blend of slapstick and martial arts like Sammo Hung and Stephen Chow. Traditional Kung-fu period pieces which take place before the 20th century, usually dealing with Shaolin Temple or Ching vs. Ming. Wuxia fantasy Kung-fu which includes a lot of flying, supernatural powers, sorcery, chivalry, and demons. These are the modern day superhero stories of China and are only limited by the imagination. Mainstream Modern Kung-fu, the contemporary action films of Bruce Lee, Jackie Chan, and Jean-Claude Van Damme in which heroes have to deal with modern problems like guns, drugs, and mobsters. Don't be surprised to see a few kicks performed by women, children, the elderly, monsters, ghosts, a disembodied hand or the family pet. Want kung-fu animals, watch Carter Wong dispatch martial arts gorillas in Shaolin Invincibles.

Martial arts was invented in Asia, branched into a variety of styles, and has been a part of physical training and combat for many centuries. Each country has developed their own unique styles which have become a proud part of their cultural heritage. Kung-fu (called Wushu in China) and its many derivatives are popular in China; Karate, Judo, Aikido, Ninjutsu are Japanese styles; Tae Kwon Do, Tang Soo Do, Hapkido are Korean, and there are plenty more around the world, like Thai kick boxing, Savate in France, Arnis in the Phillipines, and Capoeria in Brazil.So don't be too hasty to group all martial arts films into one category and assume them to be redundant or insignificant.

BULLETS AND BLOOD - HONG KONG CRIME FILMS

The Gun-fu Pics are a category of films that have supplanted the popularity of martial arts films, though in my opinion momentarily, by replacing traditional weapons with guns. Popularized by directors like John Woo and Ringo Lam, the world of cops and robbers are explored from within on a deep level of honor, friendship, loyalty, betrayal, corruption, and greed. Sub-genres exist such as the "Girls with Guns" action films that feature females in the main roles, acting with the same bravado and brutality as their male counterparts albeit more scantily dressed. Unlike Western crime films based on realism, expect all forms of outlandish stunts, superhuman feats, and illogical conclusions. Violence is pushed to a new level that may at times border on comic book mayhem or superhero farce. No one is safe in the crime world where often women, children, and pets are the victims as well as the police officers and criminals. Criticized for their excessive violence and glamorization of organized crime (Triad), there has been some backlash on the genre. Rumors circulate that many films are financed by Triad members and act as glorified recruitment posters for new gang members.

HISTORICAL DRAMAS - THE BEAUTY OF GONG LI

If you polled the nation's critics and asked them to name some of the best films from Asia, there would be little surprise to recognize a recurring name, Gong Li. A beautiful and refined actress, Gong Li has appeared in some of the best films from China's hottest directors. Ju Dou, Raise the Red Lantern, To Live, Farewell My Concubine, and Shanghai Triad are just a few of the films praised by critics, filmmakers, and viewers. Her films often represent characters caught within a turbulent time in China's history, beginning in the late 1800's to the present. China was an ancient imperial dynasty suddenly uprooted from its traditional beliefs of world supremacy by foreign powers. Invading European nations forced concessions and humiliated China's decrepit ruling government. The devastating Opium Wars were followed by aggression from Japan which lasted until 1945. Internal conflicts and wars tore the country apart and caught millions of innocent people in the crossfire. The imperial government fell to the Nationalist under Sun Yat Sen and Chaing Kai Shek who later battled, allied against Japan, then fought, and finally lost to the Communist under Mao Tse Tung. When Mao came to power, conflicts with the Soviet Union and the United States continued while oppression existed from within. Even today, China is hardly the example of an open-minded, free-speaking nation and her films represent the decades of recent oppression and individual constraints on freedom. Fearing a repeat of the Tiananmen Massacre, talented people have left Hong Kong for other parts of the world to avoid China's 1997 takeover. The new millennium will be interesting to watch as China enters into a bright, but tarnished era of world prominence and notoriety.

AROUND THE WORLD – FUTURE ASIAN CINEMA

The interest in Asian films doesn't stop at Hong Kong, Japan and China which may be the forerunners, but are not the only prospering film dragons in Asia. Every country in Asia is developing film projects, and nations like Korea, Taiwan, Vietnam, Malaysia, Thailand, the Philippines, and India (which is part of the Asian continent) are producing quality productions with their own unique styles and cultures embedded into the characters and stories. Given time, more films will be translated and available in the American market and might even walk away with an international award or two.

Even Hollywood producers have capitalized on interest in the "Pearl of the Orient" and have financed a number of films dealing with Asian-American issues. I try to ignore the shallow and atrocious attempts of earlier decades, most notably the Charlie Chan and Fu Manchu films. They lacked any true attempt to represent Asians but were merely stereotypical caricatures of Asian origin. American filmmakers did try their own hand at capturing the style of Asian martial arts films, samurai films, and especially ninja films which were a popular topic to imitate in the 1980's. It may have taken a long time, but the efforts have been occasionally made with good results, and cultural awareness and non-stereotyping have become serious issues in the American film industry. The list of Asian-American produced films are growing and are available on video with the benefit of being filmed in the English language, briefly using subtitles to keep the integrity of the spoken dialogue. In many instances these films are directed and written by Asians, but can include talented non-Asians filmmakers, such as Italian director Bernardo Bertolucci 's "The Last Emperor" and John Boorman's "Beyond Rangoon".

BUYING AND RENTING AND STREAMING

Besides providing you with informative reviews and background information, Asian Films on Video can be used as a handy buyer/renter's guide. However, you may become frustrated when searching for specific titles. To ease your process, I've included some helpful information in your search for Asian films, especially for those who do not speak an Asian language and are intimidated by entering an all-Asian store. For films that are accessible in major online video-rental chains and retail stores, I have placed a VA (video available) in the information section of the film. The VA titles are your best choice for starting off, since the copies are of high quality, the prices are reasonable, and the subtitles or dubs are quite good. If you feel a little bolder, you should try to scout out your area for shops located in or near Asian communities. All large cities will have an Asian community such as Chinatown, Little Tokyo, or Koreatown with dozens of shops catering to films. Chinese video stores in general will carry a large assortment of Hong Kong titles with most films having English subtitles (British law requires all films to have English subtitles). If you're fortunate enough to own a DVD/laserdisc player, the format is very popular among Chinese viewers and DVD/laserdisc stores will carry hundreds of Asian titles in pristine widescreen formats with subtitles. Most Chinese laserdiscs will also feature separate audio tracks for Cantonese and Mandarin speakers. Show the store owner the title in the book or mention the actors involved and ask to make sure the copy has subtitles. Politeness and patience are the key and you will be well rewarded with friendly service. Also a number of Asian-American specialty stores will have sections devoted to popular genre categories: Japanime, kung-fu, samurai, Godzilla, and action films. At times it will be difficult to find a specific title and even then it may not have subtitles, but given time and effort, perseverance will pay off. Due to the global changes over time since the initial publication of this book, eBay, Amazon, and other online retailers deal directly in selling Asian films. A number of film titles, nearly all of them, are now available on different streaming services online. This is a wonderful era of international film appreciation.

CATEGORY GUIDELINES

The general format of the book is comprised of an alphabetical listing of films. This is the heart of the book and the best way to browse through films or to check on a film you are interested in buying or renting. The first section (Part I) is dedicated to Asian-made films only while the second section (Part II) includes non-Asian-made films from Hollywood and Europe. The second section films are easier to find in stores and contain original English dialogue. At the end of the book is a number of appendices designed to offer you quick reference material. Appendix 1 (Genre/Country) is a list of films broken into country and genre categories, catering to a particular interest. This way if you want to find a kung-fu movie to see, you can chose from the list. To be broader in base, I have included films that are available though not yet reviewed. Appendix 2 is a list of some of my favorite films from the book. Appendix 3 & 4 are dedicated to the talented Asian people who made these films possible and will help you track down your favorite star or director. A listing of all their films are available for quick reference with year of production. Appendix 5 (Distributors/Retailers) is a list of places that distribute and sell Asian films. One of the best available is Tai Seng Video Marketing, the largest distributor of Hong Kong films in the United States. Most recently, Tai Seng has pushed for the elimination of bootlegs videos and has entered mainstream American distribution channels. For Japanime, check out Central Park Media Corporation, the leader in Japanese animation released in the United States. I have included a number of other major distributors who will sell via mail order (online searches will better serve you now). Appendix 6 (Conventions/Internet) is a list of popular Asian-film conventions and their email address. For those of you with computer access, check out the numerous websites dedicated to Asian film topics in a list of links used for web searching. Many of them are created by dedicated fans, for non-profit, who wish to share their enjoyment of Asian films with all newcomers. Some sites include beautiful color photos, background information, and in-depth reviews. Appendix 7 is a list of Asian terminology and their layman's definition. Appendix 8 (Bibliography) is a listing of resources used in the publication of this book.

An entire book dedicated to Asian films for those who are looking for viewing choices would be incomplete without a star-rating guide. Even if you don't know much about Asian cinema, this will be an excellent place to begin your film viewing. Along the way, I highlight and go into detail on some of my personal favorites and discuss popular topics such as the Godzilla Series, Once Upon A Time In China Series, Star Blazers Series, Street Fighter Series, and so on. A ratings system would be pointless if I used purely subjective whim, so I've tried to break down my system into a very comprehensive and accurate system. All my ratings are based on a formula which I developed, combining three criteria and averaging the total. One part is based on the objective quality of filmmaking and technique, the second part is my subjective taste and enjoyment factor, and the third part is based on the film's merit within its own genre and peers. I do this because, the level of enjoyment for a specific genre (ie: horror) film will definitely be affected by your overall enjoyment of horror films in general that you've seen in the past. It's like the old adage warning, stop comparing apples with oranges, so I decided to compare apples with apples. If you love horror films and despise kung-fu films, a three-star rating for a horror film would carry different weight than a three-star rating for a kung-fu film. So don't assume that all three-star kung-fu films should entertain you as much as a three-star horror film, because of your own bias. Please keep that in mind when checking the ratings. All films are based on a four-star scale: Four (****) is the highest and refers to films of overall excellence and enjoyment. Films worth seeing and in my opinion owning. Three (***) stars represent good, entertaining films, especially for the genre they represent, I still own those films as well. Worth seeing and enjoyable for the most part, but perhaps with some minor flaws. Two (**) stars are where you should take caution and tread carefully. If you're unfamiliar with the genre, I would avoid two stars films. These are the mediocre to fair films, and usually appeal only to diehard fans of the genre. Numerous problems occur in story content, acting, editing, or the subject material leaves little to desire for viewers outside the genre. One (*) star films are at the bottom of the barrel, films that are outright poor or not worth seeing no matter how much you enjoy the genre. Even diehard fans are warned to stay away, but you may enjoy them on a campy/crappy level for their ridiculous plot elements, low budget, or horrendous acting. Films so bad, they becoming disgustingly amusing. I would avoid these films forever and check for alternative choices, there are so many great Asian films to last you a lifetime.

Here's a quick example of the rating system: a movie like "Rumble in the Bronx" would get 3 for technique (I don't take points off for bad dubbing...though that may annoy some viewers), 3 for pure enjoyment, and 3.5 for value in the martial arts genre, the total is 9.5 divided by 3 = 3.16. Rounded down, the film would get a 3 star rating. I try not to be overly subjective since my own taste will differ from other people, but after awhile you can probably gauge my personal opinions. In many instances I will watch the film on more than one occasion to reassess its merit and test its entertainment value over time, even after 40 years I still love watching Master Killer/36th Chamber. I hope my reviews and ratings guide you wisely on your quest for entertaining films.

Each film is broken down into the following format listed in the KEY section. Some films may include more information than others because of their general availability or importance in Asian-American cinema. Of course recent memory and personal favorites shall influence my time spent on a film review. All films include the title, year of release, genre, running time, country of origin, rating, and review. Due to the problems of illegal distribution and multiple distribution rights, year of release and distributor may vary from source to source. Also various countries have different editing standards and films may be re-edited for various reasons, so running times may differ. I have searched for the most accurate information, but in the case of not being able to confirm my data I have placed a question mark to approximate dates and time (ie 1980? or C-90?m). Genre represents the style of movie and should be checked. If an MPAA rating exists that has also be listed. Films from Hong Kong are based on a tri-category rating. Type I - All Audiences (equivalent to G), Type II - Not Suitable for Kids (equivalent to PG-13) and Type III - Restricted for Kids (R and NC-17). In general, most of the films listed fall in the Type II (PG-13) category, but exceptions will have the genre listing: Family (children) or Erotic (adult), reediting of a film can change the level of rating. If the film is accessible in major video chains or online streaming, I have placed a VA (Video Available), followed by the video's catalog number or product code, the film's country of origin, and suggested retail price. Prices are not set in stone and shopping around can help. As a proponent of original aspect ratios, I have included a note on the availability of widescreen/letterbox versions. If you purchase/rent blurays, laserdiscs or DVDs, widescreen is the most popular format. In the theater, movie screens are much longer than television screens and many films are cropped (sides are cut) or involve pan & scan (unnatural camera movement not originally seen) to accommodate the smaller home screen. If you don't mind black bars at the top, I do recommend widescreen versions which look gorgeous on modern LED televisions. Sometimes the subtitles are actually shown in the black bars, leaving the film's picture free of lettering, thank you Criterion Collection. The larger the number, the wider the film. Look on the box for aspect ratio, 1.85:1 or less will be fine for any size television. 2.35:1 should only be viewed on 30 inch or larger televisions. The next portion is a detailed listing of production credits, including key people involved in the directing, writing, and producing of the film. The names of actors and the characters are listed. Finally the body of the review which will include a synopsis of the film and personal commentary.

KEY:
Title   (Alternate Title if available)
(Year) GENRE   C=Color   B&W=Black & White   Running time (m=minutes)
English/Dubbed/Subtitled   MPAA Rating (if available)   VA=video available in major chains
Catalog # Number   Country of Origin
Retail Price=(prices may differ depending on the format: video/laserdisc/dvd or changing distributor. Use the price as a guideline, but shop around.)
(TBA=To Be Announced, pending release)
Widescreen (Letterbox) Availability
Dir=director Scr=screenwriter   Prod=producer   DP=director of photography or cinematographer   Ex. Prod=executive producer   Line Prod=Line Producer
Prod Design=production designer   Art Dir=Art Director
Sp. Fx= special effects director   MAD=martial arts/action director
(additional roles: editor, music, character designer, mecha(nical) designer, costumes, makeup, stunts)
PC=production company (release company) Dist=United States Distributor(s)
Cast of actors-
ACTOR   CHARACTER PORTRAYED
ADDITIONAL ACTORS LIST
[rating]
BODY OF REVIEW (Some reviews are very detailed to provide information for viewers who have already seen the film. Read with discretion, so not to uncover anything crucial to the plot.)

Joy Luck Club, The
(1993) Drama C-136m   English & Chinese with English Subtitles   R   VA
Catalog # 2291 AS   USA   Retail: $39.99 Widescreen Available
Dir: Wayne Wang   Scr: Amy Tan, Ronald Bass
Prod: Wayne Wang, Amy Tan, Ronald Bass, Patrick Markey
Ex. Prod: Oliver Stone, Janet Yang
DP: Amir Mokri   Editor: Maysie Hoy   Music: Rachel Portman
Prod Design: Donald Graham Burt   Set Design: Jim Poynter
Art Design: Diana Kunce, Kwan Kit "Eddy" Kwok, Jian Jun Li
Choreography: Michael Smuin   Costumes: Lydia Tanji, Shu Lan Ding
PC: Oliver Stone Production Dist: Hollywood Pictures
(Based on the book by Amy Tan)
Ming-Na Wen   June
Tamalyn Tomita   Waverly
Lauren Tom, Rosalind Chao, etc.
[****]
Based on Amy Tan's bestselling novel about Chinese mothers... (enjoy Asian Films on Video!)

So hopefully, I've taken part of the confusion and difficulty away from viewing Asian films. I know there's a lot to see and read, but that's the great part and it gets better and easier each year. If you're new to the field, I would stick to the three star movies and up before working downward on the genre you enjoy. Take a chance and rent some at your local video store or download online. For those of you already experts in the field, I hope my book has done justice to the field of Asian cinema and provide insight as a companion guide. I encourage any comments or suggestions which may be included in a revised addition. I review Asian films on an annual basis and will include hundreds more in the future volumes. Thank you.

You can contact me online: johndmin@gmail.com

Enjoy and prepare to enter an entirely unique world of filmmaking.

Due to time, availability, and an expanding market, no source could catalog every Asian film in existence. I excluded films that failed to meet certain requirements: no English subtitles, unavailable by legal means. If I missed your favorite, I promise to review it in the future. Please keep in mind, every review was written by myself, no staff writers, and I have done my best to avoid any errors or inconsistencies. If you wish to make comments, suggestions, or compliments, please email me. Laserdiscs are referenced but no longer commonly available, the word is interchangeable with other digital media such as Blurays, DVDs, and digital downloads.
Warning: Some reviews contain detailed plot information...read with discretion.

PART I

ASIAN FILMS MADE IN ASIA

-0~9-

(Please look under the title's phonetic spelling, ie. "3 Evil Masters" will be in the beginning section of T for 3 "Three")

-A-

Aces Go Places 5: The Terracotta Hit
(1987) Action C-103m   Hong Kong   **Chinese with English Subtitles**
Catalog #0681   Hong Kong   **Retail: $39.99**
Dir: Liu Chia Liang (Lau Kar Leung)   Prod: Karl Maka
MAD: Liu Chia Yung (Lau Kar Wing)   Dist: Facets Video/Tai Seng Video
Sam Hui, Karl Maka, Leslie Cheung, Nina Li Chi, Conan Lee, Melvin Wong, Chan Nga Cun, Danny Lee, Roy Cheung, Fennie Yuen, Willie Doxan, Maria Cordero
[**1/2]
The fifth film in a popular action-based series of slapstick adventures from Hong Kong. To garner more international appeal, non-Chinese stars were recruited into the earlier films, albeit in minor roles. The Chinese versions are called "Aces go Places", while westernized titles are commonly called the "Mad Missions". The films cater toward pure escapism and capitalize on outlandish action scenes and exotic settings similar to the James Bond adventures, but more akin to the crazed antics of Cannonball Run.
Continuing the popularity of the first few films, the fifth sequel returns to its martial arts roots with mixed results. Under the direction of veteran director Liu, the film attempts a number of film parodies and comedic kung-fu fights. The story revolves around two men who try to open a business but get framed by criminals Leslie Cheung and Nina. Supercop Conan arrives to settle things and then the whole cast becomes involved in criminal trafficking and a warehouse full of terracotta figures, ancient stone warriors of China. Though not the best in the series, it was a big hit in Hong Kong, and features an all-star cast. This time out, no major western stars were used to spice up the international appeal.

AD Police File 1: The Phantom Woman
(1990) Japanime   C-40m Dubbed/Japanese with English Subtitles   VA

Catalog # ANI ET095-012   Japan Retail: $19.95
Dir: Ikegami Takamasa   Scr: Nakazawa Takehito
Original Story: Toshimichi Suzuki, Tony Takezaki   DP: Akihiko Takahashi
Character Designs: Tony Takezaki, Oda Fujio
Planning: Toshimichi Suzuki, Unozawa Shin
PC: Artmic, Inc./Youmex Inc.   Dist: AnimEigo
Brad Moranz Leon McNichol
Regan Forman   Jeena Malso
Mark Fincannon   Dieork
Donn Ansell   Saeki
Kelly Chalaire   Phantom Woman
Trampas Thompson Alus
[**1/2]

When a series of bizarre murders are committed by beautiful women, the special branch of AD Police are sent to investigate. Blending elements from "Blade Runner", MegaTokyo's elite AD Police discover the women are actually Boomers, perfectly human-rendered androids with artificial intelligence, incredible strength, and an attitude. The year is 2027, Officer Malso and rookie Leon McNichol are on the case to prevent further outbreaks of Boomer violence which resulted in the murder of Malso's previous partner. They follow a string of leads which point to overworked and oversexed Boomers who are being abused by their owners. In the original Boomer brain design, the artificial matrix can become contaminated with past emotions and memories. To prevent the Boomer from becoming too human, they are then marked for destruction. An illegal black market has risen to recycle old female Boomers for sexual pleasures, and in most cases the memory is purged, but some of the female Boomers still retain grudges from their past existence. Overworking the Boomer can cause the suppressed memory to become active which then triggers a mad and dangerous rage. Perhaps a moral message for men not to take for granted their spouses or girlfriends. One recycled Boomer in particular who had a sexual relationship with McNichol hunts him down and confronts him. The ending is quick and direct, leaving little to ponder. She wants him to love her, but when rejected she becomes hostile. McNichol repeats his past actions and takes down the Boomer. His decision leaves him disturbed, blurring the lines between woman and machine. The animation style is intriguing and the story is mature and not intended for children. However, the short expanse of time does not truly develop the characters or provide a strong enough reason for the actions which take place. The quality animation and action pace will appeal to fans of the crime/scifi genre.

AD Police File 2: The Ripper
(1990) Japanime   C-40m Dubbed/Japanese with English Subtitles   VA
Catalog # ANI ET095-013   Japan Retail: $19.95
Dir: Akira Nishimori   Scr: Nakazawa Takehito
Original Story: Toshimichi Suzuki, Tony Takezaki
Character Designs: Tony Takezaki, Oda Fujio
Planning: Toshimichi Suzuki, Unozawa Shin
PC: Artmic, Inc./Youmex Inc.   Dist: AnimEigo
[**1/2]

A new mission for the AD Police in MegaTokyo. Officers Malso and McNichol are called on the case when a series of brutal murders are committed against prostitutes. The victims are young women who have been disemboweled. The Central Police must determine whether the jurisdiction of the case will fall to the AD Police or the normal police. Whether the killer is human or a Boomer (android) is not clear, but human police officer Ailis Kara takes an interest in the case. She follows a number of leads and comes across a beautiful female executive. To compete with her sexist male counterparts, she removed her reproductive organs and then had more android parts inserted into her body to make her stronger and more alluring. After she lost her job, she suffered emotional instability and brutally went after young and beautiful women with real human organs. Ailis bonds with the woman and tries to help her. The AD Police arrive on the scene and prepare to take down the dangerous killer. The story focuses a great deal on Ailis' character who wishes to replace her human eye with an android eye. Her eye condition isn't serious and Officer McNichol tries to talk her out of it. She argues that improving one's body with science doesn't cause a human to cease being human, or does it? When people have problems with their organs, they replace them with mechanical ones, happens all the time. If a human has 70% or more mechanical parts, he/she is no longer considered a human, but a Boomer under AD Police's jurisdiction. Morally intriguing with the same quality animation and mood presented in the first film. The series continues to offer mature enjoyment for anime fans. Officer Ailis is not able to save the woman, but with a smile on her pretty face, she decides to go through with her eye operation and must live with her decision.

AD Police File 3: The Man Who Bites His Tongue
(1990) Japanime   C-40m Dubbed/Japanese with English Subtitles   VA
Catalog # ANI ET095-014   Japan Retail: $19.95
Dir: Akira Nishimori   Scr: Nakazawa Takehito
Original Story:Toshimichi Suzuki , Tony Takezaki
Character Designs: Tony Takezaki, Oda Fujio
Planning: Toshimichi Suzuki, Unozawa Shin
PC: Artmic, Inc./Youmex Inc.   Dist: AnimEigo
[1/2]**
Third and final episode in the three-volume OAV series which focuses on android-hunting police officers and the androids known as Boomers. Based on the same world as Bubblegum Crisis, the series has its own identity without any crossover cameos and a noticeably different style of animation. The world of humans and robots are explored in further detail in the third volume which bears resemblance to "Robocop". AD Officer Billy Fanword is a heroic cop who becomes mortally wounded in the line of duty. While trying to stop a deranged Boomer, he risks his life to save others and is whisked away to a special medical center. To help create a stronger police force, the scientists use him to create a cyborg officer. Now Fanword is trapped in a world between man and machine, without a soul or true purpose in life except to follow his program to serve and to protect. Emotionally he searches for his past self to the chagrin of the scientists who created him. The title refers to Fanword's habit of biting his tongue to induce pain and convince him of his humanity. If you enjoyed the previous two volumes, the third file is worth checking out. The whole series has offered a blend of exciting crime action and thought-provoking plots on a world inhabited by humans and androids.

Akira
(1988) Japanime: Scifi   C-124m   Dubbed/Japanese with English Subtitles
VA   Catalog # 90643   Japan Retail: $19.95
Dir: Katsuhiro Otomo   Scr: Katsuhiro Otomo and Izo Hashimoto
Prod: Shunzo Kato, Sawako Noma, Ryohei Susuki   DP: Katsuji Misawa
Music: Shoji Yamashiro   Art Dir: Toshiharu Mizutani
Animation: Takashi Nakamura   PC: Bandai Visual   Dist: Streamline Productions
Voices: Mitsuo Iwara, Mami Koyama, Nozomu Sasaki, Taro Ishida
[****]

Few animated films have pushed the boundaries of animation to new heights of surrealism and controversy while establishing animation as a mature artistic medium not just for children. Visually impressive, convoluted, and grotesque, Akira is a moral tale that questions the mind's evolution beyond its social awareness of what is right and wrong. The futuristic tale follows a group of teenage gang members, social outcasts, who get involved with psychically-gifted children and covert government agents in a deadly cat-and-mouse confrontation across decaying neo-Tokyo. The heavy-handed plot may not be for all tastes, but if you're interested in incredible animation and something unique, Akira stands in a class of its own. Arguably the best known Japanese animated film, Akira is used as a benchmark film to represent the entire genre. The animated film incorporates realistic animation with a mature tale of science fiction, action, and drama. Based on a long-running comic series from Japan, the film follows the adventures of Kaneda as he attempts to stop his friend Tetsuo from achieving god-like powers and destroying the world. The title Akira refers to the name of a mythical figure who will lead the near-futuristic population to truth and enlightenment, and away from the corruption of technology and heavy-handed government control.

The government has secretly developed a program of gifted young psychics with amazing powers. One of the psychics escapes into neo-Tokyo, igniting a massive military hunt. During a protest rally, the young emaciated boy with a bluish complexion runs into the middle of the crowd. Police quickly try to repel the protestors while secretly in search of apprehending the young psychic.

Meanwhile, a bunch of young cyberpunks (street punks adept at technology) led by Kaneda drive hi-tech motorcycles and trash rival gang members. They're carefree and reckless, living from day to day with only their motorcycles as friends. In a spectacular scene, the government closes in on the psychic boy, but then his powers are unleashed and every window in a building shatters and rains glass on the crowd. While escaping, he collides with a young member of the cyberpunks, called Tetsuo, who is then contaminated with psychic energy. Huge army helicopters descend around the boys and apprehend the entire gang. Infuriated, the cyberpunk leader Kaneda demands why his friend was taken. The commander decides to arrest the whole gang under the pretense of national security. While in interrogation, Kaneda meets an alluring girl who was part of the protest. From here on the film gets complicated as various characters fade away (Kaneda's gang) and new ones (psychics) are introduced. The scientist in charge of testing Tetsuo wishes to understand his sudden exponential psychic growth while the military commander fears the uncontrollable power. The crux of the story centers around Tetsuo's psychic evolution and the government who tries to bottle his abilities. Using his new found powers, Tetsuo escapes from the government facility and goes on a psychic rampage across neo-Tokyo. The government desperately attempts to stop Tetsuo in a Godzilla-rivaling battle across the streets of neo-Tokyo. The finale is both breathtaking and disturbing, revealing the secrets of what Akira truly is and was. Only Kaneda has the courage and resolve to stop Tetsuo's rampage before he evolves into a being of immense power driven by mental madness and pain. The climatic battle in a junkyard is both wondrous and incredibly intense as both boys fight to the death while the military remain helpless in the background. A must see for any Japanimation fans - a brilliant but bizarre classic which helped launch mainstream acceptance for Japanese animation.

Akira Production Report
(1987) Documentary C-52m Catalog #SPV 90001 Japan Retail: $24.95
PC/Dist: Akira Committee/Streamline Pictures
[***]
A documentary on the creation of Katsuhiro Otomo's animated film Akira. Offers some interesting insight into one of the most famous animated films to come out of Japan. Worth checking out to gain a better perspective on the world of animation and understand the impact of Akira.

All About Ah-Long
(1989) DramaC-106m   Chinese with English Subtitles
Catalog #0758   Hong Kong   Retail: $39.99
Dir: Johnny To Kai-Fung   Prod: Raymond Wong   Dist: Facets Video/Tai Seng Video
Chow Yun Fat, Silvia Chang, Huang Kun Husen, Ng Man Tat
[***]
Chow Yun Fat has garnered a popular reputation among fans of Hong Kong action films. He is often portrayed as a stoic, clean-shaven, short-haired killing machine with dark sunglasses and a long black coat. But before his rise to notoriety as the killer, Chow appeared in numerous comedic and dramatic roles. He plays a single father released from prison, trying to raise his young son. Similar to Dustin Hoffman's role in "Kramer vs. Kramer", Chow is frustrated when his successful ex-wife returns to claim his son. After so many years, Chow is reluctant to let go of his son, but eventually wants what is best for the boy. As Sylvia fights to get the child, Chow continues his dangerous career as a motorcycle racer. Sadly, as things seem to get better and old wounds are settled, Chow suffers a serious racing accident. For his performance, Chow won the Hong Kong Academy Award for Best Actor in 1990.

All for the Winner
(1992) Action Comedy   C-106m   Chinese with English Subtitles
Catalog #1060   Hong Kong   Retail: $39.99
Dir: Yuen Kwan   Prod: Lau Chun Wai   Dist: Tai Seng Video
Stephen Chow, Ng Man Tat, Cheung Man, Sandra Ng
[1/2]**
A film reminiscent of Ray Milliand "The Man with X-Ray Eyes", but with a humorous edge. Mao is a simple village guy who visits the wild city of Hong Kong. He meets up with his street-smart cousin who represents the city mouse to Mao's country mouse. It doesn't take long before Mao reveals his amazing gift to see through objects via X-ray vision. At first used for childish pranks, his cousin encourages Mao to capitalize on his powers at the gambling venues. Things

get complicated when two rival gang leaders both want Mao alive for themselves or dead for no one. Meanwhile, the naive Mao falls for a beautiful woman named Mau who is a double agent working for both gangs. The climax centers around a big gambling duo prepped in grand martial arts fashion, and similar to the flamboyance of a God of Gamblers film.

All Men Are Brothers - Blood of the Leopard (Man of the Marshes/108 Heroes/Blood Brothers)
(1992) Kung-Fu C-90m Chinese with English Subtitles VA
Catalog #1200 Hong Kong Retail: $39.99
Dir: Chu Jing PC: HK Film Entertainment Production Co. Dist: Tai Seng Video
Tony Leung Kar Fai General Lin Ching
Joey Wong Ching's wife
Tsui Kam Kong Monk Hu
Liang Jia Hui, Lin Wei, Wu Ma
[***1/2]

A traditional martial arts epic with a moving story and strong performances from the entire cast, especially Tsui Kam Kong as the rowdy "Flower" monk Hu. The film follows the life and exploits of General Lin Ching (Leung) and his tragic downfall. General Lin is the army's personal trainer and strategist. He is under the command of the Great General of the Sung Dynasty, the military governor of the province. Lin is a brave and loyal officer who proves himself in battle and is devoted to maintaining peace. Providing beauty and balance in his life, Joey Wong plays Lin's delicate and devout wife who remains at his side. One afternoon, Lin meets a rambunctious and arrogant monk who challenges him to a battle. The monk is unruly, enjoying wine and fighting over anything else. In reality, the loud-mouthed braggart is a rebel who fights against the oppressive government. Through humorous circumstances, the two men become close friends and then blood brothers. As the two men train with each other and share their philosophical views on life, they develop admiration and loyalty for each other. When the Great General's lecherous, sniveling son attempts to rape Lin's wife, the monk comes to her rescue. In turn, the General's son is rescued by the Great General's chief bodyguard Lu Chien, a martial arts expert of low birth. Lu dreams of rising in the ranks, but his humble parentage prevents him from reaching a high rank like his friend Lin. This creates deadly ambition and jealousy within him. The Great General orders Lu to arrest the rebel monk, but Lin intercedes and helps him escape. Furious of his defiance and fearful of Lin's loyalty, the Great General frames Lin and plans to execute him. The righteous Prime Minister stops the execution and reassigns Lin to a remote post. Lin accepts his belittling fate, believing in the justice of the government's legal system, and says good-bye to his wife and pupil. Once Lin leaves, the evil Great General and his newly promoted Lu Chien assassinate the Prime Minister and Lin's wife. When Lin escapes an assassination attempt on his own life, his monk friend (Tsui) asks him to join the bandits of Liang Mountain. He graciously refuses and accepts his low-ranking position at a border outpost where he is harshly treated. Tsui frustrated at Lin's undying loyalty and subservient nature denounces their brotherhood and leaves. The Great General sends Lu Chien and his troops to kill the noble Lin. The climax is on the exaggerated side with a reluctant Lin battling an entire army of soldiers. With a cry of defiance, Tsui appears and aids his brother. All Men are Brothers combines well-crafted martial arts scenes with a character-driven story about honor, loyalty, and commitment. The bond between Lin and Wong are potent, convincing, and well-acted. So are his bonds with his brother monk (Tsui) and the government which betrays him. Everything comes within conflict as Lin struggles with what he believes is legally right and what he knows is morally right. In one of Tsui Kam Kong's finest performance, he blends humor and heart into the famous Flower monk and nearly steals the film from the straight-laced Lin. Partly based on the classic story Shui Hu Chuan, the film will appeal to traditional martial arts fans.

All the Wrong Spies (I Love Fragrance of the Night)
(1983) Action Comedy   C-99m Chinese with English Subtitles
Catalog #0337   Hong Kong   Retail: $39.99
Dir: Teddy Robin Kwan   Prod: Tsui Hark   Dist: Tai Seng Video
George Lam, Brigitte Lin, Teddy Robin, Tsui Hark
[**]
Comedies can be the most difficult films to appeal to Americans, because of the snags involved in translation and the lack of timing which is lost from the original language. I was told by native speakers that the translation was very mediocre and that a number of the jokes did not carry over from the slang and rhymes in Cantonese. The slapstick and parody start off when a Jewish spy arrives in Hong Kong to pass on blueprints of a secret weapon being developed in Germany for World War II. For those not familiar with history, China fought against Japan and her axis cohorts. Before he can hand the blueprints to his American contact, he is murdered. A detective named Yoyo (Lam) and an underground resistance force attempts to get the blueprints to the Americans, but must do so under the pursuing gaze of the German and Japanese spies. Mistaken identity, wild chases, and general slapstick pursue all parties involved while the story parodies Casablanca. A film best avoided unless you truly enjoy Hong Kong comedies. Because of the cultural differences in humor and translation, most Asian comedies will only be available through Asian importers and difficult to find in mainstream rental establishments. Director/Producer Tsui Hark has a cameo as the Japanese ambassador.

Always On My Mind (Money Grabbing Husband and Wife)
(1993) Drama C-105m   Chinese with English Subtitles
Catalog #1493   Hong Kong   Retail: $79.98
Dir: Michael Hui   Scr: Jacob Cheung   Dist: Tai Seng Video
Michael Hui, Josephine Siao
[**1/2]
A story of a man and woman in love, following the good and bad times of their family's relationship. Television anchorman Yan Wai's (Hui) daughter needs a dowry, his son suffers from love-sickness, his wife has spells, his toddler wants to know where babies come from, and now he has intestinal cancer? It's family comedy Hong Kong style, but at least it has down-to-earth humor and real characters. Director Michael Hui added a happy ending to the moribund ending, so as to put a smile back on everyone's face. The film was shot with four different endings. The theatrical ending showed Michael Hui's character getting cured. Jacob Cheung's original script had him die on the operation table, but then the response from the test-screening was not well taken. They decided to give Hui's character a second chance. In another ending, Josephine Siao's character got cancer after Michael Hui's. And the forth one: they divorced. A charming film with likeable performances from Hui and Siao.

Angel Cop Vol. 1: Special Security Force
(1989) Japanime: Action   C-30m Dubbed   VA   Catalog # MGV 635317
Japan Retail: $9.95
Dir/Original Story: Ichiro Sakano Scr: Noboru Aikawa, Ichiro Sakano
Prod: Yasushi Nomura   DP: Hiroaki Umezawa   Music: Hiroshi Ogasawara
Character Design: Nobuteru Yuki Mech Design: Nobuyasu Moriki, Masaharu Tomoda
Animation Dir:Yasuomi Umeza   Art Dir: Hiroshi Sazaki   Planning: Naotaka Yoshida
PC: Soeishinsha   Dist: Manga Entertainment

Sharon Holm	Angel
John Hunter	Raiden
John Bull	Hacker
Barbara Barnes	Peace
Bob Sessions	Taki
Danny Flynn	Tachihara

[**1/2]

The Red May, a true-life group of leftist terrorists in Japan, are the main villains of the series. Due to Japan's growing capitalist power, the Red May organization has launched a massive terrorist campaign against the United States and Japan. Using hi-tech weaponry like a missile-launching Porsche, they destroy the American Embassy in Japan. To counter their activities, a special security force is established, granted extreme powers and a license to kill. Handsome Raiden teams up with the mysterious Angel, and together they track down the Red May terrorists. Raiden's first lead turns into a bloody dead end, and you can expect the film's tone to be mature and gritty. In no time, the terrorists wage war against the security forces while trying to escape the persistent Angel and Raiden. The violent story continues in future episodes.

The series was delayed for almost five years, due to its controversial nature, portrayal of real-life issues in Japan such as terrorism and murder, and a critical backlash to animated violence. One real headlining case involved a child serial murderer, Tsutomu Miyazaki, who happened to be a diehard anime fan. Though the American version has been slightly toned down, expect a lot of profane language and sudden scenes of extreme violence. The animation style is hard-edged and mature, and may appeal to hard-boiled cop anime fans. Don't expect much humor, but expect a high body count.

Six OAV volumes are available at the same running time and price.
Volume 2: The Disfigured City
Volume 3: The Death Warrant
Volume 4: Pain
Volume 5: Wrath of the Empire
Volume 6: Doomsday

Angel on Fire
(1995) Action Kung-Fu   C-81m Chinese with English Subtitles
Catalog #1924   Hong Kong   Retail: $39.99
Dir: Philip Ko
PC: My Way Film Company   Dist: Tai Seng Video
Cynthia Khan, Waise Lee Chi-Hung

[**]

Unless you've seen all the top action films in Hong Kong and Hollywood, it's best to avoid this quick flick completely. Sub-standard action fare strings along a number of routine chase scenes, fight scenes, and explosions which don't even compare to the Jackie Chan, Jet Li, and Bruce Lee films also on the market. The only highpoint in the entire film is Cynthia Khan who makes the film bearable for fans of the "Girls with Guns" genre. Her charm, fighting abilities, and witty repartee with the local cab driver does add a bit of charm. The film begins promisingly at a Shaolin Temple where monks practice and meditate in the early morning hours. Then a mysterious woman appears and enters the inner sanctum of the temple. Part of a criminal duo, May is a beautiful Eurasian ex-supermodel, and Ko Cheng is her muscular getaway driver. They steal a priceless artifact from the mainland Shaolin Temple and plan to sell it in Hong Kong. When the artifact is lost, Boss Tony believes May is double-crossing him and orders Ko to keep a close eye on his partner. The story then routes to Manila, Philippines (a popular location for its rural setting and lower production costs). Cynthia Khan is the Interpol officer from Hong Kong assigned to capture May. Meanwhile, female inspector Wong Li from Mainland China drives around the countryside looking for leads.

Literally, the entire second half of the film is one long chase/fight scene with no attempts to bring forth a logical conclusion or develop any character growth. Through coincidence, all the villains, May, Ko, Tony, and the heroes, Cynthia Khan, the cabbie, and Wong Li meet at various instances and engage in hasty confrontations only to be separated again to fight with different opponents. For example, an African-American kickboxer is brought into the film and ends up appearing at appropriate moments to fight each of the main characters, in turn, at various locations. The police are never unified and the over-extended chase becomes ill-planned and aimless. If more money had been spent on the script and less on the generic explosions perhaps the film would have utilized Khan's talents. If you enjoy all action and nothing else, be my guest but remember you've been warned.

Animated Classics of Japanese Literature
(1986) Japanime   C-52m (each volume)   Japanese with English Subtitles
Japan Retail: $29.95 (each volume)
PC: Nippon Animation Co., Ltd.   Dist: Central Park Media
[****]

Did you ever watch animated episodes of Tom Sawyer, 20,000 Leagues Under the Sea, or Romeo and Juliet on television? Translating classic literature into animation is a common practice to introduce well-known stories to children in a light-hearted manner. This classic approach is used to recreate some of the most beloved tales of Japanese literature. The series offers a fascinating glance at Japanese animation and literature for the price of one. The quality and style of animation varies, since each episode has their own creative team. Overall the series is excellent, but with any ensemble piece, some episodes you'll love, some you'll like, and some you won't. Those who are familiar with Japanese literature will be delighted to see old characters come alive on the screen. The series is a wonderful example of Japanese animation and offers a different approach to animation than what is commonly known in the United States as "anime".

The following is a list of available episodes:
Ansunaro Story/Koyasu Do   Catalog #CPM 1149

Botchan Parts 1 & 2	Catalog #CPM 1151
A Ghost Story/The Theater of Life	Catalog #CPM 1142
The Harp of Burma Parts 1 & 2	Catalog #CPM 1140
Incident in the Bedroom Suburb/Voice from Heaven	Catalog #CPM 1154
The Izu Dance/The Dancing Girl	Catalog #CPM 1139
A Roadside Stone Parts 1 & 2	Catalog #CPM 1152
Season of Sun/Student Days/Wild Chrysanthemum	Catalog #CPM 1141
Sanshiro the Judoist Parts 1,2 & 3	Catalog #CPM 1147
The Sound of Waves Parts 1 &2	Catalog #CPM 1146
Tale of Shunkin/Friendship	Catalog #CPM 1153
The Martyr/The Priest of Mt. Kouya	Catalog #CPM 1155
Walker in the Attic/Psychological Test/Red Room	Catalog #CPM 1150
Wandering Days/Growing Up	Catalog #CPM 1143
The Wind Rises/The Fruit of Olympus	Catalog #CPM 1148

Appleseed
(1988) Japanime: Scifi   **C-68m Dubbed   VA**
Catalog #800 633 887-3   Japan Retail: $19.95
Dir/Scr: Kazuyoshi Katayama
Ex Prod: Shinji Nakagawa, Hirohiko Sueyoshi, Yutaka Takahashi
Art Director: Hiroaki Ogura   Character Design & Animation Dir: Yumiko Horasawa
Mechanic Design: Kiyomi Tanaka   Music: Norimasa Yamanaka
Theme Song: "Crystal Celebration" by Masato, sung by Risa Yuuki
PC: Gainax   Dist: Manga Entertainment, Inc.
(based on original story by Masamune Shirow)

Larissa Murray	**Dunan**
Bill Roberts	**Bularios**
David Reynolds	**Karon**
Lorelei King	**Athena**
Vincent Marzello	**Sebastian**
Julia Brahms	**Hitomi**

[***]
After the massive devastation caused by World War III, the remnants of society construct the ultimate Utopia - Olympus City. The city is glorious, a true testament of human technology controlled by a massive super-computer called Gaia. The world is a hi-tech marvel where robots and humans live side by side, but not all humans are content to live under automated control. A group of human terrorists raid a high security facility and capture the necessary information for their cause. They decide to destroy Gaia and return control to human minds. Female officer Dunan Nats and cyborg Buliarous Hekatonecles, from the Extra Special Weapons and Tactics Squad, are sent to stop the terrorists from destroying Gaia. Ambiguous moral messages and dilemmas are presented from both viewpoints, asking the viewer to make the decision for him/herself as to who are the real heroes and villains. Common Japanese themes are explored, especially the fascination with robotics technology and its influence on the human spirit. Japan is the largest user of robotics technology and one of the most advanced nations in the world with a very homogeneous society. The film explores whether technology will ever replace the

common worker whose own expressionistic spirit lags at times, acting more like a part of the system than an individual. Does mankind need to be worried about being replaced by machines or has mankind become mechanical themselves in the process by trying to compete and emulate the efficiency of robots. The animation contains violence and explicit language.

Area 88 Act I: The Blue Skies of Betrayal
(1985) Japanime: Action   C-50m VA   Catalog #USM 1529/USM 1047
Dubbed/Japanese with English Subtitles   Japan Retail: $14.95/$29.95
Dir: Eikoh Toriumi Scr: Akiyoshi Sakai Original Story: Kaoru Shintani
Prod: Yuji Nunokawa   Ex Prod & Prod Designer: Ren Usami
Character Design & Chief Animator: Toshiyasu Okada Art Dir: Mitsuki Nakamura
Music: Ichiro Nitta DP: Juro Sugimura, Hitoshi Kaneko   Sound: Shigeharu Shiba
English Version - Ex. Prod: John O'Donnell   Prod Coordinator: Stephanine Shalofsky
Translation: Neil Nadelman PC: Project 88/King Record   Dist: U.S. Manga Corps
[***]

Thus begins the saga of young pilot Shin Kazama, a man without a purpose or goal in life who finds himself in the middle of a third-world country at war. While living in Japan, his malicious "friend" Kanzaki tricks him into joining the Asran Air Force as a mercenary. Ryoko, his girlfriend, does her best to find him while fighting off the aggressive advances of Kanzaki. Ryoko's father is head of Yamato Airlines which employs Kanzaki. Shin must face the facts of his new life, and his maturity into adulthood comes at a heavy price as he learns to kill for a living. He counts the days when he can return to Japan, but only three options are available. Serve three years, pay a 1.5 million dollar penalty, or shamefully desert his outfit. As the days drag, Shin realizes there is a fourth way...death. To truly enjoy the full scope of the series, I recommend watching all three episodes. Though the animation style has become dated, genre fans will appreciate the vintage 80's look and feel of the series.

Area 88 Act II: The Requirements of Wolves
(1986) Japanime: Action   C-57m VA   Catalog #USM 1048
Japanese with English Subtitles   Japan Retail: $29.95
Dir: Eikoh Toriumi   Original Story: Kaoru Shintani   Scr: Akiyoshi Sakai
Ex Prod & Prod Designer: Ren Usami   Prod: Yuji Nunokawa
Character Design & Chief Animator: Toshiyasu Okada Art Dir: Mitsuki Nakamura
Music: Ichiro Nitta DP: Juro Sugimura, Hitoshi Kaneko   Sound: Shigeharu Shiba
English Version - Ex. Prod: John O'Donnell   Prod Coordinator: Stephanine Shalofsky
Translation: Neil Nadelman PC: Project 88/King Record   Dist: U.S. Manga Corps
[***]

The mid-story brings together a major portion of the conflict and further develops the cast of characters. Shin contemplates desertion and sneaks out of his barracks one evening. On his way to the hanger, three escape killers stop him. No one ever deserts from Asran and anyone caught trying is eliminated. Luckily, Shin's squadron rescues him and he returns back to duty. In Japan, Kanzaki continues his secret takeover of Yamato Airlines and asks for Ryoko's hand in marriage. Kanzaki's character is fueled by his ambition and jealousy toward his childhood friend, Shin. Amazingly, we see the conflict and duality within Kanzaki as he contemplates his actions. Ryoko refuses his offer and attempts to fly to Asran and look for Shin. On board a flight captained by Kanzaki, two terrorist bombs under the airplane's wings are about to explode and kill everyone, including Ryoko and Prince Vashutal of Asran. Shin and his best friend fly to the rescue and disarm the explosives in an amazing display of aerial acrobatics. The pilots then return to Asran and prepare for battle against an elite mercenary air group. The aerial battle scenes are tense and dramatic, surpassing life-action air battles in its intensity and graphic nature. The story continues to develop character motives, aspirations, and desires. Dramatically, Shin is shot down by one of his own comrades who was secretly hired by Kanzaki. Shin refuses to die, ejects from his plane, and crosses the dessert to return back to Area 88.

Area 88 Act III: Burning Mirage
(1986) Japanime: Action   C-92m VA   Catalog #USM 1049
Japanese with English Subtitles   Japan Retail: $29.95
Dir: Eikoh Toriumi   Original Story: Kaoru Shintani   Scr: Akiyoshi Sakai
Ex Prod & Prod Designer: Ren Usami   Prod: Yuji Nunokawa
Character Design & Chief Animator: Toshiyasu Okada Art Dir: Mitsuki Nakamura
Music: Ichiro Nitta DP: Juro Sugimura, Hitoshi Kaneko   Sound: Shigeharu Shiba
English Version - Ex. Prod: John O'Donnell   Prod Coordinator: Stephanine Shalofsky
Translation: Neil Nadelman PC: Project 88/King Record   Dist: U.S. Manga Corps

Kaneto Shiozawa	**Shin Kazama**
Yoshihito Yasuhara	**Satoru Kanzaki**
Sakiko Tamagawa	**Ryoko Tsugumo**
Taro Shigaki	**Saki Vashutal**
Mikio Terashima	**Ryoko's father**
Ryoko Sakakibara	**Secretary Yasuda**
Kei Tomiyama	**Mick Simon**
Hideo Nakamura	**Go Mutsuki**

[***]
The third film in a popular series which has seen life in manga/comics and animation. This time out Shin Kazama is in his final days as a mercenary pilot for Asran, a fictional country at war. The country is involved in a civil war with two opposing factions vying for control. One is the rightful heir and the other is the heir's uncle. Pilots from all over the world are recruited to fly dangerous sorties against the enemy and must commit to a standard amount of service. They are responsible for their planes and any damage repairs or fuel consumption must be paid from their own pocket. During a mission, one of the Area 88 pilots is injured and blinded. He begins to panic and fires wildly at his own comrades. Shin has no choice but to shoot down his own comrade. He is not affected by the death and begins to question his own humanity. A new hotshot pilot in the barracks taunts Shin and becomes a constant reminder of his brutality. Commander/Prince Vashutal reveals that he is fighting against his own father and believes his uncle's forces can no longer stop his father's advances. Meanwhile, Ryoko's father loses control of Yamato Airlines to Kanzaki, so she plans to sell her shares of the company and use the money to bring back Shin. The story follows the various characters and addresses a number of issues about warfare. Eventually Shin is released from active duty, but finds it difficult to live in a society of civilians. He departs back for Asran, leaving behind his girlfriend, and joins Area 88's fighter squadron for their last sortie. The film includes some very exciting aerial dog fights and a

daring operation where the jets must fly through a perilous ravine. The conclusion is a noble end to the series and worth watching. The animation style is older, but still clean and crisp. An entertaining film with some interesting moments that will appeal to anime fans.

Armour of the Gods, The - See Operation Condor

Art of Fighting
(1993) Japanime: Action   C-46m Dubbed   Catalog #USM 1493
Japan Retail: $19.99
Dir: Hiroshi Fukutomi   Scr: Nobuaki Kishima   Original Story: Ryuko No Ken
Prod: Yoshiro Kataoka (NAS), Kenji Shimizu (Fuji TV)
DP: Seiichi Morishita   Music Dir: Akira Konishi   Music:SNK Sound Team
Character Design/General Design Dir: Kazunori Iwakura
Dramatization: Yoshikata Nitta, Yorinobu Habu, Eiichi Sato, Naoyuki Kuzuya
English Version - Ex. Prod: John O'Donnell   Prod: Stephanie Shalofsky
Dubbing Manager: Peter Bavaro   Dubbing Supervisor: Anthony Salerno
PC: Fuji TV, NAS   Dist: U.S. Manga Corps
Alden Crews   Ryo
Nick Sullivan   Robert
Veronica Taylor   Yuri
Sharon Becker   King
Carter Cathcart   Lt. Toudou
Cliff Lazenby   Mr. Big
Eric Stuart   Jack/John
[***]
Recently released on video from Central Park Media, Art of Fighting is a martial arts action film in the vein of Fatal Fury and Street Fighter. Instead of a rogues gallery of fighters to befuddle the plot, the story focuses on two main characters. Ryo and Robert come from different walks of life, but are friends bonded by their mutual respect and knowledge of martial arts. They are both masters, but definitely young, reckless, and cocky. One day, Ryo is searching for a lost cat so he can collect the reward money and pay off his bills. While outside on a ledge, he drops into the apartment of a stranger. His friend Robert joins him in the apartment, but suddenly the owner rushes in chased by some killers. They become entangled in a criminal organization that kills the man. The boss, Mr. Big, wants the diamonds and kidnaps Ryo's sister Yuri. Mr. Big has a handful of top-notch fighters, including the beautiful King who flirts and fights with the debonair Robert. Retracing their steps, the duo discover the diamond hidden away in ice cubes and deliver it in exchange for Yuri. All hell breaks loose and the two fighters manage to capture Mr. Big and put an end to his reign.
The animation technique is familiar and standard, but the dialogue between the characters are humorous and the pace of the story is quick and exciting. If you enjoy fighting films without the gratuitous violence and nudity, Art of Fighting is a pleasant alternative.

Ashes of Time   (East Evil West Poison)
(1994) Kung-Fu   C-101m   Chinese with English Subtitles   Catalog #SEL0544
Hong Kong   Retail: $39.99

Dir/Scr: Wong Kar Wai   Prod: Tsai Mu-Ho   Ex. Prod: Chan Pui Wah
DP: Christopher Doyle   Music: Franky Chan, Roel A. Garcia
Chief Prod Manager: Chan Puh-Mah   Associate Prod: Shu Mei
Prod Supervisor: Norman Lan, Tsui Siu-Ming, Jacky Fang
Art Dir: William Chang   Assistant Art Dir: AlfredYau   MAD: Sammo Hung
Dist: Tai Seng Video
Leslie Cheung   Ouyang Feng
Tony Leung Kar Fai Huang Yaoshi
Brigitte Lin Ching Hsia   Murong Yin/Murong Yang
Jacky Cheung, Maggie Cheung, Carina Lau, Tony Leung Chiu Wai, Charlie Young Choi
Nei, Bai U, Su Tak Fu
[***]

One thing can be said about Wong Kar-Wai...he sure has style. Ashes of Time is a narrative tale about a group of men who live and die by the sword, featuring Hong Kong's biggest stars. They are swordsmen, hired for duties when the price is right. Leslie Cheung portrays the main swordsmen who has now become an agent (Ouyang Feng), finding jobs for other swordsmen. The story takes place mostly in the outskirts of a desert village with constant voice-over narration by Ouyang. Each warrior's story has very little to do with the previous and the tales have a dreamlike quality with no strong conventional theme or motivation. The most dominant tale is the first dealing with Huang Yaoshi, a master swordsman who drinks a magic wine to forget his violent past. Brigitte Lin who strangely became popular playing androgynous roles appears as a sword-wielding warrior with an extremely volatile personality. She plays two roles which may actually be one character. The male version is Murong Yang and the female is Murong Yin (word play on the Chinese Yin and Yang philosophy of positive/male versus negative/female). Huang promised Yang that he would marry his sister Yin, but then reneges which starts a chain of bizarre events. The second tale is brief and introduces a woman who uses eggs and a donkey as payment in search of an assassin to kill the soldiers who killed her brother. The next story has one of the more appealing characters. Hong Qi is a shoeless swordsman in search of work. Ouyang tells him a swordsman with shoes gets more respect/money than a shoeless one. Hong is also torn between traveling the dangerous roads alone or allowing his dedicated wife to journey with him. Eventually the story returns to Huang Yaoshi and his new-found friendship with Ouyang's estranged wife.

Overall, Ashes of Time is a valid attempt in transcending the boundaries of traditional kung-fu films from Hong Kong studios. Stylistically, the film rates high above the average martial arts films and is ambitious in its allegorical treatment of swordsmen and their duties in life. Director Wong uses a variety of camera speeds and angles to capture his battle scenes from unique perspectives. His shot composition is well-established and scenes of the vast desert and horizon capture a desolate feeling of isolation and serenity. A lyrical ballad rather than a straight-out action film is Wong's contribution to Asian martial arts cinema.

Astro Boy Vol. 1
(1963) Japanime   B&W-50m   Dubbed   Catalog #RS 10010   Japan
Retail: $19.95 (each episode)
Dir/Prod/Created: Osamu Tezuka English Adaptation: Fred Ladd
PC: Mushi Productions/ Video Promotions, Inc. Dist: The Right Stuff

[**1/2]
Based on one of the original animated series to come out of Japan and to find a loyal audience of American viewers, Astro Boy can be viewed on two levels. The first and most obvious is from a classic historical level. The animation style is crude and primitive by today's standards, but represents a unique chapter in Japanese animation. Watching Astro Boy is studying history and art, examining the forefathers of today's Japanese artists who were influenced by such works. Not unlike watching a classic Max Fleischer or Walt Disney reel, Astro Boy is Japan's answer to classic Betty Boop, Popeye, or Mickey Mouse. The second level is to view the animated piece for its own value. Though the story still retains its merit even today, most young anime fans or casual viewers will probably be distracted by the crude black and white animation. Since the genre has been imitated and reinvented in many forms, Astro Boy loses some of its freshness, creativity, and drama. The series is only recommended for fans of the anime genre who are interested in a historical perspective. The first few episodes deal with Astro Boy's creation and his emergence into a superhero. The story is quite mature for an early animated piece and intriguing as it deals with Astro Boy's birth, rejection, and transition into a superhero. Pinocchio parallelism are an obvious point of inspiration, but with a much darker tone.

Atragon   (Kaitei Gunkan)
(1964) Monster   **C-88m Dubbed**   **Japan Retail: $9.95**
Dir: Inoshiro Honda   **Scr: Shinichi Sekizawa**
Prod: Tomoyuki Tanaka   **DP: Hajime Koizumi Sp. Fx: Eiji Tsuburaya**
PC: Toho Studios
Tadao Takashima, Yu Fujiki, Yoko Fujiyama, Hiroshi Koizumi, Jun Tazaki, Ken Uehara, Kenji Sahara, Tetsuko Kobayashi
[**]
Fans of Jules Verne's 20,000 Leagues Under the Sea will enjoy this fanciful tale of a superpowered submarine that saves the world. An underwater race is fed up with the surface dwellers of Earth. They release giant creatures to wreck havoc on the surface of Japan. Only the crew of the powerful sub called the Atragon can save the world. With a top-notch crew and a wicked-looking submarine, the Atragon battles undersea monsters and defeats the ocean empire. There is also an animated series which takes the art-form to a different level, Super Atragon. This film delighted me as a child with the model ships and monster, but is below par in comparison to the Godzilla films.

Avenging Eagles
(1981) Kung-Fu   **C-93m Dubbed**   **Hong Kong   Retail: $19.99**
Dir: Sun Chung   **Prod: Mona Fong**   **Ex. Prod: Run Run Shaw**
PC: Shaw Brothers
Ti Lung, Alexander Fu Sheng, Ku Feng, Wang Lung Wei
[***1/2]
An excellent smorgasbord of fighting and exotic weapons grace this fast-paced classic tale of love and betrayal. Alexander Fu Sheng, before his car accident, was the upcoming super-star, a James Dean of the martial arts who could replace the vacuum created by the death of Bruce Lee. Venerable actor Ti Lung (still acting today) plays the lead role with stoic heroism and strength, continuing his brilliant career at Shaw Brothers. Though some of the weapons like the hoop and

ball may seem fanciful, the heart of the film is its story of one man's struggle against a clan he once called his family.

An evil martial arts master (Ku Feng) has created a powerful clan of criminals known as the Eagle Clan. Children are chosen from a young age and trained rigorously in martial arts, theft, and other criminals skills. Those who survive become members of the clan, those who don't die. A dozen children grow up to be warriors and specialize in different weapons. Ti Lung is a master of the three-sectional staff and an elder member of the evil Eagle Clan of bandits. During a heist Lung is injured and separated from his clan. He is brought back to health by a beautiful woman and her kind-hearted father. Lung returns to his clan, hoping to retire and marry the woman, but their next assignment is to assassinate an ex-official who had placed Ku Feng in prison. The Eagle Clan arrives at the house and guess who's there...the beautiful daughter and her father. Lung is confronted with a serious decision and desperately tries to protect the family while pleading with his clansmen not to attack. Sadly, fate intervenes and the death of Lung's beloved causes him to lash out against the Eagle Clan. Told through flashback, Lung reveals all this to a government official in disguise, Fu Sheng, who befriends Lung, but secretly vows to kill Lung for murdering his wife. The two team up and battle the remaining Clan members who are broken into three groups and attack at different times. Similar to the best westerns, brilliant fight scenes are staged in the woods, on roofs, and insides buildings with drama and intensity. Eventually Lung is tired of running and returns to face his old master. The one-armed twins try to stop Lung and Fu Sheng, but both men are fighting for the women they loved and are unstoppable. In a fantastic battle, the two heroes take on the master and after the victory must finally face each other. A great story, charismatic performances from Shaw's best, and top-notch martial arts choreography make this a definite winner. It is rare when martial arts heroes are given ample screen time to develop their characters and provide strong reasons for why they are so driven by anger and vengeance.

Avenging Quartet
(1992) Action C-96m Chinese with English Subtitles
Catalog #1449   Hong Kong   Retail: $39.99
Dir: Siu Wing   Prod: Chan Fai Ling
Dist: Tai Seng Video
Cynthia Khan, Moon Lee, Yukari Oshima, Michiko Nishiwaki, Waise Lee, Chin Ka Lok, James Ha
[**]
In the era of political correctness, women over the age of eighteen prefer not to be called girls. In Asia, the term is commonly used and films often highlight heroines who are young looking and often act very childish. At first it may seem demeaning, but Asian heroines are much better portrayed than their western counterpart. Asian women "Girls" can fight just as well as men and sometimes better, and Asian cinema isn't afraid to see women get their share of kicks, bruises, and deaths. A popular genre of films is the "Girls with Guns" genre, a series of action films in which the principle heroes and villains are women. They don't hold back, using guns, martial arts, and explosives to win. This time out, the popular gang of four are back in another film. As usual, the Japanese girls (Oshima and Nishiwaki) are the villains who plan to steal a valuable painting which contains a crucial secret. On the good side is Cynthia Khan, a beautiful Chinese police officer who joins forces with Moon Lee, a street-smart Hong Kong girl. They both protect

Waise Lee's painting, but complications arise when the two heroines fall in love with the painting's owner who is secretly a fugitive from mainland China. Cynthia's past also comes out when it is revealed she left China to come to Hong Kong to seek her past lover, Waise. Don't fret, romantic issues take a back seat to the action and mayhem when the girls battle each other. The film's plotting is thin and the film's pacing is similar to generic American action films by Van Damme, Cynthia Rothrock, and Don "Dragon" Wilson. Tread cautiously when checking out the "Girls with Guns" genre, since the appeal is based on the female leads and the level of action rather than more "serious" filmmaking issues.

-B-

Babel II, Part 1: The Awakening
(1992) C-30m Dubbed   Catalog # SPV 91003 Japan Retail: $9.95
Dir: Yoshihisa Matsumoto   Scr: Bin Namiki   Music: David Tolley
English Version - Dir/Prod: Carl Macek   Scr: Steve Kramer
PC: Sohbi Kikaku Co., Ltd. Dist: Streanline Pictures/Orion Home Video
(created by Mitsutero Yokoyama)
[1/2]**

Babel will appeal to fans of the supernatural who enjoy psychic battles and mythical creatures in modern settings. Though when watched in parts, the story seems incomplete so I recommend the Perfect Collection at $19.95. The story deals with a secret organization of psychics who plan to take control of the world. Caught in the middle of this heated psychic battle is a young high school student named Koichi. He is disturbed by strange voices and bizarre images, and unknowingly holds the key to vast psychic powers. While riding his bike home, he witnesses a dramatic battle between a U.N. Agent and a super-powerful criminal. The criminal is transporting a van of organic body parts for experiments in creating cyber-organic soldiers. When the U.N. Agent corners the criminal, he explodes in a ball of flame. Koichi continues to be disturbed by the strange voice which he discovers are from a pretty pink-haired woman with psychic powers. She is intrigued by him and purposely drops her pendant. He tracks her down and is confronted by a group of psychic assassins. He escapes their first attack and in the episode's climax unleashes the hidden power within himself. The villains look on in horror as Koichi (Babel) unleashes the power of ancient, mythical creatures.

Babel II, Part 2: First Blood (1992)   C-30m Catalog # SPV 91053 Retail: $9.95
Now that Babel has left behind his family and life, he is destined to journey to a mystical desert tower (The Tower of Babel). Joined by three powerful creatures: a dragon, a black panther, and a giant. If you enjoyed the first volume, the rest of the series will be as equally as appealing.
Babel II, Part 3: Crossroads (1992)   C-30m Catalog # SPV 91103 Retail: $9.95
Babel's journey continues around the world. This time he goes to New York City and battles Juju in a decaying neighborhood.
Babel II, Part 4: Final Conflict (1992) C-30m   Catalog # SPV 91143 Retail: $9.95
The final episode pits Babel against the deadliest of espers. He is caught in a maelstrom of battles for the fate of the world.

Babel II Perfect Collection: Parts 1-4
(1996) C-120 Dubbed   Catalog # SPV 91333 Japan Retail: $19.95

Dir: Yoshihisa Matsumoto Scr: Bin Namiki   Music: David Tolley
English Version - Dir/Prod: Carl Macek Scr: Steve Kramer
PC: Sohbi Kikaku Co., Ltd. Dist: Streanline Pictures/Orion Home Video
(created by Mitsutero Yokoyama)
[***]
Though separated into four different volumes (a popular marketing choice for OAVs), Babel is one story rather than a series of episodes. The Collector's sets includes the entire series and when watched in one sitting will have a stronger sense of continuity and character development. Many OAVs feel like a complete film when the episodes are watched in order. Based on the discounted price and seen as one program, Babel II Perfect Collection makes a stronger impression (higher rating) than watched on an individual basis. Basically you'll encounter three types of anime videos: feature-length (complete story in one film), episodic (an enclosed story, but with no major developments), and multi-part OAV's (segmented parts which tell a complete story). The latter form can truly be appreciated when seen in its entirety.

Bandit Queen
(1995) Historical Drama   C-119m   Indian with English Subtitles   VA
Catalog #15083   India Retail: $39.95
Dir: Shekhar Kapur   Scr: Mala Sen   Prod: Sundeep S. Bedi
Dist: Evergreen Entertainment
Seema Biswas Phoolan Devi
Nirmal Pandey   Vikram Mallah
Manoj Bajpai   Man Singh
Rajesh Vivek   Mustaquim
Raghuvir Yadav   Madho
Govind Namdeo   Sriram
Saurabh Shukla   Kailash
Aditya Srivastava   Puttilal
Sunita Bhatt   Young Phoolan
[***]
The setting of Bandit Queen may be northern India, but the story is reminiscent of many Chinese historical dramas. The opening passage from a religious scripture quotes that women are on the same level as animals and low-caste beggars and should be treated as such. Phoolan Devi is the Bandit Queen, a true-life bandit who waged a private war against the upper class of India. The film does not concentrate on her Bonnie & Clyde antics with her lover/bandit, but studies her entire life from a poor, uneducated child to an abused woman in a harsh male/caste-dominated society. At a very tender childhood age, she is pre-arranged to marry a man twice her age. Her parents are poor and already have a son and daughter, so they trade Phoolan for a farm animal and a broken down bicycle. Phoolan is youthfully naive and travels with her husband to his household (as is the custom with Asian pre-arranged marriages). She is chided by children for being married to an older man and insulted by older women who criticize her for being too young and a low-caste member. When her husband makes sexual advances, she escapes to live with her family again. Many years past and she is now a young women, youthful and pretty in a natural way. A member of the ruling elite caste, Thakur, makes an advance on her. She refuses and is almost raped. The Thakur then accuses her of being a trollop and forcing his way onto

him to gain a better advantage in the community. She is beaten and cast out of the village. From there on her life gets worse and one wonders how women in India have managed to endure so much for so long. Her destiny alters when she is saved by a charismatic bandit who falls in love with her. One day, he saves her from the grotesque bandit leader who tries to rape her. Phoolan's lover murders the leader and takes over the bandit group. When the main leader of the bandits discovers the treachery, he orders them both killed. They go into hiding and share some gentle moments together on borrowed time. Sadly, he is murdered and Phoolan is raped again. Rape plays a strong factor in explaining her emotional fear and hatred toward men. She sides with another bandit leader who grants her protection and supplies. She begins a successful campaign with a loyal group of men. The film may dissuade viewers from sympathizing with Phoolan's cause, since her actions are as cruel and selfish as the criminals she despised. When her antics against the Thakurs become too vengeful and focused, her faithful bandits are hunted down and killed by government troops. She eventually surrenders to the authorities and goes to prison. Her life can hardly be called inspirational, since no one would want to endure so much bloodshed, hatred, and pain in a single lifetime. Instead the film offers a disturbing and fascinating glance into another culture in a foreign world far different from our own. Based on Indian history, we realize that truth is much harsher than fiction. Some films leave an impression through the beauty of filmmaking, others leave an impression through its shocking revelation of real events. Either way, the images are not easily forgotten and a sliver of humanity becomes a precious jewel in Phoolan's harsh world. Phoolan eventually was released from prison and entered politics, securing herself a political office and the support of many of the poor women and men she represented during her bandit years. A remarkable story of survival at any cost.

Bare-Footed Kid, The   **(Bare Footed Monk/Young Hero)**
(1993) Kung-Fu   **C-90m Chinese with English Subtitles**
Hong Kong   **Retail: $39.95**
Dir: Johnny To
Ti Lung, Maggie Cheung, Aaron Kwok, Ng Sin Lin, Kent Tsui Kam Kong
[***1/2]
Many times in American action films, the stunts and special effects overshadow the characters and plot. If given enough explosions and dead bodies, producers hope audiences will forget a weak story and poor acting. This happens too often in kung-fu movies where the plot is a poor excuse to string along a number of fight scenes. What sets The Bare-Footed Kid apart from many other martial arts films is the focus on the characters and their interaction with each other. The film has a dramatic sense where the martial arts plays a part of the film, but never overshadows or undermines the characters' persona.
In what can simply be called a beautiful period-piece, a young bare-footed beggar (Aaron Kwok) enters town in search of his recently deceased father's friend. A kindly woman (Maggie Cheung in a mature role) takes pity on him and offers him some food. He discovers his father's friend, played with noble stature by veteran actor Ti Lung, who works at a local textile/dye mill run by Cheung. Her foreman is Lung and they allow Kwok to work and live at the mill. Problems arise when a powerful merchant and crime boss decides to get rid of Cheung's mill. They have a number of confrontations over different situations, but Lung and Kwok easily dispatch the villains. Kwok decides to go one step further and attacks the merchant's home. Angered by the excess violence, Lung forces Kwok to leave the mill. Kwok doesn't comprehend Lung's hostility

and bitterly leaves the mill. His need for work leads him to enter a martial arts match and then to work as a fighter who is secretly hired by the evil merchant. Meanwhile, the lovely and energetic Cheung is in love with Ti Lung, but their relationship is subtle and gentle. They maintain a respectable distance in public but secretly desire each other deeply. Gratuitous love scenes are not necessary when a single touch of the hand can express as much love and desire between two people. Ti Lung's refusal to fight is met with treachery and Kwok risks his own life to save his father's friend. The martial arts scenes appear periodically and are well-choreographed, avoiding the farcical-flying style which has become very popular. The fights are quick and exciting with only the final battle delving into a bloody bath. Aaron Kwok plays his character with charm, but the standouts are the elegant Maggie Cheung and Ti Lung, two performers who only get better with age and time.

Barefoot Gen
(1983) Japanime: Drama   C-85m Dubbed   VA
Catalog # SPV 91423   Japan   Retail: $29.95
Dir: Mamoru Shinzaki   Scr/Prod: Keiji Nakazawa
Prod: Takanori Yoshimoto, Yasuteru Iwase   DP: Kinichi Ishikawa
Music: Kentaro Hada   Art Director: Kazuo Oga
Character Design & Dir of Drawing: Kazuo Tomisawa
Dist: Orion Home Video and Streamline Pictures
English Voices: Catherine Battistone, Brianne Siddal, Kurk Thornton, Wendee Lee, Mike Reynolds, Iona Morris, Barbara Goodson, Dan Woren, Joyce Kurtz
[*1/2]**
An endearing tale of a family's life before, during, and after the atomic bomb fell on Hiroshima, Japan in August, 1945. Though animated, the reality of the family's situation in war-torn Japan will draw you into the story with amazing depth, compassion, and reality. Be warned, the scenes of the atomic bomb and the aftermath are very vivid and grisly, not for young children. The main character is a young boy named Gen who lives with his healthy family. The household consists of his father, his pregnant mother, an older sister, and a kid brother. During the closing days of World War II, Hiroshima's civilians are oblivious to the atomic bomb and the desperate state of their defeated nation. Ironically, Hiroshima was of little military importance and not frequented by bombing raids, so when the atomic bomb was dropped without warning the civilian casualty were ill-prepared to handle the aftermath. The family struggles from day to day, hoping to survive until the end of the war. Rations are low and the economy is in a dreadful state. The horrible fact is that Hiroshima is relatively unscathed by bombing raids and air strikes, so the civilians were lulled into a false state of comfort. The civilians expect their city to be spared and try their best to carry on a normal life. We follow Gen and his little brother, like typical children, they constantly fight and get in trouble, especially when they steal a beautiful carp for their pregnant mother who is undernourished. Tender and tragic moments develop between parents and children, both sacrificing their own food and comfort for the other. Then on that fateful day, August 6, 1945, the United States airplane Enola Gay drops an atomic bomb on Hiroshima. The details and visual imagery of the film are horrifying and one hopes nothing like this will ever happen again in history. Tragic loss and great suffering befall Gen and his family, but he manages to survive the aftermath. The film's antiwar tone becomes a dominant thematic force and drives the rest of the story. Many of the following scenes are incredibly moving and

disturbing, filled with visual images almost impossible to imagine in this day and age. Keep in mind that the lingering effects of nuclear radiation, the horrible fires, and panicked confusion actually killed thousands more (men, women, and children) following the bomb's initial death toll which eventually climbed to 140,000 dead by December 1945. Gen and his remaining family members struggle to survive, meeting fellow survivors and trying to comprehend the situation that befell their lovely Hiroshima. Slowly, hope returns and blossoms after a long trail of deaths and utter futility. Also look for a 90-minute OAV sequel (1986).

Battle Angel
(1993) Japanime: Scifi   C-70m Dubbed/Japanese with English Subtitles
VA   Catalog # ADV BA/001D   Japan Retail: $19.95
Dir: Hiroshi Fukutomi   Scr: Akinori Endo   Created: Kishiro Yukito
Supervisor: Taro Rin   Character Design: Nobuteru Yuki
PC: KSS Inc./MOVIC   Dist: A.D. Vision
[***]

The future is made up of two distinct societies, the have's and the have-not's. The have's carry a mark on their forehead and live in a majestic city called Zalem. The city is a giant floating metropolis that hovers over the Earth and is connected to the ground by large metallic supports. At the underbelly of Zalem, a large aperture drops the refuse onto the citizens below who live in a mecca of waste, crime, and hopelessness. For Star Trek fans, the setting is similar to "The Cloudminders".

One day while searching the discarded refuse from Zalem, a tall lanky man finds a cyborg (robotic humanoid with a combination of organic and inorganic materials). Doctor Ido discovers the young female cyborg's brain is still active and constructs a new body for her. The raven-haired beauty does not remember her past identity, so she is named Gally, a pint-sized dynamo filled with life and passion. She lives with Doctor Ido and falls in love with a local boy named Yugo. Ido is a kind, intelligent man with a soft-spoken demeanor. In a world where cybernetic implants are common, he helps the poor with his brilliant knowledge of medicine and cyber technology. The people on the ground are like slaves who struggle to live and produce resources that are then shipped to the factory which is then processed and sent to Zalem. Yugo dreams of living in Zalem and makes a deal with a mob boss for 10 million credits. Crime runs rampant as people strive to become rich through illegal ventures and escape their station in life. With the absence of police, the factory offers bounties on criminals. When Gally discovers Ido is a Bounty Hunter-Warrior, she decides to follow in his footpath. Complications arise when Yugo has a bounty placed on his head for the lucrative crime of organ stealing. Meanwhile, a beautiful comrade of Ido's reappears and begs him to return to Zalem. She is also a cybernetic doctor, but was exiled from the city. She hopes that Ido's brilliance will help them both get back into the clouds. He refuses and she becomes a deadly rival. When Yugo's life is threatened by a vicious Bounty Hunter, Gally and Ido risk their own life to save Yugo. In a dazed state of mind, the wounded Yugo attempts to scale the gigantic cables which lead to Zalem and to escape his hellish existence once and for all.

Battle Angel incorporates the popular ingredients of Japanese animation into a tightly-woven story with an engaging group of characters. Only through the technical freedom of animation could a story like this be made. The creative minds bring to full life a new world that doesn't seem to resemble anything possible in present society. Mixing elements of futuristic architecture and hi-tech machinery with an archaic western civilization, the juxtaposition of two distinct societies is realistically captured. The story is well-thought out, dealing with numerous social issues like the horrendous crime of organ stealing and class distinction. The animation style is excellent, the action scenes are tightly choreographed, and the film's pace is quick and evenly distributed. Once again, the film is for mature teenagers and not recommended for young children. The film contains scenes of graphic violence and adult nature.

Battle Arena Toshinden
(1996) Japanime: Action   C-60m Dubbed
Catalog #USM 1475 Japan Retail: $19.95
Dir: Masami Ohbari Scr: Jiro Takayama, Masaharu Amiya
Prod: Taka Nagasawa, Nagateru Kato   Ex. Prod: Masaki Itsui, Yutaka Takahashi
Music: Kensuke Shiina
Character Design, Animation, Costume: Tsukasa Kotobuki, Masahiro Yamane
PC: Animate Film   Dist: U.S. Manga Corps

Ted Lewis	**Eiji**
Hideo Seaver	**Kayin**
Alfred DeButler	**Gaia**
Emma Rayda	**Uranus**
Chris Yates	**Chaos/Sho**
Debbie Rabbai	**Sofia**
Lisa Ortiz	**Ellis**
Billy Regan	**Duke**
Apollo Smile	**Tracy**
Carter Cathcart	**Fo**
Greg Wolfe	**Rungo**

[**1/2]

Fans of video games (Sony Playstation/Nintendo) are well aware that many new anime concepts are developed from popular game titles and vice versa. Battle Arena is a popular "fighting" video game title that was first released on the Playstation to critical and commercial success. After multiple game sequels were produced, it was only a matter of time before an animated film would be made. Eiji and his friends are being hunted down by a new menace who wishes to learn their fighting styles. One by one, our favorite characters appear and do battle with the mysterious Chaos, only to lose. Of course, no one dies and later they all band together. The entire gang travels to a huge corporate facility and battle against the villains. Characters appear from the original game and its sequel. The story is straightforward and the animation is consistent with the characters appearance and abilities in the video game. Basically a sufficient plot to string along a number of fight scenes that will appeal for its crisp animation and homage to the popular game.

Battle Royal High School: Legend of the True Demons
(1987) Japanime: Action   C-60m Dubbed   VA
Catalog # ANI ET096-006   Japan   Retail: $19.95
Dir/Scr: Ichiro Itano   Prod: Sakamoto Seiichi, Miyashita Kenji
Ex. Prod: Yamashita Tatsumi   Planning: Wada Yutaka, Ogata Hideo

Music: Sagisu Shiroo   Character Design& Animation Dir: Yuki Nobuteru
PC: Tokuma Japan Communications Co., Ltd.   Dist: AnimEigo
Michael Granberry Hyoodo Riki/Byoodo
G. Brian Realmercy Yuuki Toshihiro
Paul Sincoff   Zankan
Susan Grillo   Takayanagi Yooko
Kristen Graf   Koyama Megumi
Hadley Eure   Fairy Master
Pierre Brulator   Baba
Deann Korbutt   Sandy
Eric Palsley   Byoodo's Servant
Shelby Reynolds   Nakano
[**1/2]

High school can be a troublesome time for young teenagers, especially when inter-dimensional demons and futuristic police happen to drop by every now and then. Once again the popular anime format is revisited with high school students, fast-fighting action, and supernatural/scifi mix. A young teenager is chosen by a powerful spiritual entity to be his warrior on Earth. Byoodo, the leader of the dark world, possesses the body of his human counterpart Hyoodo Riki. He enters the human realm to hunt down and destroy the parasitic demons unleashed by the Fairy Master who has trapped Byoodo in a human body and the earthly realm.

Hovering above the planet, a space continuum starship detects a hyper-psycho kinetic wave in Tokyo. Enforcer Zankan beams down to the planet and keeps a close eye on everyone involved. On Earth, demon slayer Yuuki dispatches an evil fairy and then arrives at the high school. He's a master of the sword and experienced in dealing with demons. Thirty evil fairies search for human souls to possess. Yuuki is seduced by the Fairy Master and then launches an attack against Zankan and Byoodo/Hyoodo. Zankan fails, but Byoodo manages to defeat the evil Fairy Queen and return the course of time to before the events started. The animation is mature, macabre, and devilishly imaginative. Not for the faint of heart, but full of plenty of action: hand to hand, swords, and laser weapons.

Battle Skipper 1
(1995) Japanime: Scifi/Comedy   C-30m Dubbed
Catalog #USM 1504   Japan   Retail: $12.95
Dir: Takashi Watanabe   Scr: Hidemi Kamata Original Story: TOMY
Ex. Prod: Kantaro Tomiyama, Wako Higuchi   Music: Takeo Miratsu
Planning: Toshimichi Suzuki, Tkashi Konosu   Character   Design: Takashi Kobayashi
English Version - Ex. Prod: John O'Donnell   Prod: Stephanine Shalofsky
Prod Coordinator: Edward S. Whang   Translation/English Rewrite: Jay Parks, William Flanagan, Yuko Sato Post-Prod Supervisor: Michael Alben
Prod: ARTMIC   PC: TOMY/Victor Entertainment
Lisa Ortiz   Saori (Blonde Hair)
Elisa M. Wain   Shihoko   (Blue Hair)
Kira Burke   Kanami Izaki (Auburn Hair)
Tamara Farias   Sayaka Kitaoji   (Red/Pink Hair)

Karen Smith	Rie	(Greenish Black Hair)
Nicole D'Incecco	Reika	(Dark Brown Hair)
Paul McGrane	Todo	

[**1/2]

A light-hearted romp based on the popular format of anime girls (ie Sailor Moon). Cute girls with multicolored hair, saucer-shaped eyes, girlish uniforms, and big destructive robots. This film features all the ingredients with some really cute voice casting. Not for all tastes, the series is still fun for anime fans and younger children. The series starts at St. Ignacio High School for Women, where rivals Sayaka (President of the Debutante Club) and Reika (President of the Etiquette Club) address the student body. Best friends, Saori and Shihoko, decide to join the unpopular and understaffed Etiquette Club which comprises of two returning members. They pass a few tests and are allowed to enter the club, discovering that it's actually a front for a group of girls who combat crime in super-powered battlesuits. Not surprisingly, the wealthy Sayaka also has her own team of robots and decides to stop the Exters (actually pronounced Ex-Stars) from interfering with her plans. Sayaka's right-hand man Todo sends the evil robot team to rob a bank and lure the Ex-Stars into battle. The Ex-Stars, new and old, arrive on the scene and defeat the criminal robots just in time for the police to arrive.

Battle Skipper 2
(1995) Japanime: Scifi/Comedy   C-30m Dubbed
Catalog #USM 1505   Japan   Retail: $12.95
Dir: Takashi Watanabe   Scr: Hidemi Kamata Original Story: TOMY
Ex. Prod: Kantaro Tomiyama, Wako Higuchi   Music: Takeo Miratsu
Planning: Toshimichi Suzuki, Tkashi Konosu   Character   Design: Takashi Kobayashi
Prod: ARTMIC   PC: TOMY/Victor Entertainment
English Version - Ex. Prod: John O'Donnell   Prod: Stephanine Shalofsky
Prod Coordinator: Edward S. Whang   Translation/English Rewrite: Jay Parks, William Flanagan, Yuko Sato Post-Prod Supervisor: Michael Alben
[**1/2]

More action and mayhem continue in volume two. After the Ex-Stars proved their worth in battle, the new girls become official members of the Etiquette Club and learn the secrets of the club. The rivals at the Debutante club led by Sayaka decide to teach them a lesson and the hi-tech battles continue. Meanwhile, blonde-headed Saori meets the mysterious Brother Gilbert at school. He saves her life and she develops a crush on him, but must decide whether to follow her heart or remain loyal to the Ex-Stars. Appealing series of light-hearted action anime targeted around female characters.

Battle Skipper 3
(1995) Japanime: Scifi/Comedy   C-30m Dubbed   Catalog #USM 1506
Japan   Retail: $12.95
Dir: Takashi Watanabe   Scr: Hidemi Kamata Original Story: TOMY
Ex. Prod: Kantaro Tomiyama, Wako Higuchi   Music: Takeo Miratsu
Planning: Toshimichi Suzuki, Tkashi Konosu   Character   Design: Takashi Kobayashi

Prod: ARTMIC   PC: TOMY/Victor Entertainment
English Version - Ex. Prod: John O'Donnell   Prod: Stephanine Shalofsky
Prod Coordinator: Edward S. Whang   Translation/English Rewrite: Jay Parks, William
Flanagan, Yuko SatoPost-Prod Supervisor: Michael Alben
[**1/2]
The evil Sayaka, President of the Debutante Club, orders the kidnaping of Reiki in hopes of
luring the Ex-Stars into a rescue attempt and a trap. She then attempts to break into the Etiquette
Club's underground base and steal their technological secrets. Just in time, the Ex-Stars escape
and manage to suit up and battle their opponents. The series capitalizes on cute-style animation
and plenty of non-bloody action.

Best of the Best
(1996) Action C-m   Chinese with English Subtitles   Type II
Catalog #1120   Hong Kong   Retail: $39.99
Dir: Andrew Lau   Scr: Manfred Wong, Candy Cheng
Prod: Manfred Wong   Ex. Prod: Raymond Chow
DP: Andrew Lau   Editor/Post Prod Manager: Monico   Music: Lin Che Yeung
Prod Manager: Ellan Chang   Line Prod: Ivy Wong   Art Dir: Cyrus Ho
Assistant Dir: Yip Wai Man, Cheung Siu Kin   Costume Design: Li Pik Kwan
PC: BOB & Partners Company Ltd.   Dist: Tai Seng Video
Daniel Chan, Cheung Chi Lim, Karen Mok, Annie Wu, Amanda Lee, Roy Cheung,
Michael Tse, Jason Chu, Chan Miu Ying, Cho Wing Lim, Sammy Leung, Hang Yin, Benny
Lai
[***]
The Hong Kong Royal Police proudly graduates a new class of young and talented recruits. Two
new cadets are assigned to traffic patrol, but while on duty, one of the officers is brutally
murdered.   Those same killers, Vietnamese terrorists/refugees, dissatisfied with their
confinement in a Hong Kong internment camp, decide to stage a deadly attack against the police.
They ambush the SDU officers who suffer heavy casualties which cripple the elite police force.
In the aftermath, an elite group of officers are chosen and trained from the ranks to form a new
elite Special Defense Unit. They will be the best of the best in law enforcement. What follows
is a series of training scenes in which the men fight amongst each other, but bond during their
trials and tribulations. During one daring training mission, some of the men are injured and the
new unit is in danger of being disbanded. A number of melodramatic subplots focus on the
characters and why they joined the force, including two half-brothers who hate each other. The
story climaxes in a personal vendetta against the Vietnamese terrorists who take over the refugee
camp and capture hostages. The SDU break into the complex and wage an all-out war. The
officers put aside their differences and work as a team, rescuing the hostages and ending the
terrorist reign. Standard action fare with good production value and charismatic performances
from a cast of young actors. Plenty of gun-fighting and male-bonding scenes with some
interesting characters for fans who enjoy the ensemble/team action genre. Closing credits are
humorously laced with bloopers from the film.

Better Tomorrow, A
(1986) Action C-95m Chinese with English Subtitles   Catalog #0376

Hong Kong   Retail: $39.99
Dir: John Woo   Scr: John Woo, Chan Hing Kai, Leung Suk Wah
Prod: Tsui Hark, John WooDP: Wong Wing Hung   Editor: Kam Ma
Music: Joseph Koo   Dist: Tai Seng Video
Ti Lung   Ho
Leslie Cheung   Kit
Chow Yun Fat   Mark
Waise Lee   Shing
Emily Chu   Jackie
Yung Pao I
[***1/2]

An amazing film from action director John Woo which helped spawn a whole slew of imitators in the popular Triad/gangster genre. Though not as stylish and quick-paced as The Killer and some more recent films, the film's significance should not be understated. Woo definitely makes and breaks the mold, showing his talents for creating sympathetic gangsters within a framework of loyalty and honor, and his stylish use of slow motion, camera cuts, and ultra-fast action sequences. Many fans and critics (including Chow Yun Fat) think that this is John Woo's best. It helped put Woo and Chow on the map as the premiere action/gangster film team. The main characters are Chow Yun Fat and Ti Lung who are two hitman loyal to the mob. They've worked their way through the ranks and look forward to a promising career in crime. Woo's brilliant choice of using veteran actor Ti with Chow creates an instant bond and a passing of the mantle between the two stout characters. While in Taiwan, they plan to make a routine drop off of counterfeit money, but the assignment goes wrong and the police arrive. Ho and Kit sacrifice themselves to help Shing escape. Ho is arrested and the other two make it back to Hong Kong. Many years later, Ti Lung's Ho is released from prison and relegated to working in a taxi garage full of ex-convicts. Chow who escaped is crippled and works odd jobs on the street. The man they saved during the botched up job rises to power and eventually uses the men for his own purpose. Chow is determined to seek revenge, but Lung wants to stay out of trouble, especially since his younger brother has joined the Hong Kong police force and is met with suspicion by his superiors. Both men are drawn together through circumstances and loyalty, proving they still are the best at killing. Director Woo reinvents the martial arts film into a modern setting and uses automatic weapons instead of swords and spears in an incredibly exciting and bloody thriller. John Woo's gangster film is a true breakthrough genre-founding movie and establishes many of his trademark elements. John Woo followed up his classic with two more sequels. Though not of the same caliber, they may appeal to fans of the original or action crime films.

Better Tomorrow II, A
(1987) Action   C-100m   Chinese with English Subtitles   Catalog #0394
Hong Kong   Retail: $39.99
Dir: John Woo   Dist: Tai Seng Video
Chow Yun Fat   Ken (Mark's Twin)
Ti Lung   Ho
Leslie Cheung   Kit
Emily Chu   Jackie
Dean Shek   Lung

Shing Fui On
[***]
The rule of filmmaking: if your first film is a success, make a sequel. Don't worry about how good the film will be, since people will come to see it anyway. Woo's films have been accused of glorifying violence and popularizing Triad membership (similar to Top Gun's recruiting power for the Navy) and rumored to have received financing by members of the Triads.
Using the formula of more action, less substance, ABT2 delivers in the amount of bloodshed, action, and mayhem. If you cared more for the battle sequences than the drama from the first movie, you'll probably love the second film. As the story left off, Mark is dead and Ho is in jail, while his younger brother Kit and his wife Jackie are alive and well. Hoping to advance his career and erase his past, Kit works hard in the police force and goes undercover in Lung's organization by dating his daughter Peggy. In no time, all hell breaks loose and Lung is forced to flee to New York City, leaving his daughter under Kit's protection. Lung discovers Ken, Mark's twin brother (convenient, huh?) and the two men form a bond and return to Hong Kong. Lung discovers his daughter is dead and manages to get an early release from prison. All together, the four heroes will battle against the evil Ko. I won't give away the ending, but expect a massive battle with every Woo trick in the book and plenty of bodies.

Better Tomorrow III, A: Love And Death In Saigon
(1989) Action C-114m   Chinese with English Subtitles
Catalog #0782   Hong Kong   Retail: $39.99
Dir: Tsui Hark   Dist: Tai Seng Video
Chow Yun Fat, Anita Mui, Tony Leung Kar Fai, Saburo Tokito
[***]
The odds of Mark having another twin brother were too much of a stretch for even Hong Kong filmmakers, so doing what George Lucas will do with "Star Wars", we travel back in time to younger years when Mark Gor was still alive. Set in the 1970's, Mark travels back and forth between Hong Kong and Vietnam. In Saigon, Vietnam, Gor and his cousin (Leung) fall in love with the same woman (Mui). She's pretty, tough, resourceful, and a criminal. Scenes are established to allow the audience to see the development of Chow's character with his interaction with Mui, apparently his trainer in many ways. Chow learns how to his weapons and many of his trademark habits are picked up through his interaction with the deadly Mui. The two cousins hope to get their family out of war-torn Saigon, but violence erupts when Mui's boyfriend Ho, a hardened gangster, seeks out his revenge. He murders the uncle by sending a bomb to his garage. Meanwhile, Mui and Ho's dream for fortune are ruined when they become entangled with a Vietnamese warlord. Chow and Leung return to Vietnam to seek revenge. The action explodes, and finally the dying Mui helps Chow and Leung escape Vietnam and return safely to Hong Kong. The film's tone and action style differ from the first two films, mainly because John Woo did not direct the film. If you cared more for the drama than the action in the other films, you may enjoy the third and final installment.

Black Cat
(1991) Action C-91m Chinese with English Subtitles
Catalog #1050   Hong Kong   Retail: $39.99
Dir/Prod: Stephen Shin   Ex. Prod: Dickson Poon   Line Prod: Shan Tam, Sunny

Chan
PC: D & B Films Co., Ltd. Dist: Tai Seng Video
Jade Leung   Catherine
Simon Yam   Brian
Thomas Lam   Allen Yeung
[***]
French director Luc Besson made international waves with his stylish, brilliant action film "La Femme Nikita". The story was about a rebellious young punk who is ensconced by the government and transformed into a beautiful assassin. Jade Leung is the exciting new rising star in this Asian remake of "La Femme Nikita" mirroring the original in many respects, but falling short of the mark in other ways. A good performance debut by Jade Leung who portrays a vicious killer and a sensitive woman struggling to retain her humanity. Adds just enough new twists to the story to make it interesting, but the American locales seem out of place in an Asian film, especially with the already American-remake "Point of No Return", starring Brigitte Fonda. A foxy misfit (Jade Leung) is arrested for viciously attacking a truck driver, arrested, and executed by the U.S. Government. Secretly she is revived and conditioned to be a sleek, compact killing machine dressed in trademark sunglasses and mini-skirt. She is oblivious to feminine etiquette and the real world dynamics, and her only companion is Chinese-American agent Simon Yam, her superior, who takes her under his wing and risks his own career to transform her into the agency's best killer. Her code name is Black Cat, but to the civilized world she is Erica. She enters the real world under her new identity, but when the code name Catherine is given, she must follow out murderous assignments. One involves a brutal shootout at a wedding full of guests, including women and children. During her downtime, she meets and falls in love with a wildlife caretaker named Allen. Her relationship with him jeopardizes her career and Agent Yam confronts her. Even after her string of successful assassinations, she can not escape his control and must decide between Allen and Yam. Her decision is worth contemplating and the film is worth seeing for fans of the "Girls with Guns" genre.

Black Cat 2: The Assassination of President Yeltsin
(1992) Action C-90m   Chinese with English Subtitles
Catalog #1155   Hong Kong   Retail: $39.99
Dir: Stephen Shin   Prod: Stephen Shin, Dickson Poon
MAD: Tony Poon   Dist: Tai Seng Video
Jade Leung, Robin Shou
[**]
Mediocre sequel to the first film which reintroduces Jade Leung's Black Cat assassin Erica. Her memory is given a technical enhancement and her duty includes a protection assignment for Boris Yeltsin. Yes, the Russian President Yeltsin has plenty of enemies, so why not use an Asian assassin. The Anti-Yeltsin Organization will do anything to kill their target, including the use of a special radioactive enhancement drug. Jade and her CIA employer combine forces to track down the terrorist organization without taking down any more innocent bystanders. Plenty of locale shots are intercut with Jade when she heads to Moscow, battling would be assassins and protecting Yeltsin, a lookalike of course. The film doesn't capture the emotion, brutality, and depth of Leung's original character. The film has its share of action and chase scenes, but nothing delves into new realms of originality. Sure it's nice to see Leung back in action and fans

of "Girls with Guns" will always have a good time. If you loved the first film, you may enjoy seeing Jade rough and tough it again. Also starring Robin Shou, star of "Mortal Kombat".

Blackjack Vol. 1
(1993) Japanime   **C-50m Dubbed**   **Catalog #USM 1551**
Japan   **Retail: $19.99**
Dir: Osamu Dezaki   Scr: Osamu Dezaki, Kuniaki Yamashita
Original Story: Osamu Tezuka
Prod: Minoru Kubota, Sumio Udagawa
Ex. Prod: Yoshihiro Shimizu, Takayuki Matsutani
Music: Osamu Shoji Key Animator: Akio Shugino
Executive in Charge of North America Release: John O'Donnell
PC: Tezuka Production Co., Ltd.   Dist: U.S. Manga Corps
Voices: Sean Thornton, Julie Kliewer, Jackson Daniels, Tessa Ariel, Sean Darker, Gillian Gardner, Steve Bulen, Alfred Thor, Tiffany James, Sam Strong, Joe Romersa, Doug Stone
[***]
I've seen a lot of Japanese animation in the course of my lifetime and I was delightfully surprised that Blackjack offers a new twist on some familiar themes. Instead of relying on science fiction or supernatural elements to create a story, modern medicine is the villain and hero. Dr. Blackjack is a mysterious medical ronin who is a brilliant physician/surgeon, but not legally licensed to practice. He has a special hotline that sick patients can call only when other forms of medical treatment fail to help. A rich tycoon calls him and pleads for his help. Accompanied by a young female assistant, Blackjack arrives at the island mansion and begins a series of tests. Slowly, he discovers the cause is a rare disease which can kill the infected victim. The most bizarre side effect is the constant need to drink water to ease the pain. His situation is further complicated when it's revealed that the tycoon's wife is Blackjack's past lover. She is carrying on an affair with the tycoon's assistant, but doesn't desire the tycoon's death. The island's villagers fear the disease is contagious and in a mob-like rage (ala Frankenstein) attack the mansion. Battling against time, Blackjack explores the history of the disease so he can find a cure and stop the mob. A hero in the mold of Sherlock Holmes who uses deductive reasoning and learned intelligence to deal with his cases and save the day.

Blackjack Vol. 2
(1993) Japanime   **C-50m Dubbed**   **Catalog #USM 1552 Japan**
Retail: $19.99
Dir: Osamu Dezaki   Scr: Osamu Dezaki, Eto Mori   Original Story: Osamu Tezuka
Prod: Minoru Kubota, Sumio Udagawa   Ex.   Prod: Yoshihiro   Shimizu,   Takayuki Matsutani
Music: Osamu Shoji Key Animator: Akio Shugino
Executive in Charge of North America Release: John O'Donnell
PC: Tezuka Production Co., Ltd.   Dist: U.S. Manga Corps
[**1/2]
The second volume is interesting, but lacks the depth of characters from the first film and the life-threatening stakes are on a much smaller case. Also, Blackjack's sweet little sidekick appears only briefly in the story. Instead of a deadly disease, Dr. Blackjack must stop a drug

cartel from creating a new addictive concoction. The story begins with the phone call and Blackjack's response to a medical emergency. While journeying out in the snow, he becomes lost and stops his car to ask for directions. He comes across four attractive and flirtatious teenagers from a prestigious girls' boarding school. They give him directions, but one of the girls falls into the ice and severely injures her forehead. Lucky for her, the doctor is on the scene. Time passes, and by chance, the girl and the doctor meet again. She needs his help and expresses her love for him. He discovers that her friends mysteriously died and that her own life is in danger. She and her friends accidentally came across a rare flower, grown secretly in the mountains by a drug cartel. One prick of the flower can cause a powerful addiction, resulting in a loss of perception. The criminals try to silence Blackjack and the girl, but to no avail. The heroes manage to escape and reveal their discovery to the authorities. For continuing adventures of Blackjack, also check out volume three on video.
Blackjack Vol. 3 (1993) C-50m   Catalog #USM 1553   Retail: $19.99

Black Lizard
(1968) Crime C-90m Japanese with English Subtitles   VA
Catalog # CIV-9201 Japan Retail: $19.99
Dir: Kinji Fukasaku   Scr: Masashiga Narusawa   Stage Adaptation: Yukio Mishima
Subtitles: Cinetyp, Inc., Hollywood Subtitle Editor: H. Eisenman
PC: Shochiku Corp.   Dist: Cinevista, Inc.
Akihiro Maruyama, Isao Kimura, Junya Usami, Yukio Mishima
(based on a novel by Rampo Edogawa)
[**]
The Black Lizard is a master criminal intent on kidnaping Sanae, the daughter of the wealthy Japanese tycoon, Iwase. In exchange for her safe return, she demands the priceless Star of Egypt. On the case is Japan's number one detective, Akechi. Similar themes from Rampo's other works pop up throughout the film which runs like a Godzilla subplot without the cool monster. The film shows signs of extreme camp and a dated setting for more demanding modern viewers. The action is very minimal with more emphasis on dialogue-heavy self-realizations and romantic elements between Akechi and the Black Lizard who reveals signs of androgynous behavior. Released in America in 1991, Black Lizard is an interesting film since it captures a campy time period in Japan's cinematic culture, but its cult-like appeal leaves little to desire for mainstream viewers.
The Black Lizard owns a night club where she first meets Akechi. The sexual tension is evident, but she leaves with Jun Amamiya who soon ends up dead. Akechi is then hired by Iwase to protect his daughter Sanae. Kidnap threats are in the air and the Black Lizard plays her role like a master criminal from the Batman television series. The first attempt fails, but Sanae is kidnaped on the second attempt, using a cleverly disguised trunk-couch, while under the protection of Detective Matoba who appears dazed after he discovers his hands are missing. Her father pays the ransom, but Sanae is not returned. She is transported aboard a ship, only dressed in her nightgown for the rest of the duration of the film. We discover that she is not Sanae, but her identical double Yoko Sakurayana who falls in love with Jun Amamiya while imprisoned on Black Lizard's island base. Meanwhile, Akechi has switched places with the old hunchback Matsukichi. Akechi always gets his man or woman in this campy cult classic with some high-brow poetry to boot.

Black Magic M-66
(1987) Japanime: Scifi   C-60m Japanese with English Subtitles   VA
Catalog # USR-VD6   Japan Retail: $19.95
Dir/Scr: Masamune Shirow   Original Story: Masamune Shirow
Animation Dir: Takayuki Sawaura Mecha Design: Toru Yoshida
Character Design & Direction: Hiroyuki Kitakubo   Music: Yoshihiro Katayama
PC: Bandai Visual/Movic/Seishinsha   Dist: Manga Entertainment
[***]
Recommended for fans of robot animation. This slick, fast-paced film runs along the vein of the Terminator films and features some top-notch animation and a large amount of action. A government helicopter goes down in the rural outskirts of Tokyo. The army moves in and closes off the area to the public. A hot shot reporter and her cameraman decide the story is too hot to ignore and risk their careers by entering the quarantined area. What is discovered is that the government has developed a top secret project with robotic soldiers. The two elite killing machines, one male and one female, were lost in the helicopter's crash landing and became active. Armed with the latest in stealth and combat technology, they are nearly indestructible. It is up to the government to stop the machines. A road block manages to stop the male robot, but at a terrible cost of lives. The reporter is then caught and arrested. The female robot is still loose and makes its way toward the city. The Army calls the robot's designer who had chosen his own daughter as a simulated target. The reporter escapes and hooks up with the daughter and together they struggle to stay alive. Crazy battles and wild animation flavor the entertaining film.

Black Mask (1995)   Action C-102m   Chinese with English Subtitles   R   VA
Catalog# 10172   Hong Kong   Retail: $24.99
Dir/Scr: Daniel Lee   Prod: Tsui Hark   DP: Cheung Tung Leung
Editor: Cheung Ka Tai   Music: DJ Revolution
Presented by Charles Heung
Administrative Prod: Tiffany Chen   Associate Prod: Teddy Chen
MAD: Yuen Woo Ping
PC/Dist: Film Workshop/Win's Entertainment Ltd.   Dist: Artisan Home Entertainment
Jet Li   Tsui Chik "Black Mask"
Lau Ching Wan   Inspector Shek "Rock"
Karen Mok   Tracy
Francoise C.J. Yip   Yeuk-lan
Patrick Lung, Anthony Wong
[***]
In one of the latest Jet Li films, Li follows in the footstep of another great martial arts actor by donning a mask and fighting crime. The first was Bruce Lee as Kato in the Green Hornet series, but Li doesn't play second fiddle. Li goes solo as the Black Mask, a crime fighter who fits the mold between Darkman and Captain America, two screen and comic heroes who are altered in life by biochemical engineering. Li is an elite soldier who takes part in a chemical experiment whose participants are code-named 701. The squad is injected with chemicals directly into the spinal nerve which makes them impervious to pain or life-threatening injuries. On top of that,

they seem to possess incredible strength, agility, and speed. The soldiers are also trained in weaponry, stealth, and technology. Elite killing machines who soon become too hot to handle and feared by the government who created them. When the operation is canceled, all the test subjects are slated for elimination. Jet Li leads his unit in a daring escape from the covert government complex. He is separated from the rest of his unit and goes into hiding. Time passes, Jet Li is an innocuous introvert working at a library. He assumes his comrades are dead and doesn't expect much to happen in his quiet life. His co-workers wonder about his odd behavior, does he gamble, does he drink, is he gay? One of the female co-workers takes an interest in the bookish Jet Li, but life takes a deadly turn when Hong Kong's drug lords are killed one by one. Li's only friend is chess-playing Officer Shek who becomes involved in the brutal crime wars which pulls Li in to intervene and to save the life of his police friend. When Li discovers his old unit is behind the crime, he is torn between loyalty to his new friend and his old friends.

Though there is plenty of explosions and fights, the majority of scenes take place in darkened and bizarre areas to create a macabre mood along the lines of a dark tragedy like the Phantom of the Opera, even including an underground sewer scene. The heroism is subdued and Jet Li's costume consists of a black suit, a hat, and an eye mask that looks like it was carved off a storm drain. Unlike the Batman films, Jet Li does not rely too heavily on vehicles or gadgets, but only the fists and legs of his body. The film's story moves at a smooth pace with a number of action scenes building to the climax. Nothing in particular shines except Li, but the film is a fun alternative to Triad gangster films and traditional kung-fu epics. A brutal film with elements of Heroic Trio, but within a more mainstream Hollywood mold without the wild supernatural elements.

Black Rain
(1988) DramaB&W-123m   Japanese with English Subtitles   VA   Japan
Dir: Shohei Imamura   Scr: Shohei Imamura, Toshiro Ishido   Prod: Hisa Iino
DP: Takashi Kawamata   Editor: Hajime Okayasu   Music: Toru Takemitsu
Art Design: Hisao InagakiDist: Fox Lorber Home Video
(based on a novel by Masuji Ibuse)

Yoshiko Tanaka	**Yasuko**
Kazuo Kitamura	**Shigematsu**
Etsuko Ichihara	**Shigeko**
Shoichi Ozawa	**Shokichi**
Norihei Miki	**Kotaro**
Keisuke Ishida	**Yuichi**

[***]

A moving tale filmed in beautifully textured black and white about a young woman who suffers from the aftermath of the Hiroshima atomic bomb. Yasuko is a young woman who survives the atomic blast and fortunately does not suffer from any obvious illness or radiation sickness. However attitudes change as people believe she is tainted and treat her differently. She desperately tries to resume a normal life, which includes finding a husband but her Hiroshima past makes it difficult. Yasuko does fall in love with a man who does love her, but he is considered beneath her and of an unworthy background. Imamura does not attempt to make an antinuclear film or demand apologies for the atomic bomb, instead he uses the radioactive fallout as a catalyst for the scrutiny of Japanese social values and prejudices. Many Japanese, even today, have certain taboos or stereotypes about certain groups of people which have created barriers and downright discrimination to various groups living within Japan. This subtle racism runs deeply and goes beyond physical appearance.

Blade (Dao)
(1996) Kung-Fu   **C-112m**   **Chinese with English Subtitles**
Catalog #2075   **Hong Kong   Retail: $79.98**
Dir: Tsui Hark   **Scr: Tsui Hark, So Man-Sing, Koan Hui   Prod: Tsui Hark**
PC: Film Workshop Dist: Tai Seng Video
Zhao Wen Zhou (Chiu Man Chuk), Hung Yan Yan (Xiong Xin Xin),
Sang Ni, Moses Chan Ho, Austin Wai Tin-Chi, Valerie Chow Kar-Ling
[***]
A revisionist martial arts film that uses a classic kung-fu story with more emphasis placed on characterization and thematic mood. The Sharp Manufacturing Company is an elite sword-making company in a far western province of China. The daughter of the company's master is in love with two men, On and Iron Head. Ling wishes to pit the two friends against each other and will put her affection toward the victor. Both men refuse to play her games and visit the local town. Meanwhile, a powerful monk helps some women who are being accosted by bandit hunters. The hunters are defeated, but return in force and murder the honorable monk. On and Iron Head are repulsed by the injustice of the monk's death and decide to wage a war against the bandits. On becomes reluctant and sides with the master's decision not to interfere. This begins a bitter confrontation between On and Iron Head. When On is chosen as the new master of Sharp Manufacturer, the other workers plan to boycott his leadership. On decides to avoid internal dissension and leaves to search for his mysterious roots. The rest of the film is slightly uneven in its treatment of the characters, we flip back and forth between On and his new life with an orphan called Black Head, glimpse the wicked lives of the nomadic bandits, and the pursuit of On initiated by Lung and Iron Head. The film begins with a realistic approach to martial arts, but as the tension develops, the drama switches to more special effects-laden battles in an all-out finale.

Blade of Fury
(1993) Kung-Fu   **C-112m**   **Chinese with English Subtitles**   **Catalog #1371**
Hong Kong   Retail: $39.99
Dir: Samo Hung   **Prod: Lo Wei MAD: Samo Hung**
Dist: Tai Seng Video
Ti Lung, Rosamund Kwan, Cynthia Khan, Ngai Sing, Samo Hung
[*1/2]**
An excellent effort to recapture the excitement of traditional kung-fu movies from actor/director Samo Hung and veteran producer Lo Wei. Hung has an exciting cameo as a noble prison guard in a brief action sequence. Incorporating a talented cast, a strong story, and well-defined characters, Blade of Fury is a turn of the century tale about friendship and the country's reformation. The action is fast and furious with a number of flying scenes and quick decapitations. Ti Lung is a traveling scholar named Tan who is visiting the capital with his colorful colleague Cynthia Khan. There relationship is platonic, and the wily Khan dresses and

acts like an impetuous man. When they arrive in a remote village, they discover a group of bandits planning to attack a military convoy. They help the convoy and meet the great General of the Green Army and a fellow freedom fighter named Wu who was working as the town's blacksmith. Wu was part of the elite Black Tower resistance army that fought bravely against the Japanese occupation as shown in the opening action sequence. The men become friends and travel to a city outside the capital. As time passes, Tan's influence with the emperor thrives, while the General becomes closer to a high official who has his own ideas on running the country. The stoic Wu opens a martial arts academy and comes into conflict with the high official and defeats his best fighters, including his ruthless son. Wu then insults him further by refusing to join the high official's kung-fu society which also includes a Japanese samurai. The high official uses the General to capture Wu, but he is saved by Tan's quick involvement. Rosamund Kwan plays a courtier/musician who befriends and helps Wu and his friends. When Tan publishes a book on reforming the nation, he, Wu, and the General decide to lead a revolt against Empress Dowager and reinstate the young emperor as supreme ruler. The General of the Green Army betrays his friends and Tan is executed as a traitor, becoming a martyr to his colleagues. In a classic finale, Wu and his surviving allies attack the General and his men in a brutal battle for their cause. The ending is not a happy one, but marks the grief and struggle China had endured for many centuries as it fought for unity and freedom. A fine cast of action stars and strong martial arts sequences abound in this well-crafted turn of the century epic.

Bloody Friday
(1996) Thriller　　　**C-94m Chinese with English Subtitles**　　**Type II**
Catalog #2070　　　**Hong Kong**　　**Retail: $79.98**
Dir: Danny Ko　　　**Scr: Danny Ko, Yeung Kei**　　　**Prod: Simon Wong, Shirley Yu**
DP: Keung Kwok-Man　　　**Editor: Ma Chung-Yiu**　　**Music: Tommy Wai**
MAD: Lee Chi-Kit　　　**PC: Simpson Performance & Productions Co., Ltd.**
Dist: Tai Seng Video
Simon Yam, Loletta Lee, Ada Choi, Au Kam-Tong, Kwan Po-Wai, Gary Chan, Shirley Yu
Tsui Kam Kong, My Leung, Emana Leung, Joey Yeung, Winnie Wong
[***]
A deadly motorcycle-riding killer is on the loose for young female victims. The only one capable of stopping him is a dedicated cop named Officer Ko. What may seem to be a standard crime thriller has more twists and turns than most American films of similar nature. The story has a dark psychological tension which revolves around Officer Ko who spirals downward into despair and futility since he can't crack the case. His family life is in jeopardy and so is his career unless he stops the murderer who only strikes women on Friday.
When a string of prostitutes are brutally murdered on the streets of Hong Kong, Chief Officer Tsui Kam Kong assigns Officer Ko to lead the manhunt. Ko is a seasoned veteran, confident, experienced, and well-liked by his peer. He's given plenty of manpower, but somehow the killer is always one step ahead of him and more victims die. When the killer moves away from prostitutes, Ko is desperate to try anything to capture the Friday Killer. He befriends a key witness, a prostitute who survived an attack. Given a few clues, Ko plays a cat and mouse game with the killer who then threatens his family. A well-crafted thriller with a good dose of Hong Kong-style action and suspense. The characters are entertaining and Simon Yam does a specially good job, portraying his character with a human angle rather than the typical

superhuman cop.

Blue Kite, The
(1993) Drama C-138m   Chinese with English Subtitles   VA
Catalog #67511   China Retail: $29.95
Dir: Tian Zhuangzhuang   Scr: Xiao Mao   Prod: Luo Guiping, Cheng Yongping
DP: Hou Yong   Editor: Qian Lengleng
Music: Yoshihide Otomo   Art Design: Zhang Xiande Set Designer: Li Gang
Makeup: Hao Xia, Wu Yeyao   Costumes: Dong Juying
Dist: Kino on Video

Yi Tian	Tietou (infant)
Zhang Wenyao	Tietou (child)
Chen Xiaoman	Tietou (teenager)
Lu Liping	Mum (Chen Shujuan)
Pu Quanxin	Dad (Lin Shaolong)
Li Suejian	Uncle Li (Li Guodong)
Guo Baochang	Stepfather (Lao Wu)
Zhong Ping	Chen Shusheng
Chu Quanzhong	Chen Shuyan
Song Xiaoying	Sis
Zhang Hong	Zhu Ying
Liu Yanjin	Shujuan's Mother
Li Bin	Granny
Lu Zhong	Mrs. Lan
Guo Donglin	Liu Yunwei
Wu Shumin	Street Committee Officer

[***1/2]
One of the many new Chinese films that have arrived in America due to the brilliant "Fifth Generation" of filmmakers in mainland China. Tian Zhuangzhuang's controversial drama deals with the Chen family and their lives during the Chinese revolution and counter-revolution. The fifteen year ordeal focuses on the affects the revolution has on the family members, especially the mother and her unruly son, Tietou. The family lives in a small apartment in Beijing, China's capital. Their father is a librarian who is accused of being a reactionary and sent away for reconditioning. Through tragedy and events beyond their control, Tietou and his mother struggle on with their lives. She marries again to a soldier-friend of the family and then to a kind intellectual. The hectic life of ordinary citizens are thrown into a whirlwind of drama as correct ideologies change from year to year and friends become persecutors. Banned in China, this naturalistic film is emotionally engaging despite its slow pace and dreary topic. Until recently mainland China was not seen as the forerunner of Asian films, taking second place to Japan and Hong Kong. But keep in mind that individual freedom and financial wealth were not common for most Chinese filmmakers. China is a vast country with a rich history and culture only now being able to tell its cinematic tale.

Blue Seed Vol. 1
(1995) Japanime   C-60m Dubbed/Japanese with English Subtitles

Catalog # ADV BS/001D   Japan Retail: $24.95
Dir: Jun Kamiya   Prod: Naohiro Hayashi, Masaki Sawanobori, Yukinao Shimoji
Original Story & Character Design: Yuzo Takada   Series   Planning: Naruhisa Arakawa
Ex. Prod: Hidetoshi Shigematsu, Mitsuhisa Ishikawa, Yutaka Takahashi
Script Dir: Masaharu Amiya   Character Design: Kazuchika Kise, Takayuki Goto
Music: Kenji Kawai   English Version - Prod: A.D. Vision Inc. Ex.   Prod: John Ledford
Written, Prod, Dir: Matt Greenfield   International Coordinator: Toru Iwakami
Translators: Masako Arakawa, Chris Hutts
PC: Production IG/Ashi Production   Dist: A.D. Vision
(based on the graphic series by Take Shobo)
Amanda Winn   Momiji Fujimiya/Kaede Kunikida
Jason Lee   Mamoru Kusanagi
Carol Amerson   Moe Fujimiya/Akiko
Sharon Shawnessey Grandma/Azusa Matsudaira
Rob Mungle   Daitetsu Kunikida
Marcy Rae, Tiffany Grant, Kurt Stoll, Aaron Krohn, Rick Peeples, Jane Angus
[**1/2]
At a massive construction site in Tokyo, dozens of police cars cordon off the area and remain helpless as a young girl disappears into the darkness. She was their last hope, but then it is revealed that there is another girl...Momiji Fujimiya. An ancient race of parasitic plant-like creatures called the Aragami prepare to take over the planet Earth. To stop them, a special Japanese agency (TAC) is established and include a diverse group of officers. Of course, their best hope lies within a girl, Momiji who is the last descendant of a race of princesses who were used as sacrifices to stop the Aragami. Meanwhile, she is followed by Mamoru, a supernatural creature created by the Aragami. His original task was to protect Momiji from bodily harm since her death would negate the Aragami. Hoping to release himself from his Aragami master, he plans to betray and murder Momiji. At first, his intentions seem hostile, but he finds it difficult to kill Momiji and finally becomes the girl's guardian. The Aragami manifests itself into the vegetation of the planet and attack Momiji at her school. The story basically includes a lot of screaming and whining as Momiji escapes the monstrous pursuer. In what can best be described as juvenile perversion, Momiji is half-naked and constantly put into uncompromising positions. The film does feature some good animation, an eclectic cast of characters (likeable), and plenty of supernatural action. A short spoof film appears at the end of the video, but once again caters toward juvenile perversion with Playboy-like photos and cross-dressing. If you enjoy the comical, irreverent side of animation with a dose of action and violence, then try Blue Seed.
More episodes are available and hopefully the series will develop the characters and take new avenues in the plot's development.

Bodyguard from Beijing, The   (Chung Nam Hoi Bodyguard/Jet Li's The Defender)
(1994) Kung-Fu   C-90m Dubbed   Hong Kong   Retail: $19.95
Dir: Cory Yuen   Scr: Gordon Chan, Chan Kin Chung   DP: Tom Lau
Prod: Jet Li and Eastern Production Ltd.   Dist: Golden Harvest
Jet Li Lian Jie   Alan Hui

Christine Chung   Michelle Yeung
Kent Cheng, Ngai Sing
[**1/2]
A standard action film, but entertaining and definitely worth seeing if you're a Jet Li fan. This is the Chinese reply to the American film "The Bodyguard", starring Kevin Costner and Whitney Houston. Moving away from traditional kung-fu roles, Jet Li grows his hair and carries a gun and badge in this contemporary film about a dedicated security officer from the People's Republic of China. He is sent on assignment to Hong Kong to protect a wealthy and beautiful woman, Michelle Yeung (Chung) who is the key witness to a murder against a powerful crime boss. Michelle's influential and wealthy boyfriend requests the elite bodyguard while away on a business trip. Inspector Alan Hui (Li) arrives in an immaculate suit and takes charge of the house defenses. He dismisses the entire security group except for two cops, Fatso Charlie Leung and his skinny pal. To complicate matters, Michelle rebels against Li's authority and her little brother wants to fool around with real guns. Li doesn't get to portray his lighter side of acting, instead he is stiff and serious as the no-nonsense officer of the people. Initially, his stiff mannerism annoys everyone, but then his devout dedication warms everyone around him. Slowly losing interest in her boyfriend, Michelle becomes attached to him and Fatso starts to respect his mainland-style tactics. The film comprises of a number of action scenes where Jet Li must defend Michelle and her brother from would be assassins. The story is familiar ground and Jet Li doesn't express much range, but the fight sequences are entertaining for action fans. The American version is entitled Jet Li's The Defender and widely available.

Born Invincible   (Shaolin's Born Invincible)
(1976) Kung-Fu   C-85m Dubbed
Catalog #0067   Hong Kong   Retail: $39.99
Dir: Joseph Kuo   Scr: Joseph Kuo, Yau Ching Kang Prod: Kwok Nam Ku
DP:Wo Kuo Hsiau   Editor: Fang Chiu Kuei   Music: Chen Shiun Chi
Dist: Tai Seng Video
Carter Wong, Nancy Yan, Lo Lei, Chen Pei Ling, Long Hsu Chia, Tie Kuo Li, Wang Chu Liang
[**]
A good sign of whether a kung-fu movie is worth watching can be told from the fight scenes. Poor editing and choppy fight scenes indicate haste and low-production value. Even though the actors and fighting is good, bad editing can distract the viewer. Born Invincible is a good example. A little more financing and better editing, and the film could have been quite good. The actors involved are all very talented and the story does some interesting things. Those who are fans of Carter Wong (he's Thunder from "Big Trouble in Little China") will be interested to see him playing such a minor role in the film which bills him as the star. Though he receives top billing and is in the opening credit sequence, he doesn't carry the film, but rather plays the boss villain. The story premise starts off rather quickly as two villains attack and beat up an old man and his daughter. They're not too bright, since they decide to beat the two in front of a martial arts class training outside. The two top students can't sit by and watch such injustice. They attack the villains, but lose. They call their master for help which starts a chain of events, pitting the good school against the evil Wong and his followers. Wong proves too powerful and the entire school is disbanded with the heroic students going underground to secretly train separately

on their own. The interesting part is that there is no fixed hero as different students train to seek vengeance and to beat their opponents. The film needed tighter structuring and more character development, but a few of the fight scenes are entertaining. Carter Wong as a white-haired laughing villain is mildly amusing.

Bride with White Hair, The (White Hair Witch Legend/ Jiang-Hu [River Lale]: Between Love and Glory)
(1993) Fantasy Kung-Fu   C-89m Dubbed/Chinese with English Subtitles   VA
Catalog #34803   Hong Kong   Retail: $24.95
Dir: Ronnie Yu   Editor: David Wu   MAD: Kuo Chui   Dist: Tai Seng Video
Brigitte Lin   Lien Ni Chang
Leslie Cheung   Cho Yi Hang
Elain Lui, Ng Chun Yu, Nam Kit Ying
[*1/2]**
Popular fantasy film recently remastered and released on DVD, VHS and laserdisc by Tai Seng Video. An excellent example of fantasy kung-fu and a great film to judge whether they're your cup of tea. Keep in mind that Chinese folklore and legend differ greatly from western concepts of fantasy.
A small group of officers from the Imperial Court trek to a barren peak. The General and his men are looking for a special flower to heal the dying emperor. The set pieces and cinematography are art personified, exuding brilliant colors and shadows. Imagery is key over realism in this beautifully crafted film. High atop a precipice in an icy cold daze, a man sits alone with no shelter. He refuses to relinquish the rare flower and kills the contentious officials. We discover the reason behind the swordsman's hostilities by looking into his forsaken past. As a child, Yi Hang learned the Wu Tang sword style and grew up a carefree master. During his encounters, he helps a couple escape from a ruthless band of killers from the Mo Cult, led by the hideous Chi Wu Shuang, literally back-to-back attached brother/sister Siamese twins. A mysterious woman, Lien, also helps the couple and admires the swordsman's noble bravery. At first their relationship is tenuous, but Lien develops an admiration for the determined warrior, their sexual passions beautifully unfolding in a pool of shimmering water. Unknown to Yi, she is a powerful servant of the evil Mo Twins. The fierce Lien attempts to leave the Mo Cult and join Yi, but to leave the Riverlake she must offer herself to Brother Chi Wu. Sister Chi Wu despises Lien's newfound emotions and frames her for the massacre of Yi's Chung Yuan Clan. The duped Yi does not accept Lien's claims of innocence and becomes belligerent toward her and the Mo Cult. Wrongfully forsaken, Lien is driven to madness and her hair turns ghostly white because of Yi's betrayal. In remorse, he exiles himself on a cold mountain peak -- the only place that grows the flower he had once promised in love to her. Between sensational flying and fighting scenes, there's a strong emotional current and poignant drama that unfolds in this romantic tale of love and betrayal. The film's heavy-handed visual treatment and dark fantasy elements will differ greatly from those who are used to seeing Jackie Chan and Bruce Lee films, a totally different perspective and not for everyone.

Bride with White Hair 2, The
(1993) Fantasy Kung-Fu   C-80m Chinese with English Subtitles   VA
Catalog #32223   Hong Kong   Retail: $79.95

Dir: Dist: Tai Seng Video
Brigitte Lin   Lien Ni Chang
Leslie Cheung   Cho Yi Hang
Christy Chung   Moon
Joey Meng
[***]

An extremely entertaining sequel that follows events established from the first film. However, Lin and Cheung are relegated to secondary roles while a new cast of characters enter the story. Cheung doesn't appear until the very end of the film, while Lin lacks any emotional development or character growth. She's the one-dimensional super-powerful villain who kills with a glance and a flick of her web-like hair. Then again, you can't blame Lin since her fans love to watch her in this set role. Thankfully, the new characters are quite entertaining and charming in their own respect. The last descendant of Wu Tang (the clan that betrayed Ni Chang) is attacked on his wedding night and his bride is kidnaped. Ni Chang and her army of disgruntled female warriors live in a castle and torture their male prisoners. They brainwash the lovely bride and command her to kill her own husband. Underneath Ni Chang are two mysterious and beautiful women who were scorned by past male lovers. One acts as an advisor while the other woman portrays a captain of the guard. A colorful band of heroic warriors led by Granny infiltrate Ni Chang's palace and attempt to rescue the bride. The standout is Chung's Moon, a fiery tomboy, who battles alongside the best men and holds a hidden love for the hero. They fail with high casualties and retreat, but hope to recruit Master Cho who is hidden in the mountains. Ironically, the sequel takes less risks than the original film and tones down some of the kaleidoscopic imagery. The story will appeal to contemporary fans who enjoy a straightforward quest story of good versus evil. If you enjoyed the bizarre imagery of the first film and the unbridled love between Lin and Cheung, you will most likely be disappointed with the less passionate stance taken in the sequel. The fight scenes are shot in trademark slow-motion and blurred imagery, and are quite abundant throughout the film. Only Ni Chang possesses outlandish abilities while the rest of the characters battle on a lesser level. A fun film with a good blend of martial arts and fantasy elements.

~BRUCE LEE CLONE FILMS~

In any human endeavor, certain names come instantly to mind for their great achievements, amazing charisma, and unbounded talent. Boxing has Muhammad Ali, basketball has Michael Jordan, physics has Albert Einstein, music has Elvis Presley, and Hollywood has the likes of Marilyn Monroe and Marlon Brando. In the field of martial arts movies, there is only one champion, one actor who broke race/culture barriers and jumped to superstardom with his very first picture. I doubt anyone like him will ever arrive again in my lifetime...the immortal Bruce Lee The following is a selected list of films made after Lee's death, including Lee-imitation films which never did the actor justice. This is only a small sampling of the hundreds of low-quality clone films that surfaced in the wake of Bruce Lee's death. Perhaps you've seen some of them, but it is best to avoid the low-rated titles or any other clone film with Bruce Lee "something" in the title as a last resort. On top of being insulting clone films, the era of the 1970's produced some of the worst kung-fu movies ever made. The low-production value, the hasty writing, the laughable acting, the ingratiating music, the horrible bell-bottom pants and polyester shirts are a must to miss. Unless you watch them for bad humor, try to avoid: Bruce Le's Greatest Revenge, Bruce Lee's Ways of Kung Fu, Bruce the Superhero, Bruce's Deadly Fingers, Bruce's Fists of Vengeance.

Bruce Lee: A&E Biography Series
(1993) Documentary C-50m English   USA   Retail: $19.95
Dir: Ruben Norte
[***]
Not a clone film. If you are familiar with the A&E channel's Biography series, you know they're entertaining and informative programs. The Bruce Lee (& Jackie Chan) biography is part of the expansive series, offering behind the scenes clips and a fascinating overview of the legendary martial arts star.

Bruce Lee Fights Back from the Grave
(1976) Kung-Fu   C-97m Dubbed   R
Dir: Umberto Lenzi   Dist: Warner BTV
Deborah Chaplin, Anthony Bronson
[*]
The entire look, sound, and feel of this film will have you in shock and disbelief. After the mysterious death of Bruce Lee, rumors abound that he is still alive. Well, the new Lee rises from the grave and does battle with a host of villains, ala the Village People. The mysterious Black Angel of Death awaits Lee for the climatic battle, but can Lee beat death twice?

Bruce Lee: His Last Days, His Last Nights   (I Love You, Bruce Lee)
(1975) Kung-Fu   C-90m Dubbed   R   Hong Kong   Retail: $9.99
PC: Shaw Bros.
Danny Lee, Betty Ting Pei
[*]
One of the better known Bruce-clone films, since it claimed to be the true story of Lee's death. Sadly the name of Bruce Lee can not rest in peace as numerous exploitation films try to cash in on his worldwide fame. Actress Betty Ting Pei is no exception as she stars in this film based on her life with Bruce Lee. Betty was the actress who socialized with Bruce Lee during his success in Hong Kong and was the woman who found Bruce Lee's dead body. After work, Bruce had gone to her apartment to rest awhile and asked for some medicine for a headache. He went to sleep and never woke up according to her testimony. The film revolves around supposed fights with Bruce Lee and gangsters while showing sleazy sexual romps with Betty. Many fans and critics see this film as the ultimate insult, blaming Ting Pei for trying to make a quick buck. Not an easy film to watch, the flavor of the seventies loses any charm. In modern comparison, the look of the film gets worse with every passing year.

Bruce Li in New Guinea
(1980) Kung-Fu   C-90m Dubbed   VA   Catalog #4061-B
Hong Kong   Retail: $9.99
Dir: Kong Hung   Scr/Editor: C.Y. Yang   Prod: Kwok Po Luen

Supervisor: Keung Chung Ping   PC: Ocean Shores Limited Dist: Simitar
Bruce Li, Cheng Sing, Bolo Yeung
[*1/2]
This is one of many Bruce Li titled films that were popular in the late 70's and early 80's. The amazing thing is that Bruce Li is more than just another Bruce Lee clone, he is quite a talented and a muscular athlete with a good deal of charm and humor. When given a good role, his films are quite entertaining. This isn't one of his best films, I'd recommend Dynamo or The Three Avengers, but Bruce Li can even make the worst of his films somewhat enjoyable for genre fans. The opening starts with Li training on a mountain and performing some kicks while the villain also demonstrates his skills. Cut to Hong Kong, Chin Seng (Bruce Li) and his friend Kwan Lee the anthropologist leave for Snake Worship Island in New Guinea. They hope to study the native customs and the local martial arts (the natives know kung-fu!). On the remote island, Seng and Lee are escorted by two bumbling guides and run across an old acquaintance who is after the natives' sacred Snake Pearl. Meanwhile, political turmoil has erupted on the loincloth natives since the Snake King died and the evil Wizard takes over the tribe. He decides to capture the Snake princess Ankawa, but she is saved by Seng and Lee. The heroes must defend the princess, fight off the greedy treasure hunter, and stay ahead of the deadly Wizard and his minions. Low-budget couldn't even describe the film and most of the fight scenes take place outdoors with choppy editing and crude techniques.

Bruce Li the Invincible
(1980) Kung-Fu   C-90m Dubbed   VA   Catalog #4061-A
Hong Kong   Retail: $9.99
Dir: Law Kai Shuk Scr: C.Y. Yang   Prod: Keung Chun Ping
Ex. Prod: Kwok Po Luen   PC: Ocean Shores Limited Dist: Simitar
Bruce Li, Cheng Sing, Chen Wai Man
[*1/2]
It's tough to totally discredit Li's films, since the actor's physical skills and charisma are quite enjoyable. The fault lies in the dated look of the film and low production values. Kung-fu expert Chang Li Ching uses his skills for crime and murder. He promises his forgiving master to go straight and leaves for Malaysia. Shin San (Li) arrives in Malaysia to help his uncle and attractive cousin, but Chang is up to his wicked ways again and kidnaps Shin's cousin. Shin must recruit some help and use his martial arts to save his cousin. Only violence can end Chang's tyranny.

Also see "Dragon: The Bruce Lee Story", "Fist of Fear, Touch of Death" and "The Real Bruce Lee"

Bubblegum Crisis (8 episodes)
(1987-1991)   Japanime: Scifi   Dubbed/Japanese with English Subtitles   VA
Japan Retail: $19.95/$24.95 (each episode)
Dir: Katsuhito Akiyama (1-3), Hiroki Hayashi (4), Masami Obari (5,6) Fumihiko Takayama (7), Hiroaki Goda   Scr: Kenichi Matsuzaki, Hideki Kakinuma, Shinji Aramaki, Katsuhito Akiyama, Emu Arii, Hidetoshi Yoshida
Planning & Original Story: Toshimichi Suzuki

Character Design: Kenichi Sonoda, Satoshi Urushihara   **Music: Kaoji Makaino**
PC: Artmic/Youmex   Dist: AnimEigo
[***]
If you've been a fan of Japanime during the 80's, then you've probably heard of the Knight Sabers. A popular group of female anime characters that helped usher in the age of cyberpunk and brought a dark, rough-edged tone to girls in anime. The episodes feature hard-rocking musical scores (which seem dated by today's standards), since Priss is the leader of a rock group called Priss and the Replicants. The time is the late twentieth century in Japan where machines and technology are a staple of life. In a world of Boomers and AD Police, the four sexy Knight Sabers led by Priss sport shapely battlesuits in their pursuit to destroy the evil GENOM Corporation. They'll kick anyone's butt who gets in the way, but they're always ready to battle, party or blast a rock tune.
The episode are all available for individual sale:

Episode 1: Bubblegum Crisis	C-53m	Catalog #ANI ET091-001
Episode 2: Born to Kill	C-30m	Catalog #ANI ET091-002
Episode 3: Blow Up	C-30m	Catalog #ANI ET091-003
Episode 4: Revenge Road	C-40m	Catalog #ANI ET091-004
Episode 5: Moonlight Rambler	C-45m	Catalog #ANI ET091-005
Episode 6: Red Eyes	C-45m	Catalog #ANI ET091-006
Episode 7: Double Vision	C-49m	Catalog #ANI ET091-007
Episode 8: Scoop Chase	C-50m	Catalog #ANI ET091-008

Bubblegum Crisis Collector Suite
(1987-1991)   Japanime: Scifi   C-342m   Japanese with English Subtitles   VA
Catalog #ANI AS095-011   Japan   Retail: $190.00
[***]
For hardcore fans who are not content on just renting the series, the entire eight episodes are available in a nice slipcase for your collection.

Bubblegum Crash Volume 1: Illegal Army
(1991) Japanime: Scifi   C-45m   Japanese with English Subtitles
Catalog #ANI ET092-001   VA   Japan Retail: $24.95
Dir/Scr: Hiroshi Ishiodori   Planning and Original Story: Toshimichi Suzuki
Character Design: Kenichi Sonoda Animation Dir: Noboru Sugimitsu
Art Dir: Yumiko Ogata   Music: Takehito Nakazawa
PC: Artmic, Inc.   Dist: AnimEigo
[***]
Three volume follow up series to the popular cyberpunk adventure Bubblegum Crisis. Some fans were disappointed with the new entry into the Knight Sabers, but then loyal fans are always somewhat hard to please. If you enjoy the antics of Crisis and AD Police, there's still plenty action and smart animation in these cybertech adventures. Life has moved on for the Knight Sabers and though they're still close, they have gone onto new career paths. Linna is a successful stock broker, Priss gets a singing break, Nene's at AD Police, and Sylia is doing well too. She calls the other girls to a private dinner and announces that instead of breaking up permanently, they take advantage of the new technology in combat and help hunt down a renegade army of

Boomers led by Colonel Lando. A group of military soldiers were killed in combat, but have somehow reappeared in MegaTokyo as high-tech criminals. Using advanced weapons, they are unstoppable to the AD Police. The Knight Sabers move into action and stop the culprits who were secretly controlled by an advanced AI (artificial intelligence) program.

Bubblegum Crash Volume 2: Geo Climbers
(1991) Japanime: Scifi   C-45m   Japanese with English Subtitles
Catalog #ANI ET092-002   VA   Japan Retail: $24.95
Dir: Hiroyuki Fukushima   Scr: Emu Arii
Planning and Original Story: Toshimichi Suzuki
Character Design: Kenichi Sonoda Animation Dir: Noboru Sugimitsu
Art Dir: Yumiko Ogata   Music: Michihiko Ota
PC: Artmic, Inc.   Dist: AnimEigo
[***]
The brilliant Dr. Hayes invites his colleague Dr. Yuri to his advanced testing facility. Carrying on the work of Dr. Stingray (Sylia's father), Hayes has created a new Boomer with the same personality and intelligence of a human being. Yuri is impressed, but admits his jealousy and hatred of Dr. Hayes. The main doors open and a commando team of Boomers take out Hayes and his team. Yuri steals the prototype boomer ADAMA and plans to advance his own Boomer designs. The Knights Sabers are on the case and so are the AD Police under Officer Leon.

Bubblegum Crash Volume 3: Meltdown
(1991) Japanime: Scifi   C-45m   Japanese with English Subtitles
Catalog #ANI ET092-003   VA   Japan Retail: $24.95
Dir: Hiroshi Ishiodori   Scr: Emu Arii
Planning and Original Story: Toshimichi Suzuki Art Dir: Yumiko Ogata
Character Design: Kenichi Sonoda Animation Dir: Yasuyuki Noda
Music: Takehito Nakazawa PC: Artmic, Inc.   Dist: AnimEigo
[***]
The foreman of a construction site tells his Boomer to get to work. Suddenly, the machine's eyes light up and he yells, down with humans. It re-programs other Boomers and all hell breaks out. The AD Police arrive and take out the renegade Boomer, but more will arise from the ashes as the mysterious AI "Voice" activates more deadly machines. The Knight Sabers must go out once more to stop the tide of renegade Boomers and prevent them from destroying the fusion nuclear reactor.

Bullet in the Head
(1990) Action C-118m   Chinese with English Subtitles
Catalog #0980   Hong Kong   Retail: $39.99
Dir/Prod: John Woo Scr: John Woo, Patrick Leung, Janet Chun
Asociate Prod: Patrick Leung, Catherine Lau
DP: Lam Kwok Wa, Chan Pui Kai, Somchai Kittikun, Wong Wing Hang
Editor: John Woo   Music: James Wong, Romeo Diaz
Prod Design: James Leung Costume Design: Bruce Yiu
PC: Golden Princess Film Production Ltd./John Woo Film Production Ltd.

Dist: Golden Cinema City Video Distribution Ltd./Tai Seng Video

Tony Leung Chiu Wai	Ben
Jacky Cheung	Frank
Waise Lee	Paul
Fennie Yuen	Jane
Simon Yam	Luke
Yolinda Yam	Sally

[***1/2]

A vintage John Woo film that traces the lives of three close friends and the reason for their bitter separation. Woo deftly mixes his classic elements of friendship shattered by greed and money while forging a bond of mythical proportions between betrayal and loyalty. The year is 1967, a lively tune explodes onto the screen as street punks battle each other with baseball bats, tire arms, and chains. Out of the rough carnage, three victors emerge with boyish grins and a carefree attitude. They're young, impulsive, and daring without a care in the world. This sets the pace for Ben, Frank, and Paul, three childhood friends who live the life of the petty crook. Hoping to increase their fortunes, they plan on going to Vietnam and capitalize on the chaotic situations caused by the civil war. Ben is reluctant to go since his life improves with his marriage to Jane. Frank (the cute one) borrows some money to offer Ben a wedding gift. Along his way home, Ringo and his gangsters demand the money. Frank pleads with Ringo who violently beats him and takes the money. The bloody and wounded Frank makes it to the wedding and barely holds back his tears. United, Ben and Paul kill Ringo which force the trio to leave Hong Kong for Vietnam until the situation cools down. With a farewell kiss to Jane, Ben joins his friends and meets up with Shing who gives them a job transporting valuables to crime boss Leong. The situation in war-torn Vietnam is turbulent and the trio are arrested as Vietcong terrorists. When the real culprit is caught, they're released and hook up with Leong's man Luke. The four men bond and take on the powerful gang boss who betrayed Luke. In a drastic struggle that needs to be seen on the big screen, the four battle in Leong's place and barely escape with the gold and a beautiful singer (Yam). While the group try to escape with their lives on a boat, Paul is more concerned with the box of gold strips. During an elaborate prison break, Paul believes Frank will reveal their position and cause them to be recaptured. Motivated by greed and personal survival, Paul shoots his friend Frank, injuring him to the point of mental vegetation. The friends escape their sadistic prison captors and make their way back to safety. Many years later, Paul uses his wealth to become an influential crime boss in Hong Kong. Frank is nothing more than a mental idiot and suffers a beggar's life. Discovering the truth, Ben decides to settle old scores, find justice for Frank, and confronts Paul in the climatic showdown. Filmed during the Tiananmen Square massacre of 1989, Woo was inspired and incensed to include more vivid and brutal scenes of violence in his film to express his own personal expressions. Scenes such as when the friends are captured and tortured at a jungle prison are not easily viewed. The images depicted are extremely savage and may disturb sensitive viewers. A powerful film of friendship and betrayal, showcasing the classic elements of John Woo's style of filmmaking.

Burn Up!
(1991) Japanime: Action   C-50m Dubbed/Japanese with English Subtitles   VA
Catalog # ADV BU002/ADV BU001   Japan Retail: $19.95/$29.95

Dir: Yasunori Ide   Scr: Jun Kanzaki   Original Story: Yasunori Ide, Jun Kanzaki
Character Design: Kenjin Miyazaki   Art Dir: Kenji Kamiyama
Music: Kenji Kawai   PC: NCS/MRC/AIC   Dist: A.D. Vision
[**1/2]
An elite group of police officers (many who look like teenage girls) attempt to break up a female slavery prostitution ring. Focusing on the format of "Girls with Guns", Burn Up! is a quick-paced and enjoyable little action film with a minimum amount of hardcore violence. The opening credits are flashed over a high speed chase as the C.P. SWAT (City Police Special Weapons and Tactics) attempt to stop a car full of kidnapers. They stop the culprits and discover a link between a wealthy industrialist and a female slavery ring. The suspected perverts are kidnaping young girls and brainwashing them for sexual pleasures with older men of wealth and power. The C.P. SWAT team are sure of the culprits identity, but don't have any hard evidence to make a legal arrest. The trio of girls and their male counterparts go undercover at a local night club, hoping to tempt the prostitution kidnapers. The criminals use other young girls to entice new ones, so the cutest looking officer disguises herself and then gets purposely kidnaped. The rest of the police force want to raid the suspected mansion, but without probably cause their hands are tied. Breaking orders, the female partners stage a massive attack on the mansion with the rest of the police force arriving as welcomed backup. Plenty of fun and cute action animation for fans of the genre.

Burn Up W: File 1
(1996) Japanime: Action   C-35m Japanese with English Subtitles   VA
Catalog # (1) ADV BW-001D   Japan Retail: $19.95
Dir: Hiroshi Negishi Scr: Katsuhiko Kochiba, Sumio Uetake
Character Design & Animation Dir: Toshinari Yamashita
Music: Hiroyuki Nanba
PC: AIC/MRC   Dist: A.D. Vision
[**]
Five years later, a lackluster sequel to the original Burn Up! appears on video shelves. Broken into two volumes to double the profits, this time our female heroines are part of a special swat team W unit, "Warrior". Their assignments usually involve some kind of bizarre act, including a nude bungee jump to save some hostages from terrorists who took over a luxury hotel and a battle with an intelligent computer who kidnaps a sexy virtual program named Maria.
Burn Up W: File 2 (1996)   C-35m   Catalog # ADV BW- Japan Retail: $19.95

Butterfly and Sword (Comet Butterfly & Sword)
(1993) Fantasy Kung-Fu   C-87m Chinese with English Subtitles
Catalog # KRT 252   Hong Kong   Retail: $19.95
Dir: Michael Mak/Tang Chi Li   Scr: Chong Ching
Prod: Wade Yao, Pi Chien Hsin   Ex. Prod: Chu Yen Ping
Assistant Dir: Kao Sin Ming, Tsui Kwok Yin   DP: Chan Wing She
Present by Mark Wu, Jessica Hsu Art Dir: Lee Yiu Kong   Setting   Dir: Leung   Chi   Hing
Action: Ching Siu Ting   Prod Manager: Lee Ching Hsuan, Jackson Chan
Music: Johnson Lee   PC: Chang-Hong Channel Film & Video Company

Dist: Youngtze Film & Video, Inc./Tai Seng Video
Joey Wong   Butterfly
Michelle Khan   Ko
Tony Leung Chiu Wai   Sing
Donnie Yen, Jimmy Lin, Tony Leung Chiu Wai, Tsui Kam Kong, Yan Tze Tan, Tor Chung
Wah, Yip Tsuen Chin, Cheung Kwok She
[***]
Traditional kung-fu story with plenty of limb-ripping fights and flying stunts, starring Hong
Kong's A-list of performers. The tale is based on a popular sword fighting novel by Gu Long.
The emperor is in trouble when a high-ruling eunuch lord is secretly murdered and his place is
taken by an evil killer who specializes in a deadly claw weapon. Mistress Ko is ordered to
destroy a powerful general, Li Sui Chin, and his clan. Secretly, the evil eunuch imposter hopes
Ko and her fighters will also be killed with General Li, therefore, getting rid of both his rivals
and allowing him to take over the martial world. What follows is a muddled plot littered with
numerous subplots, but try to follow along and you'll be treated to some wild and crazy martial
arts. Eventually Ko, Butterfly, Sing, and the rest of the heroes discover the evil eunuch's plot
and launch a full-scale attack. Even an innocuous looking boy with a toy ball is an elite agent
from the government. When the fight scenes do appear, they are ultra fast and violent which
may appeal to fans who like flying kung-fu stunts. The hero must use his limb splitting
techniques to defeat the powerful eunuch and make China a safer country. The all-star cast is in
full-force, but are spread throughout the film.

-C-

Call Him Mr. Shatter   (Shatter)
(1974) Action C-90m English   R   Hong Kong/UK   Retail: $9.95
Dir: Michael Carreras   Scr: Don Houghton Prod: Michael Carreras, Vee King Shaw
DP: Roy Ford, Brian Probyn, John Wilcox   Editor: Eric Boyd-Perkins
Music: David Lindup   Art Dir: Johnson
PC: Avco Embassy   Dist: New Line Cinema
Stuart Whitman, Ti Lung, Lily Li, Peter Cushing, Anton Diffring, Yemi Ajibade
[**]
Exploitation film of the Seventies, attempting to mix hardcore American crime action and Asian
martial arts. Stuart Whitman is Mr. Shatter, a businessman (killer) of illegal repute who travels
to Hong Kong. He hopes to score big on a business transaction with Peter Cushing who would
prefer to see Shatter dead. To help his chances, Shatter meets an attractive Chinese woman (Li)
and hires a tough tournament fighter (veteran Lung in an early role) from the streets of Hong
Kong. Together, they're unstoppable as Shatter uses his gun and Lung uses his fists. The
climatic showdown happens on the wharfs of Hong Kong's busy seaport where Shatter and Lung
are double-crossed by the villains. An interesting cross blend of genres sponsored by Hammer
Studios of England and Shaw Brothers of Hong Kong, hoping to capitalize on the popularity of
martial arts, post-Bruce Lee. A sub-standard action film that fares poorly with time, but provides
some hardcore fight scenes and provides an interesting note in cross-cultural filmmaking. The
most intriguing aspect is the appearance of Hong Kong superstar Ti Lung in an English speaking
role.

Challenge of the Masters
(1976) Kung-Fu   C-97m Dubbed   VA   Catalog # 5038   Hong Kong
Retail: $19.99
Dir: Liu Chia Liang Scr: I Kuang Prod: Mona Fong   Ex. Prod: Run Run Shaw
Art Dir: Johnson Tsao   MAD: Liu Chia Liang
PC: Shaw Bros.   Dist: South Gate Entertainment
Gordon Liu Chia Hui, Liu Chia Liang, Liu Chia Yung, Chen Kuan Tai
[***1/2]
Enjoyable martial arts movie with less violence than the usual "chop-socky" film. Only one person dies in the entire film and director Liang again proves his versatility in telling stories and building likeable characters in a framework filled with great kung-fu routines. Director Liang always tried to break away from conventional martial arts plots and experimented with different angles to the classic kung-fu plot, creating some of the most entertaining movies to appear from the Shaw Brothers Studios. This is one of his finer examples and should be a must see for serious martial arts fans who especially do not prefer the flying/fantasy based films. Gordon Liu plays the loveable and legendary Wong Fei Hung, before he became a true martial arts master. His father, Wong Kei Ying, is the famous master of a local martial arts academy that competes in the lion dance and other festivals. A major festival is the focus of the film, since every academy in town covets the prize and honor of winning. The local "evil" academy hires a martial arts expert to help them win the tournament. In secret, the hired master is a criminal hiding from the law. Liu Chia Liang is convincing as the vile criminal who uses a deadly spear to deal with his enemies. On the trail of Liang, government official Liu Chia Yung visits Wong's Academy and befriends the young Fei Hung. Yung encourages Fei Hung's father to let the troublesome boy learn martial arts and discipline. Determined to learn, Gordon is sent to his father's own master, convincingly portrayed by Chen Kuan Tai. There he becomes a great martial artist and learns patience and maturity. He is dismayed to learn that his friend Officer Yung has been killed by criminal Liang. Fei Hung demands to go back and avenge his death, but Chen warns him not to rush in prematurely and complete his training. Fei Hung challenges the evil Liang in a bamboo grove, using the Shaolin staff against Liang's deadly spear and foot strikes. Fei Hung proves his skills and compassion by defeating the evil Liang and sparing his life in the process. Afterwards, Fei Hung joins his father's Academy and participates in the tournament against the "evil" academy. Once again, Wong Fei Hung proves his incredible skills and compassion, defeating the evil academy students who resort to using illegal weapons during the hectic festival battle. Gordon Lui's Fei Hung triumphs in an amazing display of talent and unites the various academies, bringing peace and honor to the community.

Challenge of the Ninja (Shaolin Challenges Ninja, Heroes of the East)
(1979) Kung-Fu   C-107m   Dubbed
Catalog #PEV 34091 Hong Kong   Retail: $19.99
Dir: Liu Chia Liang Scr: I Kuang Prod: Mona Fong   Ex. Prod: Run Run Shaw
DP: Arthur Wong, Ao Chih Chun Editor: Chiang Hsing Lung, LiYeh Hai
Music: Chen Yung Yu   Assistant Prod: Huang Chia Hsi
Art Dir: Johnson Tsao   Assistant Dir: Huang Pa Ching, Tang Wan
Costume: Kiu Chi Yu   Makeup: Wu Hsu Ching

MAD: Liu Chia Liang   PC: Shaw Bros.
Gordon Liu Chia Hui, Yuko Mizuno, Kurata Yasuaki, Liu Chia Liang
[***1/2]
Another Liu Brothers masterpiece, proving director Liang's inventiveness and actor Hui's charisma are an amazing combination. Typically in Chinese films, the Japanese are delegated to playing villains, but Liu decides to change the formula when Gordon marries Yuko Mizuno, a Japanese woman. Unfortunately, they both know martial arts and spend constant days testing each others skills. Yuko loses every time and gets frustrated trying a new technique. When she finally uses ninjutsu, Liu is shocked at the treachery and deceit, denouncing the style. Infuriated, she returns to Japan and meets with her sensei. In hopes of getting her to return, Gordon writes a letter to her. The letter is misinterpreted into a challenge and the sensei sends his seven best students to deal with Gordon. They include a Karate master, a Samurai, a tonfa/nunchaku expert, a sai expert, a spear expert, a judo master, and a ninja. One by one, Gordon battles them and is victorious by using a particular Chinese style to combat the Japanese technique. Challenge of the Ninja is quoted by many fans as their favorite Liang/Gordon film. It's not difficult to see why, since Liang's interracial marriage film breaks new boundaries and is unique among the formulaic martial arts films of the period. Though at first it may seem trivial, a marriage between a Japanese and a Chinese is a very big cultural gap. Asian races are very wary of interracial marriages which are not looked upon favorable. Especially the Japanese who have typically been portrayed as the villains of Asia are not a common choice for cultural union. The film explores that cultural union in the framework of martial arts which is very unique to the two countries and a matter of great pride. Instead of the Japanese hating the Chinese and vice versa, the characters develop and learn from their experiences with each other. In the end, a cultural gap is crossed and bloodshed is non-existent. The film's message and non-violent use of martial arts is very comparable to "The Karate Kid" where the film's story and characters are more important than the body count. The film features a fascinating look at the various Japanese and Chinese fighting styles and features a number of highly charged and exciting action sequences. The climatic battle between Gordon Liu and the ninja doesn't end in bloodshed, but mutual respect for the two highly-trained practitioners. Though Liang stepped out of the acting limelight in the film, his presence is very evident in the direction and excellent choreography which doesn't require too many tricks, wired flying, or special effects. The film is highly recommended and one of the best martial arts films produced from a brilliant director who has no peers.

Chinatown Kid
(1977) Kung-Fu   C-115m   Dubbed   Hong Kong   Retail: $19.99
Dir: Chang Cheh   Scr: I Kuang Prod: Mona Fong   Ex. Prod: Run Run Shaw
PC: Shaw Bros.
Alexander Fu Sheng, Wang Lung Wei, Sun Chien, Lo Meng, Kuo Chui
[**1/2]
The Chang Gang appear in a contemporary film that features Fu Sheng in the top spot and lets his talents shine. Similar to Bruce Lee's early life, Fu Sheng plays a young man from Hong Kong who gets involved with the seedier sorts on the street. He gets in trouble with a local gang and is forced to flee to San Francisco. Again he falls in with the wrong crowd and decides to capitalize on the situation using his excellent kung-fu to fight himself some respect. He climbs

the ladder of criminal success, making plenty of enemies, and gets involved with two opposing gangs. He tries to play them against each other in order to clean up the town for himself, not unlike Mifune in Yojimbo. Eventually, the moral of what goes around comes around climaxes in a showdown at Fu Sheng's private club which may resemble Pacino's last stand in Scarface. An anti-crime story with strong fight scenes for a realistic image, though the seventies motif does not fare well with today's modern setting. The focus of Fu Sheng's power and lust is symbolized in a digital watch he always wanted when he was poor. A gold band with a red display catches his eyes and he purchases one. Eventually he discovers his own fallen path and attempts to rectify his conscious, but he's in too deep. Chang's film is full of moral messages dealing with greed, power, drugs, and violence. The sets are modest, the acting is standard, and the film loses much of its original impact over time. It is somewhat interesting to see classic Shaw Brothers stars in a street-brawling action flick that often looks too staged for its own good.

Chinese Connection (original title: Fists of Fury)
(1972) Kung-Fu   C-106m   Dubbed   R   VA   Hong Kong
Catalog # 6121-85   Hong Kong   Retail: $39.95 Widescreen Available
Dir/Scr: Lo Wei   Prod: Raymond Chow   DP: C.C. Chen
Editor: Y.C. Chang Music: C.H. Ku   MAD: Han Ying Chieh
PC: Golden Harvest Limited   Dist: CBS Fox Video
Bruce Lee   Chen Jeh
Nora Miao Ker   Hsiu   Yuan
Maria Yi   Yen
James Tien   Chang
Tien Feng   Fan
Han Ying Chieh   Feng Kwai-Sher
Lo Wei   Inspector
Robert Baker   Russian Boxer
C.H. Wong, Y.C. Han, Lee Quin, Feng Yi, Tony Liu, Chin San, Hashimoto Riki, Arimura Pijun, Y.C. Lee, F.C. Cheng
[***1/2]
One of Bruce Lee's finest efforts and his purest film in the sense of traditional kung-fu. Set in foreign-occupied Shanghai of 1908, the Chinese are relegated to second-class citizens within their own city. A park sign reads "No dogs and Chinese allowed" which is strictly enforced by a burly guard. Bruce is refused admittance, but then watches as the guard allows a woman and her dog to enter the park. Bruce's facial expressions contort and in an instant his hands lash out at the guard, his legs spring into action, kicking the insulting park sign and in midair breaking it into two. This is the motto for the film, no longer will Chinese be degraded, cause this time they'll fight back and win.
In Shanghai, the two best martial arts schools are taught by a Japanese master and a Chinese master. The Japanese school is run by a ruthless tyrant who murders the master of the Chinese school. The police drop the case since the Japanese carry so much influence within the community. During the funeral for the Chinese master, the Japanese break in and destroy the banner plaque and challenge the grieving students. Not wishing to disgrace their dead master, the Chinese students refuse to fight. Bruce in classic clenched fist and gnarled mode, barely withholds his lethal fists of fury. The next day, Lee enters the Japanese martial arts school.

Alone, he carries the Japanese challenge, accepting in front of an entire class of Karate/Judo students. No one takes him seriously until he demonstrates his lethal force on an impetuous student. Lee's incredible speed, strength, and passion make it believable that he can defeat the entire school. He defeats them easily and unveils his trademark weapon for the first time, the nunchaku. Now synonymous with Lee, the nunchaku are Okinawan Karate weapons developed from farming implements. Simple in design, two pieces of wood bonded together by cord or chain, the sticks are lethal in the proper hands and illegal in many places. Lee's action sets off a chain of events that force a war between the Chinese and Japanese schools. Eventually Lee is pushed to the point of murder and is wanted by the police. He goes into hiding, expresses his love for a female student, and disguises himself to infiltrate the Japanese school who has taken on a Russian boxer of immense strength. Bruce enters the school at night and takes out his full vengeance on the Japanese villains and the Russian strongman, but then is apprehended by the local authority. In one of the great scenes of defiance, Bruce is led outside the school where a squad of soldiers take aim on him. Instead of surrendering, Bruce breaks free and charges the soldiers. He does a spectacular midair leap and the frame freezes as the sound of gunfire explodes.

Though only Bruce Lee's second film, it was clearly evident what a star he had become and what key elements appealed to audiences: nunchaku, one versus many, animal-like intensity, and no training necessary to defeat the evil masters. A classic film that captures the elements of Bruce Lee's appeal and stands out as his most convincing effort. If you watch closely, the fight scenes involving Bruce are actually choreographed differently than the fight scenes involving other members of the cast. The stunt double for the Japanese master who flies through the window and into the courtyard is none other than a very young Jackie Chan. Followed by an unofficial sequel, not starring Bruce Lee. Jet Li's remake, Fist of Legend gives Bruce a run for his money, and though Li marginally lacks Lee's intensity and charisma, the film is filled with excellent fight scenes that showcase the evolving nature of martial arts movies for the better.

Chinese Ghost Story, A
(1987) Fantasy   C-96 min   **Chinese with English Subtitles**
Catalog #0391   **Hong Kong   Retail: $39.99**
Dir: Ching Siu Ting Prod: Tsui Hark   Dist: Tai Seng Video
Joey Wong   Nieh Hsiao Tsing "Sian"
Leslie Cheung   Ning Tsai Shen
Wu Ma   Swordsman Yen
David Lam Wai   Hsiao Hou
[***1/2]
One of the best made and known supernatural films to appear out of Hong Kong and based on the Chinese classic "Strange Tales" (Liao Zhai Zhi Yi). Ning is a handsome scholar who is a little naive about the harsh world. He is a righteous traveling tax collector which places him on an unpopular and lonely road. Not a warrior, he's clumsy and easily gets spooked. While moderating a truce between two swordsmen, he visits an eerie temple and meets a beautiful woman (Wong) who lures men to their death by draining their Yang energy for her demonic lord. Wong realizes Ning is different than most men and falls in love with him. Ning discovers the truth and helps Wong escape her tortured fate. Ning and Yen battle the nasty things of the night and search for Wong's remains, hoping to reincarnate and free her from spiritual

imprisonment. They must fight her demon lord and everything it manages to send out at them. Together, the two descend into hell and fight for Wong's tortured soul in what can easily be called a bizarre, enticing, and astonishing tale from the beyond.

Chinese Ghost Story Part II, A
(1990) Fantasy   **C-103m**   **Chinese with English Subtitles**
Catalog #0930   **Hong Kong**   **Retail: $39.99**
Dir: Ching Siu Ting **Prod: Tsui Hark**   **Dist: Tai Seng Video**
Leslie Cheung   **Ning**
Joey Wong   **Windy**
Michelle Reis   **Moon**
Ku Feng   **Chu**
Waise Lee   **General Hu**
Jacky Cheung   **Autumn**
Wu Ma   **Swordman Yen**
[***]
An entertaining sequel that briefly explains the original in the opening credits, but it's not necessary to view the first film to enjoy. Scholar Ning (Leslie Cheung) returns to town, lonely and despondent over the death of his beloved Sian. While resting at an inn, he is attacked by a group of thieves and then falsely arrested by the authorities who are more concerned with bounty money than the right culprit. When life seems at its worst, Ning is slated to be executed in place of an official's guilty son. His cell mate takes pity on him and helps him escape, giving him a special medallion. Later on Ning discovers that his elderly cell mate was the great Scholar Wu. Mistaken for Wu (Wu's medallion), Ning meets up with a group of rebels and a quirky spirit-fighter called Autumn. The rebels are led by two beautiful sisters trying to free their father, Lord Fu, who was wrongly imprisoned by the emperor. The older sister is an exact twin of Sian, but claims she doesn't know the woman and shares no feelings toward Ning. At first, Ning is drawn to her but then realizes she is not a true reincarnation of Sian. At the Ten Mile Pavilion, they manage to free Fu who is guarded by a great general sympathetic to their cause, but bound to his duty. A fights ensues which erupts into a unified battle against a giant demon. Then the high monk of the Imperial Court intervenes and captures everyone except for Sian and Ning who team up with Swordsman Yen. It is revealed that the powerful monk is a demon in disguise who is trying to undermine the entire kingdom. All parties involved unite their skills and lay siege to the demon's evil pavilion. In a wild and effects-laden battle which includes a flying centipede, our heroes defeat the evil demon and his minions. Since this is a fantasy kung-fu adventure, expect plenty of flying martial arts, demonic creatures, possession, magic spells, humor, and ludicrous battles (Hong Kong-style special effects) that will appeal to fans of the genre.
Followed by a sequel with a different slant.
Chinese Ghost Story Part III, A (1991) C-109m   Catalog #1161 Retail: $39.99
If you enjoy the fantasy elements, but would like a little more spice and sex, also check out Erotic Ghost Story and its sequels.
Erotic Ghost Story (1990) Fantasy   C-84m   Catalog # 52096   Retail: $89.95
Dir: Ngai Kai Lam   Starring: Amy Yip, Chia Ling Ha, Man Su, Pal Sin, Kamimura Kiyoko

Chungking Express

(1996) Romance   C-104m   Chinese with English Subtitles   PG-13 VA
Catalog #8941   Hong Kong   Retail: $19.95
Dir/Scr: Wong Kai War   Prod: Yi-Kan Chan   DP: Christopher Doyle
Editor: William Chang, Kit-Wai Hai, Chi-Leung Kwong
Music: Frankie Chan, Roel A. Garcia, Michael Calasso
Dist: Miramax/Rolling Thunder
Takeshi Kaneshiro   First Cop
Brigitte Lin   Woman in wig
Tony Leung Chiu Wai   Second Cop
Faye Wang   Faye
Valerie Chow   Flight attendant
[**1/2]
Released under Quentin Tarantino's distribution arm Rolling Thunder, the preview would have you thinking this is another slick, sexy crime thriller in the mode of "Pulp Fiction". Well you're in for a disappointing ride, since the film isn't as sexy, violent, or brilliant. Instead, the film is a moderately cute tale about two different officers and two different women. Most of the film takes place around the Midnight Express, a fast-food eatery located in the Chungking area. The place keeps late hours and offers a selection of western dishes like salads, sandwiches, burgers, and coffee. A handsome detective has just gone through a break-up with his girlfriend May. He continues to call her and then pursues every other woman in existence, even the cute girl who works at the Express also named May. At the same time, a woman in a blonde wig, dark sunglasses and a trenchcoat has hired a family of immigrants to help her smuggle cocaine. The immigrants take off and she has to find them or else the mob will find her. Fatigued and disheartened, she meets the handsome officer in a bar and they have a one night affair. That's the end of the story. No attempt is made to delve into the character's motivations or create any additional impulses. A quick, simple, and stylistic tale of love.
The second story deals with a nightwatch officer who slowly takes a liking to the new girl at the Express. For those who find it difficult to recognize Asian faces, the sudden shift in story may confuse you. Faye likes the officer, but he has a girlfriend. The girlfriend/flight attendant decides to leave and drops off the apartment key at the Midnight Express. Faye decides to keep the breakup letter and key, helping herself into the cop's apartment and life. The second story has a sweeter charm and style to it than the first, and the likeable antics of Faye bloom on you. Listening to American pop songs, Faye cleans up the apartment, stocks the fridge, and takes care of the cop without him finding out. When the officer suspects something wrong and confronts Faye, she quits the Midnight Express and disappears. Later, she returns as a flight attendant and bumps into the officer, offering a chance to rekindle their romance. The visual style and use of camera techniques are what make this film memorable, while the actual contents of the story are cute but forgettable.

Cinema of Vengeance
(1994) Kung-Fu Documentary   C-90m English and with Subtitles   VA
Catalog #XE XA-6003   Hong Kong/UK   Retail: $9.99
Dir: Toby Russell   Scr: Toby Russell, George Tan   Prod: George Tan
Ex. Prod: George Tan, Roy McAree   DP: Kenneth L. Stipe
Editor: Gus Nunes, Phil Harding   Translator: Rachel Choi

PC: Vengeance Productions Dist: Eastern Heroes/Arena Home Video
Bruce Lee, Jackie Chan, Samo Hung, Simon Yam, Donnie Yen, Gordon Liu Chia Hui, Liu Chia Liang, Bruce Li, Chow Yun Fat, Jimmy Wang Yu, Ti Lung, Yukari Oshima, Sophie Crawford, Yuen Woo Ping, Kirk Wong, Gary Daniels
[***]
If you enjoy Hong Kong action/kung-fu films or just have a curious interest in the genre, then pick up a copy of Cinema of Vengeance, an excellent compliment to the documentary, The Deadliest Art: The Best of the Martial Arts Films (USA). Rather than showcase the flashiest and biggest scenes from Hong Kong, Cinema of Vengeance includes rarely seen clips and one-on-one interviews with the talented people in front of and behind the camera. It's evident Mr. Russell loves Hong Kong films and does his best to present an historical overview of the action genre from its earliest beginnings to the present day. Through a series of recent interviews, the genre is explored by the people who actually shaped the course of its history. For those who are long-time fans, it's truly a treat to see actors like Ti Lung, Liu Chia Hui, Simon Yam, Donnie Yen, Bruce Li, and Wang Yu being interviewed and hearing their real rather than dubbed voices, many who speak English,. The video clips include some amazing fight scenes with voiced-over narration and behind the scenes footage of filmmaking in progress. The video covers traditional kung-fu, modern kung-fu, gun-toting Triads, and "Girls with Guns" films, unfortunately many of the big Shaw Brothers productions are absent and remain to be absent from worldwide distribution even today. The selection of scenes from past action/martial arts films differ from the Deadliest Art (no repeats) and some of the choices are questionable. In my opinion, this is only the tip of the iceberg and should not be judged as the best films from Hong Kong, but a sampler documentary with a focus on the stars. Unfortunately, the film does not feature Jet Li, David Chiang, Michelle Yeoh, and a number of big Shaw stars of past decades. Then again, ninety minutes can never do justice to the history and wonders of Hong Kong cinema, but Russell does a great job and offers new insight. A must see for all fans and available in mainstream retailers. On the version I reviewed, the voiced-over narration is difficult to hear during the action scenes.

Circus Kids
(1994) Kung-Fu   C-104m   **Chinese with English Subtitles**
Catalog #ULV3402   Hong Kong   **Retail: $39.99**
Dir: Ma Sui Wai   **Dist: Universe Video & Laser Company**
Yuen Biao, Donnie Yen, Christy Cheung, Ken Lo
[**1/2]
At the beginning of WWII, a group of Chinese circus performers are forced to leave the circus and start a new life when Japanese planes attack the surrounding area. At first they decide to go their separate ways, but the father-figure of the group takes along the men as well as his own children. They sneak passage aboard a ship and travel to a Southern part of China, hoping to meet up with some relatives. With no practical skills, they manage a meek living by putting on acrobatic shows in the street. The local gangs give them a hard time and extort money, but the young men won't give in and fight back attracting the attention of a dashing police captain (Donnie Yen). Yen takes an interest in Cheung and walks a fine line between maintaining order and helping the performers. The group eventually settle down and the men get work in a factory which is secretly a drug base. The children try to find money in the street and end up meeting a

rich woman who is a close friend of their father. Life seems to get better, especially when Donnie takes a fond interest in Christy Cheung. But then problems arise when one of the circus men gets involved in the drug ring at the factory. The drug runners decide to eliminate all evidence and go after the circus kids who fight back in a humorous and clever way. Soon Donnie comes to their aid and they all merge on the gangsters at the drug factory in climatic battle fashion. There's not much new in the department of action and the film suffers from a period of slow lag which is somewhat helped along by a sturdy cast of performers.

City Hunter
(1992) Comedy Kung-Fu   C-105m   Chinese with English Subtitles
Catalog #SEL0535   Hong Kong   Retail: $39.99
Dir: Wong Jing   Prod: Chua Lam
Jackie Chan   Ryu Saeba
Joey Wong   Kaori
Chingmy Yau   Saeko
Richard Norton   Big Mac
Kumiko Gotoh   Kiyoko
Leon Lai
[***]
Japanese filmgoers love Jackie Chan, so it comes to no surprise that he plays the popular Japanese comic book character Ryu Saeba. Ryu is a wild carefree detective and mercenary who spends his days and nights dreaming of seducing women. His trademark theme, City Hunter, flourishes in the backdrop and there's a light sense of flippancy throughout the film. This is a fun film where nothing should be taken too seriously. With his bumbling assistant Kaori, Ryu is asked by newspaper tycoon Imamura to return his beautiful runaway daughter, Shizuko. The cute Shizuko has plans of her own and gives Jackie a hard time, eventually leading him onto a cruise ship. So Ryu and Kaori join other special guests which include Shizuko and an international gang of hijackers led by Colonel MacDonald of the US Commandos. Jackie hooks up with a number of beautiful women, including Chingmy Yau who plays a tough no-nonsense card shark and killer. When the hijackers take the ship, it is up to our group of heroes to kill everyone in sight and not get caught in the process. Don't let the musical number in the middle of the film get in your way, it's kind of fun. Though the film has a high parody level and silly sequences, the fight scenes are still exciting and the action is free flowing, plus the outtakes at the end make any Jackie Chan film worth the rental. Numerous highlights of the film include a fight between Jackie and Richard Norton and a chase scene with Jackie on a skateboard, chasing after Shizuko while being chased by a cadre of teenage skaters. Also a hilarious scene in the ship's arcade provides a fantasy sequence. Jackie hits his head and imagines he is part of Capcom's The Street Fighter video game. Dressed as Chun Li and others, Jackie battles a wild assortment of characters from the popular game. Another scene to look for is a homage to Bruce Lee in Game of Death, when Jackie fights a Kareem Abdul-Jabbar-like goon in the ship's theater. Plenty of action and cute performances from veterans Chingmy and Joey make this film worth watching.

Crime Story   (Serious Crime Unit)
(1993) Crime DramaC-103m   R-rated

Dubbed/Chinese with English Subtitles   Catalog #11233AS   Hong Kong   Retail: $39.99
Dir: Kirk Wong   Scr: Chun Tin Nam, Chan Man Keung, Cheung Lai Ling, Cheung
Chi Shing, Teddy Chan   Prod: Chua Lam   Ex. Prod: Leonard Ho
DP: Lau Wai Keung, Ardy Lam, Poon Hang Seng
Editor: Cheung Yiu Chung   Music: James Wong , Mark Lui
Prod Design: Tony Au, Lui Chor Hung, Luk Chi Fung
Prod Manager: Hui Chung Ming Shuen Ka WaiSue Wu, Law Sau Wai
Costume Design: Chong Chi Leung, Cheung Hok Chiu MAD: Jackie Chan
PC: Golden Harvest   Dist: Dimension Home Video/Paragon Film Ltd.

Jackie Chan	Inspector Chan
Kent Cheng	Detective Hung
Christine Ng	Lara
Law Hang Kang	Wong Yat Fei
Au Yeung Pui Shan	Wong's Wife
Phlia Leng Leng	Psychologist
Blackie Ko	Captain Ko
Wan Fat	Simon Ting
Low Houi Kang	Ng Kwok Yan
Chung Fat	Ng Kwok Wah

[**1/2]

A different style of Chan film that may disappoint fans expecting fast-paced action and comedy recently found in Rumble in the Bronx, Supercop, and Operation Condor. This direct to video release was picked up by Dimension Films, and once again features Chan as a supercop going undercover. But this time the general mood and performance by Chan are toned down and stretches a more serious side to the actor's repertoire. Based on the real-life kidnaping of Hong Kong real estate tycoon Wong Tak Fai, Inspector Chan is assigned to protect a mogul from protesting laborers and kidnapers. Wong is kidnaped, the job goes awry and two cops are injured. Chan vows to capture the crooks and begs Mrs. Wong not to pay the ransom. The criminal gang of kidnapers are led by Kent Cheng, a disgruntled cop. He plays the heavy, literally and figuratively, which differs from his usual jolly, comedic roles as the friendly fatman. Cheng gives a good performance as a jaded veteran cop turned dirty. His slutty girlfriend works in a "social" club and loves to entice Kent with hot sex, but when she becomes a potential witness, things heat up. They trace the money drop to Taiwan, so Chan and Kent head off and discover the criminals who were to pick up the bank transfer. Kent does everything possible to mess up the case and even goes as far as killing the criminal leader. Suspicions are planted in Chan, so he begins an internal investigation which leads to a few great action sequences. What the film fails to capture is a certain chemistry between the rival cops. Chan is suppose to be a parallel of Kent during his younger years on the force. Kent was once a noble supercop, a veteran officer who solved Wong's previous kidnaping. He feels he hasn't received the respect and recognition, let alone the rewards achieved by lesser men. In a desperate act, Detective Hung turns the tables on Chan and accuses him of being a dirty cop. He tries to murder Chan and shoots his own leg for sympathy. He escapes from Chan and convinces Mrs. Wong to forward the ransom money. Chan survives his near-death ordeal, tracks down Kent and beats him into submission. Dismally, Kent doesn't put up a fight and the scene lacks any drama or action until a fire breaks out in the building (convenient plot device). Chan must rescue a child and Kent tries to escape in the inferno, but is trapped under some debris. Chan can't help him, but convinces Kent to come clean and tell him where Wong is being held. The harbor patrol pick up the kidnapers and save Wong. The film fails to capture Kent's fall from grace and the two cops never form a bond or friendship to dramatically dissolve from. From scene one, Kent is the pathetic overweight (generic) character who hardly deserves any sympathy or respect. If Kent had been the good cop and Chan the corrupt one, the film might have taken an interesting turn. Still the film features a nice dramatic turn for Chan and some solid fights: an attack against the Taiwanese criminals, a rowdy prisoner, a night battle between Chan and killers on the street, and a tense standoff in an abandoned tanker.

Crossings
(1994) DramaC-94m Chinese with English Subtitles   Type II
Catalog #1543   Hong Kong   Retail: $39.99
Dir: Evans Chan   Scr: Joyce Chan, Evans Chan   Ex. Prod: Jessinta Liu
Presented by Witty Tsao   New York Unit Prod: Robin O'Hara
Associate Prod: Russell Freedman Assistant Dir: Thomas Chow, Todd Pfeiffer, Cub Chia
DP: Jamie Silverstein   Editor: Henry Chang   Music: Kung Chi Shing
Prod Design: William Chang, Deana Sidney   Costume Design: William Chang
PC: Riverdrive Productions Ltd.   Dist: Tai Seng Video

Simon Yam	**Benny**
Anita Yuen	**Mo-Yung Yuen**
Lindsay Chan	**Rubie**
Tang Wing Sun	**Mo's Dad**
Tong Yu	**Mo's Mom**
Ted Brunetti	**Joey**
Monica Ha	**Mabel**
Marian Quin	**Julie**
Toshi Chan	**Chung**

[**]
Occasionally, Hong Kong filmmakers leave the Asian mainland and fly to foreign countries to film their movies. An obvious and popular choice is the United States with California and New York being the most popular due to their high profile recognition and large Chinese-American communities. I'm all for new locales, but living right outside New York City and growing up on Martin Scorsese and Woody Allen films, the locale shooting and cinematography in many Hong Kong projects never capture the true beauty and nature of the city. With that, there's not much of an engaging story here which could easily be titled, A Chinese Alice in Wonderland. Mo-Yung is a young, innocent and pretty girl from China who alters her plans to fly to Toronto and arrives in New York City to search for her cheating boyfriend Benny (Yam). Claiming he was a friend of Mo's American friend Carmen, Benny arrives in China and asks Mo to show him around. He pretends to be a photographer and starts a torrid relationship with the young woman. They plan a trip to New York City and he asks her to take along a package for him. She arrives in Manhattan, but decides to hide from Benny after realizing his true nature. She's carrying a drug shipment and Benny will do anything to get it back. He had used Mo and tells his beautician girlfriend, Mabel, that he'll get the drugs and get rid of Mo. Throughout the film, another character (Joey) is introduced and seen in the shadows of society. An American school teacher

who takes medication and is plagued by self-doubts and a need for sex. He prowls the streets, beats up kids, lives with mom, looks for Asian prostitutes (cause they're more feminine!), and stalks pretty girls so he can push them onto subway tracks. For most of the film, his actions are outside the sphere of Mo's life and seem rather pointless. Considering the fact that he's the only Caucasian character, his hostile and perverted nature will definitely enforce stereotypes of New Yorkers being a dirty and dangerous bunch. Mo looks for her friend Carmen at her old apartment, but instead meets Rubie, a kind health worker who befriends her. When she finally confronts Benny, her old emotions are embraced and she passionately kisses him and cries about her father's recent death. He convinces Mo to tell him where the drugs have been hidden. Mo and Benny join Mabel and they pick up the drugs, but dump Mo and take off. The police are in hot pursuit, having been tipped off by Rubie. Alone, Mo contacts Rubie and tells her she wants to abort Benny's child. She waits quietly at a subway platform, waiting for her friend. Rubie rushes to meet her and the perverted stalker follows the unsuspecting Rubie into the subway, but instead of Rubie, he pushes Mo to her horrifying death. A rather depressing end to a disappointing film. If you enjoy slow-paced dramas with little substance and a dark conclusion then be my guest, otherwise I'd recommend a film that takes better advantage of the talents of Yam and Yuen.

Crouching Tiger, Hidden Dragon
(2000) Kung-Fu/Drama/Romance
C-120m   Chinese with English Subtitles   PG-13
VA=TBA   Taiwan/USA
Dir: Ang Lee Scr: Hui Ling Wang, James Schamus, Kuo Jung Tsai
Prod: Ping Dong, Li Kong Hsu, William Kong, Ang Lee, Quangang Zheng
Ex. Prod: David Linde, James Schamus
DP: Peter Pau   Editor: Tim Squyres
Music: Tan Dun   Cello Solo: Yo Yo Ma
Prod: Design: Timmy Yip
Costume Design: Timmy Yip
Visual Effects: Jonathan F. Styrlund   Action Director: Yuen Woo Ping
PC: Sony Pictures Classics, Asia Union Film & Entertainment Ltd., China Film Co-Production Company, EDKO FILMS   Dist: Sony Pictures Classics (USA)

Chow Yun Fat	Li Mu Bai
Michelle Yeoh	Yu Shu Lien
Ziyi Zhang	Jen Yu
Chen Chang	Lo
Sihung Lung	Sir Te
Pei-Pei Cheng	Jade Fox
Fazeng Li	Governor Yu
Xian Gao	Bo
Yan Hai	Madam Yu
Deming Wang	Tsai
Li Li	May
Su Ying Huang	Auntie Wu
Jin Ting Zhang	De Lu

Rei Yang	**Maid**
Kai Li	**Gou Jun Pei**
[****]	

"The faithful heart makes wishes come true."

-Lo

When I first discovered a martial arts film was to be directed by critically acclaimed Ang Lee (Wedding Banquet, Sense & Sensibility, Ice Storm) and choreographed by Yuen Woo Ping (The Matrix, Iron Monkey, Fist of Legend), starring Hong Kong veterans Chow Yun Fat and Michelle Yeoh, I knew a truly special film was in the works. A renowned Asian/American director was following his dreams of making a traditional kung-fu film based on the early novel by Wang Du Lu. On December 8th, 2000, the film graciously premiered at the New York Film Festival, and soon opened around Manhattan and other select cities. Being in the New York area, I eagerly sought out the film and sat in a crowded theater, not once but three times before writing this review.

One could argue, the film lacks the best martial artists on screen or the best story in Chinese lore or the slickest sets and effects, but CTHD supercedes the sum of its part, and the greater whole has transpired into one of the finest Asian films ever made, and most likely, the finest martial arts picture ever created. Incorporating a truly stellar blend of music, scenery, martial arts/wire work, acting, direction, and other elements, CTHD is an emotional experience into a traditional world of honor, duty, love, and friendship.

The story gently blossoms revealing characters and desires before a single drop of blood is shed. The great Wudan warrior, Li Mu Bai, has decided to retire his famed sword, Green Destiny (akin to King Arthur's Excalibur), and seek a life of tranquility with his beautiful colleague Shu Lien, the head of Sun security escort service. Chow and Yeoh are excellent in their roles, having portrayed noble warriors in dozens of previous films, but here they are allowed a moment of pause to showcase their subtle acting abilities and emotional range. As fate intercedes, a young thief steals the Green Destiny from Sir Te (Sihung, a popular actor from past Lee films) who is custodian of the ancient sword. Li and Shu realize that the sword was stolen by a disciple of Jade Fox (played by Hong Kong's first cinematic heroine Cheng Pei Pei). Going by the name of Master Long, our thief is caught between two worlds, one of finery and aristocracy, the other a world of vengeance and brutality known as the Giang Hu Underworld. Master Li and Shu must discreetly retrieve the sword, stop Jade Fox who had murdered Li's Wudan master, and help guide Long from her wicked path of destruction. For those who want to discover more of the plot, it is revealed that Long is Lady Jen, the daughter of Governor Yu, a just and noble politician who has left the western province of China for a position in Peking. He has arranged a marriage between his daughter Jen and a powerful nobleman named Gou. Under the tutelage of her governess who is secretly the Jade Fox, Jen is taught distrust and hatred for Wudan. Wudan Temple normally never accepts women, so Jade Fox stole Wudan's highest Secret Fighting Manual from Li's master and poisoned him with Purple Yin. She has been hiding for ten years studying the manual and teaching Jen. The ferocious Jen becomes confused and angered by her dutiful position in life after a police officer is murdered by Jade Fox. Through an extensive flashback, we discover she is in love with a nomadic bandit named Dark Cloud/Lo who has come to Peking to retrieve her. Her confusion and feelings of betrayal encourage her to steal the Green Destiny sword. Torn between her deep love for Lo and her noble responsibility to her family, she forsakes both lives and escape into the countryside dressed as a warrior. One of the many spectacular fight scenes include a restaurant brawl (similar to the Western barroom brawl) where a host of pompous-titled masters challenge Jen to a duel. The sisterly Shu Lien advises Zhang to stay true to her heart, even battling her to prove her point, and deeply admires the young girl's fiery persona, beautifully portrayed by Zhang with an equal duality of delicate frailty and savage power. Li Mu Bai believes the girl has potential to be the greatest Wudan fighter of all time and eagerly seeks to persuade her to leave Jade Fox's side and become his personal disciple. Jen warns that she might use the skills of Wudan to kill Li, but he is willing to take the chance. They battle atop a beautiful forest, walking and leaping from branch to branch with graceful ease and superhuman precision that defies gravity and logic. She is pursued by Master Li and Shu who stop her, defeat Jade Fox, and retrieve the sword, but at a great final cost to all the characters involved. The film's focus is on the female characters and the outstanding martial arts sequences are bountiful, truly shining when Shu Lien and Jen are on the screen. It is not unusual for female characters to play such a prominent role in Asian films, since women have historically been relegated to a subservient life which provides powerful characters often abused and underestimated by their male counterparts. In CTHD, the women are full of passion, dreams, and beliefs. The fight scenes are impeccably choreographed by Yuen with flawless wire-work, lightning-fast editing, and balletic artfulness. Ang Lee brings to life a true Chinese epic which deserves critical and financial success. Not surprisingly, the subtitled film is in a position to break a number of records and usher in a new age of martial arts/foreign popularity. Tested screen viewers often forget they are watching a foreign film and many people do not even realize they are reading subtitles, having become so involved in the film's characters and story. Tender moments are punctuated by Yo Yo Ma's elegant cello music. A combination of open-handed and weapons fighting blaze across the screen in a number of well-placed battles throughout the entire length of the film. Few movies have brought so much character to the screen and even the Green Destiny sword has a life and persona of its own. Please take heed that the martial arts sequences involve a number of flying/floating sequences which can be achieved only by master's of the highest degree.

I was very fortunate to be able to review this film for my book, and fittingly, this was my final entry before publication. As I finish this review, the film has yet to open nationwide and I wonder how the film will fare with audiences and critics alike. Since then the film has become a critical and commercial success, followed by a less than spectacular sequel.

The Crucification
(1994) Crime C-91m Chinese with English Subtitles   Type II
Catalog # 1534   Hong Kong   Retail: $39.99
Dir: Ko Lam Pau   Scr: Abe Kwong Man Wai, Chu Kang Ki
Prod: Wellson Chin Sing Wai, Joey Lau, Shirley Yan
Ex. Prod: Wellson Chin Sing Wai, Abe Kwong Man Wai
DP: Cheung Yiu Cho   Editor: Jing Ya   Music: Tommy Wai
Art Dir: Sukie Vip   Assistant Dir: Kwok Man Ki   Prod Manager: Petrina Ho Wai Yee
PC: P.U. Production Limited   Dist: Tai Seng Video
Michael Chow Man Kin, Jan Lau Kam Ling, Hilary Tsui Ho Yan, Sing Fung On, Ho Ka Kung, Liu Kai Chi, Jiang Rong, Ivy Leung, Toby the dog
[**]

While sitting on a toilet, a crook gets a pleasant visit from Inspector Ho (Michael Chow). The press compliment the ease in which Ho captured Big-Eyes, the number two criminal in Hong Kong. Affable Ho and his newly assigned female partner discover a stray dog and follow it back to its owner, Suen Tai Pang. Only problem is the owner is dead, stripped and crucified in the middle of the woods. They check out his apartment and the dog leads them to another apartment which was used for Suen's sexual liaisons. They catch a young woman in the apartment and start an investigation into Suen's past. In classic detective fashion, the police officers search for clues and question possible suspects. Armed with a handful of photos (that are the key to the mystery), they question Suen's three closest friends. Slowly, the two detectives develop a relationship with each other. They visit a Christian church and ask about the religious significance of the cross. The priests tell them about Christ and his sacrifice for forgiveness to the world. Their prying pays off and they discover the four friends had hired a sex mate called Fong who committed suicide. In remorse, Wah killed his friend Suen and planned to murder the other men to pay for their sins. He fakes his own murder in one of the most elaborate suicides imaginable. He impales his hands onto a wooden cross, sets himself on fire, and dives off a building. The police think the murderer is still on the loose, but Inspector Ho knows better. The murders do continue, but this time they catch Wah's wife who blames herself and tries to cover her husband's tracks. She struggles against Ho and his female partner. The film ends abruptly with her death and loose ends are conveniently tied up over tea on a beach patio. The film follows along the lines of a murder mystery where everyone is a suspect. Since the film doesn't feature Hong Kong's A-list of actors, there isn't much appeal for devoted fans. The actors give nice performances, but there's nothing exceptionally new or fresh to the story and forget about any slick action or tense drama. Hollywood taboos and rules don't apply to Hong Kong films, so expect quick left turns in the plot and dysfunctional logic sprinkled with sporadic violence.

Crying Freeman (5 episodes)
(1988-1993) Japanime: Action   C-50m (each episode)   Dubbed   VA
Japan Retail: $19.95 (each episode)
Dir: Daisuke Nishio Scr: Higashi Shimizu   Music: Hiroaki Yoshino
PC: Toei Video Co., Ltd.   Dist: Streamline Pictures/Orion Home Video
(based on the graphic novels by Masahiko Takasho, Kenji Okamura)
[1/2]**
Crying Freeman is definitely a popular series, appearing in manga comics and as a live-action film from French director Christophe Gans, starring Mark Dacascos and Julie Condra Douglass. A young Japanese man is kidnaped and brainwashed into a super assassin for the 108 Dragons, a secret Chinese criminal organization. The story traces his life as an assassin leader who eliminates high-profile clients. His skills border on the impossible and brutal, always shedding tears for his fallen victims. When a woman, Emu Hino, spots him after an assignment against a Yakuza boss, the Crying Freeman does not kill her and leaves the scene. The two fall in love with each other. As their bond forms, they must battle other criminal organizations and those who believe he is no longer worthy to lead the 108 Dragons. The animation style follows the line of the bizarre, mature, and down-right nasty.
Episode 1: Portrait of a Killer Catalog #SPV 90663
Episode 2: Shades of Death 1 Catalog #SPV 90733
Episode 3: Shades of Death 2 Catalog #SPV 90803

Episode 4: A Taste of Revenge Catalog #SPV 90863
Episode 5: Abduction in Chinatown   Catalog #SPV 90963

Crystal Triangle
(1987) Japanime   C-86m Japanese with English Subtitles   VA
Catalog # USM 1029 Japan Retail: $29.95
Animation Dir: Kazuko Tadano   Original Story: Seiji Okuda
Scr: Junki Takegami   Art Dir: Masazumi Matsumia   Character   Design: Toyoo
Ashida, Kazuko Tadano, Mandori Rukurabu
Prod: Yasuhisa Kazama, Nagateru Kato, Yukio Nagasaki
English Version - Ex. Prod: John O'Donnell   Production   Coordinator: Cliff   Rosen
Translation: Neil Nadelman
PC: MOVIC/Sony Video Software International Corp. Dist: U.S. Manga Corps
[1/2]**
Dr. Kamishiro and his eclectic band of archaeologists must decipher the mysterious codes set
down in the crystal triangle. Similar to Harrison Ford in "Raiders of the Lost Ark", the ancient
secret could be a key to great power and wealth. In no time, everyone is after Kamishiro's party,
including government agents and alien creatures. The secret reveals a way to avoid a deadly
astronomical disaster that plans to return to Earth and was the true reason for the dinosaur's
extinction. A typical film in the Japanese animation archives, but one that does not stand out or
truly represent the genre at its best.

Curse of the Undead Yoma
(1989) Japanime: Horror   C-90m Japanese with English Subtitles   VA
Catalog # VHSCY/001   Japan Retail: $29.95
Dir: Takashi Anno   Scr: Noboru Aikawa Original Story: Kei Kusunoki, Shueisha
Character Design: Matsuri Okuda PC: Toho Co., Ltd./MPS   Dist: A.D. Vision
[***]
Historical horror set in the 1500's during the bloody civil wars to unify Japan. The film revolves
around two characters, Hikage and Marou, two ninjas. In Japan, ninjas were comprised of close-
knit clans who lived together in remote villages, usually in the mountains or forest. There the
young would be trained as ninjas from childhood until they reached full maturity as adults and
were then assigned. Loyalty and trust were a key part in the clan where betrayal was non-
existent. Such famous clans as the Iga and Koga Ninjas emerged to battle for powerful warlords.
Hikage and Marou grew up together as boys and were the closest of friends. When Marou
betrays the clan and almost kills Hikage, a tale of revenge is set into motion. Hikage spends the
next part of his life in search of Marou. Meanwhile, the country is locked in a bloody war with
Oda Nobunaga and the Yoma (demons and the undead) rise to power from the death and
destruction. The powerful land and sea Yomas wish to combine their powers and dominate
humans. The animation is marvelous and the imagery is haunting, but the story becomes
repetitious in the fact that Hikage fights one battle after another to get closer to Marou. Along
the way, he meets two different women named Aya. The first is a kind woman that helps him
along his travels, the second is a young ninja who teams up with him. The film contains extreme
visual imagery of horrendous demons that have yet to be rivaled in brutality and originality in
American horror films. Caution to viewers, the stylish and rich animation contains a good

amount of graphic violence and nudity for mature audiences who enjoy traditional dark fantasy and samurai/ninja swordplay.

Cybercity OEDO 808: Data One
(1990) Japanime: Scifi   C-48m Dubbed/Japanese with English Subtitles   VA
Catalog # USM 1174 Japan Retail: $29.95
Dir: Yoshiaki Kawajiri   Original Idea: Juzo Mutsuki   Music Dir: Yasunori Honda
Character Design: Yoshiaki Kawajiri, Hiroshi Hamazaki, Masame Kosone
PC: Madhouse/Japan Home Video Dist: U.S. Manga Corps
[1/2]**
Highly charged, fast-paced minifilm blending action and science fiction. In 2808, aboard an orbital space prison, three criminals with multilife sentences are given a deal by the warden. Work for a special crime unit and for every criminal you apprehend, you reduce your overall prison time. The other choice, you can just rot in jail for the next three hundred years. The trio make a decision and are sworn in as special officers, but are not completely trusted by their chief. Just to make sure they don't escape, explosive collars and trackers are embedded around their throats. Plus an R2-D2 like robot follows them around, offering assistance and companionship. The trio comprise of three men: the first is the heroic handsome type, the other is the muscular, dark-skinned brute who is the computer hacker, and the third is an effeminate assassin who wears makeup and moves like a woman. Their first case deals with a super computer hacker who has taken over a spacescraper (skyscrapers built to extreme heights) in Cybercity OEDO 808. Of the three characters only the first one is developed, most likely the others are being saved for future installments. When the spacescraper's main computer vault becomes inaccessible, the hero discovers the main computer designer is preventing his entry. He is hiding in fear from an attempt on his life. In the distant past, he had killed the original creator of the city's computer and taken his spot in the corporate ladder of success. Somehow the building's computer discovered the dead corpse, absorbing his living mind and essence, and merged together, causing the computer to pursue a vendetta. The film doesn't delve deep into social issues, but entertains with a solid story and high quality animation.
The marketing of Japanese animation is very interesting, since an animated series can be viewed on two levels: individual episodes or the entire series. You don't necessarily have to watch every episode in a series to enjoy later episodes, but watch them each for their own enjoyment. However, when watched as one full-length saga, the story is best realized.
Cybercity OEDO 808: Data Two (1990)   C-48m Catalog # USM 1174 Retail: $29.95
Cybercity OEDO 808: Data Three (1990)   C-48m Catalog # USM 1174 Retail: $29.95

Cybernetics Guardian
(1989) Japanime   C-45m Japanese with English Subtitles   VA
Catalog # USM 1330 Japan Retail: $29.95
Dir: Koichi Ohata   Scr: Mutsumi Sanjo Prod: Hidenobu Ohyama
Character Design: Atsushi Yamagata   Music: Norimasa Yamanaka
English Version - Ex. Prod: John O'Donnell   Production   Coordinator: Stephanie
Shalofsky   Translation: Neil Nadelman
PC: Soshin Pictures Enterprise Company/AIC   Dist: U.S. Manga Corps
[1/2]**

The future is not a pretty place to live and officials have devised of a way to cleanse the city of Cyberwood. The crime, disease, and poverty in the slum-ridden areas of Cancer have reached chaotic proportions. The Federal government authorizes two scientists to discover a solution. The beautiful Leyla and her companion John Stalker search for a non-violent approach, using the Guard Suit. Their rival Adler will do anything to stop them and sabotages Leyla's experiment which results in the death of Stalker. He is converted into a bizarre cybernetic warrior. Hidden within the slums, a satanic group known as Doldo Brethren wait for a sign to rise up and seize power. When Stalker appears in the streets of Cancer, his violent actions unleash a deadly chain of events. The popular theme of man and machine in futuristic urban decay are once again explored in a slick and brutal style, the Japanese animation way.

-D-

Dagger of Kamui
(1985) Japanime: Action   C-132m   Japanese with English Subtitles   VA
Catalog # ANI AT093-008   Japan Retail: $39.95
Dir: Taro RinOriginal Story: Sampei Shirato
PC: Haruki Kadowawa Films, Inc. Dist: AnimEigo
[**1/2]
Overly ponderous and lengthy story of ninjas and warriors of the late 19th century. Jiro, a young boy is given the task of finding a treasure in feudal Japan that sends him traveling to Western America and back to Japan. The evil clan of the Tenkai will do anything to stop him and retain the treasure to further the Shogun's power. Along the way he meets an assortment of bizarre characters from female ninjas, Buddhist priests, and magicians who battle him to the death. As Jiro discovers the truth of his family's murder and the secret of the hidden treasure, he matures and realizes his monk/mentor was using him all this time. He meets the mighty monk and challenges him to a duel. The animation is good, but the multitude of characters and the constant shifting of setting and tone makes this film a lengthy adventure to watch under the best of circumstances.

Dangaio Volume 1
(1990) Japanime: Scifi   C-45mJapanese with English Subtitles   VA
Catalog #USR VD2   Japan   Retail: $34.95
(See "Dangaioh: Hyper-Combat Unit" for Complete Production Credit Listing)

Mayumi So	Mia Alice
Akira Kamiya	Roll Kran
Maya Okamoto	Lamba Nom
Naoko Matsui	Pai Thunder
Takeshi Ano	Professor Tarsan
Shigeru Chiba	Gil Berg
Ken Yamaguchi	Skeleton
Kenichi Ogata	Captain Galimos

[***1/2]
Highly energizing and exciting three-part series combining psychic powers with futuristic robots. One of the best shows to combine Marvel's X-men like characters with the popularity of

Japanese mechwarriors. Four young teenagers awaken aboard an abandoned space station with their memories wiped. Mia Alice, a young girl peers around in the darkness and hugs her slender body for warmth. "Where am I?" she asks when suddenly a giant battle droid advances menacingly toward her. She screams and crouches in fear about to be killed. Suddenly a ball of fire pummels into the middle of the droid, destroying it completely. The energy from the ball of fire dissipates and a teenage boy, panting, introduces himself. Soon we also meet a cute little girl named Ramba Nomio who shoots lasers from her finger and a sexy woman named Pi Thunder with the strength of Hercules. The four are told they are nothing but robots created for an evil ruler named The Bunker. At first they except their fate, but memories start to flash and Mia Alice knows she isn't a machine. The four escape, in search of the truth, and become mortal enemies with The Bunker.

Dangaio Volume 2
(1992) Japanime: Scifi   C-45m Japanese with English Subtitles   VA
Catalog #USR VD7   Japan   Retail: $34.95
[*1/2]**
The second film follows the further exploits of the Dangaio team as they try to recover their memories. This time the story focuses on the youngest member as she tries to recall her past. Ramba was a princess of a planet that was destroyed by the Bunker. The Bunker still furious at how his plans were foiled, assign a trio of assassins with superpowers to stop the Dangaio team. One of the assassins is a member of Ramba's planet and carries a personal vendetta against the princess. Her royal family refused to fight and handed control of the planet to the Bunker. On a remote planet, the two opposing teams battle to the finish.

Dangaio Volume 3
(1992) Japanime: Scifi   C-45m Japanese with English Subtitles   VA
Catalog #USR VD8   Japan   Retail: $34.95
[*1/2]**
The excellent end of a trilogy which proves that creative ideas are still a factor in action anime. The final episode follows the only male member, Roll, as he travels to do battle against The Bunker on a distant planet. Suddenly Roll has a flashback and remembers who he is. The planet he is saving is his own and he was the leader of the resistance, a warhero and an ace pilot. Ironically, his character is usually portrayed as the wimp and the pushover of the three females, but deep within him, the spirit of the team lies. As he tries to rekindle his past memories, he discovers that he was betrayed and murdered by his own friends for profit and jealousy. He then battles his friends and must also deal with the Bunker's forces to become victorious. The Bunker launch a final attack, but Dangaio disappears into the depths of deep space.

Dangaioh: Hyper-combat Unit
(1996) Japanime: Scifi   C-90m Dubbed   VA   Catalog # MGV 636239
Japan Retail: $19.99
Dir/Original Story/Character Design: Toshihiro Hirano
Scr: Toshihiro Hirano, Koichi Ohata, Noboru Aikawa   Prod: Toru   Miura,   Toshimichi Suzuki
DP: Kazu Konishi   Music: Michiaki Watanabe, Kaoru Mizuya

Art Director: Kazuhiro Arai   Creature Design: Junichi Watanabe
Mecha Design: Shoji Kawamori, Koichi Ohata, Masami Obari
PC: A.I.C./Emotion/Artmic Dist: Manga Entertainment Inc.
[***]
Compilation film which features highlights of all three Dangaio Episodes. The entire story is told from beginning to end, but in an abridged form which leaves out some of the key battles and mood setting scenes. I recommend the original episodes over the compilation version, since the pacing of the story is hectic and not as smooth as the original. Still if you rather not invest the time and money, there is still a good amount of action and character appeal in the English-language version. Dangaio is a solid representation of the wide appeal of giant robot action. The robots represent a cross breed between samurais of traditional Japan and the modern destructive power of Godzilla (also symbolic of the dangers of technology like the atomic bomb). When the heroes battle to save lives, they inevitably destroy a large portion of the city and surrounding area. Even in victory, the battles carry a high toll in lives and property. During the battles, the robots often act like martial arts warriors rather than advanced machinery. They often yell, kick, flip, and use an assortment of weapons like swords and other traditional martial arts items. Dangaio possesses all these characters and so do the villain's robots. One of the best representations of Japanese robot films, the skillful animation, dramatic themes, varied characters, catching music, and combination of supernatural and technological powers provide a treat for all animation/action fans. Emotion Productions was on a role with megahits like Dangaio and Gunbuster, but later ran into production difficulties and abruptly stopped, so copies may be difficult to obtain.

Darkside Blues
(1994) Japanime: Scifi   C-83m Japanese with English Subtitles
Catalog #USM 1557 Japan Retail: $19.99
Dir: Nobuyasu Furukawa   Scr: Masayori Sekishima
Original Story: Hideyuki Kikuchi, Yuho Ashibe
Ex. Prod: Masamichi Fujiwara, Hirokazu Takahashi, Tomoyuki Miyata
Prod: Masako Fukuyo, Tomohisa Abe   Music: Kazuhiko Toyama
Character Design/General Animation Dir: Hiroshi Hamasaki
English Version - Ex. Prod: John O'Donnell   Prod: Stephanie Shalofsky
Translation: William Flanagan, Yuko Sato
PC: Toho Co., Ltd./Akita Shoten/J.C. Staff   Dist: U.S. Manga Corps
[***]
A shadowy gothic film which explores a future Earth made up of those who have power and those who do not. The opening images will not be forgotten as they pull the viewer into a post-apocalyptic world of shattered cities and disbanded governments. In the dark future, a powerful corporation, Persona Century, has complete control over society and owns 99% of the planet. When a black hole opens up, a mysterious figure emerges on a flying horse-drawn carriage. Spouting the word "Renewal" his very presence is an enigma and his abilities defy the laws of reason. Known as Darkside, he is freed from an eighteen year imprisonment and befriends a group of people fighting for freedom in one of the last remaining 1% free zones. Known as Kabuki Town, it resides in the dark outskirts of an area once known as Shinjuku, Tokyo. A small band of rebels launch a surprise assault against the Persona's main headquarters in outer

space. Only one man survives, Tatsuya, and he escapes to Kabuki Town where he meets Mai, a streetwise leader of a gang known as the Messiah. She and her friends help Tatsuya and take him to Selia, a healer, who cures Tatsuya and hides him in a Church. Meanwhile from their orbital citadel, the rulers of the corporation muster every available soldier, psychic (enhanced human) assassin, and device to stop the rebels. Their assassins are deadly, but even the most powerful of the enhanced, Guren, falls easy prey to the powers of Darkside who can alter reality and pull an individual's mind deep into their inner consciousness. The Persona Corporation locate the rebel headquarters in the Himalayas and plan to neutralize it. With the help of Darkside, Mai, Selia, Katari, and others, Tatsuya travels to an abandoned junkyard to meet his fellow rebels. The Persona Corporation gather their forces and lay in ambush for their final battle. Darkside Blues is a fascinating and complex film which will appeal to viewers interested in the rich mature aspect of Japanese animation. The film uses a faded, washed-out style to personify the oppressive drabness of society, but is amazingly crisp and incredibly fluid. The film focuses on the story and characters, but leaves some conflicts open apparently for a sequel. Gratuitous violence and nudity are minimal to non-existent, but the mature tone is best suited for teenagers and adults.

Dark Warrior: First Strike
(1991) Japanime: Action   **C-60m Japanese with English Subtitles**
Catalog #ADV DW/001   **Japan Retail: $29.95**
Dir: Masahisa Ishida   **Scr: Yu Yamamoto**
Character Design: Kenichi Onuki
PC: Kadokawa Publishing/Daiei Co., Ltd. Dist: A.D. Vision
(created by Sho Takeshima)

Norio Wakamoto	**David Rockford**
Kazuki Yao	**Joe Takagami**
Yasunori Matsumoto	**Lloyd**
Arisa Ando	**Rosa**
Yuka Yano	**Judy**
Tetsuo Mizushima	**Detective Rudy Bochwitz**
Kotono Mitsuishi	**Pamela**
Ken Yamaguchi	**Man A**
Ryo Utsuki	**Policeman**

[**1/2]
The first in an animated OAV series dealing with genetic experimenting and creating a race of superhumans. Joe Takagami is on top of the world, a brilliant computer scientist, a handsome single man who just appeared on the cover of TIME magazine. He is head of a research department for the Rockford Corporation in sunny California's Silicon Valley. One day, while driving in his sport car, he notices a woman that reminds him of his long lost love, Judy. She didn't want to follow him to American and the two parted ways. He still loves her and uses his computer to find out her whereabouts. Strangely, the computer has no recollection of any such person. He delves deeper into his own past and discovers certain inconsistencies and an ominous project called, "System God-Blood". His close friend and confident, Lloyd, is sent to keep an eye on Joe. Lloyd and his battle goons take care of any intervention and hide a dark secret. The animation style isn't on the cutting edge, but reasonably good. The story has some intrigue as the

characters develop and change into brutal warriors. This best fits the category of fight movie, plenty of bloody action and bone-crunching fights. The gore factor in the first episode is pretty tame by anime standards, but picks up at the end and may shock younger viewers.
Followed by a second volume: Dark Warrior Part 2: Jihad   ADV DW/002

Deadful Melody   **(Magic Lyre/6-Fingered Strings Demon/Deadful Music/6-Finger Lyre Demon)**
(1993) Fantasy Kung-Fu   C-91m Chinese with English Subtitles
Catalog #1434   Hong Kong   Retail: $39.99
Dir: Ng Min-Keng   Dist: Tai Seng Video
Yuen Biao   Lun
Brigitte Lin   Snow
Tsui Kam Kong, Carina Lau Kar Ling, David Lam Wai, Wu Ma
[***]
Brigitte Lin is the beautiful and serene master of the Magic Lyre, an ancient six-stringed instrument. When played by a master musician, the lyre can create colorful sonic vibrations of unimaginable and deadly powers. Lin's father was the rightful owner, but since the Magic Lyre's powers are feared, the world's greatest martial arts masters decide to kill his family and take the lyre for the people's safety. They corner the little girl, Snow, at a majestic waterfall and demand the lyre. She refuses, backing up and falling to the rocks below. All are assumed dead and the lyre destroyed, but sixteen years later the lyre appears. A beautiful mysterious witch appears and orders the best escort/protection warrior to deliver the lyre. Yuen Biao and his father take the job, but along the way everyone tries to steal the lyre. Some of those involved in the theft were the original masters who killed Lin's parents. She plots to pit them against each other and will clean up the rest with vengeful satisfaction. She is so driven by her hatred that innocent people like Yuen are just pawns in her game. Complications arise when Lin discovers Yuen is her own brother who was saved by an eccentric monk. More problems pop up when the Fire Master's young student falls in love with Yuen and doesn't steal the lyre. Brother and sister combine forces and defeat the greedy, corrupt grand masters, but at a dear price. Brigitte Lin carries herself with mournful grief throughout the film and is seen from time to time, but the story revolves around Yuen Biao and his relationship with the other characters. A colorful costume story that meanders at times with a dozen minor characters sharing the screen, but the action scenes are fun and the fantasy elements balance well within the martial arts sequences.

Deadly China Hero (Duel of the 2 Masters/ Last Hero in China/Iron Rooster Fights Centipede)
(1993) Kung-Fu   C-102 min   Chinese with English Subtitles
Catalog #XE XA-6004   Hong Kong   Retail: $9.99
Dir: Wong Jing   MAD: Yuen Woo Ping   Dist: Arena Home Video
Jet Li, Cheung Man, Leung Ka Yan, Anita Yuen, Dicky Cheung, Gordon Liu Chia Hui
[***]
Non-Tsui Hark film that carries on Jet Li's famous role as Wong Fei Hung. Though not as well polished as Once Upon a Time in China, the film is still very entertaining and well-choreographed. Leaving out the heavy political overtones and historical reflection, Jet Li is a more light-hearted Wong worried about running his martial arts school and avoiding trouble.

There is also a glimpse of some "Drunken Master" style kung-fu which is absent in the Once Upon A Time in China films. Jet Li arrives in town to open a new branch of his famous Po Chi Lam school of medicine and martial arts. He meets three criminals and takes care of them at the station. A series of humorous problems arise when he buys a building that happens to be next to a brothel. The students become distracted and the owner wishes to become Wong's student. Also the Rebellious Boxers are using a monastery as a prostitution front to sell young girls to southeast Asia for money. They plot to overthrow British interests with their newfound wealth. Wong and his students meet a father/daughter traveler who team up with him to rescue the women from the evil monks led by Liu Chia Hui. Wong is also harassed by a vile official (actually second in command) who is a bitter rival jealous of Wong's fame and fortune. Wong and his assistants Ah-Fu and Ah-So discover the Boxers plot, but are framed by the wicked official who wants to destroy Wong's reputation. Complications arise when Wong discovers contaminated medicine that cause some children to become deaf. He samples some of the foreign liquid on himself and loses his hearing which effects his martial arts when assassins attack him. Wong and the official meet at a lion dance festival and Wong is disgraced when the official beats him with a weapon-filled centipede costume. It's the set-pieces and wild antics that make this special. In the lion-dance climax, he single-handedly battles a fire-breathing centipede while dressed as a leaping, scratching rooster. Then the battle enters a warehouse full of wine, giving Li an opportunity to demonstrate his drunken style. The film closes with a montage of comedic outtakes taken from the film. It's best to view other Jet Li-Wong films to fully appreciate the humor and style of the parody. The film does suffer at times from slapstick/lowbrow humor and obvious budget constraints on the action sequences. What makes this film particularly entertaining for Jet Li fans is the fact that his comedy is well complimented with marvelous martial arts scenes. A little warning: the release of Deadly China Hero is a truncated version of Duel of the 2 Masters, with most of the comedy dealing with the brothel edited out.

Deadly Dream Woman
(1992) Action C-95m Chinese with English Subtitles   Hong Kong
Dir: Wong Jing, Wong Tai Lai
Cheung Man, Jacky Cheung, Chingmy Yau, Yo Chok Ching, Yip Duk Han
[1/2]**
Cheung Man stars as a super elite assassin called Nightingale Wong. Nightingale, the gorgeous daughter of a triad boss, and her sister are assigned to protect their father at an organized crime meeting. Then one of their own betrays the boss and the entire family is attacked by assassins. The two women attempt to protect their father but are overwhelmed and everyone dies except Nightingale who escapes into a boat and drifts out to sea. You may be tempted to think the film is an action thriller at this point, but then the scene shifts to a luxurious boat full of gorgeous women and over-sexed men. Here the comedic elements step in as the escorts decide to swindle the men and dump then into a life raft. The women discover a boat floating toward them and discover Nightingale, injured and unconscious. Sexy Ching (Chingmy Yau) and her mother nurse her back to health, but discover the young woman has amnesia. In cute scenes, Ching and Nightingale become best friends and pseudo sisters enjoying shopping sprees and the likes. Her mother is a con-woman who is in serious debt from gambling. That's why she pretended to be a madam for escorts and also tries to fortune tell. When the thugs come to collect, she is helpless

and attacked. A memory ignites in Nightingale and she dispatches the thugs. After bumping her head again, she regains her memory and wipes out the villains with the help of some triad pals. Since it has only two well-staged fights, one at the beginning and one at the end, with only minor stunts here and there, the film does not have the full action appeal. The women involved are engaging and humorous throughout the film, especially Chingmy Yau and Cheung Man.

Deadly Mantis   (Shaolin Mantis)
(1978) Kung-Fu   C-100m   Dubbed   Hong Kong   Retail: $19.99
Dir/Scr: Liu Chia Liang   Prod: Mona Fong   Ex. Prod: Run Run Shaw
MAD: Liu Chia Liang
PC: Shaw Brothers Studios
David Chiang, Huang Hsing Hsiu, Liu Chia Yung
[***]
Many of the popular kung-fu films of the 1970's portrayed David Chiang as a weasel or scoundrel who only fought when he felt it was necessary, but later redeeming himself through heroic acts. This film features a similar character, but Chiang is not redeemed in the conclusion. This film takes a different approach to Chiang's screen charisma, while offering Chiang the solo spot in a solid and different style of kung-fu story. The time period is the Ching Dynasty ruled by the Manchus while the rebels are Mings loyal to the original Han emperor. Chiang is assigned by the Ching court to infiltrate a wealthy family and discover their true loyalties. He accepts the spying position and establishes himself as a respected scholar and gentleman within the household. As he spends time teaching, he develops a love affair with the master's daughter. Here the film cleverly takes advantage of Chiang's wily charisma, and whether or not he is truly in love or using the young woman is a mystery. However, he wishes to marry her and become part of the family. When they discover, he is a Ching spy, the couple must leave the household. The father refuses to let him leave with his daughter and a spectacular fight sequence erupts within the master's mansion. Chiang and his love fight one family member after another, making their way to the exit. Sadly, she is torn between fighting for her family and the man she loved. In a classic sacrifice, she dies at her father's hand to provide Chiang an escape. He does escape into the vast woods and while hiding from his enemies comes upon a praying mantis. He observes the insect's fighting style and invents a form of praying mantis kung-fu. He returns to the mansion and takes revenge for his wife. The film concludes at the Ching emperor's court. Chiang is dressed in formal robes and bows before the emperor, accepting praise and reward for his mission. His father who helped assign him, approaches his son and then attacks him. He claims he is also a Ming rebel, and that the actions of his son disgraced the entire nation. Ironically, Chiang is murdered by his own father as was his beloved wife, a tragic testament to Chiang's court greed and blind subservience to the Emperor. Director Liu creates a rare character in his film, where the main character is a Manchu (Chiang) and the antihero of the film, developing into the hero and villain. The downbeat ending is not uncommon for Asian films which often times prefer the martyr over the happily ever after ending commonly found in American films.

Death Chambers
(1979) Kung-Fu   C-121m   Dubbed   Hong Kong   Retail: $19.99
Dir: Chang Cheh   Scr: I Kuang Prod: Mona Fong   Ex. Prod: Run Run Shaw

PC: Shaw Brothers
Alexander Fu Sheng, Chi Kuan Chun, Ti Lung, David Chiang, Wang Lung Wei
[1/2]**
A classic Chang film portraying the final days of the Shaolin Temple before Manchurian troops burned it down. The film prequels Five Masters of Death, beginning with Fong Sai Yuk's (Alexander Fu Sheng) admittance into Shaolin temple. He and his pals train rigorously and wonder about the mysterious rebels (Ti and Chiang) who are staying in the temple. They spy on the rebels and begin to form an admiration for the men who stand-up against the Ching oppressors. Sai Yuk leaves the temple for a while, then discovers the Shaolin monks have been sold out to the government by a traitor. At the crack of dawn, the Manchurian Army gains entrance into the temple and begin to burn and pillage the temple. The high-ranking abbots decline to add to the bloodshed and retreat to their chambers and meditate as flames erupt around them. The heroic Fong Sai Yuk returns in time for the climactic battle and joins his comrades to fight with the Ching soldiers which ultimately ends with the Temple being burned and the surviving rebels escaping into the countryside. The film ends with the heroes dispersing and promising vengeance against the Chings which opens the door for Five Masters of Death, Executioners of Death, and other classic kung-fu films based on the true historical destruction of Shaolin Temple..

Demon City Shinjuku
(1993) Japanime: Horror   C-82m Dubbed/Japanese with English Subtitles   VA
Catalog # USM 1351/USM1107   Japan Retail: $19.95/$29.95
Art Dir: Yuji Ikeda Scr: Kaori Okamura Original Story: Hideyuki Kikuchi
Character Design & Dir: Yoshiaki Kawajiri   Animation Dir: Naoyuki Onda
Setting: Masao Maruyama PC: Video Art/Japan Home Video Dist: U.S. Manga Corps
[***]
A dark tale of demonic horror in modern day Tokyo, Japan. Shinjuku is an affluent district in the heart of Tokyo and is now under the dominion of a powerful demon called Levih Rah. The demon plans to spread his domain all over Tokyo, then the entire planet. If his plans are to be stopped, it must be in three days before he grasps a permanent stronghold on Earth. Sayaka Rama, a young woman enters the Demon City in search of her father and teams up with a streetwise hero called Kyoya. Together they come across a bevy of nasty demons who slither like snakes and morph out of solid objects, dripping with saliva and blood. Carefully, they battle their way to victory with a little help from a mystic called Mephisto. Dark, disturbing, with beautiful images, Demon City takes advantage of the flexibility of animation to create a demonic world beyond any image in a live-action film. A solid entry point for fans who wish to discover a slightly darker and mature side of Japanese animation.

Devil Hunter Yohko
(1992) Japanime   C-45m (each volume)   Japanese with English Subtitles   VA
Catalog # ADV Y/001   Japan Retail: $29.95 (each volume)
Dir: Tetsuro Aoki   Scr: Yoshihiro Tomita   Original Story: Juzo Mutsuki
Character Design: Takeshi Miyao
PC: Toho Co., Ltd./Madhouse   Dist: A.D. Vision
[1/2]**

Some viewers may recall the Yohko Sega Genesis game that appeared in the states before the actual film, it was based on, was released. Combining campy humor, the supernatural, and a bunch of cute high school girls, this animated series has a lot in common with Buffy the Vampire Slayer. Teenager Yohko is the 108th descendant of a great line of devil/demon hunters and since she is the freshest descendant (virgin), she is chosen to defend Earth. Initially, she is unwillingly to accept her role and suffers from doubts and inexperience. Out of dire necessity, She quickly learns to control her powers from her wise and fierce granny. In true girl-anime fashion, she is adorable, childlike, and dresses in skimpy outfits while dispatching monstrous, grotesque creatures on a weekly basis. Look for newer episodes with sharper animation in the near future.
Volume 2 Devil Hunter Yohko 2 & 3
Volume 3 Devil Hunter Yohko 4 & 5

Devilman Vol. 1 "The Birth"
(1987) Japanime   C-55m Dubbed/Japanese with English Subtitles   VA
Catalog # MGV 634791/USR DIE03   Japan Retail: $14.95/$19.95
Dir: Tsutomu Iida   Scr: Go Nagai, Tsutomu Iida
Original Work & Supervisor: Go Nagai   Character Design: Kazuo Komatsubara
Music: Kenji Kawai
PC: Dynamic Planning/Kodansha/Bandai Visual Dist: U.S. Rendtitions
[**]
From the opening sequence, beautifully but grotesquely animated, a world of fairies and demons battle in a tropical Eden-like paradise. A powerful fairy puts an end to the proliferating demons and then the world is free to blossom. Forward to the modern era where a teenager named Akira must take the mantle of power and battle off the demons.
One day while walking home from school, Akira and Miki are accosted by street punks who kill rabbits. The couple escape, but Akira's classmate appears in front of him. Ryo Asuka takes Akira to his father's home and explains to him a bizarre story. An ancient race of demons have resurfaced on the planet and can take the shape of any object. In an interesting twist, Akira must possess a powerful devil named Amon. Using the devil's power, he starts a war against the demon race.
Go Nagai's work has publicly been criticized for stretching the boundaries of good taste. The graphic violence and use of saturated colors is both mesmerizing and downright disgusting. Still with any artform, Nagai's style and technique is somewhat morbidly captivating. This series is not recommended for children and should be viewed with caution.
Devilman Vol. 2 "Demon Bird" (1987)   C-55m
Catalog # MGV 634793/USR DIE05 Retail: $14.95/$19.95

Devil's Woman
(1996) Horror   C-95m Chinese with English Subtitles   Type III
Catalog #1988   Hong Kong   Retail: $39.99
Dir: Otto Chan   Ex. Dir: Kant Leung Assistant Dir: Sunny Luk
Scr: Philip Cheng, Ring Law   MAD: Ng Cheung Pang
DP: Paul Yip   Art Dir: Ring Law   Prod Man: Arthur Wong
Music: Tang Siu Lam   Editor: Kwok Tin Hung
Ex. Prod: Eddie Wong, Otto Chan   PC:Extra Film

Dist: Universe laser & Video Co., Ltd.
Tsui Kam Kong, Maryann Chan, Ben Ng, Ivy Leung, Cammy Choi, Law Lan, Joey Wong, Chan Kwok Bong
[**1/2]

Recently Hong Kong filmgoers have enjoyed a recent surge in sexy thrillers, mixing violence with down-right pornographic elements. Similar to the cheap sexy direct-to-video films found in video stores under erotic thrillers or mature audiences, such as Stripped to Kill, Bedroom Eyes, Animal Instinct, and many others. The unusual aspect of Chinese erotic thrillers is that the film looks to have the same quality budgets, actors, and production value assigned to mainstream films. These films don't look like weekend projects made in basements, but indulge in sexual elements that border or exceed the steamiest of R-rated films and can be best categorized as NC-17 films. An attractive stewardess dressed in red walks the streets of Hong Kong. She is being stalked and suddenly attacked by a man. After being beaten, dragged, and almost killed, the director yells cut and tells her to do a better job and to stop complaining. The sadistic director makes her do the scene again and this time the young actress suffers the humiliation and abuse. The female actress decides to boost her career by seeking out a fortune teller who makes her sign a pact with the devil. Her popularity skyrockets, but she must kill anyone who gets in her way. Meanwhile Officer Lam Kwok-Kong (Tsui) is on a hostage rescue mission and watches in horror as a thug blasts a pregnant woman in the stomach, shockingly rocketing the fetus out of the womb. Traumatized, he seeks counselling with an attractive psychiatrist. He develops an interest for the psychiatrist which turns into trouble when the Devil's Woman possesses Lam to commit rape. His female partner, Cheung Si-Man keeps an eye out for him. The two police officers discover the true villain behind the Devil's Woman, a lonely man who tries to reincarnate his dead wife with the blood of innocents. In a bizarre and twisted scene, Tsui must resist possession, defeat the evil sorcerer, and save the soul of the young actress. Horror is not the easiest genre to digest and certain scenes will definitely scare off the timid with its bizarre blend of horror, sex, comedy, and the insane. Kam Kong's solid performance and the female villain's charm help to propel the story to a somewhat entertaining level for fans of the genre.

Dirty Ho
(1979) Kung-Fu   C-90m Dubbed
Catalog #KRT 224   Hong Kong   Retail: $19.99
Dir: Liu Chia Liang Scr: I Kuang Prod: Mona Fong   Ex. Prod: Run Run Shaw
DP: Arthur Wong, Ao Chih Chun Editor: Chiang Hsing Lung, LiYeh Hai
Music: Eddie H. Wang   Art Dir: Johnson Tsao   MAD: Liu Chia Liang
PC: Shaw Bros.
Gordon Liu Chia Hui   11th Prince
Yung Wang Yu   Dirty Ho
Lo Lieh   The General
Hsiao Hou, Hui Ying Hung
[***1/2]

The emperor needs to choose an heir to the imperial throne, but what happens when you have more than one son who wants the same position. Gordon Liu Chia Hui is back as the 11th prince who must survive an assassination attempt by the older fourth prince. Incognito, Gordon travels outside the palace to enjoy life and frolic at brothels. He acts carefree, a harmless playboy unconcerned with the assassination attempts. One evening while staying at a high-class brothel, a young man (Yung) impresses the women with his wealth and physical prowess. Gordon becomes jealous and uses his wealth to entice the women. The competition to entice the women continues until both men produce a box of jewels. Then soldiers arrive and plan to arrest both men, since one of the jewel boxes is stolen. In confidence, Gordon reveals his true stature and orders the young man escorted home and assures the soldiers that both boxes are his. As the film progresses, Ho decides to teach Gordon a lesson, but the two men form a loose partnership. Gordon keeps his identity a secret from Dirty Ho, while enjoying life's pleasures with his new found friend. In no time, the fourth prince orders his corrupt generals to put an end to Gordon's life. They try all manner of assassination techniques, but fail. A number of well-staged scenes follow where the 11th prince avoids assassination by pretending to do something else while secretly doing martial arts. Eventually, the prince must return to the palace for the coronation and uses Ho to help him. The generals under the fourth prince try to stop him and the action steams up in a large-scale attack against the prince and Dirty Ho. Though the end is debatable as to whether Dirty Ho receives his just award or not for helping the prince. A highly charged and fast-paced film with a decent dose of comedy and kung-fu. The humor stems from fight scenes in which the characters are fighting amongst each other while sharing tea or discussing art in front of casual observers. A definite treat for fans of Gordon Liu (with hair) and director Liang.

Dirty Pair: Affair at Nolandia
(1985) Japanime   C-57m Dubbed   VA   Catalog # SPV 90403Japan
Retail: $19.95
Dir: Mashahara Okuwaki   Scr: Kazunori Ito   Created: Haruka Takachiho
Mech Design: Studio Nue, Kazutaka Miyatake, Yasushi Ishizu
Character Design: Tsukasa Dokite Music: Yoshihiro Kunimoto
PC: Studio Nue/Sunrise Inc./NTV Dist: Streamline Pictures
[1/2]**
Here is a prime example of what most people call to mind when asked about women in Japanime. Two beautiful girls in skimpy outfits with big eyes who go on a rampage with guns and spaceships. In the process, cities are destroyed and plenty of explosions. The Dirty Pair were a popular duo of characters in a number of videos and Affair at Nolandia was one of the first available to American audiences. Kei and Yuri are agents for the WWWA, an intergalactic agency for justice. They usually play the bad cop/good cop image, but are sweet girls at heart. They are on the case and eventually board a luxury liner which is infiltrated by ruthless criminals. In classic Dirty Pair fashion, they defeat the bad guys with a little help, cause millions in property damage, and solve the case to the chagrin of their boss who must always clean up their messes. If you enjoyed their antics, check out:
Dirty Pair: Project Eden (1987)   C-80m Catalog #SPV 90813 Retail: $19.95
Dirty Pair: Flight 005 Conspiracy (1990)   C-60m Catalog #SPV 90883 Retail: $19.95

Doctor Wai "In the Scripture With No Words"   (King of Adventures)
(1996) Action/Romance   C-90m Chinese with English Subtitles
Hong Kong   Retail: $39.99
Dir: Ching Siu Tung Prod: Charles Heung, Alex Wong Jen-Ping
Administrative Prod: Tiffany Chen   Prod Supervisor: Chui Po Chu

PC: Eastern Production Ltd.Win's Entertainment Ltd.
Jet Li   Chow Si-Kit/Dr. Wai
Rosamund Kwan   Monica/Miss Cammy
Takeshi Kaneshiro, Charlie Young, Ngai Sing, Billy Chow, Law Kar Ying, Johnny Kong
[***]
A different kind of outing for Jet Li and Rosamund Kwan which borrows heavily from various film genres. This time Jet Li is a pseudo-Indiana Jones in search of treasure and adventure in the 1930's. At first, you might expect a historical action film in the vein of Once Upon A Time in China...well you are in for a surprise when Li suddenly appears in modern day Hong Kong. The story is just that...a story. Li plays a modern day writer who is working on a series of popular adventure stories. At the same time, he is having serious romantic problems with Rosamund Kwan. Too stubborn to admit he was wrong, he alienates Kwan while at the same time broods over his mistake. His subconscious mind seeps into his writings and the people in his life become characters for his book. At times, his co-workers jump into the story and re-write material to help the couple patch up their tremulous relationship. A number of gags play off the fact that what they write effects the ever changing lives of the characters in the story. The inner story takes place in the early part of the century and deals with the recovery of a mystical treasure. Jet Li is the Chinese nationalist in search of the treasure while Kwan is initially portrayed as a vile, Japanese spy bent on destroying Li. As the real life relationship improves, Kwan's spy falls in love with the heroic Dr. Wai. A number of action sequences play through the film, but the constant pulling in and out of scenes disrupts the overall flow of the film. The ruthless Japanese will stop at nothing to get the treasure and raid a Chinese establishment. Both stories are juxtaposed throughout the entire film until both issues are solved...Dr. Wai and Chow both get what they truly sought. Though there are a number of action scenes, the film has a strong romantic comedy undercurrent throughout the film. Since their charismatic pairing in Once Upon a Time in China, Jet Li and Kwan are always a pleasure to watch. However, Doctor Wai's various themes and familiar plot devices will fail to deliver pure entertainment for fans who only want solid kung-fu or solid romantic comedy.

Dog Soldier: Shadows of the Past
(1989) Japanime: Action   C-45m Dubbed/Japanese with English Subtitles   VA
Catalog # USM 1470/USM 1032   Japan Retail: $14.95/$34.95
Dir: Hiroyuki Ebata Scr: Sho Aikawa   Character Design: Masateru Kudo
Art Dir: Takuji Jizomoto   Animation Prod: Motomu Sakamoto, Nagateru Katou
PC: MOVIC/Sony Music Entertainment, Inc.   Dist: U.S. Manga Corps
(based on the comic by Tetsuya Saruwatari)
[**]
In the mold of Rambo, our hero John is an ex-Green Beret trying to fit back into civilian society. John looks like Rambo, dresses like Rambo, but thankfully he doesn't talk like Stallone! While working at a construction site with his beefy, not too bright, marine pal, the two witness a botched kidnaping. Gunfire explodes around them and John decides to get involved. John and the government agents try to help the woman escape from her kidnapers. The situation changes and the woman murders a government agent and disappears with the kidnapers. John and his friend are captured by the agents and recruited to help find the woman, the case, and the culprit. The case contains an important cure (AIDS) that could save the fate of millions of ill people.

John's past comes full circle, when it is revealed he knows the woman and the kidnaper's boss. Growing up on the harsh streets, the trio bonded together as children and became close friends. Now, John must battle his old friend for the fate of the world. Generic action anime with a good dose of violence led by a stoic hero.

Dominion Tank Police (4 volumes)
(1989) Japanime: Scifi   C-40m (each volume)   Japanese with English Subtitles
VA   Catalog # USM 1037 Japan Retail: $19.95 (each volume)
Dir: Koichi Mashimo   Scr: Koichi Mashimo
Original Story: Masamune Shirow Character Design & Animation Dir: Hiroki Takagi
Art Dir: Mitsuharu Miyamae   PC: Hakusensha/Agent 21/Toshiba Video Softwares, Inc.
Dist: U.S. Manga Corps
[1/2]**
In the future, the world's atmosphere is contaminated beyond safety limits and people must examine their radiation level before going outdoors. Most people suffer from some form of contamination, but hospitals are gathering samples of healthy people to search for a cure. An elite group of criminals, the Buaku gang, decide to steal samples of healthy urine. Thanks to the striptease antics of two minx-like twins, the gang escapes from the sex-starved police. It's up to the Dominion Tank Police to stop them in their ongoing adventures. Using heavily armored vehicles which cause more damage than help, the team will do anything to stop crime. Newcomer Leona joins the force and on her first major mission drives her commander's tank. Plenty of over the top animation and humor in the style of Police Academy crossed with Japanese animated hijinks. The style of animation is entertaining and the characters have unique appeal, but the childish antics will turn off viewers in search of something more serious or dramatic.
Volume 2   Catalog # USM 1016
Volume 3   Catalog # USM 1017
Volume 4   Catalog # USM 1018

Don't Give A Damn
(1995) Action C-95m Chinese with English Subtitles
Catalog #ULV 3447   Hong Kong   Retail: $39.99
Dir: Samo Hung   MAD: Samo Hung   Dist: Universal Video & Laser Co.
Samo Hung, Yuen Biao, Takeshi Kaneshiro, Cathy Chow
[1/2]**
Screen action/comedy veterans Hung and Biao both prove they're still kicking and having fun. The actors both play off each other's comedic skills and physical prowess, but long time fans may be disappointed with the familiar and subdued story. Samo is a cop named Pierre and Yuen is a customs officer who both start off on the wrong foot with each other. Using street contacts, Samo and Yuen set up a meeting to buy drugs from each other in a supposed undercover sting, but both end up bringing money and no drugs. Dozens of agents from both sides draw guns while a criminal pulls out a knife and mournfully stands in the middle of the crowd. During the drug sting operation, they end up arresting each other while the real criminals never get captured. When the situation is straightened out, both officers are criticized for their botched up actions.

This causes a bitter rivalry between Samo and Yuen and the two different departments they represent. Samo's problems are exacerbated when a handsome, bright officer (Takeshi) becomes Samo's new superior. Takeshi is a by-the-book officer who doesn't care for Samo's carefree, irreverent attitude. The three men end up fighting and hating each other, becoming rivals on the job and in the locker room. When Samo and Yuen decide to see which officer is tougher, the fight scene is fast, crazy, and hilarious. The three officers gradually become friends while they wine and dine some female policewomen. The film is full of flirtatious comedy with Samo falling in love with a new recruit (Cathy Chow) while being pursued by a sex-hungry officer. Then the story shifts gear when the officers have to stop a Japanese mobster from stealing some drugs. The Japanese hire a group of criminal punks skilled in martial arts to break into police headquarters and make off with the confiscated drugs. When things get too hot, the Japanese try to liquidate the punks who in turn escape. One of the punks, an African-American, is captured by the police, so his friends kidnap Samo's girlfriend and demand a trade. In the climatic finale, Samo, Yuen, and Takeshi go to the rescue and battle the punks who in turn must battle the Japanese mobsters who also battle Samo and friends. The situation is humorous and childish, but fast-paced with delightful performances from the entire cast. A bit of the African-American racial humor can be interpreted as insulting, but keep in mind this is a comedy action film from Samo Hung and that no offense was intentionally meant.

Doomed Megalopolis (4 volumes)
(1992) Japanime: Horror   C-50m Dubbed   VA   Catalog # 90603   Japan
Retail: $19.95
Dir: Rin Taro Original Story: Hiroshi Aramata   Original Scenerio: Akinori Endo
Music: Kazz Toyama   Dialogue: Ardwight Chamberlain
English Version Adapted, Produced, & Directed by Carl Macek
Prod: Toei Video and OZ   Dist: Streamline Pictures
[***]
Most Japanese animated films deal with the future or the ancient past (samurai/ninja), occasionally a filmmaker will choose a different era in Japan's rich history and the results are quite refreshing and entertaining. Early 1900's, Japan is on the dawn of military/industrial growth, preparing to put away the old culture and create a modern Tokyo to rival the cities of the world. With such ambitions come a price that can lead to destruction. An ancient spirit from Japan's legendary past has arisen from his tomb. Dressed as a military officer, Kato walks the streets of Tokyo and wreaks havoc on those who stand in his way. His finds a beautiful woman and takes possession of her soul. Her brother, her friend, and a mystical monk combine forces to stop the evil spirit and save Japan.
Well made, serious entry into the world of dark animation, Doomed Megalopolis will appeal to fans who enjoy the macabre: Mermaid's Scar, Vampire Princess Miyu, and Demon City Shinjuku. The animation technique is beautiful with surreal dream-like images, ambient music, rich color and lighting composition. Foregoing the exaggerated saucer eyes, the characters are more realistically drawn than typical anime and the horror elements do not delve into gratuitous violence and nudity. Vol. 1"The Haunting of Tokyo"
Doomed Megalopolis Vol. 2 "The Fall of Tokyo"Catalog # 90653
Doomed Megalopolis Vol. 3 "The Gods of Tokyo" Catalog # 90713
Doomed Megalopolis Vol. 4 "The Battle for Tokyo"VA   Catalog # 90743

Dragon Chronicles: Maidens of Heavenly Mountain   (Semi-Gods and Semi-Devils/
The Immortals/8 Guardians of Buddhism/Sky Dragon Eight Sections: Heavenly Mountain
Ancient Virgin)
(1994) Fantasy Kung-Fu   C-108m   Chinese with English Subtitles
Catalog # 35546   Hong Kong   Retail: $89.95
Dir: Ching Wing Keung   Dist: Tai Seng Video
Brigitte Lin, Gong Li, Cheung Man
[**1/2]
For viewers familiar with Gong Li's body of work, Dragon Chronicles is a far departure from her stoic Chinese woman of virtue and fortitude. I confess I was surprised to see Gong flying and kicking alongside Hong Kong finest kung-fu stars. Dragon Chronicles is a fantasy tale based on the works of Jin Yong and follows the exploits of near-God like characters who achieve great powers through magic scrolls, iron pots, and vital energy. The story introduces a number of characters who can fly, fire bolts of energy, teleport, and re-incarnate. For a dose of fast and flighty fantasy, Dragon Chronicles entertains with a host of lovely actresses, beautiful sets, and colorful costumes, but be warned that the story can become befuddled and puerile. The lovely actresses appear and disappear quickly while their motives lack coherency which may confuse first-time viewers. The story begins with the tale of a Magic Sect of martial artists renowned for its power. The Maidens of Heavenly Mountain comprise of three sisters: Gong Li is Mo Han Wan while Brigitte Lin plays twin sisters who both fall in love with the same man. This causes a rift among the sisters and starts a war that pulls in mortals from the human world. The evil sister teams up with an elder martial arts master of fierce power. He sets it upon himself to conquer the other martial arts schools of China and steal their treasured secrets. He has a number of apprentices under him, including a wily beauty named Purple. She decides to steal the secrets for herself and become the greatest martial artist in the world. When the Evil Sect attacks Shaolin Temple to achieve the sacred scroll, most of the monks panic and escape in the night. A few devoted monks (the pole fighting monk is noteworthy) stay and put up a grand fight but are defeated. A young apprentice monk with a facial birthmark escapes from the fallen temple with the sacred scroll. He is ordered by the head abbot to find Master Siu and give him the scroll.
Purple captures the apprentice and demands he translate the scroll. He refuses and she tempts him with plenty of vices against Shaolin doctrines. The two gradually form a bond and together they join forces with Mo who was recently defeated by the Evil Lin. The women are reunited in an underground cavern, put aside their differences, and join forces with the Shaolin apprentice (who learns kung-fu) to defeat Purple's evil master. In true Hong Kong-style fantasy, the characters use their amazing powers in a wild, energetic, and preposterous climatic showdown. The story may be difficult to follow at times, but the charismatic performances and the unique blend of fantasy, humor, and martial arts make up for any shortcomings.

Dragon Fist
(1978) Kung-Fu   C-92m Dubbed/Chinese with English Subtitles   VA
Catalog #4104   Hong Kong   Retail: $9.99
Dir: Lo Wei   Prod: Hsu Li Hwa   Dist: Parade Entertainment
Jackie Chan, Nora Miao, James Tien
[**]

A bearable film, somewhat enjoyable for Chan fans since it showcases his early talents. However the film fails to let Chan express his comedic charm and humor, limiting him into a generic revenge seeker. Throughout the entire film, Chan carries one expression/emotion on his face...hostility. He walks through the film with a scowl on his face and dispatches villains in hasty fight scenes. An older film made before Chan could express his own ideas and unique style, we experience a Chan that is generically similar to the countless other martial arts actors of the period. Chan plays Juan, the number one student of a martial arts instructor who is challenged by another master. Chan's master is killed in the duel, so he vows revenge for the death of his master. Chan, the master's widow, and her daughter visit the victorious master. Since then, the master has seen the folly of his ways and offers condolences. Instead of fighting Chan, he cripples himself and refuses to fight. His students are noble and obedient, hoping to avoid trouble with the angry Chan. The noble students of the master's clan try to capture some criminals hiding at an evil clan led by Wei. Chan's master's wife is then poisoned by Wei's evil clan who trick Chan into working for them against the good clan. Eventually Chan discovers who the real villains are and extracts his own style of revenge. A standard tale which features the usual amount of kung-fu and somewhat noteworthy for Chan's early star-making appearance. The film has seen a revival on videotape, laserdisc and dvd, but was a box office disappointment after the release of Spiritual Kung-fu. Even Jackie Chan has disowned the film for its lack of humor and levity.

The Dragon, the Hero
(1979) Kung-fu   C-80m Dubbed   Hong Kong   Retail: $19.99
Dir: Godfrey Ho   Scr: Szeto On Prod: Tomas Tang, Joseph Lai
DP: Yau Ki   Editor: Leung Wing Chan   Titles: Chung Chuen
Music: Mah Man, Chan Chung   Effects: Michael Fung
Prod Manager: George Lai   MAD: Tang Tak Cheung
Assistant Dir: William Cheung   Assistant Action Dir: Wong Chi Ming
Assistant Cameraman: Mok Chart Yen   Assistant Prod Manager: So Kwok Hung
Makeup: Choi Siu Chun   Still Photos: Lee Man
English: Vaughan Savidge   PC: An Jasso Asia Film Production
John Liu, Tino Wong, Dragon Lee (Bruce Lei), Philip Ku, Bolo Yeung (Yang Sze) Chan Lau, Alexander, Jim James, Chiang Chin, David Wu, Ellen Koon, Lui Yuk Kun, Lee Tin Ying, Li Ping Hung, Wong Chi Ming, Phor Sing
[*1/2]
This is not the worse kung-fu movie I've ever seen, but considering the fact that there are hundreds that are much better, I'd stay away from this film. A competent cast of talent is wasted in a plot that chops its way from one scene to the other without any structure or logic. You can almost sense the actor's apathy as they go through their lines, hoping for a quick kung-fu scene to end their tedium. Even John Liu, a wonderful leg-kicker, appears restrained and must share most of his time with mediocre actors. On the side of justice is Tino Wong and Dragon Lee, a popular Bruce Lee imitator, who are the descendants of a martial arts master killed by John Liu's father. The film takes place twenty years after that climatic battle, and a rivalry develops between the three men. Meanwhile, Liu pretends to be an ex-convict on the run and joins a local crime boss who searches for new fighters by offering prize money in a local bout. One of the weakest points in the film is that the villains are total caricatures: boring, idiotic, and generally offensive.

Veteran strongman Bolo Yeung pops up, but his brief fight scene does little to save this film. His fake chest hair looks awfully moronic. This is the kind of kung-fu film that litters video store shelves and gives martial arts film a bad name. The dubbing is horrible, the editing is poor, and so is the overall camera technique. Characters are introduced for comedic relief, but slow the film's pacing and adds more grimace than smile. Without giving anything away, since there isn't really anything worth giving away, the good guys win and the bad guys die, and who cares how it happens. Expect a lot of sloppy fighting to add insult to injury. An albino without testicles who enjoys fondling women, eating insects, and acting like a rabid dog is throw in for added effect. Poor comedic relief comes from a fat guy and skinny guy who do nothing for the plot. A girl escaping rape is also used as a plot catalyst for more fights. A chain-smoking old master and a pale Bruce Lee imitator is present, and an occasional breath of fresh air from Liu.

Dragon Inn   (New Dragon Inn)
(1992) Kung-Fu   C-102m   Chinese with English Subtitles
Catalog #1103   Hong Kong   Retail: $39.99 Widescreen Available
Dir: Raymond Lee   Prod: Tsui Hark   Presented by Ng See Yuen
Prod Supervisor: Ching Siu Tung   Dist: Mei Ah Laser Disc Co., Ltd
Brigitte Lin   Yau Mo Yin
Maggie Cheung   Jade King
Tony Leung Kar Fai Chow Wai On
Donnie Yen   Lord Tsao Siu Yan
Lawrence Ng, Tsui Kam Kong
[***]

Corruption and terror reign when a power-hungry Eunuch Tsao (Yen with grey hair and makeup) establishes the Eastern Chamber Sect to seize control of China. The sect incorporates the elite Black Arrow Troops, horse-riding warriors who have mastered the art of bow and arrow. They train rigorously and often use human prisoners for target practice. When the Eunuch discovers that Military Advisor Yang is trying to usurp his power with the Emperor, he captures him and tortures him to relinquish his power. The advisor is killed, but his son and daughter are spared. Yen hopes to use the children as bait to capture Yang's number one man, Chong (Tony Leung) who might muster up 800,000 troops against him. Filmed beautifully outdoors in a vast desert of mountains and dry river beds, the children are shackled and forced to march through the empty wasteland. Bandit leader Brigitte Lin, continuing her popular role as a powerful swordswoman dressed in men's clothing, is hired by Chong to retrieve the children. They do so with quick success and retreat to their designated rendezvous, the Dragon Inn. The inn is a lone oasis in a vast desert, commonly visited by border troops and wandering rift-rafts. The owner of the Dragon Inn is Jade (Maggie Cheung), an unscrupulous woman who fools around with men and occasionally kills them for profit. The dead bodies are often used as the main ingredient in the inn's pork buns. When Lin and Chong meet up at the inn, the pace slows down and the mood shifts to claustrophobic tension. In this segment, the characters banter and plot with mixed results on how to escape. The inn is surrounded by border guards and Black Arrow Troops who decide to stay at the inn when a sandstorm erupts. They are unaware of Chong and his party, which increase the comedic and sexual tension among the men and women at the inn. Jade and her butcher sidekick are the only ones who know how to escape via her secret tunnel. Enamored by his charisma, Jade demands Chong have sex with her. The honorable Chong proposes to marry her instead, but uses the marriage ceremony as a ruse to escape with the children. Brigitte Lin also falls in love with Chong and stays close to him and the children. The trio form a love triangle that culminates into a bond of friendship used to defeat the powerful Yen in a spectacular outdoor climax. Though elements of traditional fantasy are not present, the main characters still possess amazing abilities to fly, shoot arrows around corners, bend metal, and tunnel underground. The performances are good while the action is exciting and fast-paced. The outdoor scenery is impressive and a positive sign of the flourishing scope of Chinese films. The characters wear fanciful costumes from the King Tai era of the Ming Dynasty and brandish a large assortment of traditional weapons. The only portion that falters is the mid-section of the film which lags due to a heavy dose of overused situational comedy (Lin versus Jade, Chong versus Jade) while at the inn. Still a positive, entertaining, and critically acclaimed kung-fu epic from Tsui Hark, based on the original 1972 film Dragon Inn by King Hu (starring Pai Ying, Shang Kwan Ling Fung).

Dragon Lord (Young Master in Love)
(1982) Kung-Fu   C-93m Chinese with English Subtitles
Catalog #0407   Hong Kong   Retail: $39.99
Dir: Jackie Chan   Scr: Jackie Chan   Prod: Jackie Chan, Leonard K.C. Ho
Dist: Tai Seng Video
Jackie Chan, Hseuh Li, Whong In Sik, Barry Wong, Chan Wai Man, Sidney Yim
[**]
Young, innocent Chan becomes wrapped in a conspiracy ring that later appears as a story device for the vastly superior Drunken Master II. Chan is Dragon, a martial artist who discovers a plot to sell China's national treasures to foreign dealers. Using his wit and fighting skills, Chan battles the political thieves and stays ahead of their attacks. Though not on the level of Chan's later films, Dragon Lord is a significant transition film in Chan's career. Tired of his straightforward revenge roles, Chan wrote, directed, produced, and starred in a film to showcase his comedic talents and his underdog frantic fight to survive style. Given that, this film should be viewed as a stepping-stone film where Chan shows signs of what would later become his beloved trademark.

Dragons Forever   (Cyclone Z)
(1987) Kung-Fu   C-90m Dubbed
Catalog #0590   Hong Kong   Retail: $39.99
Dir: Samo Hung   Scr: Szeto Chuek Hon
Original Story: Gordon Chan, Leung Yiu Ming   Prod: Leonard K.C. Ho
Ex. Prod: Raymond Chow   DP: Jimmy Leung, Cheung Yiu Tso
Editor: Peter Cheung, Joseph Chiang   Music: James Wong
Art Dir: Horace Ma   Prod Design: Oliver Wong
Prod Manager: William Tam, Alice Chan Costume: Ingrid Kwan
PC: Golden Harvest Group   Dist: American Imperial
Jackie Chan   Johnny Lang
Samo Hung   Luke Wang
Yuen Biao   Timothy
Corey Yuen Wah   Mr. Hua

Crystal Kwok	Mary
Deanie Yip	Catherine Yeh
Pauline Yeung	Nancy Lee
Roy Chiao	Judge Lo
James Tien	Charlie Lee

Shing Fui On, Benny "the Jet" Urquidez, Wu Ma, Sam Wai
[***]

Whenever Jackie Chan reunites with his classmates Samo Hung and Yuen Biao, you can rest assured you're in for a special treat. Jackie, Samo, and Yuen must help a wealthy environmentalist trying to protect the wildlife in her lake. As usual, Jackie is the suave ladies man who happens to be a misguided lawyer for the chemical company polluting the lake. He finds himself attracted to the environmentalist's beautiful cousin who is helping her legal case to close the factory. Chan decides to recruit the aid of two friends who are oblivious of each other's involvement. Samo is a smuggler and con-artist who plays by the rules of honor. Yuen is a wild, very unstable, thief who specializes in breaking and entering into difficult places. Wanting to keep an eye on the environmentalist, Samo moves into the house next door and falls in love with the older woman while Chan wines and dines her young cousin. Poor Yuen spends most of his time with a shrink in one of the slower scenes. At times the comedy can be hilarious, but for new viewers the humor and slapstick may actually disrupt the flow of the fast-paced action. When Chan's friends confront each other, Samo assumes Yuen is a crook and gets him arrested. The predicament sets up a lot of the misunderstanding among the three men which lead to hilarious fight scenes popping up every now and then. The best includes a fight at Chan's apartment where he tries to keep Samo and Yuen hidden from his date. In the meantime, villains are using the factory as a cover for an international drug operation supervised by Benny Urquidez. The film has a slightly uneven balance as it shifts between a romantic comedy and an action film, but both elements are worth watching and excel when seen in the proper light. When Samo is captured by the villains and drugged, it is up to Jackie and Yuen to rescue him. The film showcases more of Samo's comedic talents and not his martial arts. Also Yuen fights brilliantly, but is given a smaller segment than Jackie and Samo, so he doesn't really shine until the end. (According to Yuen, this film convinced him that he needed to branch out and make his own films.) Highlights include, the trio beating up on each other, a spectacular fight aboard a luxury liner, and the amazing finale which also includes a fierce duel between Jackie Chan and world champion fighter Benny "the Jet" Urquidez.

Dragons of the Orient
(1988) Documentary
C-88m English Dubbed   NR   VA
Catalog# 34494   Hong Kong   Retail: $19.95
Dir: Rocky Law
PC: Golden Sun Film Company   Dist: Tai Seng Video Marketing
Jet Li, Terry Fan, Yang Ching, Wang Chun
[***]

Recently released documentary that capitalizes on the growing popularity of Jet Li and kung-fu films. Tourists visit Shaolin Temple in China, learn about the history of the temple, and admire the local kung-fu monks. The film is a loose connection of martial arts demonstrations and clips from early Jet Li films. Showcasing a wide variety of talented wushu practitioners from China, this provides an enjoyable look at real martial arts routines performed with a variety of techniques and weapons. Oddly, the documentary decides to speed up the movement of the demonstrators and to use traditional kung-fu sound effects which take away from the authenticity of the practitioners. Other segments follow a youthful Jet Li in his dramatic rise to superstar status and his return visit to his old master. The film peeks at future stars of kung-fu cinema and includes a number of Jet Li film trailers.

Dreams   (Akira Kurosawa's Dreams)
(1990) Drama/Fantasy   C-120m   Japanese with English Subtitles
PG   VA   Catalog #11911   Japan Retail: $19.95   Widescreen Available
Dir/Scr: Akira Kurosawa   Prod: Hisao Kurosawa, Mike Y. Inoue
DP: Takao Saito, Masahuro Ueda Editor: Tome Minami   Music: Shinichiro Ikebe
Lyrics: Mikhail Ippolitov-Ivanov   Art Design: Yoshiro Muraki, Akira Sakuragi
Set Designer: Koichi Hamamura   Special Effects: Industrial Light & Magic
Makeup: Shoshichiro Ueda, Tameyuki Aimi, Norio Sano   Costumes: Emi Wada
Choreography: Michiyo Hata   Dist: Warner Brothers
Akira Terao   "I"
Mitsuko Baisho   Mother of "I"
Toshihiko Nakano   "I" as a Young Child
Isaki   "I" as a Boy
Mie Suzuki   "I's" Sister
Mjeko Harada   The Snow Fairy
Masayuki Yui
Shu Nakajima
Sakae Kimura   Members of the Climbing Team
Yoshitaka Zushi   Pvt. Noguchi
Martin Scorsese   Vincent van Gogh
Toshie Negishi   Child-carrying Mother
Hisashi Igawa   Power Station Worker
Ikariya   The Demon
Chishu Ryu   103-year-old Man
Tessho Yamashita, Misato Tate, Catherine Cadou, Mugita Endo, Ryujiro Oki, Masaru Sakurai, Masaaki Sasaki, Keiki Takenouchi, Kento Toriki, Tokuju Masuda, Masou Amada, Shogo Tomomori, Ryo Nagasawa, Akisato Yamada, Tetsu Watanabe, Ken Takemura, Tetsuya Ito, Shoichiro Sakata, Naoto Shigemizu, Hiroshi Miyasaka, Yasuhiro Kajimoto, Makoto Hasegawa, Nagamitsu Satake, Satoshi Hara, Yasushige Turuoka, Shigeru Edaki, Hideharu Takeda, Katsumi Naito, Masaaki Enomoto
[***]
Either you'll watch the film's stunning, but slow-moving visual vignettes or you'll dream something better as you fall asleep during this cautiously-paced and uneven director's vision. Made in the director's later years, Kurosawa's film is almost a vision rather than an experience. He carefully weaves his tales with beautiful imagery, focusing on man's place in the sphere of nature. The film has an aesthetic appeal more akin to the senses rather than lengthy storytelling and dialogue. Eight tales are portrayed with a large cast of Japanese actors, and one segment

with American director/Kurosawa admirer Martin Scorsese portraying painter Vincent Van Gogh. Be warned, if you don't appreciate art galleries this probably isn't for you. However, Kurosawa remains a visionary master of Japanese cinema and his Dreams represent a late life testament to his own personal visions and dreams which will hold an artistic appeal that will be appreciated to connoisseurs of cinematic art.

Drunken Master   (Drunken Monkey in the Tiger's Eyes/Drunk Fist)
(1978) Kung-Fu   C-106/113m   Chinese with English Subtitles   VA
Catalog #EDO 5573 Hong Kong   Retail: $19.95
Dir: Yuen Woo Ping Scr: Jackie Chan   Dist: Bulldog Entertainment
Jackie Chan, Yuen Siu Tien, Hwang Lee, Dean Shek
[***]
If it weren't for Drunken Master II, Drunken Master would rank as Jackie Chan's finest performance of Chinese fighting legend Wong Fei Hung. Chan, the consummate perfectionist, proved in the sequel that he could do it even better than his earlier effort which deftly mixes comedy with kung-fu. Yuen showcases his masterful talents at action direction, working well with Chan's physical prowess and comedic timing. Though dated, Drunken Master remains a fine early effort and a very entertaining film for fans of Jackie Chan or the Wong Fei Hung films. It is not required to see the original to enjoy the sequel, but you should initially check out Drunken Master. Chan's Wong is nicknamed Naughty Panther for obvious reasons. He has raw talent, but he doesn't apply himself seriously in his father's martial arts academy. Instead, he's a dilettante who prefers careless fights, flirting with girls, and avoiding hard work. He gets into a big mess when he flirts with a girl and then fights with her mother. The mother is an expert and properly teaches Chan some manners. Angered and humiliated, Chan picks a fight with a local bully. When he returns home, he discovers the girl and her mother are his cousin and aunt, respectively. Then the father of the local bully also demands retribution. Chan's father, Wong Kei Ying makes amends and punishes his son. To learn discipline, Chan is sent to train under Beggar Su Hua Chi, Master of the Drunken Fist. Judging Su by his sloven appearance, Chan lacks respect for the elder which leads to a number of comical martial arts training scenes. Soon, Chan matures, learns the style, and returns in time to take care of the villains. A classic film and an early showcase for Chan's growing talents. Though produced sixteen years later, Drunken Master II proves how amazing Chan's physical presence is on screen, maintaining his lean, quick, and impressive physique.

Drunken Master II (Legend of Drunken Master)
(1994) Kung-Fu   C-102m   Chinese with English Subtitles   VA
Catalog #1568   Hong Kong   Retail: $39.99 Widescreen Available
Dir: Liu Chiu Liang (Lau Kar Leung)   Dist: Tai Seng Video
Jackie Chan   Wong Fei Hung
Anita Mui   Wong's Mother
Ti Lung   Wong Kei Ying
Liu Chia Liang   General Fu
Ken Lo Wai Kwong Ah Jan
Andy Lau
[****]

One of the finest Jackie Chan films produced, also marks his long-departed return to a traditional kung-fu role away from guns, explosions, and car chases. The masterpiece represents one of the best kung-fu films to be produced in Hong Kong, due in part to the directorial helm of veteran star, director, writer, choreographer Liu Chia Liang. From the beginning, Chan and Liang decided they would avoid wire-flying or trick photography in the fight scenes. The film blends comedy with action, using veteran stars as well as newer ones. Screen veterans Ti Lung and Liang lead the way with Jackie Chan and Anita Mui rounding off the superb cast. At the turn of the century, sinister profiteer Andy Lau is illegally exporting Chinese treasures overseas, and it's up to Wong Fei Hung to put a stop to it. What adds an extra does of pleasure to the film is seeing Jackie Chan portraying ubiquitous legend Wong Fei Hung with an irreverent boyish charm that differs from Jet Li's stoic superhero. Ti Lung portrays his noble father, Wong Kei Ying, and Anita Mui brilliantly shines as Fei Hung's wild mother (similar to Josephine Siao in Fong Sai Yuk). At a major train port, Wong Fei Hung, his father, and a humorous servant are waiting to take a train back home. At the turn of the century, trains are a rare luxury and the crowds are enormous. On top of that, export taxes run high and Fei Hung wants to smuggle in the medicinal herbs his father is bringing home. This causes a problem when his pouch of ginseng herbs gets confused with a pouch holding a priceless Chinese artifact which is being smuggled outside of the country. In disguise, General Fu tries to retrieve the artifact and is mistaken for a criminal by Chan. The two masters battle to a stalemate under the train and in an abandoned farm house. Fu may have the physical edge, but he's not interested in injuring the energetic youth. They each grab a pouch and amicably depart, but soon discover they have the wrong pouches.

Fei Hung returns home to a carefree life, but Andy Lau's spies desperate to find the artifact harass Wong's family. Fei Hung fights off his attackers using his drunken style which infuriates his strict father who detests the drunken-fighting lifestyle. Though his mother encourages Fei Hung's antics, his stern father is disappointed. Son and father argue and fight in a dramatic scene that cause Fei Hung to runaway from home. Fei is ambushed and brutally beaten by the villains who continue their smuggling operation at a local factory financed with foreign money. Tensions mount when Fei Hung teams up with Liang to battle an army of axe gangsters and the thieves who are smuggling Chinese artifacts to foreign powers. Liang is killed in the fray, but Chan's Wong is determined to get revenge and bring justice and the treasures back to China. Wong and his noble friends, including a fighting fisherman who initially started as Wong's rival for a girl's affection, enter the heavily guarded enemy headquarters, the massive refinery factory. In an amazing series of sequences, Chan battles one villain after another, dispatching his enemies over hot coals, on conveyor belts, and using industrial alcohol while dressed in glorious white and carrying his majestic white fan. Using drunken style, he eventually battles Ken Lo's amazing kicks in one of the best-choreographed fights in action cinema. The final battle is long and tense with Wong pushing his body to the limits. An excellent traditional kung-fu film that will appeal to fans, old and new. Director/actor Liang marked his comeback with Drunken Master 2, but left before completing the film due to creative differences in the end segment. He is still fully credited as the director and has gone on to a number of other modern projects. Drunken Master 2 went on to break records and was the highest grossing film in Hong Kong for 1994, beating out a number of big Hollywood productions. As usual, Chan ends the film with breathtaking outtakes. The film was released in the United States under the title Drunken Master with a new score, dialogue, and some clever re-editing, including the omission of the original ending which awkwardly portrays Chan as a mental vegetable as a side effect from the industrial alcohol.

Drunken Master III
(1994) Kung-Fu   C-89m Chinese with English Subtitles   Hong Kong
Retail: $39.99 Widescreen Available
Dir: Liu Chia Liang (Lau Kar Leung)
William Kwai, Andy Lau, Michelle Reis, Liu Chia Liang, Gordon Liu Chia Hui, Adam Cheng, Simon Yam
[1/2]**

Though it sounds like a sequel to Drunken Master II (same director), it is a totally different film that fails to capture the flavor and energy of its predecessor. Most noticeably is the absence of Jackie Chan (Wong Fei Hung) and Ti Lung (Wong Kei Ying), a knockout duo of stars impossible to emulate. Liang's early departure from Drunken Master 2 fueled him to create a film that would rival/surpass his Chan collaboration. Liang adds elements of comedy and action in a story that doesn't focus on Wong and his father as the main characters. This time around Liang uses his brother Gordon Liu as a military governor in charge of escorting a beautiful woman (Reis) who is betrothed to the acting ruler of China. She is beautiful, though naive, and wears a jade ring to signify her status as the future empress. The emperor is also superstitious, taking advice form a Chinese (Caucasian actor) priest who warns that the ring is important to his future success. A group of rebels who want to end imperial reign and usher in democracy decide to kidnap Reis and prevent the wedding. Andy Lau, in an important but minor role, is the dashing motorcycle-riding rebel who kidnaps the princess and her jade ring. He almost escapes from Gordon Liu, but is injured and takes refuge at a doctor's house. Of course, the doctor is Wong Kei Ying and he orders his son Fei Hung (Kwai) to take the role of protecting the princess.

While fleeing, Fei Hung and the princess arrive at a winery where the kindly owner, Liu Chia Liang, cares for unwed expectant mothers. Pretending to be pregnant, they hide there while Fei Hung learns some new martial arts techniques from Liang. It doesn't take long for the Governor and his spies to recover the princess, but then at the wedding the future-emperor learns the jade ring is broken. To avert spiritual disaster, the priest tells him to kill Reis. The finale which is the true highlight of the film features Liang, Andy Lau (who finally returns), Fei Hung and his dad battling their way to rescue Reis. Following the end, there are some cute outtakes of the film. Silly and childish at times, the film has fun with itself, but doesn't focus firmly within the story nor does it portray Wong Fei Hung as the central hero. Suffering from an overbearing amount of goofiness and blatant errors in historical consistency, the film doesn't succeed on many levels. Reis is the star of the film, appearing in most of the key sequences and her naive charm adds to the film's enjoyment. If you enjoy light-comedy kung-fu, the film is worth seeing, but the level of martial arts action does not come near the Jackie Chan and Jet Li portrayals of Wong Fei Hung.

DUBS vs. SUBS
(Dubbing and Subtitling Films)

Unless you have a master's degree and fluency in Asian languages, the only choice offered to a non-Asian speaking viewer is watching a dubbed or subtitled film. First off, not to discourage you, the best form to watch a film is in its original native language. The problem with dubbing occurs when mediocre voice actors are hired. They seldom carry the emotional weight of the original actors and don't have the on-site passion of the scene. In the case of great actors, the voice talent is a pale imitation of the true performer's original intent. Could you imagine watching Marlon Brando dubbed in Chinese in the "Godfather" or Clark Gable dubbed in Japanese in "Gone with the Wind" or even Arnold Schwarzenegger dubbed in Korean, that might be fun to laugh at, but they never can match up to the real thing. Also to properly lip-synch the lines, changes are made in the original content of the dialogue. Therefore, my preference is for subtitled films. They are always the best choice, but sometimes reading lines may be cumbersome and difficult to see. I've also seen plenty of spelling errors and incorrect grammar usage. Many Hong Kong films have very small subtitles written in hard to see white print. Especially when seen against a white backdrop, the words are impossible to read. From my experience, Japanese films have the best subtitles. They're large, easy to read, and concise...once again you will not get the full meaning of the original dialogue but an adequate amount to enjoy the film. Any film which has a major distributor will also have excellent subtitles, such as the Gong Li films from Mainland China or Asian films co-produced by American/European film companies. Many of the well-known foreign releases will have large, clear subtitles written in yellow which stand out better than the white lettering. The only time dubbing can be more entertaining is in kung-fu/action films and Japanese animation. The fortunate aspect of animation is that the American voice actors are replacing Asian voice actors, so as long as talented voice actors are hired they can capture the mannerism and nuances of the original animated characters. In Hong Kong martial arts/action films, dialogue takes a second seat to the action sequences and many times the plot is only a device used to move along to the next fight sequence. The action actor's charisma is visible through physical mannerism and attitude, so subtitling can be a distraction in a fast-paced film. No matter how ridiculous the dialogue may seem, keep in mind that due to cultural and linguistic differences, it is a very difficult task to translate from one language to another and that much can be lost in the translation. Some translating firms are more accurate and less grammatically incorrect than other firms. Look beyond the dubbed dialogue and you'll find some pretty enjoyable scenes, until then sharpen your reading skills and enjoy a good foreign film.

Duel to the Death
(1992) Kung-fu   C-90m Not Rated   Dubbed   Catalog #49893
Hong Kong   Retail: $59.95 Widescreen Available
Dir: Ching Siu Tung Scr: Kong Lung, Man Chun, David Lai
Presented by Raymond Chow   Prod Executive: Catherine Chang
DP: Li Yu Tang, Lau Hung Cheung   Editor: Cheung Yiu Chung
Music: Michael Lai Prod Supervisor: Louis Sit
MAD: Ching Siu Tung   Assistant MAD: Lau Chi Ko
PC: Media Asia Distribution   Dist: Tai Seng Video Marketing
Chui Siu Keung, Liu Sung Jen, Flora Cheong
[**1/2]
Once again, China's Shaolin Temple must battle Japan's evil ninjas to prove which country's martial arts is superior. A recently produced kung-fu film that shows technical improvements in

cinematography and visual effects, but still mired by poor plot structure, characterization, and comic book style action sequences...then again that might appeal to you. The film begins at Shaolin Temple where a group of black-clothed ninjas have infiltrated the temple and stolen manuals on China's secret martial arts techniques. They make quick copies and disappear into the night. The Shaolin monks on guard, raise the alert, and the temple comes to life. A lively battle ensues which ends in the ninjas making a last stand on the beach. Surrounded and outnumbered, the ninjas hide the copies and commit suicide. Thus begins a brutal battle between Japan and China.

This is basically a sword and slash film with very little pure, hand to hand, martial arts. Most of the action sequences are done on wires with fast editing. Ching Man is the top swordsman from China and with Shaolin's blessing attends King of the Sword's challenge. Also invited is Japan's top swordsman Hashimoto, an honorable warrior who disagrees with ninja ways. The emperor of Japan wishes to conquer China and must prove his superiority. A Japanese monk is sent to China as a spy and leader of the ninjas. With the help of a Chinese traitor, the Japanese capture all the great martial artist of China and retrieve the copied scrolls. The traitor's daughter, in love with Ching Man, help reveal her father's crime and risks her life to save the young swordsman. Meanwhile, Hashimoto rescues the Chinese fighters, preferring to kill them honorably rather than like animals. This is cause enough for a long battle in the woods as Ching and Hashimoto battle the evil monk and his ninjas. The climatic finale is between the two swordsmen atop a cliff overlooking the ocean. The end results will leave you with something to think about or not? Duel to the Death is not your father's kung-fu film, but follows the wilder format of supernatural abilities and bizarre stunts. If you love mind-bending action, plenty of flying, and little else, you'll enjoy the blood and mayhem.

Duel of Iron Fists
(1978) Kung-Fu   C-100m   Dubbed   Hong Kong   Retail: $19.95
Dir: Chang Cheh   Scr: I Kuang Prod: Mona Fong   Ex. Prod: Run Run Shaw
PC: Shaw Bros.
David Chiang, Ti Lung, Ku Feng, Cheng Kang Yeh
[1/2]**

An early Shaw Brothers classic that unites Chiang and Lung. Though not the strongest film from the duo and extremely dated, the appeal of both actors makes this film somewhat entertaining for vintage fans. The fights scenes are more gang-oriented, less sophisticated, and more brutal than traditional kung-fu films later directed by Chang and Liu Chia Liang.

After Lung's crime boss father is murdered, he takes the rap for the good of the gang and leaves town. In his place, the gang is taken over and brutally managed. When Lung returns, he discovers the gang has been taken over by corrupt people who were the cause of his father's murder. His girlfriend is forced into prostitution, and commits suicide after Lung discovers her shame. His own brother becomes a sloven drunk and is abused by the gang members. The only friend he finds is the cunning Rover (Chiang), a hired hitman, who Lung discovers was his father's paid assassin. Piecing together his life, Lung decides to settle the score. In an open courtyard, Lung and Chiang duel with each other in the pouring rain. Lung uses a pole, while Chiang is a master of the knives. Each fighter gains the upper hand, but pulls back from killing the other. They unite and fight the real brains behind the evil plot, realizing their purpose in life is akin to each other. The climax is hardly pretty, when dozens of assassins are ordered to kill the two men. One of the more violent Shaw films, Lung kills a ton of people, and nothing good ever happens to him.

Duel of the 2 Masters (see Deadly China Hero)

Dynamo
(1981) Kung-Fu   C-81m Dubbed   Catalog #FRM 4005 Hong Kong
Retail: $19.95
Dir: Hwa Yi Hung   Prod: Pal Ming
PC: World Northal   Dist: Fox Lorber/Orion Home Video
Bruce Li, Mary Han, Ku Feng, James Griffiths, George V. Yirikian, Steve Sander, Joseph Soto
[**]
If you're a Bruce Li fan, it's actually a bearable kung-fu film when seen for its fight scenes. The story revolves around Bruce Li's character, a young martial artist who hits it big by becoming a movie star. Driving the streets of Hong Kong as a taxi driver, Li is discovered by an advertising director named Mary. A number of the scenes are recreations of real Bruce Lee's movies as Li appears in films and promotions. As his fame skyrockets, so does the number of enemies he has to battle. Mary decides to get Li a martial arts instructor played well by Ku Feng. She chooses a down and out teacher who has lost the initiative to teach, since so many of his students have been a let down. He drinks, smokes, and reads a newspaper rather than pay attention to his students, but he is talented and his own drive is rediscovered with Li. He beats up the arrogant Li and tells him to attack him at any time. This allows for a number of spontaneous and entertaining fight scenes. When the time is right, Ku Feng leave Li and warns him about the price of success. The rest of the film involves a weak plot involving a rival agency who wants to steal Li or at least make sure he fails. They hire assassins and go out of their way to ruin Li's career by kidnaping his girlfriend. To ensure victory, Mary and her cohorts rekidnap Li's girlfriend and encourage him to win. It comes down to a climatic arena battle in a darkened stadium to see who truly is the best fighter in Hong Kong. Li wins his bout but realizes his price for success is not worth his happiness and pride.

-E-

18 Bronzemen
(1979) Kung-Fu   C-90m Dubbed   Catalog #0030   Hong Kong
Retail: $39.99
Dir: Joseph Kuo   Dist: Tai Seng Video
Carter Wong, Polly Shang Kuan, James Tien, Tien Pens
[*1/2]
A martial arts student must learn the ways of kung-fu to avenge his parents. Determined in his quest to become a martial arts expert, the stoic Wong trains with the Shaolin experts. His final test includes a deadly battle with 18 Bronzemen Masters of Martial Arts (actual fighters painted in bronze). Every time he hits them, a metallic sound rings out in the secret chambers. He manages to defeat them and also discovers the secret of a jade talisman given to him as a child. New lows of tedium, poor editing, and horrendous performances should be avoided at all costs.

Vulgar comedy involving bodily functions appear at the least inopportune time, but Wong's character remains serious minded throughout the film. The only minor merit is if you're a Carter Wong fan.

8th Man After Vol. 1: City in Fear
(1993) Japanime: Action   C-29m Dubbed   Catalog #SPV 90783
Japan Retail: $9.95
Dir: Sumiyoshi Furukawa   Scr: Yasushi Hirano Music: Michael Kennedy
(based on the original series "8th Man" by Kazumasa Hirai, Jiro Kuwata)
PC: TCJ Animation Center/ABC Films   Dist: Streamline Pictures
[***]
The original, black & white 8th Man series has revived itself for modern audiences, providing a crisp new animated series as well as a live-action film. The story follows elements of "Robocop" and other superhero avengers who awaken from the grave with new powers, but a loss of identity. Ex-cop, private detective Hazama is hired to investigate the theft of hi-tech equipment from Professor Tani's facilities. The hi-tech equipment is appearing on the streets as weapons and powerful modifications for criminals. Hazama meets an attractive woman and searches for any leads. His work gets him murdered, but he is recreated into 8th Man, a cyborg with amazing speed (think DC's the Flash). His first job is to protect the woman who he met during his human life.

8th Man After Vol. 2: End Run (1993)C-29m   Catalog #SPV 90783 Retail: $9.95

Eagle Shadow Fists   (Snake in the Eagle's Shadow)
(1977) Kung-Fu   C-88m Dubbed   VA
Hong Kong   Retail: $9.99
Dir: Yuen Woo Ping Scr: Jackie Chan   Prod: Hoi Ling   MAD: Hdeng Tsu
Dist: Simitar Entertainment
Jackie Chan, Yuen Siu Tien, Hwang Jang Lee, Tino Wong
[**]
Once again, the Japanese military expansion into China is the setting of the story. The fault with most of these plot lines is that the Japanese are very one-dimensional villains without any form of character development or motivation. It is assumed that the hatred for Japanese atrocities onto Chinese civilians are well-known and universally condemned. All Japanese soldiers should be seen as rapists, murderers, and criminals. Therefore, the Japanese characters are to be dealt with in the swiftest and deadliest manner. Though Chan is billed as the star, the young actor appears in a supporting role. A group of Chinese opera/theater performers are arrested by the Japanese and accused of performing indecent acts. Chan and the other performers decide to kill the Japanese soldiers. They go into hiding, killing more Japanese along the way. They finally settle in a rural community and befriend some poor people, including an elderly rickshaw puller, a school teacher who preaches passive resistance (foolish), and some poor farmers. Chan's elder brother decides to work the rickshaw to give the elder man time to rest. He gets into problems when he insults a Chinese prostitute who belongs to a Japanese Captain sent to the community to enforce the laws. The real villains aren't the Japanese, but the Chinese collaborators who sold out their own people to the Japanese. They are portrayed as vile creatures who praise the

Japanese and beg for everything. The Chinese traitors try to shake down the old rickshaw driver for past loans, but when he fails to pay, his whole family is brutally beaten. Chan and his friends preach resistance, but their actions of heroism are more like acts of stupidity which lead to grave repercussions. Their volatile actions cause the death of every character in the film, in what becomes a depressing and pointless film. The only special note is to see Chan in an extremely early and raw role. These early films attempted to capitalize on the Bruce Lee craze and were never given much time, money, or attention to develop quality productions. Even the fight scenes pale in comparison to many other films of the era. A disappointing effort best enjoyed in clips or with your fast-forward button.

Early Summer
(1951) DramaB&W-135m   Japanese with English Subtitles   VA
Catalog # CC1483L Japan Retail: $69.95
Dir: Yasujiro Ozu   Scr: Kogo Noda   Prod: Takeshi Yamamoto   DP: Takeharu Atsuta
Editor: Yoshiyasu Hamamura   Music: Senji Ito   Prod: Shochiku Co., Ltd.
Setsuko Hara Noriko
Chishu Ryu, Kuniko Miyake, Chikage Awashima, Chieko Higashiyama, Toyoko Takahashi
[*1/2]**
Noriko is a bright, attractive, cheerful 28-year old woman who has a wonderful job in Tokyo and lives with her parents. However, her life is far from perfect. In post-World War II Japan, she is more than ripe for marriage and pressure abound from members of her family. The traditional Japanese (as with many cultures) have a strong belief that women should marry and raise a family. This is very evident in Ozu's carefully constructed and sentimental look at one women's path to love and marriage. A saying in Japan calls an unmarried woman over 25 years, a Christmas Cake. This refers to cakes found after December 25th, who would want to eat a stale leftover from the holidays. Noriko resides with her brother and his wife and two sons. Also the parents live in the house. Noriko and her school friends gather at bars and restaurants to talk and gossip, but recently the friends divide into two groups: the married and the single. Prospective husbands are invited to the household and Noriko dismisses them with a childish gesture. Secretly, we discover that she is saddened by her solitude and the pressures of her situation. She does want to get married eventually, but her feelings must come from love and not duty.
One of the scene stealers is the youngest son who behaves in a very spoiled and rotten manner. Whether a precursor to a new generation that does not respect their elders or for cinematic levity, his aloof mannerism and disrespect for authority is amusing. Ozu's style has been compared against Kurosawa who carries a more western style in editing and direction. Ozu dislikes panning his camera and prefers to set his characters in still frames similar to a painter's frame. This way the observer is not swayed by the camera's movement, but focuses on a setting and the characters within that seem more animated than the non-moving sets.

Eat a Bowl of Tea
(1989) DramaC-102m   English   PG-13 VA   Hong Kong/USA
Retail: $19.99
Dir: Wayne Wang   Scr: Judith Rascoe   Prod: John   K.   Chan,   Lidsay   Law,   Tom Sternberg

DP: Amir Moki   Editor: Richard Candib   Music: Mark Adler
Art Dir: Timmy Yip Prod Design: Bob Ziembicki   Set Design: Lisa Dean
Costume: Marit Allen   Makeup: Yam Chan Hoi, Nancie Marsalis
PC/Dist: Columbia
Cora Miao   Mei Oi
Lau Siu Ming Lee Gong
Russell Wong Ben Loy
Victor Wong   Wah Gay
Lee Sau Kee   Bok Fat
Law Lan   Aunt Gim
Wai Ching Ho   Ah Song
Jessica Harper, Lee Saukee, Eric Tsang
[***]
Another delightful film from director Wayne Wang, dealing with Asian-American relationships in the 1940's. Instead of San Francisco (Dim Sum), Wang chooses New York's Chinatown for his emotional story. World War II has ended and Americans are back to a life of hard work and peace. In the crowded streets of Chinatown, Chinese immigrants are at work while teaching their children the value of American education and Asian traditions. Thanks to a more lenient immigration law, Chinese immigrants are allowed to bring their spouses into the United States (interracial marriages were very rare and often Chinese brides were sent to American). Russell Wong is Ben Loy, a returning war veteran who prefers the American way over strict Chinese traditions. He doesn't believe in pre-arranged or mail-ordered brides and decides he'll marry whoever he wants. He falls for the lovely Cora Miao, but plenty of universal problems disrupt their blissful marriage. Though the principal characters are all Asians, non-Asians will comprehend and feel compassion with familiar issues such as financial support for the family, multi-generational differences with overbearing parents, assimilation issues, and marital infidelities. Wong and Miao look for emotional support elsewhere, but they eventual reconcile their differences in a clever and sentimental manner. A well-crafted and recommended family drama with a touch of romance and comedy...just a slice of Asian-American life. The film was partially funded by the PBS American Playhouse production staff.

Eat Drink Man Woman
(1994) DramaC-124m   Chinese with English Subtitles   R   VA
Catalog #VHS 30013 Taiwan   Retail:$19.95
Dir: Ang Lee   Scr: Hui-Ling Wang, James Schamus, Ang Lee
Prod: Li-Kong Hsy   Editor: Tim Squyres DP: Jong Lin
Music: Mader   Prod Design: Fu-Hsiung Lee
Associate Prod: Ted Hope, James Schamus
Set Design: Hsi-Chien Lee   Makeup: Wei-Min Lee
PC: Central Motion Picture Corporation Production in association with Ang Lee Productions and Good Machine   Dist: Hallmark Home Entertainment
Sylvia Chang   Jin-Rong
Winston Chao   Li Kai
Chao-Jung Chen   Guo Lun
Lester Chen   Raymond

Yu Chen	Rachel
Ah-Leh Gua	Mrs. Liang
Chi-Der Hong	Class Leader
Gin-Ming Hsu	Coach Chai
Huei-Yi Lin	Sister Chang
Shih-Jay Lin	Chief's Son
Chin-Cheng Lu	Ming Dao
Sihung Lung	Mr. Chu
Cho-Gin Nei	Airline Secretary
Yu-Chien Tang	Shan-Shan
Chung Ting	The Priest
Cheng-Fen Tso	Fast Food Manager
Man-Sheng Tu	Restaurant Manager
Chuen Wang	Chief
Jui Wang	Old Wen
Yu-Wen Wang	Jia-Ning
Chien-Lien Wu	Jia-Chien
Hwa Wu	Old Man
Keui-Mei Yang	Jia-Jen

[****]

It's sometimes hard to put a label on Ang Lee's films because they skillfully blend the subtleties of human emotion: love, humor, loyalty, and sadness, into one tale. In his film after The Wedding Banquet, Lee returns to his native country of Taiwan. In the bustling capital of Taipei, a master chef and his three daughters live a quiet amicable life. None of the daughters are married, but have reached quite a respectable age. A Lee favorite, Sihung Lung plays the master chef (a familiar theme: he was a Tai Chi Master in Pushing Hands) who tragically loses his sense of taste. Now retired, he cooks elaborate meals for his daughters who do not share his culinary passions. The three daughters all share problems when dealing with romance. The oldest is the most successful, but the most reckless. The middle daughter is the conservative school teacher who never seems to have a suitor. And the youngest daughter works in a Wendy's Restaurant and passes her days in idle dreaming of her prince charming. Lee brings together the four stories, allowing them their own reflections and passions while interweaving how their lives affect each other. In a cute scene, Lung befriends a neighbor's son whose single mother doesn't cook that well. One day in school, Lung arrives bringing some of his best dishes. The entire cafeteria caught by the aroma enviously watch as the elaborate meal is laid out in front of the boy. In return, Lung eats the boy's food and doesn't mind since he can't taste it. Imagine a master chef walking into your elementary school and eating your cafeteria lunch while offering you a banquet in return. The daughters come across new changes in their lives, mostly romantic, and their attitudes toward family and life are altered. Humorous and bitter situations run into every characters' lives and when the film ends, as in real life, changes are dealt with and accepted for better or worse.

Eight Diagram Pole Fighter (Invincible Pole Fighters)
(1983) Kung-Fu   C-100m   Dubbed   Hong Kong   Retail: $19.99
Dir: Liu Chia Liang Scr: I Kuang, Liu Chia Liang   Ex. Prod: Chen Li Hua

Prod: Wong Ka Hee, Mona Fong   DP: Johnson Tsao An Hsun
Editor: Chiang Hsing Lung, Li Yen Hai   Music: Stephen Shing
Art Dir: Cheng Ching Shen, TengKuang Hsien   Effects: Li Yi Tzu
Costume: Liu Kuei Yu   MAD: Liu Chia Liang, Ching Chu, Hsiao Hou
PC: Shaw Brothers

Gordon Liu Chia Hui	Yang #5
Kara Hui Ying Hung	Yang Daughter
Alexander Fu Sheng	Yang #6
Wang Yu	Yang #1
Liu Chia Yung	Yang #2
Mai Te Lo	Yang #3
Hsiao Hou	Yang #4
Chang Chan Feng	Yang #7
Wang Lung Wei	Villain Yeh Li Lin
Lily Li	Yang Mother
Liu Chia Liang	Nomad

Chu Tieh Hu, Ku Ming, Kao Fei, Yuan Te
[***]
The noble heroes of the Yang Family meet on the field of battle (an elaborate studio set) to destroy an evil sect of martial artists led by Wang Lung Wei. The seven Yang Brothers are all masters of the spear style, but are betrayed and beaten. The only survivors are Yang #5 and #6. Gordon Liu escapes and befriends a nomad who sacrifices his life to help him escape. Fu Sheng returns to the Yang Mansion, but has been driven insane by the horrendous defeat. He spends the rest of the film in a state of rage, reliving the battle on a daily basis. Only his mother can defeat him and bring him to calm. Sadly, actor Fu Sheng was killed in a car accident during the filming of this movie. His promising career was ended and he does not appear in the second half of the film. The villain Yeh and his cohorts search for the remaining Yang brothers and even the emperor's men have turned against the Yang for failing to defeat the Mongolian invaders. Mother Yang sends her daughter Kara Hui to find the missing Yang #5. Meanwhile, Gordon Liu fights his way into Shaolin Temple, shaves his hair, and becomes a monk. He finds contentment in the monk's lifestyle and masters the pole technique using a wooden wolf with metal teeth as a training tool. When Kara Hui is captured by the enemy, only Gordon Liu can save her. Pushing a cart of bamboo spears, Gordon infiltrates the enemy stronghold and does battle on top of stacked coffins. His sister is wounded and the enemies outnumber him, but the valiant Shaolin monks come to his rescue. The film is darker than most Liu Chia Liang films, but the martial arts is top notch and the action is fast paced. Foreshadowing things to come, director Liu includes fight scenes with impressive trick stunts that resemble the modern day kung-fu movies of Tsui Hark. With some Shaw Brothers productions, the multitude of incidental characters can be confusing to viewers and the various subplots on Yang #6 fail to be resolved (due to Fu Sheng's death) and hinder the overall focus of the film.

Eijanaika
(1981) Historical Drama   C-151m   Japaneses with English Subtitles   VA
Japan
Dir/Scr: Shohei Imamura   Prod: Shoichi Ozawa, Jiro Tomoda, Shigemi Sugisaki

DP: Masahisa Imamura	Editor: Keiichi Uraoka	Music: Shinichiro Ikebe
Art Dir: Akiyoshi Stani	PC: Shochiku Co., Ltd.	Dist: Kino International Corp.

Kaori Momoi Ine

Shigeru Izumiya   Genji

Shigeru Tsuyuguchi   Kinzo

Ken Ogata   Furukawa

Yohei Koono   Hara

Minori Terada   Ijuin

Tsutomu Hiura   Sanji

[***]

Eijanaika translates to "Why Not?" and is a film that follows the exploits of Japanese peasants during the final years of the Shogun's reign of power in the mid-1800's. The film's main point of discontent follows a group of characters at a leisurely film pace without revealing much at times. Characters interact with each other and their actions cause effects within the entire scope of the story. One samurai who is on an important mission is brutally murdered while seeking passage on a boat. He does not know his killer and his death will have deeper repercussions. The lengthy finale involves a civil protest where thousands of peasants, commoners, and performers chat and dance in the streets, making their way to the lord's castle. They are ordered to stop, but peacefully push aside the samurai barricades and cross the bridge toward the castle. In acts of lurid defiance, the peasants mock the bewildered samurai, but just as peace is about to be restored, a samurai orders an attack on the peasants, killing many of them in the process. The film does have strong individual performances and the setting of the film is authentically portrayed, but for most casual viewers the film is difficult to appreciate. The multitude of subplots and the complicated nature of the story is a reflection on Japan's troubled history. Shohei also directed "Vengeance is Mine".

The Emperor and The Assassin
(1999) Historical Epic
C-161m Chinese with English Subtitles
China
Dir: Chen Kaige Prod: Chen Kaige, Shirley Kao, Satoru Iseki
Ex. Prod: Han Sanping, Tsuguhiko Kadokawa
Gong Li
[***1/2]

Chinese powerhouse director Chen (Farewell, My Concubine) delves deep into Chinese history to bring the tale of Emperor Ying Zheng who ruled the Ch'in (Qin) Dynasty from 221BC to 206 BC, the first unified period of China (China is derived from Ch'in). The film unfolds from Ying's adulthood and references his past through dialogue and character interaction. Those unfamiliar with Chinese history or culture may become lost as the story unfolds quickly into battles, betrayals, court intrigue, and a romance with Lady Zhao. Basically, King Ying Zheng of the Ch'in Kingdom (later known as Ch'in Shih Huang-ti, first Emperor of China) is set on unifying the seven kingdoms into one great nation. He slowly attacks one kingdom after another, defeating the Han, Zhao, Yan, and eventually the others. The film is shot on location throughout China, and epic efforts were painstakingly followed to help create accurate sets, costumes, and props for the film. The film is beautiful and a masterpiece of historical dramas considering the events unfolded over 2000 years ago. King Ying Zheng believes his campaign is a mandate from heaven and surprisingly, his success is unheralded, but at a great sacrifice when he uses his beloved Lady Zhao in an intricate plot to overtake one of the kingdoms. She slowly realizes the horrors of war outweigh the price of unification and doubts her allegiance to King Ying Zheng and helps in an intricate assassination attempt using a retired assassins who has forsaken his evil ways. She must convince him to perform this final assassination as an act of redemption for his past sins, the murdering of a family haunted him to quit. The two develop a strong relationship and plan the assassination while King Ying Zheng's own mother and a chief minister also plot and plan to usurp the royal throne through a right to inheritance. Zheng discovers his quest for unification must come at any price and ruthlessly destroys anyone and anything in his path. Though often seen as a ruthless tyrant, his later accomplishments include vast irrigation plans, the building of the Great Wall of China, the imperial tomb with the famed Terracotta Warriors, and a majestic palace.

Enigma of Love
(1993) Romance   C-95m Chinese with English Subtitles   Hong Kong
Dir: Sherman Wong Jing-Wa   Scr: Law Kam-Fai   Prod: Do Luen-Shun

Maggie Cheung	**Tammy Cheung**
Simon Yam	**Jacky Chan**
Wilsow Lam Jun-Yin	**David Lam**
Maria Cordero	**Kwai Fa-Pon**
Parkman Wong Pak-Man	**Officer Wong**
Yvonne Lam Yi-Lei	**Cat**

Baat Leung Gam, Hoh Gei Yung, Chan Hon Man, Ho Wing Cheung, Lam Wai Yin
[1/2]**

Tammy Cheung is a tough cop assigned to breaking up prostitution rings and gigolo shops. When she succeeds to an amazing degree, the gangs decide to teach her a lesson. They send in smooth-talking pretty boy Jacky Chan to woo her and make her fall in love with him. He starts off by following her with a video camera and drawing sketches of her. She tells him to get lost and uses her non-feminine ways of persuasion. Meanwhile, she and her other butch female officers are interested in the handsome Officer Lam in charge of their division. He and Tammy are old classmates from the police academy, but he doesn't express any interest in her macho persona. When she accidentally hits Jacky with her car, she starts to become more sympathetic and interested in him. He then reveals he is terminally ill and an artist which causes Tammy to undergo a transformation into a beautiful, sensitive woman. Perhaps, Tammy is a little too gullible, but she does fall in love with him and he eventually falls in love with her. Jacky is a romantic at heart and goes all out to surprise and delight Tammy with some nice visual surprises. He decides to tell her the truth and pull out. Meanwhile, Officer Lam, Tammy's boss, is smitten with her since her recent feminine transformation and becomes obsessively jealous of Jacky. He tells Jacky to back off, but Jacky insists on trying to regain Tammy's love and trust. In the finale which comes rather quickly and without warning, Lam turns psycho and starts beating Tammy and Jacky. He drives to a remote area, handcuffs Tammy to the car door, and plans to kill Jacky. Tammy uses her strength to break the car door free and slam Lam on the head. Later in the station, Jacky apologizes with a bouquet of flowers and a puppy while Tammy's fellow officers cheer her on. The film contains more romance than action, but will appeal to Cheung fans looking for more romance in her stories. What plagues the film is the sudden and implausible "fatal attraction" of Officer Lam. He is shown as a heroic officer with a justifiable vendetta against Jacky, a smooth-talking hustler of women. He's handsome, well-groomed, intelligent, and a nice guy. Then when his advances are rejected by Tammy, his character becomes obsessive, violent, and psychopathic. Even the fellow officers encourage Tammy to pursue Jacky (a known criminal) rather than their beloved commander. Even after the fact that Jacky started the relationship purely as a scam, no one seems to mind. If you can get beyond the awkward transition of characters and don't mind seeing the bad guy win out, then the film is worth seeing for Cheung and Yam.

Enter the Dragon
(1973) Kung-Fu   C-99m English   R   VA   Catalog #12809
Hong Kong/USA   Retail: $19.99 Widescreen Available
Dir: Robert Clouse   Scr: Michael Allin   Prod: Fred Weintraub, Paul M. Heller
Editor: Kurt Hirschler, George Watters   DP: Gil Hubbs
Music: Lalo Schifrin Art Design: James Wong Sun   MAD: Bruce Lee
PC: Warner Brothers   Dist: Warner Home Video
Bruce Lee   Lee
John Saxon   Roper
Jim Kelly   Williams
Shih Kien   Han
Bob Wall   Oharra
Ahna Capri   Tania
Angela Mao   Su-Lin
Betty Chung   Mei Ling
Geoffrey Weeks   Braithwaite
Yang Tse   Bolo Yeung Shik
Peter Archer   Parsons
[*1/2]**
Bruce Lee's American debut instantly marked its place in cinematic history, proving an Asian actor could be bankable by Hollywood standards while igniting a worldwide craze for Lee-style kung-fu films. Mentioned as one of the best martial arts movies of all time by a number of sources, it is also one of the best known, starring a cast of well known stars who are still kicking today. The film's basic plot and design suffer from age and the technical standards of action/kung-fu films have improved over the years, but Enter the Dragon still retains its mystical charm for one reason only - Bruce Lee. Sadly, Lee died a few weeks after the film premiered and never realized the film's phenomenal success. Lee had already completed three successful films in Asian and it was only a matter of time, before Hollywood begged the Asian Dragon to make American films. Warner Brothers hired American director Robert Clouse and sent a team to Hong Kong for principle filming. Though a strong effort was made by American filmmakers to capture the Hong Kong style of kung-fu films, Enter the Dragon does suffer from a number of faulty elements that carries over the campy mood of the early 70's.
Inspired by the James Bond success, the British government asks Lee to be a spy and infiltrate a remote island which they expect to be a drug smuggling operation. No one on the island carries guns, only martial arts are allowed and every year a tournament is held to recruit new members,

the participants include John Saxon, Jim Kelly, and Bruce Lee. Though John Saxon is not a martial artist, he is easily the most recognizable actor in the movie next to Lee and trained with Lee who helmed a majority of the fight choreography. Saxon's martial arts talents are minimal and will not outshine Lee, but his American character Roper plays a major role in the film. Jim Kelly, a talented Karate champion, also looks slow compared to Lee and with his afro-hair and bad-ass attitude, he seems comic bookish and disappears all too easily. Cameos abound from Samo Hung, Angela Mao Ying, and villains shine with veteran actor Shik Chek, and Yang Tse who is best known for his role as Bolo Yeung (he later legally took the name), the muscular henchman. Bolo has since gone on to star in a number of films and has broken away from his stereotypical hulking villain with little brains. Instead of a great Bolo vs. Bruce fight, Saxon stands to the plate and defeats Bolo. Angela Mao Ying, the queen of kung-fu, steps in as Lee's sister. Every Lee scene is a marvelous ballet of strength, agility, and speed which truly showcased his amazing talents and charisma. On the opposite extreme, the film suffers from a flimsy storyline filled with psychedelic images, loosely clad women, and overacting characters that try one's patience until Lee steps in and rewards the viewer with his graceful movements.

The following is an in-depth synopsis of the story and its fight scenes. In the morning quiet of a Shaolin Temple, two students approach each other for a match. One is the heavy set Samo Hung while the lithe man is Bruce Lee. He defeats Samo easily and then goes off to speak with one of his students about martial arts philosophy. Lee is then approached by a British official who recruits him into entering a martial arts tournament sponsored by a wealthy man called Han who owns a remote island. Lee is hesitant, but eventually accepts when he discovers Han's bodyguard O'Hara killed his sister. In a flashback, Lee's sister (Mao Ying) and her uncle are accosted by O'Hara and some men from the island. They touch her and fondle her, but the uncle pulls out a knife and slices O'Hara's face, leaving a permanent scar. O'Hara strikes the old man down and sends his goons after Mao Ying. She fights them off and looks for help, but the townspeople close their doors and turn a deaf ear. She is finally trapped in an abandoned warehouse and stops running when she is cornered, assuming rape, she grabs a shard of glass and plunges it into her abdomen. The next character to arrive in Hong Kong for the tournament is Roper (John Saxon) a freewheeling American who lives in the fast lane and owes the mob money. In his flashback, he is accosted on the golf course and decides to enter the tournament for money and prestige. The third is Jim Kelly who is a black activist that beats up some cops who were harassing him. The trio and other fighters arrive and take a junk (Chinese wooden boat) to Han's private island. On board the men gamble, talk, and act tough. A fighter challenges Lee, but Lee tricks him into a lifeboat and then lets it float far behind the junk. When the junk arrives, the competitors are wined and dined, plus they are provided with evening companions. Lee manages to meet one of the prostitutes who is secretly an agent working for the British government. Lee penetrates the underground base and discovers an elaborate drug operation. The next day, Han orders Bolo to kill the guards on duty who let Lee escape. The tournament proceeds with competitors dressed in yellow and Han's men dressed in white uniforms. Kelly and Roper who are old friends hustle people by betting on each other and winning during the appropriate round. The highlight is the battle between Lee and O'Hara. The two competitors square off and place their fists against each other. As soon as the signal is called, Lee strikes O'Hara with lightning quick reflexes. O'Hara attacks, but Lee drops down and kicks him in the groin. O'Hara tries to cheat by grabbing Lee's leg, but Lee does a back somersault, kicking O'Hara in the face. When O'Hara grabs some broken bottles and attacks,

Lee kills him with a massive sidekick and then a neck break. (The scene is of particular note, since actor Bob Wall used real glass bottles and accidentally cut Bruce's hand. Rumor circulated that Wall did it on purpose and that Lee was going to really kill him. The scene where Lee kicks O'Hara into the competitors is suppose to be for real.) Han then invites Kelly to his office and asks him where he was last night. Since the prostitutes vouched for everyone except Kelly who was taking a midnight walk, he is the prime suspect. Kelly is angered by the accusations and plans to leave the island. In a line that summons up the film's plot, Kelly accuses Han the Man of coming out of a comic book. Using his artificial hand like a weapon, Han kills Kelly and then asks Roper to join him. When Roper sees Kelly's lifeless body hanging by chains over a pit of murky water, he refuses to join Han. That evening Lee is captured while signaling the British government, but before being trapped he fights off an army of guards using a staff, double batons, and the trademark nunchaku in a whirling display of fists and feet. The next morning Lee is escorted to the main yard. Lee and Roper are ordered to fight each other, but they refuse. Bolo then battles Roper and loses his life. Then Han orders his men one by one to attack the dynamic duo and of course they lose to Lee and Roper. Meanwhile the British forces are on their way and the prostitute agent releases all of Han's prisoners. The island breaks into a fierce battleground while Lee and Han retreat into the mansion. In a magnificently filmed sequence, Lee enters a hall of mirrors and battles Han who attaches blades to his false hand and brutally carves up Lee's body. The battle is pretty much one-sided without any doubt to Lee's victory. A humorous note is the obvious Han mannequin that Lee violently kicks in the head. Lee destroys the mirrors and dispatches the evil Han who falls backward into a spear embedded in the wall. After Han gets the short end of the spear, the victorious Lee exits the mansion just as the cavalry arrives.

Though the film's caliber depends on your tolerance for Bruce Lee, I highly recommend this film for its significance as one of the best recognized and acclaimed martial arts film of its time.

For a brilliant parody of the film, I highly recommend the martial arts segment of "The Kentucky Fried Movie", starring Bong Soo Han and Evan Kim as Bruce Lee.

Executioners of Death (Executioners From Shaolin)
(1977) Kung-Fu   C-100m   Dubbed   Hong Kong   Retail: $19.95
Dir: Liu Chia Liang Scr: I Kuang Prod: Runme Shaw
Music: Chen Yung-Yu   Assistant Dir: Chang Pa Ching, Tang Wan
MAD: Liu Chia Liang   PC: Shaw Bros.
Chen Kuan Tai, Lo Lieh, Gordon Liu Chia Hui, Wang Yu
[*1/2]**

A Shaw production that follows the further exploits of the rebels who escaped the destruction of Shaolin Temple. An engrossing film with a high-caliber performance from Chen Kuan Tai as heroic legend Hung Hsi Kuan, a master of Tiger style. The film features a number of great fight scenes and memorable characters. Chen plays Hung Hsi Kuan, the strongest fighter to leave Shaolin and the most likely choice to beat evil priest Pai May. The opening scene in itself is fantastic as the narrator explains the situation at hand. A treacherous priest has betrayed Shaolin and challenges the head monk to a death match. The two elder masters engage each other, but the villain Pai May wins. The rebels retreat to safety, but vow to kill Pai May who has joined the Chings in hunting down the survival rebels. While escaping, the rebels are ambushed by Manchurian archers. Gordon Liu (in an excellent fight scene) sacrifices his life and fights off the soldiers and archers, so Hung and the other rebels can escape to their ships. The amazing part of the film is that martial arts doesn't play the sole focus of the story, but Hung's life is the central element and developed over the course of the film. Hung travels the countryside performing in shows and training in tiger style. Along the way he meets a beautiful kung-fu expert who performs on the street. He tries out her crane style and the two decide to work together which blossoms into marriage. They have a son, but Hung can not forget the vow he swore to the men who died under Pai May's tyranny. After years of hard training, he battles Pai May but loses and is rescued by an old comrade. He starts to retrain with a renewed passion, using a special device to discover Pai's weak point. We're sure he'll win on his second time, the heroes always win after the training sequence. A decade passes and we share Hung's joys as his son grows older and his love for his wife deepens. He decides the time has come where his martial arts will not get any better. His mature son tries to stop him from going and even attacks his father. Hung convinces his son to stay behind and in spectacular fashion battles up Pai May's monastery stairs against an army of deadly killers. Shockingly, Hung loses the fight and his life to Pai May who has perfected a style that makes his body impervious to pain except at one point which he can alter. It is then up to Hung's son who must incorporate his mother's crane and father's tiger style to defeat Pai May, only problem is that his father's tiger manual is missing a few pages. The drama takes a lighter tone as Hung's son attempts to learn tiger style with his father's manual, improvising his own techniques. He makes up the missing techniques and creates his own unique style which gives the befuddled Pai a massive headache. The final fight scene doesn't have the dramatic force or intensity of the previous fights, but manages to finish with excitement, humor, and a victorious end.

Explorer Woman Ray
(1993) Japanime: Adventure   C-60m Japanese with English Subtitles   VA
Catalog #USM 1026 Japan Retail: $19.95
Dir: Masato Sato, Haruhisa Okamoto   Scr: Masayori Sekijima
Prod: Kazuhiko Inomata, Ritsuko Kakita, Nagateru Kato   DP: Akihiko Takahashi
Music: Norimasa Yamanaka   Planning: Koniyoski Matsuhashi
Character Design: Hiroyuki Ochi Art Dir: Jyunichi Higashi
Animation Dir: Kumiko Shishido, Yutaka Arai, Jyoji Kikuchi
PC: Big Ban Limited & Animate Film   Dist: Toshiba Video Softwares Inc.
(based on comics by Takeshi Okazaki)
Mika Doi   Dr. Rayna Kizuki
Katsunosuke Hori   Reig Vader
Miki Ito   Mai Tachibana
Minami Takayama   Mami Tachibana
Tetsuaki Genda   Chief
Hajime Ozeki   Johnson
Atsushi Abe, Norio Tsukui
[**1/2]
A free-spirited tale following the exploits of Rayna Kizuki, a female explorer in search of relics and ancient cities. Intelligent, resourceful, and definitely a fighter, Rayna is a female version of Dr. Indiana Jones. Comprised of two episodes, Rayna's main nemesis and competitor is Reig Vader, a handsome archaeologist and once assistant to Rayna's father. While on location at an

archeological site, Rayna meets up with two graduate students, Mai and Mami Tachibana. The sisters at first wish to help Rayna, but then branch off on their own to search for the treasure. When they are captured by Reig and his men, the two sisters team up with Rayna and try to stop Reig. Plenty of light-hearted action and youth-oriented anime with various foreign locales. Their adventures continue in the second half of the video.

-F-

4 Assassins
(1977) Kung-Fu   C-100m   Dubbed   Hong Kong   Retail: $19.99
Dir: Chang Cheh   Scr: Chang Cheh, I Kuang
Prod: Mona Fong   Ex. Prod: Run Run Shaw
PC: Shaw Brothers
Alexander Fu Sheng, Gordon Lui Chia Hui, Carter Wong, Shih Szu, Richard Harrison
[***]
Four Chinese disciples learn special techniques (iron body, etc.) to kill the vicious kung-fu experts from the north. The story begins with the arrival of Marco Polo into China and his meeting with Genghis Khan. Polo is introduced to the Mongolian ruler who has conquered China and shows off the strength of his northern martial arts masters. Khan takes a liking to the foreigner and escorts him on his exploits against the Chinese rebels. Polo shocked at Khan's braggart behavior and brutality can only remain silent and watch his fighters murder their opponents. Only the strong will survive and I am the strongest, Khan boasts. The Mongolians kill and destroy everyone in their path, but a small group of freedom fighters escape and vow to defeat them. They meet a noble master who trains them in very specific techniques, the most memorable being iron body. The skin is constantly torn and damaged, then treated with a special salve to make the skin invulnerable. Arrows bounce off the chest and blades snap in two when placed against the iron skin. The four heroes each face an entire army and use their new skills to defeat the northern fighters. Sadly, the heroes have their own weaknesses and suffer casualties. The mighty iron body has a vulnerable weak point which archers discover is the man's abdomen. Even with a hundred arrows stuck in his gut, the Chinese hero fights on until victory. Under the new circumstances, Polo realizes who the true heroes are and returns to Europe with his wondrous tale..

47 Ronin, Part 1   (The Loyal 47 Ronin/47 Samurai)
(1941) Samurai   B&W-112m   Japanese with English Subtitles   Japan
Dir: Kenji Mizoguchi   Scr: Kenchiro Hara, Yoshikata Yoda
DP: Kohei Sugiyama Music: Shiro Fukai
Dist: Ingram International Films
(based on a story by Seika Mayama)
Chojuro Kawarazaki, Ganemon Nakamura, Kunitaro Kawarazaki, Yoshizaburo Arashi,
Kikunojo Segawa, Kikunosuke Ichikawa, Tokusaburo Arashi, Ryotaro Kawanami,
Joji Kaieda, Hiroshi Ouchi, Mieko Takamine, Utaemon Ichikawa
[***]
A classic Japanese story based on loyalty and the desire of duty above death. The faithful warriors of Lord Asano watch as their master is forced to commit seppuku (ritual suicide) by the

emperor. Another Lord had used his deceitful cunning to force Asano's death and his fall from imperial grace. Now without a master, the ronin samurais become vagabonds, but are united by their quest of revenge and justice. They maintain silent loyalty and vow to kill the evil lord at all costs. The best known and most ambitious retelling of the classic 18th century Kabuki tale from Seika Mayama. This timeless story is a mainstream classic in Japanese literature, having seen various reincarnations in film, television, books, and comics.

The second film brings the saga to a conclusion as the 47 masterless samurai have avenged their dead master. Instead of becoming outlaws and fighting the emperor, they accept their fate and prepare for seppuku - honorable suicide.

47 Ronin, Part 2 (1942) Samurai   C-108m   Japanese with English Subtitles   Japan

Fantasy Mission Force
(1979) Comedy Kung-Fu   C-89m Dubbed   VA
Catalog # VHS 9905-B   Hong Kong   Retail: $9.99
Dir: Chu Yen Ping   Prod: Shen Hsiao-Yin
Supervisor: Chian Wen-Hsiung, Shen Hsiao-Yin   Planning: Hsu Tsai-Lai
PC: Cheung Ming Film [HK] Co.   Dist: Chang Chiang Film [Taiwan] Co.
Jacky Chan, Jimmy Wang Yu, Brigitte Lin Ching Tsia, Jung Shau Chiu, Shiu Bu Lia,
Fang Jung, Sun Yuih, Tao Da Way, Gon Ling Fring, Chang Ling
[*1/2]
A talented cast does little to help savage a film that manages to simultaneously insult and bore the viewer. There is no doubt that this film stretches the word fantasy when a mission force is assigned to recover a group of allied generals under Japanese imprisonment. Though the initial setting is placed in the 1940's, World War II, the story never maintains a steady timeline and references to Rocky and James Bond sprinkle into the film. Wang Yu is an elite captain assigned by the allied powers to establish an elite commando team. He travels to various parts of the world and gather a motley crew of has-beens, ex-criminals, and bungling idiots. Jackie Chan is not part of the team. Be warned that this film is not primarily a Jackie Chan vehicle. He appears sporadically through the film and does take over the climax, but screen time is equally taken by other characters. Chan appears as a con-artist with his cute female ally. At first, he tries to rob the group, but then helps them, then fights them again, and then...well I won't ruin the surprise. Along the way, the commando group loses their captain (Wang Yu probably asked for too much money) and must fend for their own. They encounter a village of Amazon women warriors led by an effeminate male leader, and later spend a night in a house full of gambling ghosts. Eventually they find the enemy base and must do battle with pseudo-Nazis driving demolition derby style automobiles. What initially must have started off as a spoof loses its edge as the story develops into chaos. The ending is contrived, pointless, and rather distasteful. Most of the actors have gone on the better roles, and this film is a sad reminder that everyone appears in a stinker or two.

Farewell My Concubine
(1993) Drama   C-157m   Mandarin with English Subtitles   VA
Catalog # 2522 AS   China Retail: $19.95 Widescreen Available
Dir: Chen Kaige   Scr: Lilian Li, Lu Wei   Prod: Hsu Feng

Associate Prod: Ronald Ranvaud
DP: Gu Changwei   Editor: Pei Xiaonan
Sound Recordist: Tao Jing
Art Design: Chen Huaikai
Ex. Prod: Jade Hsu, Hsu Bin, Sunday Sun
PC: Maverick Picture Company and Tomson Films Co., Ltd.
Dist: Miramax Films(Based on the novel by Lilian Li)

Artistic Dir: Chen Huaikai
Music: Zhao Jiping
Art Dir: Yang Yuhe, Yang Zhanjia
Costumes: Chen Changmin

Leslie Cheung   Cheng Dieyi
Zhang Fengyi   Duan Xiaolou
Gong Li   Juxian
Lu Qi   Guan Jifa
Ying Da   Na Kun
Ge You   Master Yuan
Li Chun   Xiao Si (teenager)
Lei Han   Xiao Si (adult)
Tong Di   Xiao Si (adult)
Ma Mingwei   Douzi (child)
Yin Zhi   Douzi (teenager)
Fei Yang   Shitou (child)
Zhao Hailong Shitou (teenager)
[****]

A beautiful epic that traces the lives of two Chinese opera stars from childhood to the end of their career, magnificently captured by Chinese director Kaige. A haunting and lyrical tale of two friends named Cheng and Duan who meet and train at an opera academy and become stars over the course of five decades of turbulent times. China, once a grand untouchable majestic kingdom, was the center of the known world, but after its humiliating defeat by western powers the internal structure collapsed and created an inner turmoil that lasted nearly a century. Only recently has China moved toward capitalism and accepted western ideology, albeit cautiously, allowing a number of brilliant filmmakers to recount those torrid times in rich visual films that reflect an oppressive era that may return in China's current government.

Cheng and Duan are two young boys deposited (practically sold into slavery) at a Peking Opera School. Duan is a tall, muscular senior boy who has the respect of his peers. Cheng is the new boy, smaller and quieter, who is at first refused admittance because he has a sixth digit (an extra pinkie). In a shocking scene which reflects truth over fiction, his mother grabs a butcher's knife and cuts the finger off. She never sees her son again.

The first portion of the film explores the harsh world of traditional Chinese opera and the rigorous treatment that pushes one boy to commit suicide. Some even attempt to escape, but the world outside is just as harsh and uncaring. Supposedly Jackie Chan and many of his colleagues at a Chinese Academy suffered similar treatment while training as children. Harsh brutality and unquestioning authority force Cheng to take on feminine acting roles. Whether some would take offense, his very nature is warped into the mind of a girl and his dashing leading man is Duan, his only close friend. The film slowly and naturally develops the progress of Cheng's growing obsession and love with his friend Duan who in turn is oblivious to the romantic undercurrent.

When the two grow in to adults they become successful performers who are adored by millions. They pay their respects to their Opera Master and plan a successful career, but the political winds change and government corruption and oppression follow. In a whirlwind of historical events, the Japanese army complicate problems, then the Kuomintang Nationalists take control of China, then the Maoist Communists do, then the Red Guard reformists, and finally the more current government which closes the cycle of history. One can almost get dizzy from the myriad of opponents Zhang and Cheung try to appease and to avoid to stay alive. Along the way, Zhang falls for a prostitute played by Gong Li who becomes a thorn to Cheung's hidden passions. The emotional thrust of the film belongs to a love triangle among Zhang, Cheung, and the effervescent Li who later denounces them. Disturbing, provocative, controversial, the film doesn't move you to cheer or root for any of the characters, but causes you to reflect on the harshness and simple pains suffered by struggling individuals who only seek comfort and happiness. The film opens and closes with Cheung and Duan reunited in front of a party official. They are dressed in their original costumes and preform for the very last time. The film is ambitious in scope and the title refers to a 2000 year-old opera about an imperial concubine.

Fatal Fury: The Motion Picture
(1994) Japanime: Action   C-100m   Dubbed   VA   Catalog # VVFF 003
Japan Retail: $19.95
Dir/Character Design/Executive Animation Dir: Masami Obari
Original Concept SNK/NEO-GEO "Fatal Fury" Video Game
Music: Toshihiko Sahashi   PC: SNK/Fuji TV/Shochiku/Asatsu International
[1/2]**
Based on a popular video game by SNK-GEO, Fatal Fury is another edition into the long string of fighting games (all-Japanese) turned into major films both animated and live-action. As a straight-forward action film, Fatal Fury delivers a good amount of excitement and adventure. The quest involves a plot similar to Jackie Chan's Armour of the Gods. A ruthless millionaire, Laocorn Gaudeamus, is in search of the missing pieces of the magical "Armor of Mars" that were lost by his descendants during the Crusades. Using his three super-fighters - Jamin, Hauer, and Panni - he scours the Earth, planning to use the armor to grant him unlimited powers and extract revenge on the world. His twin sister Sulia escapes in search of the great martial artist Terry "Hungry Wolf" Bogard to defeat Laocorn and stop his mad quest. She arrives at a party, pursued, and acquires the help of Terry and his friends, Andy, Joe Higashi, and the voluptuous Mai Shiranui. Meanwhile, her brother and his elite fighters have gathered additional pieces of the armor which give Laocorn new powers. In a race that stretches across the globe, both parties try to acquire the remaining pieces of the armor. A modern fight film with slick animation and plenty of over-the-top action sequences. Similar to flying kung-fu movies, the heroes meet the enemy, lose to the enemy, readjust their situation, and then face the enemy again when the stakes are the highest...you can guess the outcome.

Fearless Hyena, The
(1979) Kung-Fu   C-97m Dubbed   VA
Catalog #VHS 3609-A   Hong Kong   Retail: $9.99
Dir: Jackie Chan   Scr: Kai Fuk Prod: James Shaw   Ex. Prod: Willie Chan
DP: Ming Luie   Editor: John Tat Mok   Music: Sung Hing
Dist: Alpha Films in Association with Aquarius Media
Jackie Chan, Luen Kan Shek, Hang Yip, Joan Wan

[**1/2]
A young man named Chen (Jackie Chan) and his grandfather live in a modest house in the woods. The grandfather is a master of martial arts who has a long rivalry with a villainous clan leader. The two practice martial arts everyday, but they are poor and Chen needs to find a job. He looks in the nearby village and doesn't come across much luck until he meets a con-artist and his goons. Chen is an excellent martial artist and decides to use his skills to make a profit. His grandfather hides his unique abilities and chides Chen for his juvenile antics. Well Chen doesn't listen and shows off to make some money which tip off the villains who recognize the style. They go to his home and murder his grandfather, but Chen meets up with his uncle and together they train to defeat the villains. Standard kung-fu train/revenge film only sparked by the energy of Jackie Chan's performance.

Fearless Hyena Part II, The
(1980) Kung-Fu   C-92m Dubbed   VA
Catalog #VHS 3609-B   Hong Kong   Retail: $9.99
Dir: Lo Wei   Prod: Hsu Li Hwa   Dist: Alpha Films in Association with Aquarius Media
Jackie Chan, James Tien, Hon Kwok Choi, Shih Tien
[**]
Sequel to the popular The Fearless Hyena in name only, but the story is similar and basically recasts the same actors from the first film. This time a rival between two clans, the good Ying & Yang and the evil Heaven and Earth result in a bloody battle. The only two members to escape are Chi Nam and Chan who each manage to rescue their sons, Ah Lung (Jackie Chan) and Ah Tong. The boys grow up to be competent martial artists, but Ah Tong is lazy and doesn't train very hard. Ah Lung, nicknamed Stone, trains diligently for vengeance against Heaven and Earth (two killers: one is white-haired and the other is dark-haired). The evil duo find and murder Stone's father. Meanwhile, the Beggar Su Clan who helped hide Ah Tong and his father are attacked by Heaven and Earth. Beggar Su is killed and his daughter tries to get help. Chan must avenge his father and all the dead who were murdered by the powerful duo.

Fighting Duel of Death
(1988) Action C-86m Dubbed   VA   Catalog # SA 1014   Hong Kong
Retail: $9.99
Dir: Kurt Wang   Prod: Tomas Tang   Ex. Prod: Lee Pao Tang
DP: Kao Lim   Editor: Leung Wing Chan   Music: Roman Tsang
MAD: Kwok Ting   Costume: Kathy Lo   Makeup: Man Sau
Dist: Saturn Productions, Inc.
Lyon Chan, Sean Lee, Mah Sah, Richard Chui, Steve Chan, Fanny Cheung, Mary Lee, Alan Kong, Lou Bing, Bill Ho, Mark Ting
[*1/2]
Charlie Chen is an ex-convict who is recently released from prison after six years and in search of a new life with his loyal wife Mei. His wife convinces him to quit the life of crime and not go after enemies like Shih. But Chen's old friend Ken has problems of his own and is murdered while trying to save his wife. Chen saves his wife, Lee, and meets the gangster Ma who he once saved back in a prison brawl and even gave him a blood transfusion, making them literally blood brothers. He releases Lee from her gambling debts and lets her go home, but when she discovers

her husband and son are dead , she goes on a vengeful murder spree, killing gangsters Tu and Fong. Ma and Chen's friendship is torn over Lee and the two men fight each other. In the brutal climax, Lee manages to kill Ma and is then arrested by the police. Chen stands in confusion wondering what friendship and honor truly mean. Low-budget action film with little to capture the imagination.

Fire Dragon (Fire Cloud/Fiery Romance)
(1994) Fantasy Kung-Fu   C-90m Chinese with English Subtitles
Catalog #1471   Hong Kong   Retail: $39.99
Dir: Yuen Woo Ping Dist: Tai Seng Video
Brigitte Lin, Benny Mok Siu Chung, Sandra Ng
[***]
Mok plays Yuen Ming, a young fortune teller who must deliver an important message to the prime minister. A previous courier is brutally murdered, but manages to hide the message which reveals Prince Wan's treachery to the emperor. Also after the letter is Lin, a high-flying, fire-shooting assassin who chases after Mok. The brave Mok manages to get the letter, but runs into complications when he meets a woman who won't take no for an answer. Keeping away from her and Lin cause plenty of moments of tension, comedy, and action. A film worth checking out if you enjoyed Lin in her other sword-flying kung-fu films.

Fire Tripper - See Rumik's World "Fire Tripper"

First Shot
(1992) Crime C-100m   Chinese with English Subtitles
Catalog #1375   Hong Kong   Retail: $16.95
Dir/Prod: David Lam   Scr: So Man Sing, Chan Kiu Ying, Wong Ho Wah
Ex. Prod: Rose Lam   DP: Wong Po Man, Lam Ah To   Editor: Poon Hung
Music: Lowell Lo   Prod Manager: Hui Chi Ho Art Dir: Bill Lui
MAD: Yuen Tak, Leung Siu Hung PC: David Lam Films   Dist: Tai Seng Video
Ti Lung   Wong Yat Chung
Simon Yam   Sam
Waise Lee   Faucet
Maggie Cheung   Solicitor Ma
Lau Shek Ming, Hui Chi On
[***]
Hollywood has long been known for supplanting foreign stories and converting them into American movies with recognizable American stars. There's nothing like taking a great story and letting your favorite stars appear as the main characters. Well the world isn't foreign to doing the same thing and many Hollywood films are remade abroad. First Shot is a prime example, but while Chinese may enjoy seeing their favorite stars, some Americans may not be as enthusiastic about seeing a familiar story where Robert DeNiro, Sean Connery, Kevin Costner, and Andy Garcia are replaced by Ti Lung, Simon Yam, and Maggie Cheung. If you can get beyond that, the movie is quite entertaining. This is a loose remake of Brian De Palma's "Untouchables", down to the smallest details. Both films deal with a historical crime setting and a powerful mob boss who controls the police and legal courts in his rich pocket.

The story begins in the early 1970's in Hong Kong where a special anti-corruption force is led by a brave officer. He is murdered by a powerful crime boss, nicknamed the Faucet. Later on, Lung is a police officer who tries to stop Faucet's organizations. He is shot by one of his fellow officers (Yam) on the take. Lung revives from a coma and joins forces with tough-minded, government solicitor (think: district attorney) Maggie Cheung who provides moral support and window dressing. A special task force is set up under Maggie Cheung and Ti Lung to deal with corruption within society. Ti Lung carries the lead role, filling the shoes of both Sean Connery and Kevin Costner. Lung is a veteran star of Hong Kong cinema who adds strength and stability to the role. Over the decades, Lung has remained a recognizable force and a welcome addition to any film.

With direct contact to the governor they form a special squad (one crack shot and another martial artist) and form the ICAC (Independent Committee Against Corruption). Ti Lung starts his one man assault against crime and breaks into Faucet's office and recovers the triad's ledger. Now they require the accountant who can decipher the coded ledger. In a cat and mouse chase where good guys are tough to tell from bad guys, Lung and his men find the accountant and bring him to court. In classic Hong Kong fashion, imprisonment isn't good enough for the villains. When certain murders are committed, Lung and his men decide to raid the factory and get entangled in an all out battle with the criminals.

First Shot suffers from deja vu, nothing in the film seems very fresh or motivating, viewers familiar with action films and who have seen "The Untouchables" will be least impressed. The film does not have the cinematic style of a John Woo film nor are there any powerhouse martial arts/gun scenes. Instead there are light touches of comedy (Bruce Lee jokes) with sporadic action scenes, and plenty of deaths. For those who don't mind a familiar story with good actors, there is solid entertainment to be found.

First Strike
(1995) Action Kung-Fu   C-110m   Dubbed/Chinese with English Subtitles
PG-13   VA   Catalog #N4556V   Hong Kong   Retail: $19.99
Dir: Stanley Tong   Scr: Stanley Tong, Nick Tramontane, Greg Mellot, Elliot Tong
Prod: Barbie Tung   Ex. Prod: Leonard Ho
DP: Jingle Ma   Editor: Peter Cheung, Chi Wai Yau   Music: J. Peter Robinson
Editorial Consultant: Michael Duthie   Prod Design: Oliver Wong
PC: Raymond Chow/Golden Harvest Prodiction Dist: New Line Cinema
Jackie Chan, Chen Chun Wu, Jackson Lou
[***]
Jackie Chan's third theatrical re-release in the United States (heavily cut from the original) continues his popular collaboration with director/stuntman Stanley Tong. Following up his beloved "Police Story" theme, Supercop Jackie Chan is on a case that will effect the safety of the entire world. This time he doesn't just save Hong Kong, but the United States and Russia as well. Assigned to follow a ring of Russian mobsters who are buying nuclear warheads from the black market, Chan is sent to the Ukraine as an observer on the trail of a Chinese operative. Jackie agrees to tail the operative and works on the case with the FSB, former KGB agents. At first all seems routine, but situations become complicated when Jackie follows a female suspect to the Chinese operative. Inappropriately dressed, Chan follows the operative to a cabin in the Ukrainian tundra. Rubbing his hands and shaking like a fish, Chan waits patiently for the backup

with only a seal cap to keep him warm. When the agents arrive and surround the cabin, Jackie notices a white shape moving in the snow. Suddenly, ninja-like troops in camouflage white explode from the snow and attack the FSB agents. The Chinese operative makes his escape with the nuclear device and a long chase ensues down a snowy crevice. In an amazing sequence, Chan avoids the ski-clad killers and dives off a cliff, catching the legs of a flying helicopter, only to drop himself into an icy lake below. Eventually Chan travels to Australia to meet the father and sister (Annie) of the Chinese operative. When the father mysteriously dies, Jackie is accused of being the prime suspect and wanted by the local police. Illegally in the country without money, Chan must hide from the local authorities and corrupt FSB agents while protecting Annie. It turns out that the Chinese operative is the good guy, an ex-CIA, and the FSB agents are Russian mobsters. Jackie is caught in the middle and fights to stay alive. Without any backup, he teams up with Annie who works at an aquarium. At first she is reluctant to help Chan for deceiving her, but then her brother appears and explains the situation. Annie's brother had given her the nuclear warhead to hide which she did by placing it underwater at the aquarium. Jackie and Annie return to the aquarium, but are pursued by the Russian mobsters who battle them underwater. In the finale, Jackie battles in and out of the water and manages to smash a car into the getaway boat. Atop a nuclear submarine, Chan is praised for his courageous service beyond the call of duty.

Filmed after "Rumble in the Bronx", Chan's evident struggle to appeal to an international audience has him filming less and less in Hong Kong and more overseas. Straight from a James Bond plot minus the sexual innuendoes, Chan starts in Hong Kong then jumps to the snow-covered Arctics of Russia and finally battles in a giant aquarium in Australia. The film lacks the true kung-fu persona of his earlier films and takes a bit of time to actually start flowing. The routine plot does little to enhance the story and many of the big action scenes are pale imitations of Bond films. When the physical/kung-fu action starts, no one can surpass Jackie Chan as his Gene Kelly-like grace, ingenuity, and choreography light up the screen. The battle between Jackie and a roomful of martial artists is amazing and is the only hardcore Chan kung-fu scene in the movie. Using an assortment of props: staff, broom, ladder, scaffolding, Chan explodes and amazes us with every trick in the book. Don't try this at home! The other highlight of the film is the finale as Jackie does underwater kung-fu while staying ahead of the man-eating sharks and the Russian goons. Here and there the film adds a bit of excitement with Chan fighting on stilts at a street festival, and his escape from two Russian killers while balancing on the ledge of his penthouse apartment equipped with a live koala bear and eucalyptus tree. A good, slightly uneven film for action/Chan fans with a family-oriented sense of adventure. Viva la Chan!

Fist of Fear, Touch of Death
(1994) Documentary C-90m English
Catalog #20053B   Hong Kong/USA   Retail: $9.99
Dir: Matthew Mallinson   Scr: Ron Harvey   Prod: Terry Levene
DP: John Hazard   Editor: Matthew Mallinson, Jeffrey Brown
Music: Keith Mansfield   Camera: Dan Decovney
Prod Supervisor: Scott D. Hello   Assistant Dir: Vincent Giordano
Makeup: Jean Morris   MAD: Ron Van Clief, Bill Louie   Dist: Quality Video, Inc.
Bruce Lee   Martial Arts Master
Fred Williamson   Hammer, the ladies man

Ron Van Clief	Boxer
Adolph Caesar	TV Anchorman
Aaron Banks	Promoter
Bill Louie	Kato #2
Teruyuki Higa	Karate Instructor
Gail Turner	Rape Victim
Richard Barathy	Stone Smasher
Hollywood Browde	Hammer's girlfriend
Louis Neglia	Middleweight Champion
Cydra Karlyn	Boxer's girlfriend
Annette Bronson	Jogger
John Flood	Cyclone
Ron Harvey	Jasper Milktoast

Mark Messina, Raymond Loperfido, George Lopez, Charles Odwin, Raymond Marinteau, Frankie Italo, Angelo Spergo, Alphonse Hewitt, David Pedernera, Danny Reilly, Glen Perry

[*1/2]

One of the worst films ever made, featuring Bruce Lee's image on the cover. Exploitation comes in many forms and this dated film touts itself as a documentary on Bruce Lee's life while using the World Karate Championships of 1979 in New York City as the backdrop of the film. Though it occasionally shows the legendary actor/martial artist, the majority of the film is spent in mockumentary speculation on Lee's death and stories of his physical prowess recreated in poorly choreographed fight routines. Adolph Caesar portrays a hard-nosed anchorman who interviews a number of people on the death of Bruce Lee. Every character asked pays homage to the great Lee, but ham up their roles with testosterone-level grunts and accusations that no one in Lee's perfect health could have died. Williamson is often seen without his shirt or with a scantily clad woman at his side. The film flips flops back and forth between the interviews and re-enactments of how martial artist use their abilities on the street. On two occasions, young female joggers are practically raped in broad daylight, only to be saved by a fake Bruce Lee. Don't expect to comprehend the logic of these scenes or be impressed by them, since the quality and appearance are akin to intoxicated friends videotaping a home movie. Towards the end, brief highlights of the tournament appear, and the film thankfully ends.

Fist of Legend
(1994) Kung-Fu   C-102m   Chinese with English Subtitles
Catalog #1762   Hong Kong   Retail: $39.99
Dir/Scr: Corey Yuen Scr: Ip Kwong Kim, Lam Kay Toa Ex. Prod: Jet Li
DP: Derek Wan   Editor: Chan Kei Hop, Cheng Chak Man   Music: Joseph Koo
Art Dir: Horace Ma   Prod Controller: Chui Po Chu   Prod Design: Lam Chiu Yin
Prod Supervisor: Julia Chu Prod Manager: Shia Wai Sum, Helen Li
MAD: Yuen Woo Ping   Martial Arts: Yuen Cheung Yan, Yuen Shun Yi, Ku Huen Chiu
Action Dir: Chan Ka Sheung   Costume Designer: Shirley Chan
PC: Eastern Production Ltd.   Dist: Tai Seng Video

Jet Li   **Chen Zhen**
Yasuaki Kurata   **General Fujiita**
Nakayama Shinobu, Ada Choi Siu Fun, Chin Siu Ho, Billy Chau, Paul Chiang, Yuen Cheung Yan
[****]

Jet Li's finest non-flying film pays homage to Bruce Lee in a powerhouse remake of The Chinese Connection. Thankfully, he doesn't try to imitate Lee but brings along his own unique brand of fighting and bravado to the heroic role. What sets this apart from many of his other roles is the sheer simplicity and beauty of the martial arts sequences. No bizarre camera angles, special effects, outlandish wire tricks, and supermen fighting abilities clutter the screen. The story is simple and direct, appealing to fans who enjoy hardcore martial arts.

During pre-WWII Japan, Chen Zhen is studying abroad at Kyoto University. He wears an immaculate school uniform and is a model student. However, the seeds of imperialism are planted in Japan's citizens and the 1920's are no stranger to prejudices. A group of bigoted Japanese bullies from the Kokuryu (Black Dragon) Academy harass Chen Zhen with racial epithets, calling him a Chi Na. Chen is forced to defend himself but soon the master of the Kokuryu enters the classroom. He stops the fight and informs Chen that his master in China was killed during a duel with a Japanese Master named Akutagawa. Chen leaves immediately to return to Shanghai, China and his school Jingwu Mun. After paying respects to Master Huo's shrine, Chen enters the Japanese school in Shanghai and challenges the powerful Akutagawa. He wins easily which sparks his suspicions of deceit in the match. An investigation of Master Huo's cadaver proves that he was poisoned.

Meanwhile, a power struggle develops between Chen and the eldest senior classmate, the son of Huo, who sees Chen's bravado and popularity as a threat to his own leadership. He decides to escape his problems by visiting a prostitute and neglecting his martial arts studies. Problems intensify when a militaristic Japanese general kills Akutagawa for his competitive failure and blames Chen for the murder. The Japanese school and Jingwu Mun tensions run high in Shanghai and the police are needed to break up the violence. A court of law eventually proves Chen innocent with the thanks of a surprise witness from Japan. Chen's Japanese girlfriend has left behind her comfortable life in Kyoto to join Chen. Racial issues are explored and many Chinese citizens shun Chen and his Japanese girlfriend. After a spectacular challenge with Huo, Chen decides to leave Jingwu Mun and find shelter in a shed near a burial tomb. Soon, it's discovered that the Japanese paid one of the students and a cook to poison the master with plans of destroying Jingwu Mun's reputation. The Japanese villains call over a master of Japanese karate (Kokuryu Master from Kyoto University) to deal with Li, but the master is also the uncle of Li's girlfriend. Though they have a spectacular friendly fight, they admire each other and do nothing to provoke additional violence. Chen then joins Huo who plans to challenge the ruthless General Fujiita and end the violence once and for all. Li and his elder classmate put aside their differences and battle the ruthless Japanese. A few elements that are different from the original Lee classic, include a rivalry between Li and the eldest senior to see who is in command, the positive portrayal of Li's Japanese girlfriend (Bruce Lee had a Chinese girlfriend), and the noble Japanese master who challenges Li and offers him advice. An excellent film for any martial arts/action fans with exceptional performances from Jet Li and the entire cast. If you enjoy the pure intensity of Bruce Lee and earlier kung-fu films, you won't be disappointed and you might just become a diehard martial arts fanatic.

Fist of the North Star
(1986) Japanime: Action   C-110m   Dubbed   VA   Catalog # SPV 90263
Japan Retail: $19.95
Dir: Toyoo Ashida   Music: Katsuhisa Hattori
PC: Toei Animation Co., Ltd.   Dist: Streamline Pictures
(based on graphic novels by Buronson & Tetsuo Hara)
[**]
Strangely this classic was remade into a live-action film with American actors. The animated story follows the quest of a young warrior who is revived with phenomenal powers of the North Star. In the post-apocalyptic future, vicious fighters roam the land and take what they want. In a powerful scene, a lone figure walks in silence, unhindered and unconcerned with any attacks. A building falls atop him, but he keeps walking right through the structure. He dispatches his mutated villains with rapid-fire punches and kicks which strike their victims who then explode in graphic clearness. He rarely cracks a facial expression and follows a determined course of violent action. The animation is fast and vulgar as heads explode and limbs fly apart at lightning speed while our hero continues his quest against the villains. Noted for its graphic violence, Fist of the North Star, received cult-like status and notoriety among early fans. Not intended for children, North Star appeals to fight anime fans who don't mind a heavy dose of extreme gore.

Fists of Chan
(1996) Kung-Fu   C-74m Dubbed   VA
Catalog #DP1350-B Hong Kong   Retail: $9.99
Creative Dir: David Hummer   Prod: Hakeem Fidel   Ex. Prod: Donald Kasen
Music: The Hip-Hop Chop Shop, The World Percusion Project "Wholistic Beat"
Dist: Parade Video
Jackie Chan
[**]
In accordance with Jackie Chan's rapid rise in American fame, a number of documentaries have been produced. Fists of Chan is more of a clipography than an actual biography. The entire tape is comprised of numerous clips from Chan's earlier films. Sporadically a narrator comments on Chan's role in the movie, but the information is minimal and not very thought provoking. The clips are only as strong as the films shown and they are collected from his earlier films which are not the strongest Chan works to date. I can recommend this only on two points. If you love his earlier traditional kung-fu films than the tape makes a nice highlight video. Second, if you want to explore some of his earlier films, check this video out first to help guide your decisions. If you don't enjoy any of the fighting highlights, better stay away from the films shown in the compilation tape.

Fists of Fury (originally titled The Big Boss)
(1971) Kung-Fu   C-101m   Dubbed   R   VA
Catalog #6122   Hong Kong   Retail: $19.99
Dir/Scr: Lo Wei   Prod: Raymond Chow   DP: Chen Ching Chu
Editor: Chang Ching-chu   Music: Ku Chih-hui   Art Dir: Chien Hsin
MAD: Han Ying Chieh   PC: National General   Dist: CBS Fox Video

Bruce Lee	**Hero**
Maria Yi	**Mei**
Han Ying Chieh	**Mi**
Tony Liu	**Mi's Son**
Malalene	**Prostitute**
Paul Tien	**Chen**
Miao Ker Hsiu	**Yuan**

Li Quinn, Chin Shan, Li Hua Sze
[**1/2]

The film that made Bruce Lee a star and introduced martial arts films to the world. Made on a shoe-string six-figure budget in a relatively short amount of time in Thailand. Producer Lo Wei banked on Bruce Lee's popularity as Kato of the Green Hornet and gave him a role in The Big Boss. When screen tests proved positive, Lo expanded Bruce's role and gave him the starring role to showcase his energy and talent. Fairly routine, the film is about a Chinese man who swore never to use his martial arts for violence, but is forced to break his family vow after corrupt villains murder his friends. Though this film holds the significance of being his first film, in many ways it is Lee's weakest film, due to the film's hurried production value and Lee's lack of control and direction.

The story starts when Lee arrives in Bangkok, Thailand in search of a job. He is a young immigrant who left China in search of prosperity and meets a group of Chinese friends who have already settled down in Thailand. He stays with the Chinese group of men and one woman who takes care of the house chores. They get him a job working in an ice factory owned by a crooked tyrant. When conditions get rough, the workers are forced to accept their fate with violence as their compensation. Bruce is reluctant to get involved since he vowed to his mother that he would cease fighting and wears a pendant as a reminder of his promise.

When two Chinese friends mysteriously disappear, the workers demand to know what is going on and refuse to work. A fight ensues, but this time Lee can't take the injustice and unleashes his fists of fury, defeating the entire gang. Here is where Lee gets to shine and prove his mettle as an action star. The boss and his son try to keep things quiet and attempt to seduce Lee into their world of sin and corruption. Their ice factory is really a cover for a drug operation and workers who stumble upon the truth, mysteriously disappear in a block of ice. When Lee's friends are murdered, he goes on a revenge spree and attacks the boss' mansion. The dogs and goons can't stop him, but the boss is an expert fighter with knives. In classic showdown fashion, the two opponents square off and battle to the death. Lee is victorious, but the Thai police arrive in force with Mei. Lee gets up with determination and walks off with the officers as the closing credits and music finish the film. The rest is cinematic history. Here are a few things about Lee's fighting style that made him unique on screen. Lee's character never needed to train or waste time finding a master, he was the master from the opening scene. Lee also used a unique set of trademark screeches, yells, and animal gestures to intimidate his opponents...it's amazing how many imitators have followed with little success. Lee has no problems with fighting dirty to get the job done: he hits the groin, bites, pulls hair, and will use anything he can get his hand on. His fights are more direct, less fanciful, and more realistic than other kung-fu films of the era. The film did cut out a few violent scenes where Lee embeds a saw into a man's skull and slices off his arm. Keep in mind the period of time, the limited budget, and the crude nature of the film, so try not to laugh too hard at the dubbing or when Lee sends a man crashing through a wall and the hole is a perfect silhouette of the goons' body. No matter how many low points the film possesses, Bruce Lee's charismatic presence still make this a noteworthy martial arts film.

Fists of the White Lotus`(Clan of the White Lotus)
(1980) Kung-Fu   C-100m   Dubbed   Hong Kong   Retail: $19.99
Dir: Lo Lieh   Prod: Mona Fong   Ex. Prod: Run Run Shaw
PC: Shaw Bros.
Lo Lieh, Gordon Liu Chia Hui, Hui Ying Hung
[***]
A followup film to "Executioners of Death", but not quite as memorable. In many ways, the film imitates the story and never creates any new motivations or background to the white-haired Pai May or Gordon Liu's freedom fighter. Once again Lo Lieh stars (and directs) as the evil priest who betrayed and destroyed Shaolin Temple. This time Gordon Liu and Hui Ying Hung are Shaolin rebels seeking revenge. Liu is not able to beat Lieh's priest until he develops a lighter style technique which he invented while practicing on paper dummies at their hidden base. He spends long hours in the night training with his fellow freedom fighters. When the time is right, Liu sneaks into Pai May's sanctuary and attacks him while he is bathing. A good kung-fu film with familiar routines for Shaw fans.

Five Deadly Venoms
(1978) Kung-Fu   C-100m   Dubbed   Hong Kong   Retail: $19.99
Dir: Chang Cheh   Scr: Chang Cheh, I Kuang
Prod: Mona Fong   Ex. Prod: Run Run Shaw   Art Dir: Johnson Tsao
PC: Shaw Bros.

Kuo Chui	**Lizard**
Lo Meng	**Toad**
Wei Pai	**Snake**
Lu Feng	**Centipede**
Sun Chien	**Scorpion**
Chiang Sheng	**Number 6**
Wang Lung Wei	**Judge**

[***1/2]
What if there was a secret style of martial arts, so deadly that the user could kill with a single blow and defy the laws of physical endurance. Now imagine an entire school dedicated to that deadly style. The Poison Clan practices just such a deadly style of kung-fu, using their incredible skills for crime and mayhem. Now, the dying master of the clan, wishing to make amends, orders his sixth and last pupil to find the five men who trained before him, each an expert in the secret styles - centipede, snake, scorpion, lizard, and toad. The toad style is powerful and impenetrable to weapons. The lizard is apt at climbing walls and flipping. The scorpion is a powerful kicker. The snake is agile and strikes with deadly blows. The centipede is lightning fast with his hands and feet. They all wore masks while training and kept their identities a guarded secret. Though the sixth student studied a little of every style, he is no match for the rest unless he teams up with another member. The dying master sends him to a town where another of the clan's leader is living in seclusion. He is the sole possessor of the clan's hidden treasure.

The sixth student arrives in town dressed as a beggar and starts to snoop around. We discover that police Captain Ma is the scorpion and the lieutenant is the lizard. The good lizard is friends with the muscular toad while a rich, lethargic noble is the snake who allies with a ruthless crook, the centipede. The snake and the centipede discover the master's house, but can not find the treasure, so they murder him and the entire family. The high official of the court sends his police officers to round up suspects. When they find a witness who points to the centipede, the police can't capture him because of his amazing abilities. The lizard cop asks his friend the toad to capture him and the centipede is arrested with a little help from the sixth student.

Meanwhile, the scorpion captain plays both sides of the track and finds the treasure map. The rich snake bribes the judge and the witness changes his testimony to accuse the toad. In a great battle, the snake and scorpion defeat the toad and kill him while the lizard was away on government business. When the lizard returns to town, he discovers his friend is dead and the centipede is a free man. Captain Ma tells him to calm down and forget about what happened. Furious, the lizard barges out of the station and drinks himself into a stupor. A few fellow officers come forth and tell him the true events of what happened while he was away. Then the sixth student reveals himself and teams up with the lizard to defeat the evil snake, centipede, and scorpion. The treasure is recovered from the wax of a candle and found on the scorpion's body. The heroes donate the money to the poor.

Few films outside the realm of Bruce Lee, Jackie Chan, and Jet Li have caught the imagination and popularity captured in Chang's Deadly Venoms. A notable film for its high energy and use of fantasy elements that appeared more American in style and could easily be digested by fans. Only a select few characters have special powers and they gained them through rigorous training scenes. The super-powered heroes wear masks and fight super-powered villains that could easily be seen as a martial arts version of X-men with characters like Wolverine, Spiderman, the Lizard, and Scorpion who appear in American comics. The great kung-fu scenes marked a highpoint in Chang's career and made stars out of the entire cast. From then on, the cast members would commonly be known as the "Venoms" and were remembered by their performances in the film, often playing similar roles. Chang and his venoms went on to make dozens of films that combined the talents of all the actors and their respective specialty: strength, kicking, acrobatics. These films became overnight sensations and were often shown on television during the kung-fu craze. Kids would dress as their favorite venom for Halloween and the film went on to be seen by millions of fans. Luckily, Chang resisted the studio's urging to put a more frivolous, comedic element into the classic film. An excellent example of Chang's talent in one of his best films to date, and notably one of the first fantasy kung-fu films universally applauded by fans.

Five Element Ninja - See Super Ninjas

Five Fingers of Death   (King Boxer/Iron Palm)
(1972) Kung-Fu   C-100m   Dubbed   Hong Kong   Retail: $19.99
Dir: Cheng Chang Ho   PC: Shaw Bros.
Lo Lieh   Chow Chi Hao
Wang Ping   Ying Ying
Gu Wenzhong   Sung Wu Yang
Tian Fong   Meng San Yeh

Nangong Xun   Han Lung
James Nam, Tong Lin
[**1/2]
The granddaddy of martial arts film and credited for beginning the kung-fu craze in America, though Bruce Lee's films brought it to full force. Handsome orphan Chow Chi Hao trains under Master Sung, hoping to master kung-fu and marry Sung's daughter. To prove himself, Chow will enter a kung-fu tournament and win the title and the hand of Ying Ying. The evil kung fu school has the same notions and its head master hires villains to brutalize any rival schools, so that his own son will face no worthy opponents. Lone survivor, Chow, must train and take revenge. The villains torture Chow and crush his hands to prevent him from learning iron palm. As in many films, the villains underestimate the mettle of the vengeful hero who does train and delivers bloody justice. One of the earliest of the kung fu films, and still one of the most relentlessly brutal and violent kung fu films out there which resulted in its infrequent appearance on television. A screen classic in many respects, but dated and crude-looking compared to more modern films. Ironically, Lo Lieh the hero would be typecast as a veteran villain in dozens of Shaw Brothers kung-fu films. He is most memorable as the white-haired priest from Executioners of Death and Fists of the White Lotus.

Five Masters of Death (Five Shaolin Masters)
(1975) Kung-Fu   C-100m   Dubbed   Hong Kong   Retail: $19.99
Dir: Chang Cheh   PC: Shaw Bros.
Alexander Fu Sheng, Ti Lung, David Chiang, Meng Fei, Chi Kuan Chun, Wang Lung Wei
[**1/2]
One of the most popular types of kung fu stories is the Shaolin Monks versus Manchurians. To briefly explain, the Manchus invaded China and established the Ching Dynasty which ruled for over three hundred years until the early 1900's. Po Yi, the character from the Last Emperor was the last Manchurian ruler. Many Chinese from the Ming Dynasty rebelled against the new Manchurian occupation. The Shaolin Temples, a place of Buddhist worship carried on a rich tradition of martial arts prowess. Legend claims that an Indian monk named Da Mo traveled to China. He was horrified at the monks poor state of health and sloven behavior. Studying certain aggressive animals, Da Mo invented a style of exercise which became a fighting style known as kung-fu. Action packed tales of Shaolin rebels battling the Manchurian government have become a main staple of Asian cinema.
After the infamous burning of Shaolin Temple by Ching Dynasty troops (an actual, historical event), five of the surviving rebels vow revenge against the troops, as well as against the monk who betrayed the temple. To track down and capture the noble rebels, the Manchurians send a team of kung-fu experts led by Wang. Each rebel is pursued by a villain who specializes in a certain technique and while many of their comrades die, the five main characters escape. Each one goes off to specialize in a specific technique to defeat the evil kung-fu experts. When the time comes, each of the five pairs meet in battle and fight to the death. Unlike mainstream American films, Asian filmmakers are not afraid to kill their heroes or torture them to death. Some of the masters of death survive while others are not as lucky. Non-flying kung-fu featuring a strong cast of performers in a classic Shaw production.

Flying Dagger

(1993) Comedy Fantasy Kung-Fu C-82 min   Dubbed   VA
Catalog #1290   Hong Kong   Retail: $39.99
Dir: Chu Yen Ping   Scr: Wong Jing   Prod: Mark Wu
DP: Chen Rong Shu Editor: Ma Zhong Yao   Music: Chang Da Li
Prod Manager: Jackson Chan, Eric Tang, Chang Shaw Ping
Planning: Pi Ji Tao, Wade Yao   Supervisor: Jessica Hsu
Art Dir: Li Yao Guang   MAD: Ma Yak Shing, Lam Tak On, Ching Siu Tung
PC: Chang Hong Channel Film & Video Co.
Jacky Cheung   Red Fox
Maggie Cheung   Flying Fox
Tony Leung Kar Fai Uncle Han
Cheung Man   Witch Sisters
Gloria Yip
Ng Man Tat, Yeun King Tam, Li Kai Tin, Law Lit, Pauline Chan, Fong Fong, David Wu
[**1/2]
When viewing this film, I shook my head and said this is going to be a tough review to write. Why? Because I enjoyed the film but at the same time I couldn't believe how silly and stupid it was. Falling into that realm of parody and bad taste, Flying Daggers is a movie that grows on you for its sheer childish silliness. Don't get me wrong, there's plenty wrong with the film and I wouldn't recommend it unless you enjoy Chinese slapstick and flying kung-fu films. Thankfully, Flying Daggers doesn't put on airs and pretend to be a serious period piece, from the beginning we're in on the joke and there's plenty of references to Madonna, the Addam's Family, and other fantasy kung-fu films. An all-star cast doesn't hurt and it's refreshing the film doesn't rely on toilet humor. Now to the story which sounds pretty serious at first. The Han Brothers (actually an uncle and nephew) are professional bounty hunters hired by a government official to capture the Red Fox. They have competition for their prize from a pair of sisters, lovingly referred throughout the film as those witches (bitches). The four pool their abilities and capture the Red Fox, but are pursued by a crazy killer named Invincible Death. They manage to beat him, but sever his hand which befriends the group of fighters. Fox's wife, Flying Cat and her kittens try to rescue him. On top of that a squad of Japanese assassins and a demonic couple merge on the inn where everyone is staying. The innkeeper and his wife pull up a seat and cheer on the battles. After killing the bad guys, the Han Brothers, the Witches, Flying Cat, Red Fox, and the innkeeper become friends and team-up against the evil government official. In true, high-flying form, the heroes merge on the outdoor court of the official and battle him to the death. The closing credits include a few light bloopers. A short film with over-the-top humor and plenty of battles, but keep in mind the dysfunctional plot and madcap hijinks are a major hurdle to overcome.

Flying Guillotine
(1975) Kung-Fu   C-100m   Dubbed   Hong Kong   Retail: $19.99
Dir/Scr: Ho Menga Prod: Mona Fong   Ex. Prod: Run Run Shaw
PC: Shaw Bros.
Chen Kuan Tai, Ku Feng, Wei Hung, Liu Wu Chi
[**]
Though Chen Kuan Tai is one of my favorite actors, I always cringe when people refer to this

film as a basis for kung-fu films. Trust me, kung-fu movies are not all that bad and even this one has been unfairly spotted as the worse kung-fu movie ever made. Though I admit time has not been kind to this film and an absurd, bloody weapon make this a difficult film to watch for most viewers. The story revolves around Chen, a family man and soldier for the emperor. A new deadly weapon is invented, the flying guillotine. This is where the askance looks and channel switching come into play, but bear with me since the film has its moments. The flying guillotine is a saucer that can be thrown like a Frisbee. Once it lands on the top of a victim's head, a veil drops around the entire head with a razor blade attached around the bottom of the veil. A long cord is attached to the flying guillotine and held by the user who pulls the cord and closes shut the blades around the person's neck, decapitating him in one move. Then the head and saucer are retrieved by the user. Depending on your tastes, the scenes can be quite gruesome or ridiculous as saucers fly in the air and pull off people's heads. What's more amazing is that the film carries a serious undertone and a convincing performance by Chen, the main fault lies in the use of an unconvincing weapon. The story lies in Chen who is a master of the guillotine but is mistrusted by a rival soldier who is jealous of his abilities. He encourages the paranoid emperor to get rid of Chen and accuse him of treason. After the accusations and unjust murders, Chen leaves for a quieter life with his family. The rival student won't let him go and sends his best guillotine users to kill Chen. Chen with his wife and newborn son must avoid the killers. He invents a clever device to counter the guillotine. A steel umbrella that opens up and cracks the blade inside the guillotine. Armed with only himself, he battles for his freedom and the life of his family. The scenes of Chen defending his family are quite dramatic, as his battle with a long-time comrade and friend. The story is quite good and has been reworked into other stories, sans flying guillotine, which have met with positive reviews. I won't fully recommend the film, since there's plenty wrong with it, but don't consider this the worse kung-fu movie ever made.

Fong Sai Yuk
(1993) Kung-Fu   C-106m   Chinese with English Subtitles
Catalog #1295   Hong Kong   Retail: $39.99
Dir: Corey Yuen Kwai   Scr: Kay On, Chan Kia Chang, Thai Kang Yung
Ex. Prod: Jet Li   DP: Jingle Ma   Editor: Cheung Yin Chang
Music: JamesWong, Romeo Diaz, Mark Lai   Art Dir: Benjamin Lau
Post Prod Manager: Angie Lam   Ex. Prod Manager: Stephen Lau
Prod Manager: Helen Li, Shia Wei Sun   Prod Coordinator: Julia Chu
Prod Controller: Chui Po Chu   Prod Design: Ann Hui
Costume: Shirley Chan   MAD: Yuen Kwai, Yuen Tak
Dist: Universe Laser & Video Co., Ltd./Tai Seng Video

Jet Li	**Fong Sai Yuk**
Sibelle Hu	**Ting's mother**
Josephine Siao	**Fong's mother**
Michelle Reis	**Ting Ting**
Zhao Wen Zhou	**Manchu Officer**
Adam Cheng	**Chen**

Chu Kong, Chan Lang
[*1/2]**
Superstar Jet Li proves his dynamic charisma and range by tackling another historical character

from Chinese folklore. Adding elements of comedy with flying martial arts, Jet Li is Fong Sai Yuk, a Chinese hero who doesn't always do things according to the book. The comedic interplay with the dramatic seriousness of the martial arts can be confusing at first, but the film offers a fine cast of memorable characters who help balance the comedy and drama. The wackiest character in the film is Fong's mother (Siao) who is one of the most memorable female fighters on screen. She looks motherly and pleasant, but will do anything for the pride of the Fong family. This gets her and Jet Li in plenty of trouble.

The Red Flower Society is a secret organization dedicated to the Han Emperor who wishes to end Ching Manchurian rule in China. The opening sequence has the Red Flower Society waging a massive attack against the Manchurian Emperor. They literally fly and glide on surfboards in their pursuit of the emperor. The emperor awakens from his nightmare and sends his top officer (Zhao) to deal with the rebel problem. Some will remember Zhao as the star of a number of martial arts films, like The Blade and Once Upon a Time in China 4 & 5. He plays a serious villain, straight and ruthless, providing a fearsome foe to the fun-loving Fong Sai Yuk.

In Canton, Fong meets the pretty Ting Ting and saves her from some cads by competing in a western style competition. Unfortunately, Ting's father is the new Manchurian governor and Fong's father is a member of the Red Flower Society. Without knowing that fact, Fong enters a competition to win the hand of the governor's daughter in marriage. He must defeat Fong's mother, a super-powerful and pretty kung-fu expert. Thinking the governor's daughter is ugly, he throws the fight. His mother, furious with disgracing the family name, dresses as a man and enters the competition to fight Ting's mother. Remember in Hong Kong films, as long as you dress like a man, you look like a man, no matter how much makeup or how beautiful you look. The clothes make the man. Fong's mom proves her martial arts prowess, but also wins the affection of Ting's mom who is unhappy in her current marriage to the governor. The challenge fight is one of the film's funniest scenes. Siao and Li are marvelous as they challenge Ting Ting's mother. The sequence combines humor, martial arts, and spectacular stunts in a dizzying array of balance, flexibility and strength. They fight on wooden platforms and literally on top of people's head. An impressive sight that must be seen to be truly believed. The governor demands that someone marry his daughter and captures Fong and his mother. Ting and Fong meet at the governor's mansion, not realizing their mutual marriage arrangement is to each other, they complain on their imprisonment and forced marriage to someone they do not love.

When the two are officially engaged, Fong and Ting discover the truth and happily accept the marriage arrangement. The governor throws a dinner party, but Zhao and his troops appear and declare them all traitors. Both families must go on the run and it is up to Fong Sai Yuk to save the day. Sometimes it is best not to think too logically when viewing flying kung-fu films, and instead enjoy the action and charisma of the characters. Fong Sai Yuk is an excellent example of the new trend of kung-fu movies which blend a lot of comedy and hi-flying martial arts into a massive costumed spectacle.

Fong Sai Yuk II   **(10,000 Warriors No Enemy (Kung Fu Emperor))**
(1993) Kung-Fu   **C-98m Catalog # 1642**   **Hong Kong**
Retail: $39.99
Dir: Corey Yuen Kwai   **Scr: Kay On, Chan Kia Chang**
Ex. Prod: Jet Li   **DP: Mark Li**   **Editor: Angie Lam**
Music: Lowell Lo   **Art Dir: James Leung**   **Prod Manager: Helen Li, Shia Wei Sun**

Ex. Prod Manager: Stephen Lau   Prod Controller: Chui Po Chu
Prod Coordinator: Julia Chu   Prod Design: David Lai
Costume: Shirley Chan   MAD: Yuen Kwai, Yuen Tak
PC: Eastern Production Ltd.   Dist: Universe Laser & Video Co., Ltd./Tai Seng Video
Jet Li, Josephine Siao, Sibelle Hu, Michelle Reis Lee, Corey Yuen, Adam Cheng Siu Choi,
Amy Kwok Oi Ming
[***]
A lot more singing and a less charismatic villain are prominent in the Jet Li sequel to Fong Sai
Yuk. Like Wong Fei Hung, Fong is a real-life character from Chinese folklore who helped
people against tyranny. Unlike Wong, the character of Fong is a practical joker and enjoys
getting into trouble. The story continues from the first film, but this time Fong becomes a
hardcore member of the Red Flower Society. The leader of the Red Flower Society is in fact a
Manchu prince. As a child, he was hidden away in Japan by his mother who feared he would be
murdered. In a concubine-dominated society, the emperor might have many heirs with different
mothers. Sometimes a power hungry mother would want to kill her son's rivals. The main
villain, a member of the Red Flower Society, wishes to oust the Manchu prince and take over the
Red Flower Society for his own personal gain. He's not too fond of Fong's eager enthusiasm and
loyalty, causing a bitter rivalry between the two men.
A special convoy from Japan has arrived in China, carrying important documents that reveal the
truth. Jet Li and his mom, dad is absent, are assigned in the task to retrieve the document.
Complications arrive when the Japanese escort includes a beautiful Manchurian princess who
falls in love with Fong Sai Yuk. The Red Flower Society instructs Fong to go undercover, woo
the princess, and retrieve the document. Fong's wife doesn't like the idea and manages to get in
the way. So poor Fong is hounded by a bevy of women: his wife, a Manchurian princess, and his
wild mother. Life can't get more complicated than three kung-fu women vying for one man's
attention. They fail to save their Red Flower leader who is imprisoned by the traitor. The villain
takes over the Red Flower Society and does all in his power to destroy Fong Sai Yuk. In true
heroic fashion, Fong must battle his way through an army of men and face down the traitor. If
you enjoy Jet Li or the first Fong film, then there's plenty of solid action and humor to make it
through the sequel. Li's boyish charm works well in the comedic moments, but his intensity and
energy (remember, real life Jet Li is a dedicated martial arts expert) can be felt in the dramatic
battles. When he blindfolds himself and asks his misguided Red Flower members to back off,
the sword-wielding Fong Sai Yuk is totally focused, serious, and ready to rumble.

The Four Shaolin Challengers
(1980) Kung-Fu   C-99m Dubbed   Catalog #4069   Hong Kong
Retail: $9.99
Dir/Scr: Wei Hui Feng   Prod: Charles Lowe, Cheng Hui Chun
Ex. Prod: Cheng Kai Ming   Presented: Ng Man Chow   Planning: Lu Kuei Hsiung
DP: Charles Lowe   Editor: Yu Tsan Feng   Music: Chen Fang Chi
MAD: Huang Mei   PC: Chin Ma Film Company   Dist: Simitar Entertainment
Bruce Leung   Devil Kick Chi
Li Jin Kun   Lin Shih Yung
Huang Yuen Shen   Ling Yun Chieh
Pai Piau   Liang Kuan

Liu Tan, Liu I Fan, Kuan Tsung, Wang Ching Ching, Kuo An Nor, Chieng Chih, Shan Kuai
[**]
Any movie that opens with the Wong Fei Hung theme music promises to be good, but this low-budget kung-fu film misses the mark. Young Lin is a disciple of Wong who fights off a group of crooks to protect his younger brother and sister. He establishes a martial arts academy to help other merchants escape the greedy claws of loan sharks who demand protection money. It doesn't take long for the boss of the gangsters to attack Lin and force him to close down. Thankfully, the wounded Lin is able to call on three of his martial arts brothers to help even out the score. Slowly, the heroes help reclaim the town and inspire the merchants to stand up for their rights. The climax features the four heroes in an open yard to challenge the gang's leader. Instead of a bloody death, the police arrive and take care of the wounded criminal. Plenty of traditional style weapons, lion dance music (Wong Fei Hung trademark), and fights spice up the mediocre story.

Frankenstein Conquers the World (Furankenshutain Tai Baragon)
(1966) Monster   C-87m Dubbed   VA   Japan Retail: $9.95
Dir: Inoshiro Honda Scr: Kaoru Mabuchi
Prod: Tomoyuki Tanaka   DP: Hajime Koizumi Sp. Fx: Eiji Tsuburaya
PC: Toho Studios
Nick Adams, Tadao Takashima, Kumi Mizuno, Yoshio Tsuchiya, Takashi Shimura
[**]
Leave it to the Japanese to reinvent Hollywood's most famous monster by unleashing him into a Godzilla-style film. Frankenstein is dead, but his heart lives on in Germany. World War II is coming to a close and the Nazis are losing. In a desperate attempt to escape and rebuilt their empire, German scientists pack Frankenstein's still beating heart and transport it aboard a Nazi U-boat. While escaping, the ship is destroyed and years later the heart finds its way to Japan, Germany's old Axis ally.
The heart may be old, but is used to create a new Frankenstein boy who grows at an amazing rate. He gets bigger and stronger, causing the authorities to fear him. The only ones who trust and love him are a core of scientists, including the female scientist who maternally bonds with the new Frankenstein. When Frankenstein gets too big, he makes an escape and is brutally hunted down. Then in the distant mountains of Japan, an entire lodge is destroyed by a giant creature. Frankenstein is blamed and a massive military hunt goes on for the monster. The female scientist tries to talk the government out of their cruel plans to hunt down and kill Frankenstein. Then another lizard-like creature is discovered to be the real culprit, and Frankenstein goes after it to clear his name. The two monsters duke it out in true Japanese-monster fashion. The scientists are helpless and view the battle from the sidelines. The film is competently directed by Godzilla-veteran Inoshiro Honda, but suffers from a dated visual setting and total campiness. Still appealing for fans of the early genre of monster films from Japan.

Full Contact   (Hero Thief Flies High/Xia Dao Gao Fei)
(1992) Action C-99m Chinese with English Subtitles
Catalog #1225   Hong Kong   Retail: $39.99
Dir: Ringo Lam   Scr: Yin Nam Editor: Tony Chow

Music: Teddy Robin Kwan PC: Golden Princess Film Production Limited
Dist: Tai Seng Video

Chow Yun Fat	**Jeff**
Simon Yam	**Judge**
Ann Bridgewater	**Mona**
Anthony Wong	**Sam**
Bonnie Fu	**Virgin**
Frankie Chin	**Deano**
Lee King Sang	

[***1/2]

A fabulous action film with excellent performances and breathtaking intensity from Simon Yam and Chow Yun Fat as a dark hero who strikes off on a vendetta of vengeance. Chow and his friends are living in the backwaters of Thailand and dream of returning to Hong Kong in style. Chow works as a bouncer at a wild club and his girlfriend Mona is a dancer at the club. His two other friends include a hot-headed fighter and a portly, glasses-wearing wimp named Sam. When Sam gets in trouble with a loan-shark, Chow saves him from getting his hands cut off. Sporting a short haircut and looking lean and mean, Chow is an intimidating and powerful fighter. He saves Sam, but makes an enemy out of the loan shark.

Elsewhere in Bangkok, a trio of flamboyant thieves have launched a series of violet robberies. The leader is the nihilistic Judge, a suave homosexual who enjoys magic tricks. His comrades include the beefy Deano and his sluttish girlfriend Virgin. Judge is an old acquaintance of Sam. Hoping to score big, Sam joins up with Judge and brings along Jeff and his friend. The two gangs plan to rob a weapons shipment from a rival gangster. Secretly, the vengeful loan shark pays Judge to bump off Jeff in the process. The gun heist goes as planned, but Jeff and his friend are betrayed. Too afraid to act, Sam huddles in shameful horror. He is forced to choose sides, betrays his dear friends, and shoots Jeff down. Desperately, Jeff seeks refuge in a Thai house which is attacked and bursts into flames. Only Jeff and a young girl survive the explosion and the rest of the family is killed.

Time passes and Jeff recovers in a Buddhist monastery, learning to shoot again with his left hand. Everyone thinks he is dead and carry on with their new lives. Sam becomes a hardened professional killer and falls in love with Mona. The two move in together and Judge continues to grow in power. When Jeff reappears, he forgives Sam but asks for a favor. We're not sure of Jeff's motives which intensifies the drama among the characters. Jeff decides to keep in the shadows, plotting his revenge, and only reveals his re-emergence to Sam. The two men team up and go after Judge, but when all seems to be working well, Jeff leaves Sam to Judge's mercy...or does he? In the new club where Mona works, the heroes and villains converge in an amazing gun battle with a clever point-of-view from the bullet's camera perspective. The climatic finale doesn't fail to impress and lovers of Hong Kong action will realize Lam gives Woo a run for his money and pushes Chow to give one of his best performances in the genre. Lam's style has a harsher, darker edge than other directors, but the action-packed film holds true to classic Hong Kong elements of betrayal, loyalty, and plenty of dead bodies. A must see for Chow/Yam fans.

Funeral, The
(1984) Comedy/Drama   C-124m   Japanese with English Subtitles   VA
Japan Retail: $19.95

Dir/Scr: Juzo Itami Prod: Yasushi Tamaoki, Yutaka Okada
DP: Akira Suzuki   Editor: Joji Yuasa
Dist: Republic Pictures Home Video/Ingram Entertainment
Nobuko Miyamoto   Chizuko Amamiya
Tsutomu Yamazaki Wabisuke Inoue
Kin Sugai   Kikue Amamiya
Chishu Ryu   The Priest
Shuji Otaki   Shokichi Amamiya
Ichiro Zaitsu   Satomi
Kiminobu Okumura Shinkichi Amamiya
Haruna Takaso   Yoshiko Saito
[***1/2]
A brilliant black comedy from Japanese filmmaker Juzo Itami. This breakthrough film for Itami firmly established him internationally as a renowned filmmaker of sharp satiric films about Japanese culture, family, and society. Using his wife (Nobuko) and screen favorite (Tsutomu), Itami explores the cultural clash between the older generation and the newer generation by gathering a variety of characters at the funeral of the patriarch of the family. The elderly man who also owned a house of ill-repute is the catalyst for various relatives to expose their true nature, whether induced by greed, lust, or hatred. Itami skillfully shows the nature of humans in a number of incidents that take place the family home. Though the film lacks the overall humor and anecdotal satire of Tampopo, the Funeral is a wonderful film that has a universal appeal to all viewers.

-G-

Galaxy Express 999: Signature Collection
(1979) Japanime: Scifi   C-120m   Dubbed/Japanese with English Subtitles   VA
Catalog # W GE-001/W GES-001   Japan   Retail: $24.95/$29.95
Dir: Taro RinOriginal Story: Leiji Matsumoto   Ex. Prod: Seiji Horibuchi
Music: Nozomi Aoki
English Version - Prod:Toshifumi Yoshida   Scr: Trish Ledoux
PC: Toei Animation Co., Ltd.   Dist: Viz Video
Saffron Henderson   Tetsuro Hoshino
Kathleen Barr   Maetel/Tetsuro's Mom/Queen Promethium
Janyse Jaud   Claire
Terry Klassen   Conductor
Scott McNeil   Harlock
Nicole Oliver   Emeraldas
John Payne   Tochiro Oyama
Paul Dobson   Count Mecha
[***]
Hauntingly elegant and a nostalgic reminder of an earlier age, the Galaxy Express 999 looks like a steam locomotive of the early 20th Century. In reality, underneath the facade is a highly-advanced spaceship that travels from one planet to another. The popular film which also sparked a television series is the tale of a young boy and a beautiful blonde woman on a quest to a far-

reaching planet. The boy's mother was killed by a ruthless Count who hunts humans and mounts them on his wall. Hoping to get revenge, he steals a pass card and boards the Galaxy Express. He wishes to travel to the outskirts of space to a distant planet which sells machine bodies. Once he gets the machine body, he will kill Count Mecha. The film explores the issues of humanity and technology, whether one loses humanity by becoming a machine or gains humanity once they lose it. The young boy wears a Clint Eastwood-style western poncho and carries a powerful lasergun given to him by a kind stranger on one of the far reaching planets. As time progresses over their travels, he masters the use of the gun and befriends the infamous space pirate, Captain Harlock. The beautiful Mattei remains faithful to Tetsuro, offering him guidance, financial assistance, and motherly protection, but keeping her own dark past a secret. Along the way, the train schedules stops over numerous planets, but only briefly and can never wait for anyone as told by the dwarfish robotic conductor. Episodic problems develop at each of their stops, but they always manage to make it back aboard the Galaxy Express. They arrive at the mechanical planet and Mattei reveals herself as a princess. When Tetsuro refuses to become a machine man, Mattei helps him escape the planet and reboard the Galaxy Express for their return trip to Earth.

Gall Force: Eternal Story
(1986) Japanime: Scifi   **C-87m Japanese with English Subtitles**   **VA**
Catalog # USM 1033 Japan   **Retail: $29.95**
Dir: Katsuhito Akiyama   Scr: Sukehiro Tomita   Original Story: Hideki Kakinuma
Character Design: Kenichi Sonoda Art Dir: Jun-Ichi Azuma
Prod: Mitsuhisa Hida, Ikuo Nagasaki, Nagateru Kato, Toru Miura
Animation Prod: Nobuyuki Kitajima, Masahiro Tanaka
EnglishVersion - Ex. Prod: John O'Donnell   Tranlastion: Neil Nadelman
Prod Coordinator: Cliff Rosen
PC: Animate Films, Artmic, AIC   Dist: US Manga Corps
[1/2]**

Based on an original story by writer Hideki Kakinuma who was inspired by Jim Cameron's The Terminator, Gall Force is a science fiction epic dealing with the possible formation of a new race. In a far away galaxy, a long time ago, two mighty armadas are battling in outer space. The war is vicious and casualties run high for both sides, the Solnoids, an all-female race (don't ask) and the bio-mechanical Paranoids. The story follows the exploits of the Solnoid cruiser Starleaf and her seven-women crew as they make their way to the planet Chaos in the 9th Star System. On the planet strange things begin to develop and the Starleaf's cute crew of girls find they are the guinea pigs of a revolutionary experiment. Hoping to end the war and bring unified peace, members from the two worlds secretly met and planned on developing a single species from the Solnoids and the Paranoids without alerting the military factions of their respective worlds. Crewgirl Patty suffers from stomach cramps and gives birth to a young boy. With the final success of a genetic union, both sides take claim of the child and attack the Starleaf's planetary station, Blossom. The Central Guard of Solnoid arrives and battles the Paranoids as well as the Solnoid faction which organized the tabooed experiment. The Starleaf refuses to hand over the boy who grows to full maturity and escapes to the planet Terra where the offsprings will be a new race known as Earthlings...the dawn of humanity with Adam and Eve. The animation style is dated and though the visual battles are still impressive, the antics of the child-like Solnoids will discourage anime fans who might be looking for something a little more mature.

Gall Force 2: Destruction
(1987) Japanime: Scifi   C-50m Japanese with English Subtitles   VA
Catalog # USM 1034   Japan   Retail: $29.95
Dir: Katsuhito Akiyama   Scr & Original Story: Hideki Kakinuma
Prod: Yasuhisa Kazama, Nagateru Kato, Masaki Sawanobori
Ex. Prod: Eiji Kishi, Yutaka Takahashi   Character Design: Kenichi Sonoda
EnglishVersion - Ex. Prod: John O'Donnell   Tranlastion: Neil Nadelman
Prod Coordinator: Stephanie Shalofsky   Subtitling: Studio NEMO
PC: Animate Films, Artmic, AIC   Dist: U.S. Manga Corps
[**1/2]
The war rages on between the all-female Solnoids and the Paranoids from the first film. In a spectacular space battle, the Solnoids unleash the star destroyer which disintegrates the Paranoid homeworld. The surviving members of both fleets pull back and head to the ninth system. Escaping from the destruction, pilot Lufy from the Starleaf joins a new crew of Solnoids who must save the planet Terra from destruction so that it is allowed to develop into Earth. Lufy befriends a group of Solnoids who break with orders and decide to save Terra. The military leaders of the Solnoids would rather see the planet destroyed than fall into the hands of the Paranoids. The fifth planet of the system is a vast weapon array aimed at the planet. Lufy and her new friends fly to the planet and do their best to take out the destructive weapon and save Terra. The constant downbeat nature of the series and scenes of total destruction carry a heavy overbearing tone of antiwar. The moral message is in full force and will not appeal to viewers looking for the lighter side of animation.
For all you Gall Force fans don't worry. Additional Gall Force episodes are available as OAV's. Look forward to the three volume Gall Force: Earth Chapter and the two volume Gall Force: New Era also available on video and laserdisc.
Gall Force 3: Stardust War (1987)   C-50m   Catalog #USM 1035   Retail: $29.95

Game of Death
(1979) Kung-Fu   C-100m   Dubbed   VA
Catalog #67839   Hong Kong   Retail: $19.99 Widescreen Available
Dir: Robert Clouse   Scr: Jan Spears   Prod: Raymond Chow
DP: Godfrey Godar   Editor: Alan Pattillo   Music: John Barry
PC/Dist: CBS/Fox Video
Bruce Lee   Billy Lo
Gig Young   Jim Marshall
Dean Jagger   Dr. Land
Hugh O'Brian   Steiner
Colleen Camp   Ann Morris
Robert Wall   Carl Miller
Mel Novak   Stick
Kareem Abdul-Jabbar=Hakim
Chuck Norris   Fighter
Dan Inosanto   Pasqual
Billy McGill   John

Hung Kim Po   **Lo Chen**
Roy Chaio   **Henry Lo**
[**1/2]

Tragically Bruce Lee died before completing "Game of Death", a film that possibly could have been his greatest piece of work based on the surviving footage and screenplay. Unfortunately, only a small percentage of the film was left in tact and the majority of "Game of Death" comprises of a Korean double and a variety of poorly-conceived cutaways to past clips. The most ridiculous scene includes a pasted photo of Bruce Lee's head over the double's head.

The film parallels Bruce Lee's life, asking what if Bruce Lee never died but actually went into hiding from the mob who extorted him and wanted him killed. The main character, Lee's alterego Billy Lo, gets involved with a powerful mob syndicate lead by an aging bald man. They try to kill Lo who fakes his death, changes his identity, and then goes on a vengeful search for the evil leader. Using disguises, a clever way to fool audience viewers, Lo tries to destroy the organization while protecting his blonde singer/girlfriend. For some reason, perhaps to attract American viewers, Lo's girlfriend and the main villains are Americans. The talented Korean actor who plays Lo performs a number of well-staged fight scenes and does his best to impersonate Bruce Lee's gestures and mannerism. But the fight scenes are stringed together for one reason, to finally bring the real Bruce Lee to the main headquarters which is completed footage shot by Lee. In a brilliant sequence, Lee lets actions speak for himself. To reach the crime boss at the top of the building, Lee must do battle with a martial arts master on each floor. The scenes are worth their weight in gold as Lee battles a Korean hapkido master, an Arnis stick-fighting master (Inosanto), the Caucasian right-hand man, and even the giant Kareem Abdul-Jabbar, the oddest looking martial artist in any film. His massive height compared to Bruce's diminutive stature is a true testament to the David and Goliath legend. The film ends with the crippled villain falling out of the top floor. The closing credits are graced by a beautiful montage sequence taken from Lee's past films, hauntingly reminding us of the greatness of Bruce Lee and how much he will be missed.

Game of Death 2   **(Tower of Death)**
(1980) Kung-Fu   **C-100m**   **Dubbed**   **VA**   **Hong Kong**   **Retail: $19.99**
Dir: Ng See Yuen
Kim Tai Chung, Huang Cheng Li, Roy Chiao, Casanova Wong
[**]

A lackluster sequel which fools the audience into believing Bruce Lee is still alive. The so-called Lee (Korean actor Kim) in the film is wanted by an underground organization, so he fakes his death on the set of a film. Before his coffin can be put to rest, a mysterious helicopter snatches the coffin and steals it. Then a new character pops up in search of the truth. Supposedly, it's Lee after plastic surgery was needed to alter his appearance and provide him a modicum of safty. Lee looks for clues at a remote monastery and keeps an eye on his rivals. The clues lead to an underground pagoda where a futuristic base is the headquarters of the enemy. Lee must battle the enemy hordes to the death and avenge his death. Though the film insults on many levels, the martial arts featured include some decent fight scenes and acrobatics from Kim.

GAMERA: THE FLYING FIRE-BREATHING TURTLE Series

A popular series of Japanese monster films designed to emulate the Godzilla films. The monster films are practically interchangeable, Godzilla is an erect lizard who breathes radioactive fire and Gamera is a turtle who breathes radioactive fire. What sets the two reptiles apart is that Gamera quickly turns into a superhero dedicated to protecting the children of Earth. Though not appealing for adults, the film captivated children along the lines of the Power Rangers TV show...and millions of kids grew up loving each and every film. The films were released under various titles in America and by current standards are quite silly and poorly produced. Though the series abruptly ended in America, many attempts have been made to revive the series in Japan and the United States. In the late 90's, a new Gamera film was released directly to the American video market with mixed success. New films have been produced in Japan, but have yet to arrive in the United States. Monster fans still hope for a day when Gamera and Godzilla will appear in a joint production.

Gamera - Guardian of the Universe
(1995) Monster   C-100m   Japan Retail: $19.99
Dir: Shusuke Kaneko   Scr: Kazunori Ito   Prod: Yasuyoshi Tokuma
Sp. Fx: Shinji Higuchi   PC: Daiei
Yasuyoshi Ihara, Akira Onodera, Shinobu Nakayama, Ayako Fujitami, Yukijiro Hotaru, Hirotara Honda
[***]
Gamera Lives! For all you fans of the flying turtle, Gamera gets a major makeover and reappears on American televisions. Over two decades ago, Gamera vs. Zigra marked the last and final film from Daiei to be released in America. Monster movies faded from popularity, but Godzilla proved that the big monster movies are still in vogue and Gamera made a comeback. Featuring better special effects, the flying turtle battles a group of ancient birds created from a long-lost civilization. The birds nest on a mysterious island and give the locals a major ecological headache. When the prehistoric birds venture to the mainland, they wreak havoc on the Japanese public. Gamera manages to beat most of them, but the lone surviving Gyao mutates into a giant creature. In a classic monster bash, Gamera and Gyao rock Japan for the title of super-monster of the week. The film maintains the classic monster-movie look and maintains a reasonable amount of tension and drama. A good sign for the future of Gamera films and definitely enjoyable for fans of the monster genre.

Gamera, The Invincible   (Gammera/Daikaiju Gamera)
(1966) Monster   B&W-86m   Dubbed   Japan Retail: $19.99
Dir: Noriyaki Yuasa Scr: Fumi Takahashi   Prod: Yonejiro Saito
DP: Nobuo Munekawa   Sp. Fx: Yonesaburo PC: Daiei   Dist: Just for Kids Home Video
Eiji Funakoshi, Harumi Kiritachi, Junichiro Yamashita, Yoshiro Kitahara
American version: Brian Donlevy, Albert Dekker, Dianbe Findley, John Baragrey, Dick O'Neill, Eiji Funakoshi
[**1/2]
The film that started it all and introduced the world to Gamera, the fire-breathing, flying turtle. The first film was shot in black and white and bares resemblance to the first Godzilla film. In

many ways it is an imitation of the Godzilla film, so your enjoyment factor depends on whether you like Japanese monsters or not. After a plane crashes and wakes up a giant creature, Gamera, it is considered a serious threat to the world. The evil monster goes on a rampage and destroys a good part of Japan. When conventional weaponry fail to destroy the creature, Japan manages to trap Gamera in a giant rocketship and blast him into outer space. The treatment of the film is serious and dramatic.

Gamera vs. Barugon (The War of the Monsters)
(1966) Monster   C-101m   Dubbed   Japan Retail: $19.99
Dir: Shigeo Tanaka Scr: Fumi Takahashi   Prod: Hidemasa Nagata
DP: Michio Takahashi   Sp. Fx: Noriaki Yuasa   PC: Daiei
Dist: Just for Kids Home Video
Kojiro Hongo, Kyoko Enami, Akira Natsuki, Koji Fujiyama, Yuzo Hayakawa
[**]
Greed sets the catalyst in motion as human villains travel to an exotic island in the Pacific. They steal a treasured opal which the natives warn possesses a curse. Ignoring them, the villains knock around the natives and attempt to sneak the rare jewel into Japan aboard a steamer. Unknown to them is that the jewel is an egg and when left under a heating lamp gives birth to a giant creature called Barugon. Luckily, Gamera escapes from his space prison and flies to Earth just in time to save the world. Barugon's unique power is to create a rainbow ray that emanates from his back and injures Gamera. The big turtle recovers in time to kick Barugon's butt. It is quickly seen that Gamera develops an affinity for Earth and becomes its biggest savior.

Gamera vs. Gaos
(1967) Monster   C-87m Dubbed   Japan Retail: $19.99
Dir: Noriyaki Yuasa   Scr: Fumi Takahashi   Prod: Hidemasa Nagata
DP: Akira Uehara   Sp. Fx: Kazufumi Fujii, Yuzo Kaneko   PC: Daiei
Dist: Just for Kids Home Video
Kojiro Hongo, Kichijiro Ueda, Naoyuki Abe, Reiko Kasahara, Taro Marui
[**]
Deep in the forests of Japan, a winged creature emerges from the darkness. The giant Gaos has emerged to wreak havoc on Japan and only Gamera can stop him. Gaos is a giant bat-like monster with a flat iron-shaped head and shoots lasers beams out of his mouth. He ends up using his slicing beams to give Gamera some really nasty paper cuts and the turtle is feared dead. Don't worry, since Gamera won't let the children of Earth down.

Gamera vs. Guiron
(1969) Monster   C-88m Dubbed
Catalog #CHE3042 Japan Retail: $19.99
Dir: Noriyaki Yuasa   Scr: Fumi Takahashi   Prod: Hidemasa Nagata
DP: Akira Kitazaki Sp. Fx: Kazufumi Fujii   PC: Daiei   Dist: Just for Kids Home Video
Nobuhiro Kashima, Christopher Murphy, Miyuki Akiyama, Yuko Hamada, Eiji Funakoshi, Kon Omura
[**]

A super campy film for Japanese-monster fans, especially since the heroes are kids and the villains are sexy women in space jumpsuits. Two young boys, a Japanese and American, are kidnaped and transported to a distant planet when they accidentally board a remote-controlled UFO. The population of the planet is long gone except for a couple of sexy women and their big bulldog. Of course the bulldog is a monster the size of a battleship with a long blade for a snout that shoots out sharp projectiles. Guiron proves his bullish mettle when he defeats Gaos who attacks the alien ghost city. The two women are very cordial to their human guests who learn all about the alien world. Gamera fearing for the children's safety flies to the alien world and does battle with the bulldog Guiron. The kids escape near death after their cookies and milk was spiked with sleeping powder. The sexy aliens wanted to digest the boys' brains and take over Earth. The boys keep their brains but one loses his hair. When their evil plans fail, the aliens try to escape in a flying saucer that is accidentally sliced in half by Guiron. Luckily, Gamera studied model building and fuses the saucer together and takes it back to Earth with the children safe inside. Major monster fighting on an alien city set instead of Tokyo. Look out for Gamera's attempt to take the gold medal in gymnastics.

Gamera vs. Jiger
(1970) Monster   C-83m Dubbed   Japan Retail: $19.99
Dir: Noriyaki Yuasa   Scr: Fumi Takahashi   Prod: Hidemasa Nagata
DP: Akira Kitazaki Sp. Fx: Kazufumi Fujii   PC: Daiei   Dist: Just for Kids Home Video
Tsutomu Takakuwa, Kelly Varis, Katherine Murphy, Kon Omura, Junko Yashiro
[**]
The entire nation of Japan is in serious trouble when Gamera gets a bad case of indigestion. A giant lizard-like monster known as Jiger makes a destructive path toward World Expo '70. Gamera flies to the rescue and a massive battle ensues. However, Jiger is able to use his deadly tail and cut Gamera's body and implant a small egg. The egg manifests within Gamera's body and hatches a nasty like surprise. Inside is a baby Jiger who starts to feed on Gamera's internal organs. It's not as disgusting as it sounds and the special effects include a cute monster wreaking havoc from within. Gamera's strange behavior confuses the military, but the kids know how to save Gamera. The classic duo of a Japanese kid and an American kid team up and save Gamera. Piloting a special mini-sub they fly into Gamera's mouth and through his body in a special effects scene reminiscent of Fantastic Voyage. Once they spot baby Jiger, the boys must neutralize the monster. They manage to kill the pest and fly out of Gamera just in time for the climatic battle. Feeling better, Gamera defends the Earth and puts big Jiger in his proper place. A fun movie for the kids and big monster fans.

Gamera vs. Viras (Gamera Tai Viras)
(1968) Monster   C-87m Dubbed   Japan Retail: $19.99
Dir: Noriyaki Yuasa   Scr: Fumi Takahashi   Prod: Hidemasa Nagata
DP: Akira Kitazaki Sp. Fx: Kazufumi Fujii, Yuzo Kaneko   PC: Daiei
Dist: Just for Kids Home Video
Kojiro Hongo, Toru Takatsuka, Carl Crane, Michiko Yaegaki, Mari Atsumi, Junko Yashiro
[**]

The fourth film in the series features Gamera fighting a disgusting insect-like creature under alien control. Now a full-fledged superhero, Gamera must defend the children of Earth by destroying the creature. By now, the series has committed itself to campy plots, big monster battles, and tons of children-focused appeal.

Gamera vs. Zigra
(1971) Monster   C-91m Dubbed   Japan Retail: $19.99
Dir: Noriyaki Yuasa   Scr: Fumi Takahashi   Prod: Yoshihko Manabe
DP: Akira Uehara   Sp. Fx: Kazufumi Fujii   PC: Daiei   Dist: Just for Kids Home Video
Reiko Kasahara, Mikiko Tsubouchi, Koji Fujiyama, Arlene Zoellner, Gloria Zoellner, Isamu Saeki
[**]
Gamera, the loveable turtle, is brainwashed by aliens who want to take over the world. The last Gamera film to be shown in the United States. This time out the popular theme is repeated to average results. A Japanese and an American boy scout are fooling around in their minisub when an alien ship captures them. They use the hostages to force Gamera to do their bidding. Either you obey us or we will kill the two boys, they threaten. So Gamera is forced to destroy Japan and kill thousands more. Meanwhile, the boys explore the alien spacecraft which seems oddly deserted. They discover an erect-standing squid trapped inside a glass object. They befriend the alien squid, thinking it is also a trapped prisoner...stupid kids. The kids escape in their minisub and rush to Gamera for help. Then the aliens in their brilliance, order Gamera to kill the two boys. Gamera does a double take, breaks free of the alien hold, and flies after the alien bubble craft. The aliens beam down Zigra (the squid who grows larger) to battle Gamera and destroy Earth. Rest assured children of the world, Gamera smashes Zigra and the giant bee-colored alien spacecraft. After a hard job, Gamera flies off into the sunset with Earth's children cheering him farewell.

Gatchaman
(1994) Japanime: Scifi   C-45m Dubbed   Catalog #UV 1003
Japan Retail: $19.95
Dir: Hiroyuki Fukushima   Scr: Emu Arii
Character Design: Yasuomi Umezu   Music: Maurice White, Bill Meyers
English Version - Dir/Scr: Steve Kramer
PC: Tatsunoko Production Company, Ltd.   Dist: Urban Vision Entertainment
[***]
Released in 1997, Gatchaman is a modern rendition of the classic television program: Battle of the Planets, known in Japan as Science Team Gatchaman. Sporting a new look, the upgraded animation and story deals with five young warriors: Ken, Joe, Jimmy, June, and Rocky who fly aboard the Phoenix and save the Earth from Galactic aliens. A giant alien menace attacks Japan and only Gatchaman can save the planet and discover the truth about their attackers. The character development is on the dry side, but a number of follow up videos plan to expand upon the characters and their background. Plenty of ship to ship action and hand to hand combat for fans of scifi/action animation. The Gatchaman team must save elite scientists of the world who are kidnaped and forced to help a secret organization bent on ruling the world. Their primary

weapon is a giant, dragon-shaped spaceship that hides behind an atmospheric disturbance and can destroy entire cities. The Phoenix engages the spaceship and the members of Gatchaman infiltrate the mechanical beast, battle hundreds of armed soldiers, rescue their leader, and save the Earth until next time.

Gate of Hell
(1953) Drama C-89m Japanese with English Subtitles   VA
Catalog #GAT 020   Japan Retail: $29.95
Dir/Scr: Teinosuke Kinugasa   Prod: Masaichi Nagata
DP: Kohei Sugiyama Music: Yasushi Akutagawa   Costumes: Sanzo Wada
PC: Shochiku Dist: Video Yesteryear
(based on a play by Kan Kikuch)
Machiko Kyo Lady Kesa

Kazuo Hasegawa	**Moritoh**
Isao Yamagata	**Wataru**
Koreya Senda	**Kiyomori**
Yataro Kurokawa	**Shigemori**
Kikue Mohri	**Sawa**
Kotaro Bando	**Rokuroh**
Jun Tazaki	**Kogenta**
Tatsuya Ishiguro	**Yachuta**
Kenjiro Uemura	**Masanaka**
Gen Shimizu	**Saburosuke**

[***]
A classic Japanese period-piece set in the Kamakura era, 12th-century Kyoto, noted for its elegance and imagery in Japan's rich history. A warrior called Moritoh is ordered by his superior to protect Lady Kesa. During an enemy confrontation, Moritoh protects and saves the life of the lord's beautiful wife. He is rewarded by the lord and granted any wish. To the shock of everyone, Moritoh demands Lady Kesa. While protecting her, Moritoh discovers an unrelenting passion for the woman. She is not as enamored by the rough warrior and is disgraced by his proposition. His own lust and desire force his tragic downfall from society. Japanese actress of Korean descent Machiko Kyo plays the lovely Lady Kesa who must resist against Moritoh's desires and maintain her respectability. One of the many post-World War II films that brought worldwide attention to Japanese filmmakers. Kinugasa uses beautiful color composition and scenic styles to establish his characters and their mood in a richly designed costume piece.

Genesis Survivor Gaiarth: Stage 1
(1992) Japanime: Scifi   C-51m Dubbed/Japanese with English Subtitles   VA
**   Catalog #ANI ET095-016 Japan   Retail: $19.95**
Dir: Hiroyuki Kitazume, Shinji Aramaki Character   Design: Hiroyuki   Kitazume
**   Animation Dir: Jun Okuda, Seiji Tanda   Mecha Dir: Hiroyuki Ochi**
PC: Artmic   Dist: AnimEigo
[**1/2]
In a far distant place and time, an alien planet (Gaiarth) has been ravaged by warfare. Pockets of civilization have developed and are guarded by mechanical warriors known as warroids (War

Androids). Our young hero (Ital de Labard) is an orphan raised in the wilderness by his own guardian and friend who is one of the last noble warroids left in the world. When his warroid is murdered, Ital leaves his isolated home and treks to the big city in search of vengeance and a new way of life in this coming-of-age adventure. He meets a group of mercenaries led by a clever woman named Sahari who takes a liking to him. Ital comes across an old warroid and reactivates it, but the warroid can only remember his name Zaxon and suffers a serious memory problem. Ital and Zaxon travel to the city and meet with the warroid leader in charge of defending the people. The warroid leader recognizes the name Zaxon as one of the great warroids of the past, but fails to believe the old warroid is actually the hero returned from the dead. The enemy strikes the city and the battle begins.

The first film is not a complete story, but rather the first part in a three-part saga. The multitude of characters are intended to have continuing adventures as the plot unfolds in crisp animation style. Similar to a Mad-Max apocalyptic world, great stretches of no-man desserts and plains separate civilization from civilization with creatures and bandits on the prowl. Ital becomes one of the guardians for peace, a standard do-gooder in a familiar story of good and evil.

Genesis Surviver Gaiarth: Stage 2 (1992) Japanime: Scifi C-46m Dubbed/Japanese with English Subtitles VA Catalog #ANI ET095-017 Japan Retail: $19.95
Genesis Surviver Gaiarth: Stage 3 (1993) Japanime: Scifi C-45m Dubbed/Japanese with English Subtitles VA Catalog #ANI ET095-018 Japan Retail: $19.95

Genocyber Part 1: Birth of Genocyber
(1993) Japanime: Horror C-46m Japanese with English Subtitles VA
Catalog #USM 1091 Japan Retail: $29.95
Dir: Koichi Ohata Scr: Noboru Aikawa, Emu Arii Original Story: Artmic
Music: Takehito Nakazawa, Hiroaki Kagoshima
Character Design: Atsushi Yamagata Prod Design: Kimitoshi Yamane, Shinji Aramaki, Koichi Ohata, Yoshio Harada, Hitoshi Fukuchi
PC: Artmic/Plex Dist: U.S. Manga Corps
[1/2]**

Ambitious in the vein of Akira, but along the way the film becomes muddled and degenerates into a super slug festival with extreme scenes of animated violence. A common theme in Japanese animation is the possible future where machines and man are joined into one. A crazed scientist is using powerful psychics to control his experiments in merging cybertechnology with human components. His daughter is the prime example and enforcer who keeps other psychics in line. When a pretty young girl breaks free, she finds a kindred spirit in an orphan boy on the streets of Tokyo. At the same time, a pair of cops are investigating the mysterious girl and the strange death of a top researcher. When the orphan boy is killed, the girl battles with the scientist's daughter, taking over her body and combining with the cyber machine to form a new entity that wreaks havoc on Japan. Definitely not for the weak-hearted or those looking for lighter entertainment along the lines of Project A-ko or My Neighbor Totoro.

Genocyber Part 2 & 3: Vajranoid Showdown
(1993) Japanime: Horror C-50m Japanese with English Subtitles VA
Catalog #USM 1101 Japan Retail: $29.95

Genocyber Part 4 & 5: The Legend of Ark de Grande
(1993) Japanime: Horror   C-60m Japanese with English Subtitles   VA
Catalog #USM 1228 Japan Retail: $29.95

Ghidrah the Three Headed Monster
(1965) Monster   C-85m Dubbed   Japan Retail: $9.95
Dir: Inoshiro Honda Scr: Shinichi Sekizawa
Prod: Tomoyuki Tanaka   DP: Hajime KoizumiSp. Fx: Eiji Tsuburaya
PC: Toho Studios
Yosuke Natsuki, Yuriko Hoshi, Hiroshi Koizumi, Takashi Shimura, Eiji Okada, Eiko
Wakabayashi, The Itoh Sisters
[**1/2]
When Godzilla's toughest space opponent returns to Earth, the titans of monster island come to
Japan's rescue.   One of the most memorable and popular Toho monsters, the gold-dragon
Ghidrah spouts electrical bolts out of his three heads and waves his two massive tails and wings.
He flies over Japan, destroying everything in its path. Godzilla, Rodan the winged-monster, and
Mothra the ugly caterpillar combine their strength to stop Ghidrah. Godzilla uses his dukes and
radioactive breath, Mothra uses her silkworm spray, and Rodan flies around and uses his sharp
talons to defeat Ghidrah. All-monster tag team adventure is enjoyable for its action and campy
visual effects, bringing together the four biggest names in Japanese monster lore. Now only if
they could get Gamera to appear in one of the Godzilla films...what a battle!

Ghost in the Shell
(1996) Japanime   C-82m Dubbed/Japanese with English Subtitles   VA
Catalog #MGV 635529   Japan Retail: $19.99
Dir: Mamoru Oshii Scr: Kazunori Ito
Prod: Yoshimasa Mizuo, Shigeru Watanabe, Ken Iyadomi, Mitsunisu Ishikawa
Editor: Shiuchi Kakesu   Music: Kenji Kawai   Art Dir: Hiromasa Ogura
PC: Kodansha Ltd./Bandai Visual Co., Ltd./Manga Entertainment
Dist: Manga Video/Pioneer Animation
[***1/2]
Despite limited theatrical release, this film was touted as the next Akira. Not quite reaching that
level of fame, Ghost in the Shell is still an interesting benchmark of Japanese animation that will
appeal to fans of anime and science fiction. The ghost refers to the soul or individual spirit that
exists within a body or shell. A powerful entity simply known as the Puppet Master wreaks
havoc on a futuristic Tokyo. Major Motoko Kusanagi is a cyborg (a human mind with robotic
components) assigned to the Puppet Master case. She and her partner chase through a world of
humans, computers, and cyborgs, eventually confronting the Puppet Master and discovering a
revealing secret. The story is convoluted at times and slow-paced, not revealing key elements
until later in the film. The visual style and technique are superb, showcasing the brilliant use of
light, shadow, camera angles, and depth of perception common in Japanese style animation. A
thought provoking story that intrigues the viewer to enter a new world where not everything is
black and white, but shades of animated grey. A film requiring multiple viewings to truly
comprehend and appreciate its depth and beauty.

Giant Robo: Volume 1 "The Night the Earth Stood Still"
(1992) Japanime   C-55m Dubbed   VA
Catalog # USR-VD20   Japan Retail: $19.95
Dir: Yasuhiro Imagawa   Original Story: Mitsuteru Yokoyama
Scr: Yasuhiro Imagawa, Eiichi Matsuyama   Prod: Yasuto Yamaki
Animation Dir: Kazuyoshi Katayama   Character Design & Dir of Illustration:
Toshiyuki Kubooka, Akihiko Yamashita   Image Concept Design: Makoto Kobayashi
Mecha Design: Takashi Watabe   Art Dir: Hiromasa Ogura   Music: Masamichi Amano
Music Performed by Polish National Warsaw Philharmonic Orchestra
English Version - Dir/Scr: Quint Lanaster Prod: Robert Napton, Ken Iyadomi
Recording, Mixing, & Additional Effects: Magnitude 8 Productions Les Claypool III
Translation: Tonghyun Kim   Consultants: Toshifumi Yoshida, Trish Ledoux
Presented by L.A. Hero   PC: Moo Film Co., Ltd.   Dist: U.S. Renditions
Voices: Steve Blum, Debbie Rogers, Keven Lee, Gary Michaels, Steve Areno, John
Santacrose, Tom Charles, Dan Martin Stevie Beeline, Lee West, Bill Kestin, Sonny Byrkett,
Hal Cleaveland, Dougary Grant
[**1/2]
Geared toward the big, powerful robot fans, Giant Robo recaptures the flavor and animation style
of an earlier decade. Fans might remember the similarity to the live-action film where Giant
Robo is controlled by a young boy who battles against alien monsters and invaders. Once again,
a ruthless organization of terrorists plan to take over the world. In the first adventure, followed
by other episodes, a team of assassins are after a man who holds important documents. A
diverse cast of heroes are on the screen, but the most impressive is Daisaku, the young boy who
controls a giant robot shaped like an Egyptian warrior. Standard action saga with the villains
getting the upper hand and the heroic robot appearing just in time to save the day.

Girl from Hunan
(1986) Drama C-99m Mandarin with English Subtitles   VA
Catalog #NYV 54892 China Retail: $29.95
Dir: Xie Fei, U Lan Scr: Zhang Xian   DP: Fu Jingshengi
Music: Ye Xiaogang   Prod Manager: Dong Yaping   Art Director: Xing Zheng
(Xiaoxia by Shen Congwen)
Subtitles: Shen Ning, Chris Berry Beijing Subtitling and Dubbing Studio
PC: China Film Import-Export, Inc.   Dist: New Yorker Video
Liu Qing, Na Renhua, Deng Xiaotuang, Yu Zhang
[***]
A simple and beautiful tale of love and betrayal in a small rural village in China. Xiaoxiao is a
pretty, but poor 12-year old girl from Hunan who is forced into a pre-arranged marriage with a
farmer's family. On her wedding day, she and her husband must pay their respects to the family
shrine, but instead of her husband, a boisterous rooster sits beside her. Unfortunately, her
husband turns out to be a two-year old baby boy who she must raise until manhood. Xiao
remains with the husband's family (as according to Chinese custom) and works hard from
morning to night. She blossoms into womanhood while her husband learns his first steps and
how to talk. A sister-brother relationship develops and Xiao is naive to the ways of the world,
but her body undergoes a womanly transformation. She does not feel any sexual attraction to her

child-husband and plays with him like a brother. One of the workers on the farm, a virile young man is attracted to Xiao and pursues her in a harmless way. They travel together to the main town where Xiao discovers the man desires her affection. On a rainy afternoon while taking cover in an empty shed, his passions take over and he forces himself on her. At first she resists, but then the two engage in mutual lovemaking. They promise to keep their secret, but Xiao becomes pregnant (keep in mind: in old China abortion was not an option and adultery was punishable by death). In true scoundrel fashion, Xiao's lover deserts her and disappears in the middle of the night. Xiao tries to hide her pregnancy, but when it's discovered, the village elders plan to execute her. She tries to escape, but is caught and severly punished. Her life is spared, her marriage annulled, and she becomes a servant in the household. When the son grows older, he is promised to a new bride through another arranged marriage. Symbolizing his depression and hatred in an archaic life, he decides to break with tradition and runs away from home. A sad testament to the traditional and cruel guidelines set down in China's culture.

God of Gamblers   (Gambling God)
(1990) Action Comedy   C-125m   Chinese with English Subtitles
Catalog #0791   Hong Kong   Retail: $39.99
Dir: Wong Jing   Dist: Tai Seng Video
Chow Yun Fat   Ko Chun
Andy Lau   Knife
Joey Wong   Jane
Cheung Man, Shing Fui On, Ng Man Tat, Michiko Nishiwaki
[***]
Director Wong mixes his trademark style of humor and action, allowing Chow Yun Fat to flex his acting talents on both levels. If you can stretch your imagination, think of gambling as a mystical style of kung-fu. Chow is Ko, the world's best gambler who can't lose. No one can defeat him, but they will try anything to win. After defeating a beautiful Japanese gambler (Nishiwaki), she asks his assistance to defeat the devious gambler Chan. Ko plans to help, but suffers an unfortunate accident which causes him to lose his memory and regress into the mind of a young child. Knife and his friends decide to help Ko Chun and nurse him back to health. In classic fashion, Ko regains his memory just in time to defeat his enemies in an important gambling match. Full of trademark silliness and outlandish action scenes from director Wong. Followed by two sequels, both directed by Wong, but Chow does not appear in the third film:
God of Gamblers II (1991)   C-103m   Catalog #1717 Retail: $39.99
Dir: Wong Jing
Chow Yun Fat, Andy Lau, Cheung Man, Ray Lui, Charles Heung, Shing Fui On, Ng Man Tat
God of Gamblers III: Back to Shanghai (1991) C-110m   Catalog #1020 Retail: $39.99
Dir: Wong Jing
Stephen Chow, Ng Man Tat, Gong Li, Ray Lui

God of Gamblers Returns   (Return of God of Gamblers)
(1994) Action Comedy   C-126m   Chinese with English Subtitles   Catalog #1717
Hong Kong   Retail: $39.99
Dir: Wong Jing   Dist: Tai Seng Video

Chow Yun Fat, Tony Leung Kar Fai, Chingmy Yau, Cheung Man, Wu Chien Lien, Wu Hsin Kuo, Xie Miao
[***]
The gang is back as Chow continues his popular character of God of Gamblers, a gambling genius who can not lose. This time out Chow has retired to the beautiful countryside of France where he lives at a magnificent chateau. He is visited by an old colleague known as the God of Guns who warns him that a rival gambler has been looking for him. Chow brushes it off and the two men go to the woods to practice shooting. While away, a swarm of men enter the chateau and murder everyone including Chow's beautiful pregnant wife. Before his wife dies, she makes Chow promise not to gamble for one year. Chow then goes into hiding until that fateful day. Along the way he meets Chingmy Yau, the daughter of a Triad boss who befriends Chow. Complications set in when the Triad boss is murdered and his son is in jeopardy, so Chow becomes the son's protector. An assortment of characters join them along their way while they maintain a distance from the killers and avoid the local authorities and the mainland police. Eventually, the one year ends and Chow reveals his true identity and enters a multimillion dollar match against his vicious rival. Even though his rival uses a psychic who can change the face of any playing card, Chow perseveres in the end. The film mixes comedy and action with much of the gags running into the realm of parody. Still the film features a great cast of characters and quality production for fans.

GODZILLA SERIES (Kaiju see Gamera too)

An extra large Tyrannosaurs-type reptile with the ability to spout radioactive fire became one of the hottest characters to be imported from Japan. The longest running film series in Japan, Godzilla has appeared in movies, cartoons, and even played basketball with Charles Barkley. Initially a villain, Godzilla gradually became less aggressive towards humans and helped defend the earth on a number of occasions, though his newer films have brought back a meaner Godzilla. Having the same popular mold as the classic King Kong, but instead of using stop-motion animation and large models, the Japanese filmmakers donned for a man in a giant rubber suit and intricate miniatures. The costs were kept low and much more flexibility was given to the character's abilities. The films are juvenile and predictable at times, but entertaining and reminiscent of the B-rated horror films of the 50's and 60's. The genre has a unique appeal and most people either love it or not, though the side stories involving human characters can become distracting at times. Be warned that by today's standards, the films are incredibly campy and may appeal only to genre fans or young children. Before the age of big budget special effects, the Godzilla/monster films were the roaming kings of scifi/fantasy/horror films. The ratings for the films reflect their past merits of popularity and additional films are available in Japan with improved effects and bigger budgets. The newer films are the post-Godzilla 1985 generation of films. The last film to appear theatrically was a sign of dying interest in the United States. However, Godzilla films enjoyed a healthy life in Japan and newer films were made with classic Toho monsters being revived with 90's style special effects. Though a far cry from Jurassic Park, the films have maintained a purist look with miniatures and non-computer generated monsters. Due to the recent growth in popularity, Sony/Tri-Star Pictures released in 1998, a 100 million dollar Godzilla film directed by Roland Emmerich and Dean Devlin (Stargate, ID4). The film brought in computer animation, Hollywood stars, New York City, and a more realistic Godzilla. Diehard fans were not pleased, but undaunted, Godzilla returned to theaters two years later in his true original form.

Godzilla 2000
(2000) Monster C-98m Dubbed VA Japan
Dir: Takao Okawara
Scr: Hiroshi Kashiwabara, Wataru Mimura, Neil Gaiman
Prod: Toshihiro Ogawa
Ex. Prod: Shogo Tomiyama DP: Katsuhiro Kato
Editor: Yoshiyuki Okuhara, Michael Mahoney (US version)
Music: Takayuki Hattori, J. Peter Robinson (additional music: US version)
Casting: Tadao Tanaka   Char Design: Hideo Okamoto
Prod Design: Takeshi Shimizu   Sound: Teiichi Saito, Darren Paskal (US version)
Spec. FX: Kenji Suzuki PC: Toho Pictures, Inc.
Dist: Sony/Columbia TriStar

Takehiro Murata	**Yuji Shinoda**
Naomi Nishida	**Yuki Ichinose**
Hiroshi Abe	**Mitsuo Katagiri**
Mayu Suzuki	**Io Shinoda**
Shiro Sano	**Shiro Miyasaka**
Makoto Ito	**Orga**
Tsutomu Kitagawa	**Godzilla**
Shelley Sweeney	**Reporter**

Satomi Achiwa, Kenichi Ishii, Yoshikazu Ishii, Daisuke Ishizuka, Sakae Kimura
[***]
All the ingredients are back for a fairly entertaining Godzilla film which was released theatrically and then on American home video. Formulaic plot is in full force and minor novelties are added to Godzilla's repertoire and the human cast. For those who have not viewed Godzilla since childhood, his appearance is much darker, his body looks atypically jagged, and his radioactive breath is a nice reddish color. The models still look like models, but the weapon effects have been juiced up and there is even a scene of Godzilla swimming underwater. The human subplot is non-existent, a brilliant scientist, Yuji Shinoda, and his business smart daughter, Io, bring along a female reporter (no romance) who wants pictures of Godzilla in action. The scientist is part of an independent Godzilla detection and research society which is at odds with the government defense organization. The government wants to destroy Godzilla while the scientist wishes to study the deadly beast. Apparently, the head of the government agency and Yuji were old colleagues who have become bitter rivals. The government also discovers a large underwater structure that could possibly be a monster or alien ship, and decide to raise it to the surface...not too wise. The alien ship uses solar energy to repower itself and fly into action, wreaking havoc on the citizens of Japan. The scientist and the reporter discover the alien was trying to convert the Earth's atmosphere into something more suitable. The ship sits atop a Japanese skyscraper, using energy tentacles to syphon off computer information. Godzilla decides to destroy the alien ship which has the physical advantage and a really nasty blaster, but it is easily destroyed under Godzilla's megabreath. From the ashes, the alien creature uses Godzilla's DNA to create itself

into an unstoppable monster with regenerative powers. Godzilla defeats the creature swiftly and returns to his underwater lair. A fast-paced Godzilla film with classic elements repackaged from previous Japanese monster films. Though the film is entertaining, the series seems to have reached a plateau in creativity and evolution. In the 24th feature film, how many times can we watch Godzilla destroy the incompetent military, bash through downtown Tokyo, outwit incompetent humans, and battle the latest monster of the week. The producers need a fresh boost of innovative development, perhaps a new race of monsters or another urban setting.

The DVD version contains a very insightful audio commentary for the production of the film that would interest Godzilla fans.

Godzilla, King of the Monsters
(1956) Monster   B&W-81m (Japanese version) B&W-98m (American version)
Dubbed   VA   Catalog #VA3010   Japan Retail: $9.99
Dir: Inoshiro Honda, Terry Morse (additional American footage)
Scr: Inoshiro Honda, Takeo Murata   Prod: Tomoyuki Tanaka
DP: Masao Tamai   Sp. Fx: Eiji Tsuburaya, Akira Watanabe, Hiroshi Mukoyama
PC: Toho Studios
Raymond Burr   Steve Martin (American version only)
Takashi Shimura   Dr. Yogami
Akihiko Hirata   Professor Sarazowa
Momoko Kochi, Akira Takarada, Fuyuki Murakami, Sachio Sakai,
[***]
The original classic that started a monster dynasty. Runs like a serious monster/disaster film with Raymond Burr as an American journalist who witnesses Godzilla's destruction. Filmed in black and white, Japan deals with its first true monster dilemma. Inspired by Japan's post-war mentality, Godzilla represents the deadly effects of war and nuclear contamination (atomic bombs) on Japan.

Off the coast of Odo Island, oceangoing ships are mysteriously destroyed and corpses are charred beyond recognition. The villagers of Odo Island claim a giant sea beast attacked the ships. The Japanese government investigates the islanders' claim which is based on their superstitious legends. Skeptical, American reporter Steve Martin and paleontologist Dr. Yogami escort a party to the island which comes face to face with the terrifying beast. The mutated result of atomic testing, Godzilla makes its way to Tokyo and does what he does best, stomping, chomping, and romping.

The Japanese military fail to stop the beast with conventional weapons and even a wall of electrical wires don't effect it. The only hope is Professor Sarazowa, a brilliant Japanese scientist, who uses his new oxygen-depriving formula to kill Godzilla. The nations of the world pull their resources to help Japan stop the monster. Once they discover Godzilla submerged under the ocean, they release the formula which reacts with the sea water and acidifies the liquid, melting Godzilla into a pile of bones. The original Japanese film did not have Raymond Burr and differs in many respects to the USA-available version.

Godzilla 1985
(1985) Monster   C-91m Dubbed   PG   VA   Catalog #8522   Japan
Retail: $9.99

Dir: Kohji Hashimoto, Robert J. Kizer (additional American footage)
Scr: Shuichi Nagahara, Lisa Tomei (American version)
Prod: Tomoyuki Tanaka, Anthony Randel (American version)
DP: Kazutami Hara, Takashi Yamamoto, Toshimitsu Ohneda
Editor: Yoshitami, Kuroiwa, Michael Spence   Music Dir: Katsusaki Nakay
Prod Design: Akira Sakuragi   Sp. Fx: Nobuyuki Tasumaru
PC: Toho Studios   Dist: New World Entertainment
Raymond Burr   Steve Martin
Keiju Kobayashi   Prime Minister Mitamura
Ken Tanaka   Reporter Goro Maki
Yasuka Sawaguchi   Naoko Okumura
Shin Takuma Hiroshi Okumura
Eitaro Ozawa Finance Minister Kanzaki
Kei Sato   Gondo
[**1/2]

A modern remake of the original film which was targeted for theatrical release. Looks fancier in some respect, but a certain nostalgic charm has faded and modern filmmaking techniques make the traditional-Godzilla techniques of models and costumes look amateurish and outdated. Raymond Burr is back, but spends most of his time in an isolated command center. Godzilla has reawakened and decides to wreak havoc on Tokyo. The standard formula is not upgraded as Godzilla stomps his way through downtown Tokyo while an army of miniature vehicles try to stop him. A secondary story about some crooks fits loosely into the story, but is of little importance. Godzilla's only opponent is Japan's secret weapon the X-1 supership. Shaped-like a horseshoe, the supership flies and carries an assortment of incredible weapons. When the ship fails, Godzilla is led to an active volcano rigged with explosives. At the correct moment, the explosives detonate and send Godzilla falling into the maul of open lava. For some reason, the humans offer revered silence for Godzilla's untimely death. This movie provided plenty of familiar action and reawakened the interest of Godzilla fans in the United States.

Godzilla's Destroy All Monsters
(1968) Monster   C-89m Dubbed   VA   Japan Retail: $9.99
Dir: Inoshiro Honda Scr: Inoshiro Honda, Kaoru Mabuchi
Prod: Tomoyuki Tanaka   DP: Taiichi Kankura
Sp. Fx: Eiji Tsuburaya, Sadamasa Arikawa   PC: Toho Studios
Akira Kubo, Jun Tazaki, Yoshio Tsuchiya, Kyoko Ai, Yukiko Kobayashi, Kenji Sahara, Andrew Hughes, The Itoh Sisters
[**]

An all-star monster cast slug it out against the three-headed dragon, Ghidrah. If you love the Godzilla movies, this one is a special treat since all the classic Toho monsters appear in one film. Mothra, Angillus, Godzilla, Rodan, Ghidrah, and the others are all under control by an alien race who wishes to conquer the Earth. They send various monsters to attack Japan, destroying railroads, cities, and harbors. Eventually the monsters of Earth break from their mind-controlling captivity and go after the aliens. The aliens ace up the sleeve is Ghidrah a three-headed, two-tailed, winged dragon who spews electrical bolts, but even Ghidrah is no match against the world's mightiest monsters. Then Godzilla discovers the spherical base of the enemy and kicks it, destroying the alien base on Earth.

Godzilla's Son of Godzilla
(1967) Monster   C-71m Dubbed   VA   Japan Retail: $9.99
Dir: Jun Fukuda   Scr: Shinichi Sekizawa, Kazue Shiba
Prod: Tomoyuki Tanaka   DP: Kazuo Yamada Sp.   Fx: Eiji   Tsuburaya,   Sadamasa Arikawa
PC: Toho Studios
Tadao Takashima, Akira Kubo, Beverly Maeda, Akihiko Hirata, Kenji Sahara, Yoshio Tsuchiya
[**]

Rather forgettable film in the Godzilla series, most humorous for its scenes of Minya, the son of Godzilla. On monster island, Japanese scientists are doing research on weather patterns. The scientists avoid the monsters but baby Godzilla likes playing with the scientists and catching fruit in his mouth. Of course, the island is full of nasty monsters including a giant spider and praying mantis who'd love to eat baby Godzilla. In a touching scene, Godzilla teaches his kid how to spout out radioactive fire, but Minya only produces smoke rings until Godzilla steps on his tail. At the end, the scientists launch a weather balloon that causes it to snow on the tropical monster island, freezing the creatures into hibernation. As the scientists leave monster island, they wave good-bye to Godzilla and Minya.

Godzilla vs. Biollante
(1989) Monster   C-105m   Dubbed   PG   VA   Japan Retail: $9.99 Widescreen Available
Dir/Scr: Kazuki Ohmori   Prod: Tomoyuki Tanaka
DP: Yoshinori Sekiguchi   Sp. Fx: Koichi Kawakita
Music: Koichi Sugiyama   PC: Toho Studios
Kunihio Mitamura, Yoshiko Tanaka, Masanobu Takashima, Megumi Odaka, Toru Minegishi
[**1/2]

The latest Godzilla movie from Japan is a direct sequel of Godzilla 1985, but was not theatrically released in America. Unfortunately, the newest film in the series is somewhat disappointing considering the long-run of the series. The film is billed as the ultimate battle between Godzilla and a rose-like creature called Biollante, a plant bred with Godzilla cells. Neither creature is the hero and Biollante is the weakest monster ever created to do battle. Basically a giant Audrey 2 from The Little Shop of Horrors, Biollante stands in the middle of a lake and waves its tentacle-like stems. A plant with no charisma that carries the dead soul of a scientist's daughter. The cast includes Middle Eastern terrorists after Godzilla's DNA, a gung-ho military advisor, and a girl with telekinetic powers who recurs in later films. She has some kind of special bond with Godzilla, though that is not explored deeply in this film. It's a shame that one of the longest-running film series in Japan has failed to breed bolder new stories. Still there's plenty of gruesome action for monster fans.

Godzilla vs. the Cosmic Monster   (Godzilla vs. Mechagodzilla)
(1974) Monster   C-80m   Dubbed   VA   Japan Retail: $9.99

Dir: Jun Fukuda   Scr: Hiroyasu Yamaura, Jun Fukuda
Prod: Tomoyuki Tanaka   DP: Yuzuru "Joe" Aizawa
Sp. Fx: Shokei Nakano   PC: Toho Studios   Dist: New World Entertainment
Masaki Daimon, Kazuya Aoyama, Akihiko Hirata, Masao Imafuku, Reiko Jajima, Hiroshi Koizumi, Barbara Lynn
[**1/2]
Godzilla defends his title against Mechagodzilla, a robotic twin. When Godzilla is seen going on a rampage, the world wonders why their favorite lizard has become hostile again. Suddenly another Godzilla appears and does battle with the first. We then discover that one of the Godzilla's is a machine created by an evil alien race who wished to defame the real Godzilla and take over the world. A local priest and his daughter help raise the spirit of a Japanese monster who comes to Godzilla's aid. Mechagodzilla is quite impressive, able to shot beams from his chest, flames from his mouth, and rockets from his fingertips. It can also fly and create a force field by spinning it head. Nearly indestructible, the Japanese heroes find the aliens underground base and pulls a few shots of their own to help Godzilla defeat the Cosmic Monster. In an upcoming Godzilla film, the government salvages Mechagodzilla and use it as a line of defense against hostile monsters.

Godzilla vs. the Destroyer
(1995) Monster   C-90   Japanese with English Subtitles   Japan Retail: $19.95
Dir: Tadao Ohgawara   Prod: Tomoyuki Tanaka   PC: Toho Studios
Takuro Tatsumi, Megumi Odaka
[**1/2]
Godzilla has finally met his match. Taken from the basic premise of the original Godzilla film, the destroyer is created from bio-organic material which was originally used to dissolve the first Godzilla (1956). The oxygen-destroyer combined with Godzilla's organic flesh creates the horrendous looking beasts. The baby destroyers attack Japan, but are fought back by the Japanese military. In no time, mommy destroyer unleashes her devastating power onto the cities of Japan. Meanwhile, Godzilla has returned to wreak havoc in Japan, mostly due to his mutated state caused by the previous film. Godzilla's ferocity and demeanor have changed for the worse and the creature is on a radioactive overload which could detonate the beast like a nuclear time bomb. Wisely, the military avoid any direct action against Godzilla. The interesting Dr. Saegusa (Odaka) returns and uses her psychic powers to call the friendly Minya, Godzilla's kid. Minya does his best against the Destroyer, but loses to the savage beast. In a touching scene (for a monster film), the maternal Godzilla is outraged and arrives to do battle against the Destroyer.

Godzilla vs. Gigan
(1972) Monster   C-89m   Dubbed   VA   Catalog #C88110
Japan Retail: $9.99
Dir: Jun Fukuda   Scr: Shinichi Sekzawa   Prod: Tomoyuki Tanaka
DP: Kiyoshi Hasegawa   Dir of Special Effects: Teruyoshi Nakano
Sp. Fx: Shokei Nakano   PC: Toho Studios
Hiroshi Ichikawa, Tomoko Umeda, Yuriko Hishimi, Minoru Takashima, Zan Fujita, Kunio Murai
[**]

Godzilla and his pal Angillus, an armadillo, talk and kick some monster butt. A tale more for the kids. In this workout film, Godzilla and Angillus can speak to each other in English and go to the rescue of Japan when some weird sonic emanations disturb them. An artist working at an amusement park discovers a plot to take over the world. At first Godzilla tries to take on Ghidrah and Gigan by himself, but the two provide to be too much of a match. All hell breaks loose when Godzilla's tag team partner Angillus lends a claw.

Godzilla vs. King Ghidorah
(1991) Monster   C-105m   Japanese with English Subtitles   Japan Retail: $19.95
Dir/Scr: Kazuki Omori   Prod: Tomoyuki Tanaka
DP: Yoshinori Sekiguchi   Sp. Fx: Koichi Kawakita   PC: Toho Studios
Anna Nakagawa, Kosuke Toyohara, Megumi Odaka, Kiwako Harada, Shoji Kabayashi, Koichi Ueda, Chuck Wilson
[1/2]**
Godzilla's greatest nemesis has returned and I don't mean the furry ape, King Kong. The three-headed golden dragon from outer space flies back into action with plenty of wild battles against the mighty Godzilla. In the future, a spaceship hovers over a spot in the ocean and recounts the death of Godzilla. The ship flies back into the past and warns the Japanese that in the next century Godzilla will decimate the entire country. Through a series of events, the Japanese people are fooled by the time travelers who leave behind another monster that turns into King Ghidorah. Ironically, the Japanese must revive Godzilla to help them destroy the new threat and save the future of their nation. Though the film features better effects and plenty of action, the film was not theatrically released in the United States and features a large amount of anti-American moments. Come on, it's a monster/scifi movie...let's not get too political and sit back and enjoy a classic grudge match.

Godzilla vs. Mechagodzilla
(1993) Monster   C-100m   Japanese with English Subtitles   Japan Retail: $19.95
Dir: Takao Okawara   Scr: Shou Mimura, Tomoyuki Tanaka
Prod: Tomoyuki Tanaka   Sp. Fx: Koichi Kawakita   PC: Toho Studios
Masahiro Takeshima, Ryoko Sano, Megumi Odaka, Daigirou Harada, Ichi Miyakawa, Kenji Sahara
[1/2]**
The mighty Godzilla has met his match against the even mightier Mechagodzilla, a robotic Godzilla from the future. A new generation of Godzilla films bring forth popular monsters from the past and reintroduce them to the big screen. In the near future, the Godzilla Defense Force must devise a way to stop the beast from ravaging the nation. They devise a plan to use Mechagodzilla to stop the real Godzilla. Plenty of big set action with a mechanical monster doing battle with a real one.

Godzilla vs. Megalon
(1976) Monster   C-80m   Dubbed   VA   Japan Retail: $9.99
Dir: Jun Fukuda   Scr: Jun Fukuda, Shinichi Sekizawa
Prod: Tomoyuki Tanaka   DP: Yuzuru Aizawa Sp. Fx: Shokei Nakano
PC: Toho Studios   Dist: New World Entertainment

Katsuhiko Sasakai, Hiroyuki Kawase, Yutaka Hayashi, Kotaro Tomita, Robert Dunham
[1/2]**
Theatrically released in America and a popular choice for children. A pair of scientists and a young boy discover a plot to destroy the world. An underground civilization frustrated at the surface world's nuclear attacks send Megalon and Gigan to destroy the surface world. The scientist and his friends create Jet Jaguar, a super robot who calls Godzilla to help save the world. Now don't expect much logic, but Jet Jaguar communicates with Godzilla through nifty hand gestures and flies him toward the monsters. Then Jet, transforms himself into a giant robot and the rumble begins. The tag team match carries most of the film and will appeal to fans of pro-wrestling. When all is done, Jet shrinks back to human size and piggy-backs the young boy on his shoulders. The scientist and his friend follow, walking off into the sunset.

Godzilla vs. Monster Zero   (Invasion of Planet X/Monster Zero)
(1968) Monster   C-93m Dubbed   VA   Catalog #2321
Japan Retail: $9.99
Dir: Inoshiro Honda Scr: Shinichi Sekizawa   Prod: Tomoyuki Tanaka
DP: Haijime Koizumi   Sp. Fx: Eiji Tsuburaya   PC: Toho Studios
Dist: Paramount Home Video
Nick Adams, Akira Takarada, Akira Kubo, Keiko Sawai, Kumo Mizuno, Jun Tazaki
[1/2]**
An entertaining Godzilla film that also brings in campy, classic B-rated scifi fun into the mix. A personal favorite since Godzilla and Rodan make an exciting duo battling Ghidrah, the three-headed Monster Zero. Nick Adams and his Japanese partner are two astronauts in an advanced space program. While exploring Planet X, they discover an alien race of Japanese who wear fancy jumpsuits and hip sunglasses. The aliens offer to help Earth advance in return for one favor. The astronauts ask what they can do to help their extraterrestrial neighbors. The aliens turn on a huge monitor and debut Ghidrah, a golden flying dragon with two tails and three heads that spit out electric bolts. Ghidrah has been destroying Planet X, forcing the inhabitants to move underground. The aliens need two of Earth's greatest monsters: Godzilla and Rodan. Peace is made and alien saucers land on Earth. The ships discover the hibernated Godzilla and Rodan from a mountain cliff and a deep lake. They revive the creatures who take care of Ghidrah and then do the Godzilla dance. Earth is happy, the aliens are happy, and all seems well. Then all of sudden, Godzilla and Rodan are brainwashed and ordered to destroy the Earth. This time it is up to a bright, but quirky inventor and the astronauts to free the monsters. The aliens have infiltrated a number of key places on Earth and capture the inventor. The inventor discovers that a device he made which creates a high-pitched sonic wave causes the aliens to go mad. Using this device, Earth fights the flying saucers and manages to beat them. Broken from the spell, Godzilla and Rodan do battle with Ghidrah who was the aliens' pet all along. Lots of fun, action, a hummable soundtrack, and campy scifi blend into an enjoyable film.

Godzilla vs. Mothra (Godzilla vs. Queen Mothra)
(1992) Monster   C-104m   Japanese with English Subtitles
Catalog #2321 D   Japan Retail: $19.95
Dir: Takao Okawara   Scr: Kazuki Omori
Prod: Tomoyuki Tanaka   DP: Masahiro Kishimoto   Sp. Fx: Koichi Kawakita

PC: Toho Studios
Keiko Imamura   Cosmos #1
Sayaka Osawa   Cosmos #2
Tetsuya Bessho, Satomi Kobayashi, Akira Takarada
[***]
Godzilla takes a back seat to Mothra who is clearly the star and hero of one of the newest films from Japan. The third film in the post-Godzilla 1985 generation. Once again, the Earth's environment has been corrupted by mankind's thirst for power and expansion. A meteor from outer space crashes into the Pacific Ocean, simultaneously releasing Godzilla and Battra from their underground prisons. According to legend, Battra is a savior of Mother Earth who awakens to rid the planet of harmful entities, in this case humans. The revolving human story involves a treasure seeker who breaks laws in order to make a profit. When he is arrested in Thailand, his estranged wife offers him a job to explore a strange island. He agrees and an expedition leads to the discovery of a hidden land with a giant egg. The group also discover a pair of tiny pixie girls known as the Cosmos (replacements of The Itoh Sisters). Soon it is discovered that Battra is a black Mothra, a dark twin of the good Mothra. Battra makes his way to Nagoya and levels the city. He then burrows underground and vanishes. Meanwhile, the egg is being transported to Japan for commercial profit. Along the way, the transport ship is attacked by Godzilla. The egg cracks and Mothra breaks free. A battle ensues, but the infant Mothra is no match for the mighty Godzilla. Then Battra appears and also attacks Mothra, but soon Godzilla and Battra begin to fight and ignore the wimpy Mothra who escapes and returns to its native island. Godzilla and Battra continue to fight in a wonderful underwater sequence with both creatures able to shoot out beams of energy. The floor of the ocean cracks and an underwater volcano consumes both creatures. Meanwhile, the Cosmos are kidnapped by Bessho who hopes to make 100 million dollars and go legit. His ex-wife and daughter team up with Miki, the psychic girl from Biollante to track down Cosmos. Mothra senses Cosmos' danger and heads straight for Tokyo, destroying everything in its path. The military try to stop the giant worm. The Cosmos girls are rescued and ask Mothra to return home, but the injured creature stops at the capital building and weaves a giant cocoon. If things weren't bad enough, Godzilla erupts out of Mt. Fuji and Battra transforms into a winged-Battra, both monsters head for Tokyo for the final showdown. Mothra emerges from its cocoon as a giant, beautiful moth with energy beams. It can also channel Godzilla's breath ray with its wings like reflective mirrors. Godzilla is pretty much in charge, but Mothra pleads to Battra for help in defeating the true threat to the planet, Godzilla. In a spectacular two on one battle, Mothra and Battra manage to carry Godzilla out into the middle of the ocean. Battra sacrifices himself by trapping Godzilla and plunging into the sea, while Mothra encircles the two monsters with an energy field. The Cosmos girls join Mothra for one final task to prevent a deadly asteroid from destroying the planet. With the people of Japan looking on in admiration, they fly out into space leaving a trail of golden stardust. Using themes from past movies, the producers recapture the charm of Godzilla and Mothra while updating the special effects for a new generation and adding intriguing elements to the overall enjoyment of the film.

Godzilla's Revenge
(1969) Monster   C-70m   Dubbed   VA   Dubbed   VA
Japan Retail: $9.99

Dir: Inoshiro Honda Scr: Shinichi Sekizawa
Prod: Tomoyuki Tanaka   DP: Mototaka Tomioka   Editor: Masahisa Himi
Sp. Fx: Eiji Tsuburaya, Teruyoshi Nakano   Sets: Takee Kita
Music: Kunio Miyauchi   Theme Song "March of the Monsters" by Crown Records
Assistant Dir: Masaaki Hisamatsu, Akiyoshi Nakano
Sound Recording: Ryder Sound Services, Inc.   Titles by CFI
Post Prod: Riley Jackson   PC: Toho Studios
Kenji Sahara, Tomonori Yazaki, Machiko Naka, Sachio Sakai, Yoshibumi Tajima, Hideyo
Amemoto, Kazuo Suzuki, Ikio Sawamura, Shigeki Ishida, Yutaka Sada, Shotaro Togin,
Yutaka Nakayama
[**]
A vastly different style of Godzilla film geared toward kids, but then again aren't they all. A
little boy parallels his own lonely life with daydreams of Godzilla's son, Minya. A clever little
story that treats Godzilla as a popular fictional character. A lonely boy growing up in Tokyo
lives a solitude live without a mother and an inventor dad who is always on the run. When he's
alone, he pretends his nifty radio is a communication device that gives him direct access to
Monster Island. He befriends the talking Minya who shows the boy around the island; the
producers use some stock footage from Son of Godzilla. The boy becomes involved with a
group of local bullies and thieves. Minya symbolically represents the boy's own courage and
doubts in a harsh world. When Minya is able to stand up and beat up a bully monster, real-life
imitates fantasy as the lonely boy knocks out the big bully and saves the day. The adults of the
story don't believe in the young boy's jaunts to Monster Island, but the movie viewers know
better. Since the film runs like a daydream fantasy and focuses on Minya, many Godzilla purists
find it to be disappointing and not a true example of a Godzilla story.

Godzilla vs. the Sea Monster
(1966) Monster   C-80m Dubbed   VA   Japan Retail: $9.99
Dir: Jun Fukuda   Scr: Shinichi Sekizawa   Prod: Tomoyuki Tanaka
DP: Kazu Yamada   Sp. Fx: Eiji Tsuburaya   PC: Toho Studios   Dist: Moore Video
Akira Takarada, Toru Watanabe, Hideo Sunazuka, Kumi Mizuno, Jun Tazaki
[**1/2]
Another campy, but entertaining film in the Godzilla series, this time Godzilla does battle with a
giant lobster called Ebirah. Two Japanese men stow away on a ship and find themselves hooked
up with a criminal. During a storm, the men become shipwrecked on a remote Pacific Island
named Letchi. The men team up together to find a way off the island. They discover that the
natives are forced into slavery by ruthless tyrants who call themselves Red Bamboo and plan to
take over the world. The only way on or off the island is by using their special ship that spays a
chemical to chase away the guardian sea monster. Without the chemical, any ship entering the
waters would be destroyed by the monster. The heroes manage to stomp the Red Bamboo
organization and convince the natives to fight back. When the last surviving tyrants decide to
flee, their ship is suddenly attacked and destroyed by the sea monster. The heroes and the
natives switched the ship's chemicals for a useless mixture. Thankfully, Godzilla is also on the
scene to put an end to the sea monster once and for all, bringing peace and prosperity back to the
island's natives.   A fun film with good underwater stunts and a classic battle for
Godzilla/monster fans.

Godzilla vs. the Smog Monster   (Godzilla vs. Hedora)
(1972) Monster   C-87m   Dubbed   G   VA   Japan Retail: $9.99
Dir: Yoshimitu Banno   Scr: Yoshimitu Banno, Kaoru Mabuchi
Prod: Tomoyuki Tanaka   DP: Yoichi Manoda Sp. Fx: Shokei Nakano
PC: Toho Studios   Dist: Orion Home Video
Akira Yamauchi, Hiroyuki Kawase, Toshio Shibaki
[*1/2]
Godzilla must endure a hippy-like environmental message and a disgusting opponent made from
sludge and pollution. The film seems dated with its psychedelic imagery and gross-out ending.
In the background, the 70's style song 'Save the World' hammers in every scene when a sludge
like creature appears from the polluted waters of Japan. An amphibian grows in size, feeding off
smokestacks and raw sewage. Changing from a tadpole-like creature to a huge pile of sludge
with eyes, it develops the power to fly and its noxious fumes cause people to die on the spot.
Godzilla covers his nose and goes about destroying the monster with the humans help. In a
grotesque scene, Godzilla disembowels the creature, making sure it will never reproduce again
and uses energy mirrors to help disintegrate the Smog Monster forever. The tone of the film is
less lighthearted and more ominously preachy.

Godzilla vs. the Thing   (Godzilla vs. Mothra)
(1964) Monster   C-88m   Dubbed   VA
Japan Retail: $9.99
Dir: Inoshiro Honda Scr: Shinichi Sekizawa
Prod: Tomoyuki Tanaka   DP: Hajime Koizumi
Sp. Fx: Eiji Tsuburaya, Sadamasu Arikawa, Akira Watanabe, Motoyoshi Tomioka,
Kuichiro Kishida   PC: Toho Studios   Dist: Paramount Home Video
Akira Takarada, Yuriko Hoshi, Hiroshi Koizumi, The Itoh Sisters
[1/2]**
Godzilla decides to terrorize Tokyo and the rest of Japan. The Japanese always use the
appearance of Godzilla to subtly blame the Americas for dropping the atomic bomb on their
country, since Godzilla is a creation of nuclear energy and attracted to the atomic radiation. In a
desperate plea for help, two tiny fairy girls call upon a giant butterfly to destroy Godzilla.
Known as The Thing, Mothra is one of the few always-good monsters that helps Japan against
Godzilla and other vile creatures. Godzilla kills the aging Mothra, but her offsprings, two cute
worms, capture Godzilla in a silk encasing and save the day. A lighthearted and pleasant film
which introduces one of the more charismatic creatures from Toho Studios.

End of Godzilla Section
For more giant monster movies from Japan - look under Atragon, Frankenstein Conquers the
World, Gamera, Ghidrah, King Kong, Mothra, Rodan, War of the Gargantuans

Go Masters, The
(1982) DramaC-134m   Chinese and Japanese with English Subtitles   VA
China/Japan
Dir: Junya Sato, Duan Jishun

Scr: Li Hong-zhou, Ge Kang-tong, Fumio Konami, Yasuko Ohno, Tetsuro Abe
Prod: Masahiro Sato, Wang Zhi-Min
DP: Luo De-an, Shohei Ando   Music: Jiang Ding-xian, Hikaru Hayashi
Dist: Ingram International Films

Sun Dao-Lin	Kuang Yi-shan
Huang Zong-ying	Kuang Yuan-Zhi
Du Peng	Guan Xiao-chuan
Yu Shaokang	Dr. Zhang
Liu Xin	Shen Guan-Chu
Kuang Aming	Mao Wei-hui
Shen Dan-ping	Kuang A-hui
Zhang Lei	Xiao A-hui
Rentaro Mikuni	Rinsaku Matsunami

Keiko Mita, Misako Honno, Tsu Kasa Itoh
[***]
Go (Paduk) is a strategic game revered in Asia on a level comparable with Western Chess. The game involves two opponents with colored stones (smooth-polished circular pieces, white and black) and a large board with hundreds of equal-sized squares. Placing one stone at a time, the object of the game is to surround your opponent and gain a strategic advantage while preventing the loss of your own pieces. The game is played on numerous competitive levels and thousands of books are sold on the subject. Go-Masters is the story of two great players, one who is Chinese and the other who is Japanese. The time period is the early 20th Century and both nations are on a course to full-blown war. We follow the story of both men as their situations are altered by political pressures around them. When they first meet, they communicate through Chinese characters and their love of the game. The road ahead for them is turbulent, but through the falling years, their true love for Go is never lost though their respective nations pull their loyalty and friendship apart. A fascinating and sad period-piece that delves into an Asian subject that is rarely explored in modern cinema. The film carries a strong dramatic undertone and questions the prejudice attitude of Asians toward each other when their cultures are so bonded in similarities.

Gonza the Spearman
(1986) Samurai/Romance   C-126m   Japanese with English Subtitles   VA
Catalog # ID8168KN Japan Retail: $39.95
Dir: Masahiro Shinoda   DP: Kazuo Miyagawa   Music: Toru Takemitsu
Dist: Kino on Video/Ingram International Films

Hiromi Go	Gonza Sasano
Shima Iwashita	Osai
Takashi Tsumura	Ichinoshin

Shohei Hino, Haruko Kato, Misako Tanaka
[***]
The title may give you the false impression that Gonzo the Spearman is a fast-paced samurai epic, but Gonzo's story is actually a romantic tragedy. Beautifully filmed in Japan around historical locations with characters dressed in period-piece clothing, the setting is the late 1600's, the Tokugawa Era of the samurai. The country has been unified, warfare is a memory of the

past, and peace reigns across the land. Samurai are no longer needed for just their military abilities, and many samurais have taken up the traditional art of the tea ceremony, painting, or literature.

Gonzo is an elite samurai, a skilled man in horsemanship, fencing, and an expert of the spear. He is handsome, dashing, and quite single to the chagrin of the rival bachelors. His chief rival is Bannojo, another high-ranking samurai who competes with Gonzo but never manages to beat him. He is the older brother of a beautiful woman named Oyuki who secretly desires Gonzo. Naturally, Bannojo would never agree to a marriage so Gonzo keeps his desires for Oyuki a secret. The chief retainer of their samurai clan calls Gonzo and Bannojo to a private meeting. In celebration of their lord, a samurai will be chosen to lead the procession. He will be given a higher rank and his reputation will rise within the clan. It is required for the samurai to be adept at the tea ceremony. Both men proudly claim they would be right for the position and will compete for the honor. Another samurai Inoshino is away from the province, but his wife and their children remain at home. His wife is skilled in the tea ceremony and possesses secret manuals on the proper procedure. Bannojo approaches her with deceitful desire, but when his advances are ignored, he plans to steal the manuals. Gonzo also approaches the woman and promises to marry her daughter Okuki. When Okuki's mother discovers Gonzo's true love is for Oyuki, she angrily confronts him and gets involved in an argument. Her clothes get ruffled and she loses her belt. Bannojo witnesses the struggle and assumes it is a lover's spat. He steals the belt as proof and warns the entire clan. Fearing strict persecution, Gonzo and the woman flee for their lives while being pursued by the entire clan. Confusion and sorry follow Gonzo as he must decide what to do with his life, having lost his position, home, Oyuki, and his honor. The warriors converge on a beautifully-crafted bridge where the final duel takes place between Gonzo and the woman's husband, Inoshino. A dramatic film which uses the samurai era as a setting for love, betrayal, and hatred. A beautifully photographed and well-crafted romantic drama. Minimal sword-fighting, not intended for action fans.

Grappler Baki
(1994) Japanime: Action   C-45m Dubbed   VA
Catalog #USM 1545 Japan Retail: $19.95
Dir: Yuji Asada   Scr: Yoshihisa Araki Original Story: Keisuke Itagaki
Ex. Prod: Seiichi Nishino, Genro Ito
Prod: Tsuneo Seto, Chiaki Yasuda DP: Yosuke Moriguchi
Sound Dir: Nobuhiro Komatsu   Music: Takahiro Saito
Character Design: Yoshihiro Umakoshi   Art Dir: Hitoshi Nagao
English Version - Ex. Prod: John O'Donnell   Prod: Stephanie Shalofsky
Dist: US Manga Corps

Carter Cathcart	**Baki Hanma/Mitsunari Tokugawa**
Leo Gorman	**Doppo Orochi**
Eric Stuart	**Announcer**
Stan Hart	**Kosho Shinogi/Seicho Kato**
Vance Acres	**Atsushi Suedo**

[**]

Fight-filled anime fashioned after the popular but brutal sport of full-contact arena fighting, such as the Ultimate Fighting Championship seen on pay-per-view channels. The sport matches fighters of any style in a ring where almost anything is legal! Young Baki, a high school student, decides to challenge the toughest fighters in Japan. He decides to enter the arena of combat at a Karate tournament where he beats the biggest and best fighters of Japan. In lengthy, graphic fight sequences, he proves himself to be the best fighter. Inspired by Karate legend/master Doppo Orochi, Baki continues his reign of supremacy by entering an underground full-contact competition. The best fighters in the world compete and anything goes. The finale pits Baki against a red-haired fighter who specializes in ripping out human nerve cords and severing them. Yes, they show everything in graphic detail, but even as Baki faces near death and undergoes excruciating pain, he manages to maintain his boyish smile and carefree attitude. There's no drama, no compulsion, no realism, the film is an animated video game where violence and torture are part of the fun. The graphic nature of the animation and one-dimensional story will have limited appeal to mainstream audiences. If you enjoy fighting, fighting, and fighting in a bloody animated style, Baki offers plenty and little else.

Grave of the Fireflies
(1988) Japanime: Drama   C-88m Japanese with English Subtitles
Catalog #CPM 1053 Japan Retail: $29.95
Dir/Scr: Isao Takahata   Original Story: Akiyuki Nosaka
Prod Designer & Ex. Prod: Ryoichi Sato   Prod: Toru Hara
Character Design: Yoshifumi Kondo   Art Dir: Nizo Yamamoto
Color Design of Characters: Michiyo Yasuda
English Version - Ex. Prod: John O'Donnell   Translation: Neil Nadelman
PC: Shinchosha Co. Dist: Central Park Media
[*1/2]**
A hauntingly beautiful and moving drama, portraying the sad life of a Japanese boy and his younger sister. The story follows the plight of Japanese citizens during World War II and the mature subject material is similar to Barefoot Gen, but the animation quality is sharper and brighter. The film opens with a young boy leaning against a pillar inside a station in Kobe. It is the end of World War II and citizens patch together the remnants of their life. He is emaciated, his eyes vacant and lifeless, and his tattered body remains motionless. No one helps or even looks toward the homeless boy. Beside him, a tin can opens and small little lights spirit outward and away. The fireflies represent the souls and dreams of the young child.
The tale flashbacks to an earlier part of the war when the boy was healthier and happier. Seita, 14 years old, and Setsuko, 4 years old, leave the plagued city and set off to find an abandoned bomb shelter near a river in the countryside of Japan. Dressed in a modest but clean uniform, Seita escorts his sister to their temporary home. The children's parents were killed during a firebomb attack and were staying at someone's house. When situations get worse, they are asked to leave and must fend for themselves. Life is tough, but Seita is resourceful and manages to meek out a meager living for both of them. As the war continues, food becomes scarce and Seita and Setsuko's health and spirit deteriorate.
In one of the saddest scenes in cinema, his sister slowly becomes ill and starves to death. Her once youthful glow and passion for life dissipates through the power of animation. There is no denying that the strong antiwar message will disturb viewers, but the film is an honest depiction of the desperation and sorrow of trapped characters who innocently suffered from the results of warfare. A haunting reminder that war effects children as deeply as adults and death does not

discriminate.

The Green Slime (Gamma Sango Uchu Daisakusen)
(1968) Monster   C-77m Dubbed   Japan/USA
Dir: Kinji Fukasaku Scr: Charles Sinclair, Tom Rowe, William Finger
Prod: Ivan Reiner, Walter Manley DP: Yoshikazu Yamasawa Editor: Osamu Tanaka
Music: Toshiaki Tsushima Costumes: Miami
Sp. Fx: Akira Watanabe   PC: Toei Studios

Robert Horton	**Jack Rankin**
Richard Jaeckel	**Vince Elliott**
Lucianne Paluzzi	**Lisa Benson**
Bud Widom	**Jonathan Thompson**
Ted Gunther	**Dr. Halvorsen**
Robert Dunham	**Captain Martin**
William Ross	**Ferguson**

Tom Scott, David Yorston, Linda G. Miller
[**]
Though the principal cast members are non-Asian, it would be an injustice to exclude this classic Japanese monster film of the 1960's. What makes this film historically notable is the dual partnership between Japanese and American talents. The first official Japanese/America co-production may have been the early inspiration for Ridley Scott's "Alien". Take a moment, notice the side-by-side comparisons of both alien films.
A space station/ship sends a team of astronauts to investigate a mysterious asteroid/planet. During the mission, one of the members is infected by the alien. The innocuous alien gets through quarantine, grows to adult size, and kills members of the crew who madly search for the alien. As more crew members die, the fierce alien(s) take over the station. The commander decides to blow up the station and make a daring escape. The aliens die and the survivors return to Earth. Sounds familiar doesn't it? Of course the special effects on Green Slime are on par with Saturday morning cartoons and suffers from dated visual effects. I'm not making a direct comparison, since the far superior Alien is a brilliant, visually impressive horror/scifi film but the similar story structure is uncanny.
Here's a more concise explanation of the original monster film. The international crew of Gamma III space station send a crew to investigate a bizarre approaching asteroid. One of the crew members unexpectantly brings back a small sample of green slime. During the decontamination period, the slime manages to grow into a blobish creature with a big eye and electrically charged tentacles, reminding me of Seymour the Sea-Monster. Every time the creature is cut or injured, it regenerates new slime monsters from its green blood. Slowly but surely, the slime monsters take over the rest of the ship and feed off the energy supply. The only choice is to evacuate, but the main shuttle doors are blocked by the creatures. In a daring attack, the two main heroes who both love Lucianne Paluzzi (sexy villain from Thunderball) risk their lives to travel outside the station and remove the slime monsters. They manage to open the shuttle doors and the survivors escape to Earth while the desserted space station crumbles and burns up. What kills this type of campy scifi film is the fact that much better films have been made since, utilizing better special effects and film techniques. Unless you're a very young child, need a good laugh, or enjoy campy scifi, it's best to stay away from this film. Like seeing

an old magic trick with less impressive results, once you've seen the elephant disappear, seeing a mouse disappear is not so exciting.

Green Snake
(1993) Fantasy   C-98m Chinese with English Subtitles   Catalog #1439
Hong Kong   Retail: $39.99 Widescreen Available
Dir/Scr: Tsui Hark   PC: Film Workshop   Dist: Tai Seng Video
Zhao Wen Zhou   Monk
Joey Wong   White Snake - Son Ching
Maggie Cheung   Green Snake
Wu Hsin Kuo Scholar Hsui Xien
[***]
Maggie Cheung is the Green Snake, a 500 year old serpent bent on living in the human world as a beautiful seductress. Her nemesis is Fa-Hai, a guardian of the human realm, who prevents non-humans from assuming human guise. Though Cheung is billed as the title character, the main story revolves around the doomed love affair of snake Joey Wong and human Wu Hsin Kuo. The tragic romance is a remake of the famous "Bai She Zhuan" ("Madam White Snake") story.

The film opens with a monk contemplating the nature of his purpose in life. Monk Fa-Hai (Zhao who portrayed Wong Fei Hung in Once Upon a Time in China 4 & 5) spots an elderly priest gliding through the air. Fa-Hai takes pursuit and flies alongside the priest. Fa-Hai questions him casually and then casts a spell to capture the false monk, revealing his true non-human form. The priest was a spider who spent 200 years attempting to become human. In the world of Buddhism, reincarnation and the eternal soul are always striving to improve. The only catch is that non-humans (animals) can not reincarnate into a human form. It is forbidden by the scriptures of Buddha and Fa-Hai is the self-righteous guardian who keeps the barrier between humans and non-humans in tact. He has the powers of a god and is nearly invincible.

When he detects a strange aura from the forest, he spots two female snakes: a green one and a white one. At first he plans to punish them for attempting to become human, but when the snakes protect a woman giving birth in the rain, Fa-Hai takes pity and leaves the snakes alone. Soon the snakes break into human guise and slither with passionate delight. Green (Cheung) is the new kid on the block and decides to have fun, crashing a party with Indian dancers and wrapping her legs and arms around the beautiful women. She then disappears and joins her sister, White Snake (1000 years old), who appears as a beautiful woman named Son Ching. Son wishes to reside in the human world and takes a human identity and gives up her snake-like habits: eating rodents, slithering on walls, and transforming back into a snake.

Son spots a handsome scholar (Wu) waiting for a boat on the docks. With a cup of wine thrown into the air, Son causes the rain to fall and offers her own boat to the scholar. Her magical powers allow her to create all forms of illusions. The two gradually fall in love, but their lives are plagued by curious browsers and the mischievous antics of Green Snake who finds it difficult to completely forego her snake-like mentality. When the scholar discovers the women are snakes, he nearly dies from fright. In an attempt to save her lover, Son and Green fly to retrieve a magic herb guarded by a Magic Crane.

Meanwhile Monk Fa-Hai meditates in his remote Golden Temple. He is tempted by Green Snake's beauty and doubts his own spiritual purity. In an act of blind fury, he vows to destroy the two snakes and unleashes his own fury which causes a catastrophic chain of events. A mystical battle takes place that can only lead to tragedy and sorrow. What makes the film entertaining is the seductive nature of Maggie Cheung and Joey Wong as they discover the passions and wonders of being human. The pacing of the film is awkward at times and the visualist Hark goes for mood over dialogue. The special effects are good for a Chinese fantasy production, but the rubber snake effects can become tiresome and constant flying may become distracting to viewers who are not familiar with Hong Kong flying films. Elements of comedic relief are introduced by a blind priest and his two child apprentices who attempt to capture the snakes. There's more to the film than what's on the surface, so keep an open mind and try to enjoy.

Gunbuster "Aim for the Top!"
(1989) Japanime   C-60m Japanese with English Subtitles   VA
Catalog #MGV 636235   Japan Retail: $19.95
Dir: Hideaki Anno   Scr/Original Story: Toshio Okada
Ex. Prod: Tadatsugu Hayakawa, Toshio Azami   Music: Kohei Tanaka
Character Design: Haruhiko Mikimoto   Mecha Design: Kazuki Miyatake, Koichi Ohata
Animation Dir: Yuji Moriyama, Toshiyuki Kubooka, Yoshiyuki Sadamoto
Planning: Shin Unozawa, Isao Senda, Toshio Okada
PC: Victor/Gainax/BMD   Dist: U.S. Renditions/Manga Video
Noriko Hidaka   Noriko
Rei Sakuma   Amano
Nobuo Iwamoto   Coach Ohta
Maria Kawamura   Jung-Freud
Tamio Oki   Toshiro
[***1/2]
Extremely enjoyable and well-crafted animation series using female space pilots, robots, and alien marauders. The animation is wonderful and the stories have a sense of maturity which cross over many decades of the characters' lives. The series captures and balances the strength of girls in anime and hardcore scifi with over-the-top action. In one of the best emotional openings, a female child's voice giddily narrates her love and enthusiasm for her brave father. We look at a loving photo of the father and his tiny daughter. Incredibly detailed newspaper clippings show the passage of time and the girl's voice matures and changes into a melancholy tone. Her father is dead, attacked by an unknown alien...and on that day she decides to join the fight and enroll in the Space Academy. At that point the catchy theme song cuts in and the adventure begins.
The future of Earth is dim as aliens from another galaxy have decimated most of Earth's fleet and killed her best space pilots. Captain Takaya is one of the great men lost in the alien's initial attack. At a women's space academy, young Noriko Takaya, daughter of Captain Takaya, is a first year cadet who gets swept into a life-long adventure when she is promoted beyond all her seniors to pilot the Gunbuster machine. The Gunbuster is a giant super robot/spaceship designed to battle the aliens. Senior ace pilot Kazumi Amano is dismayed at the choice and confronts the head coach for his rash decision in selecting a freshman. Coach Ohta is dedicated to seeing Noriko excel and owes her father for saving his life. He sticks by his choice and personally prepares Noriko for the assignment. When Noriko proves her worth by beating another top senior, she and Kazumi leave Japan to join the battleship Exelion in space.
Their deep space mission begins and new friends are made along the way. In one episode,

Noriko even discovers her father's ship. The series follows her growth and maturity as she becomes the Earth's best pilot. The aliens are never detailed, but seen more as a mysterious menace to Earth. One of the few series that uses Einstein's theory of relativity as a guidepost with cute science lessons placed in between episodes. The battle scenes with Gunbuster may get a little extravagant and over the top. The series does contain some mild nudity and violence, but should be fine for mature kids and teenagers. The majority of characters are female, but that never takes away from the action, drama, and excitement of an excellent film.

Title songs are performed by Sakai Noriko, a popular Japanese singer and actress. It is not uncommon to have popular Japanese singers perform title songs in Japanese animation which add to the overall quality of the film's soundtrack.

Gunbuster Vol. 2
(1989) Japanime   C-60m Japanese with English Subtitles   VA
Catalog #MGV 636237   Japan Retail: $19.95
Dir: Hideaki Anno   Scr: Toshio Okada   Music: Kohei Tanaka
Character Design: Haruhiko Mikimoto   Mecha Design: Kazuki Miyatake, Koichi Ohata
Animation Dir: Yuji Moriyama, Toshiyuki Kubooka, Yoshiyuki Sadamoto
PC: Victor/Gainax/BMD   Dist: U.S. Renditions/Manga Video
[*1/2]**
Noriko and Katsumi have graduated from the Academy and serve aboard the battlecruiser Exelion. In deep space, they perform a number of important missions and encounter the aliens. The series starts to explore Noriko's social life and introduces a male pilot. Many of the pilots are very young due to attrition caused by the war. Noriko and her female mates reside in a separate section of the ship, while the male pilots are stationed elsewhere. In a prank, Noriko must tie a scarf around a remote section of the gigantic spaceship. She leaves her quarters in the dark of night (station runs on a 24-hour day-night cycle) and bumps into a male pilot. The two become friends, but their relationship is disrupted when aliens attack the fleet. The aliens are fierce and destroy much of Earth's fleets. Many of the pilots shown earlier in the episode do not make it back alive, including Noriko's male friend. Emotionally devastated, it is time for Noriko to push aside her childhood, pilot the Gunbuster machine, and save Earth.

Gunbuster Vol. 3
(1989) Japanime   C/B&W-60m Japanese with English Subtitles   VA
Catalog #MGV 638305   Japan Retail: $19.95
Dir: Hideaki Anno   Scr: Toshio Okada   Music: Kohei Tanaka
Character Design: Haruhiko Mikimoto   Mecha Design: Kazuki Miyatake, Koichi Ohata
Animation Dir: Yuji Moriyama, Toshiyuki Kubooka, Yoshiyuki Sadamoto
PC: Victor/Gainax/BMD   Dist: U.S. Renditions/Manga Video
[*1/2]**
The tension gets bolder and the battles get wilder, perhaps a little overboard even for anime viewers. Earth's fleet and the Gunbuster machine enter the heart of the alien world and plan to detonate a super-bomb to end the war. Due to Einstein's Theory of Relativity, Noriko is still a young woman, but all her friends back on Earth have aged, married, raised children, and shared their lives with others. The film beautifully spends time with characters who were Noriko's friends in the first two volumes. Noriko is depressed by her loss of time spent in space, but she

is desperately needed to pilot the Gunbuster. In an artistic choice, the final episode forgoes color, the frame shifts into widescreen, and a number of key battle scenes are animated in dramatic black and white stills. The Gunbuster prepares for its final mission to save the universe. Noriko and an older Katsumi are teamed together for the final time and manage to end the war. The final scene is heartwarming and simple, but beautifully ends a marvelous three-volume series which incorporates the best of girl/robot anime with plenty of science fiction.

Gunhed
(1989) Scifi   C-100m   English & Japanese R   VA
Catalog #ALA/001   Japan Retail: $19.95
Dir: Alan Smithee   Scr: Alan Smithee, James Bannon
Ex. Prod: Tomoyuki Tanaka, Eiji Yamaura
DP: Junichi Fujisawa   Editor: Yoshitami Kuroiwa Music: Toshiyuki Honda
Prod Manager: Takahide Morichi   Art Dir: FumioOgawa
Sp Fx: Koichi Kawakita   PC: Toho Studios   Dist: ADV Films
Masahiro Takashima, Brenda Bakke, James B. Thompson, Kaori Mizuhima, Yujin Harada, Mickey Curtis, Aya Enjoji, Jiei Kabira, Yosuke Saito
[1/2]**
Basically a Japanese live-action movie that feels like Japanime, due to its large use of miniatures and computer graphics. In the future, CyboTech Corporation builds a massive industrial complex on a remote island. The complex is fully automated, but suddenly all communication stops. The story involves an elite team of soldiers sent to the remote island. They investigate the complex which is dominated by robots and artificial intelligence which act with a mind of their own. The international team is separated and must work to solve their own problems while staying alive. The heroic Japanese pilot, Brooklyn, is teamed with a powerful mech (a mechanical robot controlled from the inside by a human) who speaks English while he speaks in Japanese. Together, they travel through a vast subterranean base and battle an assortment of wily machines. The use of miniatures is impressive and the look and feel are reminiscent of Thunderbirds, but on a much higher plateau of filmmaking. The story bogs down too frequently and the characters seem as artificial as the machines, but there is appeal and plenty of action for genre fans.

Guy: Awakening of the Devil
(1990) Japanime: Scifi   C-40m Japanese with English Subtitles   VA
VHSG/001G Japan
Dir: Yorihisa Uchida   Prod: Shiu Maruyama
Music: Nobuhiko Kashihara   Character Design: Yakihiro Makino, Masami Ohari
Mecha Design: Yukio Tomimatsu, Tatsuharu Shirome
English Version - Ex. Prod: John Ledford Assoc Prod: Frank Nuccio
Written & Prod: Matt Greenfield Tranlation: Ichiro Arakaki, Dwayne Jones
PC: Studio Max/AIC/Humming/Uchu Planing/Friends/Media Station Dist: AD Vision
[1/2]**
Partners Guy (tough detective) and Raina (sexy sidekick) salvage a deserted spaceship but end up on prison planet Geo under a sadistic warden called Helga. They attempt to escape, but complications arise when the evil Dr. Vail turns the inmates into genetic monsters. Typical adult

style animation and hardcore action for anime fans, but not for young eyes.

-H-

Half a Loaf of Kung Fu
(1977) Kung-Fu   C-96m Dubbed   VA
Catalog #DP 1350-B   Hong Kong   Retail: $9.95
Dir: Chen Chih Hua Scr: Tang Min-Ji   Prod: Hsu Li Hwa   Ex. Prod: Lo Wei
DP: Chen Chin-Kui   Music: Frankie Chan   Editor: Leong Wing-Chan
MAD: Jackie Chan
Jackie Chan, Lung Juen-Er, James Tien, Li Hai-Lung, Kum Kong, Kim Ching Lan, Miao
Tien, Ma Yu-Lung, Li Ching-Luen, Shik Tien, Kao Chiang, Hsu Hang, Kim Si Yu
[**]
A young man named Jang (Jackie Chan) is desperately in search of a livelihood. He doesn't have
a formal education and lacks any useable trade skills. He tries to work at a coffin-makers, but
fails and soon departs for fresher pastures. Fortunately he knows how to fight and ends up
applying for a position as a bodyguard with a local clan. They are part of an escort service and
must deliver the sacred Soul Pills and Evergreen Jade. But word of the treasure has leaked to the
criminal world, enticing a host of villains to attack the Master and his escorts. One after another,
fights scenes are staged in the woods and most of the villains are second class fighters easily
discouraged. The villains team up and launch an all-out attack, wounding the clan's master. It is
up to Chan to complete the mission and defeat all the villains. A generic Chan film with a few
moments of early worth.

Hapkido   (Lady Kung Fu)
(1972) Kung-Fu   C-100m   Dubbed   Hong Kong   Retail: $19.95
Dir: Hwang Feng   Prod: Raymond Chow   PC: Golden Harvest
Angela Mao Ying, Carter Wong, Whong In Shik, Samo Hung
[**]
Sometimes watching a kung-fu movie is like viewing a sporting event. If your favorite
baseball/basketball/football team is playing, nothing in the world can tear you away. The same
goes for certain kung-fu movies that become viewable for your favorite stars. Angela doesn't
play her role to be cute or demean herself, she's a no-nonsense tough fighter with the spirit and
determination of Bruce Lee. She's back in high-kicking fashion in this Korean-style martial arts
film. Hapkido is a Korean-invented style that incorporates Japanese-style aikido (throws and
locks) with amazing high kicks. Angela must fight some lecherous Japanese villains who
threaten her and her friends. The film will appeal for its veteran cast, but lacks the finesse and
substance of later day martial arts films.

Hard-Boiled   (Hot-Handed God of Cops)
(1992) Action C-125m   Dubbed/Chinese with English Subtitles   VA
Catalog #1165   Hong Kong   Retail: $19.98
Dir: John Woo Scr: John Woo, Barry Wong
Prod: Terence Chang, Linda Kuk
DP: James Leung Editor: John Woo, David Wu   Music: Michael Gibbs

Prod Design: James Leung
Costume: Janet Chan   Sound: Brian Schwegmann
Visual FX: Ting Yuen-Tai   MAD: Philip Kwok
PC: Golden Princess Film, Milestone Pictures   Dist: Tai   Seng   Video/Criterion/Fox Lorber

Chow Yun Fat	Tequila
Tony Leung Chiu Wai	Tony
Anthony Wong	Johnny
Bowie Lam	Lionheart
Kuo Chui	Mad Dog
Teresa Mo Shun Kwan	Teresa

Philip Chan, Cheung Jue-Luh, Y. Yonemura, John Woo (cameo)
[****]
Arguments abound as to which John Woo film is the best, but there are no arguments that Hard-Boiled would be a top contender. After The Killer received worldwide attention, Hard-Boiled was quickly released in the United States video market. This time Chow dons a badge and fights on the side of the law, he plays a police officer who wages his own personal war against the Triads who murdered his partner. In a bloody opening sequence, Chow and his partner confront gangsters in an all out gun battle at a Chinese restaurant where patrons are allowed to bring their singing pet birds. A visual action ballet that showcases the brilliance of Woo's camera direction and choreography.   Hoping to take down the criminal organization, Chow's focus shifts onto criminal Tony Leung. He eventually discovers Tony is an undercover cop and the two hard-boiled men form a unique partnership and go after the Triad organization. The final battle which becomes dizzying and bombastic features Chow and Leung trapped in a hospital for a lengthy and non-stop action filled battle. Woo doesn't come up for air as the intensity of the finale carries a large weight of the film and presents a testament to ultra-style action..

Harmagedeon "The Great Battle with Genma"
(1983) Japanime   C-132m   Dubbed/Japanese with English Subtitles   VA
Catalog #USM 1468/USM 1038   Japan Retail: $19.95/$29.95
Dir: Taro RinScr: Chiho Katsura, Makoto Naito, Mori Masaki
Original Story: Kazumasa Hirai, Shotaro Ishimori
DP: Iwao Yamaki   Character Design: Katsuhiro Otomo   Animation   Dir: Takuo Noda
Art Dir: Takamura Mukuo Music: Nozomi Aoki Prod: Susumu Aketagawa
Ex. Prod: Haruki Kadokawa, Shotaro Ishimori
PC: Kadokawa Shoten Publishing Co., Ltd.   Dist: U.S. Manga Corps

Toru Furuya	Jo Azuma
Mumi Koyama	Luna
Masako Ikeda	Michiko Azuma
Keiko Han	Junko Sawakawa
Kaneto Shiozawa	Shiro Koda
Kenji Utsumi	Salamander
Yasufumi Hayashi	Sonny
Hideyuki Tanaka	Asanshi

Ryuji Kai	Yogin
Tomoyo Harada	Tao
Toru Emori	Vega
Akihiro Miwa	Floy
Ichiro Nagai	Zambi
Junpei Takiguchi	Zamedi

[***]

An ancient, evil power threatens the fate of the universe and heads straight for the planet Earth. To ensure it's victory, the demon hurls a meteor and destroys a commercial airliner. All on board are killed, but somehow Princess Luna is saved and teleported to a parallel dimension. There she meets a mystic named Floy who warns her of the danger to Earth and helps her enlist the aid of a powerful robot. Together, they search the world for the most powerful psychics to do battle. Their quest covers the entire planet, but focuses primarily on a teenager named Jo who is the mightiest of them all, but unaware of his powers. When the characters have gathered and are convinced to work together, they encounter the demon and take battle in a fantastic fashion.

Though the film runs over two hours, it seems somewhat incomplete and too short to properly develop the host of characters. A good deal of time is spent with Jo and his sister, but Luna's character is used as a catalyst and then wanders through the rest of the film as a figurehead. Another shortcoming is the lack of an ominous antagonist. When the villain is finally confronted, they are less menacing then imagined and make careless errors. If more time had been spent on tightening character interaction, this could have been a truly epic tale. But it still hits the mark and is quite entertaining from a visual and storytelling point of view.

Heart of Dragon   (The First Mission)
(1982) Action/Drama   C-85m Dubbed/Chinese with English Subtitles
Catalog #03493   Hong Kong   Retail: $19.98
Dir: Samo Hung   Prod: Chua Lam, Wu Ma   DP: Arthur Wong
Editor: Peter Cheung, Joseph Chiang   Music: Violet Lam
Assistant Dir: Ng Min Kan, Cheung King Bo, Chan Wui Ngai
Prod Manager: Chan Kou, Rosita Wong   Art Dir: Fung Yuen Chi
MAD: Samo Hung's Stunt Team - Yuen Kwai, Mang Hoi, Corey Yuen Wah, Chan Wui Ngai
Stunt Driver: Kao Shau Leung   Stunts: Yuen Mo, Lau Chau Sang, Pang Yun Cheung,
Dist: Tai Seng Video

Jackie Chan	Ted
Samo Hung	Danny
Emily Chu	Jenny
Man Hei	Yank
Lam Ching Ying	Swat Team Com
Chan Lung	
Corey Yuen Wah	
Ka Lok	
Yuen Kwai	
Melvin Wong	Inspector Wong
Lam Ying Fat	Edmond

Lee Ka Ho	Kid
Dennis Chan	Waiter
Ip Wing Cho	Rest Manager
Anthony Chan	Teacher
Tze Man Ha	Granny
Tai Po	Kenny
Wu Fung	Headmaster
Chan Chun Man	Kim
Chung Fat	Moose
Wu Ma	Cafe Owner
So Hang Suen	Wife

[**1/2]

One of the most recent American video releases starring the Trinity of Hong Kong superstars: Jackie Chan, Samo Hung, and Yuen Biao. The film begins with an action sequence of paramilitary units hunting for a group of men dressed in yellow clothing led by Jackie Chan. What at first seems an action film switches into a heavy dose of melodrama. Samo Hung never achieved American success on the level of Chan and his style of subdued comedy and humility does not fall into the same realm of similar large funny men like Jackie Gleason, Chris Farley, or John Candy. Jackie Chan is Ted, a successful police officer who dreams of joining the merchant marines. The only problem is that his brother Danny (Hung) is mentally handicapped and depends on Ted for protection. Samo uses his stupidity to run a number of sentimental sequences involving a group of grimy children, but the scenes lack pacing and run longer then they should. Hong Kong children characters (perhaps the dubbing) are tiresome, annoying, and constantly whine to the point their actions are no longer cute but irritating on film. At times, the brothers communicate on an emotional level, but the flow of the story never allows time to develop Jackie's relationship with his attractive girlfriend or his fellow officers. The film jumps from scene to scene and the villains of the story aren't even introduced until late in the second half of the film. A group of jewel thieves are raided by the police and one of the crooks escapes with the jewels. As he is escaping, he mistakes Samo and his toy gun for a policeman. Samo and his little friend hide the jewels, but are discovered by the kid's older brother who attempts to case the jewels. The crooks find the jewels and decide to murder any witnesses. It's up to Chan and his police friends to save the day.

Heart of Killer
(1995) Action C-92m Chinese with English Subtitles   Catalog #1903
Hong Kong   Retail: $39.99 (Widescreen Available)
Dir/Ex. Prod: Andrew Kam Scr: Chow Chun Wing, Philip Kwok, Andrew Kam
Prod: Ching Laam, Ng Hoi Shuen, Ronald Ng   Ex. Prod: Lee Kin Hing
DP: Jim Pak Hung   Editor: Shan Kan Shing
Music: Oman Mui, Sam Leung, Barry Cheung   Associate Prod: Ching Laam
Assistant Dir: Lee Ping Leung, Chan Wai Chu, Bandy Yiu
Chief Prod Manager: Ma Man Chung   Prod Manager: Arthur Wong, Ng Kit Keung
Art Dir: Lam Chun Fai, Angelo Bernardo Castilho   Gaffer: Tam Kin Fat
MAD: Hung Hsin Chun, Chan Tat Kong
PC: Fortune Stars Film Co.

Dist: Fitto Mobile Laser Distribution Co. Ltd./Tai Seng Video
Yu Rong Guang   Brother Lap
Benny Mok Siu Chung, Tung Ei Lin, Jang Rong, Wong Ting, Wong Hiu Man, Huang Hsiu Chun, Jan Rui Chao
[**1/2]
Hong Kong cinema has been influenced by the surge in popularity of Triad/gangster films. Filmmakers John Woo and Ringo Lam are legendary for their gritty, male-bonding, gun flicks. Of course, it comes as no surprise that other Hong Kong filmmakers have flocked into the market with their own versions. Heart of a Killer won't please fans who expect something on the Woo-level, but there are enough routine fight scenes and male-bonding to appeal to fans of the genre.

Screen favorites Yu and Mok are two assassins who live a meager existence outside of Hong Kong in a shack near an isolated river. Yu is the classic cool killer (ala Chow Yun Fat), tall, lean, handsome with a look of steel and reflexes of a snake. He kills without a second glance and indulges in a bottle of pure water after each kill. Mok is more of an enigma, since he doesn't act like a competent killer nor does he do much killing. While Yu maybe the Killer, Mok is the heart since his character becomes involved in a romantic interlude. The film balances back and forth between light romance and hard action. The head of a legitimate company is killed by his subordinate who plans to take over the company and make a deal with gangsters. The dutiful daughter senses wrongdoing and seizes control of the company, putting her own life in danger. While passing on a crowded street, Mok meets her and helps her with her belongings. She drops a smoking pipe intended for her father. Mok discovers the pipe and looks for the young woman. Mok finds her and establishes a relationship with the woman who is then hunted by the mob. She discovers that Mok and Yu are hired killers and that Yu was her father's assassin. She hates them and leaves both of them, but is later captured by the mob. Yu tries to convince Mok that a job is a job, and personal feelings are totally irrelevant. We know better and in no time, Mok and Yu wage a personal war against the mob.

Heaven and Earth
(1990) Samurai   C-104m   Japanese with English Subtitles   PG-13   VA
Catalog #69026   Japan   Widescreen Available
Dir: Haruki Kadokawa   Scr: Toshio Kamata, Isao Yoshihara, Haruki Kadokawa
Prod: Yutaka Okada   DP: Yonezo Maeda   Editor: Akira Suziki, Robert C. Jones
Music: Tetsuya Komuro   Prod Design: Hiroshi Tokuda
Art Design: Kazuhiko Fujiwara   Sp. Fx: Stewart Bradley
Stunts: John Scott, Brent Woolsey   Makeup: Shigeo Tamura
Choreography: Hiroshi Kuze, Jean-Pierre Fournier
Costumes: Yoko Tashiro, Wendy Partridge   Dist: Ingram International Films
(based on the novel by Chogoro Kaionji)
Takaai Enoki Kenshin Uefugi
Masahiko Tsugawa Takeda
Atsuko AsanoNami
Tsunehiko Watase Usami
Naomi Zaizen Yae
Binpachi Ito Kakizaki

Isao Natsuyagi	Kansuke
Akira Hamada	Naoe
Masataka Naruse	Okuma
Osamu Yayama	Irobe
Takeshi Obayashi	Murakami
Masayuki Sudo	Onikojima
Kaitaro Nozaki	Naya
Tatsuhiko Tomoi	Sone
Takuya Goto	Tokura
Satoshi Sadanaga	Akiyama
Hironobu Nomura	Taro
Hideo Murota	Obu
Taro Ishida	Tenkyu
Hiroyuki Okita	Kosaka
Akisato Yamada	Hajikano
Morio Kazama	Imperial Messenger
Masuto Ibu	Shoda
Yuki Kazamatsuri	Shoda's Wife
Kyoko Kishida	Servant
Hideji Otaki	Rifle Merchant
Stuart Whitman	Narration

[***]

A sweeping samurai epic from director Harokawa, not Kurosawa, who has become the main name in Japanese period cinema. The tale of two powerful warlords who battle over the control of Japan. The large-scale battles are impressive in a "Braveheart" vein and were filmed in Canada to better accommodate the filming. Though impressive in many ways, the film's large scope loses focus and shies away from the inner motivations and desires of the men who shaped Japanese history. Instead of over focusing on the large-scale costumed battles, a touch of subtlety and character interaction would have risen the film to the level of a Kurosawa samurai classic.

Here is Greenwood - Vol. 1

(1991) Japanime   C-60   Dubbed/Subtitled with English Subtitles   VA
Catalog # SSVD 9613   Japan Retail: $24.95
Dir/Scr: Tomimitsu Mochizuki   Character Design & Animation Dir: Masako Goto
Music: Shigeru Nagata   PC: Hakuensha Inc./Victor Entertainment, Inc.
Dist: Central Park Media
(based on the manga by Yukie Nasu)
[***]

A cute and light-hearted comedy about the students at Rykuto Academy, a prepatory high school with a dormitory called Greenwood. More serious minded than most anime romantic comedies, the series follows the exploits of Kazuya Hasukawa, a new student, and the ecletic friends he makes at Greenwood. When Kazuya's first love marries his brother, he decides to move out of the family home and live on campus. He tries to cope with the situation and immerses himself into the routines of Greenwood. The cast of characters are quite interesting, including a single female student, as they form lasting friendships. If you enjoy situational comedy and animation, the series is a perfect place to start viewing.

Here is Greenwood - Vol. 2
(1992) Japanime   C-60   Dubbed/Subtitled with English Subtitles   VA
Catalog # SSVD 9614   Japan Retail: $24.95
Dir/Scr: Tomimitsu Mochizuki   Character Design & Animation Dir: Masako Goto
Music: Shigeru Nagata   PC: Hakuensha Inc./Victor Entertainment, Inc.
Dist: Central Park Media
(based on the manga by Yukie Nasu)
[***]
Of the many episodes, number four is probably my personal favorite. Kazuya is now a part of the life at Greenwood and the students decide to make a film to win the festival prize and throw a smashing party. It's a medieval adventure story and they go all out trying to recruit people to star and help out. The next episode adds a supernatural twist to the lives of Greenwood. A girl named Misako is hit by a car and dies, her spirit decides to haunt the halls of Greenwood in search of a boyfriend. She decides to choose the handsome Mitsuru and begs him for a kiss. Her antics turn the dormitory upside down and her presence is more of a nuisance than a reason to be afraid. Plenty of visual sight gags and humor plague Kazuya and his friends. As the series unfolds, the characters become more familiar and enjoyable to watch. Not unlike watching your favorite sitcom, an animated Friends.
Episode 3: The Making of Here is Devilwood
Episode 4: The Phantom of Greenwood

Here is Greenwood - Vol. 3
(1993) Japanime   C-60   Dubbed/Subtitled with English Subtitles   VA
Catalog # SSVD 9615   Japan Retail: $24.95
Dir/Scr: Tomimitsu Mochizuki   Character Design & Animation Dir: Masako Goto
Music: Shigeru Nagata   PC: Hakuensha Inc./Victor Entertainment, Inc.
Dist: Central Park Media
(based on the manga by Yukie Nasu)
[***]
A two-part episode which follows the exploit of a girl named Miya form another high school. She shows up one evening at Greenwood, but the tough-minded dorm mistress won't let her in. The students manage to sneak her in anyway and decide to help her out. A rival female gang (they can be pretty vicious in Japan) has marked her for a fight and she needs backup. Mitsuru knows Miya from the past and the newly-elected dorm president, Kazuya, decides he must help her.
Episode 5 & 6: Second Love...Always Be with You, Acts 1& 2

Heroes of Shaolin
(1980) Kung-Fu   C-91m Dubbed   Catalog #4068   Hong Kong
Retail: $9.99
Dir: William Chang Scr: I Kuang, William Chang, Chang Hsing Yi
Prod: William Chang, Xie Lai He Ex. Prod: Chang Qian Xi, Chang Jen Dao

Editor: Chen Xung Min   Music: Chow Fu Liang
Prod Manager: Lee Xian Chang, Sun Bing
MAD: Yuan Kwei, Yuan Biu, Tony Tue
Dist: Simitar Entertainment, Inc.
Chen Xing, Lo Lieh, Lung Chun Erh, Wong Zheng Lieh, Chan Ming Lieh, Ding Hwa Chong
[**]
Period piece film dealing with China's battle against Manchurian invaders. On the beach, two great kung-fu warriors meet for combat. One man falls and in his dying breath, he begs the other fighter, Tu Ta Chen, to continue his cause against the Manchurians. You must help your country, he begs. Tu Ta agrees, but the only problem is that the dead warrior's son, Sa Pu, follows him and promises to kill him. The two constantly fight, but since they are now working for the same cause come to an unusual truth. Tu allows Sa Pu to follow him and even offers to teach him. When the day that Sa learns everything from Tu Ta, he can challenge him. The two men put aside their differences and fight against the Manchus. At the climatic finale, Tu Ta beats the devil-masked villain and then must battle Sa Pu. The two square off and Tu Ta sits down, leaving himself open to Sa's deadly spear. Then Sa repeats the words Tu Ta did in the beginning of the film and the warriors walk off as allies. One thing you man find immensely funny about kung-fu movies besides the dialogue dubbing is the habit of music dubbing. Popular film music of the era is often used in the soundtrack, so you may hear a familiar tune or two which may seem inappropriate for the scene. Standard kung-fu film with some good scenes mixed along the way.

Heroic Legend of Arislan, Part 1
(1991) Japanime: Fantasy   C-60m Dubbed/Japanese with English Subtitles
Catalog # USM 1110/USM 1081   Japan Retail: $ $19.95/$29.95
Dir: Mamoru Hamatsu   Scr: Tomoya Miyashita   Original Writer: Yoshiki Tanaka
Character Design: Sachiko Kamimura   Chief Animator: Kazuchika Kise
PC: Kadokawa Shoten/MOVIC/Sony Music entertainment   Dist: Central Park Media
(created by Haruki Kadokawa, Hiroshi Inagaki, Yutaka Taakahasi)
[**1/2]
The animation is captivating and the creation of a new rich land of sword and sorcery seem a perfect journey for fans of fantasy. The Heroic Legend of Arislan succeeds on some levels, but fails to capture the overall depth, style, and pacing of Record of Lodoss Wars. What lies at the heart of the problem is the slow-trodding plot that mires into melodramatic interludes and characters who don't fit any classic fantasy roles. The knight Daryoon vows to the king to protect his son, Prince Arislan. Once the kingdom has fallen and allegience sworn to the enemy, Daryoon must find safe haven for Arislan. His first stop is the effeminiate artist, Lord Narsus, and his apprentice the archer Elam. The enemy soldiers pound on Narsus' door forcing him to join up with his old friend Daryoon. Together the group search for new alliances and prepare for war against a mighty army.
Based on your appreciation of the first installment, you might enjoy the second installment.
The final volume contains episodes three and four of the series.

Heroic Legend of Arislan, Part 2

(1992) Japanime: Fantasy   C-60m Dubbed/Japanese with English Subtitles
Catalog # USM 1132/USM 1082   Japan Retail: $ $19.95/$29.95

Heroic Legend of Arislan, Part 3&4
(1993) Japanime: Fantasy   C-60m Dubbed/Japanese with English Subtitles
Catalog # USM 1444/USM 1097   Japan Retail: $ $19.95/$29.95

Heroic Trio, The
(1992) Fantasy Kung-Fu   C-87m Dubbed/Chinese with English Subtitles   VA
Catalog #44623   Hong Kong   Retail: $19.98 Widescreen Available
Dir: Johnny To   MAD: Ching Siu Ting   Music: William Hu
PC: Ching Siu Ting, Paka Hill Film Production Co.   Dist: Tai Seng Video
Maggie Cheung   Thief Catcher Chat
Anita Mui   Wonder Woman
Michelle Khan   Invisible Girl San
Anthony Wong, Damian Lau, James Pak
[***]
It's difficult sometimes to pin down a genre for a Hong Kong film, since they love mixing different elements into a single film. The Heroic Trio is a good example of the good and bad in Hong Kong cinema. The popular film is readily available on video shelves and has been shown on cable. Part fantasy, part horror, part action, part kung-fu and even a bit of comedy, Heroic Trio attempts everything but fails to soar in a single category. If you like a mixture of elements, the film will score high and features three of Hong Kong's best actresses.
Three modern day female super heroes (ala comic books) combine their skills to battle an ancient demon sorcerer who kidnaps babies in search of the one child who will become the new reigning emperor. Anita Mui, sporting a sexy haircut and tight dresses, is Wonder Woman. She's the noblest of the group and is married to a police officer who is on the baby kidnaping case. Michelle Khan, sulking and moribund, is Invisible Girl. She's the fallen character working for the evil demon and seducing a scientist to steal his secrets for the invisible suit. Maggie Cheung, gutsy and sexy, is Thief Catcher. She's the middle of the road hero, stopping criminals for a price in any manner she sees fit. She and Invisible Girl are sisters, but they were separated at a very young age.
At first, the three women battle each other. Khan kidnaps the babies while Mui and the police attempt to stop her. Thief Catcher is hired by the police commissioner who has had his own child stolen. Her reckless ways cause the death of a baby (the skull is punctured) and her mercenary tactics come in conflict with Wonder Woman. Thief Catcher eventually convinces Invisible Girl who falls in love with her ill scientist to join them and together they fight a wild, flying battle above and below the surface of Hong Kong. The heroic trio travel to the demon's underground layer and encounter some vile creatures. They will risk their lives to save the stolen babies and end the demon's reign forever. The film is stylistic, but mired with bizarre effects and dialogue-laden confessions that hinder the pace of the film. The dark nature of the film and grotesque visuals are not for mainstream viewers, but for those looking for something quirky and bizarre.
Assigned to destroy the trio is Anthony Wong, the demon's sadistic henchman who borders on absurdity and disgust. The film does feature a number of well-staged fantasy fight sequences

and is a rare opportunity to see three of Hong Kong's best heroines in action. A genre upon itself, Heroic Trio is applauded for its brashness and unconventionality.

Heroic Trio 2: Executioners (Executioners)
(1993) Scifi Kung-fu C-97m Dubbed/Chinese with English Subtitles
Catalog #31883   Hong Kong   Retail: $19.98 (Widescreen Available)
Dir/Prod: Ching Siu Ting, Johnny To   Scr: Susanne Chan   Original   Story: Sandy Shaw
Prod: Ching Siu Ting   DP: Poon Hang Sang   Music: Cacine Wong
Prod In-Charge: Yeung Kwok Fai   Prod Supervisor: Ise Cheng
Prod Manager: Brian Yip, Cora Cheng   Prod Design: Catherine Hun, Chan Pui Wah
Art Dir: Bruce Yu   Setting Design: Raymond Chan
Assistant Dir: Lo Kim Wah, Raymond Cheng
PC: Paka Hill Film Production Co. Dist: Tai Seng Video
Michelle Khan, Maggie Cheung, Anita Mui, Anthony Wong, Damian Lau, Takeshi Kaneshira, Lau Ching Wen
[1/2]**

The sequel follows the further exploits of the Heroic Trio, a film which will either appeal to you or not due to its unique style and format. From the beginning, the female trio of fighters are good friends and their problems are much more global. World War III has erupted and torn apart the fabric of civilization. In the aftermath, the most popular commodity is water (think a darker version of Tank Girl). Mui is occupied with taking care of her daughter and has given up her crime fighting days. Cheung is still the naughty girl of the group and steals water. Khan is stoically in the middle and transports water to needy areas.

Once again, the trio must don their costumes and help save the world. An evil villain is hoarding the water supply and lying about the city's water pipes. He uses henchman to consolidate his power and plans to overthrown the current president. The trio discover his plot and confront him. The battle is fast and furious, costing one of the trio her life. The villain is defeated, the president rescued, and water flows again through the pipes of the city. The film loses a few marks in originality and style from the original, but all three Hong Kong actresses do their best to entertain. If you enjoyed the first film then by all means catch the sequel.

Hidden Fortress, The
(1958) Samurai   B&W-126m   Japanese with English Subtitles   VA
Catalog #HID 030   Japan Retail: $19.95
Dir: Akira Kurosawa   Scr: Ryuzo Kikushima, Hideo Oguni, Shinobu Hashimoto, Akira Kurosawa   Prod: Akira Kurosawa, Masumi Fujimoto
DP: Kazuo Yamazaki   Music: Masaru Sato   Art Dir: Yoshiro Muraki, Kohei Ezaki
Lighting: Ichiro Inohara   PC: Toho Studios   Dist: Home Vision
Toshiro Mifune   General Rokurota Makabe
Misa Uehara   Lady Yukihime
Minoru Chiaki   Tahei
Kamatari Fujiwara   Matashichi
Susumu Fujita   Grateful Soldier

Takashi Shimura   Old General
Eiko Miyoshi   Old Woman
Toshiko Higuchi   Farmer's Daughter
Kichijiro Ueda   Girl-Dealer
[****]
You may have heard of this Kurosawa film when people refer to "Star Wars". George Lucas openly admitted he got some ideas from this masterpiece when he saw the film during his days as a student. Though the core story has similarities, Kurosawa's film is in a completely different realm of imagery and pacing. Once again, the 16th century is revisited for its turbulent civil wars and legends of samurais. A beautiful, spirited princess and her group must escape to a friendly province. They are pursued by an enemy warlord and his troops who post rewards. Secretly, the warlord desires the cache of gold, sixteen hundred pounds! She is escorted by a brave general (Mifune) and two bumbling men who are recruited as foot soldiers. One soldier is tall and his comrade is stout, they constantly bemoan their current state. The two men become separated, but later they are gladly reunited and continue their playful bickering. They are captured, but receive help from the most unlikely of places and complete their mission. The adventure sweeps you into a current of wonderful characters, tense action scenes, and an exciting period in Japan's rich history. The video is difficult to find at most retailers, but might appear at a film festival or during a course on Japanese/Kurosawa films.

High and Low
(1962) Crime C-142m   Japanese with English Subtitles   Japan
Retail: $19.95 Widescreen Available
Dir: Akira Kurosawa
Scr: Akira Kurosawa, Hideo Oguni, Ryuzo Kikushima, Eijiro Hisaita
Prod: Tomoyuki Tanaka, Ryuzo Kikushima   DP: Choichi Nakai, Takao Saito
Music: Masaru Sato   Art Design: Yoshiro Muraki   Lighting: Ichiro Inohara
PC: Toho Studios   Dist: Ingram International Films
(based on the novel King's Ransom by Ed McBain)
Toshiro Mifune   Kingo Gondo
Tatsuya Nakadai   Inspector Tokura
Kyoko Kagawa   Reiko, Gondo's Wife
Tatsuya Mihashi   Kawanishi
Yutaka Sada   Aoki
Kenjiro Ishiyama   Detective Taguchi
Tsutomu Yamazaki   Ginji Takeuchi
Takashi Shimura   Director
Susumu Fujita   Commissioner
Ko Kimura   Detective Arai
Takeshi Kato   Detective Nakao
Yoshio Tsuchiya   Detective Murata
Hiroshi Unayama   Detective Shimada
Koji Mitsui   Newspaperman
[****]
Long before Ron Howard directed Mel Gibson in Ransom, Kurosawa directed Mifune in High

and Low. A brilliant, taut story about a wealthy Japanese industrialist whose son is kidnapped by a group of criminals. Kingo Gondo is at odds with his fellow stockholders over the design of their new shoe line. In a risky move, Gondo borrows 150 million yen to buy a stock majority in National Shoes, leaving him in control of the company. On that same evening, he receives a call from a kidnaper claiming he has taken Gondo's son. The kidnaper demands 30 million yen, an amount that would ruin Gondo's plan to take over the shoe company. They are warned not to call the police and send the household into a frenzy. Then Gondo's son walks into the room and the call is considered a hoax, but is it? The son of Gondo's chauffeur is missing and was last seen wearing the same outfit as Gondo's son. A clever twist on the classic plot. Gondo calls the police and casually tells the chauffeur not to worry. As the police arrive and the investigation continues, little hope of capturing the kidnaper is available. As the chauffeur and Gondo's wife beg him to pay the ransom, Gondo refuses and the police detectives consider him heartless and greedy. Mifune is terribly torn between saving his shoe company and saving the life of a young boy who could easily have been his own son.

Rather than having the kidnaping be the primary focus of the film, Kurosawa breaks the film into two halves, before and after the ransom is paid. Once again, Kurosawa creates tension from a unique point of view. There is no high speed chase or gunfight, but the story evolves intelligently as dozens of detectives try to solve the mystery of the kidnaper. The officers admire Gondo's decision to pay the ransom, but his financial predicament has destroyed his future at National Shoes. The detectives provide around the clock protection and do their best to solve the case. An impressive scene within the police headquarters shows each division giving a thorough report about their investigation and piece together the mystery through flashbacks. Gondo's money is not retrieved in time and the bank's foreclose against his house and he loses everything. The rivals at National Shoes push him out of the company and his fortune is ruined, but Gondo maintains his humanity and dignity. His family is proud of his decision and stand by his side. Finally, the detectives get a lead and close in on their culprits. Only time will tell if they can capture the kidnapers and return the money to Gondo. A marvelous film that rivals many Hollywood productions of the era. A prime example of Kurosawa's gift with dramatic stories and his homage to America-style crime dramas. Regardless of your appreciation of Asian films, Kurosawa creates a film that will captivate and inspire any viewer.

High Risk
(1995) Kung-Fu   C-100m   Chinese with English Subtitles   Catalog #1852
Hong Kong   Retail: $79.98 Widescreen Available
Dir/Scr: Wong Jing Music: William Hu MAD: Corey Yuen
Dist: Tai Seng Video
Jet Li   Kit Lee
Jackie Cheung   Frankie Lane
Chingmy Yau, Valerie Chow, Charlie Young (Yeoh), Billy Chow, Kelvin Wong
[***]
This time Li plays second fiddle to Jackie Cheung who portrays a cocky superstar that supposedly does his own film stunts. The character is an amalgamation of movie stars Bruce Lee and Jackie Chan who really is famous for performing his own stunts. The film pokes fun at both characters while dealing up some wild action and comedy. Jackie is the hottest star in Asia, but in reality his good friend Jet Li does all the stunts while Jackie takes full credit. An attractive

reporter, the ever-lovely Chingmy Yau, tries to find and expose the truth. When her cameraman catches some video footage of a stunt, Yau notices something non-kosher. She starts to follow Jet Li around and gets in his hair on more than one occasion.

Jet Li is Kit "Guts" Lee, an ex-cop and demolitions expert who quit the police force after his son and a bus full of children were endangered. He decides to live in the shadow of superstar Jackie who once was a talented martial artist. Over time, Jackie's skills have dwindled and his confidence is non-existent. When the entire gang attends a film reception at a luxurious skyscraper, they get captured by an elite group of terrorists. Here at times, the film swings between absurdity and comic-book violence. The terrorists enter the building and kill all the reception workers and employees with a spray of machine gun fire. Cheung uses the dead bodies to cover himself from the bullets while escaping. Plenty of characters weave in and out of scenes, causing confusion among the hostages, terrorists, and film viewers. In true Die Hard fashion, Jet Li must outwit the criminals and save the hostages. In a hilarious fight, even Jackie must find it in himself to lend a hand and foot. This is Jet Li's answer to Jackie Chan's City Hunter. A complete parody of the action genre with plenty of Die Hard references which are never taken too seriously.

Hu-Du-Men   (Entrance from the Platform Side)
(1996) DramaC-100m   Chinese with English Subtitles
Catalog #ML 653   Hong Kong   Retail: $39.99
Dir: Shu Kei   Scr: Raymond To Kwok-Wai
Prod: Clifton Ko Chi-Sum   Ex. Prod: Raymond Chow
DP: Bill Wong Chung-Piu   Editor: Kwong Chi-Leung, Shu Kei
Music: Otomo Yoshihide   Sound Recordist: Tam Tak-Wing
Prod Manager: Tomme Li   Assistant Dir: Fruit Chan   Art Dir: Bill Lui
PC: Ko Chi Sum Film Co. Ltd.   Dist: Golden Harvest
Josephine Siao Fong-Fong, Anita Yuen Wing-Yee, Chung King-Fai, David Wu Tai-Wai,
Waise Lee Chi-Hung, Daniel Chan Hiu-Tung, Lee See-Kei, David Wu, Lee Heung-Gum
(based on the stageplay by Raymond To Kwok-Kai)
[*1/2]**

> "Hu-Du-Men is a term from Cantonese Opera. It refers to an imaginary line
> between the stage and the backstage area. When actors cross the Hu-Du-Men,
> they should forget themselves and become their roles."

Opening Card

Based on the opening statement from the film and the cover design, this film would seem like an exploration into the world of traditional Chinese opera theater and its enduring hardship. However, if you are looking for backstage scenes and intense training, better to check out Farewell My Concubine. Instead, Hu-Du-Men is a contemporary drama dealing with the life of female star Sum, wonderfully played by Josephine Siao.

A moving and interesting slice of life film that focuses on her private and public life behind the stage and on the stage. She is famous and best known for her portrayal of male characters. Now at 40, she ponders retirement, past decisions she made, and her family life. On stage, once she crosses the Hu-Du-Men, there are no such worries or problems. At home, her husband accuses her of being a callous wife and mother. Her step-daughter is having a relationship with another girl, but their homosexual relationship is never explored in any detail and not used as a cheap device for sexual tension. At work, a talented new actress has entered the troupe. She is touted as Sum's successor, but is troubled by an abusive father. Her boyfriend flies in from Medical School to offer support and love. He meets Sum who shockingly realizes he is the son she gave away in exchange to pursue her demanding career in theater. There won't be any revolutions, car chases, murders, or kung-fu scenes, but Siao's dynamic performance is honest, heartwarming, and vividly real. Seven years expired before the film was finally developed from Raymond To's stage play.

-I-

Iczer-One Vol. 1
(1985) Japanime   C-60m Japanese with English Subtitles   VA
Catalog #USR VD13 Japan Retail: $14.95
Dir/Scr/Character Design: Toshihiro Hirano   Original Story: Rei Aran
Music: Michiaki Watanabe   Mecha Design:Hiroaki Motoigi, Shinji Aramaki
Animation Dir: Narumi Kakinouchi, Masami Obari, Hiroaki Ogami
Art Dir: Yasushi Nakamura, Kazuhiro Arai
PC: Kubo Shoten/A.I.C.   Dist: U.S. Renditions
[***]
Japanese animation isn't for little children and I wouldn't recommend most of the titles for anyone under ten. Japanime is a mature art form that is best appreciated by teenagers and adults who are not easily offended by cultural differences. Iczer is a prime example of a good anime film that borders on American tolerance. Nudity and violence play a key part in the story as does excitement and a fast-paced story. In modern day Japan, a teenage girl named Nagisa is visited by an odd-looking woman (Iczer) with bizarre features. When the girl returns home, the planes of reality alter and creatures pour out of the wall and attack her. She runs to her parents who are brutally murdered. She starts to cry and scream as the deadly monsters approach her, but at the last minute is rescued by Iczer. The two become allies in their attempt to battle an alien race set on destroying the Earth. The Cthuwulf are led by a small glowing gold-colored child with demonic features inside an orb. Iczer and the Japanese girl must combine their life energies inside a powerful robot to save Earth. A massive battle erupts on the streets where no one is safe, but Iczer and Nagisa are determined to save the Earth.

Iczer-One Vol. 2
(1985) Japanime   C-48m Japanese with English Subtitles   VA
Catalog #USR VD14 Japan Retail: $14.95
Dir/Scr/Character Design: Toshihiro Hirano   Original Story: Rei Aran
Music: Michiaki Watanabe   Mecha Design:Hiroaki Motoigi, Shinji Aramaki
Animation Dir: Narumi Kakinouchi, Masami Obari, Hiroaki Ogami
Art Dir: Yasushi Nakamura, Kazuhiro Arai
PC: Kubo Shoten/A.I.C.   Dist: U.S. Rednditions
[***]
The second volume contains Act 3 and concludes the battle. Iczer defeats Booster Gold's minions and sets everything back to normal for the citizens of Earth. In a cute ending, Iczer reverses the flow of time and allows Nagisa to return to her everyday life without ever knowing

the truth of what happened. There are a few bizarre twists and turns which I will let you explore on your own. Though the film made splashes at anime conventions, Izcer is more than a decade old and shows signs of being outdated for modern viewers. For all you Iczer fans, you can continue their adventures in the three volume series Iczer-3 which continues the exploits of Iczer and friends as they fight the last remnants of Booster Gold's dominion who have survived and remained on Earth.

Idiot, The
(1951) DramaB&W-166m   Japanese with English Subtitles   VA
Catalog #NYV 05092Japan Retail: $29.95
Dir: Akira Kurosawa   Scr: Eijiro Hisaita, Akira Kurosawa   Prod: Takashi Koide
DP: Toshio Ubukata, Choichi Nakai   Editor: Takao Saito Music: Fumio Hayasaka
Art Design: So Matsuyama   PC: Shochiku   Dist: Ingram International Films
(based on the novel by Feodor Dostoyevsky)

Masayuki Mori	**Kinji Kameda, the Idiot**
Toshiro Mifune	**Denkichi Akama**
Setsuko Hara	**Taeko Nasu**
Takashi Shimura	**Ono, the Father**
Yoshiko Kuga	**Ayako Ono**
Chieko Higashiyama	**Satoki Ono, the Mother**
Minoru Chiaki	**Mutsuo Kayama**
Chiyoko Fumiya	**Noriko**
Kokuten Kodo	**Jyunpei**
Eiko Miyoshi	**Kayama's Mother**
Noriko Sengoku	**Takako**
Daisuke Inoue	**Kaoru**
Eijiro Yanagi	**Tohata**
Bokuzen Hidari	**Karube**
Mitsuyo Akashi	**Akama's Mother**

[***]

Director Akira Kurosawa attempts to faithfully recreate the story set down on paper by the Russian literary master Feodor Dostoyevsky. As Kurosawa maintains his faithfulness to the film, the cinematic quality of the film's narrative disintegrates into lengthy dialogues and dramatic pauses between the characters. To capture the Russian/European feel of the story, Kurosawa purposely cast northern Japan as a setting for the story. The scenic snow-covered countryside and western influences are evident in the style of architecture and dress. Kimonos give way to pants and overcoats, while tatami mats are replaced by tables and chairs. Mori is the idiot, a simple-minded man, who returns to his hometown after a stay at a mental hospital. When it is discovered that he has an inheritance, people's attitudes toward him change. His main dilemma is the desire and love he showers on a shrewd, conniving woman who seems mad and impossible to please. She expresses love and hatred for him while tormenting another wealthy and handsome suitor (Mifune). A bizarre love triangle develops which hints toward murder and betrayal. Due to the shifts in character and overbearing dialogue, the Idiot does not compel the narrative or allow the viewer to relate with characters on screen. Since the film has a drastic western appearance, the story falls short in appeal to western viewers who have seen similar stories done in a more timely fashion. The impulses and actions of the characters strike out violently and without warning, creating tense moments that lack resolve. The film lacks the nuances of humor and style which are found in other Kurosawa's films and appears to be a reflection on the director's personal attempt to be too faithful (restricted) to the story rather than let his own filmmaking style take control.

Ikiru   (To Live/Doomed/Living)
(1952) DramaB&W-142m   Japanese with English Subtitles   VA
Catalog #IKI 030   Japan Retail: $19.95
Dir: Akira Kurosawa   Scr: Akira Kurosawa, Hideo Oguni, Shinobu Hashimoto
DP: Asakazu Nakai   Music: Fumio Hayasaka   Art Design: So Matsuyama
Lighting: Shigeru Mori   PC: Toho Studios   Dist: Home Vision

Takashi Shimura	**Kanji Watanabe**
Nobuo Kaneko	**Mitsuo Watanabe**
Kyoko Seki	**Kazue Watanabe**
Miki Odagiri	**Toyo**
Kamatari Fujiwara	**Ono**
Makoto Koburi	**Klichi Watanabe**
Kumeko Urabe	**Tatsu Watanabe**
Yoshie Minami	**Hayoshi, the Maid**
Nobuo Nakamura	**Deputy Mayor**
Minosuke Yamada	**Saito**
Haruo Tanak	**Sakai**
Bokuzen Hidari	**Ohara**
Minoru Chiaki	**Noguchi**
Shinichi Himori	**Kimura**
Kazao Abe	**City Assemblyman**
Masao Shimizu	**Doctor**
Yunosuke Ito	**Novelist**
Ko Kimura	**Intern**
Atsushi Watanabe	**Patient**
Yatsuko Tanami	**Hostess**
Seiji Miyaguchi	**Gang Boss**
Daisuke Kato	**Gang Member**
Ichiro Chiba	**Policeman**
Toranosuke Ogawa	**Park Section Chief**
Akira Tani	**Old Man in Bar**

[****]

A masterpiece studying the simplicities of human nature from Japanese director Kurosawa. Very different from his standard samurai films, the story deals with a typical Japanese businessman (Shimura in a starring role) who discovers he has terminal cancer. Breaking away from his conformist life, he wishes to focus his last remaining days on building a playground for children. Ironically his death compels him to live a more rewarding and enriching life.

Kanji Watanabe is a government official who has spent the greater portion of his life working quietly at his office. He is always on time and rarely takes off for any reason. When a group of women come to his office to request a children's playground, they are dismissed to another branch office. The women end up traveling from one city bureau to another with each section chief claiming his jurisdiction didn't cover such issues. When Kanji discovers he is ill and doesn't have long to live, his entire life is suddenly transformed. He looks for compassion from the people closest to him, but his cold attitude toward life is returned onto him. His son and daughter-in-law are more concerned about borrowing money and living a better life without him and mistake his strange behavior for an illicit affair. His fellow officer workers don't offer much more compassion, except for a bubbly, cute girl who reminds you of a teenage Shirley Temple. After Kanji has stopped coming to work, she comes to his house and expresses her own desire to leave the office. He latches onto her, living off her own vivacious youth. She reveals her nickname for Watanabe, "All right...the mummy." He is shocked and saddened, realizing she is from a different generation. Eventually, Kanji looks for solace within himself, going through various stages of despondancy.

In a sudden shift, he is dead and the film's second half takes place at his funeral party and is dedicated to speculation on his recent actions. In a reflection of human society, other people take credit for the playground's accomplishment and downplay Watanabe's role. The film's second half is somber, bleak, and full of flashbacks that guide the viewer through the last remaining days of Watanabe. Only the viewer knows the truth and in the end Watanabe's legacy will pass on to the children who benefit from the playground.

Imp, The
(1996) Thriller   C-96m Chinese with English Subtitles   Type III
Catalog #2081   Hong Kong   Retail: $39.99
Dir: Ivan Lai   Scr: Sam Leong
Ex. Prod: Chua Lam Prod: Ivan Lai, Sam Leong
PC: Golden Harvest   Dist: Tai Seng Video
Peng Dan, Mark Cheng, Ruby Wong, Ishizuka Emiko, Cheung Lu, William Ho, Willie Wai, Lau Tik Chi, Ng Shui Ting
[**]

The Hong Kong film board does not use ratings classifications similar to the United States, but they do have a category class from Type I to Type III depending on the severity of nudity and violence in the film. The Imp falls in the latter category and surprisingly transforms itself from an interesting thriller into a Psycho-wannabe with an extra dose of sexual perversion which would made Alfred Hitchcock shake his head.

A beautiful woman is disturbed by dreams of her sister. She fears her sister has been murdered and traces her to the last known place. A television crew meets up with her and the group spend time together at an isolated inn in a small rural village. The crew are there to work, but tag along with the beautiful woman as she asks the locals a few questions. As the mystery unfolds, the tone of the film is eerie and creates a palpable tension. Sadly, the film's direction takes a turn for the worse and delves into a generic slasher/stalking mode. It doesn't take much time before members from the group start to disappear. In over-blown mayhem, the women are tied and raped by a maniacal doctor who dresses like his sister. The crazed sister is the innkeeper and together they teach wanderers a lesson in pain and horror. The sister tortures the male counterparts and her brother enjoys toying with the women. The end of the film has everyone captured, tied down, striped, and humiliated. Basically an excuse for sex and violence, the film will only appeal to fans of those genres. You won't find any major Hong Kong stars and the first half of the film appears tame and intriguing.

Infra-Man
(1976) Monster/Scifi C-92m Dubbed   PG   VA   Hong Kong
Dir: Hua-Shan   Scr: Peter Fernandez
Prod: Runme Shaw Editor: E.H. Glass   Sp. Fx: E.H. Glass
PC: Shaw Bros.
Li Hsiu-hsien Raymar "Infra-Man"
Wang Hsieh   Prof. Chang
Terry Liu   Princess Demon
Lin Wen-wei   Tu Ming
Yuan Man-tzu   Chan's Daughter
Tsen Shu-yi, Huang Chien-lung, Lu Sheng
[1/2]**
Decades before the popularity of Mighty Power Morphing Rangers hit the American airwaves, Asian children watched numerous shows dedicated to morphing heroes who battled skyscraper-height creatures. At first, Infra-Man may seem like a Japanese show but incorporates a lot more kung-fu than traditional Japanese scifi/monster shows. Surprisingly, this is a Shaw Brothers production that imitates the popular Japanese robot/monster movies of the era, featuring an all-Chinese cast. In the near future, the Earth is attacked by the diabolical Princess Dragon Mom who uses an army of monster mutants to subdue the planet. The relatively useless defense team of Earth creates Infra-man in a secret government laboratory. A Chinese scientist decides to risk the procedure and becomes Infra-man, a super-powerful costumed hero. He ventures out to battle an alien horde comprised of giant monsters. The sheer lunacy of giant monsters doing martial arts in colorful rubber suits make this films a hokey load of fun, especially for fans of Japanese scifi shows like Dynaman, Power Rangers and Ultraman.

In the Realm of the Senses
(1976) Drama: Erotic   C-105m   NC-17 Japanese with English Subtitles
Catalog #FLV 1031 France/Japan Retail: $19.95
Dir: Nagisa Oshima   Scr: Nagisa Oshima   Pro: Anatole Dauman
DP: Hideo Ito, Kenichi Okamoto   Editor: Keiichi Uraoka
Music: Minoru Miki Art Design: Jusho Toda
Set Designer: Shigenori Shimoishizaka, Dai Arakawa
Makeup: Koji Takemura   Costumes: Jusho Toda   Dist: Fox Lorber Home Video
Tatsuya Fuji   Kichi-zo
Eiko Matsuda   Sada
Aio Nakajima   Toku
Meika Seri   Maid Matsuko
Taiji Tonoyama   Old Beggar
Hiroko Fuji   Maid Tsune
Naomi Shiraishi   Geisha Yaeji
Kyoko Okada   Hangyoku
Kikuhei Matsunoya Hohkan

Yasuko Matsui	Manageress of Inn
Kyoji Kokonoe	Ohmiya
Kazue Tomiyama	Fat Maid
Kanae Kobayashi	Old Geisha Kikuryu
Akiko Koyama	Geisha

[**1/2]

Art or pornography...depends on your point of view in many ways. However, Oshima's film is not without controversy. Banned by certain festivals and panned by moral critics, the film has received mixed reviews throughout its lifespan. There is no denying that the film is an experiment in sexual boundaries and that the scenes are very graphic in nature and can be interpreted on various levels by the individual. What is evident on the screen is a torrid relationship between a young prostitute and her wild male counterpart. The film follows their sexual liaison over time, but what really becomes evident is that the majority of the film comprises of sexual intercourse. She is shunned by her fellow workers and enters the man's life as a sexual servant "geisha". The scenes are created to establish a certain intimacy between the characters, since their insatiable lust is fed upon from each other. When the man starts to strain, there is one scene where he rapes the old woman of the inn. She is not satisfied with sharing him with anyone and undergoes an emotional decision. In a scene familiar in tabloid papers, she removes him of his manhood. A difficult film to watch. The viewer should tread with extreme caution.

Instructors of Death (Martial Club)
(1981) Kung-Fu   C-100m   Dubbed
Catalog #SB 1040   Hong Kong   Retail: $19.99
Dir: Liu Chia Liang   Scr: I Kuang Mona Fong
DP: Ao Chih Chun   Editor: Chiang Hsing Lung, LiYeh Hai   Music: Eddie H. Wang
Prod Manager: Chen Li Hua   Art Dir: Johnson Tsao
Assistant Dir: Huang Pa Ching   MAD: Liu Chia Liang
PC: Shaw Bros.
Gordon Liu   Wong Fei Hung
Wang Lung Wei, Mai Te Lo, Hui Ying Hung, Ku Feng, Hsiao Hou, Mai Te Lo
[***1/2]

An entertaining addition into the Wong Fei Hung series by veteran director Liu Chia Liang, starring Gordon Liu as a young Fei Hung. Though hundreds of Wong Fei Hung films were produced, Liu Chia Liang realized few of them dealt with Wong as a teenager/young adult. The confrontation begins when a rival school attacks Wong's best friend's school at a lion dance ceremony. Hoping to mediate peace, Wong Kei Ying (Fei Hung's father) intervenes to bring peace between the two schools. Martial arts academies are notorious for their vicious rivalry and undying passion to be the finest. After a rough peace is established, the rival (evil) school secretly plans to get back at Wong and his best friend.

In the meantime, Wong and his friend practice, visit brothels, and try to prove who's better in kung-fu. Their friendly rivalry gets carried away when Wong's friend is almost killed. Wong is able to meet any challenge, but then the rivals recruit a kung-fu master from the North, portrayed by veteran villain Wang Lung Wei. Wang usually plays ruthless villains, but in a rare cinematic moment, his character is not a villain. Wang is a noble, misguided master deceived into performing treachery. At the end, he learns to respect Wong and calls off the fight, returning to his home in Northern China to the dismay of the rivals. Though the story doesn't contain any deaths, Liu Chia Liang proves that a high body count is not necessary to make an exciting martial arts film. The charming performances of Gordon Liu, Wang, Mai, and Ying Hung add tremendously to the enjoyment of the film which mixes comedic elements cleverly into the action scenes. The highpoint is the climatic duel between Wong and Wang which starts in an alleyway. As the fighters continue to push themselves deeper down the alley, the walls close in to a tight fit. Both fighters must adapt their techniques to fight in such a narrow berth and Wang demonstrates his flexibility by doing a horizontal split against the wall while standing on one leg. A great classic kung-fu film from Shaw Brothers and director Liang. A must see for any Wong Fei Hung/martial arts fans.

Iria: Zeiram the Animation
(1994) Japanime   C-60m Japanese with English Subtitles   VA
Catalog # USM 1369 Japan Retail: $29.95
Dir: Tetsurou Amino   Original Work: Keita Amemiya
Scr: Tetsurou Amino (Episode 1), Naruhisa Arakawa (Episode 2)
Storyboard: Gen Dojaga (Episode 2)   Visual Concept: Keita Amemiya
Original Character Design: Masakazu Katsura   Character Designer: Ryunosuke Otonashi
Music: Yoichiro Yoshikawa
English Version - Ex. Prod: John O'Donnell   Production   Coordinator: Stephanie Shalofsky   Translation: Neil Nadelman
PC: Crowd/Bandai Visual/Mitsubishi Corporation/Banpresto
Dist: U.S. Manga Corps
[***]
Iria is a bounty hunter apprentice who takes a licking and keeps on ticking. She proves herself by saving some kidnap victims and capturing their kidnappers to the chagrin of a local bounty hunter. She is tough, resourceful, and totally modern. A perfect example of a super cool heroine. The adventure of a lifetime starts when she escorts her brother, bounty hunter elite Gren, and their boss, Bob, on an important mission for the Tedan Tippedai Corporation. They board a drifting spaceship and discover a brutal massacre. In an exciting action sequence, Gren and Iria battle against an ancient and dangerous lifeform brought on board the spaceship. Escaping from the explosion on board the spaceship, Iria lands on the planet of Taowajan. She meets a group of street kids, befriends a child named Kei, looks for her missing brother, and searches for a way to get back home. Unfortunately, the monstrous Zeiram, wounded, also escapes the destroyed spaceship and lands on the planet. Iria must prove her skills and defeat Zeiram before a planet of innocent people are murdered.
The adventures don't end here, but continue as Iria battles against the indestructible Zeiram in future episodes. A compilation video is also available as one inclusive story, 162 minutes.

Iron & Silk
(1990) Drama C-94m English   PG   VA
Catalog # VHS 68982   Japan Retail: $19.95
Dir: Shirley Sun   Scr: Shirley Sun, Mark Saltzman
Prod: Shirley Sun   DP: James Hayman Editor: Geraldine Peroni, James Y. Kwei

Music: Michael Gibbs   Prod Design: Calvin Tsao   Set Design: Boryana Varbanov
PC: Shirley Sun Production in association with Tokyo Broadcasting International, Inc.
Dist: Live Home Video
(based on the book by Mark Saltzman)

Mark Salzman	Teacher Mark
Pan Qingfu	Teacher Pan
Jeannette Lin Tsui	Teacher Hei
Vivian Wu	Ming
Sun Xudong	Sinbad
Zheng Guo	Mr Song
To Funglin	Old Sheep
Hu Yun	Fatty Du
Dong Hangcheng	Teacher Cai
Lu Zhiquan	Teacher Li
Xiao Ying	April
Yang Xiru	Dr. Wang
Zhuang Genyua	Teacher Xu
Jiang Xihong	Teacher Zhang

[***1/2]
The true life story of Mark Saltzman, an American teacher, who went to mainland China and returned a master in Chinese kung-fu. The film is fascinating and has a real-life quality of kung-fu not seen in most studio productions. Before I get to far, this movie deals with more issues than just martial arts. The performances are sincere and honest. The film opens with Mark's narration and his journey into mainland China. As a child, he had a fascination with Chinese culture and martial arts, making his life a quest to learn more about the people and their history. Filled with American optimism and determination, he arrives as an English school teacher and quickly confronts an east versus west mentality. He falls in love with a Chinese woman and learns wushu (kung-fu) from a renowned master, but complications set in because of his race and the "hostile" cultural climate of the nation toward Westerners. Saltzman's narration is simple but poignant and for anyone who has ever had a fascination with Asian culture, his actions will seem very close to home. He wants to become a part of Chinese society, but because of his race, he is treated as an outsider. At one point, he is banned from meeting with his sifu since they believe martial arts is a defense secret. One of the few films to attempt to show the real side of Chinese martial arts. Definitely worth viewing for those who have an honest interest in Asian culture and martial arts and are looking for a heartwarming, down to earth tale about a man in a new country. Since it is based on a true story, the drama is subdued at times and the film does not contain wild kung-fu scenes, but the film is full of wonderful glimpses into real kung-fu from Mainland China. Extra credibility is added by real-life performances from Mark Saltzman and Master 'Iron' Pan who later immigrated to Canada.

Iron Monkey (The Young Wong Fei Hung)
(1993) Kung-Fu   C-86m English Dubbed/Chinese with English Subtitles
Catalog #1463   Hong Kong   Retail: $39.99   Widescreen Available
Dir: Yuen Woo Ping Scr: Tsui Hark, Elsa Tang, Lau Tai Mok
Prod: Tsui Hark   Ex. Prod: Raymond Chow, Wang Ying Hsiang

DP: Arthur Wong
Editor: Mak Chi Sin
Music: Wu Wai Lap, Johnny Njo
Art Director: Ringo Cheung   Prod Manager: Ho Lai Sheung
MAD: Yuen Cheung Yan, Yuen Shun Yi, Ku Huen Chiu
Dist: Tai Seng Video
Donnie Yen   Wong Kei Ying
Yu Rong Guang   Iron Monkey
Jean Wong   Iron Monkey's Assistant
Yang Yee Kwan
[****]

Excellent (unofficial) prequel to the Once Upon a Time in China series, introducing a number of elements that are relevant to later Wong Fei Hung films. There is also an older film with the same title starring Chen Kuan Tai, but has nothing to do with this film.

A talented cast of performers come together in an exciting and touching story in China before the turn of the century. Masterfully blending a strong story, endearing characters, and incredible martial arts sequences from Yuen Woo Ping and family, viewers are in for a treat when young Wong Fei Hung and his father are wrongfully arrested by the government. This leads to an adventure that will change their lives forever. A local doctor (Yu Rong Guang), known for his wisdom and philanthropy, is by night the masked hero Iron Monkey, a Chinese Robin Hood who steals from the rich and gives to the poor. A visiting doctor and kung-fu master, Wong Kei Ying, and his twelve-year old son Wong Fei Hung are arrested by the corrupt governor. After seeing Kei Ying and Iron Monkey duel, the governor orders Kei Ying to capture the criminal or his son will be branded. Nobly portrayed by Donnie Yen, Kei Ying searches for the Iron Monkey but discovers the townspeople are hostile to him and sympathetic to Iron Monkey. Despondent, hungry, and with his son imprisoned, Kei Ying's only friend is a beautiful woman who offers him a meal and a warm place to stay. She is Orchid, the kind assistant of the local doctor. The two heroes eventually team up and battle the evil monk who destroyed Shaolin Temple. Plenty of great stunts with exaggerated kung-fu mixed in with traditional kung-fu will delight you as a cast of talented stars: men, women, and children battle throughout the film. The choreography is wonderful, the use of music and leitmotifs pushes the drama with the right amount of humor and human moments transforming this film into an instant classic.

The following is a detailed review of the historical kung-fu masterpiece Iron Monkey.

In a Chinese town governed by a lecherous, lazy governor, a figure known as the Iron Monkey steals from the rich and gives to the poor. He doesn't wear green tights and shoot arrows, but he does wear ninja-black and shoots everything else: metals balls, spikes, flash powder. He especially takes delight in stealing from the cowardly governor and his bevy of concubines. Under the governor's command is a militia of soldiers and four renegade Shaolin monks, but they are no match for the Iron Monkey. The humiliated and injured soldiers seek solace at Doctor Yu's (Yu Rong Guang), a respected physician who provides medicine to the poor at no charge. The Head of the Guards, Master Fox who plays a comical and sympathetic Manchurian soldier, admires Doctor Yu very much and doubts the governor's reliability. The governor gives orders to arrest anyone who vaguely resembles the iron monkey. Humorously, men are arrested who sell monkey oil, scratch like a monkey, or have monkey written on their store signs. Wong Kei Ying, a respected martial artist and medical expert from Fushan, and his young son Wong Fei

Hung are visiting the city for supplies. A bunch of pick pockets try to steal from Kei Ying, but fail in their attempt. The soldiers amazed at the martial arts demonstration arrest the two Wongs for disturbing the peace. In the governor's court, dozens of suspects await trial. The governor plans to torture them hoping to force the real Iron Monkey to appear. Kei Ying stands firmly against the injustice and speaks out. Angered, the governor orders Kei Ying's son to be tortured. When the real Iron Monkey appears, the soldiers attack with little success. Instead Kei Ying battles the Iron Monkey to a stalemate and proves his merit to the governor. Assuming the Iron Monkey is a criminal, Kei Ying agrees to capture him in exchange for their release. The governor accepts and keeps Wong Fei Hung as collateral. Kei Ying searches the city, but discovers that the local townspeople are very hostile toward him and supportive of Iron Monkey. Not even being able to rent a room or buy some buns, Kei Ying results to eating garbage. Seeing this sad act, a young woman named Orchid offers him assistance. Meanwhile Fei Hung gets ill and is transferred to the doctor's house. Father and son are united by the doctor and his assistant, Orchid, who was saved from the brothels by Doctor Yu. Since then, he has taught her his style of kung-fu and also shows Wong Fei Hung how to use the staff. In a moment of humor, Doctor Yu and Orchid disguise themselves as government inspectors and rob the governor blind. When the real inspector arrives in town, he quickly removes the governor and takes charge. The inspector is an ex-Shaolin grand monk who betrayed and helped destroy Shaolin Temple. Using his two assistants, he sets a trap for the Iron Monkey, injures him, and follows him onto the nightly rooftops. On the rooftops, Kei Ying spots the evil monk and mistakes him for the Iron Monkey and attacks. Kei Ying, a Shaolin disciple, vows to kill the evil monk using his Shaolin Fist and famous No Shadow Kick, a recurring Wong kick in all the films. The evil monk manages to injure Kei Ying who then escapes. The injured Kei Ying and Iron Monkey both return to the doctor's hospital where Kei Ying discovers the truth. At first, he plans to arrest the Iron Monkey and clear his name, but his son and Orchid try to stop him. Slowly, Kei Ying realizes who true enemies and friends are and decides to go into hiding with the injured Iron Monkey. The soldiers search all the hospitals for any injured people, and when the renegade monks arrive at Yu's place, they start to accost Orchid. Wong Fei Hung enters the fray with a staff and beats the lecherous monks, but is then beaten himself by a female assassin working under the evil grand monk. Kei Ying, Orchid, and Iron Monkey team up to rescue Wong Fei Hung and destroy the evil monk and his cohorts. Even Master Fox refuses to torture Wong Fei Hung and allies with the heroes. There are some amazing effects/flying sequences, but they don't take away from the beautiful choreography and incredible martial arts prowess of the actors. The amazing aerial climax, one of the finest in martial arts cinema, takes place atop ten foot poles over a burning pool of fire. At the end, heroes say their fond good-byes and a young Wong turns and smiles for the adventure has brought him closer to his father. Highly recommended and one of my personal favorites. A perfect place to start watching kung-fu films, and definitely recommended as the first film to see in the Wong Fei Hung series.

Iron Monkey 2
(1994) Kung-Fu   C-93m Chinese with English Subtitles
Catalog #NCL 8010 Hong Kong   Retail: $39.99
No English Credits Available
Donnie Yen
[1/2]**

For those viewers who enjoyed the original Iron Monkey and are expecting a worthy sequel, take caution. The only similarity is actor Donnie Yen who portrays a hero named Iron Monkey which has nothing to do with the original character, time, or setting. Unfortunately, the film does not contain any historical reference to Wong Fei Hung, and though charismatic Donnie Yen supports himself well, the film is disappointing in comparison. Introducing extraneous characters slows the story's pacing and Donnie Yen only appears in brief segments of the film and doesn't shine in the limelight. Instead, the supporting characters take up a good portion of the film. The time era is moved up to the 20th Century around the 1920's. A local town is ruled by a ruthless gangster named Tiger Yu who has the local police in his pocket and the diabolic westerners as his allies. The Japanese and Europeans are seen as interloping villains who toy with the Chinese as they please, even engaging on a mad drive through town killing people for sport. It is up to Donnie Yen and his group of freedom fighters to stop Tiger Yu from terrorizing the town. This would have been a simple enough story, but then extra elements are thrown in with mixed results. A local con man and his girlfriend owe money to the mob. He pretends to be Iron Monkey to cash in on his fame and gets paid a sum of money to rid the town of Tiger Yu. The mysterious woman who hired the fake Iron Monkey pops up now and then necessitating the need for a rescue. Of course, incognito Iron Monkey sees to it that the money goes to the poor and keeps a watchful eye on the two youths. Also the son of a freedom fighter enters town in search of his blind father. The son who is a master of martial arts ends up befriending the cons who trick him with all sorts of deceit. They convince him to rob Tiger Yu's weapon shipment and attack the real Iron Monkey. Unknown to the freedom fighter, his blind father and Iron Monkey were patriots in the past who fought for a common goal. Somehow the con and his girlfriend join Tiger Yu's men, but when Yu's Japanese friends sexually harass his girlfriend he seeks the Iron Monkey and the freedom fighter for help. In traditional fashion, the heroes converge on the enemy mansion and battle to the death. Basically the film has a number of good fight scenes that are fast and entertaining with the standard hi-flying leaps and kicks. The comic moments from the con man are appealing at times, but too many additional scenes and needless characters bog down and disrupt the overall dynamics of the film.

-J-

Jet Li Collection:
Part of the Dimension Films Jet Li package, which are older films remastered and reedited for American audiences. In general, I recommend the remasters over the original versions, since they offer English dialogue over subtitles, a modern soundtrack, easier availability, lower retail cost, and often a cleaner editing style with the omission of over-the-top violence and cultural humor. Not to say Americans are more demanding viewers, but studios are well aware of what American audiences find appealing and not so appealing in their action films. Often times, a film's pleasure is enhanced when the necessity of difficult subtitling is omitted and the story is allowed to flow easily and quickly.

Jet Li's The Defender (see The Bodyguard from Beijing)

Jet Li's The Enforcer (see My Father the Hero)

Jet Li's Twin Warriors (see Tai Chi Master)

Journey of Honor
(1991) Samurai/Adventure C-107m   English   VA   Catalog #052756
Japan Retail: $19.99
Dir: Gordon Hessler Scr: Nelson Gidding Prod: Sho Kosugi
DP: John Connor   Editor: William Butler   Music: John Scott
Prod Design: Adrian H. Gorton
PC: Sho Kosugi Corporation
(based on a story bu Sho Kosugi)
Sho Kosugi   Prince Mayeda
David Essex   Don Pedro
Toshiro Mifune   Tokugawa Ieyasu
Christopher Lee   King Philip
Kane Kosgui   Yorimune
John Rhys-Davies El Zaidan
Polly Walker   Cecilia
Nijiko Kiyokawa, Masashi Muta, Ken Sekiguchi, Naoto Shigemizu, Stevan Minja
[***]
Ninja legend Sho Kosugi hangs up his black mask and dons more regal clothes for this adventurous epic on the high seas. The early 17th century in Japan was a popular period for films dealing with the Shogun, samurais, and European powers. Kosugi plays Prince Mayeda, the royal son, who must travel to Spain and purchase weapons for his father's battle for unification. This is an exciting and crucial period in Japanese history, since Japan will no longer be a loose community of warlords but a powerful nation unified under one Shogun (military general with the real power) and one emperor (figurehead). Kosugi encounters plenty of problems on his oceanic voyage and must battle the evil Don Pedro who will do anything to foil the prince's plan. Kosugi meets some helpful allies and eventually gets his weapons, but must be cautious of betrayal and counterattack. Along his journey, there are plenty of delightful cameos and interracial romance sparked by the lovely Lady Cecilia. Look for Kosugi's son Kane and Rhys-Davies as the helpful El Zaidan. Also the last time I saw Christopher Lee and Mifune in the same film together, they were wonderful in a delightful little farce called "1941". The film is a valid attempt to offer adventure and excitement without alienating viewers with too much historical drama. Plenty of lavish costumes, historical sets, high seas theatrics, and action scenes will delight viewers who enjoy the old Errol Flynn or Douglas Fairbanks pirate/swashbuckling films.

Judge
(1991) Japanime   C-50m Japanese with English Subtitles   VA
Catalog # USM 1078 Japan Retail: $29.95
Dir: Hiroshi Negishi Original Story: Fujihiko Hosono
DP: Akihiko Takahashi   Music: Toshiro Imaizumi
Art Designer: Chisato Sunakawa   Art Dir: Tetsunori Oyama Chief   Animator: Shin Matsuo
Created by Sony Music Entertainment   PC: Animate Film   Dist: Kiss Films

Kaneto Shiozawa	Hoichiro Oma "The Judge"
Miki Ito	Nanase
Tomomichi Nishimura	Defense Lawyer
Kazunari Hutamata	Koji Kawamata
Hideyuki Hori	Ryuichi Murakami

[**1/2]

A mature story dealing with the legal system from beyond the grave. A mild-mannered businessman (Clark Kent-Superman duality) is the butt of jokes and bullied for his shy demeanor. He is protected by a pretty, spunky co-worker who enjoys visiting his apartment and arguing with his pet parrot. When a woman at the company is accused of embezzlement, she leaves a message at his house to contact the branch boss. He does, but the branch boss assaults him and terrorizes him to keep his mouth shut. Later, her dead body is discovered and the unconcerned boss prepares for his trip to America. While driving his sporty Audi 80, a flock of birds crash into his windshield and his car swerves off the road. As he struggles out of the vehicle, a long-robed figure stands before him. The Judge is tall and imposing with demonic features and dark-hair. He passes his verdict and punishes the culprit in a very graphic manner. The guilt-ridden boss tries to escape, but supernatural justice has a very long arm.

Everyday life resumes, but the Judge's work is never done when he discovers the corporate head is involved in the murder of an executive. The task seems simple, but the corporate head escapes punishment through the involvement of a defense attorney who possesses spiritual powers. When the two men reach a spiritual stalemate, the Ten Kings of Hell are summoned to pass judgment. The dead are called as witnesses, but it is the corporate head's own guilt and his inner soul which causes his downfall. The Judge falls in the mid-stream of well-done and entertaining Japanime with a story that is quite clever and unique. The characters are very traditional and could have used some more development in the limited time span of the film. The character that stands out is the spiritual defense attorney who walks a fine line between profit and justice. The film contains mature elements, but is not overly violent or sexual in content. Recommended for fans of the genre who especially like topics on the supernatural.

Ju Dou
(1991) DramaC-98m Mandarin with English Subtitles   VA
Catalog # VHS 68983   China/Japan Retail: $19.99
Dir: Zhang Yimou   Scr: Lui Heng
Prod: Zhang Wenze, Hu Jian, Yasuyoshi Yokuma
DP: Gu Changwei, Yang Lun   Editor: Du Yuan   Music: Xia Ru-jin
Art Design: Fei Jiupeng, Xia Ru-jin   Costumes: Zhi-an Zhang
PC: Tokuma Shoten Publishing Co., Ltd., Tokuma Communications Co., Ltd., China Film Co-Production Corporation, China Film Export & Import Corporation
Dist: Live Home Video (Miramax Films)

Gong Li	Ju Dou
Li Bao-Tian	Yang Tian-qing
Li Wei Yang	Jinshan
Zhang Yi	Yang Tianbai as infant
Zhen Ji-an	Yang Tianbai as youth

[***1/2]

A landmark film that shook the film community and stirred up some old guard protest in China. This is the first major film to bring the beautiful Gong Li's presence to American audiences. Director Zhang shakes traditional views and pokes at old guard mentality in this passionate film. Gong Li is forced into marriage with a rich merchant who is abusive and domineering. He is much older than her and consistently approaches her for sexual favors. She turns inward, but finds love in the hands of a worker who treats her kindly and shares her dreams of a better life. The two develop a secret relationship that results in the birth of a child. The merchant is angered, but his protests are eliminated when he suffers a serious accident. The crippled merchant is left in the care of Gong Li and her lover. Roles are reversed and the master becomes the slave, but in an ironic twist of fate, situations become optimistic for the merchant when the child believes the merchant is his real father. Gong and her lover continue their love and ignore the old man who secretly plots to exact his revenge. When the son gets older, he exacts revenge on what he believes is his cheating mother and her suitor. A drama filled with passion, tension, and betrayal. Zhang carefully weaves his tale and develops his characters, so that we care and share their dreams and fears. Critically acclaimed and highly recommended.

July 13th   (1001 Ways to Kill Yourself)
(1996) Horror   C-95m Chinese with English Subtitles   Catalog #1961
Hong Kong   Retail: $79.98
Dir: Wellson Chin   Dist: Tai Seng Video
David Wu (David Ng), Michelle Reis, Wong Tze Wah
[**]
As a long-time fan of horror films, I'm always looking out for new tales of the macabre and ghastly. Unfortunately, I don't get too many chances to see any serious Asian horror films. Sure they make them, but not in the abundance of martial arts/action films or comedies/romances. Hoping July 13th would break that trend, I rented the film and sat down one evening. David Wu plays a detective investigating the mysterious suicide of a teenage girl. Tracking down clues and interviewing friends, the dead girl appeared to have a normal life. He and his cute partner who happens to be his ex-lover are on the case and find a witness to the girl's suicide. The film is promising at first, creating a chilling and mysterious sensation with the introduction of the young female witness who claims she saw an elderly woman pushing the teenage girl in front of the train. No one else has seen the woman and the officers doubt her credibility. Eerie things begin to happen and their witness is in jeopardy. After another bizarre murder, the film takes a drastic spiral into absurdity and tedium when the officers meet an ex-investigator who worked on a similar case but went insane. They follow his lead and encounter the spirits of dead women. Piecing together the clues, they realize a book was involved in all the murders and trace its purchase to a book store owned by an elderly woman. She had used the book and dark magic to create a death spell in hopes of bringing back a loved one. Overall, the film entertains in doses but fails to lock on a central theme, flipping back between horror, comedy, and romance. The constant bickering of the characters and red-herring chases get tiresome and redundant, so when the film ends it comes as a relief not a revelation.

-K-

Kabuto - See Raven Tengu Kabuto

Kagemusha (The Shadow Warrior)
(1980) Samurai   C-159m   Japanese with English Subtitles   PG   VA
Catalog #VHS 1109 Japan Retail: $19.95
Dir: Akira Kurosawa   Scr: Akira Kurosawa, Masato Ide
Prod: Akira Kurosawa   Ex. Prod: Akira Kurosawa, Masato Ide
DP: Takao Saito, Shoji Ueda, Kazuo Miyagawa, Asaichi Nakai
Music: Shinichiro Ikebe   Art Design: Yoshiro Muraki
PC: Toho-Kurosawa Production   Dist: 20th Century Fox

Tatsuya Nakadai	Shingen Takeda - Kagemusha
Tsutomo Yamazaki	Nobukado Takeda
Kenichi Hagiwara	Katsuyori Takeda
Kota Yui	Takemaru
Shuji Otaki	Yamagata
Hideo Murata	Baba
Daisuke Ryu	Oda Nobunaga
Kaori Momoi	Otsuyanokata
Jinpachi Nezu	Bodyguard

[****]

Kurosawa's dramatic and historical film revolves around the turbulent years before Japan was united into one nation under the Shogun's power. In the 1500's, Japan was a nation of one emperor and many warlords (daimyos) who fought over control of the nation. The emperor was without military power and the capital of Kyoto was vulnerable to attack. In the chaos, Takeda Shingen, arose to power as a fierce and shrewd leader. The Takeda Clan were known for its ferocity and brilliance in battle. Shingen's chief rivals are Oda Nobunaga and Tokugawa Ieyasu, actual characters from history. While attempting to capture Kyoto, Shingen steps out of his inner camp and plans to listen to a flute player within the barricaded castle. The garrison leader is a noble man, but an enemy guard takes advantage of the situation and shots Shingen. Quickly, the tides of war change and rumors circulate that Shingen is dead. The lords of the Takeda clan fear the repercussions of deflated morale among the elite troops. An idea is proposed, one that is too insane to comprehend but worth a chance in their dire situation. Earlier, a petty thief had been captured and arrested. His life was spared since he resembled Shingen. The lords decide to use this shadow warrior to rally the troops and convince their enemies of Shingen's immortality. The facade must convince everyone, including the lord's concubines, his soldiers, and even his own grandson. Not wanting to tip their position, Shingen's enemies send spies to discover the truth and they witness a bizarre burial ceremony at a quiet lake. Only time will tell if the false Shingen can hold together the mighty Takeda clan.

Kagemusha is an artistic film with the nature of classical literature. The film is not for fans of action films and though there are similarities to ""Braveheart"", most of the climatic battles take place off screen or with quick camera pans and cuts. The heart of the film is the political intrigue involving a single man, a criminal, who becomes the most powerful warlord in Japan. But his very pretense, consumes his own identity and he starts to believe in an illusion. When his disguise fails, the Takeda Clan is taken over by hot-headed Katsuyori who leads the clan into a failed military battle. This will open the historical annals and allow Oda Nobunaga and Tokugawa Ieyasu to seize power of Japan.

Kama Sutra
(1997) DramaC-113m   R   English   Catalog #VM 6478   India
Retail: $29.95
Dir: Mira Nair   Scr: Helena Kriel, Mira Nair
Prod: Mira Nair, Lydia Dean Pilcher (Trimark Pictures)
Ex Prod: Michiyo Yoshizaki   Co-Prod: Caroline Baron
DP: Declan Quinn   Editor: Kristina Boden   Music: Mychael Danna
Associate Prod: Dinaz Stafford, Tina Difeliciantonio
Prod Design: Mark Friedberg   Costume Design: Eduardo Castro
Dist: Trimark
Indira Varma   Maya
Sarita Choudhury   Tara
Ramon Tikaram   Jai Kumar
Naveen Andrews   Raj Singh
Rekha, Khalik Tyabji, Arundhati Rao, Surabhi Bhansali, Garima Dhup
[***1/2]

"The art of love is much more than the act itself."
Kama Sutra

Kama Sutra refers to the ancient Indian practice of sensual pleasure and ecstasy. Director Nair, acclaimed for her works dealing with Indian culture (Salaam Bombay, Mississippi Masala), tackles one of the most misunderstood topics to emerge from India. This film is not a sexual how-to guide or softcore pornography, but a deeply moving film about love and commitment. Beautifully photographed and authentically recreated, the film draws the viewer into another time and place, quite exotic and fascinating for the average American.

In 16th century India, Maya is a perfect girl who blossoms into a beautiful woman. Living under a wealthy household, she is raised as a servant and close companion to the master's daughter, Tara. Tara's older brother who is physically deformed loves Maya, but her feelings for him are platonic. In no time, Tara grows to despise Maya, jealous of her beauty, grace, and skills in dancing. Tara's attitude toward her long-time companion becomes cruel and antagonistic. On Tara's wedding night, Maya gets her revenge by sleeping with her husband to be...an Indian King, Raj Singh. With whispered words, Maya tells Tara, "All my life I have lived of your used things. But now...something I have used is yours forever." This captures the rift that divides the two childhood friends into bitter enemies. Maya is expelled from the mansion and meets a handsome stone-architect, Jai Kumar. He falls in love with her beauty and takes her to the home of a woman who teaches the Kama Sutra. When Jai's career is disrupted because of his love for Maya, he chooses his career over her. Distraught and tired of being used by men, she decides that she wants to use them. She studies the art of the Kama Sutra, mastering the various techniques and transforms herself. King Raj discovers her and makes her a concubine which infuriates Tara who then attempts to commit suicide. Jai and Maya rekindle their passionate romance, but when they are discovered, King Raj orders the stone-cutter to be executed. Maya tries everything in her powers to cancel the execution, but Raj's obsession with sex, drugs, and pleasures have corrupted his ability to rule. Tara's brother contacts the mighty Sultan and then leads an army against Raj's palace, hoping to save the women he loves.

Nair delicately unfolds the film by layers, allowing us to glimpse the erotic world of the Kama

Sutra, but also to touch upon deeper social issues within India. Though the time setting is quite old, the problems and issues are quite contemporary.

Kid With the Golden Arm
(1979) Kung-Fu   C-100m   Dubbed
Catalog #SB-1052   Hong Kong   Retail: $19.99
Dir: Chang Cheh   Scr: I Kuang, Chang Cheh   Ex. Prod: Runme Shaw
Prod: Mona Fong   DP: TsaoHui Chi   Editor: Chiang Hsing Lung, LiYeh Hai
MAD: Chang Sheng PC: Shaw Bros.
Kuo Chui, Chiang Sheng, Lo Meng, Lu Feng, Sun Chien, Pan Ping Chang, Wei Pai, Wang Lung Wei
[***]
Exciting and colorful Chang-gang film, reminiscent of many western classics. A shipment of gold is loaded on a wagon and escorted by lawmen to a famine plagued area for relief. Along the way a ruthless group of bandits are determined to capture the cache of gold. Each character in the film is a master of a certain style and introduced in the main credits. Lo Meng is the powerful leader of the bandits, aka the Kid with the Golden Arms. His arms are incredibly muscular and defined to the point where no blade can cut him. His lieutenants include a spear expert, a man with a metal plate on his head, and an expert with body armor and a metal fan. On the side of good, a drunken bum (Kuo Chui) follows discreetly behind the lawmen. He is a government agent in disguise. The captain of the guards and his lawmen are also escorted by a group of famous heroes. Including a Wu Tang sword expert, his beautiful female companion, and two wild ax-toting brothers. As they get closer and closer to the relief settlement, their numbers dwindle from surprise attacks and booby traps - poisoned water, spikes, and rigged landscape. It is finally revealed that the commander had hoped everyone would die so he could steal the shipment for himself. Kuo manages to beat him, but Lo is blinded which convinces him to retire and amend his wicked ways. Then he is killed by the female swordfighter as an act of revenge for the murder of her boyfriend. The film is highlighted by a number of great acrobatic fight scenes with and without weapons. Well-choreographed stunts and interesting characters make this a very entertaining adventure, especially for fans of Chang's other films.

Kiki's Delivery Service
(1989) Japanime: Family   C-102m   Dubbed/Japanese with English Subtitles
Japan Retail: $19.99
Dir: Hayao Miyazaki
Scr: Hayao Miyazaki, Jack Fletcher III & John Semper (US version)
Prod: Hayao Miyazaki
Ex. Prod: Morihisa Takagi, Yasuyoshi Tokuma, Mikihiko Tsuzuki, Jane Schonberger (US)
DP: Shigeo Sudimura   Editor: Takeshi Seyama
Music: Jo Hisaishi, Paul Chihara (English only)
Prod Design: Hinoshi Ono Sound: Shuji Inoue, Ernue Sheesley (US)
Spec FX: Kaoru Tanifuji   Character Design: Katsuya Kondo
PC: Nippon TV Network, Studio Ghibli, Tokuma Shoten
Dist: Toei Company Ltd., Buena Vista Home Video (US)
Minami Takayama   Kiki/Ursula

Rei Sakuma	Jiji
Mieko Nobusawa	Kokiri
Keiko Toda	Osono
Kappei Yamaguchi	Tombo
Haruko Kato	Madame
Hiroko Seki	Barsa
Koichi Miura	Okino

[****]

A truly entertaining story about the coming of age of a young girl who happens to be an apprentice witch. In this case, witches are just like everyone else except they have their own unique cultural heritage and abilities. And meeting a witch would be the same as meeting a Jewish girl or an Amish girl. Beautifully animated and combining a European sense of architecture, the story begins as Kiki reaches her 13th birthday. A rite of passage is necessary before adulthood, so Kiki plans to leave home and spend an year abroad on her own merits. Her parents are worried, but they and the entire village gather outside to watch her depart with words of encouragement. With broom in hand and her pet familiar, a black cat, she sets off into the great world ahead of her. She soars with power, but bounces into a tree before disappearing. Her parents share a tense look and hope for the best. From that point on, we accompany Kiki as she tries to make the best of her new life. Along the way, she meets another young witch of 13 who has almost finished her rite of passage. She is a fortune-teller and encourages Kiki to find a trade. Hoping to find a town without a witch, she flies on and lands in a bustling city, but causes a ruckus on her first day. Witches may exist, but still the sight of a girl flying on a broom during rush hour causes a few fender benders. Scolded by the local police and not sure of the strange surroundings, Kiki is despondent until a portly woman runs out of her bakery shop in search of a customer. The customer forgot her parcel and is too far to chase after. Kiki offers her services and flies back in no time. The woman at the bakery shop takes kindly to her and offers her a home and job delivering baked goods. So starts Kiki's delivery service and along the way she meets some nice people, including a boy who wants to fly. A wonderful coming-of-age story with bright, realistic characters, a heartwarming story, catchy music, and the best animation east of Disney. Highly recommend for fans of all genres and especially children.

Killer, The   (Bloodshed Brothers)
(1989) Action C-110m   Dubbed/Chinese with English Subtitles   VA
Catalog #FLV 1114   Hong Kong   Retail: $19.95 Widescreen Available
Dir/Scr: John Woo   Prod: Tsui Hark
DP: Wong Wing-hang, Peter Pao   Editor: Fan Kung-ming
Music: Lowell Lo   Theme Song Sung by Sally Yeh
Art Design: Luk Man-wah   Set Design: Dai Zhenqing   Costumes: Shirley Chan
MAD: Ching Siu Tung, Lau Chi Ho   PC: Film Workshop Dist: Fox   Lorber   Home Video

Chow Yun-Fat	Jeffrey Chow
Sally Yeh	Jennie
Danny Lee	Detective "Eagle" Li
Kenneth Tsang	Sergeant Randy Chung
Chu Kong	Sydney Fung

Lam Chung	Willie Tsang
Shing Fui-On	Johnny Weng
Ye Rongzu	Tony Weng
Yi Fanwei	Frankie Feng
Huang Guangliang	Wong Tong
Barry Wong	Chief Inspector Tu
Parkman Wong	Inspector Chan
Wu Shaohong	Hitman
Yang Xing	Bodyguard
Yan Zhaohong	Bodyguard

[****]

As haunting music plays over the rainy backdrop of Hong Kong's evening skyline, a remote Christian Church glows brightly with the calm warmth of hundreds of candles. A handsome, lone figure sits in the empty Church and reflects upon his life and future. Here he will meet a man and accept a job that will change his life forever. Here begins the story of a killer.

Arguably, the finest John Woo film to reach the American shores and definitely the most influential in his international claim for fame. Currently, John Woo is a successful Hollywood filmmaker, directing high-paced action films like "Hard Target" with Jean-Claude Van Damme [**1/2], "Broken Arrow" starring John Travolta and Christian Slater [***], and the brilliant "Face-Off" with John Travolta and Nicholas Cage [****]. Though stylish and entertaining, his American films lack the incredible energy and grace of his Triad/Cop masterpiece "The Killer". The story is about honor among two men from opposite sides of the law, a professional hitman (Chow Yun Fat) and a hard-edged cop (Danny Lee) who befriends him. They are brought together over the tragic shooting of a lovely club singer, Sally Yeh, and the obsessive vendetta of a Triad boss intent on destroying Chow.

Chow is hired by a gangster to make a hit on a rival mob leader, during the shootout Sally is accidentally caught in the crossfire and blinded. Chow takes a personal interest in helping her and decides to amend his ways and discontinue his life as a hitman. He listens to her hauntingly beautiful voice and acts as her guardian angel. Lee is a tough, no nonsense cop who is first introduced during an undercover sting operation. He and his partner meet some gangsters to sell weapons, but when a local traffic cop stops them, a battle breaks out. Determined to get his man, Lee chases the criminal into a crowded bus. This a scene in the style and presence Woo gives to his characters. The criminal and cop are both aboard the bus. With subtle precision, the sound fades until we only hear the cocking of Lee's gun. Lee is focused and through a variety of camera angles, he takes down the criminal without shooting the hostage. The hostage, an elderly woman, suffers a heart attack. Meanwhile Chow decides to take one more hit so he can afford an expensive eye-cornea operation for Sally. During a crowded festival, Chow uses a sniper's rifle and takes out a leading businessman/mob boss. Lee is on the scene and chases down Chow to a beach. Chow is ambushed and betrayed by his benefactor. Lee arrives and helps Chow, but wants to arrest him. When a young girl is shot, Chow risks everything to rush her to a hospital and makes an unusual bond with pursuing officer Lee.

Wishing to find some leads, Lee is assigned to interrogate Sally. Chow's contact man and best friend arrives at Chow's house and tries to kill him. Chow lets him live, but now he and the mob boss are bitter enemies with Lee and Sally caught in the middle. In a beautifully choreographed finale in an old Church, Woo uses slow motion, close-ups, whirling stunts, and massive explosions, but his fights never look hectic or disorganized, there's a sense of ballet-like precision and delicacy. The bloodshed reaches comic book levels as Chow and Lee battle their way to victory. A must see for all action fans who will never see crime movies in the same fashion ever again.

Killer from Shantung (Boxer From Shantung)
(1972) Kung-Fu   C-100m   Dubbed   Hong Kong   Retail: $19.99
Dir: Chang Cheh   Scr: I Kuang   Prod: Mona Fong
Ex. Prod: Run Run Shaw   PC: Shaw Brothers
Chen Kuan Tai, David Chiang
[**]
Brutal life of gangsters and their underworld existence. Chen Kuan Tai and his friend arrive in Shantung to start a new life. Unfortunately, they're penniless and lack education. One day, Chen bumps into a successful gangster, David Chiang, who impresses him. He dresses in fancy western clothes, carries a long cigarette, and rides around in luxury. He tips Chen who is outraged for being considered a beggar, but decides to follow the same career path. Chen uses his amazing fighting prowess to gain a reputation for himself and climbs the ladder of criminal success. Naive at first, Chen starts to realize the dangers that surround him. Meanwhile, Chiang is betrayed and teams up with Chen to go after the ruthless boss who tried to rule all of Shantung. A good cast in a dated and typical plot.

Killer Meteors   (Jackie Chan versus Jimmy Wang Yu)
(1976) Kung-Fu   C-94m Dubbed   Catalog #4098
Hong Kong   Retail: $9.99
Dir: Lo Wei   Scr: Wing Soo   Prod: James Shaw   Ex. Prod: Willie Chan
DP: Lo Chee Wan   Editor: Harry Forbes   Music: Michael James
PC: Lo Wei Motion Pictures, Ltd.   Dist: Simitar Entertainment, Inc./Alpha Entertainment
Jackie Chan, Jimmy Wang Yu, Doris Mei, Dina Hse
[*1/2]
Incredibly disappointing film starring Wang Yu, but billed as a Jackie Chan film to capitalize on his recent success. This is not a Chan film, he only appears three times throughout the story and he doesn't even play a hero as he does in other brief appearances (Fantasy Mission Force). Wang Yu is the Killer Meteor, a famous martial arts hero who possesses a deadly weapon that no man has ever seen. Famous criminals pay homage to him by giving up crime, cutting their fingers off, and offering him pearls to stay alive. When the kung-fu master Thunder Sword comes, he asks Killer Meteor to visit his wealthy master, Jackie Chan. He agrees and helps Chan track down his deceitful wife, a cruel vicious woman who is poisoning him. Without going into two many details, the film twists and turns with a number of subplots until we get to the climatic (disappointing) finale between Chan and Wang Yu. If you're hoping to see Chan shine, you'll be utterly disappointed. If you're looking for a generic kung-fu film from the 1970's, then you'll get mediocre fight scenes and a moronic plot.

Killer of Snakes, Fox of Shaolin
(1980) Kung-Fu   C-92m Dubbed   Catalog #4066   Hong Kong
Retail: $9.99

Dir/Scr: Man Wah   Prod: Yih San Pao
DP: Chin Tian   Editor: Chow Kwok Chung Music: Chan Kwok Man
Prod Manager: Hsu Tang   Art Design: Ong Shih Chai
MAD: Kiao Hsuen Ming, Lin Mang Hwa   Makeup: Hsien Cher Yuen
Dist: Simitar Entertainment, Inc.
Carter Wong, Moh Wun-Hsia, Kuo Wu Sing, Lily Han, Cheung Li, Cheung May
[*1/2]
Wong Pu is a clever girl, and good thing, since she has to outsmart a nasty suitor named Sing.
Lucky for her, a mysterious newcomer named Tan (Wong) offers a helpful hand. The evil Kim
is another threat, but the heroic Tan is a master of the martial arts. He battles evil villains and
spirits from the animal realm. Unknown to Tan, Wong Pu and her father use black magic to
disguise their true appearance. When Tan is injured, Wong Pu uses her magic to nurse him back
to health, risking her own life to channel energy. The process turns her hair white for 300 years.
Tan recovers and can not return his love, since in reality she is a snake and he is human. He goes
off and defeats the evil snake Sing and the wise Buddhist monk tells Wong Pu to return to her
own kind. An early fantasy kung-fu film that includes many popular Chinese legends and
predates many of Hong Kong's most popular fantasy films. The special effects are non-existent
and the poorly executed story will make Wong Jing films look like masterpieces. A Carter
Wong film that should be explored after many other choices.

Kimigure Orange Road
(1989) Japanime: Comedy   C-70m Japanese with English Subtitles
Catalog #ANI AT092-006
Japan Retail: $24.95
Dir: Naoyuki Yoshinaga, Takeshi Mori, Koichiro Nakamura
Scr: Kenji Terada   Character Design: Akemi Takada
Art Dir: Satoshi Miura   Music: Sagisu
PC: Toho/Studio Pierrot   Dist: AnimEigo
(based on characters created by Izumi Matsumoto)
[***]
A multi-volume series which highlights the social lives of a group of teenagers. The chemistry
and appeal of the show lie within a love triangle that goes on and on without ever being resolved
(until Volume 5). Of course, love matters are complicated when you come from a family of
psychics, each with their own unique abilities. Kyosuke is your average teenager who enjoys the
company of two girls, best friends Madoka and Hikaru. They both compete for his attention and
are appealing in different respects. Not wanting to ruin a good thing, Kyosuke doesn't commit
and maintains a close friendship with both girls which results in disastrous and hilarious
moments. If you enjoy Ranma 1/2, you'll probably love this series and vice-versa. The only
difference is that Ranma uses martial arts to drive the romance and comedy while KOR uses the
supernatural.
Two episodes are included, but both are equally funny. The first one involves a magic rope that
can transfer the mind of one person into the body of another. The kids don't believe that's
possible, so their grandfather demonstrates the rope. Bad luck follows when Kyosuke becomes
trapped in the body of a goldfish and later a cat. The second episode is even wilder as Kyosuke's
cousin pays a visit. She possesses the psychic ability of illusion and gets Kyosuke into plenty of

trouble with his two female friends.

Best described as a romantic comedy with a supernatural twist, KOR is pleasant viewing for all ages and genders. No overt violence or sex, but plenty of coy sexual innuendoes and childish antics.

Kimigure Orange Road: Volume 5

(1989) Japanime   C-70m Japanese with English Subtitles   Catalog #ANI   AT092-010
      Japan Retail: $24.95
Dir: Naoyuki Yoshinaga, Takeshi Mori, Koichiro Nakamura
Scr: Kenji Terada   Character Design: Akemi Takada
Art Dir: Satoshi Miura   Music: Sagisu
PC: Toho/Studio Pierrot   Dist: AnimEigo
(based on characters created by Izumi Matsumoto)

Furuya Tooru	**Kyosuke**
Tsuru Hiromi	**Madoka**
Hara Eriko	**Hikaru**
Tomiyama Kei	**Takashi**
Tomizawa Michie	**Manami**
Honda Chieko	**Kurumi**
Ogata Kenichi	**Jingoro**
Yara Yuusaku	**Master**

[***]

You're probably asking where the other three volumes are and I wish I knew myself. For some reason, distributors shipped copies of the first and last, but the other three videos have been in limbo for some time. Keep looking and you'll probably find them eventually. A special laser disc box set is available with the entire series. The fifth series is a departure from the supernatural hijinks of the first film. The characters have matured and prepare for their futures with important entrance exams. Kyosuke fondly reminisces about the past month when he made his final decision on who to date. You won't see much in the way of psychic powers, but for those who followed the series, the film is a touching way to resolve the love triangle.

King Kong Escapes

(1968) Monster   C-96m Dubbed   G   VA   Japan Retail: $9.99
Dir: Inoshiro Honda Scr: Kaoru Mabuchi Prod: Tomoyuki Tanaka
DP: Hajime Koizumi Sp. Fx: Eiji Tsuburaya   PC: Toho
Rhodes Reason, Mie Hama, Linda Miller, Akira Takarada, Eisei Amamoto

[**]

King Kong is once again in the hands of Japanese filmmakers who decide that two Kongs are better than one. A rare mineral is needed by diabolic villains in their plan to gain power and wealth. Since the machine is radioactive and volatile, machines and men are too dangerous to use for excavation. Instead, the evil conglomerate build a mechanical King Kong to help dig. When that fails, the real King Kong is captured and taken to the island for slave duty. He is equipped with a mind-controlling harness and goes to work. All works well, but Kong has some human friends who don't want to see Kong become a slave and want the evil villains to fail. Once Kong is freed, he battles the robot Kong and makes good his escape. Kong races down the island toward the docks where he makes mincemeat out of the villains' ship, sinking them and their cargo of rare ore.

King Kong Versus Godzilla
(1963) Monster   C-105m   Dubbed   Japan Retail: $9.99
Dir: Inoshiro Honda, Thomas Montgomery (additional American footage)
Scr: Shinichi Sekizawa, Paul Mason & Bruce Howard (American footage)
Prod: Tomoyuki Tanaka, John Beck (American footage)
DP: Hajime KoizumiSp. Fx: Eiji Tsuburaya   PC: Toho
Tadao Takashima, Yu Fujiki, Akiko Wakabayashi, Mie Hama, Akihiko Hirata
American version: Michael Keith, James Yogi, Harry Halcombe
[1/2]**
Though American filmmakers invented the big monster movies in 1931 with the classic King Kong, leave it to the Japanese who kept the ball running and eventually imported King Kong overseas. The rights for King Kong were borrowed by Toho Studios who featured a classic match against Godzilla. The story keeps the elements from the original King Kong film, but add the ability of channeling electricity. When Japan is besieged by Godzilla, a team of scientists and officials decide to use King Kong to battle the monster. The Japanese travel to Skull Island where Kong and other prehistoric monsters are kept. They gain the help of the local villagers who have invented a berry wine that puts Kong under the table. Kong proves he's a nice guy when he beats a giant octopus that attacks the village, a truly campy action sequence that must be seen. The Japanese capture King Kong and bring him to Japan. A fleet of Japanese helicopters airlift poor, drunk Kong to the waiting clutches of Godzilla. When the two giants meet, they come out battling and Godzilla is on the verge of winning, but a electrical storm charges King Kong and both monsters plummet into the sea. At the end, only Kong resurfaces and swims back to Skull Island. A fun movie in the monster genre and definitely a cult classic. It is reported that two endings were filmed, and America got the Kong-victory ending. Monster films are comical and juvenile in many ways with dated sets and rubber suits, but have tremendous appeal for their campy nostalgia and mock violence. Not to nitpick, but based on measurements of Kong and Godzilla from their original films, Godzilla should have been able to stomp on the tiny ape who's only a fraction of the reptile's reported height.

Kung Fu Arts
(1980) Kung-Fu   C-80m Dubbed   Catalog #4063   Hong Kong
Retail: $9.99
Dir: Lee Geo Shou, Lee Shi Giei   Scr: Shio Shai Jen   Prod: Shio Shai Liang
DP: Le Shi Gei   Editor: Chiang Kou Chien Music: Huang Mao Shan
Supervisor: M. Hui Keung Planning: Kim Young   Makeup: Chou Mei Yun
MAD: Huang Chia Da   PC: Kam Yeung Film Co.   Dist: Simitar
Entertainment
Carter Wong (Huang Chia Da), Cheng Shing, Ching Ts Ming, Sida the French Monkey Star, Ge Kung Tsong, Cheng Ming Yang, Yu Hon, Huang Huei Ling, Pan Huei Gin, Liu Wen Bing
[**]
Period piece with a royal family involved in a deadly conspiracy. Lord Kang (Wong) is

betrothed to the King's daughter, but when an assassination attempt is made on the king and the princess is poisoned, Kang becomes the main suspect. The chief advisor fears Wong is trying to usurp royal power and orders his immediate capture. He escapes and vows to find the truth. The king offers his daughter's hand in marriage to anyone who comes up with a cure. Sida the Monkey appears with a cure, wins the challenge, and gets married to the princess. The animal-human marriage ceremony disgusts the king, so he orders his daughter and her prospective husband/monkey to be banished down a stream. Meanwhile, the king's advisor is playing with the bizarre situation and acquires more power while trying to hunt down and capture Wong. The king dies and the advisor takes over, but thanks to Sida the monkey and a young Tarzan-wannabe, the two lovers are reunited in the castle's dungeon. Don't worry, they get free, fight a lot, and when the High Judge and the soldiers come in, leave it to Sida to save the day and provide the crucial document that proves who is truly innocent and guilty. If you enjoy Carter Wong or silly old kung-fu movies, this one definitely fits the mold.

Kung Fu Commandos   (Incredible Kung Fu Mission)
(1980) Kung-Fu   C-90m Dubbed   R   Hong Kong   Retail: $19.99
Dir: Chang Hsin Yi   Dist: Prism Entertainment
John Liu, Shangkuan Ling-Feng
[**1/2]
Basically a send up of The Dirty Dozen (divided by half) and replacing World War II guns with swords and kung-fu. The film's highlight is John Liu, a star who never reached Jet Li or Jackie Chan's fame or popularity but who made a number of entertaining films. If you've never seen a John Liu movie, then you're missing out. John Liu is one of the most amazing leg-kickers on screen. Known for his amazing flexibility and control, Liu can do vertical kicks and hold his leg in midair, then kick a dozen times before putting his foot on the ground. If you enjoy the power and flexibility of kicking techniques, then check out a Liu movie.
Liu is hired by a wealthy man to lead a commando team to rescue a patriotic leader who has been imprisoned by the government. The team doesn't comprise of criminals, but a motley group of fighters for profit. Ironically, they include a cook, a thief, and even a strong man from a circus. At first they don't respect Liu and fight among themselves, but he kicks them into line. In no time, the team is well trained and enter the heavily guarded enemy territory. They succeed in rescuing the patriot, but the casualties run high. Liu regrets the loss of his newfound friends, but escorts the patriot to the rendezvous. The patriot thanks him and asks who ordered his rescue. Liu reveals the name, but the patriot looks on in confusion and doesn't recognize the name. The wealthy man appears and murders the patriot. His only purpose was to kill the patriot for his own personal vengeance. Liu infuriated at the betrayal and loss of his men counterattacks. What proceeds is an amazing battle of kicks against his powerful opponent, including an unofficial record of the most kicks delivered to a single villain. Unfortunately, most John Liu movies have low-budgets and suffer from poor editing and weak filmmaking. The main strength lies in the amazing kicking abilites of the lead actor.

Kung Fu Cult Master, The (Heaven Sword and Dragon Sabre/Heaven Slaughter Dragon Story)
(1993) Fantasy Kung-Fu   C-100m   Chinese with English Subtitles
Catalog #ML 468   Hong Kong   Retail: $39.99

Dir: Wong Jing   Dist: Mei Ah Company
Jet Li, Chingmy Yau, Cheung Man, Tsui Kam Kong, Richard Ng, Tony Leung Chiu Wai
[***]
Incredibly popular fantasy tale based on the Jin Yong novels. Various versions of the story exist in print, television, and film. Major disappointment is the cliffhanger ending which was never resolved due to poor box office receipts and the cancellation of the sequel. The full story was originally planned to be completed in the second film, but still manages to be entertaining and worthwhile. Some of the most beautiful women in Chinese films star in mythical fantasies about magic swords and mystic cults.
Hundreds of kung-fu experts stand in an outdoor ceremony, waving banners and saluting the greatest martial artist and his wife. The couple possess the most powerful weapons in the kung-fu world: the Dragon Sword and the Tien-lin Sword. The narrator tells that when the swords are brought together a great power will be unleashed. At a later point in time, two factions battle for the swords and great martial arts schools are called into action to take sides. On the one side are the Chinese schools, lead by Shaolin Temple, they include the Wu Tang Clan, Ngo Mai Nuns, Kun Lun, Hung Tung, and Wah Shan. The evil sect is from Persia and is led by four rulers, each from a color: The Golden Lion, The White Eagle, The Green Bat, and The Purple Fox.
The rift starts when a student of the Wu Tang falls in love with and marries the daughter of White Eagle. He also befriends Golden Lion and hopes to bring peace to the two clans. Secretly, the Manchurian emperor has his own forces and wishes to pit the cults against each other.
The basic plot starts with Jet Li's parents dying before his own eyes and vowing revenge. They were killed by the "good" cults since they refused to reveal the identity of Golden Lion who was injured and still holds the Dragon Sword. A head nun wields the Tien-lin Sword which she uses against the evil sect in dramatic large scale battles. Jet Li is physically incapable of fighting, due to receiving the Jinx's Hand as a child, but he is cured and learns the Great Solar Stance and becomes a hero. He hooks up with Chingmy Yau who also does kung-fu and holds a secret. There are plenty of characters to follow, but it is soon learned that a traitor has caused the rivalry between the good and evil sects. Then a Manchurian princess and her troops launch attacks against the various schools to cause confusion and hatred. Not content to sit on the sidelines, Jet Li learns Shaolin kung-fu and finally tai chi (from the master who raised him, Chang San Fung) in his efforts to unite the other "cults" against the true common enemy. After defeating the masters who gave Li the Jinx palm, the film ends abruptly as the evil Manchurian princess asks Li and his allies to meet them at the imperial palace. To save the Persian Cult masters, Li received the antidote from the princess and in return owes her three favors. Not easy to follow at times, Cult Master features some wild flying, fantasy kung-fu and plenty of great action scenes from Hong Kong's best performers.

THE KUNG-FU MASTER TV SERIES

The Kung-Fu Master

The Revenge of the Kung-Fu Master

Kwaidan

(1964) Horror   C-164m   Japanese with English Subtitles   VA
Catalog #KWA01   Japan Retail: $29.95
Dir: Masaki Kobayashi   Scr: Yoko Mizuki   DP: Yoshio Miyajima
Music: Toru Takemitsu   Art Design: Shigemasa Toda
Dist: Public Media Home Video
(based on the stories of Lafcadio Hearn)

Rentaro Mikuni	Samurai
Michiyo Aratama	1st Wife
Misako Watanabe	2nd Wife
Katsuo Nakamura	Hoichi
Ganjiro Nakamura	Head Priest
Takashi Shimura	Priest
Joichi Hayashi	Yoshitsune
Ganemon Nakamura	Kannai
Noboru Nakaya	Heinai

Tetsuro Tamba, Tatsuya Nakadai, Keiko Kishi
[***1/2]
The Japanese culture is rich with tales of the supernatural and bizarre. Traditional horror stories have been popular for centuries. Kwaidan is a compilation film of four classic horror tales. Incorporating classic literature with beautiful visual imagery, Kwaidan tells the tale of ghosts and their dealings with humans. Each story has a dreamlike quality and an eerie sense of dread. Those familiar with Japanese literature will recognize some of the stories, while newcomers will be introduced to an entirely new realm of horror. Atmosphere and a sense of melancholy play key elements over gore and violence found in many contemporary horror films. One of the better known stories concerns the life of a young monk (Hoichi) who lives at a Buddhist monastery. He is a gifted musician and is visited at night by some warriors. They take him to an outdoor palace courtyard where he performs for the nobles and warriors. Each night he is called, but the head monks discover that he is playing for a dead lord and that eventually his soul will be lost to the spirits. In an attempt to save the young man, Buddhist scriptures are painted all over his body. When the spirits arrive, the writings make the man invisible. However, the monks forgot to cover his ears and so the spirit spots a pair of ears floating in midair. The spirit warrior angered, grabs the ears and tears them off his body. He is no longer bothered again, but must live his life in a state of deafness never to hear the beauty of his own music. Other stories revolve around women who have been scorned and return to life as ghosts, including one story of a female spirit in a lone house in the middle of a snow storm and a long-haired wife who faithfully waits for her missing husband. Culturally different and more casually paced than Hollywood films, Kwaidan stresses art and style over blood and horror. A fascinating look at what goes bump in the night at a Japanese home.

-L-

LA Blue Girl (6 volumes)
(1992) Japanime   C-45m (Vol. 1-5) C-60m (Vol. 6)   Rated - Anime 18   VA
Dubbed/Japanese with English Subtitles   Japan Retail: $29.95 (each volume)
Dir: Kan Fukumoto Scr: Megumi Ichiyanagi   Original Story: Toshio Maeda

Prod: Rusher Ikeda   Character Design: Rin Shin Art Dir: Taro Taki
Music Dir: Teruo Takahama   English Version - Ex. Prod: Humphrey G. Kumano
PC: Daiei Co., Ltd.   Dist: Central Park Media
English Version:

S. Watkins	**Miko Mido**
Bat Mackeral	**Nin-Nin**
Hannah Hartz	**Baba**
Wendi Talker	**Yaku**
Crystal Shipp	**Kamiri**

[1/2]**

Warning - Adults Only. Not for children! As the tidal wave of Japanese animation pours into American video stores, all types of titles have recently been released.   Unlike American animation which is mainly perceived as children's cartoons, large portions of Japanime are targeted for adult only viewing and contain explicit scenes of pornography and violence. LA Blue Girl is part of the adult anime market where sexual content plays a major portion of the film's theme. The story follows the exploits of a young school girl and her special gifts. For fans of erotic anime, the story's animation is well done and there are plenty of cute high school girls and demons having sex in the wildest settings. In particular is a cute, but super horny ninja teddy bear called Nin-nin. He provides comic relief and is a helpful, albeit annoying, sidekick to the main girls. If you like the childish antics of girls in anime and if softcore animated imagery, this series will entertain you. Again I stress this series is not for children and those who are offended by pornographic animation.

Last Emperor, The
(1987) Historical Drama   C-160m   English and Mandarin with English Subtitles
PG-13   VA   China/Italy/UK
Dir: Bernardo Bertolucci   Scr: Mark Peploe, Bernardo Bertolucci, Enzo Ungari
Prod: Jeremy Thomas   DP: Vittorio Storaro Editor: Gabriella Cristiani
Music Dir: Ray Williams   Music: Ryuichi Sakamoto, David Byrne, Cong Su
Prod Design: Ferdinando Scarfiotti
Art Design: Gianni Giovagnoni, Gianni Silvestri, Maria Teresa Barbasso
Special effects: Gianetto De Rossi, Fabrizio Martinelli
Makeup: Fabrizio Sforza   Costumes: James Acheson   Dist: Columbia
(based on Pu Yi's autobiography From Emperor To Citizen)

John Lone	**Aisin-Gioro "Henry" Pu Yi**
Joan Chen	**Wan Jung, "Elizabeth"**
Peter O'Toole	**Reginald Johnston**
Ying Ruocheng	**The Governor**
Victor Wong	**Chen Pao Shen**
Dennis Dun	**Big Li**
Ryuichi Sakamoto	**Masahiko Amakasu**
Maggie Han	**Eastern Jewel**
Ric Young	**Interrogator**
Wu Jun Mei	**Wen Hsiu**
Cary-Hiroyuki Tagawa/Chang	

Jade Go	Ar Mo
Fumihiko Ikeda	Yoshioka
Richard Vuu	Pu Yi, Age 3
Tijger Tsou	Pu Yi, Age 8
Wu Tao	Pu Yi, Age 15
Fan Guang	Pu Chieh
Henry Kyi	Pu Chieh, Age 7
Alvin Riley III	Pu Chieh, Age 14
Lisa Lu	Tzu Hsui, The Empress Dowager
Hideo Takamatsu	Gen. Ishikari
Hajime Tachibana	Japanese Translator
Basil Pao	Prince Chun
Jian Xireng	Lord Chamberlain
Chen Kai Ge	Captain of Imperial Guard
Zhang Liangbin	Big Foot
Huang Wenjie	Hunchback
Liang Dong	Lady Aisin-Gioro
Dong Zhendong	Old Doctor
Dong Jiechen	Doctor
Constantine Gregory/Oculist	
Soong Huaikuei	Lung Yu
Shao Ruzhen	First High Consort
Li Yu	Second High Consort
Li Guangli	Third High Consort
Xu Chunqing	Grey Eyes
Zhang Tianmin	Old Tutor
Yang Baozong	Gen. Yuan Shikai
Cai Hongxiang	Scarface
Yu Shihong	Hsiao Hsiu
Wu Jun	Wen Hsiu, Age 12
Lucia Hwong	Lady of the Book
Cui Jingping	Lady of the Pen
Wu Hai	Republican Officer
Gu Junguo	Tang
Xu Tongrui	Captain of Feng's Army
Li Fusheng	Minister of Trade
Chen Shu	Chang Chinghui
Cheng Shuyan	Lady Hiro Saga
Zhang Lingmu	Emperor Hirohito
Luo Shigang	Chang Ching Hui's Secretary
Zhang Daxing	Tough Warder
Zu Ruigang	Second Warder
Jin Yuan	Party Boss
Akira Ikuta	Japanese Doctor
Ma GuangCui Xinmin/Japanese Bodyguards	

Li Zhenduo	Dignitary
Yang Hongchang	Scribe
Wang Biao	Prisone

[****]
If a title can actually reflect a film's significance in cinematic history, then The Last Emperor would reign as the supreme ruler of Asian films. The only Asian film to win the Academy Award for Best Picture (1987), The Last Emperor went on to win additional awards and received critical praise. A visual masterpiece of multi-national filmmaking helmed by Italian director Bernardo Bertolucci. Based on true events, the epic follows the life of Pu Yi, the last Manchurian emperor of China before the Nationalist usurped his imperial power. The epic is told through a series of flashbacks from the point of view of an older Pu Yi played by John Lone. The adult Pu Yi has been arrested by the Communist government and accused of treason due to his alliance with the Japanese forces during World War II. He attempts suicide by slicing his wrist, but is discovered and taken to a hospital. Slowly his story unfolds and glimpses into another world are seen for the first time. As a young child, Pu Yi became an emperor of a country who no longer needed an emperor. Secluded and surrounded by eunuchs, his only solace is a British scholar played charmingly by Peter O'Toole who teaches him to be a free-thinking man. Pu's attempt to escape the Forbidden Palace are stopped and he remains a prisoner, a puppet figure, within his own palace. The next decades are turbulent times for China as the Imperial Ching Dynasty of the Manchus fall and a new democratic government replaces it. Then war with Japan breaks out and Pu is reinstated as the puppet dictator of Manchuria, occupied by the Japanese who call it Manchuko. Pu convinces himself that he has regained authority and turns a blind eye to Japanese control. His wife (Chen), once in love with him, is jaded and sick of how controlled their life has become. When Japan loses the war, China is thrust into a brutal civil war by men who had once worked as allies. Mao's communists defeat the Nationalist and Pu becomes a symbol of a decadent past and is imprisoned and re-educated for his sins. His life unfolds until his death and we are left wondering what kind of man he was and how anyone could have lived with his responsibilities being the ruler of the largest population of people on the Earth. Bertolucci deftly weaves his tale through flashbacks that bring the story up to full speed and never fails to show the man before the emperor. A review doesn't do this film justice, since it also explores numerous facets of China's past. The film never tries to glorify the main characters, but focuses on their motivations and desires. Much can be said about the technical brilliance of the film, from its period costumes, rich musical score, and grandiose sets which include actual footage of the Forbidden Palace in Beijing. Cinematically beautiful and well-crafted, the film is a historical testimony to a great dynasty now long gone. Performances are strong overall, but most credit can be given to Lone and Chen's performance as the ill-fated emperor and empress.

Last Hurrah for Chivalry
(1979) Kung-Fu   C-108m   Dubbed   Catalog #49903   Hong Kong
Retail: $59.95
Dir/Scr: John Woo   Assistant Dir: Chin Po   Associate Prod: Louis Kit
MAD: Feng Ke An   MAD Assistant: Huang Ha, Hsu Chung Hsin
Prod Coordinator: Catherine Cheung   Dist: Media Asia Distribution/Tai Seng Video
Wei Pai, Liv Sung Ren, Lee Hoi San

[**1/2]

All the ingredients are in place for a top-notch kung-fu epic, following the format of the Shaw Brothers classics. Super-director John Woo directed and wrote the screenplay, casting a host of veteran players. However, Woo's film lacks any of the chemistry and dynamic tension created by his Triad action films. Instead, we are given a good-looking film without much charisma, action, or drama to hold the viewer. The story follows the exploits of a muscular villain who kills off a rival school. He commands ninjas and a group of elite killers with various weapons. Two men cross paths, one is a student vowing for revenge while the other is a hired mercenary ordered to kill the hero. The plot follows along the standard kung-fu format: father/master gets killed, son/student trains, and gets revenge in the end. The two men fight, but eventually pool their resources and work to destroy the true enemies. Faking the death of the hero, the mercenary returns to collect his reward but is betrayed in the process. He realizes his mistake and suddenly the hero appears and joins him. They kill the elite fighters first and then battle the master. The film's major problem is the introduction of supporting characters who slow down the pacing of the film. Minimal wirework is used, but none of the fight scenes are particularly refreshing or innovative and for fans who are familiar with Jackie Chan, the stunts look rather dull and slow. What it comes down to is a mediocre kung-fu film that looks better than most, but suffers from the same faults and contrivances. Sadly, there are no hurrahs for this early John Woo film and much of the rating goes toward effort not achievement.

Laughing Target - See Rumik's World "Laughing Target"

Legacy of Rage
(1987) Action C-86m Chinese with English Subtitles
Catalog #0292   Hong Kong   Retail: $39.99
Dir: Ronnie Yu   Prod: Dickson Poon Dist: Tai Seng Video
Brandon Lee, Michael Wong, Regina Kent, Bolo Yeung, Ng Man Tat, Mang Hoi, Whan Wei Man
[***]

Brandon Lee is a naive young man, framed by his close friend, Michael Wong. Lee ends up serving eight years in jail and must endure the hardship of prison. In the meantime, Wong is hitting on Brandon Lee's girl. Michael does more bad stuff, Brandon gets out of prison, and learning of his friend's betrayal, goes after him, seeking revenge. Armed with an arsenal of weapons and his martial arts prowess, Lee succeeds in getting his revenge. A decent action film with a number of positive aspects. Mostly of note, since it is the only Hong Kong film to star Brandon Lee (son of Bruce Lee) who wished to avoid undue comparisons between his father and him. Bruce Lee became a super-star after appearing in Hong Kong films, but Brandon's effort failed to launch him into the same status. Brandon kept making American films and the Crow was his big box-office breakthrough. Sadly, he was accidentally killed on the set of Crow 2 when fragments of metal were propelled from a handgun used on the set. Brandon died mysteriously like his father, but unlike his father Brandon never received the fame in films, dying five years younger than his father.

Legend of Crystania: The Motion Picture
(1998) Fantasy Anime

C-85m Dubbed   Catalog #VHSLC/001D   Japan
Retail: $19.95
Dir: Nakamura Ryutaro Original Story: Mizuno Ryo   Prod: Yokoyama Kazuo
Ex. Prod: Kadokawa Tsuguhiko   Planning: Tamiya Takeshi
Character Design: Takaraya Yoshifumi, Sato Hiroshi   Art Director: Gary Dehan
PC: Kadokawa Shoten, Narubeni, Victor Entertainment, Tokyo Television
Dist: ADV Films
[***]
The long-awaited sequel to Record of Lodoss Wars is not a true sequel, but rather a remote spin-off with a few characters from the original and a sparse connection in story. For fans hoping for a justifiable masterpiece, this is not the film and will disappoint completely. As a standard animated fantasy film, Legend of Crystania is enjoyable, though the animation style fluctuates in the film with moments of excellence and mediocrity. The characters are also a mix of routine, curious, and engaging. The story takes place 300 years after the Lodoss Wars, though not much has changed from a technological and economical point of view. The evil prince Ashram and the dark elf Pirotesse have survived their supposed death and now lead a group of survivors in search of a new home. Ashram's fleet comes upon a new land, but he becomes trapped and his soul is under the control of Bardas, an evil entity bent on becoming the Gods King. Centuries of imprisonment later, Pirotesse comes across a motley group of heroes led by Redon who help her free Ashram and defeat Bardas. Though fantasy based, there is less emphasis on classic European fantasy and more of a free-wheeling spirit to the characters and monsters portrayed. Once again, our hero is a young, impetuous, but incredibly brave lad who is bent on avenging the death of his parents and saving the day. He is accompanined by a band of heroes who all have their own past and their own unique abilities. A tight standard story of good and evil and love and death for fans of fantasy based animation. Hopefully, Record of Lodoss Wars the true sequel will appear on shelves in the near future.

Legend of Drunken Master (see Drunken Master II)
Once again, Dimension Films has repackaged a classic Jackie Chan film for American audiences with a new dubbed-tract, new music, and some re-editing for an October 2000 release. Thankfully, they edited out the last sequence which showed a bewildered Wong Fei Hung suffering from the effects of his last battle.

Legend of the 7 Golden Vampires   (The 7 Brothers Versus Dracula)
(1973) Horror Kung-Fu   C-90m Dubbed   Hong Kong/UK
Retail: $19.95
Dir: Roy Ward Baker   PC: Shaw Brothers & Hammer Studios
David Chiang, Peter Cushing
[*1/2]
The Chinese love to cross genres and I support the concept, but when you cross genres, culture, and continents, the results can be ludicrous and insulting. The popular kung-fu movie format is crossed with the popular Hammer-horror film style of the 1970's. Count Dracula assumes the identity of a Taoist priest and flees to China, where he resurrects an army of zombies. Hot on his tail is Dr. Van Helsing (Cushing), who is aided by a family of kung fu heroes led by Chiang. They provide Helsing with cultural guides into the heart of China, leading the heroic party to

Dracula's temple. An interesting attempt and noteworthy for its novelty, the film suffers greatly over time, continuity errors, and a ridiculous premise. The Hammer actors can't do kung-fu and the Shaw actors must lower their skills a notch to coincide with the English actors' abilities. Only recommended if you enjoy watching bad Christopher Lee vampire films and cheesy kung-fu films from the 1970's.

Legend of the Liquid Sword
(1993) Kung-Fu   C-85m Chinese with English Subtitles   Hong Kong
Dir: Wong Jing
Aaron Kwok, Tsui Sui Keung, Liu Chia Hui, Chingmy Yau
[**]
The liquid sword refers to a weapon created by the powers of the Sacred Water. When Batman (a flying kung-fu master who sucks blood) steals the water, he is bent on destroying all those who oppose him. A brave fighter and his three annoying sisters/beauties make the trek to the Sacred/Secret Water and warn the high priestess. Along the way, they meet another warrior who is amazing at kung-fu and can perform all sorts of tricks like burrowing underground. At first the warrior and the party fight, but soon they become allies. He falls in love with the three beauties and they string him along appropriately to further their own gains. On their quest, they met a con woman and save her from an angry mob. The group then arrive at the Sacred Water's hidden palace. The high priestess doesn't believe them, but when one of her own pupils betrays her, she helps them battle Batman. The combination of flying kung-fu, plenty of sped up scenes and slapstick comedy never click together in a disjointed and meandering film farce. An overly familiar premise that has cluttered the Hong Kong fantasy kung-fu market.

Legendary Weapons of Kung Fu
(1982) Kung-Fu   C-100m   Dubbed   Hong Kong   Retail: $19.99

Dir/Scr: Liu Chia Liang	**MAD: Liu Chia Liang**	**Ex. Prod: Run Run Shaw**
Prod: Mona Fong	**Art Dir: Johnson Tsao**	**PC: Shaw Bros.**
Liu Chia Liang	**Lei Kung**	
Liu Chia Yung	**Lei Yung**	
Gordon Liu Chia Hui	**Monk Ti Tan**	
Hui Ying Hung	**Monk's Niece**	
Alexander Fu Sheng	**Con man**	
Hsiao Hou	**Tieh Hou**	

[***1/2]
Without a doubt, samurai movies owe a lot of their popularity to Japanese director Akira Kurosawa, and the same could be said about the kung-fu genre to Hong Kong director Liu Chia Liang. A pioneer filmmaker, Liu delved away from the classic revenge/training films and created some of the best kung-fu movies ever made, starring in many of them. Legendary Weapons of Kung-fu is considered by some critics and fans as one of the greatest kung-fu movie ever made. Not for the martial arts alone, but the subtext and multi-layered story that focuses on China's changing heritage toward martial arts and on a deeper level the film industry's changing attitude toward martial arts movies. There are plenty of elements that make it a great film, but to western audiences a number of the films key elements may seem foreign and not as engaging. Once again, multi-talented Liang stars, directs, writes, and choreographs a film that satirizes

martial arts films while presenting an action-paced drama about China's dawn into the modern era and the ebbing of traditional martial arts. At the turn of the century, numerous clans of martial artists practice magic and search for ways to become invulnerable to foreign guns (Boxer Rebellion). One group led by Master Lei Kung is disbanded and the members are warned of the impossibility of fighting a bullet. Kung is concerned about the welfare of his students and decides to leave the world of martial arts. He disappears and retires to the countryside. Of course, this would have the same implications as Einstein saying the world is flat in a martial arts versus science context. His word's of doubt fuel a hunt for him by other martial art schools. The fiercest is his own brother (played by his real brother Yung) who uses black magic and tricks. Also sent are a Shaolin expert Ti Tan, a female expert played by Hui, and a powerful young fighter named Tieh Hou.

Meanwhile, an imposter (here is where the film may become confusing) played by Fu Sheng appears and claims that he is Lei Kung. Acting flamboyant and bragging about his skills, he easily dispatches any challengers. Secretly, Lei Yung staged the whole event in hopes of flushing out the real Lei Kung. Needless to say, fighters not in on the scam follow Fu Sheng to an outhouse over a stream. Without going into vulgar details, Tieh Hou falls into the foul water and becomes deadly ill. The real Lei Kung and Hui (who comes to believe in Kung's cause) help him to recover. Kung pretends to be a simple peasant with no martial arts talent, but Tieh discovers the truth and tries to kill him. His weakened behavior is met by kindness, a bowl of medicine, and a friendly nod. In no time, Kung's whereabouts are known and the Shaolin Monk Ti Tan arrives. It takes a combined effort to beat him by attacking his vital points in his ear. He accepts defeat and returns to Shaolin for meditation. A group of night assassins also fail and the recovered Tieh Hou is now on Kung's side completely. The final battle showcases Yung and Kung, battling with all eighteen legendary weapons of kung-fu. One of the few films were older masters battle each other in combat rather than a master versus a young disciple. Liu Chia Liang proves again that a high body count are not necessary to make a wonderful and exciting martial arts film.

Lensman
(1984) Japanime   C-107m   English   VA   Catalog #SPV 90015
Japan Retail: $29.95
Dir: Yoshiaki Kawajiri, Kazuyuki Hirokawa   Scr: Soki Yoshikawa
Prod: Hiroshi Suto   Character Design: Yoshiaki Kawajiri, Kazuo Tomizawa
PC: MK Company   Dist: Streamline Pictures
English Voices: Kerrigan Mahan, Tom Wyner, Greg Snegoff, Michael McConnohie
(based on original concept E.E. "Doc" Smith)
[**]
Billed as Star Wars for the animation crowd, Lensman never delivers on its promise as it wavers between Japanese and American animation styles. The use of computer animation is a novel prospect, but appears out of place and Titan AE is a far better effort. Based on the E.E. "Doc" Smith novels and boasting ground-breaking traditional animation with computer animation, Lensman is the ponderous tale of Kimball Kinnison who becomes a Lensman, guardian of the universe. When space pirates known as the Boskande threaten the civilized universe in the 25th century, it is up to young Kimball and his band of followers to stop the marauding fleet. Through trials, Kimball matures into a seasoned warrior, meeting along his way a fuzzy bear

(Chewbacca clone), a woman (Princess Leia), and an old mentor (Obi-Wan Kenobi). They battle their way to the enemy base and destroy the entire planet, flying out of the exploding core and joining the ally fleet. On paper, elements of the story do show signs of promise, but Lensman never "clicks" into an engaging film. The characters and plot actually becoming boring and predictable without the exciting shine found in other animated films.

Lightning Swords of Death
(1974) Samurai   C-83m Dubbed   R   VA   Japan Retail: $19.95
Dir: Kenji Misumi
Tomisaburo Wakayama, Masahiro Tomikawa, Goh Kato
[**1/2]
Classic samurai action vehicle known by numerous titles and incarnations, though I personally refer to it as the Babycart from Hell or the Lone Wolf and Cub series which has been remastered and recently released in a special collection. Basically the story and its many sequels and re-incarnations deal with a samurai and his baby son (in a babycart) who travel around Japan and kill everyone in their way. The discredited samurai roams medieval Japan pushing his young son ahead of him in a baby cart equipped with weapons and gadgets. He is hunted by a powerful lord who wants him dead and all sorts of assassins are sent to kill the dynamic duo. Basically little plot and plenty of action in Japan's answer to the Hong Kong kung-fu films. Unendingly bloody, but beautifully-crafted sword fights and melodramatic standoffs similar to other mind blowing genre films: crime - "The Killer" and western - "The Wild Bunch".

Love Among the Triad
(1993) Crime/Romance   C-90m Chinese with English Subtitles
Catalog #1330   Hong Kong   Retail: $39.99
Dir: Andy Chin   Scr: Andy Chin, Joey Cheung, Elizabeth Lau
Producer: John Hau DP: William Yim
Gaffer: Y.C. Wong   Music: Johnny Chen
Coordinator: Chong Yeuk   Stunt Coordinator: Tung Wai
Prod Ddesign: Joey Cheung Prod Manager: Y.S. Chow
Assistant Dir: Elizabeth Lau, L.L. Chung Art Dir: John Hau
PC: Prairie Productions Co. Ltd./Flying Colour Film Productions Co. Ltd.
Dist: Long Shore Pictures Ltd./Lui Ming (International) Film Enterprises
Simon Yam, Rosamund Kwan
[***]
A multilayered romance set in the underworld of Chinese crime lords. A beautiful club singer, Cecilia, is the focus of two young men who belong to the Triads of Hong Kong. Ching (Yam) has returned to help with the business. In charge is Chun, a handsome but ruthless boss who carries on a relationship with the singer and keeps his beautiful wife, Sue, in the dark. Ching is also attracted to Cecilia, but he stays away from her out of loyalty to his friend. Chun begins his ruthless consolidation of power by taking out his rivals and confiscating a club. His work is important, but the film doesn't focus on the criminal aspects of his life. Instead, the film is an intriguing drama which portrays the men and women involved in romance. Problems arise when Chun's wife confronts his mistress and the rival gangsters try to assassinate Chun and Ching. Chun enters dangerous waters when he begins to cheat on his mistress and wife with a new

woman. His friend Ching helps him through the tough moments. Ching also meets a smart, conniving woman named Ms. Kwok (Kwan). At first their relationship is superficial, but develops into real romance for the one-woman Ching. In the end, relationships are resolved and the men continue their loves and careers in crime.

Luna Varga: Vol. 1
(1991) Japanime: Fantasy   C-60m Japanese with English Subtitles
Catalog #ADV LV/001   Japan Retail: $29.95
Dir: Shigenori Kageyama   Scr: Aki Tomato, Yumiko Tsukamoto
Original Story: Toru Akitsu
PC: Kadokawa Shoten/NEXTART Dist: A.D. Vision
[1/2]**
Female fantasy heroics meets Godzilla-style ally in this wild and wacky series. Luna is a young woman with special powers who can summon a giant beast from her body. When the monster appears, she is attached to the head of the creature while in a sitting position. The sexual implications notwithstanding, Luna and her friends battle against evil wizards, monsters, and armies. The film has a strong medieval setting and plenty of traditional fantasy elements. Expect a lot of pratfalls and slapstick style humor along the way.
Followed by more episodes and wild antics from Luna and her friends. The series has some appeal and if you liked the first, you'll probably have some fun with the second volume.

Luna Varga: Vol. 2
(1991) Japanime: Fantasy   C-60m Japanese with English Subtitles
Catalog #ADV LV/002   Japan Retail: $29.95

-M-

Machine Robo
(1986) Japanime: Scifi   C-125m   Japanese with English Subtitles
Catalog #SSVS 9701 Japan Retail: $24.99
Series Dir: Hiroshi Yoshida Scr: Hideki Sonoda
Ex. Prod: Toshihiko Sato   General Prod: Kazuo Shimamura, Hiroshi Kato
Prod: Hyota Ezu, Minoru Ono, Masaru Umehara
Music: Tachio Akano   Character Design: Nobuyoshi Habara
Art Dir: Toshihide Tojo, Yoshito Watanabe
English Version - Ex. Prod: John O'Donnell   Prod: Stephanie Shalofsky
PC: Ashi Productions Co., Ltd.   Dist: Software Sculptors

Kazuhiko Inoue	**Rom Stol**
Yuko Mizutani	**Leina Stol**
Shinya Otaki	**Blue Jet**
Koichi Hashimoto	**Rod Drill**
Toshiharu Sakurai	**Triple Jim**
Junichi Kagaya	**Kirai Stol**
Shigezon Sasaoka	**Gadess**
Minoru Inaba	**Grujious**

Hiroko Takahashi Diondora
Susumu Hayami Narrator
[**1/2]
Packed with five episodes, Machine Robo is vintage Japanese animation that will appeal to fans of robot shows like Voltron and Tekkaman. Based on episodes, the series follows the struggle of rebels on the planet Cronos who have been attacked by the Gandorans under the leadership of Lord Gadess. His space armada positions itself above the planet and sends his monsters to retrieve the sacred Hyribead. They hunt down Master Kirai and murder him. His son (Rom) and daughter (Leina) vow to defend the planet. They leave their home accompanied by a group of transforming robots and join forces with other freedom fighters scattered across the planet. Their quest is to search for the various pieces that make up the sacred Hyribead. Heroes and villains are locked in a desperate search to find the remaining pieces. Whenever the villains encounter the heroes, a fight ensues with similar results in each episode. Enjoyable for fans who enjoyed the episodic adventures of earlier animated television shows.
Episode 1 - Rising Storm! - The Fighting Style of Justice!
Episode 2 - Wolf Sword! Call Forth the Thunder of Courage!
Episode 3 - Steal the Metal Laster!
Episode 4 - Devil Trap - The Enslaved Village!
Episode 5 - Hot Fight at Absolute Zero!

Macross II "Lovers Again" (3 Volumes)
(1992) Japanime: Scifi   C-40m Dubbed   VA   Catalog #USR VD11
Japan Retail: $24.95
Dir: Kenichi Yatagai Character Design: Haruhiko Mikimoto
Mecha Design: Koichi Ohata, Junichi Akutsu, Jun Okuda
Art Dir: Hidenori Nakahata   Music Dir: Yasunori Honda
PC: Big West/LA Hero   Dist: U.S. Renditions
[**1/2]
Though the Macross II title gives the impression this is a sequel, the story is more of an alternative reality to the original Macross Saga. It can get pretty confusing, but the story features some familiar elements including the Zentraedi, Robotech style mechas, and plenty of singing. A plot device that can become tiresome if you don't like the particular style of music. A cocky reporter named Hibiki Kanzaki will do anything for a story and gets in trouble with the military and his boss when he pulls a surprise interview. An alien fleet approaches Earth; the Zentraedi splinter group called the Marduk have arrived to lay waste to the Earth. To counter the Earth singer Lynn Minmay who sings her enemies to peace, the Marduk have their own singers called "emulators" led by the beautiful Ishtar. A massive battle occurs in space and Hibiki teams up with a veteran war correspondent to cover the breaking news. The reporters manage to capture the injured Ishtar and bring her back to Earth. The Marduk make pursuit and a massive land battle takes place for Ishtar. Hibiki's attitudes toward journalism mature and he meets up with the ace pilot Slyvie Gena. Additional episodes follow in what can best be described as space/soap opera.
Volume 1 - Contact/Ishtar
Volume 2 - Festival/Marduk Disorder
Volume 3 - Station Break/Sing Along

Macross Plus - Part 1
(1994) Japanime: Scifi   C-40m Dubbed/Japanese with English Subtitles   VA
Catalog # LD80064   Japan   Retail: $14.99
Dir: Shoji Kawamori   Co-Dir: Shinichiro Watanabe   Scr: Keiko Nobumoto
Original Story: Studio Nue / Shoji Kawamori
Prod: Kaya Ohnishi, Minoru Takanashi, Yoshio Tsuda, Akira Inokuchi, Hirotake Kanada
Ex. Prod: Yoshimasa Ohnishi, Takashi Mogi, Hirohiko Sueyoshi, Tatsuo Miyata, Isamu Asami
Mechanic Design: Shoji Kawamori Character Design: Masayuki
Sound Dir: Masafumi Mima   Dir of Animation: Atsushi Aono
Music: Yoko Kanno with Members of the Israel Philharmonic Ochestra
PC: Big West/Macross Plus Project/Hero Co., Ltd.   Dist: Manga Entertainment, Inc.
[**1/2]
Macross and its numerous reincarnations run along the lines of a soap opera rather than an animated feature. Macross is a small universe in the phenomenal and successful world of Japanese animation. The series has taken on various incarnations in films, television series, comics, and video games. In the Macross future (2040 AD), the colony of Eden is beautiful and peaceful. Pilots Isamu Dyson and Guld, past friends, become bitter rivals over the love of Myung. They are opposing pilots in an important government contract to develop new transforming planes, Project Super Nova. Meanwhile Myung manages Sharon Apple, a virtual reality singer, who is the hottest thing around. Dyson and Guld battle with their fists, mind, and heart as well as their planes to win the affection of Myung and seal the government contract.

Macross Plus - Part 2
(1994) Japanime: Scifi   C-40m Dubbed/Japanese with English Subtitles   VA
Catalog # LD80064   Japan   Retail: $14.99
Dir: Shoji Kawamori   Co-Dir: Shinichiro Watanabe   Scr: Keiko Nobumoto
Original Story: Studio Nue / Shoji Kawamori
Prod: Kaya Ohnishi, Minoru Takanashi, Yoshio Tsuda, Akira Inokuchi, Hirotake Kanada
Ex. Prod: Yoshimasa Ohnishi, Takashi Mogi, Hirohiko Sueyoshi, Tatsuo Miyata, Isamu Asami
Mechanic Design: Shoji Kawamori Character Design: Masayuki
Sound Dir: Masafumi Mima   Dir of Animation: Atsushi Aono
Music: Yoko Kanno with Members of the Israel Philharmonic Ochestra
PC: Big West/Macross Plus Project/Hero Co., Ltd.   Dist: Manga Entertainment, Inc.
[**1/2]
Japanese animation falls into many different realms which will appeal to a variety of genre lovers. Macross is best suited for those who enjoy science fiction, romance, and soap operas that develop slowly over time. Continuing the love triangle of Guld, Dyson, and Myung, nothing too drastic develops in the second volume which ends on a cliffhanger note. The virtual program Sharon Apple is wowing audiences and selling out stadiums, but Dyson and his technonerd pal try to break into Sharon Apple's AI and take control of the program. Meanwhile, Myung is depressed and spends time with one of her old friends. She drops by her office late at night where an arsonist tries to burn down the facility. Luckily, Guld who has Zentraedi blood

receives a mysterious warning and manages to save Myung and win her affections. Hotshot Dyson isn't too happy with the outcome and decides to teach Guld a lesson. Both men pilot their robot/planes and take to the Earth, but the routine test match gets ugly and personal. Macross features some top-notch animation, a multicultural cast, and plenty of subplots, but can not be enjoyed in just one sitting or per episode basis. Unless you plan to devote time to the entire series, you'll never fully appreciate the ongoing story. Followed by:
Macross Plus - Part 3
(1994) Japanime: Scifi   C-40m Dubbed/Japanese with English Subtitles   VA
Catalog # LD80064   Japan   Retail: $14.99

Maddox-01: Metal Skin Panic
(1991) Japanime   C-50m Dubbed/Japanese with English Subtitles   VA
Catalog #ANI ET095-011   Japan Retail: $19.95
Dir/Scr: Nobuyuki Aramaki   Ex. Prod: Yoshida Hisatake, Maruyama Hidetoshi
DP: Okino Masahide   Music: Yashima Ken   Art Dir: Nango Yoichi
Character Design: Hideki Tamura
Mecha Design: Nobuyuki Aramaki, Kimitoshi Yamane
PC: FujiSankei Communications, International   Dist: AnimEigo
Matsumoto Yasunori   Sugimoto Koji
Asakami Yoko   Ellie Kusumoto
Sogabe Masayoshi   1st Lt. Kilgore
Ishida Yukiko   Nagura Shiori
Ikemizu Michihiro   Ellie's Superior
Hase Arihiro   Onose Haruo
[***]
Watching the first five minutes of this film will give you an understanding of why Japanese animation is so admired and loved by millions of fans all over the world. The incredible animation and the amazing attention to detail and technological viability help create a realistic world in rich colors. The Maddox-01 is the ultimate hi-tech weapon designed by the government. An enclosed battlesuit, the prototype proves itself brilliantly against a squad of tanks to the chagrin of the gung-ho tank commander. During transport, the suit accidentally lands near a gifted mechanic named Sujimoto Koiji. His curiosity gets the better of him and he becomes trapped in the suit. Simple events of life like eating and using the restroom become grand chores. Failing to remove himself from the suit, Koiji manages to operate the suit and proceeds to rendezvous with his waiting girlfriend. Of course, his antics cause a destructive rampage while he travels and tries to disengage himself from the suit. The military tank commander who sees the suit as a threat to his way of warfare takes a personal interest in destroying the young man and the suit completely. His antics go overboard as he battles against the suit in the heart of Tokyo. The end of the video is followed by a mini-documentary on the real weapons of modern warfare. Maddox-01 is a one-shot OAV film with no planned follow-ups. The reliable story is constrained in its time frame and doesn't shoot beyond any new bounds of animation. A quick and entertaining tale that will appeal to fans of anime mayhem and tech battles without the gratuitous blood and sex found in other titles.

Magic Crane, The

(1993) Kung-Fu   C-92m Chinese with English Subtitles
Hong Kong   Retail: $39.99
Dir: Benny Chan   Prod: Tsui Hark   PC: Film Workshop
Anita Mui   Tien "Butterfly" Lam
Tony Leung Chiu Wai   Kwun Mo
Rosamund Kwan   Pak Wan Fai
Lawrence Ng
[**1/2]
While watching Magic Crane, a strange sense of deja vu creeps into your thoughts. The story looks vaguely familiar and the actors portray clichéd characters that have appeared in countless pictures. If you enjoy wild, fanciful martial arts fantasy films, then Magic Crane will have moments of entertainment, but does not stand above other Hark productions and in many ways is a rehashing of various fantasy period-pieces.

On his way to a congress of kung-fu masters, an initiate (Leung) falls from a high cliff, only to be rescued by lovely Butterfly Lam who rides a huge crane. The famous martial arts school of the world gather for a special conference, but a villain amongst their midst poisons the masters and takes over the world of martial arts. He and his seductive sister are then defeated by a powerful master who uses a giant bell to ring his foes to death. The rest of the movie features plenty of battles between the warring martial arts factions, an equally fierce rivalry between Butterfly and Pak Wan Fai who believes Butterfly killed her father, Master Pak. Of course, there's the Magic Crane who provides transportation and friendship. When the truth is discovered, the heroes ban together and defeat the evil bell master. Pak and Kwun Mo return to Tein Chong Mountain, while Butterfly disappears into the sky.

Martial Arts: The Chinese Masters
(1981) Kung-Fu Documentary   C-53m English Narration
Catalog #PAVR-569
Prod: Roger Morris Ex. Prod: Anthony Delano DP: Jim Thomas
Cameraman: Ron Tufnell   Editor: Neville Donoghue, Robin Parsons
Design: Jerry Takigawa   Dist: Pacific Arts Video Records
[***]
A documentary about traditional Chinese Martial Arts, sponsored by the London Daily Mirror. Properly known as wushu (kung-fu) in China, this video highlights various routines performed by a touring troupe of experts. The video is divided into segments with demonstrations on weapons, mind over matter, combat katas (routine), and free forms. No wires are used nor is there any trick photography, you are actually seeing a recording of the live demonstrations which are performed by a talented troupe of men and women from China. The video also provides split-screen viewing to allow various camera angles on the screen. The demos are pretty standard and not intended to imitate any Hong Kong kung-fu films. Instead, the video provides a fascinating glimpse into real martial arts for those who have an interest in an ancient discipline.

Martial Arts Master Wong Fei Hung
(1994) Kung-Fu   C-94m Chinese with English Subtitles
Catalog #1519   Hong Kong   Retail: $39.99
Dir: Hwang Hang Lee   Dist: Tai Seng Video

Chin Kar Lok, Lam Ching Ying
[**1/2]
Though not in the league of a Tsui Hark's Wong Fei Hung films, Lok provides a solid performance in this good non-flying martial arts film. A lighter, simpler version of a young Wong Fei Hung and his adventures. This time Wong is a little more carefree and not as serious in trying to change the country or getting involved in societal woes. He's young and wants to have a good time, spending most of his time gambling with fighting crickets and beating up thugs. All his father wants in life is for Wong to be serious and take care of the family business, Po Chi Lam. Wong continues his reckless ways, but then his father passes on and his life changes. Rival Lo Wai doesn't want Wong to take over the business so he challenges him. Wong manages to win and along the way meets a very attractive Japanese woman. She is the sister of a Japanese warrior who is traveling around China and challenging the great martial arts masters of the land. He has yet to lose a fight and plans to return to Japan, but then hears about Wong Fei Hung and can't resist the challenge. The Japanese woman falls in love with Wong. She is torn between her love and her loyalty to her brother. In the finale, the two masters duel to the death.

Martial Arts of Shaolin 1, 2, 3
See Shaolin Temple 1, 2, 3
A series of films about Shaolin disciples, starring a young and whimsical Jet Li (Li Lian Jie).

Martial Club - See Instructors of Death

Mary From Beijing (Awakening)
(1992) Romance   C-103 min   Chinese with English Subtitles   Type I
Catalog #1370   Hong Kong   Retail: $39.99
Dir/Scr: Sylvia Chang   Prod: Hon Pou Chu Ex. Prod: Anthony Chow
Associate Prod: Victor Chu   Executive in Charge of Prod: Zhang Yimou
DP: Christopher Doyle   Art Dir: William Chang   Editor: Yu Shum, Kong Chi Leung
Music by Music Factory   Assistant Dir: Bill Yip, Crystal Kwok
Prod Manager: Jessinta LiuProd Supervisor: Lo Fook Yuen
Dist: Universe Laser & Video Co. Ltd.
Gong Li, Kenny Bee, Wilson Lam, John Kiang, Cynthia Cheung, Jan Lam, Bao Wan, Nanette Chu Mu, Pao Fong, Lawrence Ahmon, Cheng Chen Yiu, Melvin Wong
[***]
Gong Li continues her acting career outside the realm of Chinese epics with this simple, but likeable little film. Gong Li is Ma Lei, a newly arrived immigrant to Hong Kong from mainland China. Though she spent the majority of her life in China, she was born in Hong Kong and hopes to get an identity card to work and reside permanently. Since her Chinese name sounds like Mary, the Chinese L sounds like an R, people wrongfully call her Mary. She is hired by a jeweler, Peter, and soon moves in with him. He takes care of her and supports her, but is not quite ready to show Mary to his parents. His excuse, wait until you learn more Cantonese or English. Meanwhile, he continues his own lecherous lifestyle filled with parties and loose woman while devoted Mary stays home alone and walks the dog.

Mary eventually bumps into her new next door neighbor, a handsome young man named Wong Kwok Wai. Unknown to Mary, he is a wealthy man in the process of a divorce with his socialite wife Elizabeth. Slowly, but surely the romance develops and there is a strong mutual attraction between both characters. When Mary decides to leave Peter, he tries to win her back with material possessions. There's nothing overtly unique or breathtaking about the film, but the down to Earth elements of romance and love are well portrayed by Gong Li and the cast.

Master, The   (Master Wong Fei Hung 92)
(1989) Kung-Fu   C-91m Chinese & English with Chinese Subtitles   Type II
Catalog #SEL 0487   Hong Kong   Retail: $39.99
Dir: Tsui Hark   Prod: Anthony Chow & Michael Lai   Prod Supervisor: David Lo
PC: Film Workshop
Jet Li, Jerry Trimble, Corey Yuen, Crystal Kwok, To Wai Woo, Lam Ping Hong
[**]
Basically a fish out of water story and reminiscent of Paul Hogan's "Crocodile Dundee". Hoping to cash in on the early success of Jet Li, Tsui Hark casts him as a young martial artist visiting his uncle in Los Angeles. Unfortunately Jet Li can't speak a word of English and runs into trouble as soon as he gets off the airplane. Though set in modern-day Los Angeles, this is definitely Li's weakest film to date. Chuck (Li) arrives in America to visit Uncle Tak who is running a medicine clinic and teaches students kung-fu, a take off of Po Chi Lam in the Wong Fei Hung clinic. A cocky American named Johnny wants to shut Tak down and control all the business. He uses his gang of thugs to terrorize Tak and eventually must face Li. On top of a skyscraper, they battle to the finish.

Master Killer, The   (36th Chamber of Shaolin)
(1978) Kung-Fu   C-115m   Dubbed   Hong Kong   Retail: $19.99
Dir: Liu Chia Liang (Lau Kar Wing)   Scr: I Kuang
Prod: Run Run Shaw, Mona Fong
DP: Huang Yeh Tai Editor: Chiang Hsing Lung, Li Yen Hai   Music: Chen Yung Yu
Art Dir: Johnson Tsao   Lighting: Chen Feng
Associate Prod: Huang Chia Hsi   Assistant Dir: Huang Pa Ching, Tang Wan
Makeup:: Wu Hsu Ching   Props: Li Wo MAD: Liu Chia Liang
PC: Shaw Brothers
Gordon Liu Chia Hui   San Te "Master Killer"
Liu Chia Yung, Wang Yu, Lo Lieh, Yu Yang, Wei Hung, Hua Lun, Chen Szu Chia
[****]
People often ask me what's my favorite martial arts film? Though I can think of a dozen personal favorites, I usually answer with one or two films. Those who are familiar with the genre will easily remember Master Killer, one of my all-time favorite martial arts films. A movie used as a personal benchmark for rating other kung-fu films. From the opening scenes, you sense that this is not your run of the mill chop-socky film. Lightning flashes and the music begins under the opening credits. Gordon Liu in monk mode - bald, shirtless, looking deadly - stands erect with hands clasped in a praying stance. Suddenly he explodes into action performing with his hands and a variety of weapons, demonstrating his prowess and skills.
Though I don't give many kung-fu movies four stars, I did with the Master Killer because it is a

perfect representation of the genre's appeal and its positive strengths. I've seen this kung-fu film more than any other and I still enjoy it time after time. The fight scenes are brilliantly choreographed and not a single element is treated with triviality. Noted by fans and experts as the classic Shaw Brothers film that ignited the popularity in post-Bruce Lee martial arts movies and helped garner respect for the genre. The film made Liu Chia Hui a superstar in Asia, second only to Jackie Chan. Even today, Liu portrays his image of a Shaolin monk in films. Enough said, just go and see the film. The following is a detailed review.

The story revolves around the never ceasing battle between the Manchurian Chings and the Chinese Mings. A Ming general, played by Liu Chia Yung, is discussing his plans with a teacher/patriot in a Canton inn. Yung is determined to end Manchurian tyranny and will ambush the Lord General when he visits Canton. The Ming general launches his attack, but the Lord General is not there...it's a trap. He battles with General Ting and is executed.

After the fight, we are introduced to the main character, Liu Yu Te (Gordon Lui). He doesn't know any martial arts, but is an intelligent philosophy student studying the annals of Confucius and other great scholars. His teacher/patriot is disturbed at the killings and encourages his students to always stand against injustice. One student asks "What can one man do, they're so many?" The teacher replies calmly, "One can do a little, but when united with others, they can accomplish anything." Liu and his two classmates visit the teacher and join the rebellion. When a crackdown occurs, his teacher and classmates are all executed. Even Lui's family is wrongfully imprisoned and murdered while trying to help him escape. Liu and his friend escape into the countryside, but only Liu barely makes it to Shaolin Temple.

The wounded Liu is nursed back to health and ordered to leave the temple. A high-ranking abbot believes Liu is deceitful and dangerous and that Shaolin should avoid entanglement with the outside world. The chief abbot takes pity on Liu and allows him to remain at the temple. The high-ranking abbot consents, but with reservations toward Liu who changes his name to San Te. A year passes and Liu has adapted to the tranquil life of a Buddhist monk. He wants to learn martial arts and is told that thirty-five chambers of kung-fu exist. He asks his superior which one is the best...the highest is the sacred thirty-fifth chamber. Liu agrees to start there and enters a chamber filled with senior monks reciting scriptures from the Sutra. What kind of kung-fu is this, Liu asks. The head of the chamber ejects Liu who runs to his immediate superior. "That's the highest form you'll ever see, the ultimate chamber," he replies to the confused Liu. In defeat, Liu agrees to start one down at the thirty-fourth chamber. Smiling, his superior takes him to the first chamber which appears to be nothing more than a log floating in a pool of water.

In one of the best training sequences of any film (half the film is dedicated to it), we watch Liu train from a novice to a master killer. The film does not trivialize the importance of training and spends detailed time. There is no secret scroll, super potion, or magic stance. No do-it-yourself book or learn to fight in ten easy steps. Liu must train hard from morning to night in an environment that can only breed excellence. He has the best teachers, each a master of an individual technique, and trains with excellent students. Liu masters the basics, developing balance, arm strength, wrist strength, leg strength, speed, eye coordination, and endurance. After completing the ten basic chambers in record time, he proceeds to learn fighting forms, kicking styles, and then weaponry. Having trained in kung-fu for many years, I can honestly say the training scenes are truly motivating, fascinating, and practical. In an excellent montage, we see San Te's progression through all the upper chambers. After completing a difficult test to graduate to the next level, the chamber master smiles and says, "San Te, you're not bad."

Five years later, San Te becomes a head priest and allowed to teach his own chamber. The high-ranking monk from the beginning worries that San Te has been promoted too quickly and shows signs of ambition and aggression. He challenges San Te to a competition which will test his skills. San Te loses twice to the monk who is a master of the butterfly swords. Despondent, San Te wanders in the bamboo yard late at night. While practicing, he comes up with a new weapon and invents the three-sectional staff.

After winning, he proposes to open a new chamber, the thirty-sixth which will be dedicated to teaching commoners kung-fu and how to defend themselves. Angered by his words, the chief abbot expels San Te who returns home to bring justice in Canton. In a scene that may confuse casual viewers, he recruits a number of pupils in Canton. These characters are legendary heroes who will later continue the legacy of Shaolin. For those waiting to see San Te's training in action, you won't be disappointed. Skills from each chamber are put to the test. San Te defeats the General's top fighters in heroic fashion. General Ting is determined to destroy the rebels and assembles an army to attack Shaolin Temple. The army is ambushed by a shower of rice and thrown into disarray. General Ting rides after San Te who stops atop a beautiful scenic hilltop. Confident and poised, San Te draws his three-sectional staff and challenges General Ting's double swords. A fantastic film for martial arts/action fans and a great kung-fu tale about Shaolin Temple with Hong Kong's best loved monk, Gordon Liu Chia Hui.

Master Wong Vs. Master Wong
(1993) Comedy Kung-Fu   C-95m Chinese with English Subtitles
Catalog #1270   Hong Kong   Retail: $39.99
Dir: Lee Lik Chee   Dist: Ocean Shores Video, Ltd./Tai Seng Video
Alan Tam, Carol Cheng, Anthony Wong, Teresa Mo, Ng Man Tat, Eric Tsang, Do Do Cheng
[**]
Sherlock Holmes, Robin Hood, King Arthur, and Wong Fei Hung may all be great heroes, but that doesn't make them immune to parodies. The film runs like a bad Mel Brooks' movie. The Once Upon A Time In China movies are the guidelines for spoofing Wong Fei Hung, Auntie Yee, and Wong's students. The story starts off with a grandfather telling a group of children about a Wong story that is unknown to all. Supposedly Wong is a con-artist who capitalizes on his fame by selling souvenirs, knick-knacks, and rigging demonstrations. His reputation does exist, but more through luck and false circumstances. He knows kung-fu by accident, performing his famous no-shadow kick only when under duress. He is invited to Canton to make money by an unscrupulous business man. In Canton, he meets a beautiful martial artist who wishes to challenge Wong Fei Hung. A movie best viewed for those familiar with the Wong Fei Hung character and appreciate parodies, because the few good jokes center around past film references.

M.D. Geist: The Most Dangerous Ever
(1986) Japanime   C-45m Dubbed/Japanese with English Subtitles
Catalog #USM 1507/USM 1024   Japan Retail: $19.95/$29.95
Dir: Hayato Ikeda   Original Story/Assistant Dir/Mecha Design: Koichi Ohata
Scr: Riku Sanjo   Animation Dir: Hiroshi Negishi
Character Design: Tsuneo Ninomiya   Art Dir: Yoshinori Takao

PC: Nippon Columbia Co., Ltd.   Dist: U.S. Manga Corps
[**1/2]

> "Geist-02: Second Most Dangerous Soldier developed under the MDS Program.
> A genetically-engineered soldier, Geist possesses superhuman physical abilities
> and extensive combat skills. Performed beyond expectations in combat. Subject
> evaluated too unstable to be integrated into society. Permanently imprisoned aboard
> an orbital satellite."
>
> From M.D. Geist

The future is a dark place for mankind in this scifi adventure which features a good dose of violence and action. The M.D.'s are the most dangerous soldiers ever created, biologically and genetically altered with vast superpowers and capabilities. One of them known as Geist escapes from his orbital confines and isn't in the best of moods. He lands on the planet Jerra and spots a battle suit. While attempting to confiscate it, a gang of marauders attack him. He kills their leader without batting an eye and joins the marauders, who are now led by a young woman who tries and fails to seduce the enigmatic Geist. He joins forces with the military to prevent the release of the Death Force which could possibly annihilate ever human being on the planet Jerra. Geist and the heroes infiltrate the Brain Palace citadel of the Nexrum invaders to stop the doomsday project from activating in less than twelve hours. Geist is left with the decision to stop the doomsday device or let it runs its course and destroy the people who imprisoned him. If you really must know the outcome, then read the review for the sequel. The version I reviewed includes five additional minutes of footage filmed by Koichi Ohata.

M.D. Geist II: Death Force
(1996) Japanime   C-45m Dubbed   Catalog #USM 1508 Japan
Retail: $19.95
Dir: Koichi Ohata   Scr: Riku Sanjo   Music: Yoshiaki Ouchi
PC: Nippon Columbia Co., Ltd.   Dist: U.S. Manga Corps

Jason Beck	**MD Geist**
John Hollywood	**MD Krauser**
Joan Baker	**Vaiya**
Greg Stuhr	**Breston**
David Fuhrer	**Eagle**
Vincent Bagnall	**Major**
Howard Glassroth	**Non-Comm.**

[**1/2]

Ten years later, a sequel is created from the original MD Geist. This time creator Ohata (Genocyber) helms the latest adventure. Ohata enjoys blending images of carnage from human, animal, and robotic elements into bizarre, twisted creatures. Geist has sided with the death force and turned his back against humanity. The years have gone by and the unleashed death force are waging a war against humankind. They appear in various forms, but are intent on destroying all human life. In a desperate attempt to stop them, the survivors valiantly search for a hero and make a last stand at a giant fortress commanded by warlord Krauser. He is the original MD prototype, Geist-01 and vows to destroy Geist for its actions against humanity. Their creator, Dr. Breston has his own plans to destroy both MD's and rule the planet Jerra.

Mermaid Forest   (Rumik World: Mermaid Forest)
(1991) Japanime: Horror   C-56m Dubbed   VA
Catalog #USM 1453 Japan Retail: $14.95
Dir: Takaya Mizutani   Scr: Masaichiro Okubo
Character Design: Sayuri Ichiishi Art Dir: Katsuyoshi Kanemura
Music: Kenji Kawai   PC: Shogakukan/Victor Musical Industries Inc.
Dist: U.S. Manga Corps
(created by Rumiko Takahashi)
[***]
Those who eat the forbidden mermaid's flesh will either die a horrible death or be cursed to live for eternity. Based on that simple premise, we follow the story of a boy named Yuta and his adventures. Having been turned into an immortal, Yuta searches Japan and wanders for centuries. He encounters all sorts of characters, but finally bonds with a girl named Mana. The film provides background material on Yuta and Mana, but lacks the overall tightness and intensity of the second film. The film still has a fascinating story and offers character development to help enhance the second film.

Mermaid's Scar
(1992) Japanime: Horror   C-50m Dubbed   VA
Catalog # VV MS-001   Japan Retail: $19.95
Dir: Morio Asaka   Character Design and Animation Dir: Kumiko Takahashi
Art Dir: Hidetoshi Kaneko Music: Norihiro Tsuri
PC: Shogakukan, Inc.   Dist: Viz Video
(based on the comics by Rumiko Takahashi)
[***1/2]
A wonderful combination of fantasy and horror set in a small ocean town in contemporary Japan. A young teenage boy, Yuta, and girl, Mana, quietly travel around the countryside. They seem carefree and calmer than the years they represent. In reality, they are immortals cursed for eating Mermaid's flesh. The rare flesh will cause most people to go insane and mutate into a hideous creature, but for a few individuals they are granted immortality as their curse. Having lived for hundreds of years trapped in a youthful body may sound wonderful, but time can pay a horrible price on the mind. Their adventures bring them to a house near the ocean where a young boy and his mother live comfortably. Appearances are deceiving and strange things start to happen. When it is discovered the boy is a mermaid eater, centuries old, problems arise. He is older than Yuta and Mana, corrupted by his wisdom and the hatred of his childlike body. He attempts to feed his female companion the Mermaid's flesh, but she mutates into a horrible creature. Only Yuta and Mana are left to stop the evil child. A dark moral tale from the mind of manga genius Takahashi.

Merry Christmas, Mr. Lawrence
(1983) War   C-124m   English   R   VA   Catalog #VHS 80049
Japan/UK
Dir: Nagisa Oshima Scr: Nagisa Oshima Prod: Jeremy Thomas, Paul Mayersberg
DP: Toichiro Narushima   Editor: Tomoyo Oshima   Music: Ryuichi Sakamoto
Prod Design: Shigemasa Toda   Art Dir: Andrew Sanders   Dist: MCA/Universal

(based on the novel The Seed and the Sower by Laurens Van Der Post)

David Bowie	Celliers
Tom Conti	Col. John Lawrence
Ryuichi Sakamoto	Capt. Yonei
Takeshi	Sgt. Hara
Jack Thompson	Hicksley-Ellis
Johnny Okura	Kanemoto
Alistair Browning	DeJong
James Malcolm	Celliers' Brother
Christopher Brown	Celliers at Age 12

Yuya Uchida, Ryunosuke Kaneda, Takashi Naito, Tamio Ishikura, Rokko Toura, Kan Mikami, Yuji Honma, Daisuke Iijima, Hideo Murota, Barry Dorking, Geoff Clendon [**]

Intended to bring new light to Japanese and British relationships during World War II, Merry Christmas, Mr. Lawrence is a ponderous, lengthy film that will have little appeal outside of viewers who might enjoy prison films on World War II (Bridge on the River Kwai, King Rat, Empire of the Sun, Return to the River Kwai). Even then, the film fails to deliver coherency as an odd relationship develops between the Japanese in charge and their British prisoners. The Japanese camp commander, Yonei, and Sergeant Hara are portrayed as one-dimensional sadist who relish in over-dramatic statements and physical punishment. On the other hand, the British soldiers maintain their dignity and rationale, never quavering under stress or torture. Though produced in Japan, the film's message seems anti-Japanese and doesn't do much for the notion of Japanese conformity.

The year is 1942, World War II in the Pacific is running full steam and Japan's blitzkrieg has resulted in thousands of allied prisoners. At one prison camp in Java, the Japanese soldiers brutalize their prisoners . The majority of the film involves torture and punishment which will not appeal to the faint of heart. Though Japan's atrocity to prisoners is a true fact, the film seems like a lesson in cruelty rather than a portrait of determination and strength found in similar prisoner of war films. Homosexuality in the prison also play a significant role as does past memories and torments.

A new prisoner is transferred, Bowie, and the commander takes a special interest in him. Bowie refuses to bow to conventions and a severe dispute is created between the Japanese and English. In addition, the commander demands to know the names of prisoners who are ammunition/weapons experts, but the prisoner commander refuses and a battle of wills develop which poorly imitates the brilliant intensity found in Bridge on the River Kwai. Then the film's focus shifts to a lengthy flashback of Bowie's childhood life and his relationship with his younger brother. The director/writer's intent is befuddled and the film fails on a number of levels, lacking a big budget and high-profile actors, there's little appeal. Director Oshima is not a mainstream filmmaker, as proven in his other film, In the Realm of Senses.

Even with a fondness and knowledge of World War II, expect to a film that fails to capitalize on developing characters and focusing on a central theme. At numerous points, the film could have ended with a fade to black, but continues on with its meandering story until the war's end.

Midnight Angels
(1996) Action Kung-Fu   C-87m Dubbed   Catalog #21203

Hong Kong   Retail: $9.99
Dir/Scr: Teresa Woo Presented by Sally Aw   Prod: Garry Chan, Amy Choi
DP: Sander Lee   Editor: Norman Wong   Music: Richard Lo
Prod Designer & Associate Prod: William Yuen Prod Supervisor: Margaret Cheung
MAD: Leung Siu Hung
English Dialogue & Post Prod: Larry Dolgin
PC: Molesworth Limited   Dist: Eastern Heroes/Arena Home Video
Cynthia Luster (Yukari Oshima), Moon Lee, Elaine Lui, Alex Fu, Hideki Saijo, John
Keung, Hwang Jang Lee, Yeung Kwan, Jimmy Wang Yu
[**]
More Angel madness (Angel on Fire, Angel 1 & 2) from Hong Kong's hottest girls with guns.
These films are pretty much cut from the same mold and you'll either love them or hate them.
Just think of a Charlie's Angels re-run and you get a good idea of what you're going to get. The
Angels are an elite group of crime fighting detectives. Though they're not police officers, they
work with the law and outside when legal methods don't work. Times have changed and the
Angles have some male members in the squad, they all answer to their slick-dressed boss played
by Wang Yu. Most of the action takes place in the beginning and the end while the middle
section of the film plods along at a slow pace. The Angels must keep an eye on some criminals
who have established a base at a nearby construction site. In one silly scene, the Angels know of
the villains whereabouts at a mansion and must rescue some agents. They try to infiltrate the
mansion, but manage to get captured in the process. Next the villains plan a daring armored car
heist, but one of the male Angels is inside the car. The car is heisted and then buried at an open
spot at the construction site. The driver, in on the scheme, is murdered and the armored car dug
out. Luckily, the hero has survived and takes on the villains until the police arrive. In true camp
fashion, the last scene showcases the entire cast gathered around a hospital bed. One of the
angels slips on a banana peel, the cast breaks into laughter, and the frame freezes. Thus ends
another madcap adventure for the midnight angels.

Mishima
(1985) DramaC/B&W-120m   Japanese with English Subtitles   R   VA
Catalog #11530   Japan/USA   Retail: $19.95
Dir: Paul Schrader   Scr: Paul Schrader, Leonard Schrader (conceived in collaboration
with Jun Shiragi, literary executor of the Mishima estate)
Prod: Mata Yamamoto, Tom Luddy   Ex. Prod: George Lucas, Francis Coppola
DP: John Bailey   Editor: Michael Chandler, Tomoyo Oshima Music: Philip Glass
Prod Design: Eiko Ishioka   Art Design: Kazuo Takenaka
Set Design: Kyoji Sasaki
Makeup: Yashuhiro Kawaguchi, Masayuki Okubi, Noriyo Ida
Costumes: Etsuko Yagyu
PC: Zoetrope Studios/Filmlink International/Lucasfilm Ltd.   Dist: Warner Home Video
Ken Ogata   Yukio Mishima
Masayuki Shionoya Morita
Hiroshi Mikami   Cadet No. 1
Junya Fukuda   Cadet No. 2
Shigeto Tachihara   Cadet No. 3

Junkichi Orimoto	Gen. Mashita
Minoru Hodaka	Ichigaya Colonel
Go Riju	Mishima, Age 18-19
Yuki Nagahara	Mishima, Age 5
Kyuzo Kobayashi	Literary Friend
Haruko Kato	Grandmother
Kimiko Ito	Grandmother's Nurse
Hideo Fukuhara	Military Doctor
Yosuke Mizuno	"Yukoku" Producer
Yuichi Saito	Student
Bando	Mizoguchi
Hisako Manda	Mariko
Naomi Oki	Girls
Miki Takakura	
Imari Tauji	Madame
Koichi Sato	Kashiwagi
Shinji Miura	Pavilion Acolyte
Sawada	Osamu
Reisen Lee	Kiyomi
Setsuko Karasuma	Mitsuko
Tadanori Yokoo	Natsuo
Yasuaki Kurata	Takei
Mitsuru Hirata	Thug
Sachiko Akagi	Thug's Girl Friend
Sachiko Hidari	Osamu's Mother
Tsutomu Harada	Romeo
Mami Okamoto	Juliet
Nagashima	Isao
Hiroshi Katsuno	Lt. Hori
Hiroki Ida	Izutsu
Jun Negami	Kurahara
Ryo Ikebe	Interrogator
Shoichiro Sakata	Isao's Classmate
Naoya Makoto	Kendo Instructor
Kojiro Oka	MP

[***]

On Nov 25, 1970, a small group of men barricaded themselves within a military office and demanded Japan return to a more imperial/military society. If their demands were not met, the group leader would commit seppuku, ritual suicide. As history shows, the government did not give in and the man did commit suicide. Perhaps the true-life incident would have been forgotten, but the man was none other than Yukio Mishima, one of Japan's best-know modern writers.

A highly ambitious and stylized biography of Japan's most controversial post-WWII author, playwright, actor, director, and militarist. The film is a biographical interpretation of Yukio Mishima's life, full of allegory in reference to his literary career. Mishima led an unsuccessful coup against the government, hoping to revitalize Japan's warrior-like heritage. When his demands weren't met, he committed traditional seppuku, suicide with a knife. His misguided passion to merge life and art led to a number of famous books. Scene's of Mishima's actual life (shot in black & white) are contrasted with vivid dramatizations (in opulent color) of key fictional works that grappled with his emotional crises and homosexual urges. The film is artistic and delves slowly into Mishima's world, at times trying the patience of contemporary filmgoers. I would not recommend this film unless you are an admirer of the author's works (which are referenced to frequently) or interested in Mishima's life which should be researched before seeing the film.

Monster City - See Wicked City

Mortal Combat	**(Crippled Avengers)**		
(1978) Kung-Fu	**C-100m**	**Dubbed**	**Hong Kong Retail: $19.99**
Dir: Chang Cheh	**Scr: Chang Cheh, I Kuang**		
Prod: Mona Fong	**Ex. Prod: Run Run Shaw**	**PC: Shaw Bros.**	
Kuo Chui	**Blind Peddler**		
Chiang Sheng	**Retarded Swordsman**		
Lo Meng	**Deaf Blacksmith**		
Sun Chien	**Legless Fighter**		
Chen Kuan Tai	**Nobleman**		
Lu Feng	**Noble's Son**		

[***]

A group of handicapped heroes seek vengeance on an evil master who crippled them. Director Chang incorporates the talented Venom gang with veteran star Chen Kuan Tai in an unusual, but action-packed martial arts tale of justice and revenge. Chen Kuan Tai is a noble master who returns home one evening to discover a ruthless attack on his family. His wife is murdered and his son's hands have been chopped off...American versions have toned down the graphic violence. In an act of anger, he murders the attackers and slowly descends into a void of callousness and hatred for healthy people. He teaches his crippled son (Lu Feng) kung-fu and equips him with two metallic hands. Together, they become vicious bullies who terrorize the town.

Through separate events, the father and his son manage to cripple four different men for getting in their way. A true underdog mentality follows the heroes of the film, for even in victory, they will never regain their full health. A noble swordsman enters the town and demands justice. He attacks Chen's mansion, but is beaten and mentally tortured until he becomes a human vegetable. The other crippled avengers take the retarded swordsman to his master's home. The cripples team together, study under the master, develop unique styles which take advantage of their handicap, and return to town for revenge. Meanwhile, Chen has invited a number of great martial arts masters to celebrate with him and his son. Tragically, the masters do not realize the evil descent of Chen's ways and fight against the crippled avengers. A good number of noble fighters are unnecessarily killed, especially the iron body fighter whose body is incredibly powerful, but not a match against the metal legs of Sun Chien. Some of the training methods and scenes involving the handicap will be a bit of a stretch, but provide plenty of acrobatic energy and unseen excitement.

In standard Chang form, the fight scenes are fast, energetic, and clever with hardly any use of wire-work or camera trickery. The site of handicapped warriors mixes pathos with humor, but should not be considered an offense to the handicapped population. An enjoyable film with charismatic portrayals from the entire Chang gang.

Mothra   (Mosura)
(1961) Monster   C-100m   Dubbed   Japan Retail: $9.99
Dir: Inoshiro Honda, Lee Kresel (American version)   Scr: Shinichi Sekizawa, Robert Myerson (American version)   Prod: Tomoyuki Tanaka, David Horne (American version)
DP: Hajime KoizumiSp. Fx: Eiji Tsuburaya   PC: Toho Studios
Frankie Sakai, Hiroshi Koizumi, Kyoko Katawa, The Itoh Sisters
[**]
"Don't mess with mommy, especially if she weighs over 100 tons!" The characters in Spielberg's Lost World should have watched Mothra and taken warning. A group of scientists and entrepreneurs (a popular combo in monster films) discover a giant egg and decide to study it and reap profits from its discovery. Of course, mother Mothra, a giant multi-colored butterfly, doesn't take kindly to her children being in show business at such an early age. She intervenes and terrorizes Tokyo. The film spends a considerable time in the battle sequences, until the egg hatches and the baby caterpillars return to their mother. Mothra is never portrayed as a pure villain, but more of a concerned mother. She gladly returns to her island with her children. A beloved member of the pantheon of Godzilla-like monsters but who has a heart of mommy gold. Plenty of action, neat sets, models, and appeal for vintage monster fans.

My Father is A Hero   (Jet Li's The Enforcer)
(1995) Kung-Fu   C-98m Chinese with English Subtitles   Catalog #1767
Hong Kong   Retail: $39.99
Dir: Yuen Kwai   Scr: Sandy Shaw   Story: Wong Jing
Prod: Wong Jing, Tiffany Chen   Ex. Prod: Charles W.K. Meung, Jimmy W.S. Meung
PC: Win's Entertainment Ltd.   Dist: Tai Seng Video
Jet Li, Anita Mui, Xie Miao
[***]
Another excellent Jet Li action film for fans who prefer a contemporary setting. In modern-day Peking, Jet Li is a local crook who gets involved with a gang of criminals. His seedy work keeps him away from his devoted wife and son (Xie Miao), a young martial arts champion in China. His son is disappointed with his father's lack of time and indifference, but still loves him deeply and the bond is evident on screen. The poor family live in a small home and Li's reputation makes his son a target of local school bullies. One day while coming home, Li is arrested in front of his family and dragged off. Gossip and distrust befall upon Li's family and his son sheds tears for his father. While in prison, Li hooks up with a criminal and they both escape to Hong Kong and join a ruthless syndicate.
The martial arts dynamics between Jet Li and his son are electrifying as well as emotionally engaging (Also see New Legend of Shaolin). At times the film does delve into the melodramatic and features a brutal torture scene with Li's son. However, the film's focus on the father and son relationship create a wonderful impulse for the martial arts action. Supporting characters also

play a strong part in the film. There's a few twists and turns, so don't keep reading if you enjoy surprises.

At an enormous Beijing arena, Xie and hundreds of children perform amazing wushu (kung-fu) techniques at a national competition. Li does appear at the tournament, but instead of as a spectator he gets involved in a violent fight with some criminals. Eventually Li is arrested by the police and torn away from his family. In reality, Li is an undercover officer who must go deep into the organized crime world of Hong Kong. He and a fellow criminal (Uncle) escape from the Chinese prison and travel to Hong Kong where they meet up with a ruthless crime boss. Anita Mui is the Hong Kong police officer who encounters the crime boss and Jet Li during a brazen double-cross against some foreign weapons dealers. The criminals escape, but Li and Mui confront each other. In the confusion, Li doesn't kill Mui, but actually saves her life and maintains his undercover. Mui is intrigued by Li and starts an investigation that leads her back to mainland China. She meets Li's wife and son. Li's wife is heartbroken and ill, her health doesn't recover and she places her son in Mui's hands. Mui and the boy travel back to Hong Kong where they become separated. Li's son is captured by the criminals and used as leverage. Li reveals he is a police officer and must battle the criminals. His criminal friend (Uncle) risks his life to save Li's son and turns against the vicious crime boss. The climatic showdown draws Li, his son, and Mui to a ship rigged with explosives and full of wealthy patrons who are taken hostage. In over-the-top Hong Kong style, the action explodes and the heroes risk all to stop the villains.

My Lucky Star
(1985) Comedy Kung-Fu   C-99m Dubbed   Catalog #XE XA 2071
Hong Kong   Retail: $9.99
Dir: Samo Hung   Scr: Barry Wong   Prod: Leonard K.C. Ho
Ex. Prod: Raymond Chow
DP: Ngor Chi Guan, Arthur Wong Editor: Peter Cheung, Joseph Chiang
Music: Michael Lai Prod Manager: Amy Chin
Art Dir: Eddie Ma, Fung Yuen Chee   Makeup: Wong Yuk Ting
Dist: Hong Kong Connection/Arena Home Video

Jackie Chan	**Muscles**
Samo Hung	**Kidstuff**
Yuen Biao	**Ricky**
Sibelle Hu	**Officer Woo**

Lam Ching Ying, Richard Ng, Eric Tsang, Charlie Ching, Fung Shui Fan, Wu Ma, Paul Chang, Michiko Nishiwaki, Dick Wei, James Tien, Tso Tat Wah, Lau Kar Wing
[**1/2]

Samo heads an all-star cast in this comedy and action caper that revolves solidly around two main thematic points. Childish, perverted humor and fast-paced action. Jackie Chan and Yuen Biao lead the way in action, but their scenes are bookended throughout the film. The main core is the comedy with Samo and his lucky star troupe. Samo's group of kooks, cons, and perverts were close friends during their childhood orphanage days. They're pretty harmless (like Paulie Shore/Chris Farley/Bud Abbott), but troublesome, juvenile, and annoying. For some reason, the Hong Kong police believe they can help solve a major crime problem. Officers Chan and Biao are on mission to Tokyo to capture a crooked Hong Kong cop who ran off with evidence equaling a hundred million dollars. While chasing the crooks in a Japanese amusement park (broad daylight), Chan and Biao are ambushed by a clan of colorfully-dressed ninjas. Yuen is captured and Chan is really depressed. Why not send re-enforcements or ask the Japanese police for help? That won't be necessary. Instead, the next hour of the film deeply focuses on the antics of Samo and his foibled friends. First, Samo has to convince them to join the police mission, then they have to spend some time groping Sibelle Hu with childish pranks. The humor can be funny at times, but slapstick mayhem is more like it. The gang finally arrive in Japan and help Chan. Pretending to be criminals from Hong Kong, Samo and his gang penetrate the ninjas hideout at the amusement park. In no time, everyone is running around, chasing each other, and fighting. A hit-and-miss comedy with some of the hottest Hong Kong stars acting pretty darn silly.

My Neighbor Totoro (Tonari no Totoro)
(1993) Japanime: Family   C-87m Dubbed/Japanese with English Subtitles
G   VA   Catalog # 4276   Japan Retail: $19.95
Dir/Scr/Prod: Hayao Miyazaki   Ex. Prod: Yasuyoshi Tokuma
Music: Jo Hisaishi   Art Design: Kazuo Oga
Animator: Yoshiharu Sato   Prod Camera Supervisor: Hisao Shirai
PC: Studio Ghibli   Dist: Fox Video
English Voice Actors:
Greg Snegoff, Lisa Michaelson, Kenneth Hartman, Natalie Core, Cheryl Chase
Japanese Voice Actors:
Masahiko Tsugawa, Mayumi Oogawa, Tetsuro Tamba, Nenji Kobayashi, Isao Hashizume, Junko Sakurada
[****]
Immensely entertaining and clever story about Japanese spirits who take kindly to a pair of girls. One of the few Japanese films that give Disney a run for its money as wholesome family entertainment. The imagery and odd-looking spirits have a Japanese feel to them, but give it a chance and be open-minded. The unique story, crisp animation, and rich characters will grow on you and your children. I highly recommend this animated film along with Kiki's Delivery Service for family viewing.
Satsuki and her younger sister Lucy move into the countryside with their kind father, taking up residency in an old house. Their mother is ill and remains at a nearby hospital. Satsuki tries to keep Lucy's spirits up by playing with her and exploring the house and surrounding countryside. The girls sense something is bizarre from the first day when a room covered with black soot suddenly becomes spotless as the soot separates into little balls and run for cover. With plenty of time on their hands, the two girls embark on a wonderful adventure with a magical creature called Totoro, a combination of a big puffy rabbit with catlike whiskers, short ears, and big round eyes. Lucy gets lost in the countryside after trying to deliver a ear of corn to her sick mother. Neighbor Totoro calls a giant Cheshire cat with multiple legs and a body similar to that of a bus to help Satsuki. She and the cat rescue Lucy and deliver the ear of corn to their mother who is starting to feel better.   Similar to Alice's trip in Wonderland, seeing is better than describing, in a rich and wholesome adventure for children of all ages. The beautiful animation of the wild forest characters are truly enchanting and the music is delightful.

Mystery Files
(1996) Thriller   C-83m Chinese with English Subtitles   Type II
Hong Kong   Retail: $39.99
Dir/Scr: Kam Tin Yat   Prod: Leung Hung Wah
DP: Wong Ka Fai   Editor: Wong Wing Ming   Music: Mak Chun Tung
Prod Manager: Kannex Wong   Art Dir: Chu Kin Sun, Adeline Lo
Prod: Canaan Film Production Ltd.
Andy Hui Chi On, Edmond Leung Hon Man, Vivial Lai, Cheong Wei Yee, Ada Choi Siu Fun
[1/2]**
What do you do when the police are baffled and not a suspect is in sight...why you call in a private crimebuster. If you're a fan of the Hardy Boys or Nancy Drew you might find inspiration in this average attempt to capitalize on youth-oriented mysteries. The film is divided into three cases involving a young man, who in desperate need of money, travels to mainland China to help the local authorities solve some crimes and earn reward money. He has a reputation for keen observation and a sixth sense. Teamed with a police officer, the two travel together on a variety of crime scenes. The first involves a bizarre love triangle and murder. The second mystery is also easily wrapped up. The final story takes place on an ocean liner while traveling back home.

Mystery of Rampo, The   (Rampo)
(1994) DramaC-101m   Japanese with English Subtitles   VA
Catalog #80053   Japan Retail: $19.99
Dir: Kazuyoshi Okuyama   Scr: Kazuyoshi Okuyama, Yuhei Enoki
Original Story: Edogawa Rampo   Prod: Yoshihisa Nakagawa, Yoshinobu Nishioka
DP: Yasushi Sasakibara   Editor: Akimasa Kawashima   Music: Akira Senju
Prod Design: Kyoko Heya   Dist: Samuel Goldwyn/Evergreen Entertainment
Naoto Takenaka   Edogawa Rampo
Michiko Hada   Shizuko
Masahiro Motoki   Kogoro Akechi
Mikijiro Hira   Marquis Ogawara
Teruyuki Kagawa   Masashi Yokomizo
[***]

"I once heard the story of a desert traveler...whose steps were off
by a mere one centimeter. He walked around in a circle forever..."
                                                        Opening card
As the film images unfold, a bright red chest dominates the screen. The narrator calls it a hope chest "nagamochi" and throughout the film, the chest represents the inner mind and desires of Rampo. The story is a fictional account of the life of noted writer Edogawa Rampo.
The film has a strong visual presence over the narrative, and images are used as a key driving force in the story. For those of you who are not familiar with foreign "art-house" films, you should be warned that Rampo is not a standard tale in the Hollywood sense.
The time is Imperialist Japan before the dawn of World War II. Rampo's story "The Appearance of Osei" is banned by the government for its inappropriate portrayal of the female heroine who murders her aging husband. Rampo who is a quiet and hermit-like author doesn't dispute the ruling, but recedes deeper into his own personal writings. His agent and friend, Yokomizo,

escorts him to a debut party where Rampo's story has been made into a film. The audience is not concerned with Rampo's feelings and his story is altered to a mainstream generic action film. As his life seems to lose purpose, Yokomizo shows him a newspaper of a strange event. While a sickly man was playing hide and seek with his children, he accidentally locked himself in a red chest and suffocated. The survivor is his wife Shizuko. The real life event is exact in every detail to Rampo's unpublished story. This starts a chain of events when Rampo's real existence blends with the fictional existence of his stories and characters. His alterego is the handsome and dashing Detective Akechi who follows Shizuko to a splendid mansion by the ocean owned by Marquis Ogawara. Shizuko is shunned by Japanese society who accuses her of murdering her husband. The Marquis marries the scorned woman, but then subjects her to a bizarre ritual of cross-dressing and bondage to arouse his sexual drive.

The original film was altered by the producer who hired a new director and reshot sixty percent of the film. An interesting expression of art and literature in a uniquely Japanese film.

My Young Auntie
(1981) Kung-Fu   C-115m   Dubbed   Hong Kong   Retail: $19.95
Dir/Scr: Liu Chia Liang   Prod: Mona Fong   Ex. Prod: Run Run Shaw
Editor: Li Yen Hai, Chang Hsing Lung
Music: Eddie W Wang   Art Director: Johnson Tsao
MAD: Liu Chia Liang, Ching Chu, Hsiao Hou   PC: Shaw Bros.
Liu Chia Liang, Hui Ying Hung, Hsiao Hou, Wang Lung Wei, Tang Wei Cheng, Gordon Liu Chia Hui, Tsao Ta Hua, Chuan Yung Wen, Yuan Tei, Mai Te Lo
[***]

A highly entertaining and charming film from Hong Kong master Liu Chia Liang. This film incorporates a number of western-style sequences and is universally appealing for its theme of old culture versus new for the roles of women versus men. Director Liu's personal protégé (real life interest as well) Hui Ying Hung is the heroine of the film. She's an expert martial artist, but from a rural province in China and unaware of the modern changes in the world. Cars, neon lights, and nylon stockings are all new to her when she moves to a province outside Shanghai. The story begins with the symbolic marriage of Hui to a wealthy merchant who wants Hui to legally inherit his fortunes and prevent the misuse of his wealth. Hui's youthful is complicated when the wealthy man passes away. His greedy brother played by Wang Lung Wei, a popular villain, wants the property and fortune to expand his personal empire. Instead, the entire fortune is passed on to one of his nephews played by director Liu Chia Liang. Wang is frustrated and sends his adopted son to retrieve the deeds from Hui and Liu. What follows is a hilarious and action-packed film where Hui legally becomes Liu's auntie. Meanwhile, Liu's son (Hsiao Hou) returns from Hong Kong with his westernized thoughts and attitudes, taking an instant disliking to his pretty, young grand-aunt! A number of humorous scenes follow, revolving around Hui's age and place in the family order. Eventually, the whole Liu team join forces to battle Wang and his men for the rights to the deed. Liu is a true innovator and a director who saw beyond the mere need to show martial art movies as only martial arts movies of vengeance and training. Very much like the popular Karate Kid films, Liu's martial arts films are a vehicle for engaging characters and interesting plots where the fantastic martial arts never supplant the human drama and humor.

Naked Killer, The
(1992) Action C-88m Chinese with English Subtitles
Catalog #ML 394   Hong Kong   Retail: $39.99
Dir: Clarence Fok Yiu Leung   Scr: Wong Jing   Prod: Wong Jing
MAD: Lau Shung Fung   Dist: Mei Ah Company
Chingmy Yau Kitty
Simon Yam   Officer Tinam
Svenwara Madoka   Cindy
Carrie Ng   Princess
Kelly   Baby
Johnny Lo Hwei Kong
[**1/2]
Oddly, it took a trip to the adult section of a video store to finally track down this popular Chingmy Yau release. At first, it seemed Yau had switched to making X-rated films, and though it contains a deal of nudity, there is no pornography at all. The film has NC-17 elements with numerous scenes involving lesbian sex and extreme violence...an over the top film not for everyone. Chingmy Yau is a beautiful woman who seeks revenge on a lying bastard. She ends up shooting him and the entire office. While making an escape, she is attacked by a horde of gun-toting thugs. She is saved by a mysterious older woman who helps her convalesce and begins to train her in the art/business of assassination. The cop on the case falls in love with Yau and tries to convince her to go legitimate. Another female assassin decides to put Chingmy and her mentor out of business, permanently. She and her lesbian lover battle in all sorts of fanciful ways to kill their rivals and anyone who gets in their way. The film is a wild and irreverent attempt to blend action and gratuitous sex in what is popularly known as the "Girls with Guns" type film. The film does entertain on a certain level and Chingmy Yau fans are in a for a treat, but I'd tread cautiously if this does not sound like your typical film for enjoyment.

Neon Genesis Evangelion - Genesis 0:1
(1995) Japanime: Scifi   C-60m Dubbed   Catalog #ADV EV/001D   Japan Retail: $24.95
Dir: Hideaki Anno   Original Story & Planning: GAINAX
Character Design: Yoshiyuki Sadamoto   Mecha Design: Ikuto Yamashita, Hideaki Anno
Art Dir: Hiroshi Kato   Music: Shiro Sagisu
PC: GAINAX Dist: A.D. Vision
[***]
Incredibly popular, ongoing series which helped renew interest in the anime industry in Japan, solidifying Gainax's position in the field. Shown on television, NGE has been the biggest smash since Sailor Moon and quickly gained attention in the United States. All the episodes are slated for release and expect to see some full-length feature films. Capitalizing on the big robot theme, NGE also includes some behind the scenes subplots involving the main characters, and an intriguing dose of in-house humor for anime fans.
In the year 2015, an alien race known as the Angels have attacked Earth. In response, defenses have been created to ward off the creatures, but only the Evangelion robot and her pilots can stop

the threat. Strangely, only a few select children (14 years old) who were born nine months after a meteoroid landed can handle the controls of the Evangelion which was created by Shinji's father. Well animated, interesting film that promises a lot of character development and plenty of anime action in future volumes.

Neon Genesis Evangelion - Genesis 0:2
(1996) Japanime: Scifi   C-60m Dubbed   Catalog #ADV EV/001D   Japan Retail: $24.95
Dir: Hideaki Anno   Original Story & Planning: GAINAX
Character Design: Yoshiyuki Sadamoto   Mecha Design: Ikuto Yamashita, Hideaki Anno
Art Dir: Hiroshi Kato   Music: Shiro Sagisu
PC: GAINAXDist: A.D. Vision

Spike Spencer	**Shinji Ikara**
Allison Keith	**Misato Katsuragi**
Sue Ulu	**Ritsuko Akagi**
Tristan MacAvery	**Gendo Ikari**
Amanda Winn	**Rei Ayanami**
Guil Lunde	**Fuyutsuki**
Brian Granveldt	**Hyuga**
Kendra Benham	**Ibuki**
Jason Lee	**Aoba**

Joe Pisano, Kurt Stoll, Carol Amerson, Rick Peeples
[***]
Shinji's adjustment has not been easy and his life hits another low point when he gets beat up at school. Basically, the second volume focuses on Shinji's doubts about being a pilot. Even though he does well in training, his next encounter with an Angel leaves him confused and afraid. He runs away from his apartment and wanders the city aimlessly. Meanwhile, his two male classmates are concerned about his well being and pay a visit. When Shinji is found, it is decided he be terminated from the program. The NERV agents escort him to the train station. Shinji must decide whether he will stay and fight or leave forever.
Though I have yet to see every episode in the series, I'm impressed and look forward to reviewing upcoming episodes. Due to the popularity of the series, more episodes have been released and are available for purchase at the same suggested retail price.

New Fist of Fury
(1976) Kung-Fu   C-114m   Dubbed   VA   Catalog # 3608-A
Hong Kong   Retail: $9.99
Dir/Scr: Lo Wei   Prod: Hsu Li Hwa   Ex. Prod: Lo Wei
Dist: Simitar Entertainment, Inc.
Jackie Chan, Nora Miao, Chan Sing, Chang King, Lo Wei
[**]
Sequel to the classic Bruce Lee film Fist of Fury (American title: The Chinese Connection) in which Japanese aggression is unleashed upon a Chinese martial arts schools. The film casts Jackie Chan in the lead role as Bruce Lee's successor, but the film's overall quality doesn't compare to the original. Jackie Chan is too young and lacks the experience and charisma to

ignite the screen as Lee did. Instead, Chan is a bumbling small-time thief who lives with his uncle in Japanese-occupied Taiwan. The survivors from the original film (Bruce Lee was shot) under Miao's leadership hope to establish themselves with friends in Taiwan. At the harbor, Chan steals Miao's bag. He ends up returning her bag and apologizes, changing his criminal ways after witnessing Japan's brutality. Only during the end of the film does Chan decide to learn martial arts and fight the imperialist Japanese. The Japanese and their Chinese cohorts crack down on the rebels who must then go into hiding. They buy passage on a escape boat and plan to flee. In a very uninspiring ending, they are ambushed and suffer a massive defeat. The film leaves little to cheer and even less to inspire martial arts fans.

New Legend of Shaolin   **(Legends of Shaolin/Hung Hei Koon: Shaolin's 5 Founders)**
(1994) Kung-Fu   **C-95m Chinese with English Subtitles**
Catalog #1497   **Hong Kong**   **Retail: $39.99**
Dir: Wong Jing   **Dist: Tai Seng Video**
Jet Li   **Hung Shi Kwan**
Xie Miao   **Man Ting**
Chingmy Yau   **Con Artist**
Wong Jin
[***]
Superstar Jet Li is teamed up with an unlikely partner in this fast-paced, traditional kung-fu adventure. In the world of martial arts cinema, anyone and anything can possess incredible skills. During a deadly massacre, Shaolin expert Hung Shi Kwan arrives just in time to save his son, Man Ting, but loses the rest of his family to vicious killers. In a classic scene similar to Lone Wolf and Cub, Li forces the child to choose between a toy rocking chair and a weapon. If he chooses the toy, he would be killed for showing weakness. Luckily, Man picks the weapon, so father and son journey on a long road filled with revenge and danger. The villains are after an important map which is tattooed onto five Shaolin boys. The boys meet Xie and Li, so there's plenty of childish humor and slapstick-style fights to go along with the more serious sequences. Xie maintains his intensity and fights with adult-like bravado, a miniature Jet Li, while the other boys provide comedy and child action. The heroic group also meet a pretty con artist and her incorrigible mother. The female duo cause problems and add to the subtle humor of their situation, but join the group's cause and help battle the villains.
Jing's movie is full of wonderful action scenes, but in his trademark manner the director precariously balances drama and comedy, flip-flopping at a hectic pace with uneven results not for all tastes.

Ninja Films - See Ninjamania under Part II

Ninja Scroll
(1993) Japanime: Fantasy   **C-94m Dubbed/Japanese with English Subtitles**
VA   **Catalog #800 634 813-3**   **Japan Retail: $19.99**
Dir/Scr: Yoshiaki Kawajiri   **Character Design & Animation Dir: Yutaka Minowa**
Art Director: Hiromasa Ogura   **DP: Hitoshi Yamaguchi**   **Sound**   **Dir:**   **Yasunori Honda**
Ex. Prod: Makoto Hasegawa, Masamichi Fujiwara, Yutaka Takahashi

PC: Mad House/JVC/Toho Co. Ltd./MOVIC Inc.   Dist: Manga Video
Rudy Luzion, Dean Elliot, Wendee Day, Richard George, Alfred Thor, Doug Stone, Jenny Haniver, Ed Mannix
[***]
A slick animated film not intended for kids or the faint of heart. Set in feudal Japan during the time of the samurai and ninja, this epic film follows the path of Jubei, a masterless ninja who works as a mercenary. He is on a quest to defeat an evil master who sends a gallery of bizarre assassins to kill him. Along the way, he meets a monk who poisons him and demands his help. Jubei initially refuses, but their common goal brings their efforts together. They are joined by a female warrior with unique magical powers. Her mystic abilities come in handy when dealing with the bizarre killers, including a dwarf with a body full of insect hives. The inventive and bizarre characters must be seen to be believed. The film combines elements of history, sword-action, and dark magic in a lush, dark world of beautiful animation. Ninja Scroll stands as a prime example of the deft way to mix various genres and create something utterly innovative.

No Retreat, No Surrender
(1986) Kung-Fu   C-85m English   PG   VA
Catalog #90003   Hong Kong/USA   Retail: $9.99
Dir: Corey Yuen   Scr: Keith W. Strandberg   Original Story: Corey Yuen, Ng See Yuen
Prod: Ng See Yuen   DP: John Huneck, David Golia   Editor: Dane A. Davis, James Melkonian, Alan Poon   Music: Paul Gilreath, David Spear
Makeup: June Brickman, Sher Flowers   Sp. Fx: John Ting
PC: Cannon   Dist: New World Video

Kurt McKinney	Jason Stillwell
J.W. Fails	R.J. Madison
Jean-Claude Van Damme	Ivan the Russian
Ron Pohnel	Ian Reilly
Tim Baker	Tim Stillwell
Gloria Marziano	Mrs. Stillwell
Kim Tai Chung	Bruce Lee
Peter Cunningham	Frank
Dale Jacoby	Dean
Kent Liphan	Scott

[**]
Given enough time, filmmakers will think of new possibilities on how to capitalize on Bruce Lee's popularity and immortality. Modeled after Rocky and Karate Kid, a teenager named Jason moves into a new town and befriends a nice loser while making enemies with the popular (karate students) kids. The highlight of the film is the appearance of Jean-Claude Van Damme as Ivan and KimTai Chung, an accomplished Korean martial artist who plays Bruce Lee's spirit. The young boy and his father move into the new town after his father's martial arts school is shut down by a ruthless mobster and his vicious Russian kickboxing goon, Van Damme. Embarrassed and injured, the boy's father quits martial arts for a quieter life. His son still wishes to train, but makes enemies when he helps a black boy being harassed by bullies led by an overweight jerk. The next day, the two new friends visit the local martial arts school. The chubby bully who is a student (pathetic one at that) at the school tells one of the black belts that

the new kid and his black friend are trouble makers who are looking for a challenge. The black belt beats up on the new kid (not a good thing for business) and unfairly alienates him from the local martial arts school. He continues to train on his own with little result, but does manage to visit Bruce Lee's grave site. In the evenings, the spirit of Bruce Lee appears and begins him on a rigorous training program. Whether the apparition is real or his imagination is left to the viewer. The mobsters arrive in the new town and have sights on taking over the local martial arts school. When the local martial arts masters are called to challenge Van Damme, they lose in an exciting tournament-fight sequence which showcases Van Damme's potential. Jason enters the ring and proves himself a hero in front of friends, father, and the local martial arts school. The end of the film has a particularly good number of fight scenes for a low budget film and marked Van Damme's first break. The popularity of the film carried onward to a number of mediocre sequels, even starring Cynthia Rothrock. Directed by Hong Kong veteran Ng who like many of his peers has branched out into American-style action films.

-O-

1:00 AM
(1995) Horror   C-86m Chinese with English Subtitles
Catalog #1792   Hong Kong   Retail: $39.99
Dir: Andy Chin   Dist: Tai Seng Video
Anita Yuen, Veronica Yip, Wong Yiu Ming, Tsui Kam Kong
[1/2]**

An anthology of three supernatural tales which bears resemblance to the Twilight Zone and Amazing Stories series on television. All the supernatural events take place around 1:00 am and involve human ghosts. Chinese culture is rich in tales of spirits and their relationships with living beings. The ghost tales go more for chills and never attempts to delve into gratuitous violence or profanity. The stories are light-hearted and enjoyable for all ages, but are rather routine for viewers familiar with this type of entertainment. When singing sensation Sunny Wong goes into a mysterious coma, he is placed under the care of Hong Kong's best physicians and nurses. One of the nurses helps him recover while working the graveyard shift. Sunny's soul is being held captive by the ghost of a fan who died during his concert. She's loves him and blames him for her death. The nurse senses the girl's despair and also shares her interest in the singer...a supernatural love triangle. The second story involves a meek college woman who buys a used car. She tends to show off and speak boldly, so her friends decide to play a practical joke. She gets stranded at night on a lonely road where a mysterious spirit scares her to death. The final story which is the most entertaining, revolves around two police officers. Action veteran Tsui Kam Kong plays the tough cop. They are both assigned a late night job of monitoring speeding drivers on a lonely stretch of road. When their speed camera goes off in the middle of the night, they don't discover a car in the photo but a ghostly figure of a woman. The officers try to find the reason for the spirits existence and help her soul find eternal peace. In a cinema world of blood, sex, and gore, it's refreshing to find an occasional horror tale that deals with the supernatural elements and not a body count. Most of the ghostly imagery comes from mental imagination and there's practically no effects elements. A simple, likeable ghost tale with a talented cast of Hong Kong stars. If you enjoy the film, check out more ghost stories in the aptly-titled sequel, 2:00 am.

Odin: Photon Space Sailer Starlight
(1985) Japanime: Scifi   C-139m   Japanese with English Subtitles
Catalog #USM 1050 Japan Retail: $29.95
Dir: Toshio Masuda, Takeshi Shirado, Eiichi Yamamoto
Scr: Kazuo Kasahara, Toshi Masuda, Eiichi Yamamoto
Original Story: Yoshinobu Nishizaki
Ex. Prod: Yoshinobu Nishizaki   Prod: Tomoharu Matsumata
Music: Hiroshi Miyagawa Art Dir: Geki Katsumata, Tadano Tsuji
PC: West Cape Corporation   Dist: U.S. Manga Corps

Toshio Furukawa	Akira Tsukuba
Hideyuki Hori	Mamoru Nelson
Keiko Han	Sarah Cyanbaker
Goro Naya	Boatswain Shonosuke Kuramoto
Gentaro Ishida	Asgard
Tessho Genda	Belgel
Noboru Matsuhashi	Cyborg
Takeshi Kato	Capt. Takeshi Suzuka
Toru Furuya	Jiro Ishige
Noriaki Wakamoto	Naoki Ryuo

[***]
The year is 2099, a beautiful starship with majestic sails and a long bow, reminiscent of sailing ships of the 1800's, prepares for a historic launch into deep space. The history-making starship is the Starlight and takes off on its maiden voyage. Before it leaves for deep space, a rogue pilot joins the crew. While exploring the galaxy, they come across a graveyard of ships and a lone survivor, the beautiful Sarah Cyanbaker. She talks about a mystic planet known as Odin. The Captain orders the ship to return to Earth, but Tsukuba and the crewmen are driven by the desire to see Odin and stage a mutiny. Their flight leads them into a hostile armada commanded by a giant artificial intelligence known as Belgel. A spectacular space battle between the Starlight and Belgel takes place. By capturing a wounded cyborg, the truth of Odin is revealed. Created by Nishizaki, the genius behind the phenomenal Starblazers/Yamato Series, the blatant similarity to the Spaceship Yamato series are incredibly eerie and offsetting. The entire look and feel of the film could easily be mistaken as an alternate version or a spinoff series. Unfortunately, the epic grandeur of the original Yamato series is lost and comparisons would be unjust. Fans of the Yamato-style animation will find this version entertaining and complimenting.

Once a Thief
(1991) Action Comedy   C-107m   Chinese with English Subtitles
Catalog #0979   Hong Kong   Retail: $39.99 Widescreen Available
Dir: John Woo   Scr: John Woo, Clifton Ko, Janet Chun
Prod: Linda Kuk, Terence Chang   DP: Poon Hang Seng
Editor: David Wu   Music: Violet Lam   Prod Manager: Fanny Leung
Art Dir: James Leung   Costume: Shirley Chan   MAD: Cheung Jue Luh
PC: Milestone Pictures   Dist: Tai Seng Video
Chow Yun Fat   Joe

Leslie Cheung   Jim
Cherie Chung   Cherie
Kenneth Tsang Kong, Declan Michael Wong
[***]

If you're expecting a film along the lines of The Killer or Hard-Boiled, this action comedy might leave you a little disappointed. Made for the Chinese New Year/holiday season, the film is molded toward light-hearted comedy, romance, and action with a self-deprecating parody of Woo's more intense films. Similar in vein to the Bruce Willis action-comedy Hudson Hawk, director Woo offers better pacing than Hudson Hawk and a solid dramatic story at the heart of its whimsical tale. The story begins with three dashing characters visiting an exclusive Paris museum. Chow Yun Fat, Leslie Cheung, and Cherie Chung are the criminal trio who specialize in stealing rare artwork in well-staged, non-violent capers that remind the viewer of The Thomas Crown Affair. They manage to steal a valuable painting from a French security truck in a slick and quick manner, celebrating their accomplishment afterwards. The slapstick among the three are harmless but utterly juvenile which is explained by a well-timed flashback of the three youths. The trio were orphans raised by a crook (think Oliver's Finnegan) who teaches them the art of thievery. Kenneth Tsang is the teacher/crook and is ruthless in his determination to make them master criminals. Luckily, the trio are caught stealing from a Hong Kong police officer who adopts the children under his own wing and attempts to reform them. Now adults, the trio are constantly engaged in thefts and wild antics focusing on the two male rivals vying for Cherie's affection. Cherie wants the group to stop their criminal actions and retire to a safe life. Leslie and Chow almost agree, but a rich foreigner offers them two million dollars to steal a valuable painting. Leslie goes off on his own to take the painting, but is betrayed and attacked. Chow comes to his rescue, but is later killed during the operation in a spectacular chase sequence. Leslie and Cherie escape to Hong Kong, fall in love, and eventually get married. Meanwhile, the painting is handed over to Kenneth Tsang who orchestrated the double-cross.

Two years later, a crippled Chow miraculously reappears in Hong Kong, asking his old mentor for some money. Instead, Tsang pushes Chow's wheelchair down a flight of stairs and ridicules him. Chow plans a way of exacting revenge on his old mentor and teams up with Leslie Cheung. Unfortunately, Cherie is reneged to a supporting role and appears briefly from here on. Ultimate revenge is achieved when Tsang is arrested and beaten, while the priceless painting is destroyed. Then in the closing montage, Chow is seen as a nanny/housemaid who takes care of Leslie and Cherie's children.

In many ways, this film was a breath of fresh air after the ever intensive and violent action films of the era. Woo, hoping to assuage his more moderate audience, cleverly teams the charismatic Chow with Leslie Cheung, a youthful handsome actor, and the effervescent Cherie Cheung. Relying on the comedic antics of the trio who squabble and joke like schoolyard children, they also manage to perform amazing acts of theft while battling large assortments of enemies. Though the cross genre might turn off action fans who want more killing and comedy fans who want less, the balance easily shifts from humor to violence and will be enjoyable for fans of combining genres. Overall, the film is entertaining and cute, providing a showcase for the trio of actors and Woo's direction.

An American version of this movie with the same title has been produced, so be careful which version you are renting or buying.

WONG FEI HUNG SERIES

ONCE UPON A TIME IN CHINA

China at the close of the 19th Century.
Humiliating defeat in the Opium War had opened
the doors of the Middle Kingdom to Western trade,
ideas, religion, and intervention. With technology
- electricity, the telegraph, the steam engine -
came the firearm. Western firepower began to
upset the traditional order - the might of the gun
threatened the very existence of the martial arts.
Amid these turbulent times, one man dared to
speak out for the people, dared to stand up for
what he believed. He was an intellect, a healer, a
martial artists - one of the greatest patriotic
figures in Chinese folklore. This is the legend of
Wong Fei Hung...

Opening from "Once Upon A Time In China"

Known also as the Wong Fei Hung movies, this epic series traces the life and times of Wong Fei Hung during the turbulent period of Western Occupation in China and the downfall of the Imperial Family. Though the films are fictional in scope, the character of Wong Fei Hung and many of the people he met are based on historical figures while the general backdrop of the film is historically accurate. The real Wong Fei Hung was born in Canton in 1847 and died in 1924. He studied martial arts under his father's master Luk Ah Choy, even though his own father, Wong Kei Ying, was a master of Hung's Fist and one of the legendary Ten Tigers of Kwantung (Canton) heroes. Wong Fei Hung mastered Hung's Fist, studied Chinese medicine, and practiced the southern Chinese tradition of Lion Dancing. Many of his students became experts and taught others who are still alive and kicking. Wong's life was mainly established on screen in ninety-nine black-and-white films, starring Kwan Tak Hing, which set the pace and popularized the famous Wong theme music heard in every film reincarnation (the music is so synonymous with Wong that it's used even when Wong's name is mentioned, similar to the famous Bond-theme found in every James Bond appearance). The Cantonese tune developed from the song, "Under the General's Orders" and can be heard in various versions.

Based on a long running series of plays and films, the fictional Wong Fei Hung is the quintessential super-hero of Chinese folklore and entertainment, having appeared in hundreds of incarnations since the beginning of China's film industry. Producer Tsui Hark decided to recreate Wong's early adult to mid-age life and started a series of films (and television episodes in Hong Kong) which are now considered the new standard for all Wong films. The martial arts scenes are an excellent blend of realism and the impossible. Certain scenes with Wong and other masters include amazing feats of acrobatics and skillfully choreographed flying stunts via wires which add to the mythical legend of Wong. The following characters are integral to the series and reappear from time to time in other films as well.

Wong Fei Hung - the main character and central hero of all five Hark films, portrayed by Jet Li and Zhao Wen Zhou. The best martial artist in China/World from Fu-Shan Province, he is a gentle kind-hearted scholar experienced in Chinese medicine. Though ignorant of Western culture, he is willing to adapt and monitors the fate of his nation and its people. He is the perfect well-rounded hero, a humble man who runs a martial arts academy and a medical facility called Po Chi Lam.

Wong Kei Ying - Also a scholar of medical profession and a master of martial arts. He is Wong Fei Hung's caring father and appears in a number of films. In Hark's version, Wong Fei Hung's mother is not present and presumably passed away.

Foon Leung - A central character to all five films. Foon plays the classic side-kick, offering comedic moments, and is nicknamed Owl because of his wide eyes. His kung-fu is excellent, but he tends to be a trickster and gets in trouble while goofing off.

Aunt Yee (Thirteenth Aunt) - A modern, beautiful woman who is Wong Fei Hung's single aunt through legal marriage. She is actually Wong's age and very much smitten with the hero. He cares for her also, but is rather shy in the ways of love.

Aunt May - Sister of Aunt Yee and introduced in the fourth movie after Jet Li and Rosamund Kwan left. She appears with Rosamund in the fifth movie.

Club Foot - Originally a villain from OUTC 3, Club Foot was the leader of a gang of rickshaw drivers known for their amazing kicking abilities. His leg is healed by Wong and he joins their martial arts academy. Club Foot becomes one of Wong's most loyal disciples and is often seen as a counterpart to Foon Leung's humorous antics.

Porky Lang/Fatty Wing - overweight, but powerful and loyal student to Wong. He is the most renowned of Wong's students. A butcher by trade, he later opened a real academy in Hong Kong.

Ah So - several variations, but a member of the Wong group and very loyal. He is nicknamed "bucktooth" and sometimes the character is over-exaggerated for comedic relief. He has spent time in Europe and is able to read English and is adept at Western ways.

In-depth reviews are given for each of the six epic films. All take place in China, except the sixth film which was shot in Texas and once again reunited Tsui Hark with Jet Li as Wong Fei Hung

Once Upon a Time in China (Wong Fei Hung)
(1990) Kung-Fu   C-134m   Dubbed/Chinese with English Subtitles
Catalog #SEL0385   Hong Kong
Retail: $39.99   Widescreen Available
Dir/Prod: Tsui Hark Scr: Tsui Hark, Yuen Kai Chi, Leung Yiu Ming, Tang Pik Yin
Editor: Mak Chi Sin Music: James Wong   Ex. Prod: Raymond Chow
MAD: Yuen Chong Yan, Yuen Shun Yi, Lau Kar Wing Dist: Golden Harvest
Jet Li   Wong Fei Hung
Rosamund Kwan   Auntie Yee
Yuen Biao   Foon Leung
Kent Cheng   Porky Lang
Jacky Cheung, Yang Yee Kwan
[****]

A heavy drum beat slowly resonates against a black screen as an introductory passage scrolls onto the screen (US version only). It speaks of a time when China is in turmoil and the inventions and the influences of the Western World have forever changed traditional China. From that era, a hero of the people arose. A scholar, a healer, and a martial artist who cared for all people. When the words end, the music tempo picks up and waves crash upon a shore as the title burns in bold red letters, then the morning sun rises. The morning beach provides a training ground for Wong Fei Hung and his elite students. The classic Wong Fei Hung music used in almost every Wong film is the background music as hundreds of students run behind Master Wong (Jet Li) on a beautiful beach at dawn. The scene is both impressive and inspiring as the entire school follows the movements of their master and mentor.

This is Tsui Hark's Once Upon A Time In China, a film that reminds viewers of the wonder and majesty of traditional martial arts. Director Tsui Hark creates a spectacular effort which is often considered the definitive portrayal of Ching Dynasty's legendary hero, Wong Fei Hung, starring Jet Li and Zhao Wen Zhou. The film carries a political overtone and warns of the influence Western culture has had on China's proud heritage. The film may appear to be anti-Western and pro-Chinese which is understandable since the hero is of Chinese origin, but Wong is an open-minded hero who does not completely condemn Western technology and ideas, but warns they should be adopted gradually and not replace traditional ways. In many scenes Wong makes an attempt to try Western ways under the guidance of the foreign-traveled Aunt Yee.

In the late 19th Century, Chinese port cities have been open to American and European trade and investment. Master Wong Fei Hung, a respected scholar and leader of the local militia, is concerned with European influence, especially after Chinese civilians are accidentally shot and illegally kidnaped. He attends a meeting at a European-style restaurant and meets General Wickens, the leader of the British forces, Jackson, the head of an American conglomerate, and the Chinese high official who wishes to maintain strong ties with the Western powers. Meanwhile, a local worker named Foon escapes from a ruthless gang and befriends Fatty Wing and the Wong militia. This starts a feud between the gang and Wong Fei Hung which results in the destruction of Po Chi Lam and the wrongful arrest of Wong's students.

Meanwhile, Master Yim, a penniless master of martial arts, arrives in the city to make a name of himself. Though he is incredibly skilled, he is unknown and lives in utter poverty. Initially, Foon wanted to become a student of Wong, but through misunderstood circumstances becomes an enemy of Wong Fei Hung. Foon becomes a student of Master Yim who challenges Wong Fei Hung in a truly stylistic and beautiful rain-drenched fight sequence whose choreography compares to Gene Kelly's Singin' in the Rain dance sequence. Master Yim and Foon join the Chinese gang, but Foon soon realizes his place is with Master Wong.

Wong and his students battle the ruthless gang who hide aboard the American ship under the command of the evil Jackson and his killers. Wong must free Aunt Yee and a group of women who were kidnaped to be used as prostitutes. After Wong saves his life, the Chinese high official clears him of all charges and apologizes for his lack of faith. Hark's film creates a wonderful springboard into the world of kung-fu's greatest hero, Wong Fei Hung. These films can best be described as The Godfather and Gone with the Wind epics of martial arts.

Once Upon a Time in China 2
(1991) Kung-Fu   C-109m   Dubbed   Hong Kong
Retail: $39.99
Dir: Tsui Hark   Scr: Tsui Hark, Chan Tin Suen, Cheung Tan
Prod: Tsui Hark, Ng Sze Yuen   Ex. Prod: Raymond Chow

DP: Wong Ngor Tai Music: Richard Yuen, Johnny Njo
PC: Film Workshop Dist: Golden Harvest
Jet Li, Benny "Max" Mok, Rosamund Kwan, Donnie Yen, John Chiang, Zhang Tie Lin
[****]
A spectacular sequel to Tsui Hark's first masterpiece and well worth seeing just for Donnie Yen and Jet Li's climatic battle. Wong battles the White Lotus sect, a group of anti-western cult members who believe all western influences are evil and that Chinese kung-fu is invincible. They summon up false magic powers to make themselves invulnerable and cheat members into believing they are immortal. When innocent Chinese people are killed, Wong decides to unveil their lies and end their cult.
The year is 1895, Imperial China is in a downward spiral littered with corruption and misguided leaders. At a medical convention in Canton, the legendary Wong Fei Hung befriends Dr. Sun Yat Sen who is the leader of a national movement toward democracy. Wong listens to the techniques of Western medicine and also introduces his knowledge of Chinese medicine and acupuncture with the help of Dr. Sun. The lecture hall is attacked by the White Lotus, forcing Wong and Sun to join together and help find a safe haven for the foreigners and the children from the Western School. They find refuge in the British Embassy, but are surrounded by White Lotus members and corrupt government troops. Wong and his friends defeat the Lotus assassins, but military troops surround them and aid the Lotus members who make good their escape. Wong joins forces with Sun's friend and the two men enter the heart of the White Lotus Cult and engage in an incredibly elaborate battle. Meanwhile, the military officer in command (Donnie Yen) attempts to capture Sun's patriotic followers and overthrow Wong's influence and fame. He corners Wong, Sun's friend, and Leung in a granary and battle them into a narrow alleyway. Wong is victorious and delivers the important package to Dr. Sun which unfurls into a flag representing the new democratic China...a theme that would not be too popular with mainland China. The film is electrifying in its pacing, martial arts, and the characters' performances. Unlike make martial arts films where the plot is just a flimsy vehicle to string along fight scenes, the historical backdrop and moral implications of the plot are true reflections of a nation's entire entity. Jet Li is outstanding, a true physical and acting pleasure to watch on the screen. As with the rest of the films, the undercurrent of political and moral messages may lose viewers not familiar with the era and is best understood when viewed against China's historical perspective.

Once Upon a Time in China 3
(1992) Kung-Fu   C-102m   Chinese with English Subtitles
Catalog #1443   Hong Kong   Retail: $39.99
Dir: Tsui Hark   Prod: Tsui Hark, Ng See Yuen   Presented by Raymond Chow
PC: Film Workshop Dist: Golden Harvest/Tai Seng Video
Jet Li, Rosamund Kwan, Benny Mok Siu Chung, Lau Shun, Hung Yan Yan, Chiu Ghun
[***1/2]
Slightly uneven film that features a number of lion-dancing and chase sequences which shifts the political undertone of the film into a more generic action plot. Then again if you love lion-dancing and kung-fu action combined, you are in for a treat. The film is highly rated for the introduction of two wonderful characters to the Wong series: Wong Kei Ying and Clubfoot. Wong Kei Ying is Fei Hung's father and a master of the martial arts. Clubfoot is a highly charged and popular new character who steals a number of scenes from the ensemble cast.

Played by Hung Yan Yan, Clubfoot is the leader of a gang of rickshaw pullers hired to kill Wong Fei Hung. He is renowned for his amazing kicking abilities and his ruthless determination to win. The period is still the troubled late 19th Century, Empress Dowager and her favorite eunuch Li Hung Cheung sponsor a Lion Dance Competition to bolster the morale of Chinese martial arts.

Instead of unifying the nation, the competitive Martial Arts (Lion Dancing is an integral part) Academies use the competition as an opportunity to boost their individual prestige and presence. Academies battle each other and sabotage the intricate and ornate lion heads and costumes of their competitors. Wong Kei Ying is involved in a number of enterprises that manufacture lion costumes. His business is attacked by a ruthless boss, Clubfoot, and his gang. Wong Kei Ying battles Clubfoot, but the younger man's ferocity beats the venerable Kei Ying. Luckily, Wong Fei Hung has traveled to Peking to visit his father and decides to unify the Academies and bring to justice the ruthless boss. Clubfoot is assigned to kill Wong, giving him a tough time. During an open-air festival, Clubfoot is crippled by a horse and unable to kick. He returns to his evil boss but is thrown out as a useless fighter. Wong Fei Hung takes him in, helps him to recover, and changes his outlook toward life. Gradually, Clubfoot would become one of Wong's most loyal pupils, never forgetting his kindness. The evil boss demands a truce and even tries to get Clubfoot to rejoin him. Wong attends a dinner, but is betrayed when the floors are soaked with oil and assassins use shoe spikes to move around. An incredible and creative battle ensues, but Wong is not so easily defeated. At the same time, the Russians have planned to assassinate Lord Li Hung Cheung during the Lion Dance Competition and the key assassin happens to be an old friend of Aunt Yee who once gave her a movie camera. Wong Fei Hung enters the Lion Dance Competition to keep an eye on Li Hung's safety and to defeat the evil boss from winning the prize. Most of the climatic battle takes place in lion costumes atop a large bamboo tower holding the prize. The fight scenes are truly amazing and the introduction of new characters help breathe new life into the adventure. The original version was re-edited several times after the premiere, alternate versions range from 90 minutes to 2 hours plus in length.

Once Upon a Time in China 4
(1993) Kung-Fu   C-102m   Chinese with English Subtitles   Hong Kong
Retail: $39.99
Dir: Yuen Bun   Prod: Tsui Hark
PC: Film Workshop Dist: Tai Seng Video
Zhao Wen Zhou, Jean Wong, Benny Mok, Chin Kar Lok, Xiong Xin Xin
[***1/2]

Sadly, superstar Jet Li and creative genius Tsui Hark disputed over a number of issues which caused the parting of ways, due to financial and creative differences. Could Hark find someone to replace Jet Li and continue the series?

Well Zhao is a very talented actor who shares a striking resemblance to Jet Li in appearance and martial arts style, but his first outing seems to lack the confidence, poise, and humor of Li. However, his physical talents are impressive and the film features a number of well-staged martial arts sequences. The story follows a similar theme from the third film as European powers attempt to overthrow the Imperial reign and install a more democratic rule sympathetic to their own ventures. Wisely, Tsui Hark reused the entire cast from the third film except for Rosamund Kwan's Auntie Yee who is replaced by her sister Auntie May, so the love-play relationship is toned down. Wong Fei Hung is caught in the middle between the Europeans and the Chinese Red Flower Sect, an elite group of women who want to see the destruction of European influences in China. Adding a bevy of female fighters to the plot was a cute idea. They wear bright red, pink, and white costumes, carry flower lanterns, and use an assortment of weapons and tricks. During a parade, they attack the German Consulate and plan to burn the European residents. Wong enters the battle, uses a whip to stop them, and saves the Europeans. His own help is met by foreign distrust as he and a member of the Red Flower are arrested by German soldiers. A priest helps the two escape and she befriends Wong and leads her to the Sect's secret headquarters. As retribution, the Sect capture Wong's friends. It is up to Wong Fei Hung to bring peace back to the nation and save his friends.

Once Upon a Time in China 5 (Dragon City's Cruel Tyrant)
(1994) Kung-Fu   C-95m Chinese with English Subtitles
Catalog #1632   Hong Kong   Retail: $39.99
Dir: Tsui Hark   Prod: Tsui Hark, Ng See Yuen
Presented by Raymond Chow
PC: Film Workshop   Dist: Tai Seng Video
Zhao Wen Zhou (Chiu Man Chuk), Rosamund Kwan, Jean Wong, Benny Mok Siu Chung, Hung Yan Yan
[***1/2]
The series started to slip slightly in the mid films when Jet Li was replaced in Part 4. Just as questions of the series viability arose, the latest installment brings back our favorite characters in an exciting story dealing less with politics and more with classic villains...pirates. A free-spirited adventure with less historical overtones, but plenty of great martial arts sequences. Following the fourth film, Peking is in chaos, the Imperial government has fallen, and the Nationalist battle for power. Wong Fei Hung and his friends decide to leave China and head for quieter venues in British controlled Hong Kong. They arrive at a local port town and meet up with the rest of their comrades. For the first time, the entire gang is all present and the fun starts. With the disintegration of the Imperial government, the local port town is in economic and social ruin. Coastal pirates rule the sea and kill travelers and shippers, while townspeople tremble in their homes. When a local grain baron suspects a crook has been to his warehouse, he orders his men to follow a stranger who arrives at the same time. They follow him to a broken cart and an amazing battle in the rain takes place. The grain workers are all injured and return to the warehouse. The strangers aid the injured men and reveal their true identities: Wong Fei Hung and friends. Wong and his friends help catch the real crook and take him to the police. When they discover the crook is a police officer who was starving, they realize the sad state of the town. Wong and his friends take a ship, confront the sea pirates and arrest the captain called Flying Monkey. They discover the secret headquarters and battle the wizened leader Cheung and his vicious daughter Ying. The pirates are arrested and their treasure confiscated. When the leader's son Cheung, Jr. discovers the attack, he raids the town during a victory festival. An army of pirates come to town, but the heroes await them and plan a lavish ambush in a spectacular cinematic fashion. Though the film plays out like a generic action film, the familiar performances of Zhou and his ensemble cast bring forth energy, charisma, and martial arts excitement. Hopefully, the sixth film will be even better in this highly energized and exciting series from the master of traditional period-pieces, Tsui Hark.

Once Upon a Time in China 6   (Once Upon a Time in China and America)
(1997) Kung-Fu   C-96m Chinese with English Subtitles   Hong Kong
Retail: $39.99
Dir: Tsui Hark   Prod: Tsui Hark, Dick Tso Presented by Charles Heung
DP: Walter Gregg   Editor: Angie Tam   2nd Unit Dir: Lau Ka Wing
Administrative Prod: Tiffany Chen   Costume: Willian Tung
MAD: Samo Hung
PC: Win's Entertainment Ltd.   Dist: China Star Entertainment Ltd.
Jet Li, Rosamund Kwan, Hung Yan Yan (Xiong Xin Xin), Chan Kwok Wong, Jeff Wolfe,
Joe Sayah, Chrysta Bell Eucht, Patrick Lung, Richard Ng
[***]

Yes, Jet Li made amends with Tsui Hark and returns as Wong Fei Hung in the newest Once Upon a Time in China. Shot on location in parts of Texas, Wong and the beautiful Auntie Yee arrive in the United States to help support a branch of Po Chi Lam, led by the Americanized Dr. So. The opening scene will surprise many kung-fu purists as stagecoaches, wide open prairies, and gun-toting cowboys grace the screen. The subtitled version I reviewed is difficult to read, so hopefully a remastered version will soon be available. Though the film is enjoyable to watch, it suffers from routine martial arts sequences and does not rate as highly as any of the previous films. The novelty factor wears off quickly and the story is all too familiar and predicable, see Jackie Chan's Shanghai Noon. Basically there are two plot elements within the film, the first involves Jet Li and Kwan who share an onscreen romance. Their traveling party is attacked by savage Indians, and Wong is separated from the rest of the group and loses his memory. He falls in a river, but is rescued by a peaceful tribe of Indians who raise him as their own. Even though Li has forgotten his memory, he still retains his natural instincts to heal and fight. He soon becomes the medicine man and falls in love with a squaw (Star Trek fans, think Captain Kirk in Paradise Syndrome). Auntie Yee and her friends finally find Wong and must beat some sense into him. Then the next story involves the ruthless merchants of the town who have made a pact with some bandits. The bandits rob the bank and the local Chinese are blamed for the theft. They are betrayed by one of their own and Wong and his friends are slated to be hanged. Luckily, one of the American deputies believes their cause and tries to help. He's an expert gunslinger who befriends Wong and learns a few kicks in the film. The finale has the entire Wong gang battling the evil merchants and the bandits who decide to ride into town for revenge. One aspect which weakens the film is that none of the opponents know martial arts. Seeing Wong fight against Indians and cowboys is a novel concept, but lacks any martial artistry or opportunities for high-flying action. In fact, placing Wong in a familiar Western setting gives more cause to re-examine the fantasy aspects and shatters the illusion of disbelief. Westerns have lost much of their popularity and charm in the United States, so a pedestrian western plot with martial arts is an old idea that seems behind the times and fails to compliment either genres. A less that spectacular comeback for Jet Li's Wong Fei Hung. Hopefully, the producers will return to a more traditional Wong and set him back in China for the seventh film. Unfortunately, Jet Li's popularity has skyrocketed and his Hollywood schedule will curtail him from doing anymore Wong Fei Hung films in the near future.

Once Upon a Time a Hero in China

(1991) Comedy Kung-Fu   C-90m Chinese with English Subtitles
Catalog #1098   Hong Kong   Retail: $39.99
Dir: Lee Lik Chee   Dist: Tai Seng Video
Alan Tam, Eric Tsang, Tony Leung Kar Fai
[*1/2]
Warning - This film is not part of the Tsui Hark series and should be best avoided. Don't confuse this juvenile parody of the Once Upon a Time in China movies with the real thing. Alan Tam again plays a goofy master cook, Wong Fei Hung. Also included are parodies of his daffy kung fu pals Ah-So, Leung Foon, and Porky Wing. The whole team must battle against drug traffickers led by Bad Egg Ken (Leung Kar Fai). As usual, Wong's fame precedes him and he doesn't know any martial arts but gets by through luck and sheer bungling (think of Peter Sellers in the Pink Panther films). He does manage to fight in a kitchen to his advantage with flying butcher knives and a Hissing Fart. Unless childish foreign slapstick is your forte, best steer clear of the parody films.

Once Upon a Time a Hero in China II - See Master Wong vs. Master Wong

Operation Condor 2: The Armour of the Gods   (The Armour of the Gods)
(1986)
Action Kung-Fu   C-89m Dubbed   R
Catalog #14807   Hong Kong   Retail: $19.99
Dir: Jackie Chan   Scr: Edward Tang, Szeto Chuek-Hon, Ken Lowe, John Sheppard
Original Story: Barry Wong   Prod: Jackie Chan, Leonard K.C. Ho, Chua Lam
Ex. Prod: Raymond Chow
DP: Peter Ngor, Robert Thompson, Arthur Wong, Cheung Yiu Jo
Editor: Peter Cheung   Music: Michael Lai
MAD: Jackie Chan   PC: Dimension Films/Media Asia Group
Dist: Tai Seng Video (HK)/Dimension Films (USA)
Jackie Chan   Asian Hawk
Rosamund Kwan   Laura
Alan Tam   Alan
Maria Delores   May
Ken Boyle, Lola Forner, Bozidar Smiljanic, John Ladalski, Robert O'Brien, Boris Grregoric
[***]
Though entitled Operation Condor 2, this is actually the first Operation Condor film, but was released as the sequel in the United States. Admiring the success and action brilliance of the "Indiana Jones" films, Jackie Chan hoped to recapture the magic by creating his own adventurous modern-day treasure hunter. However, Jackie falls short of Dr. Jones, lacking the sophistication and nobility of Harrison Ford's character. Instead, Chan's character cares more for profit and excitement, terrorizing whoever gets in his way. Though ambitious in scope with various locales, non-Asian actors, and an incredibly large budget for a Hong Kong film, Armour of Gods never captures the awe, wonder, and excitement of "Raiders of the Lost Art". Part of the problem is the situational comedy that sneaks back in every ten minutes, but we'll get back to that later. Still seen on its own, a number of the action sequences are exciting and Chan's screen

persona does have appeal for fans.

The opening begins with Jackie decked in camouflage fatigues stealing an ancient artifact from the top of a stone statue. The primitive natives aren't too happy and decide to go after him. Sounds like the opening in "Raiders of the Lost Ark'. Well he makes his escape and avoids the hostile natives in a clever manner, using his martial arts abilities and a can of beer to escape. The escape scene marks an infamous stunt in which Jackie Chan almost died. The scene where he jumps to catch a tree branch and escape, nearly cost him his life. A relatively simple jump for Chan, the branch broke and he plummeted to the rocks below. He ended up puncturing his skull and was rushed to the hospital. He survived, but still carries a scar and a hole in his skull which he occasionally allows people to touch. Like a true trooper, Chan never lets an injury stop his production and the outtakes at the closing credits are his testimony to bravery, dedication, and foolhardiness.

Unfortunately, the rest of the film carries through at an uneven pace, mixing mundane comedy with mainstream action. Chan shines when he lets his body and fluidity carry the action, but instead often opts for standard car chases, big gun battles, and puerile bits. The main scene after the escape teaser is a jumble of juxtaposing cuts of a rock singer screaming away, while a fashion show is going on simultaneously elsewhere. Later the significance of the scenes play together, but for now confusion explodes as assassins enter the fashion show and go on a rampage with rock music blaring in the background. The assassins go through all that effort to kidnap a young woman named Lorelei. Afterwards, Jackie is in an auction room where he comes across the path of a wealthy and attractive European woman. There is some romantic cat play but nothing ever develops. Soon Jackie meets his old friend Alan who was the rock singer from the beginning. Now here's where the befuddled love triangle plot comes in and mars the entire film. Supposedly, the trio (Jackie, Alan, Lorelei) were in a rock band together and Jackie loved Lorelei, but now Alan loves her and she loves Alan....or so she thinks for now. The killers kidnaped Lorelei to force Jackie to steal a priceless relic, The Armour of God.

Jackie needs five pieces of the Armour of God to rescue Lorelei, so he promises wealthy collector Bannon to return the borrowed pieces and come back with the entire set. Bannon agrees and supplies him with equipment and his daughter, the attractive woman at the auction. They finally trace the kidnaper's path to what seems to be a Franciscan brotherhood that regularly induces local prostitutes. Under the cover of whores, the trio break in and wander around aimlessly. They manage a goofy escape, but not before Lorelei is brainwashed and then they're back at the castle. Finally after an hour of screen time, the film picks up toward its climatic conclusion. Chan takes on the fake monks, battling throughout the monastery. The bizarre climax has Jackie entering a room with four African-American women warriors. They're dressed in fetish like black one-piece bathing suits, black stockings, and black high heel shoes. Amazons in comparison, Jackie battles them in a superb fight scene that doesn't really require an explanation. Soon the group is happily united and the film ends. Perhaps Chan was too ambitious in his quest for international visibility or perhaps a solid story wasn't worked out during preproduction. Whatever the case, Chan shows promise and entertains, but the film is hardly a masterpiece or one of his best efforts. The above review was originally based on the 100 minute Hong Kong version, the 89 minute American version is slightly better with a tighter plot and a lot of the slapstick humor re-edited or cut out completely.

Operation Condor   **(The Armour of the Gods 2/Operation Eagle (in Japan))**

(1991) Action Kung-Fu   C-92m PG-13 Dubbed   VA   Catalog #12687
Hong Kong   Retail: $19.99
Dir: Jackie Chan   Scr: Jackie Chan, Edward Tang
Prod: Jackie Chan, Leonard K.C. Ho   Ex. Prod: Raymond Chow
DP: Wong Ngok Tai   Editorial Consultant: Rod Dean   Music: Stephen Endelman
Art Dir: Oliver Wong, Yui Man, Lam Chun Fai, Eddie Ma Pun Chiu
Prod Supervisor: Willie Chan, Edward Tang
PC/Dist: Dimension Films in association with Media Asia Distribution
Jackie Chan   Asian Hawk
Carol Cheng, Eva Cobo Garcia, Shoko Ikeda, Aldo Sanchez
[***]
Sequel to the popular film, Armour of Gods, but released in American as a solo film entitled Operation Condor. Better than the original which explains its earlier release, it continues the exploits of Chan's treasure hunter/martial artist named Asian Hawk. The fight scene at the end is amazing and incredibly inventive, plus the search for Nazi gold is more of a worthy theme than a cult finding five pieces of armor to rule the world. Also the comedic side kick, Alan, is given a rest and this time Jackie is escorted by three attractive women of very different backgrounds across the Sahara Desert.

Once again, Chan bothers some natives by stealing their artifact and proving how stupid they are and how clever he is. Amazingly, Chan escapes in a giant plastic bubble and roles down the side of a mountain. I don't know if he was actually involved in the stunt, but nevertheless the scene is still breathtaking.

Then Jackie crosses paths with millionaire Bannon who wants him to search for a cache of Nazi gold hidden in the desert. Instead of an irritating friend and a childish romantic triangle, Jackie teams with three attractive and resourceful women who provide comedic interplay and sweet charm. One includes an arrogant historian, a Japanese wanderer, and the German granddaughter of the Nazi solider who hid the gold. The female trio may delight for their visual comedy, but may also fluster true martial arts afficionados since the women lack any fighting prowess. Meanwhile, another treasure seeker in a wheelchair is also after the fortune and sends his goons to delay Jackie's party and find out what they know. The middle of the film does spend considerable time with the three women getting into trouble, but the scenes are cute and Chan's frustration is comical as he defends the women while fighting their attackers at the same time. Soon they reach the underground base and discover the gold. The film is pure excitement from here on and the sets are impressive for any film, let alone a Hong Kong movie. A massive underground base, more impressive than the Nazi island base in Raiders of the Lost Ark, rests hidden underneath the desert. Jackie's group is captured by the villains and also pursued by aggressive desert bedouins. In the mind-blowing climax, Jackie battles thugs on top of generators, moving platforms, around dark corridors, on steel gratings, and even in a giant wind tunnel designed for secret jet experiments. The inventive wildness of the film is full force and Chan easily redeems the slights from the first film. The American release edited out many of the additional comic routines provided by Chan and the women, including a sexually suggestive attempt to share drinking water. Either version is worth the effort and should be available in local video stores.

Operation Scorpio

(1991) Kung-Fu   C-95m Dubbed   Hong Kong   Retail: $19.95
Dir: David Lai   Scr: Chan Che Wei, Barry Wong, Lui Sau Fung
Ex. Prod: Leonard Ho   MAD: Liu Chia Liang
PC: Shaw Brothers
Chin Kar Lok, Liu Chia Liang (Lau Kar Leung), May Lo, Yuen Chun, Wu Fung
[***]
Chin Kar Lok is an idealistic dreamer who enjoys drawing comics over listening to his professor's lectures. He doesn't know martial arts, but he illustrates comics of heroes who are masters of kung-fu. His life takes a dramatic turn when he gets involved with an escaped house servant/slave of an evil merchant who demands sexual favorites. The tyrant's son who is proficient in scorpion style takes on all comers in a beautiful display of acrobatics and kinetic footwork. The illustrator makes a few friends and starts to train in martial arts. Different off-the-wall martial arts philosophies are explored when the illustrator hooks up with masters of two completely different styles: the muscular master focuses on power/strength and the elder master focuses on "Wok-Washing" techniques. The heroes combine their forces and invade the villain's mansion, opening the film to an exciting series of action sequences in which the villains strike back. The young hero masters martial arts, incorporating both fighting styles with his own variation based on his knowledge of the scorpion fighter. Teaming up with the "Wok-master" (Liu Chia Liang), the two men defeat the powerful scorpion fighter and send his evil father over the edge. The movie never takes itself too seriously, spicing the action with humor. The film may not have the polished look of other kung-fu films with veteran stars, but there's enough in the story, characters, creative choreography, and stuntwork to make for a fun feature worth checking.

Organized Crime & Triad Bureau
(1993) Action C-101m   Chinese with English Subtitles
Catalog #35273   Hong Kong   Retail: $79.95
Dir: Kirk Wong   Dist: Tai Seng Video
Danny Lee, Anthony Wong, Cecilia Yip
[**1/2]
A rather interesting film in the sense that it promotes police brutality and shows the vicious killers in a sympathetic light. A dedicated cop, played by Danny Lee (cop from "The Killer") is obsessed with capturing a ruthless killer on the loose. The whole movie follows the exploits of Lee and his special crime unit trying to capture the killer and his girlfriend. Every now and then, a suspect is tortured and beaten while CAPO (Citizens Against Police Organization) try to stop the brutality. When the police discover the criminal couple on an island, they plan an elaborate manhunt that takes up a good portion of the film. The crook (Wong) who normally sleeps around with other women bonds with his loyal girlfriend (Yip) in their fugitive-like ordeal, providing some nice romantic moments (ala Bonnie & Clyde). They finally escape to the city, but are cornered by Lee and his determined police officers. Lee goes through the motions of hunting down the couple, but the dramatic climax lacks the style experienced in other crime/action films. A rather uninspired film with standard action scenes placed every ten minutes, but engaging for its acting performances.

Otaku no Video

(1993) Japanime   C-100m   Japanese with English Subtitles   VA
Catalog # AT093-002   Japan Retail: $29.95
Dir: Mori Takeshi   Scr: Okada Toshio   Story Outline: Gainax
Character Designs: Sonodo Kenichi   Technical Director: Masuo Shooichi
DP: Sano Sadashi   Art Director: Nagao Jin   Animation Dir: Honda Takeshi
Music: Tanaka Kohei   Prod: Inomata Kazuhiko, Kanda Yoshimi
Planning: Maruyama Yoshio, Okada Toshio
PC: Gainax in Association with Studio Fantasia   Dist: Toshiba Video Soft, Inc.

Tsujiya Kooji	Kubo
Sakurai Toshiharu	Tanaka
Kobayashi Yuuko	Fukuhara Misuzu
Amano Yuri	Satoo Yuri
Nakahara Shigeru	Hino
Morikawa Tomoyuki/Iiyama	
Kikuchi Masami	Miyoshi
Tobita Norio	Yamaguchi
Takagi Wataru	Kitajima
Umeza Hideyuki	Shao Bai Lung
Ootsuka Akio	Banker & Narrator

[***1/2]

Otaku no Video is a fascinating and disturbing look at ultra-fans of Japanese animation and manga (print comics). Similar to Trekkers/Trekkies (Star Trek fans) and Rocky Horror Picture Show fans, otaku no videos are people dedicated to the genre to the extent of extreme fanaticism. They dress like their favorite characters, wait in overnight lines for their favorite movies, memorize dialogue, spend tons of money on related merchandise, and in general live and breathe the genre.

The film follows the fictional life of Kubo, a normal Japanese college guy, who gets sucked into the world of the otakus when he meets an old high school classmate, Tanaka. Tanaka (typical nerd/geek) is an overweight, glass-wearing, single guy who introduces Kubo to the world of otakus. The film can be seen from two points of view, a humorous and biting satire of extremist fans or a depressing social commentary on the dangers of anime saturation. Throughout the animated story, live-action interviews take place of real (perhaps staged) otakus who live in Japan. In general, they are twenty-somethings and live a sheltered existence with no social female companionship. Most otakus are male and it is obviously stressed how anime and manga feature scantily clad girls to appease the lonely male fans.

Once Kubo meets Tanaka, he quits the tennis club and stops seeing his girlfriend. He becomes a true otaku, spending hours and millions of yen on becoming the ultimate otaku - the otaking! The two friends start their own company and become extremely wealthy and powerful until there company is taken over. Then the story moves into the future as they plan a comeback and end their lives with success. The final scene is both a homage to the genre of anime and a stab at it. Providing both an entertaining anime story and a mockumentary, Otaku no Video leaves you smiling, but also asks you to examine your own passion with anime and manga.

In the course of the story, actual historical events are documented as well as key events in the history of anime. A number of subjects are dealt with that are particular to otakus, including minor sub-branches such as Science Fiction clubs, Godzilla fans, garage kit model fans, military buffs, cel (an individual frame or picture from an anime or manga) collecting, and many others with statistical graphs and questionnaires. For relevance, I'd recommend this film only after you're more familiar with the satirized genre.

Outlanders
(1986) Japanime: Scifi   C-50m Dubbed   Catalog #USR DIE07
Japan Retail: $19.95
Dir: Katsuhisa Yamada   Art Dir: Yusaku Saotome
Character Design & Animation Dir: Hiroshi Hamazaki
Music: Megumi Wakakusa PC: Hakusensha/Tatsunoko Production/ Victor
Dist: U.S. Renditions
(based on the comic by Johji Manabe)
[1/2]**
If you can get beyond the devilish appearance of Kahm with her bold, big eyes, wild-colored hair, and outlandish outfit, you might enjoy this silly, but cute anime film. Kahm is a powerful alien princess assigned to conquer Earth for her father, the Emperor of Santovsaku. Dressed in a sexy outfit and carrying a huge sword, she is unstoppable. Of course, she's all set to do the job when she runs across average Japanese student Tetsuya (I can't help thinking this must be the fantasy of every anime writer). Well instead of subjugating the humans, she takes an interest in Tetsuya and brings him back to her home world, whether he likes it or not. The emperor is displeased that she failed in her mission and more than amiss that she wants to marry a barbaric human. Kahm is used to getting her way and poor Tetsuya is caught in the middle as all hell breaks loose. Kahm recruits two of her friends who help Tetsuya escape, but the brave Japanese teen challenges the alien in a battle to the death. An older film, but silly and fun for fans of girls in anime.

-P-

Pat Labor 1: Mobile Police
(1989) Japanime: Scifi   C-100m   Dubbed/Japanese with English Subtitles   VA
Catalog #MGV 634801/MGV 635485   Japan Retail: $19.99/$24.95
Dir: Mamoru Oshii Scr: Kazunori Itoh   Concept: Masami Yuki
Character Design: Akemi Takada Mecha Design: Yutaka Izubuchi
Animation Prod: Studio Deen
PC: Headgear/Emotion/TFC   Dist: Bandai Co., Ltd./ Manga Entertainment
[*1/2]**
In the near-future of 1999, the world has reached the age of robot technology. Giant mechanized robots called Labors are used in place of heavy machinery and hi-tech equipment. The efficiency, mobility, strength, and versatility of the Labors have revolutionized modern industry, but with the price of improvement comes a sacrifice. The wonderful machines can also be used for massive destruction and corruption in the wrong hands. Regular police are no match and only a more advanced Labor can take out a renegade Labor, therefore, Pat Labor is created. A special police branch to monitor and patrol the use of Labors.
The Pat Labor officers must investigate a mysterious case of runaway Labors who go berserk for no reason. The opening credits are interspersed with an amazing and realistic army maneuver to

hunt down and destroy a renegade Labor. The truth leads officers Noah Izumi and Azuma Shinohara to the massive Babylon Project Labor construction site positioned out on Tokyo bay. The brilliant scientist who committed suicide created the complex so that wind would create a high-pitch frequency throughout the building and cause Labors to go mechanically wild. With an impending storm with strong winds approaching, all eight thousand Labors in the entire city could go on an automated rampage. Desperate to prevent the catastrophic carnage, the dedicated officers of Pat Labor must figure a way to save the day. Fighting off the internal defenses of Babylon Project Site, the Pat Labor team moves in an attempts to stop the Bable virus from unleashing itself. A technically mature style of animation involving a humanistic approach to animated characters and an intriguing premise crossing robotic action and crime dramas.

Pat Labor: The Mobile Police - The New Files Vol. 3
(1992) Japanime   C-90m Japanese with English Subtitles   Catalog #USM 1541
Japan Retail: $29.95
Dir: Yasunori Urata, Yasunao Aoki, Nana Harada
Scr: Mamoru Oshii, Michiko Yokote, Kazunori Itoh
Character Design: Akemi Takada Mecha Design: Yutaka Izubuchi, Yoshinori Sayama
Music: Kenji Kawai
English Version - Ex. Prod: John O'Donnell   Prod: Stephanie Shalofsky
Translation: David Fleming
PC: Headgear/Emotion/TFC   Dist: U.S. Manga Corps
[***]
Based on episodes from the television series rather than theatrically tailored for release. The video comprises of episodes with a strong sitcom flavor rather than hard-packed action found in the full-length feature films. Very little mech action takes place and most of the interaction is internal, between members of the Pat Labor force. This is only one volume reviewed in a series of volumes to be released, so new releases may differ in story style and content. Check out the full-length features, before deciding whether or not the characters will appeal to you on a daily dose. The first episode involves a civil war within SV2's maintenance crew and the head chief. The chief is disturbed with his men when he discovers a large amount of pornography and other items of distraction. He bans the material and sets his crew to work long shifts without the pleasures of life. The chief's second-in-command assumes a police state mentality and Nazi-parodies run sky high as the crew rebels against authority. The second episode involves a rivalry between female Officers Kanuka and Takeo. While on vacation, the two females compete in a variety of ways to determine who is the better officer. Their antics drive the rest of the squad up the wall. The third finds Ohta on the run from the law when he is accused of viciously murdering his fellow officers from Pat Labor. His memory is blurred of the events that led to the carnage and only with the clothes on his back, he hides in the city and finds help in the least likely of places. In no time, the humorous truth is revealed and everything works out well for the next adventure to follow.
The three episodes in volume three are entitled:
Episode 8: The Seven Days of Fire
Episode 9: Versus
Episode 10: It's Called Amnesia

Peace Hotel
(1995) Action C-86m Chinese with English Subtitles
Catalog #1737   Hong Kong   Retail: $39.99
Dir/Scr: Wai Ka Fai   Original Story: Chow Yun Fat, Wai Ka Fai
Ex. Prod: Tsui Hark   DP: Wong Wing Hang   Editor: Tony Chow, Chan Kei Hop
Music: Cacine Wong, Healthy Poon   Prod Manager: Chin Wing Wai
Line Prod: Woo Ping   Art Dir: Yee Chung Man, Yau Wai Ming
Costume: Ng Li Lo   MAD: Yuen Bing
PC: Cassia Hill Production Ltd.   Dist: Tai Seng Video
Chow Yun Fat, Cecilia Yip, Ng Sin Lin, Chin Ho, Lau Shun, Annabelle Liew, Hedy Chang, Mickey Ng
[***]
One of the newer films from Tsui Hark, starring Chow Yun Fat and Cecilia Yip. The film captures an element of an American early western frontier. When Chow's beautiful mistress is murdered, he goes wild and massacres everyone in the hotel, gaining the nickname, "King of the Killers". The last survivor is a young teen who begs for mercy and runs up the stairs. Chow slices his ear and is about to kill him when sunlight pours in and a dove flies past him. He decides to amend his brutal ways and quits killing. He opens a hotel, called the Peace Hotel, and will give sanctuary to anyone who enters its door. When a young woman arrives being chased by a ruthless gang, Chow must decide whether to protect her (as he promises to all) or to battle the horse-riding marauders. Visually impressive film with less action than you might expect. The film has a very strong stylistic stamp with black and white flashbacks, slow motion scenes, rapid cuts, and angular setups. Expect a heavy does of romance, since the story focuses on Yip and Chow. What adds a plus to the film is Cecilia Yip's performance as a lying, conniving, club girl who tries to muscle her way into Chow's life by pretending to be his dead mistress. She gets what she deserves and though she is a cheat, her perseverance and strength turns you (and Chow) to her side. An entertaining film that combines style, action, humor, and romance.

Peacock King Spirit Warrior 1: Revival of Evil
(1994) Japanime   C-49m Dubbed   Catalog #USM 1549 Japan
Retail: $19.99
Dir: Taro Rin Scr: Kazuhiro Inaba, Tatsuhiko Urahata
Original Story: Makoto Ogino
Character Design: Ken Koike, Hisashi Abe   Animation Dir: Hisashi Abe
Music Dir: Masafumi Mima   Music: Toshiyuki Abe
English Version - Ex. Prod: John O'Donnell   Prod: Stephanie Shalofsky
Dubbing Manager: Oeter Bavaro   Dubbing Supervisor: Anthony Salerno
Translation: William Flanagan, Yuko Sato
PC: Mad House/Shueisha/Pony Canyon/Pioneer LDC   Dist: U.S. Manga Corps
Ed Garland   Kujaku
Michael Schwartz   Onimaru
Matthew Harrington/Jiku
Aussa Stein   Asura
Dan Truman   Kaiho Ko

Martin Epstein	Head Priest
Denise Gottwald	Tsukuyomi
James Stanley	Siegfried
Jon Avner	Haus'Hoffer
Ed Kissel	Nikko

[***]

Though Japanese animation covers many genres, it can still be divided into two major categories: serious and comedic. Peacock King is a very serious story that deals with the forces of good versus evil. The globe-hopping story follows the mad exploits of a Neo-Nazi leader bent on reigniting a new reign of darkness. Lord Siegfried von Mittgard must find the mystical dragon orb and reunite the orb with a special woman who will become the new dark regent. Battling all over the world, four warriors from different backgrounds gather to stop Siegfried's plan. Acting under his clan's orders, Kaiho Ko is a mystical warrior from the Sendo Clan of China. He must recover the dragon orb at any cost and uses a magical energy sword. Onimaru is a master of the black arts and summoning. Nikko is a powerful leader in Buddhist exorcism. But the true hero is Kujaku, a young man unsure of his apprentice level abilities. While riding home on the bus, Kujaku and his female companion Asura are accosted by demonic zombies. Kujaku is the classic fantasy/quest hero who must develop his skills and mature over time until the day he can defeat the enemy and save the world. They join forces with the other heroes in an attempt to protect the orb and save Kujaku's sister, Tomoko. The film ends with a Nazi attack on the holy monastery which gives them possession of the dragon orb and poor Asura.

Peacock King Spirit Warrior 2: Rumbling Kunlun Mountain
(1994) Japanime   C-48m Dubbed   Catalog #USM 1550 Japan
Retail: $19.99
Dir: Taro Rin Scr: Kazuhiro Inaba, Tatsuhiko Urahata
Original Story: Makoto Ogino
Character Design: Ken Koike, Hisashi Abe   Animation Dir: Hisashi Abe
Music Dir: Masafumi Mima   Music: Toshiyuki Abe
English Version - Ex. Prod: John O'Donnell   Prod: Stephanie Shalofsky
Dubbing Manager: Oeter Bavaro   Dubbing Supervisor: Anthony Salerno
Translation: William Flanagan, Yuko Sato
PC: Mad House/Shueisha/Pony Canyon/Pioneer LDC   Dist: U.S. Manga Corps
[**1/2]

The hunt for power and control continue in the second volume which continues the violent and dramatic tone of the first series, but lacks the globe-hopping quest aspect. If you enjoyed the first installment, the second will also be appealing and brings to conclusion the supernatural saga. Sendo warrior Ko has infiltrated the Nazi castle and searches for the dragon orb. Injured, he is brought back to health by Tomoko who sacrificed her freedom in return for Ko and Asura's safety from the powerful Siegfried. It is revealed that he is not human and his own Nazi ambitions are betrayed by Hoffer who commands the now-possessed Tomoko to raise an ancient citadel from the ground. The other heroes find Ko and Asura, join forces, and battle the enemy. Sadly, Tomoko must fulfill her tragic destiny and battle her own brother, Kujaku, for the fate of the world. Their history is revealed in flashbacks which sets the tone for their climatic confrontation. The two battle on a Tibetan mountaintop and represent the reincarnated gods of ancient past, Kujaku-Oh and Tenja-Oh.

Phantom Lover
(1995) Romance   **C-102m**   **Chinese with English Subtitles**   **VA**
Catalog #1857   **Hong Kong**   **Retail: $79.98**
Dir: Ronnie Yu   **Scr: Ronnie Yu, Raymond Wong**
Prod: Michael Ng, Raymond Wong, Leslie Cheung
Ex. Prod: Li Ming, Raymond Wong   **Prod Design: Eddie Ma**
Dist: Tai Seng Video
Leslie Cheung   **Song Dan Ping**
Wu Chien Lien   **Du Yu Yan**
Huang Lei, Liu Lin
[1/2]**

As I watched the film, I was truly awed by the beauty of the sets, lighting, and shot composition. Yu and his film crew really go all out to make a rich, lush-looking period piece. So it struck me as odd that I found myself falling asleep as the story slowly unfolded. The story is framed in two time settings and shot with two different lighting approaches: the main story is shot in faded colors, approaching an almost grey hue which captures the ambience of the early century. The inner story is a series of flashbacks on the life and death of Song and Du Yu, during their torrid romance at the opera house. The cinematography is breathtaking with vibrant colors and lush sets. A group of Chinese performers arrive in town to open up a show. They take over the abandoned opera house which has been forsaken since a horrible fire destroyed the building and killed the famous singer, Song Dan Ping. Soon the spirit of Song helps the novice troupe succeed. Then the past ignites into the presence as Song reveals he is still alive and never perished in the fire. He demands revenge against his attackers, but what price will the characters have to pay. Yu's film was eagerly anticipated as an Asian rendition to the classic Phantom of the Opera, but where Yu succeeds in visuals, he fails in storytelling. The character seem as ghostly and insubstantial as the spirits they represent. None of the characters personas jumps alive on the screen and challenges the viewers to identify with them.

Picture Bride
(1994) Romance   **C-90m PG-13**   **English & Japanese with English Subtitles**
VA   **Catalog #5445 AS**   **Japan Retail: $19.99**
Dir: Kayo Hatta   **Scr: Mari Hatta, Kayo Hatta**   **Prod: Lisa Onodera**
Ex. Prod: Diane Mei Lin Mark
DP: Claudio Rocha   **Editor: Lynzee Klingman, Mallory Gottlieb**   **Music: Mark Adler**
Prod Design: Paul Guncheon   **Costume: Ada Akaji**
PC: Thousand Cranes Filmworks   **Dist: Miramax**
Youki Kudoh   **Riyo**
Akira Takayama   **Matsuji**
Tamlyn Tomita   **Kana**
Cary-Hiroyuki Togawa/Kanzaki
Toshiro Mifune   **The Benshi**
Yoko Sugi   **Aunt Sode**
Lito Capina   **Augusto**

[***1/2]

"At the beginning of the 20th century, photography
modernized the tradition of arranged marriages in Asia.
In place of face-to-face meetings, families and matchmakers
and photographs to introduce prospective couples living
in different parts of the country or even across the ocean.
Between 1907 and 1924, more than 20,000 young Japanese,
Okinawan, and Korean women journeyed to Hawaii to
become the wives of men they knew only through photographs
and letters. They were called "picture brides."
This film is based on their stories."

Opening Card

Based on true accounts, Picture Bride is a delicate, heartwarming, and beautiful film dedicated to the women who left Asia in search of new lives in a new world. Many Japanese men who left for new parts of the world such as Hawaii and California to work and seek fortunes soon wanted to establish permanent residence and raise a family. Interracial marriages were unheard of during the turn of the century, so most wrote to relatives or friends in Japan who helped set up pre-arranged marriages or mail-brides. Letters were exchanged as were photos of prospective spouses and if the match was compatible, the women would venture across the sea to meet her husband. Picture Bride follows the exploits of young Riyo, a virginal teenager who imagines a life in Hawaii with a strong, young man. When she arrives, her dreams are shattered when her husband turns out to be her father's age. His photo was dated and the letters never mentioned his true age. Dismayed and without a knowledge of English or enough money to return home, she unwillingly stays with him but refuses to commit herself to him. He gently acquiesces to her wishes and attempts to win her heart with romance and kindness. The two are brought together through their mutual hardship and desire to build a future for themselves. They maintain a close tie to fellow Japanese within the Hawaii community and also run into trouble with other ethnic groups. Riyo starts to learn English and befriends a resourceful woman named Kana. A film that offers insight into a part of Japanese-American history filled with emotions that are true for people from every point in time. The viewer realizes that love and age should not be restrictive, since dreams and passions are shared by all people, regardless of race, age, or sex. Beautifully filmed on location with a stellar cast of Asian actors. Highly recommended for all viewers.

Plastic Little "The Adventures of Captain Tita"
(1994) Japanime: Scifi   C-50m Japanese with English Subtitles   VA
Catalog #ADV PL/001D   Japan Retail: $29.95
Dir: Kinji Yoshimoto   Scr: Masayori Sekimoto
Prod: Kazuhiko Ikeguchi, Hideaki Fujii   DP: Akihiko Takahashi
Character Design, Key Illustration & Direction: Satoshi Urushihara
Art Dir: Tsutomu Ishigaki   Original Creator: Kinji Yoshimoto, Satoshi Urushihara
Planning: Masaki Sawanobori, Mitsuhisa Hida   Music: Tamio Terashima
Created by Sony Music Entertainment   PC: Animate Film   Dist: Kiss Films
Yuriko Sezaki   Tita
Hekiru Shiina   Elysse
Norio Wakamoto   Balboa

Kappei Yamaguchi	Nichol
Takanori Nakao	Roger
Shou Ohtsuka	Mikhail
Keiko Yokozawa	Mei
Hiroshi Iknaka	Guizel
Yosuke Akimoto	Nalerof

[**1/2]

Compact story with a good dose of action, science fiction elements, and top-notch animation from the mind of Satoshi Urushihara (2nd major animated project). Titu is the captain (taking over for her dead father) of a marine pet hunting ship. A submersible ship that captures rare aquatic specimens for laboratories and institutes. Her entire crew is extremely loyal and experienced, some even have military training. While docked at port, Titu comes across a young girl running for her life. She is pursued by a military faction within the government ruled by a tyrannical dictator. The dictator killed the girl's father after he discovered his plans to destroy the city. She was given the access codes to the explosive devices and told to escape. Titu and her crew help the girl and take on the military faction. There is no doubt that the animation is a pleasure to view, but what holds back the story from truly entertaining fans of Japanime and science fiction is a plot filled with inconsistencies that take forever to build. When the climax is finally reached, the confrontation between Tita and Guizel is anti-dramatic. A good deal of the plot is spent on Tita and Elysse's budding friendship which includes a prolonged nude scene in a bathing room with ample scenes of teenage breasts. The nudity is also complemented with violence but not on a grotesque level. A stronger, tighter plot mixed into a formula that already has wonderful animation and a good blend of characters would have made Plastic Little a much more memorable and repeatable outing.

Pole Master
(1980) Kung-Fu   **C-100m**   **Dubbed**   **Hong Kong**   **Retail: $19.99**
PC: Shaw Brothers
Ti Lung, Ku Feng
[***]

Ti Lung never looked better as he speaks softly and wields a big staff. Lung is a master of the Shaolin pole, basically a simple bamboo staff six feet in length and anywhere from an inch to two inches in diameter. He is the master of a local martial arts school with dedicated students. A rival master (Ku) offers him money to teach at his Academy. Ti Lung politely refuses. Ku is angered at Ti's arrogance and refusal, but fears the master's famous pole style. He hires a man and woman to teach Ti a lesson. In a crowded marketplace, she throws herself at Ti, claiming to be his mistress. Onlookers laugh, but the woman's brother appears and demands Ti marry his pregnant sister (all a ruse). He refuses and a fight breaks out. Ti accidentally injures the woman's brother who fakes his death and later disappears. Unknowingly, the evil master framed Ti Lung and forces his school to shut down. In desperation, Lung seeks out Ku and takes his offer. He becomes the evil school's teacher, but is dismayed at the cruel nature of the students. A long bitter rivalry exists with another school and a line is drawn in the middle of the town. Anyone caught crossing it will be punished, usually by cutting off their arm or leg. When a young student crosses the line to talk to Ti Lung, he is captured. Ti saves him from losing a leg and disassociates himself with the villains. The young student secretly watches Ti train and so does the evil master who hopes to learn his secret. During his training, Ti always stops at the end of his kata and doesn't continue. The evil Ku believes Ti has reached the end of his technique and is no longer necessary. Ti and his newly trained disciple challenge and defeat the evil master and his school. Pole Master is a strong example of a more accurate and realistic portrayal of martial arts. Unlike the Japanese who honor the sword, Chinese and Hong Kong films have a myriad of popular weapons. For showcasing the power and practicality of the staff, there are few movies as entertaining and insightful as the Pole Master. Veteran Ti Lung plays his role with little humor and plenty of conviction.

Police Story (Police Force)
(1985) Action Kung-Fu   **C-106m**   **Dubbed**   **VA**
Catalog # DP1350-A   **Hong Kong**   **Retail: $9.99**
Dir/Scr: Jackie Chan   **Prod: Jackie Chan, Leonard K.C. Ho**
PC: Golden Harvest   **Dist: Parade Video, Inc.**
Jackie Chan   **Officer Chan**
Brigitte Lin   **Selina**
Maggie Cheung   **May**
Cho Yuen, Bill Tung, Kenneth Tong, Lam Kok Hung
[****]

Dated by Chan standards, still an excellent example that combines Chan's amazing physical abilities and comedic presence. A personal favorite of many viewers, this is one of the first modern Chan films to be released in America, dubbed into English, and accepted at film festivals. Entertainment Weekly rated it as one of the best action films of all times and so do I. The role started a series of popular sequels in which Jackie is a cop trying to do the right thing at the wrong time. The opening scene features an amazing car chase sequence which demolishes an entire hillside town. Jackie is a cop involved in a sting operation to nail a top ranking triad boss in Hong Kong. The police set up an undercover raid unit and watch a major deal going down, but are betrayed by one of their own officers. The boss' girlfriend is Brigitte Lin who stays in the car while the action abounds as the police desperately try to regain control of the situation. The boss is captured by the police and his trial date is set. The only way to win the case is to convince Lin to become a state's witness, but she refuses and is released under Chan's protection. Meanwhile, adorable Cheung is planning a surprise birthday party for her boyfriend Chan and catches (jumping to conclusions) the two together. Desperately, Chan must save his relationship and his career. In a number of humorous scenes, Chan must convince Cheung that Lin is only an assignment and means nothing to him. On the other hand, Chan tries to convince Lin that her boss is trying to execute her and even stages an elaborate mock assassination attempt. When the real assassins appear, Chan is in for a big dose of trouble. Lin discovers the first attempt was a hoax and returns to her boss' side. The court case falls through and the crime boss goes free, but he decides to frame and murder the meddling Chan. They kill the crooked cop and kidnap Lin, planting evidence that frames Chan for the murder. Chan must flee from his own officers, rescue Lin, and find evidence to convict the crime boss. With Lin's help, they print up some incriminating information and go on a wild cat-and-mouse chase through a department scene. The action is fast and furious, but in the end Chan always gets his man and woman.

An excellent film that showcases some great fights, witty humor, and amazing stunts. Check out the outtakes at the end of the film where one of the stunts went wrong. The bus scene went horribly wrong. The two stuntmen who went through the windshield were supposed to land on specially padded cars, however the bus stopped short and they landed on the road. It may not sound serious, but it was a double-decker bus and the stuntmen were on the second level. For modern martial arts action, Chan delivers a high dose and maintains his family friendly style.

Police Story 2
(1988) Action Kung-Fu   C-90m Hong Kong
Dir/Scr: Jackie Chan   Prod: Jackie Chan, Leonard K.C. Ho
PC: Golden Harvest
Jackie Chan, Maggie Cheung, Bill Tung, Lam Kwok Hung, Charles Chao, Crystal Kwok, Cho Yuen, Henny Ho
[***]
Jackie Chan's Police Story received fantastic reviews in Asia and American, making it a natural to continue in a series of sequels. Following his adventures as a Hong Kong supercop who does his best, but still gets in trouble, Chan is demoted from detective to traffic cop. He has plenty of enemies and decides to take some time off from police work, but gets involved with a ruthless gang behind a wave of bomb threats. Cute and lovable May (Maggie Cheung), Jackie's girlfriend, plays a more substantial role in the second film. Their relationship is still full of humor, love, and misunderstanding. When Chan gets in the way of the criminals, they kidnap May to keep Jackie under control. Pushed to supercop limits, Chan rides atop a bus, crashes through windows, and looks for May. He confronts the gang in a giant warehouse where the nasty explosive experts use firebombs to heat things up. The climax is a true showstopper as Chan and May must avoid the ruthless criminals and a warehouse full of deadly pipes, scaffolding, walkways, and aerial drops. Plenty of top notch fighting and great scenes where Jackie and May escape from an army of thugs. Maggie Cheung's role in the film was reportedly shorter than the original script due to an accident suffered on the set. A must see for all action/Chan fans.

Police Story 3: Supercop   (Supercop)
(1991) Kung-Fu   C-96m Dubbed   R
Catalog # VHS 9678/CC1479L   Hong Kong   Retail: $19.95
Dir: Stanley Tong   Scr: Edward Tang, Fibe Ma, Lee Wai Yee
Prod: Willie Chan, Edward Tang   Ex. Prod: Leonard Ho, Jackie Chan
Prod Supervisor: Barbie Tung
DP: Ardy Lam   Editor: Cheung Yiu Chung, Cheung Kar Fei   Music: Joel McNeely
Prod Manager: Peggy Lee, Cheung Shun Sun, Chan Wai Yeung, Lee Bing Wan
Art Dir: But Yiu Kwong   Make-up: Lo Shui Lin
MAD: Tang Tak Wing, Sze Chun Wai, Chan Man Ching, Wong Ming Sing
PC/Dist: Dimension Films in association with Media Asia Distribution
Jackie Chan   Kevin Chan "Supercop"/Lin Fu-Sheng
Michelle Yeoh   Chief of Security Yang
Maggie Cheung   May
Ken Tsang   Chaibat
Corey Yuen Wah   Panther
Bill Tung   Uncle Bill

Josephine Koo   Chaibat's Wife
Wong Siu, Lowei Kwong, Philip Chan, Law Lit, Shum Wai, Hon Yee San
[***]
The second Jackie Chan film to be released after Rumble in the Bronx is actually an older film dubbed into English with a new musical score and a few scene cuts to allow better pacing and get rid of any references to previous films.

Jackie Chan is a top Hong Kong detective working undercover in cooperation with the Chinese police who have captured Panther, a leading member of a major criminal organization. Panther knows the details of the gang's operations. Jackie and Michelle befriend Panther and organize his escape to Hong Kong where he meets Chaibat, the head of the gang, face to face. Now in the gang's confidence, Jackie and Michelle (pretending to be siblings) go along with them to negotiate a major drug deal and get into an explosive jungle battle. The two work well together, each officer is at the top of their game. With business matters completed, the entire gang fly to Kuala Lumpur and plan to breakout Chaibat's wife who might just testify if pressured by the authorities. Unfortunately, Jackie's girlfriend May is staying at the same hotel and mistakes Michelle for Jackie's mistress. A common scene of misunderstood humor that is quickly resolved. At the last moment Jackie is exposed and captured, but escapes in time to foil the breakout and hitch a ride on Chaibat's escape helicopter which crash lands on a Malaysian locomotive. Not to be outdone, Michelle hops on a motorcycle, joins Jackie, and participates in an energetic and exciting finale.

An ambitious entry in the series, highlighted by exotic locales, bigger stunts, and the beautiful Michelle Yeoh (Khan) who returns to the movie business after a brief retirement due to marriage. Among the many action scenes is the training duel, prison break, restaurant fight, an out of control helicopter with Jackie hanging onto its rope ladder, and Michelle's amazing motorcycle jump onto a moving train. The outtakes showcase most of the dangerous stunt work. Though the film has a slower start than Rumble in the Bronx, in many ways, Supercop is a better film with wilder stunts performed in exotic Asian environments and a strong supporting cast. The biggest highlight is the beautiful Michelle Yeoh who is the first women to appear in a Chan film who can hold her own ground and doesn't need Chan rescuing her. An exciting and welcomed entry into the Chan library.

Police Story 4: Project S   (Once a Cop/Supercop 2)
(1993) Action C-109m   Chinese with English Subtitles
Catalog #SEL 0608   Hong Kong   Retail: $39.99
Dir: Stanley Tong
Michelle Yeoh (Khan), Yu Rong Guang, Chu Yun, Yukari Oshima (cameo), Eric Tsang (Cameo), Jackie Chan (cameo)
[***]
Following up her successful stint as Jackie Chan's sidekick in Police Story 3 (American title: Supercop), Michelle Khan shines as the star of this film. If you're hoping to see a good deal of Jackie Chan, forget about it. Chan plays a small cameo role that has nothing to do with the main plot. He appears dressed as a woman shopping for jewelry, but is operating as an undercover cop. A cute, silly, and extremely quick cameo.

The film opens in mainland China where Khan is still an active police officer. A group of criminals have taken hostage a number of civilians in a skyscraper. The elite police are on the job and Khan is sent in disguised as a doctor. One of the hostages is a security guard (Yu) who helps foil the criminals. Yu and Michelle are close friends, but he returns to Hong Kong to find different work. They say their good-byes and Michelle returns to work. Her new assignment includes a trip to Hong Kong and she joins forces with the Hong Kong police. Through a series of clues, they are hunting down a gang of ruthless thieves who plan to rob the Central Bank of Hong Kong. A key member is Yu who has joined their organization, but refuses to kill Michelle at a crucial moment. He tries to visit her and learn how much she knows about his new life. She teams up with some Hong Kong cops and go inside the top security bank. Yu and his pals are double-crossed by their partners and barely escape with their lives. Khan and her fellow cops also have plenty of problems keeping alive. Poor Khan comes face-to-face with a giant killer (think Bruce Lee versus Kareem Abdul-Jabbar) who puts her through the ringer and then some. She manages to beat him and goes after Yu who escapes into an underground tunnel system. In an emotional and dramatic scene, she must convince Yu to surrender or take him down the hard way. The mid part of the film slows down in action as romantic plot elements develop between Khan and Yu. All in all, an enjoyable action film with plenty of charisma and kung-fu from Khan and Yu.

Princess Mononoke (Mononoke Hime)
(1997) Japanime: Fantasy/Adventure
C-133 English Dubbed   Japan
Dir: Hayao Miyazaki   Scr: Hayao Miyazaki, Neil Gaiman (US version)
Prod: Toshio Suzuki
Ex. Prod: Yasuyoshi Tokuma   DP: Atsushi Okui
Editor: Hayao Miyazaki, Takeshi Seyama   Music: Jo Hisaishi
Sound: Kazuhiro Wakabayashi
Animation: Masashi Ando, Yoshifumi Kondo, Kitaro Kosaka
PC: Dentsu, Nippon Television Network, Studio Ghibli, Tokuma Shoten
Dist: Toho Company Ltd., Dimension/Miramax Films (US)
Gillian Anderson   Moro
Billy Crudup   Ashitaka
Claire Danes   San
Keith David   Okkoto
Minnie Driver   Lady Eboshi
Billy Bob Thorton   Gonza
[*1/2]**

A wonderful new entry form the world of Japanese animation, available in English at major video retailers. Master animator Hayao Miyazaki, an inspiration for many American/Disney animators, introduces his newest and boldest film. Hayao's previous works have reached a mainstream audience and are available in English, such favorites as My Neighbor Totoro and Kiki's Delivery Service. An all-star cast of Hollywood voices replace the original Japanese voices in a critically acclaimed and enchanting adventure into a unique world of fantasy. In a truly fantastic opening, a savage boar crashes through the forest and attacks a village. This is no ordinary boar, but a mythical creatures which is covered with thousands of moving lesions, undulating and transforming around the husk of the gigantic creature. The hero, a young warrior named Ashitaka, takes down the boar, but is injured in the process. His arm is infected by a deadly disease that spreads throughout his body. The village elders discover a bullet lodged in the boar which drove it mad and twisted its physical presence. Ashitaka must discover the source of the bullet, prevent it from happening again, and discover a cure before it is too late. So begins his epic journey, one that will lead him on a wild and dangerous adventure where he will meet an assortment of characters who have individual needs and desires. He becomes embroiled in a complex war between the mystical forest creatures and the gun-toting humans who wish to conquer the forest. Somehow, he must bring peace to both groups without getting himself killed in the process. Critically acclaimed film, highly recommended for all anime/adventure viewers.

Private Psycho Lesson Vol. 1 & 2
(1996) Japanime: Erotic/Mystery   C-60m Japanese with English Subtitles   Japan
Retail: $29.95
Dir : Tetsuro Amino   Scr: Nagareboshi   Original Story: Yujin
Prod: Yoshinori Chiba, Tomohisa Abe   Ex. Prod: Hiroshi Yamaji
DP: Jin Kaneko   Character Design: Makoto Takahoko
Design Dir: Shinichiro Minami   Art Dir: Yoshinori Hirose
PC: J.C. Staff/Blue Mantis   Dist: Central Park Media
Hirori Mori	**Sara Iijima**
Syo Mineta	**Tamine**
Tozainanboku	**Dr. Chan**
Kotomi Ryuguden	**Yuri Saito**
Rumi Goto	**Erika Shimada**
Sojiro Okise	**Alex**

[**1/2]
As a film critic, there are certain genres of film that are inherently offensive to the general public. Gratuitous violence and nudity, sexual exploitation of minors and pornography-related films hover on the outskirts of mainstream tolerance and depending on your social/religious/political slant, those types of films may be worth burning and banning from society. So keep in mind, these films are made for those who enjoy the erotic genre of anime. When dealing with pornographic/erotic films a certain sense of artistic license must be taken. If material as such offends you, no matter how well made, you won't enjoy the film. On the other hand if erotic material entices you, no matter how poorly the film is made, you may find enjoyment. Private Psycho Lesson is a well-animated and interesting film that tones down the sexual exploits of other erotic anime to a more acceptable level for casual adult anime viewers. The main character is a woman who helps poor lost souls. She uses her massive breasts, swirling them, to hypnotize people and counsel them. A teenage girl is murdering people and prostituting on the side. We discover she is obsessed with beautiful breast and bodies, since she suffers from a lack of emotional self-confidence. In the next story, Sara and her old friend Erika battle each other. Suffering from past abuse, Erika has invented a method to turn people into mindless zombies. She uses her zombie army to take care of Sara and her partner. Only if Sara can rip off her blouse and rotate her breasts will she be able to save the day. Another erotic genre lovers only film with cute animation and plenty of sexual escapades.

Professional, The: Golgo 13
(1983) Japanime: Action   C-94m Dubbed   VA   Catalog #SPV 90703

Japan Retail: $19.95
Dir: Osamu Dezaki   Scr: Hideyoshi Nagasaka
Music: Toshiyuki Omori
PC: Saito Productions/Tokyo Movie Shinsha   Dist: Streamline Pictures/Orion Home Video
(based on the graphic novels by Takao Saito)
[**1/2]
Leonard Dawson is a rich industrialist who hires hitman Duke Togo, the Professional. Something goes wrong and Dawson's son is killed. Blaming Togo, Dawson uses his entire fortune to kill Togo. The film meanders through a number of chase scenes where Togo survives and his opponents die. Trying to capture the essence of the antihero popularized by Clint Eastwood, the subtle nuance is lost in Togo's calm appearance. The animation is good and the action is hard, but the characters lack depth and emotion. Togo kills and moves through the film with icy compassion, his movements and actions are too mechanical. For those who like the one-dimensional killer who doesn't break a sweat, shed a tear, or blink, there may be something here. The seriously animated film has a good share of nudity and violence.

Project A
(1983) Kung-Fu   C-106m   Chinese with English Subtitles   Hong Kong
Retail: $19.99
Dir/Scr: Jackie Chan   Prod: Jackie Chan, Leonard K.C. Ho
PC: Golden Harvest

Jackie Chan	Dragon Ma
Samo Hung	Fei
Yuen Biao	Inspector Tzu
Bill Tung	Captain Chi
Dick Wei, Isabella Wong	

[***1/2]
A wonderful period piece set in Hong Kong at the turn of the century. Chan is Sergeant Dragon Ma, an officer of the Hong Kong Coast Guard. Chinese pirates terrorize the South Seas and British ships are easy prey. The film is broken into two segments, the first deals with Chan and his maritime guards while the second half focuses on the pirates. With many of Chan's films, there is a lot of comedic elements and less action in the first half as opposed to the second half. Chan and his friends are chided by the military establishment in Hong Kong. The pirates flourish and government resources dwindle. Chan requests more ammunition for his men, but is rudely denied. While drinking away his problems with his friends, the mainland police force start to accuse the coast guard of squandering money that should be used to give them raises. The police under their commander, Yuen Biao, start a barroom fight between both sides. The fight is wild and wonderful with bodies, chairs, and pasta flying across the room. In no time, the whole lot are arrested and reprimanded by their superiors. The coast guard is disbanded and the members are put under Biao's command. This gives pause in the film's action pace, providing a stretch of comedy and playful antics against their superior officer. In the backdrop, the town's crime boss has made a deal with the pirates. He in turn makes a deal with a corrupt police officer. Money for the exchange of 100 police rifles. Chan with the help of his con-man friend Samo, steal the guns for themselves. Samo plays both sides and tries to make a deal with the

mobsters, but fail. This sets up for a number of clever and fast-paced chase scenes as the mobsters try to capture Chan and Samo. In particular note, a bicycle chase scene, Chan's climb up a flag pole and into a clock tower, and Samo and Chan's fight in a small restaurant are well worth the admission. The second half of the movie kicks in and focuses on the pirates. The pirate junk (Chinese boats) attack a British schooner and kidnap all the delegates. The military governor decides to make a deal for the hostages in exchange for the guns, but Chan's rousing speech convinces him to do otherwise. In full dress uniform, Chan and his coast guards are reinstated and go off to pursue the pirates. Chan disguises himself as the mob boss and with Samo as a pirate infiltrates the secret island hideaway. The rest is pure action when Yuen Biao arrives with the calvary and wage full-out war against the pirates.

Project A 2
(1987) Kung-Fu   C-108m   Dubbed   Hong Kong   Retail: $19.99
Dir/Scr: Jackie Chan   Prod: Jackie Chan, Leonard K.C. Ho
PC: Golden Harvest
Jackie Chan   Dragon Ma
David Lam   Officer Chun
Rosamund Kwan   Miss Pai
Bill Tung   Captain Chi
Maggie Cheung, Carina Lau, Tsui Kam Kong
[***]
The sequel to the popular Project A continues the further adventures of Inspector Dragon Ma, a turn of the century law enforcement officer in Great Britain's occupied Hong Kong. The major change of course is the exclusion of Samo Hung and Yuen Biao. Depending on whether you like Samo and Biao, this movie will appeal to you less or more. One positive note is the introduction of an attractive cast of co-stars, including Chan favorite Maggie Cheung and Kwan. What hurts Project A 2 the most is the over-abundant introduction of too many villains. Simplicity can be a blessing in an action film, but Chan tries for a little too much which causes a definite loss of momentum and tension within the body of the film. Throughout the film, Chan is fighting against renegade pirates, corrupt cops, gangsters, Imperial spies, Nationalist revolutionaries, and his own bosses. The main villain is Superintendent Chun, a high-ranking official suspected of corruption. The Hong Kong authorities place Chan in charge of one of Chun's sections. Chun is not too happy and plans an intricate way to discredit and arrest Chan. At a party, Chan is accused of stealing the Governor's jewelry and then arrested. Don't fret, because Chan is used to playing the underdog and figures out a way to clear his name and arrest the guilty. The last portion of the film contains a wild, raucous battle throughout the streets of Hong Kong with a fabulous array of stunts.

Project Girls in Japanese Animation

PROJECT A-KO Series

What makes Japanese animation so adored throughout the world with legions of dedicated fans? Perhaps the high quality animation, the beautiful art designs, the mature stories, or exciting high-paced action. For many, it is a love of everything mentioned above and then some, but dissecting the genre would be like pondering why people love Italian food more than Chinese...everyone's subjective reasons for enjoying Japanime or Italian cuisine are somewhat different. Animation is an under-appreciated medium that is not limited by live-action problems such as outdoor lighting patterns, weather conditions, set construction constraints, or zoning rules. In many ways, the freedom of animation surpasses live-action and is a perfect medium for fantasy, horror, science fiction, and the truly bizarre. The only limitation of animators is their own creativity and patience.

If you're new to the genre then get ready for a wild ride, if you're a veteran viewer, you know what I'm talking about. Project A-ko is an excellent example of the unique characteristics that set Japanese animation apart from western/Disney animation. The entire series focuses on three major characters: A-ko Megami, B-ko Akagiyama, and C-ko Katsubuki. That's right, those are the names of the main characters in a very enjoyable, albeit off the wall, series of Japanese animated films that will introduce you to the lunacy and excitement of Japanime.

Before you get too confused, let's explain a few things. Ko (literally means child) is a very popular feminine ending in Japanese. Asian names are comprised of characters and the formation of characters produce names like Reiko, Yumiko, Keiko, Mariko, and Yuko which are standard staple female names in Japan. Sometimes the ending is overdone and every daughter in the household will be named this-ko or that-ko. Hence the spoof on A, B, C, and even D-ko. Another popular element is the use of female characters, usually very young, sexy, and tough. In this case, the girls are students of Graviton High School, Japan. Female heroines are a popular character choice in anime which tends to be drawn by males and viewed by males. Discussions about sexual undercurrents and fantasy elements are best left to the sociologists. There is a stronger sense of victory (and humor) when an underdogged girl saves the world instead of a muscle-bound Schwarzenegger, Stallone, or Van Damme. Intelligent, powerful, resourceful heroines can be found in hundreds of Japanese animated films and television shows, but the characters always manage to maintain their feminine charms and are subject to the woes of women.

There are five other traits that are commonly found among the girls in anime. Big eyes, colorful hair, high-pitched voices, school-like uniforms, and nudity. Big eyes are based on an influence from older animated films from the United States (Betty Boop and Disney). Eyes are the windows of emotion and expression. Larger eyes allow for more creative freedom and offer a psychological parallelism with Asian and Western views of beauty. Multicolored hair and wild hairstyles help animators differentiate between characters and add personality traits. High voices are a trademark for what is considered alluring by Japanese culture. Women in Japanese society often raise their voice to appear cuter and more docile. Uniforms have been adopted in Japanese schools and have remained commonplace for over a century. The sailor uniforms are also popular due to Japan's island status and naval pride. Nudity is an accepted form of animation in Japanese culture where community bathing is very popular and as a harmless alternative to erotic expression. However, pubic hair is not allowed and often banned in live films, magazines, and Japanese animation. (For more heroines see: Battle Skipper, Bubblegum Crisis, Burn Up!, Dangaio, Dirty Pair, Gall Force, Gunbuster, Iczer, Silent Moebius, The Slayers, Tenchi Muyo).

The most obvious (initial) attraction is the high quality animation which incorporates stylistic elements unseen in American animation. Over time, the viewer will discover unique and clever techniques such as the use of black and white animation with color, slow motion, stills, swirling camera angles, ghosting effects, lighting and shadow effects, depth of perception, multiframing in one shot, background dissolves, rack focus, and more than one can discuss in a unique world that goes beyond mere two-dimensional animation. Another exciting element is the creativity which goes into the projects: warriors and ninjas battle alongside demons and aliens from all times and worlds. The subject material never fails to amaze viewers. Project A-ko was an early Japanese animated movie that caught my attention, my initial impression was bewilderment and shock which eventually became love for the entire series. Dubbed versions of the films are available, but I personally enjoy the subtitled versions.

Project A-Ko
(1986) Japanime: Scifi   C-86m Dubbed/Japanese with English Subtitles   VA
Catalog #USM 1015 Japan Retail: $29.95
Widescreen Available
Dir: Katsuhiko Nishijima   Original Story: Katsuhiko Nishijima, Kazumi Shirasaka
Scr: Katsuhiko Nishijima, Yuji Moriyama, Tomoko Kawasaki Prod: Kazufumi Nomura
Character Design & Dir of Animation: Yuji Moriyama Art Dir: Shinji Kimura
Ex. Prod: Naotaka Yoshida
English Version - Ex. Prod: John O'Donell   Translator: Matt Thorn
PC: Kobayashi Productions/Soeishinsha Co., Ltd.   Dist: U.S. Manga Corps
Miki Itoh   A-ko Megami
Emi Shinohara   B-ko Akagiyama
Michie Tomisawa   C-ko Katsubuki
Tetsuaki Genada   Agent D
Shuichi Ikeda   Captain
Asami Makodono   Miss Ayumi
[*1/2]**

"Yatta! Yatta!" screams C-ko (a spoiled Shirley Temple lookalike) as the superpowerful and sexy redhead, A-ko, punches the lights out of rival B-ko who is dressed in her favorite cyber-bathing suit. Around them the city is in flames, but these high school girls don't care about global destruction, only who will win the affection of C-ko. To many casual viewers, you will probably totally disregard and despise this series. For those who are anime fans and open-minded to clever, satirical cross-genre masterpieces, look no further. This is an excellent film which spoofs the world of anime on various levels, so a number of the scenes will hold particular reference to long time Japanime fans. Juxtaposing dramatic scenes in outer space with technical realism and high school girls performing wacky and wild antics is a brilliant blend of tense action and cute comedy. The story follows the exploits of A-ko, a 16 year old high school girl who happens to have the strength of Superman and Wonder Woman rolled into one (look for the reference at the end). Her best friend is C-ko, a cute, whiney blonde who can't cook to save her life. The nemesis is the beautiful and powerful B-ko and her girl gang. B-ko is infatuated with C-ko (don't ask why) and wants to destroy A-ko. The carefree A-ko acts like a regular high school teenager and her only concern is to get to school on time. She often uses her supersonic speed to pull along C-ko just before the bell rings, of course, her run can tear up sidewalks, smash through walls, and crash through other people's houses. The rich and brilliant B-ko (think Lex Luthor) manages to create wave after wave of powerful robots to challenge A-ko. Meanwhile, an alien ship fashioned after the Yamato commanded by a Captain Harlock lookalike battles Earth's Defense Forces. The space scenes are animated in top-notch dramatic fashion and offer plenty of excitement for serious anime lovers. The aliens have come to retrieve C-ko who is a long lost space princess. The alien spaceship enters the atmosphere and launches a wave of attack spider-ships which invade the city. Meanwhile A-ko and B-ko are still fighting, oblivious to the alien threat, and knocking out anyone who gets in their way. Flying in a peddle-powered helicopter, B-ko's gang watches the battle erupt on a massive scale. When C-ko is kidnaped by the alien Agent D, A-ko and B-ko join forces and attack the alien spaceship. The climax won't disappoint anime fans. The film is twisted in its pursuit for mayhem and fun and bends the rules to delightful lengths. Don't take the film seriously and sit back and enjoy the comedic hijinks, excellent music, quality animation, and girl-on-girl battles. Followed by a string of sequels which never lived up to the original film.

Project A-Ko 2: Plot of the Daitokuji Financial Group
(1986) Japanime   C-70m Japanese with English Subtitles   VA
Catalog #USM 1102 Japan Retail: $29.95
Dir/Original Story/Character Design & Dir of Animation: Yuji Moriyama
Scr: Takao Koyama Prod: Naotaka Yoshida, Hisatoshi Maruyama
DP: Norihide Kubota   Art Dir: Junichi Azuma   Music Dir: Yasunori Honda
English Version - Ex. Prod: John O'Donell   Translator: Pamela Ferdie, William Flanagan
Rewrite: Jay Parks
PC: Soeishinsha Co., Ltd.   Dist: U.S. Manga Corps
[***]
The entire gang is back, but a certain element from the first film is lost, especially when juvenile romance becomes the key motivation. This time around B-ko's dad plays a key part in the story. The A-ko crew enjoy their summer vacation and soak up the rays. A number of scenes highlight the A-ko characters romping around a pool and having careless fun. For the next three films, the A-ko story takes a different tone, stressing less combat and focusing more on the hijinks of the three Ko's. Following events from the first film, B-ko builds a powerful anti A-ko robot to once and for all deal with the pesky redhead, A-ko. We are also introduced to B-ko's father who starts to enter the plot as the villainous corporate head of Daitokuji Financial Group. After stealing his daughter's brilliant blueprints, he sends a group of soldiers to attack the enemy spaceship and salvage all her secrets. His secret weapon is the Daitokuji Intercept Special Reserve Golden Cherry Blossom Mark-111 robot, lovingly known as Marilyn. Lucky for the surviving aliens that A-ko and C-ko plan to help them get home. When Mr. Daitokuji's plan fails, he reveals his own B-ko battlesuit and engages the opponents first hand to the utter embarrassment of his daughter. The actual length of the film is shorter, the rest of the video is full of trailers, clips, and a music video.

Project A-Ko 3: Cinderella Rhapsody
(1989) Japanime   C-50m Japanese with English Subtitles   VA
Catalog #USM 1103 Japan Retail: $29.95
Dir/Character Design & Dir of Animation: Yuji Moriyama
Scr: Tomoko Kawasaki   Original Story: Katsuhiko Nishijima, Kazumi Shirashi, Yuji Moriyama

DP: Norihide Kubota   Art Dir: Satoshi Matsudaira   Music Dir: Yasunori Honda
English Version - Ex. Prod: John O'Donell   Prod Coordinator: Stephanie Shalofsky
Translator: Pamela Ferdie, William Flanagan   Rewrite: Jay Parks
PC: Soeishinsha Co., Ltd.   Dist: U.S. Manga Corps
[**1/2]
I don't know why the writers decided to move away from the original formula of the first film, but A-ko 3 is even a farther departure than the sequel. Turning the series into a soap opera, the entire film deals with the affection of a handsome young teenager named K who rides a motorcycle and gets involved with all three girls. A-ko and B-ko battle for his affection in typical romantic sitcom flavor. The final scene does include a battle atop a fancy restaurant in the sky, but it comes too late and seems out of place with all the romantic interludes. The film's lacks the excitement and brilliant satire of the first film.

Project A-Ko 4: Final
(1990) Japanime   C-59m Japanese with English Subtitles   VA
Catalog #USM 1104 Japan Retail: $29.95
Dir/Scr/Character Design & Dir of Animation: Yuji Moriyama
Original Story: Katsuhiko Nishijima, Kazumi Shirasaka, Yuji Moriyama
DP: Tadashi Hosono Art Dir: Junichi Azuma   Music Dir: Yasunori Honda
English Version - Ex. Prod: John O'Donell   Prod Coordinator: Stephanie Shalofsky
Translator: Pamela Ferdie, William Flanagan   Rewrite: Jay Parks
PC: Soeishinsha Co., Ltd.   Dist: U.S. Manga Corps
[**1/2]
The final film in the series ends with a whimper not a bang. If you're a fan of the series you might find some entertainment as C-ko's true princess nature is revealed when her mother lands on Earth. Deep in the desert, an archeological team unearths a strange hexagram embedded into an ancient wall. The music pounds and the men are frightened to death and flee. Deep in outer space, a giant armada approaches Earth and the same hexagram adorns their spaceships. This episode focuses on Miss Ayumi, the school teacher, who plans to get married. Mr. Daitokuji introduces her to prospective husbands, but her demeanor strike the girls as bizarre. She holds a pendant and mysteriously vanishes to chat in a hypnotic state. When the girls discover K is the prospective mate, they try to put an end to the marriage. Once again, the action is downplayed for more mundane sitcom-styled hijinks.

Project A-Ko Versus Battle 1: Grey Side
(1990) Japanime: Scifi   C-54m Japanese with English Subtitles
Catalog #USM 1105 Japan Retail: $29.95
Dir: Katsuhiko Nishijima   Scr: Katsuhiko Nishijima, Tomoko Kawasaki
Original Story: Katsuhiko Nishijima, Kazumi Shirasaka
DP: Takafumi Arai Character Design & Dir of Animation: Hideyuki Motohashi
Art Dir: Mitsuharu Miyamae   Music Dir: Yasunori Honda
English Version - Ex. Prod: John O'Donell   Prod Coordinator: Stephanie Shalofsky
Translator: Pamela Ferdie, William Flanagan   Rewrite: Jay Parks
PC: Final-Nishijima Dist: U.S. Manga Corps
[***]

My second favorite A-ko film since the original Project A-Ko. This film is a total departure from the original story and may dismay purists. Katsuhiko Nishijima, the creative mind behind the first A-ko film left the series, but returns in full force. This is a parallel universe and not a sequel to the originals. This time, A-ko and B-ko are friends and partners. The characters stay true to their former selves, A-ko is tough and irreverent, B-ko is bossy and smart (minus battlesuit), and C-ko is the spoiled cry baby princess. C-ko is kidnaped from her wealthy parents by a pair of crooks: Liza, a female butch with super-strength, and Gail, a handsome hotshot pilot. There spaceship suffers damage and C-ko is jettisoned into the desert and lands on top of A-ko's giant supply pack. To help them, Maruten, a six-inch high member of the Space Patrol, offers advice and guidance. Together they pursue the kidnapers and help rescue C-ko. Plenty of action and comedic interplay amongst the three Ko's.

Project A-Ko Versus Battle 2: Blue Side
(1990) Japanime: Scifi   C-52m Japanese with English Subtitles
Catalog #USM 1106 Japan Retail: $29.95
Dir: Katsuhiko Nishijima   Scr: Katsuhiko Nishijima, Tomoko Kawasaki
Original Story: Katsuhiko Nishijima, Kazumi Shirasaka
DP: Jin Kaneko   Character Design & Dir of Animation: Katsuhiko Nishijima
Art Dir: Yoji Nakaza   Music Dir: Yasunori Honda
Planning: Naotaka Yoshida
English Version - Ex. Prod: John O'Donell   Prod Coordinator: Stephanie Shalofsky
Translator: Pamela Ferdie, William Flanagan   Rewrite: Jay Parks
PC: Final-Nishijima Dist: U.S. Manga Corps
[***]
Though separated onto two volumes, this continues the exploits of Grey Side. A lot happens and most of the scenes are rough and tumble action. A-ko, B-ko, and Maruten are after the dreaded 3-headed dragon. It doesn't help that they must fight through Gail and Liza. Situations even get worse when Poor C-ko is possessed by the dark spirit of master Xena and goes about her path of destruction, starting on her father's fleet. Meanwhile B-ko's weapons and ingenuity fall prey to Gail's charm and good looks. It takes everything A-ko and B-ko have to free C-ko and save the universe from mass destruction. Hopefully, this will not be the end of the Ko girls.

Pushing Hands
(1995) DramaC-100m   English and Chinese with English Subtitles   VA
Dir/Scr: Ang Lee   DP: Jong Lin Music: Xiao Song Qu
Dist: Triboro Entertainment Group
Sihung Lung   Mister Chu
Deb Snyder   Martha
Bo Z. Wang   Alex
Lai Wang
[***]
Director Ang Lee achieved critical (and Hollywood's Academy) respect with his Jane Austen adaptation of Sense & Sensibility. Long before he made a romance about British women, Lee created a strong reputation with films dealing with families issues. Pushing Hands is a light, small-budget film that explores interracial as well as multigenerational issues. Though the film

has a documentary-like feel and low-key performances, the film shines on a number of levels which will play special relevance to those who have experienced racial issues within the family. Sihung Lung is a Chinese widower who leaves Beijing and moves in with his son, his American wife, and their son in suburban New York. Sihung can not speak English (guide book phrases don't count) and his daughter-in-law (Deb Snyder) can't speak a word of Chinese. Languages are the least of their cultural problems, both she and Sihung stay home all day and seem to get in each other's way. Sihung is a master of Tai Chi and his practices and nuances drive the attractive writer up the wall. To avoid problems, Sihung volunteers at a local Chinese recreation center where he meets a kind widow. When marital problems increase at home, Sihung is blamed for the tension and hostility.

In a particularly moving scene, Sihung runs away from home and works as a dishwasher in a Chinese restaurant. He lives in a hovel and doesn't get any respect from the Chinese-American owner. Sihung refuses to leave and runs into problems with the local authorities who are amazed at his martial arts abilities. His son bails him out and through much talking, they resolve their differences and establish a compromise. A small, but moving film from a master storyteller of human life. Though martial arts is present and portrayed realistically, this is in no way a martial arts film.

-R-

Raise the Red Lantern (Big Red Lantern [Dragon] High High Hang)
(1991) DramaC-125m **Mandarin with English Subtitles PG VA**
Catalog #VHS 5068 China Retail: $19.95
Dir: Zhang Yimou Scr: Ni Zhen
Prod: Chiu Fu-Sheng Ex. Prod: Hou Hsiao-Hsien
DP: Zhao Fei, Yang Lun Editor: Du Yuan Music: Zhao Jiping
Prod Manager: Feng Yiting
Art Design: Cao Jiuping, Dong Huamiao Costumes: Huang Lihua
(from the novel Wives and Concubines by Su Tong)
PC: Era International (HK) Ltd. in association with China Film Co-Production Corporation
Dist: Orion Home Video

Gong Li	Songlian
Ma Jingwu	Chen Zuoqian
He Caifei	Meishan, Third Wife
Cao Cuifeng	Zhuoyun, Second Wife
Jin Shuyuan	Yuru, First Wife
Kong Lin	Yan'er, Maid
Ding Weimin	Mother Song
Cui Zhihgang	Doctor Gao
Chu Xiao	Feipu
Cao Zhengyin	Old Servant

[****]
A beautiful and deftly-crafted drama about a young woman's induction into a wealthy man's cadre of concubines who bitterly strive for his attention. The title represents the process by

which the master calls for one of his concubines. In the evening, he raises a red lantern (a symbolic color of fertility and passion) in front of the chosen concubine's private chambers, where after she enters the main bed chamber. Once again, the effervescent beauty of Gong Li is juxtaposed with the cruel and repressive ways of Chinese culture. Director Zhang Yimou focuses the story from Gong Li's point of view. She is the newest concubine, the fourth and prettiest to enter the household. A certain hierarchy of jealousy exist among the other women. The first wife is the eldest and the least threatened in position, she has experience and title so no longer desires her husband's physical touch. The second wife at first takes a liking to Songlian (Gong Li) and takes her under her wing while the third wife who until recently was the youngest and prettiest bitterly resents Songlian. Then there are whispers of a past wife who caused problems and was removed to a shed atop the roof. Headstrong Songlian enters the household against her will, but she is educated, and thinks herself ready for any new experience. But her mother betrays her, selling her as a concubine with no freedom, and soon her world is no larger than the millionaire's vast house. Its living quarters are arrayed on either side of a courtyard. There is an apartment for each of the wives and a vast number of servants and a doctor who caters to their illness. Songlian is quietly informed on how the way things work. A red lantern is raised each night outside the quarters of the wife who will be honored by a visit from the master. Remember the rules and all will be well. At first, she is not eager to satiate the rich old man, but as pressures surmount, she uses her feminine ways only to become trapped in a web of deception, vying for attention against her rival concubines. These women never realize who their true oppressor is and live in a secluded world of gossip and tedium which only their master husband can relieve. Only tragedy befall those who pursue a world beyond the red lanterns. A brilliant and deeply moving picture that is recommended for any serious film viewer.

Ran
(1985) Samurai   C-160m   Japanese with English Subtitles   R   VA
Catalog #3732   Japan/France Retail: $29.95
Dir: Akira Kurosawa   Scr: Akira Kurosawa, Hideo Oguni, Masato Ide
Prod: Masato Hara, Serge Silberman
DP: Takao Saito, Masaharu Ueda, Asakazu Nakai
Editor: Akira Kurosawa   Music: Toru Takemitsu
Prod Design: Yoshiro Muraki, Shinobu Muraki   Art Design: Yoshiro Muraki
Set Designer: Tsuneo Shimura, Osami Tonsho, Mitsuyuki Kimura, Jiro Hirai, Yasuyoshi Ototake   Makeup: Shohichiro Ueda, Tameyuki Aimi, Chihako Naito, Noriko Takamizawa
Costumes: Emi Wada
PC: Greenway Film/Herald Ace, Int./Nippon Herald Films, Inc.   Dist: CBS/Fox Video
(based on King Lear by William Shakespeare)
Tatsuya Nakadai   Lord Hidetora Ichimonji
Akira Terao   Tarotakatora Ichimonji
Jinpachi Nezu   Jiromasatora, Oldest Son
Daisuke Ryn   Sahuro, Youngest Son
Mjeko Harada   Lady Kaede, Taro's Wife
Yoshiko Miyazaki   Lady Sue, Jiro's Wife
Kazuo Kato   Ikoma

Masayuki Yui	Tango, Hidetora's Servant
Peter Kyoami	The Fool
Hitoshi Ueki	Fujimaki
Hisashi Igawa	Kurogane
Takeshi Nomura	Tsurumaru
Jun Tazaki	Ayabe
Norio Matsui	Ogura
Kenji Kodama	Shirane
Toshiya Ito	Naganuma
Takeshi Kato	Hatakeyama

[***1/2]
Grand samurai epic that bears more than a passing resemblance to Shakespeare's King Lear, but given a unique Japanese/Kurosawa overhaul. An aging warlord, Hidetora Ichimonji, suffers a disturbing nightmare and decides to split his kingdom among his three sons. The youngest son, Saburo, ridicules the idea and insults his father for misguided weakness. Saburo is banished and the kingdom is given to the two older sons, Taro and Jiro, who gladly accept the castles and responsibility. Soon the lust for power drives loyalty away, and Hidetora's own troops are driven away from his son's castles. Behind the scenes, Taro's wife Sue (whose parents died under Hidetora) manipulates Taro and demands he take action against his father. His second son also refuses to aid Hidetora against the treachery of his eldest son and daughter-in-law. Though Jiro's wife does not bear any ill will to the warlord, she is helpless in swaying her husband's decision. The two sons battle to overthrow their father permanently and seize the entire kingdom, but Saburo returns and struggles to redeem his father's honor. Taro is killed and his wife Sue demands Jiro marry her, announce his leadership, and continue the battle against Hidetora. A tragic chain of events which leave Hidetora heartbroken and ruler over a decimated kingdom. Classic imagery and beautiful sets compliment the film's dramatic energy and timeless story of power, greed, and betrayal.

Ranma 1/2 - TV Series Volume 1
(1989) Japanime: Comedy Martial Arts   C-50m Dubbbed
Catalog # VVRT-001 Japan Retail: $29.95
Dir: Tsutomu Shibayama   Prod: Hidenori Taga
Series Dir: Tomomitsu Mochizuki Music: Eiji Mori
Character Design: Atsuko Nakajima   DP: Mitsunobu Yoshida
English Version - Prod: Seiji Horibuchi   Assoc. Prod: Satoru Fujii
Prod Coordinator: Toshifumi Yoshida, Trish Ledoux
Translation: Toshifumi Yoshida   Scr & Lyrics: Trish Ledoux
Art Dir & Package Design: Yoshiyuki Higuchi
Viz Video Logo Animation: Will Culpepper II   Dubbing & Post Prod: Ocean Studios
PC: Fuji TV and Kitty Film Dist: Viz Video
(based on the comic by Rumiko Takahashi)
[***1/2]
In the pouring rain on a side street of Tokyo, citizens walk with umbrellas and parcels minding their business. Suddenly, a giant panda erupts onto the street and a tiny, redhead girl does a flying side kick into the panda's face, slamming him against the wall. The panda regains its

stance, performs some martial arts, and slams the girl in the head. Confusing? Or just another father and son discussion in the ongoing series Ranma 1/2.

From the brilliant creator Takahashi, Ranma 1/2 falls into the category of Japanese humor, romance, and martial arts action in an extremely delightful, imaginative, and fast-paced series of episodes and films. The title refers to the two sides of Ranma Saotome, a young martial artist, who is betrothed to a beautiful Japanese martial arts expert. While Ranma and his father were on a trip visiting a holy shrine in China, he slips and falls into a magical pond. (The secret: when exposed to cold water, you physically transform into the person/animal who drowned in the pool.) Now, whenever Ranma is exposed to cold water and then hot water, his sexual identity changes from a black-haired boy (normal) to a red-haired girl and vice-versa respectively. Takahashi creates a great deal of possibilities as the female and male Ranma both end up with social relationships and problems, while trying to find a cure and stay out of trouble. Even more humorous is Ranma's grouchy dad, Genma Saotome, who doesn't change into a girl, but a giant panda bear. The wild comedy isn't for all, but it pleases on a number of levels and is cause for much entertainment. Similar to the appeal of The Three Stooges or The Marx Brothers, but with much more dramatic substance, the comedy builds upon the characters wild irreverent attitude toward each other. The first video follows the origins of Ranma and his father who come to Japan and visit and old friend, Master Soun Tendo of the "Tendo Anything Goes Martial Arts Training Hall". Tendo has three cute daughters: Kasumi 19, Nabiki 17, and Akane 16 years old. Ranma must marry Kasumi, but their relationship gets off on the wrong foot and ignites the story. Quickly, a host of additional characters are introduced that produce a number of irreverent and humorous love triangles.

Episode 1: The Strange Strangers from China

Episode 2: School is No Place for Horsing Around

Ranma 1/2 - TV Series Volume 2
(1989) Japanime: Comedy Martial Arts   C-50m Dubbed
Catalog # VVRT-002 Japan Retail: $29.95
Dir: Tsutomu Shibayama   Prod: Hidenori Taga
Series Dir: Tomomitsu Mochizuki Music: Eiji Mori
Character Design: Atsuko Nakajima   DP: Mitsunobu Yoshida
English Version - Prod: Seiji Horibuchi   Assoc. Prod: Satoru Fujii
Prod Coordinator: Toshifumi Yoshida, Trish Ledoux
Translation: Toshifumi Yoshida   Scr & Lyrics: Trish Ledoux
Art Dir & Package Design: Yoshiyuki Higuchi Viz   Video   Logo   Animation: Will Culpepper II Dubbing & Post Prod: Ocean Studios
PC: Fuji TV and Kitty Film Dist: Viz Video
(based on the comic by Rumiko Takahashi)
[***]

Every day at school, Swordsman Kuno challenges Akane to a fight, so he can win her hand in love. Now his passions are divided when he meets a fiery redhead who proves she can fight as well. Of course, the redhead is the female Ranma who has no intentions of getting involved with the arrogant Kuno. Matters become complicated when Nabiki sells alluring photos of the female Ranma and Akane to the love-stricken Kuno. Ranma tries to reveal the truth to Kuno, but he accuses Ranma of using black magic and kidnaping the beautiful redhead. More of a distraction,

Ranma and Akane beat up Kuno and go on their way, proving that their teamwork is a lethal combination.
Episode 3: A Sudden Storm of Love...Hey, Wait a Minute!
Episode 4: Ranma and...Ranma? If it's Not One Thing, It's Another

Ranma 1/2 - TV Series Volume 3
(1989) Japanime: Comedy Martial Arts   C-50m Dubbed
Catalog # VVRT-003 Japan Retail: $29.95
Dir: Tsutomu Shibayama   Prod: Hidenori Taga
Series Dir: Tomomitsu Mochizuki Music: Eiji Mori
Character Design: Atsuko Nakajima   DP: Mitsunobu Yoshida
English Version - Prod: Seiji Horibuchi   Assoc. Prod: Satoru Fujii
Prod Coordinator: Toshifumi Yoshida, Trish Ledoux
Translation: Toshifumi Yoshida   Scr & Lyrics: Trish Ledoux
Art Dir & Package Design: Yoshiyuki Higuchi
Viz Video Logo Animation: Will Culpepper II   Dubbing & Post Prod: Ocean Studios
PC: Fuji TV and Kitty Film Dist: Viz Video
(based on the comic by Rumiko Takahashi)
[***]
The exploits continue as Akane hits Ranma, sending him to chiropractor Dr. Tofu. The smart Tofu enjoys Akane and Ranma's company, but his attitude changes when Akane's sister pays a visit. Smitten with love, Tofu goes into a trance and is oblivious to the world around him. He manages to misdiagnose Ranma, grabs his skeleton Betty, and jogs around the city for hours. Meanwhile, Genma councils Ranma that Akane is really a nice sweet girl. Ranma shows signs of romance for Akane, but their playful bickering attitude towards each other mask their true feelings. Plenty of fights and situational comedy are all part of the ongoing story.
The world of Ranma 1/2 is an incredibly popular and long-running series. This only represents a small sampling of the series which is available on video. The first season includes 18 episodes total, while all 22 episodes of the second season are also available. You can also get the third season and a bunch of specially made OAV and theatrical films which introduce a wonderful world of new characters and situations.

Raped by an Angel   (Naked Killer 2/Super Rape/Legal Rape)
(1993) Action C-95m Chinese with English Subtitles
Catalog #1301   Hong Kong   Retail: $39.99
Dir: Ricky Lau   Prod: Wong Jing   Dist: Tai Seng Video
Chingmy Yau, Mark Cheng, Simon Yam
[**]
A loosely-based sequel to the popular The Naked Killer with the same cast as the original film. Amazingly, Asian sequels do not have to logically precede or follow the story of the original film. They may have the same characters and settings, but consistent logic are not necessary. Therefore, an entire cast may die in the first film, but then miraculously reappear for the sequel just in time to die all over again. Entertainment and a familiar formula are the main ingredients that drive action films in Hong Kong. Due to its extreme content, the film went though a number of changes due to censor problems. Mark Cheng portrays the Jekyll/Hyde villain who emanates

charm and gentleman-like refinery, but in reality is a cold, brutal rapist. Disturbing scenes visualize Cheng's elaborate rape methods and his cunning ability to blackmail his victims into silence. A highlight of the film is actress Chingmy Yau, a ravenous beauty who combines Demi Moore's sensuality with Meg Ryan's adorability. After Cheng rapes and kills Yau's best friend, she vows revenge and performs her Yuk-Jing's striptease to lure him into a trap. The film quickly devolves into a predictable and tasteless film (but fun for fans) as the heroine lets Mark Cheng rape a woman with AIDS just for poetic retribution. Not an exemplary film and best avoided, but Chingmy's presence always adds a bit of charm.

Rashomon
(1950) Samurai　　**B&W-87m**　　**Japanese with English Subtitles**　　**VA**
Catalog #6109　　**Japan Retail: $29.95**
Dir: Akira Kurosawa　　**Scr: Shinobu Hashimoto, Akira Kurosawa**
Prod: Jingo Minoura　　**DP: Kazuo Miyagawa**
Music: Fumio Hayasaka　　**Art Design: So Matsuyama**
PC: Toho Inc.　　**Dist: Embassy Home Entertainment**
(based on the short story "Yabu no Naka" and the novel Rasho-Mon by Ryunosuke Akutagawa)

Toshiro Mifune	**Tajomaru**
Machiko Kyo	**Masago**
Masayuki Mori	**Takehiro**
Takashi Shimura	**Firewood Dealer**
Minoru Chiaki	**Priest**
Kichijiro Ueda	**Commoner**
Fumiko Homma	**Medium**
Daisuke Kato	**Policeman**

[****]

Rashomon is a fascinating and deceptively simple film that utilizes multiple points of view to reveal the story. Whose point of view is correct is not as important as Kurosawa's intriguing use of characterization and plot development. Based on the critically-acclaimed writings of Ryunosuke Akutagawa (1892-1927). Though the film stars Toshiro Mifune and takes place in the feudal era, this is not an action samurai film, but rather a tale of morality and truth. On a rainy day under a dilapidated gate (Rashomon), travelers wait under the dry arch for the wet weather to end. A traveler stops and finds an old woodsman and a Buddhist priest solemnly standing. The traveler is talkative and discovers the two witnessed a bizarre murder. Slowly, the story is revealed from various points of view with different outcomes. The truth is never established, though each teller claims his/her version is accurate.

The film wowed the critics and helped establish Kurosawa's reputation as a filmmaker. A rogue samurai (Mifune) is arrested when he is accused of raping a woman and attacking her escort. Witnesses are called and the story is repeated numerous times from various viewpoints: woodsman, woman, rogue, and a spiritual medium. Though the overall length of the film is short, the film comprises mostly of the witnesses' accounts and re-enactments of the crucial event. A theme now overused in many sitcoms and dramas. After the story ends (it is a loose adaptation from the works of Akutagawa), the weather clears and the men find an abandoned baby. The woodsman decides to shelter the child as his own and walks away from the other men who ponder the moral implications of the past events.

Raven Tengu Kabuto   **(Kabuto)**
(1992) Japanime: Fantasy   **C-45m Japanese with English Subtitles**   **VA**
Catalog #USR DIE01   **Japan Retail: $19.95**
Dir/Scr: Buichi Terasawa   **Ex. Prod: Kazuo Suzuki**
Animation Dir: Hisashi Harai
PC: L.A. Hero / Dark Image Entertainment   **Dist: Nippan, Kiss Films**
[***]
An exciting story mixing historical samurai action with supernatural horror and technical mayhem. Raven Tengu Kabuto is a mystical samurai with a magical sword called "Hiryu". Once he was human and a retainer for a wise lord and his daughter. He returns to his hometown and discovers a new evil has taken over the area. Samurai warriors loyal to the lord help escort the daughter to safety, but their party is attacked. The lord has been replaced by an evil woman and her gifted sidekick who can create mechanical marvels that rely on traditional know-how, but seem futuristic by even today's standards. Kabuto must save the daughter and battle the evil Tamamushi and her minions. With magical wings and martial arts skills unmatched, he defeats her powerful samurai warrior and dozens of wicked ninja warriors. He finds the lord's daughter and rescues her from Tamamushi's flying palace, revealing the true secrets of their dark powers. The story features creative animation, sword action, and interesting characters in a popular theme of good versus evil. Creator Buichi is also the mind behind Space Cobra and Midnight Eye, Goku.

The Real Bruce Lee
(1994) Kung-Fu   **C-100m**   **Dubbed**   **Catalog #20053A**   **Hong Kong**
Retail: $9.99
Dir/Editor: Jim Markovic   **Scr: Lerry Dolchin**
Presented/Prod: Serafim Karalexis
PC: Madison World Films   **Dist: Quality Video, Inc.**
Bruce Lee, Bruce Li, Dragon Lee
[**]
This is actually two films in one, the first portion of the video features early films of Bruce Lee. Before Lee came to America, he was a child actor in numerous Hong Kong films and on stage under the guidance of his father. This video offers a fascinating glimpse at his early career by showcasing four scenes from his childhood career as far back as 1947 (Kid Cheung, The Bad Boy, Carnival, Orphan Sam). Then the film shifts gears and features two of Bruce Lee's better known clones: Bruce Li and Dragon Lee. This is where the film suffers and you sit and watch a bad Bruce Lee clone at work. While clips are featured for Bruce Li, an entire Dragon Lee film is included. Most likely, the distributors only had thirty minutes of Bruce Lee footage and needed more to market the video as a full-length feature film. They obtained the rights to a poor Dragon Lee film and included it to create a longer running time.

Rebel From China
(1988) Action C-97m Chinese with English Subtitles   **Type II**
Catalog #1061   **Hong Kong**   **Retail: $39.99**

Dir: Li Wai Man   Scr: Ringo Lam   Dist: Tai Seng Video
John Woo, Wan Yeung Ming, Patrick Tse
[***]
Chen Hsiang Ming is a young, disillusioned private in the People's Liberation Army of China. After hearing about his father's forced suicide due to political pressures, Chen and his brother flee to Hong Kong for a better life. Unfortunately, life on the other side of the border isn't always greener. An honest life is too tough for the brothers, so they turn to crime. However, their plans to become smugglers are thwarted by Marine Police. Then trouble comes from the other side of the coin, as a ruthless Triad gang boss plans to redevelop the apartment block where Chen lives. Even though Chen realizes he is fighting a futile battle against the law and the Triad, he is determined to fight until the end. Like many Chinese characters, they realize the inevitable outcome is death, but are determined to fight as long as they take their oppressors with them.

RECORD OF LODOSS WAR (JAPANIME MEETS WESTERN FANTASY)

Record of Lodoss War: Vol. I-6 Box Set
(1990) Japanime: Fantasy   C-355m   Dubbed/Japanese with English Subtitles
VA   Catalog #USM 1273 Japan Retail:$99.99/$124.99
Dir: Shigeto Makino (1), Akinori Nagaoka (2), Katsuhisa Yamada (3), Taiji Ryu (4,7,9-11), Kazunori Mizuno (5), Akio Sakai (6), Hiroshi Kawasaki (8), Akinori Nagaoka (12,13)
Scr: Mami Watanabe (1-8, 10-13), Kenichi Kanemaki (9,11)
Original Story: Hitoshi Yasuda, Ryo Mizuno
Music: Mitsuo Hagita   Character Design: Yutaka Izubuchi, Nobuteru Yuki
PC: Group SNE/Kadokawa Shoten/Marubeni Corp/Tokyo Broadcasting System
Dist: U.S. Manga Corps
[****]
Two deluxe box sets are available for purchase and are cheaper than buying the tapes individually. The outside box design is different and comes in a collector's holding case. The dubbed version sells for $99.99 while the subtitled version is $124.99. For those who own DVD players, the set will be released on dvd with both versions available for one price.

Record of Lodoss War: Vol. I
(1990) Japanime: Fantasy   C-90m Dubbed/Japanese with English Subtitles   VA
Catalog #USM1274 Japan Retail: $19.95 (Subtitled Version: $29.95)
See Box Set for Complete Credits
[****]
The Record of Lodoss Wars is an impressive and dedicated effort to portray traditional European fantasy in a Japanese animated format. In my experience, no other film or series (Asian or non) has better captured the essence and wonder of fantasy, in what many consider the quintessential fantasy epic. The only films that have come close in scope are The Lord of the Rings animated films and the upcoming live-action epics. The story is rich and complex, but easily digestible for any viewer and expands over five hours of animation in a thirteen volume series: sold in six separate tapes. The opening montage explains the great Lodoss Wars that torn the land apart. After many years of peace, war is brewing again and a classic group of warriors band together to

aid in the battle. The six heroes are Pahn, the young knight in training, Deedlit, a sprite female elf warrior, Ghim, a burly dwarf, Slayn, the wise wizard, Etoh the cleric, and Wood(chuck), the thief. The six characters are drawn together for different reasons, but unite under one cause to stop the destruction of the world. The story begins with a mini-quest against a mighty dragon. This is a future scene in which the party is already formed and work well together. After that adventure, the story will fall back in time and explain their origins and continue from that point on. The first video is an excellent deal for your money and will set the pace for whether you will enjoy the series. Other episodes follow, comprising two episodes each.

Episode 1: Prologue to the Legend
Episode 2: Blazing Departure
Episode 3: The Black Knight
Plus the mini-documentary "The Making of Record of Lodoss War"

Record of Lodoss War: Vol. 2
(1990) Japanime: Fantasy   C-60m Dubbed/Japanese with English Subtitles   VA
Catalog #USM1275 Japan Retail: $19.95 (Subtitled Version: $29.95)
[****]
Now the stages of war have been set and our band of brave warriors join the forces of good King Fahn. The stronghold of Myce falls to evil Emperor Beld's dark army which employs monsters and mercenaries. Parn and his friends join forces with King Fahn and attend a banquet in honor of King Kashue, the Desert King. Meanwhile, the warriors stop Karla's plan to kidnap Princess Fianna.

Episode 4: The Grey Witch
Episode 5: The Desert King

Record of Lodoss War: Vol. 3
(1990) Japanime: Fantasy   C-60m Dubbed/Japanese with English Subtitles   VA
Catalog #USM1276 Japan Retail: $19.95 (Subtitled Version: $29.95)
[****]
The tragedy of war takes its toll as more strongholds fall to Beld's growing army. Parn and his five friends return from the Sage Wort who explains to them that Karla is the descendant of an ancient kingdom of sorcery and bent on her own ambitions. At the palace, King Fahn is proud of their success and bravery, offering Parn a knighthood in the Holy Knights of Valis. Parn's father was a knight and his childhood memories of his father disappearing to war haunt his dreams. He denies politely, but will serve the king alongside his friends. The mighty dwarf Ghim becomes restless and separates from the party.

Episode 6: The Sword of the Dark Emperor
Episode 7: The War of Heroes

Record of Lodoss War: Vol. 4
(1990) Japanime: Fantasy   C-60m Dubbed/Japanese with English Subtitles   VA
Catalog #USM1277 Japan Retail: $19.95 (Subtitled Version: $29.95)
[****]
In a dramatic turn of events, the six heroes are divided and must join again to defeat the evil Karla. On their way to join Ghim and Slayn, the heroes meet Shiris and Orson, the berserker,

who mistake them for enemies and attack. The misunderstanding is resolved, but Ghim can no longer wait and enters the ominous castle of Karla. He realizes Karla is using the body of High Priestess Leylia who once saved Ghim's life. Sorceress Karla mocks the mighty dwarf warrior and toys with him. Ghim's friends arrive in time and help him save Leylia, but pay a drastic price in return. Ghim falls in his final victory and Wood is corrupted by the spirit of Karla's circlet.

Karla is temporarily halted, but the evil Ashram with the support of the dark elf Pirotess and the wizard Wagnard search for the Scepter of Domination hidden within the Fire Dragon Mountain.

Episode 8: Requiem for Warriors

Episode 9: The Scepter of Domination

Record of Lodoss War: Vol. 5
(1990) Japanime: Fantasy   C-60m Dubbed/Japanese with English Subtitles   VA
Catalog #USM1278   Japan Retail: $19.95 (Subtitled Version: $29.95)
[****]
The great dragon, Shooting Star, defends the Scepter of Domination and wreaks havoc on the people of Lodoss. The dark God Kardis prepares to awaken with the traitorous help of the Wizard Wagnard who has forsaken all and seized power for himself. The heroes must find a way to stop the tide of evil, before it is too late.

Episode 10: The Demon Dragon of Fire Dragon Mountain

Episode 11: The Wizard's Ambition

Record of Lodoss War: Vol. 6
(1990) Japanime: Fantasy   C-60m Dubbed/Japanese with English Subtitles   VA
Catalog #USM1279   Japan Retail: $19.95 (Subtitled Version: $29.95)
[****]
By now, you're either a dedicated fan or utterly confused. The epic saga comes to a close and the final battle will be held on the dark island Marmo. Ghim has fallen, Wood is under the spell of Karla, and Deedlit has been captured by Wagnard and scheduled to be sacrificed for Karlis. The remaining heroes break into Wagnard's citadel and must battle their way to the core of the wizard's domain. On the outside, the last remaining armies of Lodoss battle to the death. Evil dragon Narse attacks the heroic armies who have joined forces, but will perish if Karlis is released.

Episode 12: Final Battle! Marmo, The Dark Island

Episode 13: Lodoss-The Burning Continent

Red Dust
(1990) Romance C-94m   Chinese with English Subtitles   Catalog #1211
Hong Kong   Retail: $39.99
Dir: Yim Ho Scr: Echo Chen de Queri, Yim Ho   Prod: Hsu Feng
Ex. Prod: Jessinta Liu   Music: Shih Jei Yong
DP: Poon Hang Seng Editor: Chow Cheung Gun
Art Dir: Jessinta Liu, Edith Cheung   Art Dir Consultant: William Cheung
Costume Designer: Edith Cheung
Production Coordinator: Hsu Jye Coordinator/Prod Supervisor: Hsu Bin

Preseted by Tong Cun Lin PC: Pineast Pictures Production
Dist: Ocean Shores Video Ltd.
Chin Han, Lin Ching Hsia, Maggie Cheung, Richard Ng, Ku Mei Wah, Yim Ho
[***]
In the mold of "Doctor Zhivago" but on a much quieter and smaller scale, Red Dust is a tragic romance between a man and woman separated by the changing tides of civil disorder. Though instead of seeing the story from a male point of view, the film unfolds from a woman's point of view. Shen Shao-hua is a talented writer who falls in love with a man during World War II's occupied China. Though he is Chinese, he works for the Japanese government to help maintain order within the city. His influence is helpful to Shen and her friends, but she feels a certain hesitation toward a man who is helping the enemy occupy her country. Her memories float back to her past when her parents refused to let her see the boy she loved. Locked away like a prisoner, she tried to escape and commit suicide. She turned her thoughts toward writing and away from male companionship, but now she finds herself drawn to the man. Though he works for the occupying Japanese forces, he secretly is sympathetic to the Chinese people. When the war ends and a new government takes over the country, Shen and her lover are both in trouble for war crimes. He is accused of being an enemy of the people and must hide in the country. Meanwhile, Shen's friend (Cheung) and her lover are part of a resistance group and end up being killed. Cheung's role is small, but her appearance and charm are undeniable as she offers comfort and advice to Shen. The tides of change sweep across the nation as Nationalists fall to Communists. Shen leaves the city and travels to the country to be with her exiled lover. Together they attempt to flee the nation, but are separated in the vast flood of escaping bodies. Shen remains in the country and continues her writing. Many years after her death, her lover returns to China and discovers her beautiful writings. A delicate film that offers a reflection into the life of a woman who loved a man, regardless of what people or the government told her.

Red Firecracker, Green Firecracker
(1993) Romance   C-116m   Chinese with English Subtitles   R   VA
Catalog # VHS 80043   China Retail: $19.95
Dir: He Ping Scr: Da Ying   Prod: Yung Naiming, Chen Chunkeung
DP: Yang Lun   Editor: Yuan Hong Art Dir: Qian Yunxiu
Music: Zhao Jiping
(based on novel by Feng Jicai)
PC: Yung & Associates Co.   Dist: October Films/Evergreen Entertainment
Ning Jing   Chun Zhi ("The Master")
Wu Gang   Nie Bao (Painter)
Zhao Xiaorui Mr. Mann
Gao Yang   Mr. Zhao
Xu Zhengyun Mr. Xu (One-Armed Master)
[***]
Chinese romantic dramas are in popular demand due to the masterpieces of Chen Kaige and Zhang Yimou. Though not on that level, Red Firecracker, Green Firecracker is an interesting film that takes place in a remote village in northern China before the 1911 revolution ended Imperial reign. The Cai family, a wealthy family specializing in the creation of fireworks, is under the rule of Chun Zhi (Jing) the only living heir who happens to be a woman. A difficult

position since most businesses are run by males who can continue the family name and bear heirs. To placate her life, she dresses and acts like a man in charge of the family. When a poor artist Nie Bao (Gang) with a rebellious spirit is hired, he adds complications to Chun's life. Once again the secluded world of a female yearning to be an independent woman is explored. This time what bounds her is her duty to family and the business. Gradually, she visits the painter and admires his work. She fights her own blossoming love for him, denying him at times while pursuing him viciously. The two decide to marry, but to prove his worth he must perform in a dangerous fireworks competition. The local elders who disagree with the marriage support the foreman of the business to compete against the artist. In the vein of many Chinese films, the ending is poignant and tragic. Love can only be achieved at great personal cost and the price is often eternal separation.

Red Lion   (Akage)
(1969) Samurai   C-115 Japanese with English Subtitles   VA
Catalog #VA-18   Japan
Dir: Kihachi Okamoto   Scr: Sakae Hirosawa, Kihachi Okamoto
Prod: Yoshio Nishikawa, Toshiro Mifune DP: Takao Saito
Music: Masaru Sato Art Dir: Hiroshi Ueda
PC: Toho   Dist: Ingram International Films

Toshiro Mifune	**Gonzo**
Shima Iwashita	**Tomi**
Etsuji Takahashi	**Hanzo**
No Terada	**Sanji**
Yunosuke Ito	**Magistrate**
Shigeru Koyama	**Staff Chief Aragaki**
Takahiro Tamura	**Sozo Sagara**
No Terada	**Sanji**

Nobuko Otowa, Yuko Mochizuki, Ai Okada, Tokue Hanazawa, Mori Kishida
[***]
Red Lion is an interesting film that takes a popular genre and adds an element of humor and quirkiness to the main characters. It reminded me of films like "The Inspector General" and "The Court Jester" with Danny Kaye, and "Support Your Local Gunfighter" and "Support Your Local Sheriff!" with James Garner. The Kaye films add humor to the swashbuckling European adventures, while the Garner films add mirth to the popular western genres. In both sets of films, the main characters are not who they seem and solve the town/people's problems in less than traditional heroic ways with a cast of classic characters who personify the genre. Though the character is portrayed in a humorous manner, the story is fraught with tragedy and historical drama. Toshiro Mifune plays Gonzo the Red Lion, a simple horse-trainer who returns to his village as a great warrior and representative of the Imperial Government. The title Red Lion is somewhat misleading and the true translation should be Red Hair or Red Mane which describes a brightly colored Red Wig that is worn by Mifune to represent his status and position in the army. The time period is the mid-19th century, a crucial era in Japanese history and foreign policy. The three century reign of the Shogun Tokugawa is coming to an end, replaced by Imperial reign. As the changing fervor sweeps the nation, commoners chant "Eijanaika!" and prepare for an improved society. This film should be viewed before the film Eijanaika, since it also deals

with the subject of reformation and takes a more light-hearted approach to the complex political and social changes. The Imperial army is marching through the countryside, taking one city after another with little resistance. Gonzo begs his commander to let him ride into his own home town and secure it for the army. He convinces his commander, borrows his Red Lion wig, and proudly rides into town, bearing the crest of the Emperor. Since he represents the might of the Imperial army, the corrupt magistrate and crime boss don't put up a fight and try to appease the warrior. But Gonzo is not your typical heroic soldier and appears bumbling, misguided, and insecure about his status. Slowly, his brave nature does appear and he can handle a sword like a master. He helps the villagers, but the evil magistrate hires a samurai to kill Gonzo and attacks his followers. When everything seems to be working on Gonzo's side, he sends his men to deliver a chest of gold to his commander. The four men ride into camp, but discover an internal conflict has resulted in the execution of the Red Lion commander and his troops. The White Lion wig commander orders the men killed, but the pickpocket manages to escape and warn Gonzo. The White Lion army marches into town and battles against forces loyal to the Shogun and Gonzo. A bittersweet film that will appeal to those who enjoy films about Japanese history or samurai lore.

Red Rose, White Rose
(1994) Romance   **C-112m**   **Chinese with English Subtitles**
Catalog #L1030   **Hong Kong**   **Retail: $39.99**
Dir: Stanley Kwan   Scr: Edward Lam   Prod: Wong Hei, Wu Koo Hsiung
Ex. Prod: Wong Cheuk Han, Yang Teng Kuei
DP: Christopher Doyle   Editor: Brian Schwegmann
Associate Prod: Benny Wong
Prod Designer: Pan Lai   Music: Johnny Chen
PC: Golden Entertainment Co. Ltd./Golden Flare Video Ltd./First Organization Ltd.
Dist: Warner Brothers
Winston Chao   Zhao-bao Tung
Joan Chen   Jiao-rui Wang
Veronica Yip Yen Li Tung
(based on a story by Eileen Chang Reyhen)
[1/2]**
A romance set in the early part of the century. Zhen-bao is a handsome, charismatic man who is plagued with too many women in his life. Ze hong is one of the women he meets and falls in love with, but their relationship is tenuous. Zhen is a man of little patience and when he feels a relationship has come to an end, he packs up and leaves. His next relationship is with the wife of his friend Wang. This part of the story is the longest with a torrid passion of rejection, guilt, and betrayal. Though it sounds steamier than it is, most of the action is subdued and the characters never captivate the passions of the viewer.
Shot in widescreen, the subtitles are shown in the black bar portion. The print is green, large, and easy to read. Hopefully, more Asian-subtitled films will follow this format. Though the story may appeal to fans of the romance genre, the flow of the story is casually paced with written intermissions to further advance the plot.

Red Sorghum

(1987) DramaC-91mChinese with English Subtitles   R   VA
Catalog #NYV 55992China Retail: $19.99
Prod/Dir: Zhang Yimou   Scr: Chen Jianyu, Zhu Wei, Mu Yan
DP: Gu Changwei   Editor: Du Yuan   Music: Zhao Jiping
Prod. Designer: Yang Gang PC: Xiian Film Studio   Dist: New Yorker Video
Gong Li   Nine, the Grandmother
Jiang Wen   Yu, the Grandfather
Liu Ji   Their Son
Cui Cun-hua Sanpao, the Bandit Chief
Teng Rijun   Luohan
[***1/2]

The period is the late 1930's and Gong Li is sent off to marry an old, brutish leper who owns a winery in the countryside. The film has a brutal style and at times, it seems that we are watching through a window in time to a place that really existed. Li's husband dies and she quickly takes over the floundering business. She falls in love with a man who had once accosted her, but had saved her life in the past. One night, he urinates in the wine and successfully improves the vintage. Life seems to get better, but the Japanese invade China and subjugate the population. Against superior odds, Gong Li leads her people to fight against the barbaric cruelty of the Japanese soldiers. The film doesn't hold back the horror peasants suffered at the hands of the Japanese. In one scene, a Japanese soldier forces a Chinese peasant to skin alive his comrades. A certain savagery and visual disturbance explodes on the screen as if the ghosts of the dead were screaming to have their tale told. Beautifully shot in technicolor and another example of China's maturity into the realm of filmmaking. The pace and setting represent a simple peasant life and does lack the grandeur of period epics like Farewell My Concubine, but the impact of the story and performances are extremely effective and memorable.

Remember, Remember Me
(1995) DramaC-90mChinese with English Subtitles   Type I
Catalog # OL 494   Hong Kong   Retail: $39.99
Dir: Charlie Tak   Scr: To Kwok Wei   Prod: Steven K.S. Lo, Chan Ka Ling
Ex. Prod: Chan Ka Ling   Ex. Dir/DP: Tam Chi Wai   DP: Mark Lui
Art Dir: Bill Lui   Prod Manager: Wong Shiu Hung, Yeung Ka Sing
Costume Dir: Nelson Chung, Chik King Man
PC: Regal Film Co. Ltd.   Dist: Ocean Shores
Chu Yin, Ng Kai Loon, Chu Kin Kwan, Ko Chun Hsiung, Hui Fan, Elaine Wu, Lau Sung,
Fu Yuk Ching, Lee Fong, Lo Suet Ling, Liu Oi Ling
[**1/2]

A simple story with a bit of charm, dealing with friendship and success. Nothing really stands out in the plot, but a few of the scenes are humorous and engaging. The opening credits end and we see a large building owned by Chu Ah-chai. Though young, he is extremely wealthy and famous. A female reporter wishes to interview him and ask about why he is in search of a one thousand note Hong Kong bill. He is reluctant, but after treating the weight-conscious reporter to cake and milk he goes into his story. His beginnings are humble as he grew up in a household of sisters. He has three sisters, a grandmother, and his parents. Unfortunately, the women in the family are very ugly and troublesome. His mother chides him for not being a financial success, since it is his duty to find eligible husbands for his sisters. His father is not mentally fit, since he believes he can summon up spiritual powers and practices chi exercises. Most of his time is spent taking care of his invalid grandmother. Even in school, his teacher Mrs. Yu harasses him. She is secretly called Stone Fish by the students because of her unattractive appearance, hard demeanor, and lonely attitude. When a new student from Taiwan enrolls, he and Chu become good friends. Ricky is wealthy, laid back, and very generous to Chu. In typical teen fashion, the two talk about girls, what to do in the future, and just hang out at the beach. There they met an unattractive fat girl (running theme) who happens to be friends with a really cute girl named Ching. Both men fall in love with Ching who turns out to be Stone Fish Yu's only daughter. In a quick turn of events, Ching leaves Hong Kong to pursue a singing career. Her mother goes insane, fatty girl disappears, and the boy's leave school. When Ricky's father demands he enroll in a law program in Canada, Ricky runs away from home and stays with Chu. The two work at odd jobs, but financial success evades them. Then one day, Ricky gives Chu a one thousand note with a happy birthday message written on it. Since Chu's is desperate for money, he photocopies the good luck bill and spends it. Now that Chu is successful, he wishes to retrieve the special note that turned his life around. The paths of the characters briefly touch at certain events, but do not add much to the predictable conclusion.

Return of the Dragon
(1974) Kung-Fu   C-91m Dubbed   R   VA
Catalog #6123   Hong Kong   Retail: $14.95
Dir/Scr: Bruce Lee   Prod: Raymond Chow
DP: Ho Lang Shang Editor: Chang Yao Chang   Music: Ku Chia Hui
Art Design: Chieng Hsin   Costumes: Chu Sheng Hsi
Dist: CBS/Fox Video
Bruce Lee   Tang Lung
Chuck Norris   Kuda
Nora Miao   Chen Ching Hua
Huang Chung Hsun Uncle Wang
Chin Ti   Ah K'ung
Jon T. Benn   Boss
Robert Wall   Robert
Liu Yun, Chu'eng Li, Little Unicorn, Ch'eng Pin Chih, Ho Pieh, Wel P'ing Au, Huang Jen Chih, Mali Sha
[***]
Bruce Lee's third feature film and his directorial debut is highlighted by the famous battle between Lee's character and karate champ Chuck Norris. Chinese kung-fu expert Tang Lung arrives from China and lands at an airport in Rome. He is wearing traditional Chinese clothes, baggy cotton pants, and a buttoned down jacket with a shirt underneath. Being my first Bruce Lee film, I was initially amazed at how simple and peasant-like he appeared. He looked harmless, small, thin, and naive while quietly waiting for his ride. It doesn't take long for Lee to take off his jacket and prove my impression was wrong. He has arrived to help a group of Chinese immigrants run a restaurant. The film may seem ludicrous by today's standards; why would the mafia go through that much trouble for a Chinese restaurant and where are the police?. Why would the mafia use a roguish assortment of Americans, Italians, Indians, and African-

Americans as their thugs? And why does everyone speak English but need a translator? And why doesn't anyone just shoot Lee? Let's not ponder on the details or the second unit shots of Rome, and focus on Bruce Lee's graceful fury and power. Lee singlehandedly frustrates the mob boss and his effeminate Chinese translator, so they bribe one of the Chinese workers to betray the rest of the group. Using lightning fast moves, his trademark nunchakus, and throwing darts, Lee takes care of the goons in every scene while teaching his fellow Chinese the beauty of Chinese gung-fu (as they pronounce it). The scenes are merely stepping stones for the violent escalation that forces the mob boss to call in martial arts experts: a Japanese, an American, and Chuck Norris. Bruce easily dispatches the first two and then battles Norris in Rome's Coliseum in what can best be described as one of the greatest matches on film. Norris was a champion tournament fighter who studied the Korean style of Tang Soo Do. Bruce Lee believed in bringing using real fighters and realistic style fighting moves in his films.

Return of the Master Killer (Return to the 36th Chamber)
(1980) Kung-Fu   C-100m   Dubbed   Hong Kong   Retail: $19.95
Dir: Liu Chia Liang Prod: Mona Fong   Ex. Prod: Run Run Shaw
Art Dir: Johnson Tsao   MAD: Liu Chia Liang   PC: Shaw Bros.
Gordon Liu Chia Hui   Wang Lung Wei
[***]
Don't be misled by the title, this is not a true sequel to the Master Killer nor does Gordon Liu reprise his role of Shaolin monk San Te. Interestingly, this is a light-hearted parody of the Master Killer with plenty of in-jokes at how kung-fu stunts are performed and Liu even pokes fun at his own persona. Gordon Liu is the local village con-man and beggar who impersonates Shaolin monk San Te, hero of the first film. Most of Liu's friends are employees at a dye factory owned by Manchu bullies. They enforce harsh rules, slash wages, and beat up anyone who gets in their greedy way. Gordon and his friends fool the thugs into believing he is the real Monk San Te and the tides turn albeit temporarily in favor of the workers. When his bluff is eventually called by the Manchu boss and top fighter (venerable Wang), Gordon is beaten to a pulp and cast out. Conditions worsen at the dye factory, so the guilty Liu decides to give up his lazy and shallow ways. He must learn real kung-fu quickly and decides to go to Shaolin Temple. Once again this may mirror the original Master Killer, but budget, development, and plot are greatly simplified. He enters Shaolin through deceit and the monks refuse to train him, but the real San Te takes a liking to him and lets him work around the temple. While working as a carpenter, Gordon learns martial arts while watching the monks and mimicking their behavior. In traditional Shaw ingenuity, Liu develops his own style of scaffolding martial arts. San Te tests his new skills, and then tells him to leave Shaolin Temple and seek his own path. At first Liu believes he hasn't learned any true martial arts, but a quick toss of his friend convinces him otherwise. Proudly dressed in monk attire, Liu enters the dye factory and heroically dispatches the villains. The fight scenes are well choreographed, entertaining, and family friendly without a single fatality. However, the training scenes are not nearly as good as the first film and the style and drama are much weaker. Rather disappointing if you expect a sequel to the spectacular Master Killer, but fine for a comedy kung-fu film with plenty of charm from our favorite Shaolin monk, Gordon Liu.

Revenge of the Ninja - See Ninjamania Section

Rhapsody in August
(1991) Drama   C-98m PG   Japanese with English Subtitles   VA
Catalog #5062   Japan Retail: $19.95
Dir: Akira Kurosawa   Prod: Toru Okuyama, Hisao Kurosawa
Scr: Akira Kurosawa   (from the novel Nabe-no-Naka by Kiyoko Murata)
DP: Takao Saito, Masaharu Ueda Music: Shinichiro Ikebe
Art Design: Yoshiro Muraki   Dist: Orion Home Video

Sachiko Murase	Kane - the Grandmother
Hisashi Igawa	Tadao - Kane's Son
Narumi Kayashima	Machiko - Tadao's Wife
Tomoko Ohtakara	Tami - Tadao's Daughter
Mitsunori Isaki	Shinjiro: Tadao's Son
Toshie Negishi	Yoshie - Kane's Daughter
Choichiro Kawarasaki	Noboru - Yoshie's Husband
Hidetaka Yoshioka	Tateo - Yoshie's Son
Mie Suzuki	Minako - Yoshie's Daughter
Richard Gere	Clark - Kane's Nephew

[***]

After completing Dreams and Ran, Kurosawa quickly went to work on his next project. A film closer to the heart of his life and more contemporary in topic. The film was not as praised as his earlier films and criticized for its handling of certain topics and its simplicity. Unfortunately, genius can sometimes be a curse and critics often demand more from veteran directors. But life is not comprised of all high points and awards. Simple stories are sometimes the purest. The story is seen through the eyes of four children who are spending their summer vacation at their grandmother's rural home outside of Nagasaki.

The film's primary focus is on the grandmother who represents the old Japan that suffered under military rule and defeat. Kurosawa is not trying to exemplify the actions of militarism and denounce the Americans, but strives to capture the common person's point of view. In war, it is the civilian who is caught in the middle and suffers the most. The four children are more concerned with frivolous topics and enjoy reading their parents postcards who are in Hawaii visiting a wealthy relative. Supposedly, their grandmother has a brother who immigrated to the United States and his child married a Caucasian which gives birth to Clark (Gere) and his half-Asian siblings. The grandmother doesn't recall her brother and she begins a painful exploration into her past. Meanwhile, the children discover their own spiritual awakening as they visit the ruins of Hiroshima (World War II atomic bomb site). The parents return to Japan and Clark is with them, paying his respects and apologizing for America's wartime actions. The film's theme falters on questioning the circumstances of World War II and shoulders the blame from both perspectives. The children and parents try to encourage grandmother to fly to Hawaii and visit her brother, but sadly the circumstances turn for the worse. Lost in confusion and depressed, the grandmother stands defiant against the imagery of the sky, rushes outdoors, holding an umbrella, and walks through the pouring rain with her four grandchildren running after her.

Richard Gere was in Japan when he met Kurosawa who still had an uncasted part. Perhaps having such a well-known actor detracted from the body of the film, but Gere was more than eager to play the part. When the film is mentioned to people, they respond, "Oh, the Richard

Gere film where he plays a half-Japanese." This is hardly a Richard Gere film, his appearance is brief and only in the latter portion of the film. A personal film from a director who has given the cinema world so much.

Riding Bean
(1989) Japanime   **C-48m** **Dubbed**   **VA**
Catalog #ANI ET094-001   **Japan**   **Retail: $19.95**
Dir: Yasuo Hasegawa   **Original Story & Character Design: Kenichi Sonoda**
PC: Youmex, Inc.   **Dist: AnimEigo**
[1/2]**
None of the main characters are purely righteous in fact they're criminals, but then again they have a roguish appeal. Chicago's Bean Bandit is a professional getaway driver who charges a minimum of forty-five thousand a job. He's a seasoned criminal and doesn't bat an eye when a cop gets killed or innocent victims get run over. He's cool under pressure, confident, and extremely strong. A Chicago detective has it in for him and buys a Cobra to chase him down on the streets. Of course, Bean has a fast car that can do a few tricks of its own. Complications start when a pair of lesbian criminals frame Bean and threaten the life of a young girl and her father. Bean and his sexy partner, who wants to go straight one day, are hired to deliver the girl to safety. When they're framed for her kidnaping, everyone goes after them, while Bean goes after the real crooks. When he gets mad, he's deadly and he sports an arsenal of weapons and wears bullet-proof clothes. Fast action-paced animation with little else.

Robot Carnival
(1987) Japanime: Scifi   **C-91m** **Dubbed**   **VA**
Catalog #BFV 958   **Japan Retail: $19.95**
Dir: Katsuhiro Otomo, Atsuko Fukushima, Kouji Morimoto, Hiroyuki Kitazume, Mao Lamdo, Hidetoshi Ohmori, Yasuomi Umetsu, Hiroyuki Kitakubo, Takashi Nakamura
PC: A.P.P.P. Co. Ltd.   **Dist: Streamline Pictures**
[*1/2]**
An excellent compilation of animation dealing with robots and technology. Nine of Japan's finest animators collaborated to direct eight short stories on a variety of robotic subjects using their own style of animation and discretion. The stories range from futuristic to historical, colorful animation to black and white, romance to comedy, and everything in between. The stories vary greatly in content and style, therefore may not hit the mark with all viewers, but is a great place to sample your viewing appreciation for Japanese animation. Some of the highlights include: "Nightmare," in which a drunk awakens to discover his city overrun by mechanical creatures, and "Presence," about a scientist falling in love with his female robot...interestingly the majority of stories have minimal to no dialogue with the stories told through music and visual imagery. Other stories include a action-packed scifi tale of a cyborg who must save a girl from evil robots. Two young teens who meet an interesting robot at an amusement park. A historical tale of the first robot built in Japan using pulleys, bamboo, and gears. All in all, the film is fascinating from an artistic point of view and as a whole delights from different perspectives.

Rodan
(1956) Monster   **C-74m** **Dubbed**   **Catalog #33828**   **Japan Retail: $9.95**

Dir: Inoshiro Honda Scr: Takeshi Kimura, Takeo Murata
Prod: Tomoyuki Tanaka   DP: Isamu Ashida   Sp. Fx: Eiji Tsuburaya
PC: Toho Studios
Kenji Sahara, Yumi Shirakawa, Akihiki Hirata, Akio Kobori, Yasuko Nakata, Minosuke Yamada
[**1/2]
One of the earliest monster movies to come out of Japan following the success of Godzilla. Similar to the original Godzilla film (though shot in color) in many ways, but Rodan plays more like a traditional American horror/scifi film of the 1950's. When H-bomb testings unleash an ancient pterodactyl it soon rises out of its subterranean home to wreak havoc on the world. The first person to discover the creature is a Japanese mine worker who gets trapped deep in a subterranean pocket. He manages to survive but discovers a large egg which hatches. The military tries everything to stop the supersonic monster especially when two of them appear in the air. Good monster action and less camp than other films of the genre.

The Romance of the Vampires
(1994) Horror   C-98m Chinese with English Subtitles   Type III
Catalog #1514   Hong Kong   Retail: $39.99
Dir: Ricky Lau Kwun Wai
Scr: Joey Cheung, Ricky Lau, Ricky Ng, Victor K.O. Yeung
Prod: Victor K.O. Yeung, Robin Yeung   DP: K.C. Ma   Music: Lennon K.C. Li
Prod Coordinator: Ip Wing Cho, Victor K.O. Yeung
PC: Sunton Films Production Ltd.
Ben Lam, Yung Hung, Mondi Yau, Louie Yuen
[**1/2]
Most Asian horror films tend to focus on camp or downright blood and gore, occasionally some films try to be more sensitive and stand out. Though Romance of the Vampires has its share of nudity and violence, the tone of the film is more along the lines of a romantic drama. Rainbow is a beautiful woman (similar to Sally Yeh in The Killer) who was blinded by a vicious gangster. Now she desperately needs money for an eye operation and works as a high class prostitute. The opening shots of the escort agency are silly, but are quickly glossed over to Rainbow and Cheung's relationship. Cheung is the male escort who delivers the prostitutes and takes care of them. He takes a personal interest in Rainbow, helping her and living with her as a guardian. He secretly loves her, but she views him as a brother and caretaker in a completely platonic relationship. One evening, the gangster who was put away by Rainbow tries to extract revenge. He kidnaps her and plans to gang rape her. A handsome, mysterious stranger arrives and saves her from the gangsters. She develops a relationship with Fung, a wealthy man who visits her only in the evening. Fung and his companion Moon are vampires who have settled in Hong Kong to indulge in sex and murder. The female vampire, Moon, loves Fung and loves to kill men. Fung falls in love with Rainbow, since she reminds him of a past love. A common thread in vampire movies. The film has few action scenes and focuses on the love triangle between Moon, Fung, and Rainbow and also among Fung, Rainbow, and Cheung. This film won't win any awards or break any new ground, but the down-to-earth performances and the softer pace is a welcome change in the gore-filled world of horror.

Roots Search
(1986) Japanime: Scifi   C-45m Japanese with English Subtitles
Catalog # USM 1025 Japan Retail: $34.95
Dir: Hisashi Sugai   Scr: Mitsuru Shimada   Ex. Prod: Hiromasa Shibazaki
Character Design & Animation Supervisor: Sanae Kobayashi
Art Dir: Yoshinori Takao
English Version - Ex. Prod: John O'Donnell   Translation: Alara Rogers
Prod Coordinator: Cliff Rosen
PC: Nippon Columbia Co., Ltd.   Dist: U.S. Manga Corps
[**1/2]
There is no denying that in the realm of science fiction, many films are imitated for their visual style, mood, or intriguing theme. Such classics as "Star Wars", "Blade Runner", and "2001: A Space Odyssey" have been imitated by countless filmmakers but never surpassed and rarely rivaled. Roots Search also carries the torch of imitation by bearing a strong resemblance to the Ridley Scott classic scifi/horror film "Alien". But die-hard scifi/horror fans may recall a smaller film called "Galaxy of Terror" which was also inspired by "Alien". Roots Search resembles the schlock scifi/horror adventure "Galaxy of Terror" (starring Ray Walston and Erin Moran) since the alien creature in both films had the power to create illusions and manipulate through persuasion. Deep in space, a ship comes out of warp and is on a direct course to Tolmeckius Research Institute, a space station dedicated to the research of espers. On board, a young woman named Moira is undergoing experiments due to her powerful esper/psychic abilities. She has strange visions of an alien creature and her fellow crew members being killed. On cue, the spaceship crashes into the station with only one survivor, Buzz. He reveals that the spaceship was overtaken by an alien who can read human minds and use their darkest regressions as weapons against them. Quickly, the crew jettison the alien body out into space and quarantine the derelict spaceship. However, the alien manifests itself in the space station and murders the crew members one by one. Efforts to communicate with the creature are in vain and the crew pull out weapons to kill the monster. The alien claims to be the messenger of God on a mission to purify the universe of human sins. Only the resourceful Buzz and the female psychic survive. The ending is up to interpretation and may leave viewers scratching their heads or not.
Nothing new is added to the genre and the animation style is not as crisp as newer films. If the story appeals to you, the film's pace is quick enough not to bore even casual fans.

Roujin Z
(1991) Japanime: Scifi   C-80m Dubbed   PG-13   VA
Catalog #USM 1292   Japan Retail $19.99   Widescreen Available
Dir: Hiroyuki Kitakubo   Original Story, Scr & Mechanics Design: Katsuhiro Otomo
Prod: Yoshiaki Motoya   Original Character Design: Hisashi Eguchi
DP: Hideo Okazaki   Chief Dir: Hiroyuki Kitakubo
Art Dir: Hiroshi Sasaki   Mechanical Design: Mitsuo Iso   Art Design: Satoshi Kon
Assitant Dir: Toshiaki Hontai   Animation Dir: Fumio Lida
Music: Bun Itakura English Version - Ex. Prod: John O'Donnell
PC: Tokyo Theaters Co., Inc./The Television Inc./MOVIC Co., Ltd./TV Asahi/Sony Music Entertainment (Japan) Inc.   Dist: U.S. Manga Corps
English Voices:

Allan WengerTerada
Toni Barry	Haruko
Barbara Barnes	Nobuko
Adam Henderson	Maeda
Jana Carpenter	Norie
Ian Thompson	Takazawa

[***1/2]

In the not so distant future, a brilliant administrator presents a lecture to a group of high officials and scientists. He proposes to introduce a machine that will take care of the elderly and reduce the expensive cost on in-patient, hands-on care. The idea is met with enthusiasm since the machine can take care of all his medical, physical, and mental needs. Then a young woman asks what about his spiritual need, what about his need to be touched by a human hand, and to be loved. The administrator becomes flustered and accuses the girl of stopping progress. This is the interesting dilemma proposed in an intelligent film from the creator of "Akira", Katsuhiro Otomo.

The story focuses around the administrator and his quest to end the needless time and money spent on caring for the elderly. His research creates an advanced machine that will take care of the elderly. The machine/computer is called the Z-100 and looks like an oversized coffin. An elderly Japanese man is chosen as the first test subject and whisked away from his small tenement where a kindly Japanese nursing student had taken care of him. Through incidents explained, the elderly man and Z-100 merge into one entity and goes on a rampage to maintain its freedom. The old man is driven by his desire to see his past wife at the beach while the nurse and her friends are moved by compassion to save him. The administrator and the authorities are desperate to stop the Z-100 and keep things quiet from the concerned public. Tamer than most Japanese animated films, the story still contains a dose of outlandish action scenes, mild nudity, adult content, and a thought provoking theme.

Rumble in the Bronx

(1995) Kung-Fu   C-105m   Dubbed   R   VA
Catalog # ID 3378LI   Hong Kong   Retail: $19.95 Widescreen Available
Dir: Stanley Tong   Scr: Fibe Ma, Edward Tang
Prod: Barbie Tung, Roberta Chow Ex. Prod: Leonard Ho
DP: Jingle Ma   Editor: Michael Duthie, Peter Cheung   Music: J. Peter Robinson
Prod Design: Oliver Wong   Stunt Co-ordinator: Jackie Chan, Stanley Tong
PC: Golden Harvest   Dist: New Line Cinema

Jackie Chan	Keung
Anita Mui	Elaine
Françoise Yip	Nancy
Bill Tung	Uncle Bill
Marc Akerstream	Tony
Garvin Cross	Angelo
Morgan Lam	Danny
Kris Lord	White Tiger

[***]

Ironically, I viewed Rumble in the Bronx on video before its theatrical release. When I first watched the original film, I was rather disappointed. The subtitles were difficult to read, the quality murky and cropped, and the pacing seemed off. So I didn't really feel strongly about the film. When the film was released in the United States (months later) I viewed the theatrical version and was surprised at how much better it looked and sounded, proving that Chan's films are best seen on the big screen. Chan's films are shot in widescreen film ratios that are cropped in television and video versions. In general, I believe in the merit of subtitles over dubbed versions, but in the case of martial arts movies, a dubbed film frees the viewer to watch the action on screen.

Re-edited and given a new soundtrack, Jackie Chan hit the American audiences with a lively, contemporary film set in New York City - the Bronx. In reality, Vancouver was the backdrop and becomes quite apparent in certain scenes: look for the Rocky Mountains in the climax with the hovercraft. At first the dubbing seems atrocious and very anti-American, but when Chan starts to move his body, just sit back and expect the amazing. He jumps, kicks, and glides into action, and if that wasn't enough, he'll do the action on refrigerators, through shopping carts, on stairs, and just about anywhere you can stand. Keep in mind that he does his own stunts and was around forty years old during the filming and you can truly respect his amazing physical conditioning and real screen bravery.

The story is simple in scope and runs like a loony tune cartoon with simple characters in very confined roles who are the props needed for Chan's energetic style. Jackie is visiting New York City to attend the wedding of his uncle. His uncle owns a convenience store in the Bronx, but sells the place so he can marry an African-American woman. The new owner is lithe, nerdy Anita Mui who dreams of making the place a real winner. Jackie decides to stay and help her out. When Chan beats up some shoplifters from a local gang, he becomes their number one target. Soon the gang, the police, and Chan are mixed up with organized mobsters after a pouch of stolen diamonds. The film's wild stunts are highlighted in outtakes at the end of the film. Familiar to on-set injuries, Chan broke his ankle while jumping onto a moving hovercraft and completed the film wearing a cast. A star who loves to give his audience one hundred percent and proves that even over forty he is still the best. A fun, enchanting film that will appeal to the younger crowd and martial arts viewers looking for something a little less serious.

Rumik World: Fire Tripper
(1985) Japanime   C-50m Dubbed/Japanese with English Subtitles
Catalog #USM 1456 Japan Retail: $14.95
Dir: Osamu Uemaru Scr: Tomoko Konparu
Character Design: Katsumi Aoshima   Art Dir: Torao Arai
Music: Koiichi Oku
PC: Shogakukan   Dist: U.S. Manga Corps
(based on original work and design by Rumiko Takahashi)
[***]

Part of the Rumiko Takahashi series of animated film, Fire Tripper is a wonderful little tale that mixes supernatural elements into a time-traveling love story. In feudal Japan, bands of mercenaries terrorize the countryside and prey on poor victims. A young teen defends his family from the bandits, but in the process his home is burnt and his younger sister is trapped in the flames. He tries to rescue her, but a smoldering log cracks from the roof and plummets toward her. In an instant, horror crosses his face, but disappears into shock as she vanishes in thin air.

Thus begins a clever tale of time travel and romance in a memorable story. Time travel is tricky, so don't read any further or you might regret knowing too much about the plot. This story would translate favorably to live-action as well as animation and should be considered recommended viewing for non-anime fans as well. The frightened child arrives in modern day Tokyo and is adopted by a caring couple who soon have a child of their own. On an uneventful day, she and her younger brother are walking home and a refinery explodes. They are both engulfed in flames, but again her mysterious powers ignite, shooting them back into the past. She awakes to find herself under attack by bandits, but is rescued by a brave teen warrior. He takes her to the village and plans to marry her. One night, he gets drunk and even tries seducing her before passing out. Soon a relationship develops, but she is disturbed by past images presented when she meets his younger sister. Somehow, she has traveled back to the days preceding her own disappearance. In what may confuse some, she is now the older sister of her older brother, but discovers that he is actually her younger brother from the future. When they leaped back in time, he jumped a decade earlier than she did. So in reality, she was born in the past and he was born in the future, but in both time lines they are adopted brother and sister. With no blood ties between them, they succumb to their love for each other and decide to choose one time to live the rest of their lives. The animation is crisp but casual, the focus is drawn towards the characters and not the visuals. We care for the characters and their predicament. This is not a story full of wild animation and bizarre color schemes, but an engaging and heart-warming tale of love that complements Takahashi's talents as a leading creator of stories dealing with romance and comedy.

Rumik World: The Laughing Target
(1987) Japanime: Horror   C-50m Dubbed/Japanese with English Subtitles
Catalog #USM 1455 Japan Retail: $14.95
Dir: Toru Matsuzono   Scr: Tomoko Konparu, Hideo Takayashiki
Character Design: Hidekazu Obara   Art Dir: Torao Arai
Music: Kawachi Kuni
PC: Shogakukan   Dist: U.S. Manga Corps
(based on original work and design by Rumiko Takahashi)
[***]
A dark romantic fantasy from the brilliant mind of Takahashi. Incorporating elements similar to Mermaid's Scar and Fire Tripper, romance is given a new twist. Two young cousins are betrothed to be married at a very early age. There is charm in the two children as they share their loving bonds. Many years later, the male cousin has grown up and leads a happy life at school and with a new girlfriend. When his fiance's mother dies, she is sent to live with him. His fiancé is not happy with any female rivals and bizarre events start to happen.
Takahashi's films are not meant to be big explosive, cutting edge animated films. Instead, the animation is used as a tool rather than a distraction for the film's wonderful story and multidimensional characters. Due to her amazing popularity, more titles are being distributed in the United States and complete copies of the original manga (comics) are available in book stores.

Rumik World: Maris the Chojo
(1986) Japanime: Comedy   C-50m Dubbed/Japanese with English Subtitles

Catalog #USM 1455 Japan Retail: $14.95
Dir: Kazuyashi Katayama, Tomoko Konparu   Scr: Hideo   Takayashiki,   Tomoko Konparu
Ex. Prod: Taga Hidenori
Character Design: Rumiko Takahashi, Katsumi Aoshima Art Dir: Toran Arai
PC: Shogakukan   Dist: U.S. Manga Corps
[**1/2]
Now for something completely different. Maris incorporates much more humor and slapstick visuals than previous works under the Rumik World title. Maris is a Thanatosian, a powerful being six-times stronger than a human. To compensate for her great strength, she must take pains to restrain herself with humans. Needless to say, she gets in trouble constantly and her superpowers cause plenty of damage which she must cough up and pay. Hoping to end her financial woes, she volunteers to save a rich kid who has been kidnaped. Armed with her sidekick who can morph into any creature and then make multiple duplicates, the two discover the whereabouts of the kidnapers. Maris battles the woman and the man. Soon she discovers the man is actually the kidnaped victim and has fallen for his kidnaper. Poor Maris isn't left with any rewards and must go back to the drawing board.
This may not be for all tastes, but those who enjoy the wacky girls of anime will find this a refreshing way to wind down after a long day and let the brain have a break.

Rumik World: Mermaid Forest - See Mermaid Forest

-S-

7 Blows of the Dragon
(197?) Kung-Fu   C-90m Dubbed   Hong Kong   Retail: $19.95
Dir: Chang Cheh   Scr: I Kuang, Chang Cheh Prod: Run Run Shaw
Assistant Dir: Ho Chih Chiang, Wu Yu Shen
DP: Kung Mu To   Editor: Kuo Ting Hung, Jeff Young, Barbara Pokras
Music: Chen Yung Yu   Art Dir: Johnson Tsao
Set & Costume Design: Kamber Huang   Sound: Wang Yung Hua
English Version: Lisa Lu   MAD: Pao Hsueh Li, Feng Wu Ma
PC: Shaw Bros.   Dist: New World Pictures

David Chiang	Young Dragon
Lily Ho	Tigress
Ti Lung	Magic Sword
Wang Chung	Fearless One
Chin Feng	Clever Star
Ku Feng	Welcome Rain
Yueh Hua	Leopard Man
Tetsuro Tamba	Jade Dragon
Toshio Kurozawa	Golden Spear
Nan Kung Hsun	General Wen
Fan Mei Sheng	Black Whirlwind
Tien Ching	Steward Li Ku

Ling Ling	Lady Lu
Li Yun Chung	Governor Liang
Ching Miao	Master Chen
Tung Lin	Heavenly King
Chen Kuan Tai	cameo

[**]

Vintage story of loyalty and betrayal in the Sung Dynasty 960-1126 AD. An early classic that suffers from age and staleness in comparison to modern martial arts movies. Based on the tale All Men are Brothers, this film is similar to the modern remake All Men are Brothers - Blood of the Leopard. The remake is a much finer version, but the original film's martial arts are more down to Earth and may appeal to fans of early Shaw Brothers stars. The plots are similar, but the main fault is the introduction of too many characters without developing any true heroes within the film. Also a lack of female presence and solid villains give the film a mechanical feel as one fight scene follows another with no tension. The 108 Bandits are attacked and one of their members is killed by a General. The Bandit leaders want to get revenge, but requires someone with martial arts skills that rival all. They send Black Whirlwind and his mentor to the home of a respected martial artist and scholar.

He is a noble man, but does not wish to get involved with the bandits. When the government discovers he harbored bandits, he is arrested and slated for execution for treason. The rest of the film is littered with mediocre fight scenes as various escape attempts are foiled. Eventually, an escape works and the two generals, once friends, must battle each other to the death. There aren't too many surprises and stars like Ti Lung may get top-billing, but hardly express more than a grunt throughout the entire film. This is director Chang's early effort and his latter films are much more entertaining, fast-paced, and colorful.

The Saint of Gamblers
(1995) Action Comedy   C-96m DIC 6145 with English Subtitles   Type II
Catalog #1882   Hong Kong   Retail: $79.98
Dir: Wong Jing   Dist: Tai Seng Video
Got Man, Fai, Chingmy Yau, Donnie Yen
[**]

Slapstick film molded after the God of Gamblers series. The action scenes are quite good, but the rest of the film is marred by childish slapstick and a routine plot that plods slowly. The God of Macau Gamblers is entering the world gambling competition, dueling with the likes of gamblers from America, Japan, India, and Thailand, all appropriately stereotyped and dressed for the part. When Ray Thai discovers a naive Mainlander named God Bless You, he sets him up as the new Saint of Gamblers. God and his profit-hungry discoverer Uncle San team up with Ray Thai. But Thai is part of the Japanese triads and plans to bum God off and win the tournament. Lovely Yau and her spunky brother switch sides and join God Bless You. In the predictable finale, God arrives just in time to enter the competition and play to victory. The films shifts carelessly from well-choreographed action/fight scenes to rough and tumble slapstick in the mold of the Three Stooges.

Salaam Bombay
(1988) Drama C-114m   Indian with English Subtitles   Catalog #70172

UK/India   Retail: $19.95
Dir: Mira Nair   Scr: Sooni Taraporevala   Prod: Mira Nair
DP: Sandi Sissel   Editor: Barry Alexander Brown
Music: L. Subramaniam   Prod Design: Mitch Epstein
(based on a story by Nair and Taraporevala)
Shafiq Syed   Krishna/Chaipau
Sarfuddin Qurrassi   Koyla
Raju Barnad   Keera
Raghubir Yadav   Chillum
Nana Patekar   Baba
Aneeta Kanwar   Rekha
Hansa Vithal   Manju
Mohanraj Babu   Salim
Chandrashekhar Naidu   Chungal
Ramesh Deshavani, Anjan Srivastava, Chanda Sharma
[****]

Bombay, India is not a city for the weak or naive, let alone an eleven-year boy without a family or home. Salaam (Hello/Greeting) Bombay is an emotionally dramatic portrayal of life in the underbelly of Indian society. A young boy named Krishna is the main character who is abandoned by his family at a circus. The reason, he destroyed his brother's bike and must come up with 500 rupees before he can return. One day while running an errand, the boy returns and finds the circus has packed and moved. With a handful of canned massala and a few rupees, he buys a ticket to the nearest major city, Bombay. It doesn't take him long to find a niche in life, since survival is in his nature and Krishna is a resourceful, clever boy. Nicknamed Chaipau, he works as a tea-boy at a streetside shop owned by Chacha. The shop is located next to a brothel where Boss Baba runs a drug ring and lives with his prostitute/wife. A new girl (virgin) is brought into the brothel and Baba is hired to break her into the ways of prostitution. While the daughter, Manju, of a kindly prostitute provides companionship. A drug runner named Chillum befriends the young boy, providing a surrogate older brother, but when situations worsen for the misguided Chillum, Chaipau becomes the older brother and tries to help his friend. In the end, Chaipau is betrayed by the people around him and sinks deeper into a life of poverty and despair. At the end, Nair dedicates the film to the children of India, but her beautiful and touching portrayal of hardship is a loving tribute that applies to all the downtrodden children of the world. Nominated for the Best Foreign Film 1988 Academy Award.

Sam the Iron Bridge (Champion of Martial Arts)
(1993) Kung-Fu   C-92m Chinese with English Subtitles
Catalog #1506   Hong Kong   Retail: $39.99
Dir: Fung Pak Yuen Prod: Steven Shin   Dist: Tai Seng Video
Too Siu Chun, Christy Cheung, Yu Hai, Lilly Li
[**1/2]

A rather different type of kung-fu movie over your standard fare. The film has an impressive cast and location, parts of Kwantung province and the Forbidden Palace. A great period movie with a cast of hundreds if not thousands shot on location in or around the Forbidden City and parts of Kwantung province. Sam is a powerful young martial arts expert who wins a championship and the adoration of everyone in town. But he goes against an evil sect who wishes to profit on the European opium trade. Though his martial arts prowess is respected, he runs into complications. A straight forward plot and good fight scenes for martial arts fans.

THE SAMURAI TRILOGY (The Story of Miyamoto Musashi)

It would be unheard of to watch Japanese samurai films and not recognize the historical name of Miyamoto Musashi. A samurai living in the 16th century, Musashi gained legendary status through his amazing exploits. How much is true and how much is fiction is difficult to say, but he was a master of the sword and did win a number of challenges, often estimated at sixty personal duels. Born around 1584 in either Mimasako or Harima province, he started his career at age thirteen and took his surname from the birthplace of his father and died in the service of Lord Tadotoshi Hosokawa in 1645 and is buried in Kyushu. He also spent time ink painting and writing a journal of his philosophies titled "The Book of Rings". Many scholars admire his gentle side, but the films and books of his life emblazoned his legend as a master swordsman. Similar to Wyatt Earp in Western mythology, his fame grew through word of mouth and the exciting stories of writers. Historically, his place in Japanese culture/history/folklore will always be firmly established and his portrayal in movies, television, books, and just about everywhere else remains in strong stride. The trilogy is based on the popular Eiji Yoshikawa novels. Director Inasaki and actor Mifune created the definitive mold of the life and times of Japan's greatest swordsman.

Samurai, The: Musashi Miyamoto
(1954) Samurai   C-92m Japanese with English Subtitles   VA
Catalog #CC1328L   Japan Retail: $49.95
Dir: Hiroshi Inasaki Scr: Tokuhei Wakao, Hiroshi Inagaki
Prod: Kazuo Takimura   DP: Jun Yasumoto   Music: Ikuma Dan
Art Dir: Makoto Sono   Lighting: Shigeru Mori   Sound: Choshichiro Mikami
PC: Toho   Dist: New Line Home Video/Ingram Internation Films
(based on the novel by Eiji Yoshikawa, adapted by Hideji Hojo)
Toshiro Mifune	**Miyamoto Musashi**
Rentaro Mikuni	**Honiden Matahachi**
Kaoru Yachigusa	**Otsu**
Mariko Okada	**Akemi**
Kuroemon Onoe	**Takuan Osho**
Mitsuko Mito Oko	

[****]
The first film in the brilliant Samurai Trilogy which follows the exploits of Miyamoto Musashi and his rise to fame. In 1598, the crucial Battle of Sekigahara ends and Japan is unified under one lord, Tokugawa Ieyasu. By 1600, the Tokugawa era will begin and no longer will civil wars be a part of Japan's history. A teenager named Musashi is on the losing side. He escapes from the war and seeks solitude in the mountains, perfecting his two sword techniques: Enmyo-ryu and Niten-ryu. He then travels throughout Japan eager to prove his merit in any duel. Winner of Best Foreign Film 1955 Academy Award.

Samurai II, The: Duel at Ichijoji Temple
(1956) Samurai   C-102m   Japanese with English Subtitles   VA
Catalog #CC1329L   Japan Retail: $49.95
Dir: Hiroshi Inasaki Scr: Tokuhei Wakao, Hiroshi Inagaki
Prod: Kazuo Takimura   DP: Jun Yasumoto   Music: Ikuma Dan
Art Dir: Makoto Sono   Lighting: Shigeru Mori   Sound: Choshichiro Mikami
PC: Toho   Dist: New Line Home Video/Ingram Internation Films
(based on the novel by Eiji Yoshikawa, adapted by Hideji Hojo)

Toshiro Mifune	Miyamoto Musashi
Koji Tsurata	Sasaki Kojiro
Sachio Sakai	Honiden Matahachi
Akihiko Hirata	Seijuro
Yu Fujiki	Denshichiro
Daisuke Kato	Toji
Eijiro Tono	Baiken
Kaoru Yachigusa	Otsu
Mariko Okada	Akemi
Kunimori Kodo	Priest Nikkan

[****]
An arrogant monk challenges anyone to test his skills. A samurai decides to challenge him, but then a man gently whispers in his ear, that's Miyamoto Musashi. The monk's face turns white and he lowers his grip. This is the kind of respect and awe that Musashi's legend created and this reverence is passed onto the viewer as we follow the continuing exploits of Musashi and his growing fame. The second film continues his love relationship while showing his famous duel against an entire Samurai school. In the background, Musashi has made enemies as well as friends. The character of Sasaki Kojiro is introduced. He is a feared master of the sword and considered the only rival to Musashi.

Samurai III, The: Duel at Ganryu Island
(1960) Samurai   C-102m   Japanese with English Subtitles   VA
Catalog #CC1330L   Japan Retail: $49.95
Dir: Hiroshi Inasaki Scr: Tokuhei Wakao, Hiroshi Inagaki
Prod: Kazuo Takimura   DP: Kazuo Yamada Music: Ikuma Dan
Art Dir: Hiroshi Ueda, Kisaku Ito Lighting: Tsuruzo Nishikawa
Sound: Masanobu Miyazaki
PC: Toho   Dist: New Line Home Video/Ingram Internation Films
(based on the novel by Eiji Yoshikawa, adapted by Hideji Hojo)

Toshiro Mifune	Miyamoto Musashi
Koji Tsurata	Sasaki Kojiro
Kaoru Yachigusa	Otsu
Mariko Okada	Akemi
Michiko Saga	Omitsu
Takashi Shimura	Nagaoka Sado

[****]

The final film in the Samurai Trilogy, focusing on Miyamoto Musashi's classic duel with Kojiro Sasaki. A powerful samurai with a giant sword who challenges the famous Musashi. The film builds toward the climatic battle as friends warn Musashi not to go. He travels by boat to a deserted beach and is armed only with a wooden sword. With the sun on his back, Musashi meets his greatest opponent and forever locks himself into Japan's history and folklore. Since the series is based on true events and historically recreated, the life and times of Musashi transcends beyond mere fiction (Bond, Tarzan, and Sherlock Holmes). Samurai is a great film about a great man, unfolding gently for the audience to fully appreciate the magnificent story. Highly recommended and an excellent spot to begin your journey into Japanese samurai films.

Sanjuro
(1962) Samurai   B&W-94m   Japanese with English Subtitles   VA
Catalog #6063   Japan Retail: $29.95
Dir: Akira Kurosawa   Scr: Ryuzo Kikushima, Akira Kurosawa, Hideo Oguni
Prod: Ryuzo Kikushima, Tomoyuki Tanaka   DP: Fukuzo Koizumi, Koichi Saito
Editor: Akira Kurosawa   Music: Masaru Sato   Art Design: Yoshiro Muraki
PC: Toho Studios   Dist: Embassy Home Entertainment
(based on the short story "Hibi Heian" by Shogoro Yamamoto)

Toshiro Mifune	**Sanjuro**
Tatsuya Nakadai	**Muroto**
Takashi Shimura	**Kurofuji**
Yuzo Kayama	**Iori Izaka**
Reiko Dan	**Koiso**
Masao Shimizu	**Kukui**
Yunosuke Ito	**Mutsuta the Chamberlain**
Takako Irie	**Chamberlain's Wife**
Kamatari Fujiwara	**Takebayashi**
Keiju Kobayashi	**Spy**

Akihiko Hirata, Kunie Tanaka, Hiroshi Tachikawa, Tatsuhiko Hari, Tatsuyoshi Ebara, Kenzo Matsui, Yoshio Tsuchiya, Akira Kubo
[*1/2]**

Companion film to Yojimbo, following the further exploits of Mifune's scruffy rogue samurai. A clean-cut group of young samurai meet at an abandoned temple to secretly pledge an alliance. Led by the chamberlain's nephew (Kayama), they are rebuffed at the cavalier attitudes of the older lords. They are idealistic, passionate men who chant in unison and brandish their swords. A laughter pierces the night air and ronin Mifune mocks the nine warriors. The contrast in appearance and attitude are striking, but appearances are deceiving which set in work the moral of the film. Mifune's character is scruffy, sloven, and embarrassing, but his character possesses knowledge of life and understands the truth of corruption and power. He helps guide the naive samurais in their quest to end corruption and bring justice into their community. Together they must rescue the kidnaped chamberlain and his family from the power-hungry superintendent. Kurosawa laces his film with satirical comments delivered by the deadpan ronin, Mifune, while delivering fast-paced sword battles in this clever and entertaining period piece. In the end, Mifune is sick of the bloodshed and chides the samurais for admiring his deadly skills. Hoping to teach them a lesson, Mifune turns on them and says, "Shut up. What was so great about that?

He was exactly like me - a drawn sword. Your old lady was right. Really good swords are kept in their scabbards. Yours better stay in yours. And don't try to follow me or I'll kill you. Goodbye." Another samurai masterpiece from the men who did it best.

Sansho the Bailiff
(1954) DramaB&W-125m   Japanese with English Subtitles   VA
Catalog #CC1375L   Japan Retail: $69.95
Dir: Kenji Mizoguchi   Scr: Yahiro Fuji, Yoshikata Yoda Prod: Masaichi Nagata
DP: Kazuo Miyagawa   Editor: Mitsuji Miyata
Music: Fumio Hayasaka, Kanahichi Odera, Tamekichi Mochizuki
Art Design: Kisaku Ito   PC: Daiei   Dist: Ingram International Films
(based on the story "Sansho Dayu" by Ogai Mori)
Yoshiaki Hanayagi   Zushio
Kyoko Kagawa   Anju
Kinuyo Tanaka   Tamaki, Zushio's Mother
Eitaro ShindoSansho
Akitake KonoTaro
Masao Shimizu   Masauji Taira
Ken Mitsuda   Prime Minister Morozane Fujiwara
Chieko Naniwa   Ubatake
Kikue Mori   Priestess
Kazukimi Okuni   Norimura
Yoko Kosono   Kohagi
Kimiko Tachibana   Namiji
Ichiro Sugai   Minister Of Justice
Masahiko Tsugawa   Zushio as a Boy
Naoki Fujiwara   Zushio as an Infant
Keiko Enami   Anju as a Girl
Ryosuke Kagawa   Ritsushi Kumotake
Kanji Koshiba   Kaikudo Naiko
Shinobu Araki   Sadaya
Reiko Kongo   Shiono
Shozo Nambu   Masasue Taira
Ryonosuke Azuma   Manager of a Brothel
Teruko Omi   The Other Nakagimi
[****]
A classic in Japanese cinema and much praised in the world film community as one of Japan's finest films.   The peasant life of 11th century feudal Japan is the backdrop and director Mizoguchi carefully blends the environment into the lives of his characters. Young Zushio, his mother Tamaki and his sister Anju journey in search of their exiled father. While traveling in the woods, they are captured by bandits and sold into slavery. Mother Tamaki is forced into prostitution and exiled to the faraway Sado Island, while the children are sold as servants to Sansho the bailiff. He is a man of power and cruelty, not to be taken lightly. Zushio grows into a man and after ten years, he has become an overseer for Sansho. Disheartened by his own cruelty and place in life, he plans a daring escape with Anju. Heroically, she sacrifices her life in

order for him to escape. Hoping to quell his disturbing images of his dead father and mother, he arrives in Kyoto where his father's deeds have become legendary. Zushio's popularity help to obtain a governorship and respect. Using his new found prestige and influence, he ends slavery and banishes the evil Sansho. Zushio hopes to find his mother and discovers her alone, blind, facing the beautiful crashing ocean. A quiet end to a long life full of hardship and death.

Savage 5
(1979) Kung-Fu   C-90m Dubbed   Hong Kong   Retail: $19.99
Dir: Chang Cheh   Scr: I Kuang, Chang Cheh   Prod: Mona Fong
Ex. Prod: Run Run Shaw   PC: Shaw Brothers
Ti Lung, David Chiang, Chen Kuan Tai, Danny Lee
[*1/2]**

A classic kung-fu movie of the seventies, combining the talents of the early Chang gang of superstars. Lung, Chiang, and Chen are residents of a small Chinese town in a remote part of China. Similar to the old west, the town is a walled-in community mostly made up of farmers, merchants, and tradesmen. Everyone knows each other and secrets are not very common among the peaceful townsfolk. The next nearest village is days away and the law is even further. The villagers must band together and fight when a marauding group of bandits take over the country town. Similar to the Seven Samurai, except the heroes are found from within. The film begins pleasantly as the local town thief is caught and tied to a tree. He is harmless, stealing food and small items more for fun and the villagers aren't too worried when he escapes. A large group of bandits arrive in town and take it upon themselves to rape and pillage the villagers. Slowly, the villagers fight back, but are defeated when a new group of bandits arrive with guns. The local thief reveals his true identity, he is the notorious King Bandit and duels with the evil bandits. King Bandit and a handful of brave villagers challenge the entire gang. Asian filmmakers are not afraid to sacrifice their heroes and through much bloodshed the village is freed of the bandits. A raw, non-flying kung-fu film that may lack the finesse of modern martial arts movies, but possesses a raw energy and strength often missing in today's action films. One of my personal favorties and remains a Shaw classic even today.

Scarred Memory
(1996) Romance   C-90m Chinese with English Subtitles   Type II
Hong Kong   Retail: $39.99
Dir: Ray Leung   Scr: Ray Leung, Wong Sa Fai, Au Kin Cheong, Hsu Jen Tu
Prod: Ma Fung Kwok   Ex. Prod: Wellington Fung
DP: Miu Kin Fai   Editor: Yiu Tin Hung   Music: Wan Ho Kit, Lee Hon Kam
Art Dir: Ken Chiu   Prod Manager: Peggy Cheung   Line Prod: Raymond Fung
Prod Co-ordinator: Tomous Leung   MAD: Kong Tao Hoi
PC: Media Asia Films Production
Simon Yam, Veronica Yip, Farini Chang, Gilbert Lam, Almen Wong, Peter Ngor
[1/2]**

The lovely Veronica Yip is a top-notch surgeon who suddenly feels empty and misguided in her life at the hospital. Her lapses almost cause the death of a patient, so she decides to pack up and take a leave of absence. Her road leads to a wild life of partying and having fun. She recognizes a slightly retarded fellow (Simon Yam) and takes an interest in him. When she was at the hospital, he was brought in by police officials. He is a notorious gangster who has lost his memory and become retarded. She finds a common bond within the simple man and takes it upon herself to help him recuperate. When her lapse of judgement almost results in the death of a patient, she leaves the hospital and enjoys life on the wild side. One day, she bumps into the retarded man and begins a relationship. Suddenly, the film takes a drastic turn as Simon remembers his past and goes off to fight in a gang war. Perhaps a little more development would have been nicer than a pointless and sudden turn toward violence.

Scent of Green Papaya, The
(1993) DramaC-104m   **Vietnamese with English Subtitles VA**   **Catalog #74343**
France/Vietnam   **Retail: $19.95**

Dir/Scr: Tran Anh Hung	**Prod: Christophe Rossignon**
DP: Benoit Delhomme	**Editor: Nicole DeDieu, Jean-Pierre Roques**
Prod Design: Eric Dangremont	**Set Design: Alain Negre, Claude Sune**
Sp Fx: Cleo Daran	**Makeup: Amelie Rouffio**
Costumes: Jean-Philippe Abril	
PC: Les Productions Lazennec	**Dist: Columbia Tristar Home Video**
Tran Nu Yen-Khe	**Mui Age 20**
Lu Man San	**Mui Age 10**
Truong Thi Loc	**The Mother**
Nguyen Anh Hoa	**Old Thi**
Vuong Hoa Hoi	**Khuyen**
Tran Ngoc Trung	**Father**
Talisman Vantha	**Thu**
Souvannavong Keo	**Trung**
Nguyen Van Oanh	**Mr. Thuan**
Neth Gerard	**Tin**
Do Nhat	**Lam**
Vo Thi Hai	**Grandmother**
Bui Lam Huy	**Doctor**
Nguyen Xuan Thu	**Antique Dealer**

[***]

Sensual film about a young woman growing up in 1950's Vietnam. Mui is a 10 year old peasant girl sold into servitude who spends the next ten years blossoming into a woman. She spends her life in a troubled family and must avoid advances while obeying her duties. Eventually she finds romance with her new employer, a young pianist. Hung's directorial debut and based on his childhood accounts filmed in France. An enchanting romance from a country remembered best for its war and not its cinematic presence in the world.

Secret Rivals
(1976) Kung-Fu   **C-90m Dubbed**   **Hong Kong**   **Retail: $19.99**
Dir: Ng See Yuen   **Dist: Tamo Video**
John Liu, Wong Tao, Huang Cheng Li, James Nam
[**1/2]

Director Ng proves that you can make entertaining kung-fu movies without the massive sets, costumes, and extras found at giant studios like Shaw Brothers. John Liu plays a mysterious character who befriends a young martial artist and saves his life. The martial artist is in search of killers who murdered his colleagues. He meets a beautiful Japanese/Chinese woman who heals him after he was injured in a fight. Meanwhile, Liu tracks down the killers and uses his amazing kicks to take care of any villains. In the climactic battle, the two join forces to defeat the evil master. The film's story is weak at times with mediocre acting, but if you admire martial arts, Liu's kicking skills truly shine in this film. A classic example of an entertaining genre film, where good martial arts over everything else saves the film. Liu is the standout and his fights with a pair of weapon-wielding killers and against the evil master are quite memorable. Also a training scene with Liu will appeal to fans of kung-fu films.

Seven Samurai
(1954) Samurai   B&W-203m   Japanese with English Subtitles   VA
Catalog # SEV 080   Japan Retail: $34.95
Dir: Akira Kurosawa   Scr: Shinobu Hashimoto, Hideo Oguni, Akira Kurosawa
Prod: Shojiro Motoki   Editor: Akira Kurosawa
DP: Asakazu Nakai
Music: Fumio Hayasaka   Art Design: So Matsuyama
PC: Toho   Dist: Public Media Home Vision

Takashi Shimura	**Kambei**
Toshiro Mifune	**Kikuchiyo**
Yoshio Inaba	**Gorobei**
Seiji Miyaguchi	**Kyuzo**
Minoru Chiaki	**Heihachi**
Daisuke Kato	**Shichiroji**
Ko Kimura	**Katsushiro**
Kuninori Kodo	**Gisaku**
Kamatari Fujiwara	**Manzo**
Yoshio Tsuchiya	**Rikichi**
Bokuzen Hidari	**Yohei**
Yoshio Kosugi	**Mosuke**
Keiji Sakakida	**Gosaku**
Jiro Kumagai	**Gisaku's Son**
Haruko Toyama	**Gisaku's Daughter-in-Law**
Fumiko Homma	**Peasant Woman**
Ichiro Chiba	**Priest**
Tsuneo Katagiri	**Peasants**
Yasuhisa Tsutsumi	
Keiko Tsushima	**Shino**
Toranosuke Ogawa	**Grandfather**
Gen Shimizu	**Masterless Samurai**
Jun Tasaki	**Big Samurai**
Isao Yamagata	**Samurai**
Jun Tatari	**Laborer**
Atsushi Watanabe	**Vendor**

Yukiko Shimazaki	Rikichi's Wife
Sojin Jr.	Minstrel
Shimpei Takagi	Bandit Chief

Eijiro Higashino, Kichijiro Ueda, Akira Tani, Haruo Nakajima, Takashi Narita, Senkichi Omura, Shuno Takahara, Masanobu Okubo, Eijiro Tono

[****]

If a survey was taken by filmmakers and critics to list the best foreign films in cinema history, Seven Samurai would surely be reserved a spot. One of Kurosawa's finest film which translates into one of the finest films to be produced in Japan. The story is simple, a timeless classic, but under Kurosawa's direction and brilliant performances by Shimura, Kimura, and Mifune has transcended beyond the action genre. In the 1600's, Japan is unified under one lord, Shogun Tokugawa Ieyasu, and many samurai find themselves unemployed and without service. These masterless samurai "ronin" traveled the country in search of a livelihood. An aged veteran of the wars, Kambei, arrives at a small town populated by simple farmers. The villagers are wary of the strange samurai and live in a state of poverty and fear. Kambei discovers that the villagers are repeatedly attacked by a group of well-armed bandits. The penniless samurai strikes a deal with the village leaders and sets off to recruit warriors to defend the village. One by one, the samurais are gathered in the village, help train the villagers, and prepare for war. Some of them like Katsushiro fall in love with a local woman, while the other warriors maintain a professional distance, or squabble amongst themselves. The seventh samurai is Kikuchio, played with bravado and energy by Mifune. He's a hot-headed braggart who despises the villagers' cowardice and walks proudly among the samurai. In reality, he is the son of a farmer. He resents and disguises his shameful past. In the end, four of the warriors fall in the battle and the villagers resume their normal lives. A must see masterpiece and one of the greatest samurai films ever made. The film is shot in black and white, and quite lengthy, so two separate sittings may be required. The familiar story was remade into the western "The Magnificent Seven" and the scifi piece "Battle Beyond the Stars".

Shadow of China

(1991) DramaC-100m   PG-13   Japan
Dir: Mitsuo Yanagimachi   Scr: Mitsuo Yanagimachi, Richard Maxwell
Prod: Elliott Lewitt, Don Guest   Ex. Prod: Satoru Iseki
DP: Toyomichi Kurita   Editor: Sachiko Yamagi   Music: Yasuaki Shimizu
Prod Design: Andrew McAlpine   Costume: Sandy Powell
PC: Marubeni/Nippon Herald Films/Fuji/Nissho Iwai/Sunrise, Inc.
Dist: New Line Cinema
(based on the novel "Snake Head" by Masaaki Nishiki)

John Lone	Henry
Vivian Wu	Moo-Ling
Sammi Davis	Katherine
Koichi Sato	Akira
Roland Harrah III	Xiao Niu
Roy Chiao	Lee Hok Chow
Colin George	Burke
Kenneth Tsang	Mr. Lau

Dennis Chan   **Mr. Wu**
Fredric Mao   **Chi Fung**
[***]

"October 1976
The violent political in-fighting that took
place after Mao Tse-tung's death ended with the
arrests of the Gang of Four. Some were forced to
flee China after fierce armed battles. And some left
because their idealistic revolution had collapsed."

Opening Card

An interesting film that never garnered much publicity or attention in the United States. The film opens with disturbing, true-life images of mainland China's oppression and emotional sorrow. John Lone and Vivian Wu are two young Chinese patriots protesting against communist oppression. The two are putting up anti-government leaflets when the police crack down on them. They both attempt to escape to Hong Kong, but Vivian sacrifices herself to allow John to escape. He does so and many years later, he becomes a rich industrialist in Hong Kong. In the meantime, Vivian spent many years in a re-education camp and comes to Hong Kong. Old memories start to stir and both characters have new feelings for each other and secrets which they must keep in the past. A Japanese photojournalist takes an interest in Lone's life as well as falling for the charms of Vivian. Lone's life is changed and he senses responsibility for his actions. Realizing he can not escape his past, he leaves behind his fortune and he returns to mainland China. Based on the Japanese bestseller Snakehead.

Shall We Dance?
(1996) Romance/Drama
C-118m   **Japanese with English Subtitles**   **PG-13**
Japan
Dir/Scr: Masayuki Suo
Koji Yakusho   **Shohei Sugiyama**
Tamiyo Kusakari   **Mai Kishikawa**
Naoto Takenaka   **Tomio Aoki**
Eriko Watanabe   **Toyoko Takahashi**
Yu Tokui   **Tokichi Hattori**
[***1/2]

A delightful film about a typical Japanese businessman who decides to stir up his life by enrolling in ballroom dancing classes with a beautiful instructor. The plight of his life may seem familiar, he has the wife, child, the job, the picturesque life, but the sign from the dance school draws him like a voice in his soul. He develops an infatuation with his dance partner and befriends the eclectic group of other students. Pleasant, artfully directed, and engaging characters from beginning to end but the nuances of Japanese salarymen lives might not translate for all audiences. A fairly good Hollywood remake starring Richard Gere is available.

Shanghai Grand   **(New Shanghai Bund)**
(1996) Crime C-107m   **Chinese with English Subtitles**   **Type II**
Catalog #ML 679   **Hong Kong**   **Retail: $39.99**

Dir: Tsui Hark   Scr: Sandy Siu Lai-king, Matthew Poon Man-kit, Chow Hoi-kwong
Leslie Cheung, Andy Lau, Ning Jing, Amanda Lee Wai-man, Wu Xingguo, Liu Xun
[***]

A lush, opulent-looking film set in Shanghai before the start of World War II. Based on a television series; therefore, dedicated purists might be disappointed with the new reincarnation. On its own, the film is an interesting blend of action and romance broken into a storybook format. The film is divided into three chapters, dealing with each of the main characters involved in a love triangle. Leslie Cheung and Andy Lau are both in love with the same woman, a wealthy daughter of a maniacal Shanghai Triad boss. The film does seem to waver in its commitment of romance versus a seedy film involving the criminal world. Scenes pop into the film which seem akin to fantasy kung-fu films and may leave some wondering what's happening to the contemporary plot. Veteran Tsui Hark is trying to appease both sides of the coin, mixing genre elements, and falls into the loophole of not completely appeasing the action fans or the romance fans. Still, Shanghai Grand is a beautifully shot film with vintage costumes, sets, and atmosphere. The charm of the actors do reach beyond the misguided story direction and allows the viewer to be entertained in their complicated circumstances.

Shanghai Triad
(1995) Crime DramaC-109m   Mandarin with English Subtitles   R   VA
Catalog #VHS 11853China Retail: $19.95
Dir: Zhang Yimou   Scr: Bi Feiyu
Prod: Jean-Louis Piel   Ex. Prod: Zhu Yongde, Wang Wei
Produced for the UGC Yves Marmion
PC: Shanghai Film Studio, Alpha Films, UGC Images and Le Sept Cinema
Dist: Sony Pictures Classics

Gong Li	**Xiao Jingbao**
Li Baotian	**The Godfather**
Li Xuejian	**Liu Shu**
Wang Xiao Xiao	**Shuisheng**
Shun Chun Shusheng	**Number Two**
Jiang Baoying	

[***1/2]

American audiences familiar with actress Gong Li will be exposed to a different side of her acting persona. Instead of a strong, noble peasant woman, Gong is a seductive nightclub singer involved with the Chinese mob. In the seventh collaboration between Li and director Zhang Yimou, the story unfolds from a boy's point of view who recently arrives in Shanghai. Because his last name is the same as the triad leader, his uncle recruits him into the organization. His task is to serve the leader's pampered mistress, a wily, hot-tempered singer. At first, Gong Li seems superficial, a beautiful woman with a powerful lover who has a life of luxury; her own home, servants, a fancy car, clothes, jewelry, and wealth. She treats the new boy harshly (Cuihua) and scolds him for the simplest mistake. He keeps quiet, but a streak of defiance gets him into trouble with the mistress. Slowly, he learns that the mistress is having an affair with one of the leader's lieutenants. Situations heat up when a gang attacks the Shanghai Triad, killing Cuihua's uncle and injuring the triad leader. The wounded leader, his mistress with Cuihua, and his entourage decide to escape the city and let situations cool down. On a remote island, Gong reawakens her rural past and realizes her wrongful path. She hopes to find new purpose in her life, but is unaware that the triad leader has discovered her relationship with his lieutenant. A tragic end befalls the lovers and the world of crime wins a round in life.

Director Zhang's film is a brilliant study of humanity and spheres of influence. Lives are affected and subjugated by the powers around us. The cinematography and technical splendor of Shanghai and the countryside are the finest offered on film and the story's subtle but powerful emotions swirl with deceit, passion, and the loss of humanity.

Shaolin Challenges Ninja - See Challenge of the Ninja
Shaolin Deadly Kicks
(1980) Kung-Fu   C-91m Dubbed   Catalog #4065   Hong Kong
Retail: $9.99
Dir: Wu Ma   Scr: Chu Hsiang Kan   Prod: Tung Chen Ching
Editor: Ko Tan Hung   Music: Chow Fook Leung
Prod Manager: Chen Man Chi   Supervisor: Kuan Shan
Planning: Wang Feng   MAD: Huang Lung   Makeup: Wu Mai
PC: Wha Tai Motion Picture Co.   Dist: Simitar Entertainment, Inc.
Tan-Tao Liang, Lo Lieh, Wang Hop, Lung Kuan E, Kam Kong, Lo Dak, Choi Hung
[**]
The ruthless Eight Dragons gang have pulled the biggest job of their criminal life. They decide to separate and reunite later when the police heat goes down. A paid stool pigeon tells the officer, he'll find the dragons at Eagle Gorge at noon. Of course it's a trap, and dozens of bamboo spears fall down on him. He fakes his own death and goes undercover as a criminal to get closer to the dragons. Veteran villain Lo Lieh is the final dragon who manages to get all eight pieces of the map. Using his chain claw, he battles the officer and his girlfriend in the woods. Generic martial arts and action film that loses quite a bit over time.

Shaolin Handlock
(1981) Kung-Fu   C-93m Dubbed   Hong Kong   Retail: $19.99
Dir: Ho Menga
David Chiang, Chen Hui-Min, Chen Ping, Lo Lieh
[**]
A contemporary action plot that uses a physical gimmick as the main focus of the story. An evil master murders his rival and takes over his assets and marries his wife. The children are brought up by the master, but one son is separated and vows vengeance. He develops a special technique called the Shaolin Handlock which is nothing more than a throat lock with leverage placed on the side of the head and back. This lock is supposedly unbreakable and can kill its opponent instantly. Chiang plans to use the lock on the evil master, so he infiltrates the villain's headquarters. However, his own brother stands in the way and believes the evil master is his real father. Their mother tells her misguided son the truth, that his stepfather killed his real father and forced her to become his wife. Now reunited, the family vows to kill the villain, trapping him in a warehouse and using the dreaded Shaolin handlock. The evil master aware of the deadly technique uses hidden knives inside the elbows of his jacket. The two brothers manage to use their martial arts in unison and win the day. An average film from the early eighties with a low budget appeal, but interesting for David Chiang's charisma and the campy use of the Shaolin

Handlock.

Shaolin Invincibles
(1977) Kung-Fu   C-90m Dubbed   Hong Kong   Retail: $9.99
Dir: Cheng Hou, Yuen Cheung Yeung   Scr: C.Y. Yang, Wei-Min Chiang
Dist: Simitar
Carter Wong, Judy Lee Chia Ling, Tan Tao-Liang, Lung Chung-Erh
[*1/2]
You may recognize Carter Wong, the muscular star of many martial arts films. Brother and sister warriors set out on a quest to battle an evil martial artist. They finally find him at an enormous palace and battle all over the surrounding terrain. The most notably funny (worse scene) is when the duo are walking through the fields and are attacked by wild gorillas. Carter uses his kung-fu to dispatch the primates, but then the apes (monkey see, monkey do) come back at him doing martial arts. They flip, kick, and chop their way into battle. A few decent fight scenes pop up but the film is rather forgettable and poorly produced by today's tastes. Only recommended for campy and worse films made lovers.

Shaolin Kung-fu Kids
(1995) Comedy Kung-Fu   C-92m Chinese with English Subtitles
Catalog #1783   Hong Kong   Retail: $39.99
Dir: Peter Yuen   Dist: Tai Seng Video
Roger Kwok, Chu Yan
[1/2]**
This is a perfect example of how Chinese films blend a variety of genres into one. Part romance, part comedy, and all kung-fu grace this "Home Alone" inspired film. A group of Shaolin kung-fu experts are invited to perform an exhibition in the United States. The head abbot and the junior monks escort a dozen boys adept at Shaolin kung-fu. One of the students is a young boy who likes to fool around and not train too hard. He gets separated from his fellow monks while on a journey to Hong Kong. Alone and with no money, he befriends a young woman and a young man. Coincidences befall every character in the film, but there is a sense of childish charm to the film. The young woman and the young man both claim to be police officers, one is from Hong Kong, the other is from China. They both try to help the lost kid and bring him home. There they discover their single parents are long-lost lovers. They were to meet at a rendezvous point, but got the times mixed up and never saw each other again. They spend the entire time fighting, blaming each other, and falling in love again. So do their kids which are from separate and ended marriages. Along the way, the spoiled fat kid tries to make life tough on the perfect Shaolin kid. The fat kid joins a gang, gets kidnaped, and causes problems for everyone. In true Hollywood fashion, a crucial ball game is rescued from defeat when the Shaolin kids enter the competition. At first they play by the rules and lose, but they win by using their martial arts skills in the game. Cute, harmless fun targeted toward children.

Shaolin Plot
(198?) Kung-Fu   C-102m   Chinese with English Subtitles   Hong Kong
Retail: $19.99
Dir/Scr: Huang Feng

James Tien, Casanova, Samo Hung, Yuen Biao (cameo), Wang Hsia, Yung Wen, Yuan Sheng, Li Yiu Ken, Chin Kang, Kuan Shan
[**1/2]
Though dated by modern film standards, Shaolin Plot is a familiar story with some good martial arts scenes. Especially delightful is Samo Hung (an early role) as a ruthless and despicable monk, and Biao's brief cameo in the beginning of the movie. The story is all too familiar and the film suffers from some loose editing, over-zooming, and a poor print transfer. The High Prince Dalgen of the Imperial Manchurian Dynasty is a despot bent on learning every martial arts style in China. Fighting techniques are written down in manuals, coveted and guarded as valuable heirlooms among the various martial arts sects. When the Prince is foiled by patriotic Chinese who despise Manchurian involvement, violence is the only solution. James Tien plays the son of the master of the Wu Tang School. His master is killed and the manual stolen by the evil monk (Hung). Tien is saved by a Shaolin grandmaster who is blinded in the battle. Tien then carries on in traditional fashion of training, but ironically disappears for a good portion of the film and doesn't even play a major part in the final battle. Instead, the film shifts over to the last remaining school of martial arts, Shaolin Temple. Prince Dalgen is denied the manual, so he disguises himself as a deaf and mute monk with a really bad plastic eyeball. While living at Shaolin, he secretly reads the Shaolin manuals and kills anyone who gets in his way. Tien discovers the plot, but the monks are not enthusiastic about his presence and engage in a long fight. The fact that every Shaolin disciple is a master of martial arts raises the stakes. When it is discovered Tien is the student of the Shaolin grandmaster, they let him pass, but are too late. Prince Dalgen has taken hostage the Head Abbot and retreats to his well-guarded palace. Tien and an elite group of monks travel to do battle and free their master. Shaolin Plot may be more of a running gag than a title, since hundreds of movies have been made with similar stories, but for some reason, the fascinating aspects of Shaolin and the large cast make this film somewhat entertaining for fans.

Shaolin Temple
(1980) Kung-Fu   C-90m Dubbed   Hong Kong   Retail: $19.99
Dir: Chan Hsin Yeh
Jet Li, Yu Hai, Yu Cheng Hu
[***]
The film that launched Jet Li's career and sparked two sequels. Produced in mainland China, Jet Li was part of the National Wushu team and a natural choice for the lead role. Young, energetic, charismatic, with a whimsical smile, he brought a unique sense of charm and had amazing martial arts skills to boot. Jet Li is a young Shaolin monk who gets in trouble because of mischief, but eventually redeems himself in the eyes of his master. Typical scenes of monks training, getting in trouble with the head abbot, and fighting when necessary. Plenty of wonderful training scenes within Shaolin Temple, also avoids the use of special wire techniques more commonly seen in Jet Li's newer films. It is a pleasure to see Li at an early age, showcasing his amazing physical prowess.

Shaolin Temple 2
(1983) Kung-Fu   C-102m   Dubbed   Hong Kong
Dir: Chan Hsin Yeh

Jet Li, Wong Chiu Yin, Din Nan
[***]
Jet Li is just your average Shaolin monk who happens to have a vendetta against a ruthless and powerful lord who murdered his father. The abbot took pity on Jet Li and raised him within the temple. When the lord regains his status in the court, Jet Li breaks away from the temple and goes after revenge. He leaves Shaolin with the help of some young children and disguises himself as an entertainer. He attends the evil lords birthday party and plans to assassinate him. At the same time, a group of rebels plan the same thing and everyone's paths get crossed and the assassination fails. The troops move in, and in the panic, everyone flees. While fleeing, Jet Li teams up with two of the rebels. Unbeknownst to him, one of the rebels is disguised as a female. The trio have their differences and bicker, but eventually team up when they discover their common cause. Along the way, a love triangle develops and Li discovers he was originally betrothed to the female rebel. Torn between his love for her and his faith to Shaolin (monks must be unwed), he allows the other rebel warrior to win her hand. They attempt to escape to Shaolin Temple and fight troops along the way, including border guards at the Great Wall of China. The impressive climatic battle takes place atop the evil lord's floating palace. Not only does Jet Li and his friends fight hundreds of well-armed soldiers, but a brigade of Shaolin monks enter the hi-paced battle and twirl their staffs and save the day in true Hollywood cavalry fashion. Almost any film starring Jet Li promises to be action-packed and quite entertaining...this film is no exception. A worthy addition to the Shaolin Temple series.

Shaolin Temple 3
(1985) Kung-Fu   C-100m   Dubbed   Hong Kong
Dir: Liu Chia Liang
Jet Li, Yu Hai, Yu Cheng Hu
[**1/2]
Don't laugh, but this is a family kung-fu film with lots of little girls and boys performing flips and doing kicks. The opening credits are animated with a fairytale like song explaining the classic rivalry between Shaolin and Wu-Tang Schools of martial arts. On one side of the river, a group of boys study Shaolin and the girls, on the other side, study Wu-Tang sword style. Conveniently, the children range in all ages and make a perfect Brady Bunch matchup for each other. The two groups bicker and fight, always trying to prove which style is superior and just being kids. As the kids get older, love is in the air and matches are made. The boys are all orphans raised by a kind monk who saved them from death. He teaches them Shaolin kung-fu and prepares for the day to take revenge against their oppressors. The girls are from a wealthy family and their father is not so approving of their relationship with the Shaolin boys. The villains who murdered the orphans' real parents track down the surviving Shaolin kids and plan to extract revenge through ploy and tactics. They use the Wu Tang clan to their advantage, but their plot is revealed and both sides join forces and attack the villains. A lot of fun martial arts and a charismatic cast of kids makes this film different than the average film.

Shaolin Traitor
(1982) Kung-Fu   C-94m Dubbed   Hong Kong   Retail: $19.99
Dir: David Lin   Scr: Chou Kao   Prod: Li Chia Hsin
DP: Huang Yen Pei Editor: Huang Chiu Kuei   Music: Chou Fu Liang

MAD: Ko Pao   Prod Manager: Cheung Kuo Lien
Prod Designer: Liu Ni Tsu   Stage Supervisor: Liang Tung Lang
Camera: Chung Shen   Effects: Wang Shih Ni   Technician: Lin Chang Lien
Continuity: Chen Chun Yu Makeup: Cheung Pi Yung   Costume: Sun Chih Yung
Dist: Video Gems
Carter Wong, Lung Chun Erh, Cheung I, Chiang Nan, Lao Ping, Lung Fei, Chuan Yuan,
Nan Shao Fu, Su Chen Ping, Liu Yen Kao, Liu San
[**]
Someone is killing the monks of Shaolin Temple, and all evidence points from within the temple.
Heroic Shaolin monk-in-training Carter Wong (with hair) is always at the wrong place at the
wrong time. He is caught red-handed on numerous murders and blamed for the murder of the
Shaolin monks. In a desperate attempt to clear his name, he escapes from Shaolin Temple and
searches for the real killer. Meanwhile, the rare jade staff is stolen from Shaolin Temple. It was
a gift from the Manchu Emperor who sends his daughter to find out its whereabouts. If the
monks can not recover the rare gift, they will commit mass suicide as penitence for their loss. A
pretty stiff penalty which will cause the end of Shaolin Temple. The new Head Abbot puts a
bounty on Carter's head and a bevy of kung-fu experts attack under all guises. Carter eventually
hooks up with a cute woman who believes his cause. She has been sent by an ex-renegade
Shaolin monk who once trained Carter. The story loses some points as the film's plot meanders
and no clear cut villain electrifies the story. If you want a somewhat confused surprise, don't
read any further. Carter and his female friend go after the true Shaolin killer, a top-ranking
monk who is not a Buddhist but a spy sent from the Dali Lhama to infiltrate and destroy Shaolin
for their disgraceful lost. He had secretly made plans with the emperor, but betrays both sides.
He escapes into the Shaolin Temple's room of torture and traps, but is killed by Carter's renegade
master. Then the master attacks Carter revealing that he is a traitor who conspired to destroy
everyone from the start. Okay, if that's what he says, we'll take him word for it. Regardless of the
reason, master and student must battle each other to the death. At this point, I must confess that
this film does not rate too high in plot or character development. Most martial arts films from
this era follow a very set pattern of style and quality. If you are a Carter Wong fan, which I am,
there are some scenes of entertainment. The martial arts is standard, but decent, and there is a
nice little cat fight between the female hero and the evil princess.

Shaolin Wooden Men   (36 Wooden Men/Shaolin Chamber of Death)
(1976) Kung-Fu   C-103m   Dubbed   Hong Kong   Retail: $9.99
Dir: Lo Wei Prod: Hsu Li Hwa
Jackie Chan
[**]
A warrior undergoes a deadly test at the hands of his Shaolin teachers, in order to discover
whether or not he has the skills needed to avenge the death of his father. As a young child, the
mute Chan witnesses the murder of his father. He then seeks guidance under the Monks of the
Shaolin Temple. However, he finds the training too slow, so he trains under the guidance of a
prisoner at the Temple. His loyalties are then tested when his new master escapes and starts
killing people. A fairly standard film with the usual amount of kung-fu.

She Shoots Straight

(1990) Action C-90m Chinese with English Subtitles   Hong Kong
Dir: Corey Yuen   Prod: Samo Hung
Joyce Godenzi   Mina Kao
Tony Leung Kar Fai Tsung Pao
Carina Lau, Corey Yuen Wah, Agnes Aurelio, Samo Hung, Sandra Ng
[**1/2]
When first reviewing this movie, I did not have the luxury of subtitles and required the helpful
assistance of a Chinese-speaking friend. So my review may be slightly biased in that sense, but I
was reassured that a subtitled version is available. So check before you pick up this girls with
guns film. The film opens with a beautiful wedding between two police officers, Mina and
Tsung. Since Tsung and Mina are both officers in the line of duty, there is a serious fear that one
of them will be killed before they have a chance to raise a family. Situations are complicated
when Mina's heroic efforts give cause for some crooks to extract some revenge. The leader
(Yueh) lures Mina, Tsung, and fellow officer Carina to the edge of a forest and unleashes a
bloody ambush of traps. Tsung does not survive the ordeal, but Yueh eventually gets captured.
His girlfriend (Aurelio) tries to free him, but Mina and her officers are on the scene. In a brutal
and lengthy fight, Mina and Aurelio battle each other in an abandoned stockyard. Samo Hung
appears in a small role as the police chief. In real life, he married Godenzi in 1995. Entertaining
film of the Hong Kong girls with guns genre.

Shogun's Ninja
(1983) Samurai   C-115m   Dubbed   VA   Japan Retail: $9.99
Dir: Noribumi Suzuki   Scr: Takahito Ishikawa, Fumio Koyama, Ichiro Otsu
Ex. Prod: Shigeru Okada   Associate Prod: Goro Kusakabe, Tatsuo Honda
DP: Toro Nakajima, Shin Ogawahara   Editor: Isamu Ichida
Music Prod: Masakatsu Suzuki   Art Dir: Yoshikazu Sano
Set Design: Genzo Watanabe   Costume: Mamoru Mori, Masakatsu Suzuki
MAD: Sonny Chiba   PC: Toei Studios   Dist: Media Home
Sonny Chiba, Henry Sanada, Sue Shiomi, Shohei Hino, Yuki Ninagawa, Noribumi Suzuki,
Kazuma Hase, Go Awazu, Kumiko Hidaka, Maki Tachibana, Katsumasa Uchida
[***]
Shogun's Ninja is a fictional account of the historical ninjas who were involved in the unification
of Japan in the late 1500's. The story attempts to border between historical intrigue and martial
arts action while succeeding and failing at various points. The musical score is mired in over-
jazzed tunes that seem inappropriate, but overall the film is an entertaining vehicle that explores
a fascinating era in Japanese history. The film contains realistic and fantasy-levels of skills with
ninjas flying through trees and performing amazing feats, but the battles are fast and well-
choreographed with an interesting blend of characters. When Toyotomi Hideyoshi seizes power
of Japan, he orders his general (Chiba) to kill a powerful rival lord and confiscate his gold.
Chiba uses his ninjas (two ashen-haired twins) to murder the lord and family. In tragic tradition,
the dead lord's wife commits suicide and leaves behind a bloody flute. A loyal retainer helps the
lord's only son escape from the murderous ninjas. They escape to China where the young boy
grows up to become a master of Chinese and Japanese martial arts. Years later, Sanada is the
young hero who returns to Japan. He begins his quest for vengeance and joins a group of rebels.
Somehow, none of the original villains have aged over time and still resort to their bloody

methods of torture and assassination. Sanada fights his way into Chiba's camp, but is captured and tortured. The torture scenes should not be viewed by children. Sanada refuses to reveal the whereabouts of his family fortune which is desperately needed by Hidoeyoshi to finance his Korean campaign. Following Sanada from China is a female martial artist and her loyal companion. Sanada also discovers a Japanese woman who was part of his father's household as a child and possesses his mother's flute. She was rescued and adopted by ninja master Hattori Hanzo (true-life, famous ninja) who despises Hideyoshi and Chiba. A brief love triangle develops, but Sanada doesn't have time for romance as he plans his next move. United with a small contingency, six heroes armed with different weapons ambush Chiba and his entire army in a deep Japanese forest. An amazing battle of swords, shurikens, samurais, ninjas, arrows, and kicks erupts the countryside to the pleasure for fans of action, historical, and martial arts films. The finale is fast and furious with a good dose of camp and tragedy. Sanada discovers the two short swords he wielded contain hidden maps of his father's treasure. Rather than surrender the treasure to Hanzo, he casts the swords into the sea and rides off into the sunset with the girl of his dream.

Silent Mobius: The Motion Picture
(1991) Japanime: Scifi/Horror   C-60   Dubbed/Japanese with English Subtitles
VA   Catalog # 90793   Japan Retail: $24.95
Dir: Michitaka Kikuchi   Scr: Kia Asamiya   Music: Kaoru Wada
Art Dir: Norihiro Hiraki   PC: Kadokawa Publishing Co. Ltd.
Dist: Streamline Pictures
[***]
A clever mixture of supernatural witchcraft and cop-action in the hi-tech world of Japan. In Tokyo, 2028, a young woman, Katsumi Liquer, returns from American to visit her ill mother. While walking down a side street, Katsumi discovers a hidden past which draws her into a battle between humans and a demonic power from the beyond. The head demon, Lucifer Folk, senses her gifts and attempts to devour her life force. At first, she is skeptical and helpless to use her own powers, but eventually joins forces with the psychic police force. She parters with a spiritual healer dressed in a traditional kimono and a tough modern woman with cybernetically augmented strength. A number of supporting characters are also present, all women who possess skills adept at fighting the demons. The story is skillfully told through flashbacks and shows Katsumi as a naive woman and then an experienced AMP officer. The series is broken into two volumes which can be purchased separately and run sixty minutes each. The first volume is the most important, since it contains background information and a stronger story than the second which continues their adventures. The animation is of high quality and the childish antics of many animated films are absent in this serious combination of drama and horror. A personal favorite and not recommended for young children due to its satanic references and animated violence.

Silent Mobius 2
(1992) Japanime: Scifi/Horror   C-60   Dubbed/Japanese with English Subtitles
VA   Japan
Dir: Yasunori Ide   Scr: Michitaka Kikuchi
Goro Naya, Lisa Ann Beley, Don Brown

324

[***]
A commendable sequel, but not as memorable as the original film. Silent Mobius 2 follows the further exploits of Katsumi Liquer and her battle against demons from another world. The first film deals with Katsumi in her present position as an AMP officer and flashbacks to her arrival in Japan to see her mother. As a young woman, her mother sacrificed her life to help Katsumi beat the demons. The second film follows the days after those flashback events and stays within one framework of time. What the film mostly focuses on is background information on why Katsumi stayed and her new found friends who become life-long teammates in the first film. The film doesn't have the emotional impact of the first film nor the life and death struggle against the demon lord, Lucifer Folk. Back again is Kiddy the muscular cyborg and Nami the psychic priest. Also the Chief and Lebia get their share of action. Special attention is focused on Yuki who befriends Katsumi. Once again, two demons from Lucifer Folk are still present in the Earth's spiritual dimension and resonant around an old suspension bridge. They sense the power of Gigelf within Katsumi and wish to subvert it for their own use. Katsumi who has gone through the shock of demonic horrors and the death of her mother just wants to return to Hawaii and get on with a normal life. The AMP officers revoke her rights and force her to stay in Japan while keeping an eye on her. An elderly man and a beautiful girl take residence in Katsumi's mother's old house. Katsumi is drawn to the house and eventually must face her fears and overcome her doubts. The entire AMP team try to fight off the two demons, but it is only Katsumi who can defeat them. The closing is a montage of scenes as Katsumi grows into a veteran AMP agent, fighting against demons with resounding courage. A sequel is promised and eagerly waited.

Slaughter in San Francisco
(1981) Kung-Fu   C-92m English   R
Dir: William Lowe   Dist: Rhino Home Video
Don Wong, Chuck Norris
[*]
Sub-standard Hong Kong-style action film set in San Francisco, capitalizing on Chuck Norris' growing fame (Bruce Lee's nemesis in Return of the Dragon). Don Wong is the typical action hero who decides to stand up against the corruption and murder plaguing the streets of San Francisco. He's assigned to take down the ruthless Norris who walks with emotionless ease, knocking down opponents with a backward glance of his fist. The hero gets a few licks, but when the climax roles around there is no doubt to who's the victor.

Slayers, The: Volume I
(1995) Japanime: Fantasy   C-100m   Dubbed/Japanese with English Subtitles
VA   Catalog # SSVD-9410   Japan Retail: $19.95
Dir: Takashi Watanabe, Makoto Noriza, Osamu Yokota, Masato Sato
Original Story: Hajime Kanazaka, Rui Araizumi
Scr: Hajime Kanazaka, Rui Araizumi   Prod: Zen Enoki, Kazuto Imanishi
PC: TV TOKYO, SOFTX   Dist: Software Sculptors
[**1/2]
The first volume is a compilation of four episodes based on the Japanese animated series The Slayers. A number of other volumes exist which also contain multiple episodes continuing the

story. Fantasy based, the story deals with Lina Inverse, a perky female sorceress who happens to be a thief and a warrior. The action is fast-paced, but a heavy does of comedy also lends itself to immature slapstick. Lina spends much of the time in off-camera comments and vainglorious narration. Her misadventures start when she attacks the Fang Gang and relieves them of some of their treasure. One of the items is a cursed blade and the other is a statuette. One of them holds a key to releasing a demonic power and is being pursued by minions of the demon lord. Lina teams up with a young, not-so-bright, warrior with blonde hair. For profit and fun, the two battle dragons, zombies, bandits, and the evil minions who hope to steal the magic artifact under Lina's possession. Along the way they meet one of the five great sorcerers (Rezo) who helps them on their exciting adventure. A fun mix of comedy and fantasy. In general, I prefer subtitled versions that maintain the original voice soundtrack, but in this case the dubbed version is done very well and the English voices seem appropriate to the characters portrayed.
Episode 1: ANGRY? Lina's Furious Dragon Slave!
Episode 2: BAD! Mummy Men Aren't My Type!
Episode 3: CRASH! Red and White and Suspicious All Over!
Episode 4: DASH! Run for it! My Magic Doesn't Work!

Slayers, The: Volume II
(1995) Japanime: Fantasy   C-75m
Dubbed/Japanese with English Subtitles   VA   Japan
VA   Catalog # SSVD-9411   Japan Retail: $19.95
Dir: Takashi Watanabe, Makoto Noriza, Osamu Yokota, Masato Sato
Original Story: Hajime Kanazaka, Rui Araizumi
Scr: Hajime Kanazaka, Rui Araizumi   Prod: Zen Enoki, Kazuto Imanishi
PC: TV TOKYO, SOFTX   Dist: Software Sculptors
[1/2]**
Only three episodes on volume two which basically carry the same style of humor, though elements are not as fresh. Continues the wild adventures of Lina Inverse and her friends who battle against Rezo, the Red Sorcerer. Lina and her friends discover the truth about their magical relic and must stay away from Rezo who reveals his true purpose. The band of heroes are pursued by all types of monsters and wizards, but manage to win and stay ahead of their captors. The episodes are full of situational comedy and visual sight gags which border on the juvenile. The series is hardly over and if you like the first few episodes, other episodes are available in English or Japanese.

Snake and Crane Arts of Shaolin
(1977) Kung-Fu   C-93m Dubbed   VA
Hong Kong   Retail: $9.99
Dir: Chen Chih Hua Prod: Hsu Li Hwa   Ex. Prod: Lo Wei
Prod Designer: Chu Shih-Mei   Prod Manager: Li Hsien-Chang
MAD: Jackie Chan, Du Wei Her   PROD: Lo Wei Productions, Inc.
Dist: Entertainment Programs International
Jackie Chan   Su Yin Fong
Nora Miao, Kum Kong, Kim Ching Lan, Lee Yung Kun, Liu Ya Ying
[1/2]**

Throughout Chinese films and novels, Shaolin Temple is well known as a Buddhist place of retreat for its monks and a training ground for the best martial artists in China. Eight grandmasters of Shaolin kung-fu have gathered to combine their knowledge into inventing a powerful style known as the "Eight Steps of the Snake and Crane". They are secretly poisoned and their bodies disappear, as does the manual containing the Snake and Crane style. Much later, a strange young man appears with the lost kung-fu manual. Jackie Chan plays Su Yin Fong and unlike many of his earlier films, he doesn't require any training already excelling in martial arts. One by one, assassins and masters from other kung-fu clans: Black Dragon, Flying Tiger, Beggars and Wu Tang attempt to steal the manual. Chan also befriends a dirty beggar named Wong Chu who secretly is a woman and the daughter of the master of the Flying Tiger. If you want little plot and lots of action, this Chan film delivers plenty of enjoyable martial arts sequences throughout the film. Eventually the good clans team up with Chan who is in search of the true killer of the eight Shaolin grandmasters. This time out Chan avoids the classic training-plot and moves through the story with a high number of energetic fight scenes with a variety of performers. The fun and the excitement never slows down.

Snake Fist Fighter
(197?) Kung-Fu   C-83m Dubbed   VA
Catalog # 3608-B   Hong Kong   Retail: $9.99
Dir: Chin Hsin   Prod: Lee Long Koan
MAD: Chan Yuen Lung, Se Fu Yai   Dist: Simitar Entertainment Inc.
Jackie Chan, Juan Hsao Ten, Shth Tien, Han Kuo Tsai, Yuen Bill, Chang Chin, Kuen Yung Man
[**]
In this film, Chan's training scenes are shown as flashbacks when he was a very young child. What is suppose to be seen as scenes of endurance and training could easily be interpreted as child abuse, brutality, and depravity. The young Chan is tortured by an old beggar who uses some very bizarre techniques to teach martial arts. The lessons/tortures pay off and Chan becomes a talented martial artist. He is a waiter who befriends a local pickpocket and comes into conflict with the boss. As in most martial arts stories, one beating leads to the next. Conflicts escalate when the gangsters decide to kill the pickpocket and get their revenge on Chan. None of the fight scenes really carry any of the Chan trademarks and are rather mediocre. A long line of fight scenes follow in which Chan keeps running into the gangsters. The end is followed with the climatic showdown between Chan and the main villain.

Snake in the Eagles Shadow(The Eagle's Shadow)
(1978) Kung-Fu   C-97m Hong Kong   Retail: $9.99
Dir : Yuen Woo Ping   Script: Jackie Chan
Jackie Chan, Juan Jon Lee, Simon Yuen, Shi Tien Chiu Chi-Ling, Chen Hsia, Wang Chang, Louis Feng
[**1/2]
The last remaining master of the snake style of kung-fu, decides to take on a student to ensure the survival of his style of combat. Chan accepts the role with hesitancy, but performs with bravado when villains appear, hoping to kill his master. A vigorous blend of kung fu and comedy, the first film of this type starring Jackie Chan.

Sohryuden: Volume 1 "Legend of the Dragon Kings"
(1991) Japanime   C-97m (each volume)   VA
Japanese with English Subtitles   Catalog # USM 1324   Japan Retail: $29.95
Dir: Shigeru Ueda, Yoshihiro Yamaguchi
(based on the original novel by Yoshiki Tanaka published in Japan by Kodansha)
Music: Susumu Aketagawa Art Dir: Shichiro Kobayashi   Sound Dir: Osamu Dezaki
Character Design: Shunji Murata Ex. Prod: Hidenori Taga, Koichi Murakami, Sosaku Miki
English Version - Ex. Prod: John O'Donnell   Prod Coordinator: Stephanie Shalofsky
Subtitling: Studio NEMO   Tranlastion: William Flanagan, Yuko Sato
English Rewrite: Jay Parks
Lyric Rewrite: David Mayhew   Package Design: Mark Weiss
PC: Yoshiki Tanaka/Kitty Films/Fuji TV/Kodansha
Dist: Central Park Media Corporation (US Manga Corps)
[**1/2]
In modern Tokyo, the handsome Ryudo brothers live a life of luxury and ease. Then they're accused of murdering their uncle's family and go on the run from the law and a mysterious figure named Kamakura no Gozen. In truth, the four Ryudo brothers are descendants of the lengendary Dragons Kings and possess amazing physical and psychic powers. Even when caught in death, their bodies transform into gigantic dragons which then re-incarnate back into their human form. Gozen uses his connection and powerful influence to lure the brothers into a military training site where he attempts to kill them and drain their dragon's blood. The brothers manage to escape the dragon-demon Gozen and his deadly red beret troops. Then they're off to Tokyo Fairyland for a little rest and relaxation, but a powerful organization sends their henchman to capture the four brothers and their sweet cousin. In the background, Lady L watches and waits for the perfect opportunity. The Ryudo's are separated at the amusement park and must battle animal-costumed killers, before they escape on a boat and use their powers to take care of the killers once and for all. The series is paced like television episodes with a new threat introduced in each episode which is then solved at the end. Cousin Matsuri Toba provides narration and introduction of key elements in the story. Interesting with a number of well-developed characters and subplots which are further developed as the series goes on...Lady L. The animation isn't quite as polished as modern full-length features or OAV's.
Episode 1: The Four Brothers Under Fire
Episode 2: The Legend of Dragon Springs
More volumes have been released.
Sohryuden: Volume 2   Catalog # USM 1325   Retail: $29.95
Episode 3: Black Dragon King Revealed
Episode 4: Tokyo Bay Rhapsody
Sohryuden: Volume 3   Catalog # USM 1326   Retail: $29.95
Episode 5: The Graceful Agent
Episode 6: Skyscrapers and the Red Dragon
Sohryuden: Volume 4   Catalog # USM 1327   Retail: $29.95
Episode 7: Revenge of the Four Brothers
Episode 8: Rampage of the Iron Dragon

Sohryuden: Volume 5   Catalog # USM 1328   Retail: $29.95
Episode 9: Storm of the White Dragon
Episode 10: The Brothers' Great Escape
Sohryuden: Volume 6   Catalog # USM 1329   Retail: $29.95
Episode 11: The Soaring Blue Dragon King
Episode 12: The Four Dragon Kings Take to the Sky

Sol Bianca
(1990) Japanime: Scifi   C-60m Japanese with English Subtitles   VA
Catalog # SB/001   Japan Retail: $29.95
Dir: Katsuhito Akiyama   Scr: Mayori Sekijima   Original Concept: Toru Miura
Character Design: Naoyuki Onda   Mecha Design: Atsushi Takeuchi
Art Dir: Shigemi Ikeda   Music: Toru Hirano
PC: NEC Avenue/Pony Canyon   Dist: A.D. Vision

Yohko Matsuoka	**Feb**
Rei Sakuma	**April**
Minami Takayama	**Janny**
Yuriko Fuchizaki	**June**
Miki Itoh	**May**
Daisuke Namikawa	**Rim**
Tesshou Gendo	**Dr. Delopez**
Tomomichi Nishimura	**Lind**
Takeshi Aono	**Batros**
Rokuro Naya	**Gavance**

[***]
The all-female crew of the Sol Bianca are the sexiest pirates in outer space. They're all named after months in the year and each have unique personalities and different color hair. Janny, Feb, April, May, and June. During a clever and quick raid of a merchant spaceship, they discover a young stowaway who wishes to go to the planet Tres. Rim wants to go home, but a ruthless tyrant has taken over the planet and launches an all out attack against the underground resistance. Of course, they taunt him with threats of expelling him into outer space unless they are rewarded with the sacred Golden Box. Life gets complicated when the planet's tyrant decides to take action against the heroes.When half the Sol Bianca's crew are captured, the dictator wants their ship and their aid, but they refuse. Slated for execution, they are rescued and leave the planet for good. Poor Rim is stuck behind and it doesn't take long for the crew of Sol Bianca to turn back and change the tides of war. The female pirates act tough, but really have a heart of gold (think Han Solo).
Sol Bianca tales elements of science fiction, action, and girls in anime, but balances them in a proper mixture while favoring a more realistic approach and eliminating the ultra hijinks and childish antics of Project A-ko and Battle Skipper. Instead, we are treated to a mature story, top-notch animation, and a lovable group of female characters.

Sol Bianca 2
(1991) Japanime: Scifi   C-60m Japanese with English Subtitles   VA
Catalog # SB/002   Japan Retail: $29.95

Dir: Hiroki Hayashi Scr: Mayori Sekijima   Original Concept: Toru Miura
Character Design: Naoyuki Onda Mecha Design: Atsushi Takeuchi
Planning: Toru Miura
Art Dir: Shigemi Ikeda   Music: Kosei Kenjo
PC: NEC Avenue/Pony Canyon   Dist: A.D. Vision
[***]
The crew of the Sol Bianca are back. They hope to become wealthy and retire to a life of comfort. Their newest scheme involves pasha, the most valuable substance in the known galaxy. They plan to corner the market, but along the way other parties become interested in the pasha and the women of Sol Bianca. The valiant, sexy crew are more than ready to match wits with any opponent and after all money is not as important as friendship and loyalty. An enjoyable sequel for fans who enjoyed the first film.

Space Warriors
(1989) Japanime   C-80m Dubbed   VA
Catalog #USM 1531 Japan Retail: $19.95
Dir: Tetsu Kimura   Scr: Takeshi Hirota
Prod: Ken Matsumoto, Michio Kato, Yasuhiro Tazaki
Ex. Prod: Katsushi Murakami, Koichi Motohashi   Art Dir: Motoyuki Tanaka
Character Design: Masahiro Sekino   Planning: Shin Unosawa, Shoji Sato
PC: Bandai/Nippon Animation Co. Ltd.   Dist: US Manga Corps
(based on original manga by Yuki Hijiri)
[**1/2]
In the future, a new breed of space warrior has emerged. The psychic warrior, a person possessing unique abilities. A space pirate and a space warrior match each other's psychic abilities. The pirate is the survivor of an assassination attempt on his life and vows to kill the man who murdered his family. While he terrorizes his enemies, his sister remains home safe and oblivious to his doings. The warrior is assigned the task of taking down the pirate and resuming order within the intergalactic community. He visits the pirate's sister and befriends the woman. Later he confronts the brother and ends his reign, though he senses a kindred spirit.

Spearmen of Death
(1980) Kung-Fu   C-100m   Dubbed   Hong Kong   Retail: $19.99
Dir: Chang Cheh   Scr: Chang Cheh, I Kuang Prod: Mona Fong
Ex. Prod: Run Run Shaw   Art Dir: Johnson Tsao   PC: Shaw Bros.
Kuo Chui, Chiang Sheng, Lo Meng, Lu Feng, Sun Chien
[**1/2]
Another Chang-gang film, starring the heroes and villains of Five Deadly Venoms. This time the story revolves around the brothers of a Spear Style School. The head master is killed and revenge is inflicted on the enemies, but the local authorities are looking for a scapegoat. An elder brother (Kuo Chui) of the Spear School takes the blame and flees. He leads a poor existence, but discovers the truth. One of the students set up the murder and scapegoat to seize control of the school. Kuo gathers help from the few remaining loyal students and wages an all out war against the new master. The plot bears a strong resemblance to Duel of the Iron Fists, an earlier Chang film. Though a major difference is the style of martial arts. The previous Chang

actors relied more on strength and brutality while the new group of stars are highly acrobatic, performing amazing gymnastic fight routines with minimal to no camera trickery. The most memorable aspect of this film is the spear techniques used by the actors. To create a dazzling effect, colorful flags are attached to the end of the spears. When whirling and twirling the weapons, the flag spears create a fast and colorful new fighting device for the actors to block and dodge. The amazing talents are incredible. Entertaining retread of the story will appeal to fans of the genre.

Spirits of Bruce Lee
(1980) Kung-Fu   C-92m Dubbed   Catalog #4062   Hong Kong
Retail: $9.99
Dir/Scr: Shang Lang Prod: Chui Cheung Lum
DP: Wong Yat Ping Editor: K.K. Chiang Music: Wong Ju Yan
Supervisor: Lee Tsai Fong   MAD: Ching Tung Yee
PC: Mirabelle International Production   Dist: Simitar Entertainment, Inc.
Michael Chan, Sue Chia, Long Poon Lok, Wong Tip Lan, Guh Men Tong, Chan Fei Lung
[*1/2]
This film has nothing to do with Bruce Lee, but capitalizes on the namesake. The story is a low-budget action flick set in Thailand. Two brothers are involved in the lucrative business of jade importing. When brother Chang Fan disappears during a business trip, Chang Chen Wai decides to search for his missing brother and the lost jade. He crosses the path of Li Pai Yu who offers him a helping hand. Local gangster boss Ming Pan Tin is behind the murder and plans to shut up any nosy people. The two friends fight off his assassins and go after Ming, teaching him a deadly lesson. Not much can be said about the hundreds of kung-fu movies that popped up in the '70s and '80s, all featuring subpar filmmaking techniques, quickie production values and stories/titles that tried to capitalize on Lee's fame.

Spiritual Kung Fu   (Karate Ghostbuster)
(1978) Kung-Fu   C-96m Dubbed   VA
Catalog #4110   Hong Kong   Retail: $9.99
Dir: Lo Wei   Prod: Hsu Li Hwa   DP: Chen Yung Shu   Editor: Liang Yung Chan
Scr: James Tien   MA: Jackie Chan   Prod: Lo Wei Productions
Dist: Entertainment Programs International
Jackie Chan, Kao Chiang, Wang Chin, Shih Tien
[*1/2]
Jackie Chan is a martial arts student at Shaolin Temple (only monks have to shave their heads). When a mysterious Ninja steals a special scroll of martial arts called the "7 Fists", Chan and others are punished for not preventing the crime. The man who stole the scroll, learns the "7 Fists" and begins a reign of terror. He challenges all the masters of the famous clans, beating them and taking over their clans. All looks lost, but then a meteorite crashes into Shaolin Temple, releasing five ghosts who haunt the temple. The spirits look like Raggedy Ann and Andy dressed in all-white ballerina outfits and horrendous red wigs. They are the guardians of the "Five Style Fists" book which is the only technique that can counter the deadly "7 Fists". Chan takes it upon himself to learn the five animal styles: snake, crane, tiger, leopard, and dragon. What may have been an attempt at creativity, sinks this picture into new realms of inane

humor and insult. The temple is thrown into chaos when one of the Shaolin abbots is murdered and another is accused of the crime. Chan and a group of friends attempt to discover the true culprits. Finally, Chan shows moments of stardom and the last portion of the film is quite entertaining. But a large portion of the film deals with 1940's sight gags and low-brow jokes surrounding the ghosts.

STAR BLAZERS SAGA

(SPACE CRUISER YAMATO SERIES)
(1974 - 1980 TV Series)   (1977 - 1983 Movies)
An entire book should be dedicated to the phenomenal success of the "Star Blazers" television series and the popular movies based on them. In the late 1970's, a very unique series was introduced to American audiences as a daily 30-minute cartoon. Rather than your run of the mill story with nonlinear episodes, the Yamato dealt with the voyages of the Yamato Crew/known as the Spaceship Argo in English. They helped defend Earth and through incredible odds always succeeded in their missions. For American television, the names of characters and certain items were changed to more westernized names. Also certain scenes were edited and changed for the different formats, a common practice for Asian programs introduced into a Western market. The series could be seen on numerous level, grand space opera, incredible animation, or pure entertainment. Characters matured, fell in love, died, and changed as the series kept pace with the season in time. A wonderful series with a timeless appeal, though keep in mind the animation technique is quite dated.

Originally three series were made: Quest for Iscandar and The Comet Empire which were widely shown on American television and are the best known and loved, while the third series the Bolar Wars had a very limited release. The entire collection of films and episodes are now available on video from the Voyager Collection. The original Japanese films are available individually or in a special collector's set.

Japanese Character	Americanized Name
Admiral Okita	Captain Avatar
Susumu Kodai	Derek Wildstar
Daisuke Shima	Mark Venture
Yuki Mori	Nova
Dr. Sado	Dr. Sane
Leader Dessler	Leader Desslock
Queen Stasha	Queen Starsha

Star Blazers - First Season "Quest for Iscandar"
(1974) Japanime   C-572m   Dubbed   VA   Catalog #80506-
Japan Retail: $19.95/volume (13 volumes)$159.95 for complete season
See Films for Complete Credits
[****]
Though dubbed in English and edited for tamer, American audiences, the only way to fully capture and admire the depth of the series is to view the entire 26 episodes covered over a 13 volume set of videos. Earth is mysteriously attacked by the Gamelons and only the Argo can

save the planet. See the film reviews for more information.

Star Blazers - Second Season "Comet Empire"
(1978) Japanime   C-572m   Dubbed   VA   Catalog #80505
Japan Retail: $19.95/volume (13 volumes)$159.95 for complete season
See Films for Complete Credits
[****]
The second season introduces a host of new characters, plus familiar ones from the original season are back. A new more powerful menace roams the galaxy...the Comet Empire.

Star Blazers - Third Season "Bolar Wars"
(1980) Japanime   C-572m   Dubbed   VA   Catalog #80504
Japan Retail: $19.95/volume (13 volumes)$159.95 for complete season
PC: Office Academy Co. Ltd.   Dist: Voyager Entertainment
[***1/2]
The infrequently seen, mysterious third season which received limited air-time is now available on video tape. Unfortunately, most video rental places only carry the first two seasons which were the most popular and best known. A new alien threatens the galaxy.

Space Battleship Yamato
(1977) Japanime   C-135m   Japanese with English Subtitles   VA
Catalog # VEI 6003   Japan Retail $29.95
Dir: Toshio Masuda Scr: Keisuke Fujikawa, Eiichi Yamamoto
Concept, Original Story, General Direction: Yoshinobu Nishizaki
Prod Design: Leiji Matsumoto   Music: Hiroshi Miyagawa
PC: Office Academy Co. Ltd.   Dist: Voyager Entertainment
[****]
This is the film that let's you relive it all, sparking a series of films and television episodes seen around the world. From the dramatic music to the technical designs of the engine, meticulous detail was put into every aspect of the film. Ambitious in scope, the series garnered critical admiration and inspired legions of imitators from all over the world. In the 22nd Century, Earth is locked in a desperate losing battle with a warlike planet of aliens known as the Gamelons who have expanded into the universe, subjugating all planets within their path. Earth puts up resistance and the Gamelons launch a full scale attack on the Milky Way Galaxy. Planet after outer planet falls until the Gamelons establish a base on Mars and initiate the extermination of the human race. (Parallels between World War II Japan and the United States are brilliantly incorporated within the framework of the story, but do not mar the overall pacing.) Large radioactive meteorite bombs destroy the surface of the Earth until life is forced to move underground. Great tragedy befalls the planet when radioactive levels reach a point that will no longer sustain life on Earth. On Mars, an alien spacecraft crashes and a beautiful woman dies delivering a message to Earth. If Earth can fly to Iscandar (a cure for the radioactivity) and back to Earth in one year (the length of a television season), the planet can be rebuilt to its former beauty. There's not enough time to build a spaceship, so the Earth forces take the hull of the Yamato (largest battleship ever built) and convert it into a spacecruiser. The only problem is that the Gamelon homeworld resides next to Iscandar, so the Yamato crew must fight every mile of

the way.

Farewell to Space Battleship Yamato: In the Name of Love
(1978) Japanime   C-151m   Japanese with English Subtitles   VA
Catalog #80569   Japan Retail $29.95
Dir: Toshio Masuda   Concept, Original Story, General Direction: Yoshinobu Nishizaki
Scr: Toshio Masuda, Keisuke Fujikawa, Hideaki Yamamoto
Prod: Toru Yoshida   Music: Hiroshi Miyagawa   Art Dir: Tomoharu Katsumata
Prod Design: Leiji Matsumoto   Costume: Yukiki Hanai
PC: Office Academy Co. Ltd.   Dist: Voyager Entertainment
[*1/2]**
The second film is a re-edited compilation of the second Star Blazers series. Though excellent in many ways, the compilation film leaves out a lot of important detail only seen in the series. Due to the constraints of telling a complete story in one film, many characters and plot elements are altered in this film. The Yamato crew must battle a deadly new enemy, the Comet Empire. A floating moon/palace that can accelerate through the cosmos like a burning comet. They plan to destroy Earth and use Desslock as an ally. Earth, now rebuilt to full glory, sends a space fleet to do battle. The entire fleet is defeat and victory seems eminent for the Comet Empire. The Yamato crew are given advice from Desslock who no longer wishes to battle with Earth. With the new knowledge, the Yamato penetrates the Comet Empire and enter the heart of the palace and destroy it. An exciting entry into the Yamato saga with most of the cast from the first film.

Space Battleship Yamato: The New Voyage
(1979) Japanime   C-93m Japanese with English Subtitles   VA
Catalog #80578   Japan Retail $29.95
Concept, Original Story, General Direction: Yoshinobu Nishizaki
Prod Design & Editor: Leiji Matsumoto   Music: Hiroshi Miyagawa
PC: Office Academy Co. Ltd.   Dist: Voyager Entertainment
[*1/2]**
A continuation of the events after the second film, focusing on the Gamelons who aided the Yamato Crew. Though aggressive and arrogant, Lord Desslock has found a certain amount of compassion and admiration for earthlings and the Yamato crew. While visiting his dead planet, he discovers an alien racing tearing the planet apart. He engages in battle and eventually teams up with the Yamato crew to battle their new enemy. The core characters return and pay tribute to the heroes who died in the first two films in a moving ceremony at a memorial grave. Once again the amazing depth and character of the show captures the viewer's attention.

Be Forever Yamato
(1980) Japanime   C-149m   Japanese with English Subtitles   VA
Catalog #80509   Japan Retail $29.95
Concept, Original Story, General Direction: Yoshinobu Nishizaki
Scr: Toshio Yoshida, Keisuke Fujikawa, Hideaki Yamamoto
Music: Hiroshi Miyagawa   Prod Design: Leiji Matsumoto
PC: Office Academy Co. Ltd.   Dist: Voyager Entertainment

[***1/2]
The aliens from the third film return and take over the Earth. In a massive surprise attack, the Dark Empire cripple Earth's defense system and arm the hyperon bomb. A gigantic weapon so deadly it can destroy the entire planet. The only hope is the Yamato crew who must travel back in time to defeat the enemy and deactivate the bomb. The alien leaders demand the wherabouts of the Yamato, but no one on Earth will reveal the location of the famed spacecruiser. Due to the death of past characters, a host of new characters are introduced and join the fray, including the daughter of Starsha. Meanwhile on Earth, Yuki is caught by an alien officer named Alphon and remains at his side. Kodai and the crew release the Yamato from its asteroid base and enter the enemy realm, a vast swirling cosmos of energy and are warped into the future, 200 years after the invasion. For some reason, the film alters into a widescreen format as the Yamato crew arrive on a futuristic Earth controlled by the aliens' ancestors. The valiant crew realize what they must do to stop the Dark Empire once and for all.

Final Yamato
(1983) Japanime   C-163m   Japanese with English Subtitles   VA
Catalog #80570   Japan Retail $29.95
Dir: Yoshinobu Nishizaki, Tomohara Katsumata Scr: Leiji Matsumoto
Concept, Original Story: Yoshinobu Nishizaki
Adapted: Hideaki Yamamoto   Music: Hiroshi Miyagawa
Prod Supervisor: Toshio Masuda   Chief Prod: Masahisa Saeki
Associate Prod: Eiichi Yamamoto Prod Design: Leiji Matsumoto
PC: Office Academy Co. Ltd.   Dist: Voyager Entertainment
[***1/2]
The final film is also the grandest in scope and character development, while the animation is appropriately raised to a new level of quality and crispness. The film reunites the entire crew for their final journey aboard the Yamato. Slated as the last film, the Yamato Crew faces a powerful, new race whose home planet was destroyed by a water planet. The water world is entirely comprised of liquid and collides into other planets, flooding the entire population. The Yamato attempts to rescue one of these planets, but only saves a single boy. He is the son of the ruler of the new race who uses his massive battlefleet to conquer the universe. It is up to the Yamato and her crew to stop the new race and save Earth from the water planet. The film closes the final chapter in the saga, but as seen in previous films, death is not the end of a story. Possibilities of a new Yamato film may materialize in the near future.

Yamato Box Set
(1977-1983)   Japanime   C-660m   Japanese with English Subtitles   VA
Japan Retail: $99.95
[****]
All five feature films in a collector's box released from Voyager Entertainment. Definitely worth the price for any anime fans. Since then a live-action film was released and additional titles in the anime series.

Story of Qiu Ju, The
(1992) DramaC-100m   Chinese with English Subtitles   PG   VA

Catalog #65696　　China　Retail: $19.95
Dir: Zhang Yimou　　Scr: Liu Heng　　　Prod: Ma Fung Kwok
Editor: Du Yuan　　DP: Chi Xiao Ling, Yu Xiao Qun　Music: Zhao Ji Ping
Art Design: Cao Jiuping　　Dist: Columbia
(from the novel The Wan Family's Lawsuit by Chen Yuanbin)
Gong Li　　　　　　Wan Qiu Ju
Lei Lao Sheng　　　　Wan Shantung 'Village Head'
Liu Pei Qi　　　　　Wan Qing Lai 'Husband'
Yang Liu Chun　　　Meizi
Ge Zhi Jun　　　　　Officer Li
Zhu Qanqing, Cui Luowen, Yang Huiqin, Wang Jianfa, Lin Zi, Ye Jun
[***]
A fascinating and frustrating story about the squabbles of peasant life and honor in China's countryside. Gong Li portrays a non-glamorous wife obsessed with justice for her injured husband. The film shows the frustration and determination Gong Li goes through to bring the local village chief to justice. At times the viewer may become frustrated at the woman's resilience, but admire her at the same time as she travels painstakingly back and forth from the capital to her local village.
In a small remote village outside Beijing, a young peasant woman and her husband farm red peppers. During an argument the local village chief and Gong's husband have a quarrel. The village chief ends up kicking the husband in the genitals and injuring him. This starts a catalyst of actions that force Gong to pursue judicial action against the local chief. At first, she demands an apology and reparation. The chief mocks her and insults her pride. It is evident that both she and the chief are stubborn and want to win without losing any face. Costs are not the matter, but pride is the goal. The tension of hostility are evident when Gong Li pays a cordial visit to the chief's house and rests her pregnant body. What if my husband can never have children again, she says out loud. Then adds insultingly, not all of us can be so lucky to have so many children. The chief who has daughters and is disgraced by not having a son is offended. (Unfortunately in Asian tradition, the value of a male child is extremely important for carrying on the family heritage and assuming control of the extended family. It is not uncommon to see a couple with four daughters while the fifth and final child is boy. Reports have circulated that under the one child policy in China, couples are murdering their babies if they are not boys.) She goes to the local police and soon her demands lead to Beijing (China's capital, once known as Peking) where she talks to higher officials and eventually forces the issue in Chinese court. Adapted from Chen Yuan Bin's novel "The Wan Family's Lawsuit".

Stray Dog　　(Nora Inu)
(1949) Crime DramaB&W-122m　Japanese with English Subtitles　　VA
Catalog #K0657　　Japan Retail: $29.95
Dir: Akira Kurosawa　　Scr: Ryuzo Kikushima, Akira Kurosawa
Prod: Sojiro Motoki　　DP: Asakazu Nakai　Editor: Yoshi Sugihara
Music: Fumio Hayasaka　　Art Design & Direction: So Matsuyama
PC: Shintoho Production, acquired by Toho in 1959　　Dist: Sony Video Software Inc.
Toshiro Mifune　　　　Murakami
Takashi Shimura　　　Sato

Ko Kimura	Yuro
Keiko Awaji	Harumi
Reisaburo Yamamoto	Hondo
Noriko Sengoku	Girl

[****]
World renowned director Kurosawa may best be remembered for his powerful samurai films, but if questions arise whether he can do modern dramas then just point them toward Stray Dog and doubts will no longer exist. Stray Dog is an excellent film that places Mifune in a more modern role (keep in mind the film was made over fifty years ago) as a young detective in the big city. It is only a few years after Japan's defeat in World War II and life has just started to return to normal. The country has adopted a western concept of capitalism and Mifune wears a tailored suit and carries a Colt pistol. The film is very western in presentation (some accuse Kurosawa of being too western) and the film could easily be remade by Alfred Hitchcock with the handsome Mifune played by Gregory Peck. The story revolves around the loss of Detective Murakami's handgun while riding a crowded trolley. Japan is a much more gun-restrained country than the United States and handguns were very rare during that time period. When a series of murders are committed and the bullets are identified as Mifune's, he is compelled to take full responsibility and seek out the murderer. His quest becomes an obsession as he searches the city for any possible leads. His superior sees this as over-zealous behavior and reassures the new detective it was a mistake and that guns don't kill people, but people kill people. Still Mifune blames himself and follows up a number of leads that brings him closer and closer to the culprit. A veteran detective named Sato is assigned to help him . He is the father-figure for Mifune, an officer of the law who has seen it all and still maintains a shred of decency and humanity. In one touching moment, Sato calls over Mifune to proudly show his sleeping children. Through a series of leads, the two detectives discover the identity of the culprit and come into contact with a variety of characters representing Japanese society: the girlfriend, the parents, and the friends. As the detectives get closer to the culprit, Mifune discovers the criminal is similar to him in many ways. Here the film captures the parallelism between Mifune and the criminal.
Mifune (Murakami): "During the war I saw how easily good men turned bad. Perhaps it is the
        difference in our ages, yours and mine - or perhaps the times have changed, but..."
Shimura (Sato): "You understand him too well."
Both men are products of the defeated post-World War II Japan, but have taken totally different paths. Their decisions effect the lives of everyone around them and carry heavy repercussions.
Though the film may be technically dated, it still retains a powerful narrative and progressive pace. Keep in mind that Kurosawa made the film only a few years after Japan was totally decimated by American military forces. In that respect, Stray Dog is a classic masterpiece that still retains it's dramatic force and universal story. I saw the film recently again, 58 years after it was initially released, and was amazed at how well the story kept its form. Classic films don't get older, they just get better. For those unfamiliar with Japanese films, Stray Dog is a perfect place to start viewing Asian films, especially the works of Akira Kurosawa.

Street Fighter II: The Movie
(1994) Japanime   C-96m Dubbed   VA   Catalog # SMV 49756   Japan
Retail: $14.95
Dir: Gisaburo Sugil Scr: Kenichi Imai, Gisaburo Sugil

Music: Cory Lerios, John D. Andrea   PC: Capcom Co. Ltd.
Dist: Sony Music Video
[**1/2]
For fans of the Capcom Video Game Series, Street Fighter II is a more serious adaptation which in many ways surpasses the live-action film "Street Fighter", starring Jean-Claude Van Damme. The entire gang from the video game is on screen for battle, though the myriad of characters can be slightly confusing for viewers who are not familiar with the background. The main character is Ryu, not Guile, who travels the world in search of martial arts competitors. He meets a strange assortment of people - good and bad. Meanwhile, Guile and Chun Li are on a mission and must stop the evil leader from taking over the world. The high-quality animation features plenty of solid fight sequences enhanced by lighting techniques and contemporary American music. If you enjoy the characters from the video game and serious-minded action anime, then SF2 is a worthy addition to your collection.

THE STREET FIGHTER Series (Sonny Chiba)

Japan's knockout answer to Bruce Lee came in a powerhouse brute named Sonny Chiba. Though never achieving the fame and legendary status of Bruce Lee, Chiba enjoys a dedicated cult following with high profile fans like Quentin Tarantino. Sonny played Terry Sugury, an anti-hero of Chinese/Japanese heritage who is scorned by either society. He relies only on himself and his superior skill, seeking money for violent jobs though he does possess his own code of honor. The films range in quality from cheesy to sloppy, and expect plenty of common theme music and over dramatized facial expressions from Chiba and his opponents. Be warned, the films are very dated and reminiscent of exploitation films of the 1970's. A big favorite of American director Quentin Tarantino (Reservoir Dogs) who used Chiba references in the opening of True Romance.

Street Fighter, The
(1975) KarateC-91m Dubbed   R   VA   Catalog # N4301V
Japan Retail: $19.99 Widescreen Available
Dir: Shigehiro Ozawa   Scr: Koji Takada, Steve Autrey
PC: Toei Studios   Dist: New Line Cinema
Sonny Chiba   Terry Sugury "Street Fighter"
Milton Ishibashi   Junjo
Masafumi Suzuki   Masaoka
[**]
After the tragic death of Bruce Lee in 1973, a tidal wave of enthusiasm for martial arts films was left void. Company after company, actor after actor rushed into capture the magical success of Lee's onscreen magnetism. Needless to say, Lee remains in a class of his own. Toei Studios of Japan had their own Bruce Lee clone, a hulkish, brute with monkey-like grace and a horrible scowl. His name was Sonny Chiba and he became the Street Fighter Terry Sugury. Depending on your taste for exploitation films, you might enjoy this film or despise it for its low-production value, poor editing, and nonsensical plot. I do warn that the film is molded after the 70's style of low-budget filmmaking with brutal fights, bizarre sound effects, and costumed faux pas. Terry is

a half-Japanese, half-Chinese assassin for hired. He helps breakout a vicious convict, but then Terry is double-crossed and never paid. This starts a chain of events where Terry kills everyone who crosses him, leading to a deeper dive into the world of crime. He eventually befriends a Karate Master which is the best aspect of the film. The tiny rotund master (based on true-life master Mas Oyama) teaches Terry the qualities of humility and honor. The finale has Terry battling for his life against the vicious criminal he helped release.

Return of the Street Fighter
(1975) KarateC-88m Dubbed in Extended Play Mode   R   VA
Catalog #N4300E   Japan Retail: $19.99
Dir: Shigehiro Ozawa   Scr: Koji Takada, Steve Autrey   DP: Teiji Yoshida
Art Direction: Tokumichi Igawa   M: Tony Sushima   PC: Toei Company, Ltd.
Dist: New Line Cinema

Sonny Chiba	**Terry Sugury "Street Fighter"**
Yoko Ichiji	**Kitty**
Milton Ishibashi	**Junjo**
Masafumi Suzuki	**Masaoka**
Donald Nakajimi	**Otaguro**
Zulu Yachi	**Yamagumi**
Claude Cannyon	**Don Costello**

[**1/2]
More enjoyable than its predecessor and recommend you watch it first. You won't lose much in continuity since the preview on the first tape gives away most of the film. If you enjoy this film then it might be worth seeing the original. If you don't, you best stay away from the series. Sonny Chiba is back from the first film and still up to his hired-gun/foot ways. Japanese Yakuza boss, Otagura hires Sonny to perform a number of jobs. Sonny does so easily, always with his sidekick Kitty, dressed like Sugar Bear from Starsky & Hutch. In the meantime, the Yakuza are planning a major takeover of martial art schools around the world, using Masaoka's name as a cover. When Masaoka discovers the criminal conspiracy, he confronts the villains and demands they stop using his name. The criminal boss hires Terry to kill Masaoka, but he decides money is not worth a great man's life (humbled from the first film) and tells Masaoka of the assassination attempt. The men join forces, and Terry goes after the Yakuza boss who is really only a puppet to a Mafia boss.

Street Fighter's Last Revenge
(1979) KarateC-80m Dubbed in Extended Play Mode   R   VA
Catalog #N4384E   Japan Retail: $19.99
Dir: Shigehiro Ozawa   Scr: Koji Takada, Steve Autrey   Dist: New Line Cinema
Sonny Chiba, Milton Ishibashi, Masafumi Suzuki
[**]
Sonny Chiba is back, bigger, better, and badder than ever! This time Chiba is a modern day Batman, with his own hidden closet full of neat supplies. A local political upheaval has affected labor workers and Chiba is hired by a wealthy businessman to release a man carrying a valuable tape formula to increase the value of narcotics. In true mercenary fashion, Chiba performs his job easily but is soon betrayed by the monsters who hired him. Having had enough of the

underworld, Chiba stages a one man assault against the Yakuza.

Sister Street Fighter
(1978) Karate C-80m Dubbed in Extended Play Mode   R   VA
Catalog #N4302E   Japan Retail: $19.99
Dir: Shigehiro Ozawa   Scr: Koji Takada, Steve Autrey   Dist: New Line Cinema
Sonny Chiba, Milton Ishibashi, Masafumi Suzuki, Sue Shiomi, May Hayakawa, Harry Kondo
[**]
The Street Fighter films have to be seen to be believed - a high level of unintentional camp, the dubbed dialogue, the hectic fight scenes, and the silly plot. Bad movies can be categorized as bad movies that bore (the worst type) and bad movies that are so bad they're actually fun. Sister Street Fighter is the latter and for all its misgivings, can be quite entertaining if seen as a campy karate film of the 70's. In Sonny Chiba's final Street Fighter film, he plays a minor role to the lead female character. She joins the police and goes undercover to Yokohama, Japan to search for her missing brother, Li Long. She joins some other people (Chiba) and must fight to stay alive, save her brother, and defeat the evil Hammerhead and a rogues gallery of fighters.

Street Gangs of Hong Kong
(1974) Kung-Fu   C-105m   Dubbed
Hong Kong   Retail: $19.95
Dir: Chang Cheh   PC: Shaw Bros.
Betty Lu Ti, Lily Li, Wang Chung
[*]
This film holds a very special place in my memory...a painful place. This is one of the worst kung-fu movies ever released in the states. The entire composition of the film is dreary and insipid, emphasized by poor acting, ill choreographed fight scenes, and a dated appearance. But there's also a personal reason I despise the film, because I've seen it so many times. After the kung-fu craze died, martial arts film became difficult to find on television. Late night was the only spot available and television networks loved putting Street Gangs on way too frequently. Hoping to find some hidden merit, I would watch the film again and again. A young man's father is killed by a brutal gang. Though he's a loner and misguided, he vows to avenge his poor father. He joins a vicious gang, gaining their confidence and secretly finding out who killed his father. Though Liu Chia Liang received some credit for choreography, it didn't help much since the fights are quite choppy and the ugly decor comprised of garish shirts, bell bottoms, and gold medallions.

Suikoden - Demon Century
(1993) Japanime   C-45m Dubbed   VA   Catalog # ADV SU/001D   Japan Retail: $29.95
Dir: Hiroshi Negishi   Scr: Masayori Sekijima   Originally   Created: Hitoshi Yoshioka
Prod: Haruki Kadokawa, Makoto Hasegawa, Tomoyuki Miyata
DP: Akihiko Takahashi   Music: Yoichiro Yoshikawa
Art Dir: Osamu Honda   Character Design: Nobuyuki Tsuru

Line Prod: Nobuhisa Abe
PC: Kadokawa Shoten/Nippon Victor/JC Staff   Dist: A.D.Vision

Spike Spencer	Takateru Suga
Aaron Krohn	Miyuki Mamiya
Jason Lee	Ryo Hamura
Rob Mungle	Owen O'Brien
Brett Weaver	Masaru Ohshita
Tristan MacAvery	Kyoichi Amamoto
Jeff Gardner	Takayuki Kurihara
Robert Peeples	Agu
Traci Shannon	Saeko Kishima

[***]

Bearing resemblance to the classic tale "The Water Margin", a group of heroes are gathered together by fate to save a group of orphans from a ruthless corporate leader. A young man enters a seedy bar and demands information from the bartender. The bartender refuses, not so politely, and gets into a scuffle with the young man. The bar's patron, muscular Ryo, decides to teach the young guy a lesson, but in less than a minute the two men become fast friends. Takateru has come to search for his missing sister who was kidnapped by the criminal organization Koryukai who is led by a boss taking orders from a demonic statue. They have kidnapped Takateru's sister and are also trying to muscle out a Christian orphanage supervised by Father O'Brien, once a mercenary known as the Killer Wolf. Ex-mercenary Ryo is recruited by his detective friend and join O'Brien's plight against the Koryukai and their deadly sword-wielding minions. Meanwhile, Takateru accidentally befriends a transvestite named Miyuki who attempts to work his/her charm on him. She/he is an excellent fighter, extremely spirited, and a well-drawn character in more ways than one. The heroes are pre-destined to unite together and defeat the evil Koryukai. Images of an ancient war blossom into the memory of Takateru who leads the heroes on an attack against the Koryukai stronghold. In a fashion that goes to the extreme, Rambo-style, the forces of good and evil encounter each other in a destructive battle of firearms, missiles, and feet. The combination of characters are quite interesting and given their own unique style and appearance. The story follows a standard quest/revenge format, but includes a few interesting turns and developments. Solid animation and a slick, quick story that most likely will leave you entertained.

SuperBook (26 episodes)
(1982) Japanime: Religion   C-40m (each volume)   Dubbed   Japan
Retail: $9.99 (each volume)
Dir: Kenjiro Yoshida, Masakazu Higuchi Scr: Akiyoshi Sakai
Character Design: Akiko Shitamoto   Music: Masahito Maruyama
PC: CBN/Tatsunoko Productions   Dist: Tyndale Family Video
[***1/2]

Ironically, one of the most entertaining and informative animated series on religion is created by a nation where the practice of Christianity is almost non-existent. The animated exploits follow a young girl and boy who are magically transported to the old testament era where a friendly robot guides them through the great biblical stories. They can interact with the characters, but are swept along the currents of history and can not alter the outcomes. A clever and enjoyable

way for children of all ages to sit back, join the ride, and learn about Christianity.
For those of you familiar with biblical stories, I have included a list of all the stories that the series have portrayed.

Vol. 1 Adam & Eve	Vol. 2 Noah & the Ark	Vol. 3 Moses & the Miracles
Vol. 4 David & Goliath	Vol. 5 Abraham & Isaac	Vol. 6 Joseph & His Dreams
Vol. 7 Samson & Delilah	Vol. 8 Esther & the King	Vol. 9 Jonah & the Big Fish
Vol. 10 Nehemiah & the Wall	Vol. 11 The First Easter	Vol. 12 The First Christmas
Vol. 13 Elijah, True Prophet	Vol. 14 Abraham & Lot	Vol. 15 Isaac & Rebekah
Vol. 16 Joshua the General	Vol. 17 Deborah & Barak	Vol. 18 Samuel:Hearing God's Voice
Vol. 19 David & Jonathan	Vol. 20 Hezekiah & Isaiah	Vol. 21 Joseph & His Brothers
Vol. 22 Moses & the Burning Bush		
Vol. 23 Moses & the Plagues		
Vol. 24 David: Shepherd Boy		

Supercop
See Police Story 3: Supercop
The second major Jackie Chan/Hong Kong film to be released in the American market in 1996 after the success of Rumble in the Bronx. You may have seen this Jackie Chan and Michelle Khan film in your local theaters, but this is actual a re-release of an older Hong Kong film.

Super Dimension Century Orguss
(1983) Japanime   C-80m VA   Dubbed   Catalog # USR-VD10   Japan Retail: $19.95
Dir: Noboru Ishiguro, Yasuyoshi Mikamoto   Original Story: Studio Nue
Prod: Toshitsugu Mukaitsubo
DP: Masahide Ueda   Music: Kentaro Haneda   Music Direction: Seiji Suzuki
Character Design: Haruhiko Mikimoto   Art Direction: Yoshiyuki Yamamoto
Ex. Prod: Yutaka Fujioka, Yoshimasa Onishi   Dist: U.S. Renditions/L.A. Hero
English Version - Prod: Ken Iyadomi   Associate Prod: Robert Napton, Upton S. Redmondton
English Scr & Voice Dir: Raymond Garcia   Supervising Dir: Quint Lancaster
Prod Coordinator & Casting: Victor Garcia   Research & Story Consultant: David Keith Riddick
English Voices: Steve Blum, Tom Charles, Melissa Charles, Dorothy Melendrez, Bill Kestin, Debbie Rogers, Gary Michaels, Patricia Vega, Victor Garcia, Lucy Vargas, Mimi Davies, Yutaka Maseba, Dougary Grant
[**1/2]
In the year 2062, two advanced worlds are battling for control over the orbital elevator in hopes of gaining an advantage in the war. Ace pilot Kei Katsuragi flies his ship into the thick of the battle and activates the super dimensional space/time oscillator bomb which throws him into a time warp. He appears in an alien world which bears make similarities to his own, but as for the time and place, it is alien. He meets up with a group of female pilots who help him and save his life on a number of occassions. He returns the favor and together they battle a tyrannical leader on an episodic basis.
Over time, animation suffers from a dated appearance as new techniques and styles develop

which leave old animation shows looking old. Orguss has an interesting premise, but the older style of animation may not appeal to modern viewers. The story's lengthy development looks rich and there are plenty of novel characters and more introduced, including a female cyborg. The series is quite lengthy and other volumes are available. If you like the first, you may like the others, but keep in mind the series has the look and feel of old television shows.
Episode 1: Space/Time Collapse
Episode 2: Lonely Wolf
Episode 3: Pretty Machine

Super Dragon's Dynamo
(1982) Action C-82m Dubbed   VA   Catalog # VHS 33050
Hong Kong   Retail: $9.95
Dir/Scr: Joseph Chung   Prod: Harry Sin
DP: King Chano Dung   Editor: Leung Wing Chan   Music: Lawrence Chan
Prod Design: Jackson Wu   Prod Manager: Ma Ming Chi
MAD: Alfred Chow Supervisor: Joseph Lai   Assistant: Stephen So
PC: IFD Films   Dist: Alpha Video Distributors, Inc.
Champ Wang, Sherman Chow, Shelly Yim, Samuel Lee, Liu Tan, Chang Chong, Wang Shan, Tin Ching, Faye Ding
[*1/2]
Another subpar action film from Hong Kong, riding on the tidal wave of Bruce Lee and Jackie Chan films in the United States. A bad film made over fifteen years ago, time only intensifies its shortcomings and the cast will not be recognized by modern action fans.
Tang Shih Hai is a wealthy businessman in Hong Kong, but encounters a serious problem when his officials are murdered. He decides against using his lazy, gambling son, Champ, and appoints Cheng as his general manager. Secretly, Cheng is a member of the International Criminal Group and uses his power to murder Tang and take control of the company. Champ is wrongly arrested and serves two years of hard labor in prison. When he gets free, Champ is a changed and searches for the man who murdered his father and sent him to jail. Cheng doesn't want Champ to regain control of his father's company or reveal the truth, so he hires some men to take care of him. When Champ's woman is beaten and borders on death, he takes the law into his own hands and battles Cheng in a empty warehouse late at night.

Super Ninjas (Chinese Super Ninjas/Five Element Ninja)
(1982) Kung-Fu   C-100m   Dubbed
Catalog #KRT 117   Hong Kong   Retail: $19.99
Dir: Chang Cheh   Scr: I Kuang, Chang Cheh Ex. Prod: Run Run Shaw
Prod: Mona Fong   PC: Shaw Brothers
Cheng Tien Chi, Lo Meng, Lung Tien Hsiang, Chen Hui Min, Chen Pei Hsi, Wang Lieh, Chu Ke
[**1/2]
Though made around the same time period as the kung-fu craze in America, Super Ninjas didn't enjoy the airplay that other Chang films did due to its heavy dose of graphic violence. A powerful kung fu clan is destroyed by band of Japanese ninjas. The ninja then destroy the people who imported them and set themselves up as rulers of the martial world. The lone survivor of

the ninja's initial attack,
Only one man, a survivor of the ninja's first attack, can defeat them, and he does so by teaming up with some other guys and learning the tricks of the ninja himself. A masterpiece of kung fu, and possibly one of the goriest kung fu films of the earlier years. One scene has a man stabbed through the abdomen, and as he keeps on fighting, his intestines slowly seep out of his belly. He is killed when he accidentally steps on his own innards and trips. In the end, the heroes pull the villain in two with their bare hands.

Swordsman   (Laughing and Proud Warrior)
(1990) Fantasy Kung-Fu   C-119 min   Chinese with English Subtitles
Catalog #0851   Hong Kong   Retail: $39.99
Dir: King Hu Prod: Tsui Hark   Dist: Tai Seng Video
Sam Hui, Cecilia Yip, Fennie Yuen, Cheung Man, Rosamund Kwan, Michelle Reis, Wu Ma, Jacky Cheung, Lam Ching Ying
[**1/2]
Patience is the key to enjoying the first film in the Swordsman series based on a story by Jin Yong.   Sort of an all-star film - co-directed by legend-from-the-past King Hu, plus Tsui Hark, Ching Tsui Ting and others - the result is very confusing for anyone who doesn't know the Jin Yong novels it's based on.   But perseverance pays; watch it a few times and you'll understand most of it.   The story begins at the library of the imperial palace where a sacred scroll is kept.   A thief enters the library and steals the scroll.   The Chief Eunuch in charge decides to keep the theft a secret from the emperor and orders his men to discreetly search for the scroll.   The prime suspect is Lord Lam who retired from the court around the same time.   The Eunuch's troops surround Lam's estate and call in Master Zhor and his men.   Ling and Kiddo arrive to aid Lord Lam.
A solid story with many interesting characters, but the special effects which mostly take place at night and the multilayered plot might be confusing to many viewers who also may fin it difficult remember who's who. Jacky Cheung won a Golden Horse award for Best Supporting Actor for his role in this film.   This is Tsui Hark and King Hu's interpretation of a well-known romantic and action-filled novel.

Swordsman 2 (Laughing and Proud Warrior: East Direction Not Fail/Laughing and Proud Warrior: Invincible Asia)
(1991) Fantasy Kung-Fu   C-108m   Chinese with English Subtitles
Catalog #1173   Hong Kong   Retail: $39.99
Dir: Ching Siu Ting   Prod: Tsui Hark   Dist: Tai Seng Video

Jet Li	**Ling**
Rosamund Kwan	**Ying**
Brigitte Lin	**Invincible Asia**
Michelle Reis	**Kiddo**
Fennie Yuen	**Blue Phoenix**
Lau Shin	**Wu**
Waise Lee	

[***]
Another well-made fantasy martial arts epic teaming Jet Li with a bevy of beautiful female

fighters. Jet Li is a master of the sword, but seems distanced and jaded with life. His life is complicated when he meets a beautiful woman who always maintains a silent demeanor. Doesn't sound like such a bad thing, but then again the woman is a man who is turning into a woman because of the magical powers of the Sacred Scroll. Though Brigitte Lin is gorgeous, her girlfriend doesn't take kindly to the sexual transformation. Meanwhile her troops are rallying to destroy everyone in their path and action scenes abound.

Considered by many to be the definitive "flying people" movie. A must see for the Essence Absorbing Stance alone. Based on a story by Jin Yong. Jet Li plays the boozy blademaster who once again finds himself involved in the quest for the magical Sacred Scrolls. Brigitte Lin stars in a tailor-made role as a villainous sorcerer who slowly transmogrifies into a woman as the story progresses! The object, magical Sacred Scrolls which bestow untold power upon their possessor. Brigitte owns the scrolls, of course, and suspicion draws him/her into inevitable violence.

Swordsman 3: East is Red   (The East is Red/East Direction Not Fail: Wind Cloud Again Rises
(1992) Fantasy Kung-Fu   C-108m   Chinese with English Subtitles
Catalog #1401   Hong Kong   Retail: $39.99
Dir: Tsui Hark   Prod: Tsui Hark   Dist: Tai Seng Video
Brigitte Lin   Invincible Asia
Joey Wong   Snow
Yu Rong Guang   Officer Koo
[1/2]**

The third installment in the Sowrdsman series has less to do with a swordsman and more to do with Asia the Invincible, the character popularized by Brigitte Lin in the second film. Asia the Invincible was originally a male martial arts master who learned the secret style of the Sacred Scroll which altered his/her sexual identity, since the practitioner had to be castrated. The film includes a long introduction describing events in a quick and loose manner leading to Asia's demise. The heroes from the second film, the swordsmen led by Jet Li, lay siege to Asia's Black Cliff fortress and battle her to the death. When the credits finally role and end, a Spanish warship appears in the horizon, sailing along the Black Cliffs. The emperor has assigned Officer Koo to escort the Spanish ship to the sunken site of a Dutch merchant ship. The Spanish captain inquires about the legendary Asia the Invincible and requests a trip to the abandoned fortress. Curious himself, Koo agrees to the expedition. Officer Koo is escorted by Ling and Chin, two loyal subordinates, the Spanish captain, and a squadron of Spanish soldiers. When they discover an elderly groundskeeper, they demand to see the burial site of Asia the Invincible. The Spanish then reveal their true intents and desecrate the grave in search of the powerful Sacred Scroll which gave Asia her amazing powers. The groundskeeper reveals himself as Asia the Invincible and rescues Koo, but tortures him for discovering her ruse. He pleads with her to return to the world of martial arts, since charlatans claiming to be Asia are deceiving the people and causing conflicts. Asia agrees and starts her violent rampage of death and destruction. Initially, she promises to be just and her character is treated with sympathy which is quickly thrown out to focus more on a story full of graphic violence and death. Along the way, a cult of Japanese warriors enter the battle and so does Asia's ex-lover Snow (Joey Wong) who is leading the remnants of Asia's previous army, the Sun Moon Sect. Wong's Snow is one of the film's highlights as she first imitates Asia and her deadly sewing needles, but then repents for her deception. She is in love with Asia and also develops a bound with Koo who saved her from the deceived members of the Sun Moon Sect. Asia decides to kill all her imitators and conquer the world, calling herself Asia and Europe the Invincible. She bestows mystical powers to challenge Officer Koo who has fallen in love with Snow and Asia. He tries to convince her to give up her violent ways and battles her atop a sinking ship. Asia refuses, driven by her insane lust for violence and ends up causing the death of every character in the film, before finally floating away with the dead Snow on a ship's sail.

Elements common in Chinese fantasy include mystical martial arts abilities, wild acrobatics, strange creatures, beautiful sets, and lavish costumes. East is Red has all the elements, but in such a hectic abundance that the film seems a parody within itself. The plot and character development lacks tight cohesion, shifting focus on wild battles and then dramatic confessions. The lunacy doesn't stop there as most of the film takes place outdoors and on the sea with warring models ships led by Asia the Invincible, the Spanish, the Ming government and Koo, and the Japanese who actually have a submarine with mines. Along the way, Asia rips out the hearts of her enemies, frolics with prostitutes, rides a marlin on the sea, battles a grey man-ninja, curses Catholicism, and kills the Japanese leader who dressed in imposing samurai armor is actually a dwarf (similar to Master Blaster for those familiar with Mad Max 3: Beyond Thunderdome). The entire story follows a vengeful Asia who is pursued by a righteous Koo and a dying Snow. It seems the film studios decided to capitalize on a visual film with little substance, hoping loyal fans would flock to any picture where Lin is dressed in traditional garb and wielding a sword and magical powers.

-T-

301, 302
(1996) Thriller   C-98m   Korean with English Subtitles
Catalog #ID3355HL Korea Retail: $39.99
Dir/Prod: Chul Soo Park   Scr: Suk Goon Lee   Ex. Prod: Yong Man Kim
DP: Eun Gil Lee   Editor: Gok Ji Park Art Dir: Jung Who Choi
Set Design: Yung Sam Cho
PC: Arrow Releasing, Inc.   Dist: Evergreen Entertainment
Eun-jin Bang, Sin Hye Hwang, Chu Ryun Kim
[***]
A contemporary Korean film that made its American debut at the Sundance film festival. A murder thriller with visual scenes that will delight Hitchcock aficionado and provide a unique glance into the obscure world of Korean filmmaking. The numbers represent two women who live across from each other in an apartment complex where a murder occurred, and the next door neighbor may know a thing or two. One day a man visits and sits down with the woman in apartment 302. He is looking for the woman in 301 who has mysteriously disappeared. The two young women lived in apartments opposite each other and developed an unusual friendship, thus beginning their journey of self-realization and spiritual freedom.

The woman in 301 is a writer who lives an introverted life and finds difficulty in digesting food. The woman in 302 is the new neighbor on the block, recently divorce, she hopes to start a new life and loves to cook. At first, Hwang (302) attempts to be courtesy with Bang (301) by bringing over some of her best dishes. When Bang keeps refusing, Hwang is compelled to force her to eat even if it kills her. Slowly the women reveal their own pasts and how they have come to their bizarre attitudes toward life. This is not a film for the kids, since the macabre film deals with numerous mature subjects and contains nudity. The dishes prepared by Hwang are a culinary delight and becomes the catalyst of the film's theme. The film's pacing is not overly quick and major portions of the film will fall into flashbacks when you least expect it. Eventually the women come to grips with their own problems and undergo a bizarre transformation which is best seen and not described in this review. A moody thriller which focuses on the tension of the two women and the claustrophobic mood created by their proximity to each other on the same floor. A fine example of the talented growth of Korean filmmakers, and my only complaint involves the dialogue sound. Whether caused by microphone placement or a bad sound mix, at certain points the dialogue fades in intensity. If you're watching the film for subtitles that shouldn't be a problem, since the music and effect sounds are fine. A quirky, dark story that expresses the intensity of individual moods over expensive budgets and gory effects.

36 Crazy Fists
(1977) Kung-Fu   C-91m Dubbed   VA   Hong Kong   Retail: $9.99
Dir: Chen Chih Hua Scr: Szu Tu An   Prod: Chang Kit
DP: Chen Ching Chu   Music: Wu Ta Chiang   MAD: Jackie Chan
Dist: Parade Video
Hsiung Kuang, Liu Chia Yung, Jen Shin Kuan, Ku Feng, Mi Hsueh, Chin Pei, Feng Ko An, Shan Kuai, Chen Liu, Chiang Cheng, Li Wen Tai, Pe Sha Li, Ma Han Yuan, Hsieh Ti
[**]
Billed as a Jackie Chan film, the video release has an introduction with Chan practicing the martial arts scenes he choreographed in the film. This is the last and only time you will see Jackie Chan. Instead the film focuses on Wong Tai Kwon (Hsiung Kuang), as the distributors were purposely misleading you to take advantage of the recent surge of Chan's popularity. Hsiung is an accomplished martial artist, but lacks the charisma and energy of Chan. The story follows a classic training/revenge format. Two Shaolin monks are visiting a small town and spot Wong being beaten up by a gang of thugs. They rescue him and take him home to his beautiful sister. From her, they learn their father was forced by the thugs to pay protection money. When he refused, they beat the old shop owner who eventually died from his injuries. Wong wishes to take revenge and begs the monks to help him. They return to Shaolin Temple, but the head abbot (who has a bizarre tick) refuses him admissions. The two monks then flatter another abbot who does take Wong as his student. From here the film hops onto a merry-go-round and never develops any further. Wong learns some martial arts, beats up his opponent, and then gets beat up by a stronger opponent. This prompts him to train some more and then the cycle repeats a few times until the end of the film when the villainous white-bearded master Ma Man Tang challenges him. A few interesting fight scenes pop up here and there, and eventually Wong meets the drunken beggar (actually a kung-fu master) who helps him learn the crazy fist techniques.

3 Evil Masters
(1980) Kung-Fu   C-95m Dubbed   Hong Kong   Retail: $19.95
Dir: Lu Chun Ku   Scr: I Kuang Prod: Mona Fong   Ex. Prod: Run Run Shaw

Editor: Chiang Hsing Lung, Liu Shao Kuang
Music:Eddie H. Wang   Art Dir: Johnson Tsao   MAD: Hsu Huang
Planning Coordinator: Huang Chia Hsi
PC: Shaw Brothers
Chen Kuan Tai, Chiang Lin, Yuan Tak, Wang Lung Wei, Lin Hui Huang, Kuang Feng
[***]
Venerable Hong Kong star Chen Kuan Tai is a heroic master of the martial arts who decides to bring to justice three evil masters led by Wang Lung Wei. In the amazing credit teaser, one of the best openings of any martial arts film, Chen invites the three infamous killers to a roadside inn. He casually greets them while enjoying his tea. Wang politely asks why they were called, since the evil masters respect Chen's skills and have never insulted him. Chen chastises them for their evil behavior and plans to end their careers. Wang laughs and then attacks with his two allies. The credit starts and a wonderful battle occurs in which Chen is winning the battle. The innkeeper is injured and Chen goes to his rescue. Then Chen is betrayed and stabbed by the innkeeper. Chen is forced to retreat and goes into hiding at a nearby martial arts school. A student finds him and takes care of him, while learning martial arts from Chen. The student's teacher is not a reputable martial arts instructor and abuses his power and position. When the student beats his own instructor, the arrogant teacher becomes furious and plans to expel him. Chen appears and warns the teacher who had been injured by Chen in a long ago fight. Still vengeful and petty, the teacher and his school injure Chen and cast him out. Chen is alone and the three evil masters are in search of him. When Chen is out of the way, the three evil masters go on a criminal spree and take over the arrogant teacher's school. It is up to Chen's new student to defeat the evil masters one by one in traditional fashion. Chen really shines as the noble hero, but his student lacks the charisma and presence of a heroic character. A number of scenes involve comedic antics between Chen's students and a pair of jealous nitwits at his school. The fight scenes are well-choreographed and the film's overall strength is added by Chen who disappears in the second (weaker) half of the film. Still a worthwhile martial arts film for fans who prefer more realism than fantasy.

Tai Chi Master (Tai Chi-Legend of the Octagon/Tai Chi Zhang San Feng)
(1993) Kung-Fu   C-109m   Chinese with English Subtitles   VA
Catalog #1513   Hong Kong   Retail: $39.99
Dir: Yuen Woo Ping Dist: Tai Seng Video
Jet Li   Junbiao
Johnny Chin Sui Hao   Tienbiao
Michelle Khan, Samo Hung
[***1/2]
A fictional period-piece about the inventor of Tai Chi Chuan, played by Jet Li. An all-star cast joins Jet Li as he demonstrates his amazing ability and boyish charm. Following up his popular role as a Shaolin monk, Junbiao and Tienbiao are two young disciples who get into too much trouble. They are cast out of Shaolin during a training exercise when the hot-tempered Tienbiao strikes out against a chief abbot. Junbiao comes to his brother's (many Asian films refer to close friends as brothers though no hereditary bond exists) aid and together they battle a squad of Shaolin pole experts. The two escape due to the kindness of an abbot and venture out into the real world. Poverty-stricken and lacking practical skills, the two try to perform in the streets and

run into more trouble. Michelle Khan and some of her friends are rebels and befriend the two ex-monks. Tienbiao unsatisfied with running and hiding, proposes he joins the army to infiltrate their ranks. At first his loyalty to his friends exist, but is gradually weakened as the power of success corrupts him. He climbs quickly up the ranks and becomes the second in command to the ruling eunuch. (Males who resided in the imperial palace were castrated to avoid contaminating the royal blood line, many powerful eunuchs arose in China.) Tienbiao is more ruthless than his predecessors and forces his soldiers to train under harsh methods. His excuse, only the best will live. Unable to beat his friend, Junbiao escapes to an isolated area and slowly loses his mind. Michelle Khan keeps an eye on him, but then Junbiao observes nature and his surrounding terrain. Gradually, he devises a new style of martial arts applying pressure against pressure, hence inventing Tai Chi. When he regains full strength, he plans to challenge Tienbiao and to bring him to justice for betraying the rebellion and their friendship. The film is highlighted by a number of spectacular fight scenes, involving hundreds of extras with elaborate weaponry and flying (via wires) acrobatics. Though the film never attempts a fantasy image, the martial arts experts perform incredible skills in elaborately constructed sets while dressed in historical costumes. The action seldom slows down and is a definite treat for fans of Jet Li, Chin, or Michelle Khan, three of the best martial arts talents from Asia.

Tai Chi II
(1996) Kung-Fu   C-95m Chinese with English Subtitles   VA
Catalog #46113   Hong Kong   Retail: $79.95
Dir: Yuen Woo Ping Dist: Tai Seng Video
Jacky Wu, Christy Cheung, Mark Cheng, Sibelle Hu Hui Chang
[***]
A master of Tai Chi tries to sway his son (Wu) away from the life of martial arts and toward a respected, scholarly field. He obeys, but secretly learns martial arts with his cousin. His mother knows the truth and feigns ignorance to avoid family confrontation, always trying to appease her stern husband. Hoping to impress a sophisticated woman (Cheung), Wu adopts a Western name, Jacky, and shows off his athletic prowess. Cheung takes an interest in him, but so does a local government official who views Jacky as a threat to his courtship of Cheung.
The true villains throughout this period-piece are the Europeans who have invaded China to force opium into the market. They establish opium dens and bribe corrupt Chinese officials. Not all the officials take kindly to western infringements and a young official makes a stand against the European opium merchants. When that same government official challenges Jacky to a duel, he loses. He admits his defeat and while walking home is attacked by the European opium dealers who see him as a threat to their plans. They kill him and blame Jacky for the murder.
Jacky, his girlfriend, and her freedom-rights friends team up to reveal the true culprits and free China of its oppressors. The Opium War was a serious part of China's sad past and appears as a plot theme in a number of recent films. Basically the drug was imported from India and other parts of Asia, refined, and then sold into China. European powers, such as the British, amassed large fortunes off the addicting drug. When China tried to ban the drug, a war was started to maintain the flow of opium in China. Even the Empress Dowager succumbed to opium smoking as did many high officials and respected scholars. The film addresses the issue of drug abuse and its harmful repercussions. An enjoyable film with good martial arts sequences and engaging performances from Jacky Wu and Christy Cheung.

Takegami
(1990) Japanime: Horror   C-43m Dubbed   Catalog #USM 1620
Japan Retail: $19.95
Dir/Scr/Original Story: Osamu Yamazaki   Ex. Prod: Makoto Hasegawa, Tomoyuki
Miyata   Prod: Shigeaki Komatsu, Nobuhisa Abe   Music: Seikou Nagaoka
Character Design: Masami Ohbari, Kenichi Onuki   Master Design: Masami Ohbari
English Version - Ex. Prod: John O'Donnell   Prod: Stephanie Shalofsky
Dubbing Manager: Peter Bavaro   Dubbing Supervisor: Anthony Salerno
Translation: Kevin McKeown
PC: Minamimachi Bugyosho/J.C. Staff   Dist: U.S. Manga Corps
[**1/2]
An ancient demon has arisen in modern day Japan and only a young man can stop the dragon demon from dominating the world. To enter the human world, the demon needs a host body in which to manifest. He chooses a young high school girl who happens to have a crush on our hero. She is unknowingly possessed while visiting a religious shrine to pray to the gods to make her prettier and more desirable. Feeding on her frailties and desires, the evil demon takes over her body. The good spirit bonds with the hero, destroying previous demons that have incarnated. When the hero confronts the girl/demon, he finds he can not kill her. Though not in love with her, he is aware of her feelings toward him and feels compassion for the lost girl. The good demon encourages him to attack the girl, but the moral crisis gives the evil demon an advantage. Only by using his powers of compassion and love can the evil demon be vanquished and the girl saved. Standard anime fare that will appeal to fans who enjoy the supernatural high school setting. Not for young children.

Tampopo
(1986) Comedy   C-114m   Japanese with English Subtitles   VA
Catalog #24050   Japan Retail: $29.95
Dir: Juzo Itami   Scr: Juzo Itami   Prod: Yasushi Tamaoki, Seigo Hosogoe
DP: Masaki Tamura Editor: Akira Suzuki   Music: Kunihiko Murai
Art Design: Takeo Kimura Dist: Republic Pictures Home Video
Ken Watanabe   Gun
Tsutomu Yamazaki Ooro
Nobuko Miyamoto   Tampopo (Dandelion)
Rikiya Yasuoka   Pisken
Kinzo Sakura Shohei
Koji Miyamoto   Man in White Suit
Koji Yakusho, Shuji Otaki
[****]
Few movies transcend cultural boundaries as easily and cleverly as Tampopo, a brilliant comedic satire of Japanese society and human nature. For viewers who are familiar with classic Japanese films from Kurosawa, Ozu, and Mizoguchi, Itami's film is as different as night to day.
From the beginning scenes, we realize this is not going to be an ordinary movie, but one that defies classification and plays with the boundaries of filmmaking and storytelling. A handsome gangster (Miyamoto) in an impeccable white suit enters a darkened theater followed by his goons

and a bubbly female. The film is about to start, but then someone chews on his snacks a little too loudly for Miyamoto. He takes care of the rude viewer and then addresses the screen. He talks about his love for movies and invites you to join him in the theater. Through the film, Miyamoto is a representation of our own dreams and desires to play a character in film. He floats in scenes where he makes love, touches innocence, and gets locked into a gun battle. But this satiric element does reflect the Japanese attitude toward perfection, no matter the subject. Plus there's nothing in the world like a good bowl of noodles. When the Zen noodle master sits at the counter with his student, reminiscent of Jedi maser Yoda and Luke Skywalker from Empire Strikes back. He educates the student with grave seriousness and deep mental concentration on the proper procedure for eating the noodles. For fans of Asian martial arts movies where training scenes are a rigorous part of life will see similarities in Tampopo.

In classic western/samurai fashion, Gun is the mysterious stranger who arrives in town on a dark and stormy night. Accompanied with his lanky sidekick, he wears a cowboy hat, has a rugged jaw, a stoic glint in his eyes, and drives a truck. He first comes to attention to a small noodle shop owned by a widow named Tampopo (dandelion). He helps her fight off some bullies, but gets beat up in the process. He wakes up the next day and offers to help her improve her business. Quite frankly, your noodles stink, he informs her. Tampopo accepts Gun as her mentor and begins a long and arduous road to becoming a noodle master. Not wanting to give away too much of the film, her quest introduces her to a marvelous group of characters.

If you were limited to only one or two films from Japan, I'd put Tampopo at the top of your list.

Taxing Woman, A
(1987) Comedy   C-126m   **Japanese with English Subtitles**   VA
Catalog #FLV 1900 Japan Retail: $19.95
Dir/Scr: Juzo Itami Prod: Yasushi Tamaoki, Seigo Hosogoe
DP: Yonezo Maeda   Editor: Akira Suzuki   Music:Toshiyuki Honda
Dist: Orion Home Video/Fox Lorber Home Video
Nobuko Miyamoto   Ryoko Itakura, Tax Inspector
Tsutomu Yamazaki Hideki Gondo
Masahiko Tsugawa Assistant Chief Inspector Hanamura
Hideo Murota   Ishii, Motel President
Shuji Otaki   Tsuyuguchi, Tax Office Manager
Daisuke Yamashita Taro Gondo
Shinsuke Ashida, Keiju Kobayashi, Mariko Okada, Kiriko Shimizu, Kazuyo Matsui, Yasuo Daichi, Kinzo Sakura, Hajimeh Asoh, Shiro Ito, Eitaro Ozawa
[***]
An intelligent satirical film from Japanese director Juzo Itami. This time his wife is a hard-nosed, determined tax agent, Ryoko Itakura, who purses Hideki Gondo. Gondo is a gangster who tries to keep his finances a secret from the government tax collectors. Itakura and Gondo start off as opponents, but a bizarre relationship develops between the two. Both characters are persistent in beating the other side and they establish a mutual admiration for their cunning. In the end, Itakura always gets her audit and Gondo resigns with a subtle nod.

Taxing Woman's Return, A
(1988) Comedy   C-127m   **Japanese with English Subtitles**   VA   Japan

Dir: Juzo Itami   Scr: Juzo Itami   Prod: Yasushi Tamaoki, Seigo Hosogoe
Editor: Akira Suzuki   DP: Yonezo Maeda   Music: Toshiyuki Honda
Dist: New Yorker Video/Ingram International Films
Nobuko Miyamoto   Yuoko Itakura
Rentaro Mikuni, Masahiko Tsugawa, Tetsuro Tamba, Takeya Nakamura, Mihoko Shibata, Toru Masuoka, Hosei Komatsu
[**1/2]
Sequel that continues the comedy and drama from the original, but carries the worn formula a bit too long for its own good. After seeing Tampopo, The Funeral, and A Taxing Woman, Itami retreads previous material and moves along with a relaxed tempo. A forgettable film that marked a decline in Itami's overseas popularity. Nobuko is back, but long time costar Yamazaki is sadly absent. She's still a top notch tax investigator and battles politicians, industrialists, and swindlers set on inflating Tokyo's land value and making a killing in the market.

TELEVISION PROGRAMS FROM ASIA - Special Section –

My book is dedicated to films from and about Asia, but I wanted to take a little time out and discuss the availability of television programs from Asia, also available on video. Many of the Japanese animated videos are actually television programs originally aired on public television. You may notice the commercial break points, the shorter running times, and the use of common television themes: never dying characters, repeated stories, etc.
Asian countries are rich producers of films, but their television markets are much larger and play a dominant role in the entertainment field. In Hong Kong alone, the Shaw Television Branch produces over 6,000 hours of television every year which equals more than 3,000 full-length feature films. If you happen to live near a major city or a region with a large foreign population, your access to Asian television programs become a possibility. I must warn that in the majority of cases, English subtitles will not be available, but for people who speak the language or are learning, this will become a good chance to practice your language skills. Many Asian food stores or centers will rent videos featuring films and television programs. I have visited Chinese, Indian, Japanese, and Korean stores with a large selection of videos available for rent. Since my language background is Korean and Japanese, I have had the privilege of seeing many television programs which I enjoyed immensely.
If you happen to look on television, many UHF stations offer foreign programming which showcase Asian programs. Many of them will include subtitles and cover a wide range of shows, from animation to dramas. Of particular interest is Japanese programming which include exciting samurai shows, quirky comedies, and endearing dramas. The miniseries is a popular format and continuous episodes are shown on a weekly basis. As I write, I am following a Korean program which appears every Saturday and Sunday night at 9pm eastern standard on Channel 63. The show is called There is a Bluebird and features a wonderful cast of Korean characters. The show is being carried for the entire year, so you may be able to catch it if you are from the NY/NJ region. Don't limit yourself to movies, for television programs also offer a wonderful world of entertainment at a more leisurely pace.

Temptress Moon   (The Wind and the Moon)

(1996) Romance   C-115m   R   Mandarin with English Subtitles
Catalog # ML 636   Hong Kong/China   Retail: $39.99
Dir: Chen Kaige   Scr: Shu Kei   Original Story: Chen Kaige, Wang Anyi
Prod: Tong Cunlin, Hsu Feng (Miramax Films)
Ex. Prod: Sunday Sun   Production Supervisor: Jade Hsu
DP: Christopher Doyle   Editor: Pei Xiaonan
Art Dir: Huang Qiagui
Music Performed: Central Philharmonic Orchestra, Chamber Orchestra of the Central Music Academy
Dist: Miramax Films

Zhou Yemang	Pang Zhengda
Leslie Cheung	Yu Zhongliang
Gong Li	Pang Ruyi
He Saifei	Xiuyi

Kevin Lin, Zhang Shi, Lin Lianqun, Ge Xiangting, Xie Tian, David Wu, Zhou Jie,
[***]
Released theatrically in America in 1997, Temptress Moon reunites director Kaige with the beautiful Gong Li. The film lacks the grandeur and historical scope of other Gong Li films, but returns more to a straightforward dramatic romance. Zhonglian is a servant in a powerful noble's mansion. His boyhood task is to take care of the master's young daughter, the mischievous Ruyi who runs around disrupting mah-jongg games. She and her older brother Zhengda enjoy a life of ease and sin. Zhengda discovers opium and encourages his sister to become an addict. The sinful life causes Zhongliang to escape his position and he disappears for twenty years, living in Shanghai. He changes his name to Xiao Xie and works his way through life as a playboy and con man. He discovers master Pang has died and must return to the mansion. Things have changed greatly, but one thing remains, Ruyi still loves him. Zhengda has become a mental vegetable and unable to speak or function. In his place, Ruyi has become master of the household with a cousin, Pang Duanwu, as her assistant. A whirlwind of passions erupt and Li struggles with her emotions and duties to the household. In time, Ruyi follows Zhongliang to Shanghai and discovers his true nature.
All in all, Tempest Moon is a beautiful-looking film with a misty glow and features some fine performances. What fails to entice is the drama of the story, on many levels the long film does not move with any energy or passion. The characters go through their roles, but lack the dynamic chemistry of earlier films. I recommend the other Gong Li films and as you enjoy them, you can save this film as an alternative choice.

Tenchi the Movie: Tenchi Muyo in Love
(1996) Japanime   C-95m Dubbed/Japanese with English Subtitles   VA
Catalog # PI VA-1390D/PI VA-1390S   Japan Retail: $19.95/$24.95
Dir: Hiroshi Negishi Scr: Ryoei Tsukimura, Hiroshi Negishi
Character Design & Animation Dir: Hiroyuki Horiuchi Direction: Koji Masunari
Animation Dir: Takahiro Kishida, Kazuya Kuroda, Michiyo Suzuki
Art Dir: Torao Arai Music: Christopher Franke
PCDist: AIC/Tenchi muyo Committee/Pioneer Entertainment
[***]

Based on a popular series, Tenchi Muyo is a full-length film based on the exploits of Tenchi and his unique friends. The film's appeal lies within the characters who bicker while saving the Earth. A super criminal named Kain escapes from a maximum security prison in space and sets off for Earth. Two cute Galaxy Police detectives are on a routine patrol of the Earth sector when they detect the escape and destruction of the police center. It takes no time for detectives Mihoshi and Kiyone to meet up with Tenchi and his friends so that they can stop the evil Kain. Meanwhile, Kain wants to destroy the house of Jirai, so decides to travel in time to kill off Tenchi's bloodline. Tenchi and his friends, a unique group of individuals made up of teenage girls with unique abilities stop Tenchi from disappearing by disrupting the time line. They travel back into time and do battle with Jirai. Tenchi is united with his mother and father when they are young. The film has a fanciful element, never taking itself too seriously and demonstrating the superb nature of Japanese animation. Quite entertaining, the raucous characters will delight, but very young children might find some of the imagery scary. In general Japanese animation is designed for older children in junior high and above. However the underground appeal exists in all ages, especially among college-aged students.

As Japanese animation gains more admirers in the United States, we are treated to the popular shows in Japan. Some programs like Sailor Moon, Star Blazers are picked up for national syndication while others are available on video for rental or purchase. Plenty of more Tenchi episodes are available.

Ten Tigers of Kwantung
(1979) Kung-Fu   C-100m   Dubbed   Hong Kong   Retail: $19.95
Dir: Chang Cheh   Scr: I Kuang Prod: Mona Fong   Ex. Prod: Runme Shaw
PC: Shaw Brothers
Ti Lung, Alexander Fu Sheng, Kuo Chui, Chiang Sheng, Lo Meng, Lu Feng, Sun Chien
[**1/2]
The Ten Tigers of Kwantung (Canton) were a famous group of historical heroes who defended the poor and oppressed. They were experts in martial arts and well-respected among their peers. Director Chang Cheh attempts to create a martial arts masterpiece, featuring Shaw Brothers most talented stars. Instead, the film is mired by its extensive cast and lack of serious confrontations, primarily focused at the beginning and end of the film. The Ten Tigers of Kwantung must defend the peace and battle Manchurian oppression. The film has a passing of the torch element, introducing a number of younger stars who carry off all the battles at the end. Ti Lung is the majestic leader and the group run around Cantion, but are too powerful for anyone to handle, so there's no true confrontation. Just as fights are about to break out, the villains pull back and avoid contact. At the end, the villains decide to corner and kill their opponents in elaborate ambushes. The one-on-one fights fill the film's end and highlights an entertaining battle between a weapon's expert and a hero who uses anything as a weapon. All in all, the deaths of the heroes do not carry any weight or significance to the viewer while the big name stars stay in the background.

Tetsuo: The Iron Man
(1992) Scifi   B&W-67m + 25m (for DrumStruck)   Japanese with English Subtitles
Catalog #FLV-1078 Japan
Dir/Scr: Shinya Tsukamoto

Dist: Fox Lorber Home Video
[**]
Experimental films are prone to be interpreted by individual viewers, expressing bizarre thoughts and images which can not be defined by casual references. One man's garbage is another man's treasure, so without sounding too harsh I give warning that Tetsuo is a very difficult film to appreciate and by standard terms is quite degrading, obscene, ridiculous, and over the top.
The film is a shocking experiment into the realm of man and machine, a popular theme among Japanese writers. The stark black and white footage and experimental filmmaking style reminded me of avant garde German films, but exaggerated to new levels (think Mike Meyers' Sprockets from Saturday Night Live). There are some disturbing and fascinating imagery, but the films descent into stop-motion perversion and violence will turn off the most ardent viewers. The film's imagery explodes onto the screen as a bizarre operation on a man's leg occurs in the middle of a cluttered area filled with metallic parts and refuge. An average Japanese man discovers a metallic object growing out of his face. The mechanical parts grows and consumes the man's identity. Images of another man controlling the device are intercut. A woman is killed while examining a metallic object and begins to pursue the Japanese man. He escapes and engages in a sexual relationship with a woman that turns violent. Both he and she are warped by the metal and he pulls out a giant penis drill and starts to ram it into her body. Needless to say, the film becomes a bizarre jumble of images until its climatic end. The video also includes a short American film entitled DrumStruck, directed by Greg Nickson, starring Anthony Bevilacqua, Markus Greiner, Lia Nickosn

They Were 11
(1986) Japanime: Scifi   C-91m Dubbed/Japanese with English Subtitles
VA   Catalog # USM 1469/USM 1028   Japan Retail: $19.95/$39.95
Dir: Tetsu Dezaki, Tsuneo Tominaga   Scr: Toshiaki Imaizumi, Katsumi Koide
Character Design: Akio Sugino   Art Dir: Junichi Azuma
PC: Kitty Enterprises, Inc./Victor Company of Japan Ltd.   Dist: U.S. Manga Corps
(based on the comic by Moto Hagio)
[***1/2]
Recently, I had the opportunity to view Robert Zemeckis' "Contact", starring Jodie Foster. I was very impressed with the film's serious treatment of possible contact with extra-terrestrial life. Too many science fiction programs deal with science farce rather than science fact. Such inspirational, thought-provoking, and wondrous films like "2001: A Space Odyssey" and "Close Encounters of the Third Kind" were rare glimpses into our possible future. This led me to recall an animated film which deserves special attention for its attempt to create a realistic story in a futuristic setting. In the future, humans (Terrans) and other races have survived through space exploration, warfare, and misunderstanding. Now the surrounding star systems have resolved their differences and are part of one federation. At the prestigious Cosmo Academy, a training ground for the best students from every planet, talented cadets gather for a rigorous schedule of exams. To successfully graduate would guarantee a secure future. The final exam involves a group of ten students to board an un-manned derelict spaceship. They must fix the ship, get it running, and survive for an extended period of time: 53 days. The only problem is that aboard the spaceship there are 11 instead of 10 cadets. This causes paranoia and doubt among the cadets as they resolve to salvage the ship while learning to work with each other and trust each other.

Hagio was inspired by a classic Japanese folktale from Kenji Miyazawa (the Jules Verne of Japan) about eleven children who discover that one of them is a monster.

Three Avengers
(1980) Kung-Fu   C-93m Dubbed   R
Catalog #FRM 4004 Hong Kong   Retail: $19.95
Dir: Wong Wah Kay Scr: Wong Ching, Wong Wah Kay
Ex. Prod: Pal Ming
PC: World Northal Corporation   Dist: Fox Lorber/Orion Home Video
Bruce Li   Hung Tack
Michael Winston, Chien Yuet Sun
[1/2]**
Bruce Li is back and though the film has a rough, low-budget edge, it's actually an entertaining film and one of Li's better kung-fu adventures. If you like realistic, non-wire flying kung-fu then this film features plenty of action and a charismatic host of characters. Li is the closest thing to Bruce Lee in power and entertainment. Just take the bad with the good and enjoy yourself. Hung Tack and his best friend Mok are part of a Chinese Opera Troop where martial arts and acrobatics play a big part of the performance. They are excellent fighters, but a bit on the wild side. When a gang of punks start harassing the performers, Bruce and his pal decide to teach them a lesson. They win but the mayhem causes damages to the theater. Embarrassed, the master of the Opera Troop expels Bruce and his friend. The two buddies decide to strike it out on there own, but trouble befalls them when a rich developer starts to threaten Bruce's aunt and cousin. An interesting segment develops when an American fighter visiting China battles Bruce and is defeated. Instead of coming back for revenge, the American admires Bruce and becomes his student. The three friends manage a martial arts school, but the evil land developers frame Li and his friends. The injured Mok takes the blame and goes off to prison, while Li is discovered by a talent scount and becomes a big star. In many films, their friendship would fail to be developed, but Three Avengers follows the careers of both men and how they have changed. Mok still wants revenge for the setup and his master's death, finding his American friend, they search for the bald-headed killer. Li also decides to put fame and fortune aside, realizing friendship is more important than money. The fight scenes are all well choreographed and the story moves smoothly with down to earth characters being developed over a course of time. Except for the rough edges in filmmaking, the film works on a number of levels and stands as one of the better kung-fu films of that decade.

Thunderbolt
(1995) Kung-Fu   C-100m   Chinese with English Subtitles
Catalog #ML 614   Hong Kong   Retail: $39.99
Dir: Gordon Chan   Ex. Prod: Leonard Ho
MAD: Coord: Samo Hung
PC: Golden Harvest   Dist: Mei Ah Company
Jackie Chan, Anita Yuen, Michael Wong, Kayama Yuzo, Ken Lo Wai Kwong
[***]
The cover of the video gives you the impression that Jackie Chan is a hot shot driver trying to emulate Tom Cruise from "Days of Thunder". Though racing does play a big part of the film,

there's enough kung-fu and action without wheels to please the best of fans. Surprisingly, the film emphasizes less trademark comedy/slapstick than his past projects and focuses more on dramatic action within the story. The opening scene introduces us to the Mitsubishi Motors Training Facility, an advanced site dedicated to the improvement and development of automobiles. (Mitsubishi is an official sponsor for Jackie Chan, so you'll see their products in all his films) Jackie is a Hong Kong student studying at the facility and gets to show off his Japanese with an attractive woman. Quickly he returns to Hong Kong where his father owns a large garage repair facility and a fleet of tow trucks used by the traffic police. Continuing with the international flavor of the film, an international villain named Cougar kills an undercover cop in the United States and flees to Hong Kong. He's definitely one of the weaker Chan villains to appear on screen. Wearing a black helmet, he roars down the streets of Hong Kong, drag racing with Chan and other police cars that fail to capture him. Even when he's finally caught, there's not enough direct evidence to convict him. Cougar decides to teach Chan a lesson and brutally attacks his father's garage, nearly killing his cute sisters. The total carnage and energy of the fight scene is definitely a high point and when Chan returns the favor by battling in a crooked pachinko parlor, it's true action delight. Chan decides the only way to beat Cougar is by racing him. They both arrive in Japan for a prestigious race. Chan's confidence is boosted with help from workers at the garage who modify his car. When the car is destroyed, Chan's Japanese female friend comes to the rescue with two brand new Mitsubishi race cars. The race begins and you should race out and catch this film.

Tigers
(1991) Action C-108m   Chinese with English Subtitles   Hong Kong
Dir: Eric Tsang   Scr: Nam Yin, James Yuen
Prod: Miu Kiu Wai Ex. Prod: Wallace Cheung Kwok Chu
DP: JingleMa Editor: Kam Ma   Music: Tats Lau, Patrick Lui
Art Dir: Lee Chi Ngai   Prod Manager: Jessinta Liu
Assistant Dir: Ng Hon Keung, Leung Chun Kwon
MAD: Tung Wai, Yuen Tak, Leung Siu Hung
PC: Movie Impact Limited
Dist: Ocean Shores Video Ltd.
Andy Lau, Wong Yat Wah, Tony Leung Kar Fai
[**]
Standard cop/crime fare without the charisma and style of Hong Kong directors John Woo and Ringo Lam. Five Hong Kong police officers are involved in a corruption scandal by accepting bribes from a powerful crime boss. The film focuses on the individual characters and explains their motives and reactions. Two of the officers, Ming and Tau Pi try to get revenge by murdering the criminal Fong Tung who is under witness protection. The film is full of a series of rough and tumble fight scenes and minor gun battles. The witness who doesn't want to be turned over for police protection, due to the fact they've beaten him and tried to kill him, breaks free of his protectors and makes a run for it in a high scale hotel. The two hot head cops are on his lead and battle him every inch of the way. There are some nice stunts as men fall down a few stories and battle in elevators, but when the police arrive on the scene. The only solution is death.

To Kill with Intrigue
(1977) Kung-Fu   C-107m   Dubbed   VA
Catalog #9902-B   Hong Kong   Retail: $9.99
Dir: Lo Wei   Scr: Ku Lung Ex. Prod: Lo Wei   Prod: Hsu Li Hwa
DP: Chen Chung Yuan   Editor: Kuo Ting Hung   Music: Chen Fang Chi
Prod Manager: Li Hsien Chang   Prod Design: Chu Shih Mei
MAD: Chen Hsin Ie, Chen Wen Lung
Dist: Alpha Film & Video Inc. 1984 ZIV Entertainment
Jackie Chan, Chu Feng, Shen Ie Leng, Yu Ling Lung, Wang Kuo, Tung Lin, Ma Chi,
Chang Ching Hsia, Chen Hui Lou, Li Wen Tai
[**]
Jackie Chan's earlier films were mostly low-budget generic action flicks that lack the humor, style, and excitement of Chan's modern films. If you've seen his newer films made in the late 1980's and 1990's, don't expect the same quality or entertainment. A costume piece with Chan playing a very straight role as the wronged hero seeking revenge. Chan is the son of Master Lei, a martial arts master who is celebrating his birthday. That evening, the Lei family is attacked by the Killer Bees who stab people with cute charm-like daggers. The daughter of the Killer Bees' deceased master wants revenge on Lei for killing her family. Everyone is killed, but she takes pity on Chan and spares his life. After all, he had nothing to do with the murders. Before the battle, Chan had sent his lover, Chin Chin, the maid, away to safety. She is carrying their unborn child and meets with Chan's friend Chin Chun. Chan searches for Chin Chin, but she has disappeared with Chin Chun. Meanwhile a number of other things complicate matters. One of the better characters in the film is Third Dragon, an elderly martial arts master who takes Chan under his wing. He is the leader of the Dragon Escort Company that was recently robbed. They suspect Chin Chun and with Chan search for the man. They hire mercenaries from the Bloody Rain Clan to find Chin Chun, but the mercenaries betray the Third Dragon and attempt to murder him and Chan. With the help of Miss Killer Mee, they beat the killers, but Chan is mortally wounded.

Tokyo Decadence
(1991) Erotic Drama C-92m Dubbed/ Japanese with English Subtitles
NC-17 VA   Japan
Dir/Scr: Ryu Murakami   Music: Ryuichi Sakamoto
Dist: Triboro Entertainment Group
Miho Kikaido, Tenmei Kano, Yayoi Kusama, Sayoko Amano
[*1/2]
The first thing that catches your eye is the erotic cover of a Japanese woman dressed in sexy lingerie leaning against the window of a penthouse apartment. The erotic cover caught my eye, since Japanese sexual culture is a fascinating topic that differs greatly from western values. The story follows the life of Ai (love), an attractive high-paid prostitute. She works for a Tokyo agency that specializes in sado-masochistic fantasies. We follow her kinky escapades from one hotel room to the next, while she searches for a client she is in love with. However, the film hardly explores the culture and opts for lurid and humiliating sex scenes involving bondage. It fails to explore the young woman's inner feelings and shed any light into her exploits in a decadent world of prostitution and sorrow. The film actually doesn't attempt to build a coherent

plot or create any motivations for the characters who act with puppet-like passion. A film that fails on a number of levels, providing little interest for fans who are looking for Japanese dramas or sexual voyeurism. Adapted from Murakami's own novel "Topaz".

Tokyo Olympiad
(1966) Documentary C-170m   Japanese with English Subtitles
Catalog #CC1227L   Japan Retail: $99.95
Dir: Kon Ichikawa   Dist: Voyager Entertainment
[1/2]**

A long and ponderous special dedicated to Japan's hosting of the 1964 Summer Olympics. After the ravages of World War II, Japan was modernized and rebuilt into a powerful ally of the western world. As a symbol of its renewed pride, Tokyo was the official site of the 1964 Summer Olympics. The document was made to highlight the events that took place during the Olympics, but definitely has a Japanese bias. Interesting from a historical point of view rather than entertainment.

Tokyo Story
(1953) DramaC-134m   Japanese with English Subtitles   VA   Japan
Dir: Yasujiro Ozu   Scr: Yasujiro Ozu, Kogo Noda   Prod: Takeshi Yamamoto
Editor: Yoshiyasu Hamamura   DP: Yushun Atsuta
Music: Takanobu Saito   Prod. Designer: Tatsuo Hamada, Itsuo Takahashi
Art Design: Tatsuo Hamada, Itsuo Takahashi   Costumes: Taizo Saito
Dist: New Yorker Video

Chishu Ryu	**Shukishi Hirayama**
Chieko Higashiyama	**Tomi Hirayama**
So Yamamura	**Koichi**
Kuniko Miyake	**Fumiko**
Haruko Sugimura	**Shige Kaneko**
Nobuo Nakamura	**Kurazo Kaneko**
Kyoko Kagawa	**KyokoYounger Daughter**
Setsuko Hara	**Noriko**
Shiro Osaka	**Keiso**
Eijiro Tono	**Sanpei Numata**
Teruko Nagaoka	**Yone Hattori**
Zen Murase	**Minoru**
Mitsuhiro Mori	**Isamu**
Hisao Toake	**Osamu Hattori**
Toyoko Takahashi	**Shukichi Hirayama's Neighbor**
Mutsuko Sakura	**Patron of the Oden Restaurant**
Toru Abe	**Railroad Employee**
Sachiko Mitani	**Noriko's Neighbor**
Junko Anan	**Beauty Salon Assistant**
Yoshiko Togawa	**Beauty Salon Clients**
Ryoko Mizuki	

[****]

Ozu's masterpiece of family drama is a countless favorite among film professors and critics. An elderly couple leave the country and travel to Tokyo to visit their children and grandchildren. Though they have sacrificed so much to bring their children up, the adults find little time to take care of their aged parents. A simple reflection into life which carries a deep moral message. Ozu is well-known for his use of static camera work and simple angles to frame the rudimentary life of the average Japanese person. Differing greatly in style from Kurosawa, Ozu's films stress patience and serenity within a smaller realm of life.

To Live
(1994) DramaC-132m   Mandarin with English Subtitles   VA
Catalog #VHS 90013 China   Retail: $19.95
Dir: Zhang Yimou   Scr: Lu Wei, Yu Hua
Prod: Chiu Fu-Sheng   Ex. Prod: Christophe Tseng, Kow Fuhong
DP: Lu Yue   Editor: Du Yuan   Music: Zhao Jiping Sound: Tao Jing
Prod Manager: Hu Shaofeng, Zhang Zhengyan   Associate Prod: Barbara Robinson
Prod Design: Cao Jiuping   Makeup: Sun Wei   Costumes: Dong Huamiao
(based on the novel by Yu Hwa)
PC: Samuel Goldwyn Company presents an Era International (HK) Ltd. Production in association with Shanghai Film Studios
Dist: Hallmark Home Entertainment

Ge You	**Fugui**
Gong Li	**Jiazhen**
Niu Ben	**Town Chief Niu**
Guo Tao	**Chunsheng**
Jiang Wu	**Wan Erxi**
Ni Dahong	**Long'er**
Liu Tianchi	**Adult Fengxia**
Zhang Lu	**Teenage Fengxia**
Xiao Cong	**Fengxia_as a child**
Dong Fei	**Youqing**
Zongluo	**Fugui's Father**
Liu Yanjing	**Fugui's Mother**
Li Lianyi	**Lao Quan**
Zhao Yuxiu	**Dr. Wang**
Zhang Kang	**Mantou**

[****]
An excellent film about a family caught up in the tides of Maoist change during the Chinese revolution. Director Zhang reunites with his lovely leading lady, Gong Li as she plays the wife of a wealthy man who loses everything through his vices. In a subdued, but winning performance Ge You is Gong's husband, a thin middle-aged man with a long face and a bewildered look, who falls victim to make situations. He is quiet and harmless, not very sharp and we witness his downfall in a local gambling den. He sits opposite his friend who in reality desires Ge's beautiful home. After a string of losses, Ge is ordered to pay the bill or lose his house. He has no choice and is forced into instant poverty, but events seem fortunate when communists seize power and treat the upper class with disdain and violence. Ge is separated

from his wife and swept into a military life switching sides when convenient. He doesn't care about idealogy, but is concerned with survival and peace. The tides of change sweep him and his wife from one situation to another, but fortunes look good when their mildly retarded daughter is betrothed to a Communist official. The film doesn't let you for once think life is so sweet and easy, and when the Youth Guard sweep throughout China and arrest everyone who is a scholar over the age of thirty, the country is placed into turmoil. Ge's daughter who suffers a pregnancy complication dies in the hospital, since all the doctors have been arrested. Her child survives and grows up under their guidance.

An artistically memorably film with a moving element that won awards at the British Academy Awards and the Cannes Film Festival and received nominations at the Golden Globe and the Academy Awards. Adopted from Yu Hwa's novel "Lifetimes".

Tora! Tora! Tora!
(1970) War   C-143m   English   PG   VA
Catalog #27370   Japan/USA   Retail: $19.95
Dir: Richard Fleischer, Toshio Masuda, Kinji Fukasaku, Kinji Fukasuku
Prod: Elmo Williams   Scr: Larry Forrester, Hideo Oguni, Ryuzo Kikushima
(based on Tora! Tora! Tora! by Gordon W. Prange and the Broken Seal by Ladislas Farago)
Editor: James E. Newcom, Pembroke J. Herring, Inoue Chikaya
DP: Charles F. Wheeler, Shinsaku Himeda, Masamichi Sato, Osami Furuya
Music: Jerry Goldsmith   Dist: CBS/Fox Video

Martin Balsam	**Admiral Kimmel**
Soh Yamamura	**Adm. Yamamoto**
Jason Robards Jr.	**General Short**
Joseph Cotten	**Henry Stimson**
Tatsuya Mihashi	**Cmdr. Genda**
E.G. Marshall	**Lt. Col. Bratton**
Takahiro Tamura	**Lt. Cmdr. Fuchida**
James Whitmore	**Adm. Halsey**
Eijiro Tono	**Adm. Nagumo**

[***]

Ambitious attempt to recreate and capture the drama of the attack on Pearl Harbor, Hawaii, which ignited America's entry into World War II. The well-documented screenplay provides character and plot development from both points of view and show the major and minor blunders from both sides. Japanese fimmakers were used to create the scenes involving Japanese characters and American filmmakers captured the American side. The majority of film follows the political events leading to the actual conflict which is showcased in the latter portion of the film. The re-created attack on Pearl Harbor is amazingly accurate and relies on footage shot for the film using detailed miniatures and actual locations. On December 7, 1941, Japanese carrier-based planes launched a massive air attack against the American Pacific Fleet harbored at Pearl Harbor, Hawaii. The Japanese used a number of codes, including Tora! Tora! Tora! when preparing for attack. In English, Tora mean tiger. Dozens of ships were sunk or damaged, including the Battleship Arizona with over a 1000 men lost. The American carrier fleet, on maneuvers, escaped damage. The all-star cast and detail may appeal more to fans of historical dramas and military buffs than casual viewers. The tension and drama are felt from both sides with Oscar-winning special effects. The film Midway starring Toshiro Mifune and Charlton Heston was another attempt to recreate the Pacific Conflict on the big screen.

Twilight of the Cockroaches
(1990) Japanime/Live-Action   C-105m   Dubbed   VA   Catalog # 90273
Japan Retail: $19.95
Dir/Scr: Hiroaki Yoshida   Animation Design: Hiroshi Kurogane   Music: Morgan Fischer
PC: TYO Productions Inc./Kitty Films Inc.   Dist: Streamline Pictures
Kaoru Kobayashi, Setsuko Karamsumarau
[**1/2]
A combination of Japanese animation and live-action, predating Joe's Apartment. Mr Saito is a lonely bachelor who lives in disarray and apathy. His home is infested with a community of intelligent cockroaches who have had a wonderful peaceful existent with their human neighbor. Everything in the human world is live-action while all the cockroaches are animated. Life suddenly takes a turn for the worse when Saito falls in love with a neighborly woman who moves in and decides to add a feminine touch which includes the elimination of the insects. The film at times ponders while the cockroaches philosophize and debate whether to leave their home. An interesting attempt in the world of anime to experiment and try something different.

Twin Dragons, The (Double Dragon)
(1992) Kung-Fu   C-100m   Dubbed   VA   Catalog # EDO 5713
Hong Kong   Retail: $9.95
Dir: Tsui Hark, Ringo Lam Scr: Barry Wong, Tsui Hark, Cheung Tung Jo, Wong Yik
Prod: Teddy Robin Ex. Prod: Ng Sze Yuen   Presented by Teddy Robin
DP: Wong Wing Hang, Wong Ngor Tai   Editor: Mak Che Sun
Dist: Edde Entertainment/Ace Video
Jackie Chan, Maggie Cheung, Teddy Robin, Nina Li Chi
[***]
Just like the title says, there's two Dragons in the film both played wonderfully by Jackie Chan. Co-directed by Ringo Lam and Tsui Hark, Chan was asked to help make a movie to benefit the Hong Kong Directors Guild. The story is similar to Jean-Claude Van Damme's "Double Impact" where two twin brothers are separated at birth but rejoined later in life to fight a common enemy. There the comparisons end and Twin Dragons takes off in full comedic force. The mistaken identity scenes are funny while the fight scenes are terrific, allowing Chan to flex his humor and power into two separate roles. The separation at birth is inconsequential and rather ridiculous. A criminal grabs one of the newly born children as a hostage and drops it off in a park. A drunk prostitute finds the baby boy and raises him as her own while the despondent parents move to America. The two grow up: one becomes a tough auto mechanic while the other is a concert conductor. The auto mechanic gets into trouble when his best friend tries to save a pretty lounge singer, Maggie Cheung, from a gang of thugs. The thugs go after him, but mistake the composer and end up threatening the lives of both brothers. Only united can they stop the gangsters and save the women they love, now only if the women could decide which hero they truly love.

Twin Warriors (see Tai Chi Master)
Part of the Dimension Films Jet Li package, which are older films remastered for American audiences. In general, I recommend the remasters over the original versions, since they offer English diaolgue over subtitles, a more modern soundtrack, and at times, cleaner editing and the omission of over-the-top violence.

Twinkle Twinkle Lucky Stars   (Target, The)
(1985) Comedy Kung-Fu   C-95m Dubbed   Catalog #0470
Hong Kong   Retail: $39.99
Dir: Samo Hung   Prod: Leonard K.C. Ho   Dist: Tai Seng Video
Samo Hung, Jackie Chan, Yuen Biao, Righard Ng, Fung Shui Fan, Andy Lau, Richard Norton, Sibelle Hu, Rosamund Kwan, Michelle Khan
[**]
If it weren't for a few saving fights, this film would rate even lower. Sadly the talents of Jackie Chan and Yuen Biao are secondary in the film, while the majority of action focuses on the My Lucky Stars gang led by Samo Hung. A group of lecherous clods who grope and come close to raping young women. In a modern world of sexual equality and harassment laws, films of this nature will send dangerous messages if taken in the wrong context. Samo and his friends taking a vacation in Thailand after the success of their previous case. Back in Hong Kong, Jackie and Yuen are cops on a hot trail and get involved in some spectacular fights, but the film quickly returns to Thailand for the majority of the film. Samo is the good one and pretty much keeps to himself, moping because he can't win the affections of a woman. The rest of the gang make wild faces and chase after everything on two legs. They even go to the extent of using voodoo magic and starting a fire in their apartment to catch poor Rosamund nude. These men act like the worst perverts you could hardly imagine and personally lack any charm or decency. They get caught up in a gang war and discover deadly assassins are planning to kill a Hong Kong drug lord.
They all rush back to Hong Kong and team up with Jackie who now must protect the vile drug lord. A few fight scenes are sprinkled in to keep the action flowing, but they come too late and too short. Richard Norton has a fight scene in which he beats Jackie Chan. Originally, Chan was suppose to have a climatic battle at the end with Norton. Chan injured himself so Samo fills the role in one of his best fights. The scene leads with the heroes battling the villains in a hotel. Samo takes on a sai master only equipped with two tennis racquets. Hilarious. Then Samo dukes it out with Richard Norton, proving no pain no gain. If you do want to see the film, keep in mind Jackie Chan has a small supporting role while Samo is the star. The women art cute and well-known stars but are treated more like sex objects. Rosamund with her short hair is adorable and gives a cute scene as a blind woman in the ladies bathroom to avoid Richard Norton. However her innocence and naivete is used as a way for the men to crop feels and look down her shirt.

Two Shaolin Kids in Hong Kong
(1994) Kung-Fu   C-95 min   Chinese with English Subtitles
Catalog #1699   Hong Kong   Retail: $39.99
Dir: Yip Tin Hang   Dist: Tai Seng Video
Anita Lee, Liu Chia Hui
[**]

One of the slapstick martial arts comedies from Hong Kong's tiny duo. They're like the little rascals, but a lot wilder for the 90's. Fatty is the portly one who goes for the laughs and gets in trouble while his sidekick is the straight no-nonsense one who's a great fighter. The martial arts scenes can actually be quite entertaining, but much of the humor is extremely juvenile with a mix of mild perversion, slapstick comedy, and ludicrous fights scenes. A fun duo in the vein of Abbott and Costello as kids, but don't anticipate much in the plot and character development.

-U-

U-Jin Brand
(1991) Japanime: Romance C-45m Japanese with English Subtitles
VA   Catalog # USM 1075 Japan Retail: $29.95
Creator: Hideo Takano   Original Writer: Yujin   Planned by Takumi Ogawa
Prod: Soichiro Harada, Nagateru Kato
Scr: Satoru Akahori Dir: Osamu Okada
Chief Animator: Yumi Nakayama DP: Akihiko Takahashi
Music: Nobuo Ito   Music FX: Atsushi Watanbe   Dir Music: Naohisa Hayakawa
Music Prod: Animate Film Ex. Prod: Michihisa Abe   Ass. Prod: Koichi Kikuchi
Editors: JAY FILM, Toshio Henmi, Mitsuteru Okada
Co-Prod: J.C. Staff   PROD: Animate Film   Created by SEIYO
English Version - Ex. Prod: John O'Donnell   Prod Coordinator: Stephanie Shalofsky
Subtitling: Studio NEMO
Tranlastion: William Flanagan, Hisako Ikeuchi   English Rewrite: Jay Parks
Lyric Rewrite: David Mayhew   Package Design: Mark Weiss
PC: Yujin/SEIYO/Animate Film Co. Ltd.
Dist: Central Park Media Corporation (US Manga Corps)
[1/2]**

An anthology of stories surrounding relationships within the business community of one corporation. The film contains a mature style of animation and storytelling, but leans toward a lecherous and voyeuristic side. Tsurujiro Kazama is a handsome, talented 28 year old songwriter who loves to compose music for the hottest teen stars in Japan. Since he is in such demand, he makes his own hours and keeps to himself in a tiny little apartment overlooking a girl's school. He spends most of his time eyeing the teenagers and fantasizing about them. When a new client comes, he forces her into his room and has sex with her. He never pursues a serious relationship, having been heartbroken from a past love affair. His childhood sweetheart is Akiyo and the new girl bares a resemblance to her, but can he cope with his past feelings of love.

In the second story, co-worker Sachiko is in love with the handsome Nakadai. However Nadakai has met a new woman named Hitomi and no longer pays any attention to Sachiko. The word gets around the office that Hitomi is a bitch who is pretending to be a sweet virgin. The boss, Toyama no Benbei, decides to act upon the situation for the good of the company. Secretly, he lives a dual life which no one knows about...the respected corporate boss and the sexual avenger. The solution he decides upon is to rape Hitomi and prove that she is no longer a sweet virgin. Seemingly, rape is not that serious an offense in Japan (In reality rape is very serious, but animation has had a long standing of depicting rape scenes - be careful on your viewing preference).

The final story deals with a husky, bearish worker named Iwata who is having sex with a wild slut named Tomoko. Tomoko is the daughter of a section leader. Meanwhile, Iwata spends secret time with the gentle Kyoko. Toyama decides to solve the problem by raping Tomoko! In the end Kyoko reveals her true love for a richer more powerful man, while Tomoko dumps the pathetic Iwata for his failed betrayal. The story content is serious in nature with occassional humor, but the film's main driving force is sexual eroticism which stems from a fascination with young women (teenagers) and forced sexual situations (rapes which the women enjoy). Not intended for minors and geared towards fans of the adult erotic genre.

Ultimate Teacher
(1988) Japanime   C-57m Dubbed/Japanese with English Subtitles
Catalog #USM 1471/USM 1030   Japan Retail: $14.95/$29.95
Dir: Toyoo Ashida   Scr: Monta Ibu
Character Design: Atsuji Yamamoto   Art Dir: Setsuko Ishizu
PC: Movic   Dist: U.S. Manga Corps
[**]
Every now and then I come across a film that just seems a little too overboard, extensively silly, grotesque, insane, and difficult to watch. Then the next day, I'll bump into someone who loved the same film. I'll point out all the faults and they'll enthusiastically agree, but counter that the film was purposely done that way as a super spoof, a loving parody of an existing genre. Well, take it as you may, the fact remains that you better know what genre the film is spoofing or you're in for a miserable time. Ultimate Teacher spoofs the fights and comical high school antics of girls found in Project A-ko, but on a much cruder and bolder level. Tokyo's Emperor High School is the worst school in the city, looking like a combat zone with a rowdy bunch of students who don't look half as bad as a Los Angeles gang members. An eccentric new school teacher, Ganpachi, arrives with the promise of turning the school around no matter what he has to do. Part tyrant, part super-hero, and a complete fool, he starts fights with the students, wears female panties, and organizes his own gang. In reality, he's a genetic cross between a man and a cockroach, and yes, he has the proportionate strength of a human-size cockroach. The only thing that stands between him and total supremacy is the leader of one of the gangs. A cute, tough girl named Hinako Shiratori is the school's best fighter, but loses to Ganpachi when her weakness is discovered. To fight effectively, she must wear blue "Lucky Kitty" gym shorts. As a child when she fought, she was traumatized by little boys mocking her visible panties. By wearing gym shorts, she didn't mind boys seeing up her skirt and could fight effectively. She attempts to battle Ganpachi with regular panties, but her powers are diminished and she almost loses. With the help of her gang friends and a mysterious stranger, they put an end to Ganpachi's reign. In one bold move, Ganpachi's burly gang members dress in female "Lucky Kitty" shorts and sexually taunt Hinako, with a blatant "Schwing, schwing!" This scene will either have you laughing on the floor or reaching for your fast forward button, but then again comedy is always subjective.

Unbeatable Dragon (Shaolin Invincible)
(1978) Kung-Fu   C-100m   Dubbed   Hong Kong   Retail: $19.95
Dir: Chang Cheh   Scr: I Kuang Prod: Mona Fong   Ex. Prod: Runme Shaw
Art Dir: Johnson Tsao   PC: Shaw Bros.

Kuo Chui, Lo Meng, Chiang Sheng, Lu Feng, Sun Chien
[***]
Another entertaining film from director Chang and his talented ensemble group (the Chang Gang). The Manchurian court has requested martial arts experts from North Shaolin and South Shaolin Temple to demonstrate and teach their skills. One group performs with excellence, but the other temple has tepid results. That temple does not plan to teach the Manchurians and sends only their novice instructors.
The Manchus fear the growing rebellion within Shaolin and decide to pit one temple against the other. They encourage the two groups (of three) to spar, then murder the losing instructors and blame the others. When word gets back to the temple, they send real experts to exact revenge. But first they must train in special styles with humorous results: Lo Meng's egg training scene is one of the most memorable. He does finger push-ups over raw eggs and every time he breaks one he has to eat it. He likes eggs until he eats them morning, noon, and night for a few weeks, but the master won't let him have anything else. When they perfect their techniques, they beat the other Shaolin instructors but discover it is really the court who has set them up and band together in a final effort to win. History loves to play with tragic figures, and China was never able to defeat the Manchurians so Chinese films tend to have a martyr-toned end. The cast is full of veteran Chang actors who put up a great job performing acrobatic and powerful martial arts techniques with and without weapons. A weapon featured but not often seen is the long staff with a nunchaku-style end.

Urotsukidoji 1: Legend of the Overfiend   (The Wandering Kid)
(1993) Japanime: Erotic Horror   C-108m   Dubbed/Japanese with English Subtitles
NC-17   VA   Catalog # A18 1072   Japan Retail: $29.95
Dir: Hideki Takayama   Scr: Goro Sanyo, Noboru Aikawa, Michael Lawrence
Original Story: Toshio Maeda   Music: Masamichi Amano
PC: JAVN/West Cape Corp.   Dist: Anime 18 (Central Park Media)
[**1/2]
The animation is beautiful, the action is high-paced, and the characters are interesting, but the story focuses more on extreme scenes of violence and explicit sex: lesbian scenes, violent rapes, bodily mutilations, and demons. Unless you find these topics interesting, I'd stay away from the film since subtlety is not an issue. The most popular and well-known of the X-rated Japanese animated films to come to America, the film is easily accessible in video stores. The story follows Amano Jyaku and his sister Megumi who know that every 3,000 years the realms of demon and humans merge into one reality. Being demons, they aren't too kind to humans and can assume human appearance. The duo track the demonic Overfiend and confront him at Myojin University, Japan. Along the way, Akemi Ito and Tatsuo Nagumo encounter some nasty surprises as they join the struggle against the evil Overfiend and his minions who wreck havoc on the souls of the young. Sexual penetration plays a key part to the demons domination of human beings. Here's a brief scene from the movie (take caution): a young high school girl is asked to go to a teacher's office. The young girl is dressed in a tight gym suit and glistens from her work out. The older female teacher dressed in a sharp suit invites her in and then rapes her. She tears apart her gymsuit and performs oral sex in a very graphic manner. Then the teacher's body rips apart and transforms into a slithering demon that rapes the teenager. Soon the wandering kid enters and violently destroys the demon.

Urotsukidoji 2: Legend of the Demon Womb
(1993) Japanime: Erotic Horror   C-88m Dubbed/Japanese with English Subtitles   NC-17
VA   Catalog # A18 1073   Japan Retail: $29.95
Dir: Hideki Takayama   Scr: Goro Sanyo, Noboru Aikawa, Michael Lawrence
Original Story: Toshio Maeda   Music: Masamichi Amano
PC: JAVN/West Cape Corp.   Dist: Anime 18 (Central Park Media)
[**1/2]
Sequel to the first film with the same form of adult animation and graphic content. The story
continues the exploits from the original and many other sequels follow part two. The series has a
strong appeal due to its slick animation and combination of supernatural elements, using sex and
violence. After all, wouldn't real demons indulge in sex and violence? The films have travelled
the anime circuit and are easily found for rental or purchase. Only for fans of the first film.

Urusei Yatsura: Movie 1 "Only You"
(1983) Japanime: Scifi Comedy   C-100m   Japanese with English Subtitles   VA
Dir/Scr: Mamoru Oshii   DP: Wakana Fumio
Character Design: Kazuo Yamazaki   Animation   Dir: Kazuo   Yamazaki,   Yuji
Moriyama
Art Dir: Shichiro Kobayashi
PC: Kitty Films   Dist: AnimEigo
(based on manga characters by Rumiko Takahashi)
[**1/2]
Popular, long running Japanese TV series based on characters created by the legendary
Takahashi, also available are video tapes featuring the 197 television episodes and the 11 OAV
episodes. The versions most commonly found in retailers are the six Urusei Yatsura movies.
Ataru Moroboshi is loved by Lum and Elle, two alien women with very stubborn attitudes about
dating. Ataru's main squeeze is the feline space princess Lum, but Elle claims that Ataru
promised to marry her. In a flashback sequence eleven years ago, two children are playing with
each other. Ataru steps on the shadow of Elle which in her culture means she is caught and will
be his future bride. Not satisfied with the decision, Lum kidnaps Ataru and takes him back to her
planet. Her father isn't too happy with his daughter marrying an inferior human and all hell
breaks loose on the planet.
The series lacks the freshness and appeal found in newer animated films based on Rumiko's
works, perhaps the characterizations are a bit too bizarre and the animation style seems dull and
shallow. The relationship between Lum and Ataru never found its mark with me. As the film
delves deeper into a realm of lunacy, the film becomes tedious and lacks the high-powered
muscial score, slick animation, and chemistry found in similar films.

Urusei Yatsura: Movie 2 "Beautiful Dreamer"
(1984) Japanime: Scifi Comedy   C-90m Japanese with English Subtitles   VA
Dir/Scr: Oshii Mamoru   Character Design: Kazuo Yamazaki
Animation Dir: Kazuo Yamazaki, Yuji Moriyama
Art Dir: Shichiro Kobayashi
PC: Toho   Dist: U.S. Manga Corps

(created by Rumiko Takahashi)
[**1/2]
The series continues with the entire gang trapped in a time loop that causes them to relive the day before the School Festival. Lum leads the way in hijinks and trouble. Plenty more videos are available for fans.

Urusei Yatsura: Movie 3 " Remember My Love"
(1985) Japanime   C-93m Japanese with English Subtitles
Urusei Yatsura: Movie 4 " Lum the Forever"
(1986) Japanime   C-94m Japanese with English Subtitles
Urusei Yatsura: Movie 5 " The Final Chapter"
(1988) Japanime   C-90m Japanese with English Subtitles
Urusei Yatsura: Movie 6 "Always My Darling"
(1991) Japanime   C-77m Japanese with English Subtitles

-V-

Vampire Hunter D
(1985) Japanime: Horror   C-80m Dubbed   VA
Catalog # SPV 90023 Japan Retail: $19.95
Dir: Toyoo Ashida   Character Design: Yoshitaka Amano
Music Direction: Noriyoshi Matsuura
PC: Epic/Sony, Inc. Dist: Streamline Pictures
(based on characters created by Hieyuki Kikuchi)
[***]
Horror master Kikuchi's best-known work in the United States is the tale of a rogue Vampire Killer named D. (Kikuchi also created Wicked City, Demon City Shinjuku, A Wind Named Amnesia) Interesting and somewhat exciting blend of horror and adventure with animated scenes of extreme violence and grotesque humor. A popular Japanese animated film within the American community and easily found in video stores and animation clubs. In the future, vampires roam the world in dominance and only a handful of human survivors live day by day. A young girl is wanted by Count Magnus, the despotic vampire ruler, who demands her life and blood in sacrifice. He is supported by a plethora of demonic henchman and the town's people are fearful to get involved. A solitary figure enters the town riding on a horse. He is similar to the Clint Eastwood loner in the Sergio Leone spaghetti westerns, a man without a name and place, riding from one town to the next. Well he stops and reveals himself as a vampire hunter, and now he's come for Magnus. Armed with weapons and a talking hand, he battles the forces of darkness and reveals his own dark secret. A clever blend of horror and action in standard quality Japanese animation. The elements of fantasy and horror blend conventional western concepts with more outlandish Asian elements.

Vampire Princess Miyu: Volume 1
(1988) Japanime   C-50   Dubbed/Japanese with English Subtitles   VA
Catalog #AT092-004 Japan Retail: $19.95/$24.95
Dir: Toshihiro Hirano   Scr: Noboru Aikawa Character Design: Narumi Kakinouchi
Storyboards: Narumi Kakinouchi Animation Dir: Narumi Kakinouchi

Art Dir: Yoji Nakaza
Music: Kenji Kawai
PC: Soeishinsha/Pony Canyon   Dist: AnimEigo

Watanabe Naoko	Miyu
Koyama Mami	Se Himiko
Shoo Mayumi	Ranka
Horikawa Ryoo	Yuzuki Kei
Ueda Toshiya	Shiba
Asai Toshiko	Kei's Mother

[***]

In the quite town of Kyoto, a series of mysterious murders have circulated rumors of vampires. The victims are all women and were found drained of blood. A beautiful woman named Himiko is a spiritual healer hired to help a young girl who has entered a deep coma. Himiko discovers that the girl is possessed by a vampire. She then meet Miyu and Larva, ancient vampires with supernatural powers from a dark realm. They are not your classic vampires, since they can survive in sunlight and are immune to crosses, holy water, and garlic. Himiko does her best to stop them, but the vampires shrug aside her defenses and warn her not to get involved. She then learns that Miyu and Larva are not the vampires involved in the murder, but are actually there to stop renegade vampires from committing any more. The illusions are dropped and Himiko witnesses the amazing powers of Miyu as she defeats the evil vampire and sends it back into the dark realm. Episode two continues the exploits of Vampire Miyu, a guardian who dispatches renegade vampires in the human realm. Himiko better understands Miyu's attempts to stop the evil creature and provides assistance. An evil creature has taken the form of a schoolgirl and traps her victims in a lifeless state. They are turned into macabre dolls and collected in her barren home. Her newest victim is a boy who falls in love with the evil creature and together they must decide what fate will best suit their lives. A serious animated film with haunting images and a dark tale of the supernatural. Recommended for horror fans, but children should be supervised while viewing.
Episode 1: Unearthly Kyoto
Episode 2: A Banquet of Marionettes
More episodes in the continuing saga of Miyu and Himiko.
Vampire Princess Miyu: Volume 2 (1988)   C-50m Catalog #AT092-005 Retail: $19.95/$24.95
Episode 3: Fragile Armor
Episode 4: Frozen Time

Velvet Gloves
(1996) Action C-94m Chinese with English Subtitles   Hong Kong
No English Credits Available
[**1/2]

A group of young women enroll in the government's elite special police unit for females, hoping to become the best of the best among the Hong Kong police. Similar to American training films like "An Officer and a Gentleman," "Top Gun", and "Feds" in which young recruits go through all rigors of physical and academic exams to become the best and join a proud branch of the government services. Eventually the recuits bond together in friendship, help each other out, and become true leaders. Velvet Gloves takes the same ingredients, but introduces an all-women cast and since this is a fictional film, the women are all young, attractive, and act like cute school girls. But when the time comes, the women don red berets, military fatigues, bullet-proof vest, and carry automatic weapons. They can shoot, kick, and fight with the best of any terrorist or drill sergeant. The main story focuses around three of the cadets, Feng Tin, Mindy Li, and San Wang. Feng Tin is the most attractive and takes the lead position as the most serious and well-minded of the cadets. Her father is a high-ranking officer who lost his son in a military conflict. Hoping to replace her brother the warhero/soldier, Feng is determined to join China's elite crime unit. Mindy Li is the impoverished girl who had to work hard her entire life. Her father is an ex-captain, but their family is poor and lives in the rural countryside of mainland China. San Wang is the cute wisecracker and provides some light moments of humor. The film starts off with a fast pace as the women engage in actual combat with well-armed kidnapers. The main body of the film delves into rigorous military-style training with some moments of relief when the parents visit and the girls go shopping. A few mistakes almost expel some of the cadets, but they all prove themselves under fire in a final confrontation with terrorists. The end is a classic Hollywood-style scene when the cadets graduate in front of their parents and loved ones. Though the film was not initially made as a comedy, the act of young girls beating up brutish killers and training drills with weapons adds a bit of humor in the vein of Goldie Hawn's "Private Benjamin". The characters are likeable and the film never attempts to get overly lewd, violent, or preachy. Instead the characters have fun and train hard, hoping to graduate on time. A likeable film with familiar elements that doesn't quite excite, but neither bores.

Venus Wars
(1989) Japanime   C-104m   Dubbed/Japanese with English Subtitles   VA
Catalog # USM 1071/USM 1046   Japan Retail: $19.95/$29.95
Original Story, Dir, Scr: Yoshikazu Yasuhiko   Character Design: Hiroshi Yokoyama, Yoshikazu Yasuhiki Art Dir: Shichiro Kobayashi
PC: KugatsushaGakken/Shochiku/BandaiDist: U.S. Manga Corps
[***]
In the future, people from Earth have colonized Venus after the planet-altering collision of an ice asteroid. Quickly, Venus is terraformed into a liveable world with two nations arising, Ishtar and Aphrodia. In a spectacular opening sequence, Aphrodia launches a major invasion by land and air onto the unsuspecting Ishtar. The city is overrun and hostility erupts into a devastating war. A young group of kids who love to ride speed-cycles are trapped in the middle of the confrontation. The hot-shot cycler Hiro Seno and a few of his friends survive the devastation and decide to fight against the invaders. Hiro climbs the ranks and joins a desert battle unit. Along for the war, Earth journalist Susan Somers is caught in the whirlwind of pointless destruction and betrayal. If you've ever seen the spectacular opening sequence which is shown in previews and on montage tapes, you might be forewarned that the rest of the film is not filled with large scale battles and non-stop action. A solid animated entry into the world of science fiction and action.

Victory
(1994) Comedy   C-105m   Chinese with English Subtitles
Catalog #1673   Hong Kong   Retail: $39.99
Dir: Chin Wing Keung   Dist: Tai Seng Video

Yee Tung Sing, FanYick Man
[**1/2]
A fun-spirited movie about a group of college volleyball players and their quest to win the championship. You've seen the plot a dozen times, the underdog team goes up against an incredible team only to be humiliated, but through the right coach and proper motivation (final round speech) they win or at least try their best. This time it's an elite women's volleyball team made up of attractive women from all backgrounds. The film does spent a lot of time with the girls and their hijinks, but focuses mainly in their training. When the team is beaten by a rival college made up of Amazons (incredibly tall Chinese women), most of the members quit including the coach. The dean is embarrassed and the program is slated to be cancelled. But a core group of girls decide to stick together and keep playing, though undermatched and much smaller than their opponents, they pull together and entice a meek professor with no volleyball knowledge to be their coach. After long practice sessions, they pull off an amazing victory. Along the way romance and friendship are tested as one of the girls develops a crush on the professor and the ace player holds a grudge against the new girl.

Visionary by U-Jin Vol. 1
(1995) Japanime: Erotic   C-40m Japanese with English Subtitles
Catalog #A18-1623   Japan Retail: $29.95
Dir: Teruo Kogure   Scr: Toyohiro Ando Original Story: U-Jin (Shuberu Publishing Co.)
General Prod: Seiichi Nishino   Prod: Shigeyuki Hasegawa
Dramatization: Teruo Kogure (Story 1), Ichizo Kobayashi (Story 2)
English Version - Ex. Prod: Humphrey G. Kumano
Translation: nDa Language Services
PC: Knack   Dist: Anime 18/Central Park Media

Satomi Korogi	Doreimon
Shohei Yamaguchi	Ujita
Mika Kanai	Reiko
Kozo Shioya	Daimajin
Kosuke Okuno	Tanuo
Naoko Matsui	Sayuri
Hiroyuki Oshida	Maejima

[**1/2]
A compact erotic tale mixed with humor and romance. Please keep in mind that this film is not intended for children and is specifically geared toward erotic anime lovers. If you enjoy softcore pornographic elements and the romantic humor found in mainstream titles, Visionary 2 will be quite entertaining. Computer nerd Ujita manages to tap into another dimension and pull knockout Doreimon into his bedroom. She's adorable, sports a tale, and doesn't take kindly to his sexual advances. In return for some sweet potatoes, she uses her alien powers and grants him wishes. A nice erotic twist on the Aladdin tale. His first wish involves turning into a baby squirrel so he can stay with dream babe Reiko. Rivals Daimajin and Tanuo decide to set up Ujita and make him lose face in front of Reiko. Though Ujita is the consummate nerd, big-glasses, small penis, bowl-shaped haricut, and no self-esteem, Reiko and the other girls in the flower arrangement club decide to forgive him for his past transgressions and accept his friendship. The second episode jumps to their college days, keeping the entire cast in tact. Ujita wants to go after

Sayuri and Reiko, but he feels a little under-manned and asks Doreimon to increase the size of his penis. Using her magic powers, Doreimon gives him more than he bargained for. Old-time rival Daimajin decides it's time to drop pants and prove who really is the biggest dick on campus.
Episode 1: SM Snake
Episode 2: Miracle Alien

Visionary by U-Jin Vol. 2
(1995) Japanime: Erotic   C-75m Japanese with English Subtitles
Catalog # A18-1624 Japan Retail: $29.95
Dir: Teruo Kogure (Story 1, 2), Taichi Kitagawa (Story 3)
Scr: Toyohiro Ando (1,2), Ryo Saga (1-3) Prod: Shigeyuki Hasegawa, Noriko Nishino
General Prod: Seiichi Nishino   Character Design: Jun Yoshida, Takaharu Osumi
Dramatization: Jirou Sayama (1), Taichi Kitagawa (2)
English Version - Ex. Prod: Humphrey G. Kumano
Translation: nDa Language Services
PC: Knack   Dist: Central Park Media Corporation
[**1/2]
More erotic tales from those "dirty little" minds of U-Jin. If you enjoy erotic animated tales, then U-Jin is a nice departure into adult animation without the excessive violence and gore found in other adult titles. Volume 2 contains plenty more tales of eroticism laced with comedy and horror. Appealing for fans of the genre, the series is not intended for anyone under eighteen. The stories are self-explanatory and usually result in sexual situations among the young cast members. They involve two childhood friends, Koban and Sameo, who share girlfriends in a unique arrangement. Koban falls in love with 19 year-old Shiori when he rescues her from a would-be rapist. The shy Koban can't confess his love for Shiori until they both decide to go skydiving with a little help from Sameo. The second story involves Mai, an attractive woman, who'll do anything to get ahead in the entertainment field. The final story features a bizarre erotic tale of vampires at St. Stoker University. Once again, a 19 year-old female (Kanna) transfer student from Europe must solve the strange disappearances and discover the truth.
Story 1: Skydiving in Love
Story 2: New Century Queen
Story 3: The Vampire Tradition

Voltage Fighter Gowcaizer
(1996) Japanime: Action   C-45m Dubbed   Catalog # USM 1628 Japan   Retail: $19.95
Dir: Masami Ohbari Scr: Kengo Asai
Prod: Yoshinori Chiba, Shinichi Hirai, Tomoko Kawasaki
Ex. Prod: Hiroshi Yamaji, Yoshimasa Ohnishi
Character Design & Storyboard: Masami Ohbari   Art Dir: Hiroshi Kato
English Version - Ex. Prod: John O'Donnell   Prod: Stephanie Shalofsky
Dubbing Manager: Peter Bavaro   Supervisor: Anthony Salerno   Translation: Kevin McKeown
PC: J.C. Staff/GAGA Communications, Inc./Big West
Dist: U.S. Manga (division of Central Park Media Corporation)

[**1/2]
The newest release from Central Park Media Corporation is an action-paced film from the director of Battle Arena Toshinden and Fatal Fury. Set at the beginning of the 21st century, the story follows the exploits of high school students at an elite academy for the brightest students in Japan. Professor Fudo suspects the Belnar Institutes leader, Shizuru Ozaki, is behind the massive earthquakes that have destroyed Tokyo. Young student Isato Kaiza is trapped in the middle of events when his friend Kash (Hellstinger) gives him a Caizer Stone which enables him to transform into a superbeing called Gowcaizer. What follows is a string of bizarre battles between students who also possess powers that allow them to transform into powerful beings with battlesuits. The most bizarre is the Asahina twins: brother and sister team who morph into one entity with bizarre physical results. The characters are drawn in a stringy style and the film features plenty of hardcore action. The women are exceptionally thin with lavish eyes and giant breasts that bulge out of their skimpy outfits, but the fights are left to the big boys. Nothing new, but definitely something familiar for anime fans who like their action loud and fast.

-W-

Wandering Kid, The
See Urotsukidoji   -   Japanime

Wanna-Be's
(1986) Japanime   C-45m Japanese with English Subtitles   VA
Catalog # USM 1031 Japan Retail: $34.95
Dir: Yoshiharu Shimizu   Scr/Planning: Toshimichi Suzuki
Prod: Eiji Kishi, Yutake Takahashi
DP: Masahide Okino   Music: Hiroshi Arakawa
Art Dir: Masamuzi Matsumiya   Character Design: Yoshiharu Shimizu
Mecha Design: Shinji Aramaki   Animaton Dir & Character Design: Yoshiharu Shimizu
PC: MOVIC/Sony Entertainment (Japan) Inc.   Dist: U.S. Manga Corps
(based on the comic by Toshimichi Suzuki)

Eriko Hara	Miki Morita
Miki Takahashi	Eri Kazuma
Shuichi Ikeda	Tetsuma Kidou
Akio Nojima	Sonada Oki
Eiko Yamada	Bloody Matsuki
Urara Takano	Buster Horiguchi
Shouza Itzuka	Dr. Sawada
Yusaku Yara	Joe Taguchi

[**]
For fans who remember GLOW (Gorgeous Ladies of Wrestling), this animated tale features two attractive women in the world of Japanese female wrestling. The story is straight-forward and zips by in a predictable fashion. Eri and Miki are the Wanna-Be's, two cute Japanese women who become popular wrestlers. Secretly, their debt-ridden coach has volunteered them to be guinea pigs for a genetic experiment. The girls who want to party every night start a strict regiment of training while being genetically altered into superhumans with steroid-like

responses. They challenge the dominant Foxy Ladies team, a pair of monstrous and brutal world champions. When the Wanna-Be's are under physical duress, they undergo a metamorphosis which increases their strength and aggression. Eri and Miki confront their coach and discover the truth. They hunt down the corporate head who used them as a test to attract lucrative investors. What results is a standard battle scene between the Wanna-Be's and a gruesome genetic monster created by the corporate head. The film features a number of physically violent fight scenes in the wrestling ring and brief nudity. The animation is good, but nothing above the average and the story does not question morality or any deep issues. If you enjoy wrestling or female heroines, the film may appeal to you, but lacks the action, charm, and energy of other girls in anime films. However, the topic of steroid testing is explored in athletics which proves the expansive scope of Japanese animation.

War of the Gargantuas (Furankenshutain No Kaiju - Sanda Tai Gailah)
(1970) Monster C-92m Dubbed VA
Japan Retail: $9.95
Dir: Inoshiro Honda Scr: Inoshiro Honda, Kaoru Mabuchi
Prod: Tomoyuki Tanaka DP: Hajime Koizumi Sp. Fx: Eiji Tsuburaya
PC: Toho Studios Dist: Paramount Home Video
Russ Tamblyn, Kumi Mizuno, Kipp Hamilton, Yu Fujiki, Kenji Sahara, Jun Tazaki
[**]
Imagine your surprise when you spot American actor Russ Tamblyn in a Japanese monster film. For those of you who aren't musical fans, Russ starred in a number of popular films including "Seven Brides for Seven Brothers", "West Side Story", "Hit the Deck", and "Tom Thumb". Russ plays an American in love with beautiful Kumi Mizuno who happens to care for a giant monster called Gargantuan. Created around the same mold as the Godzilla films by veteran Honda, Gargantuan is a towering ape with scraggly hair and a monstrous face. The Gold (or Brown) Gargantuan befriends Kumi and Russ, but is frightened of the human world and goes into hiding in the mountains and forests of Japan. When hikers start disappearing and bones pop up, Gold Gargantuan is the prime suspect. Meanwhile, Gold Gargantuan meets a fellow super bigfoot called Green Gargantuan and the two become friends until table etiquettes get in the way. Green Gargantuan likes to eat humans and does so with relish, entering a city and chewing up some innocent civilians. This forces the two Gargantuans to battle to the death while Russ and Kumi helplessly follow and tell the authorities not to shoot at the Gold one. Needless to say, the army fires on both until Japan is monster free once again. For the time, the film's effects were adequate, but age and an unfamiliar monster has shelved the Gargantuans into relative obscurity. Enjoyable for nostalgic reasons, the film still holds an entertaining spot for monster buffs.

Warrior From Shaolin
(1981) Kung-Fu C-90m Dubbed **Hong Kong Retail: $19.95**
Dir: Liu Chia Liang (Lau Kar Wing) **Prod/MAD: Liu Chia Liang, Liu Chia Hui**
Dist: Ocean Shores Video Ltd.
Gordon Liu Chia Hui, Lily Li, Liu Chia Yung
[**1/2]
Gordon Liu (the Master Killer) is back as a Shaolin monk who must deliver a precious chest to another Temple. In reality, the chest is just a front, actually containing plans for patriotic rebels.

Their courier was ambushed and makes it to Gordon's temple before passing out. The monks decide to help and assign Monk Gordon Liu to the heroic task. He comes across two small-time crooks who at first want to rob him, but then befriend him and join his cause. The two crooks are played for comedic relief (ala Abbott and Costello) but rather than hinder the plot they work well against Gordon's honesty and naiveness. The heroes are pursued by a wonderful husband and wife villain team that are perfect foes to Monk Liu and his two friends. They try to help Gordon by joining the local police force, but when Gordon is captured and tortured, they throw away their police armbands and join the patriotic rebels. The heroes are outnumbered and cornered which leads to a well-paced battle sequence that ends on a road near an outdoor shop. The villains have injured Gordon's two friends, so he uses his deadly Shaolin techniques and manages to beat the deadly duo who relied on a shoe knife and gun. Though be warned, the film has a rough low-budget edge, not nearly as impressive as Liu's other films with brother/director Liu Chia Liang. But somehow, Gordon brings a charismatic presence to the film and makes it enjoyable for kung-fu fans. A number of highlights include a humorous scene involving a prostitute and Gordon, another scene where Gordon is attacked by villagers who think he is an evil sorcerer, a fight against zombies, and the climatic end where Gordon loses his temper and fights like mad. Overall this film isn't a piece of art, but captures the right blend of fun and fighting. The talent in the martial art scenes are evident, due in part to the brilliant work of Liu Chia Liang. When their contract ended at Shaw Brothers, the Liu Brothers went on to make their own films. What they lack in budget, they make up in raw talent.

Warriors of the Wind   (Nausicaa of the Valley of the Wind)
(1985) Japanime: Fantasy   C-95m Dubbed   VA   Catalog # USM 1046
Japan Retail: $19.95
Dir: Kazuo Komatsubara, Hayao Miyazaki   Scr: Hayao Miyazaki
Prod: Isao Takahata Music: Jo Hisaishi
Animation: Takashi Nakamura,Tsukasa Tannai
PC: Tokuma Shoten   Dist: New World
[*1/2]**
An excellent anti-war story with characters drawn in a pleasant American fashion. The dubbed version would be impossible to tell as a Japanese import, and has been shown on American television in a variety of edited formats. In the distant future, the world is recovering from centuries of deadly plague and warfare. A young princess and her father govern over a beautiful village in a verdant valley full of windmills. The wind comes from the ocean and pushes back the poisonous air from the deadly dunes and the toxic jungle. The princess is a strong-willed intelligent warrior adept at flying a windrider, dealing with strange insects, and fighting. At her side is the mysterious and deadly Lord Yappa who travels the vast deserts and preaches peace and unity. One day, an enormous airship crashes outside her quiet village. Aboard the wreckage they find a young princess from another kingdom and a large pulsating egg. The mysterious princess and all aboard pass away, but the crimson egg continues to grow and beat. Suddenly a flying armada attacks the village and enslaves all the inhabitants. The conquering queen demands complete subservience and orders the princess to be returned to her empire as a hostage. The princess must stand strong for her people and accepts her new fate, but during her escort to the palace, the queen's airships are attacked by a warrior from a rival kingdom. He and the princess combine forces and make their way back to the valley of the wind. The militaristic

queen is after the ancient embryo which possesses one of the demon beasts. She unleashes the devastating demon beast to stop a horde of giant monsters from attacking the village, but the ancient creature is unstable and dissolves into a massive blob of plasma. Only the princess' love and sacrifice can save the villagers and the queen's army from total annihilation. Valley of the Wind enjoyed extreme popularity in Japan, but never achieved the same in the United States probably due to its lack of distribution and the maturity of the film's subject. Though dated by animation standards, the story is full of wondrous art while depicting a world of strange creatures and archaic weaponry mixed with modern. Some material may be unsuitable for very young children, but the film is quite tame in Japanese standards and will entertain all age groups. A highly recommended film for all lovers of animation or fantasy-related stories. The original version was edited down from its 120 minute running time which is still available on laserdisc.

Warriors Tragedy, A
(1993) Kung-Fu   C-90m Chinese with English Subtitles   Hong Kong
Dir/Scr: Frankie Chan
Ti Lung, Frankie Chan, Andy Lau
[1/2]**
Unusual looking martial arts fantasy from the mind of Frankie Chan (kind of a Mongolian Dragon Inn). A group of heroes gather in a small village to settle the score for a tragedy that took place 20 years before. Ti Lung is the troubled warrior out for revenge who opens the film in a beautiful snow-covered set where he refuses to fight a duo (male/female) of warriors who want his head.
Similar in style to rogue western films or the samurai epics, Ti Lung wanders alone and comes into contact with a wide assortment of characters. He and his fellow fighters are invited to a powerful master's mansion where a series of intrigues and befuddled plot developments arise. Someone tries to murder the master, but who is his real enemy and what is his motivation. The female characters also provide plenty of chemistry as relationships devlop between various pairs. Though the film features a number of dated-wire scenes and less than imaginative fights, Warriors Tragedy attempts to surpass typical martial arts films with more attention spent to landscape design, characters caught in self-realizations, and numerous plot twists and turns which actually mire the film's overall pacing and dramatic effect.

Warriors Tragedy 2, A
(1993) Kung-Fu   C-90m Chinese with English Subtitles   Hong Kong
Dir/Scr: Frankie Chan
Ti Lung, Frankie Chan, Andy Lau
[***]
Apparently filmed in unison with the first film, the story is a direct continuation of the exploits of Ti Lung and Frankie Chan. What makes this film more interesting than the first is the lack of an over-complicated subplot and the multitude of fringe characters portrayed in the first film. Also, the first film warms you up to the visual style and the motivations of the characters. Given more breath of freedom, the story focuses on Ti Lung and the woman he loves. There are touching scenes as Ti is torn between a peaceful family life and his hardened warrior's life. While traveling, he comes under attack by a clan robed in white robes. Ti refuses to fight, but the entire clan, men, women, and children, demand his head and advance against him. He attempts to

scare them off, but a young child bravely approaches him and harmlessly attacks. Then a hidden assassin kills the child and the shocked Ti is forced to battle the clan. He can not escape his warrior's past and must confront the evil master in a climatic showdown. Meanwhile, Chan is also doing his best to stay alive and engages in an outdoor chariot match. The heroes get the job done and prepare to part company, but in a final nod to campiness, Chan warns Ti of AIDS, and Ti yells that in this time period there is no AIDS!

Wedding Banquet, The
(1993) DramaC-109m   English & Cantonese with Subtitles   R   VA
Catalog #8170-85   Taiwan   Retail: $19.95
Dir: Ang Lee   Scr: Ang Lee, Neil Peng, James Schamus
Prod: James Schamus, Ted Hope, Ang Lee   DP: Jong Lin
Editor: Tim Squyres Music: Mader   Art Design: Rachel Weinzimer
Prod Design: Steve Rosenzweig   Set Design: Amy Silver   Costumes: Michael Clancy
PC: Central Motion Pictures Corporation Dist: Fox Video

Winston Chao	**Wai Tung**
May Chin	**Wei-Wei**
Ah-Leh Gua	**Mrs. Gao**
Sihung Lung	**Mr. Gao**
Mitchell Lichtenstein	**Simon**
Neal Huff	**Steve**
Jeffrey Howard	**Street Musician**
Anthony "Iggy" Ingoglia	**Restaurant Manager**
Dion Birney	**Andrew**
Jeanne Kuo Chang	**Wedding Guest**
Ang Lee	**Wedding Guest**
Chung-Wei Chon	
Tien Pien	

[***]

A pleasant, witty film about a modern Chinese male living with an American man in Manhattan. Notably, Ang Lee's first major breakthrough film in the American film community. Handsome yuppie Wai Tung has a great job, a nice apartment, wonderful friends, and a male lover named Simon. What could possible go wrong in his idyllic open-minded world of Manhattan? Well old values still live in Taiwan where his parents are oblivious to the fact that he's gay. They harass him about their need for a grandchild and send him information about eligible females. Wai decides to get his parents to back off and makes up a story about his engagement with a woman. His traditional parents decide to visit from Taiwan when their son announces he is marrying a beautiful Chinese woman. A charade is put on for their benefit, but problems increase when a real relationship develops between man and woman. It's hard to resist the beauty and charm of May Chin who needs to get married so she can legally stay in the United States. All kinds of situational probelms arise from the wedding ruse and director Ang Lee skillfully crafts the material into a presentable and touching story about honesty, love, and relationships. In the end, everything works out for the best when old and new generation come to grips with the truth.

When Tae Kwon Do Strikes

(1983) Kung-Fu   C-95m Dubbed   R   Catalog #FRM 4006
Hong Kong   Retail: $19.95
Dir: Huang Feng   Scr: Chu Yu   Prod: Raymond Chow
DP: Li Yu Tang   Editor: Chang Yao Chung   Music: Li Shao Hua
Jhoon Rhee, Angela Mao Ying, Carter Wong, Whong In Sik, Kenji Kazama, Anne Winton,
Andre Morgan
PC: Golden Harvest International   Dist: Fox Lorber/Orion Home Video
[**]
Korean-American Tae Kwon Do Master Jhoon Rhee shows off his brutal skills in this action-
packed film about Chinese and Koreans fighting against brutal Japanese oppression. No one in
Asia is very fond of the Japanese who are frequently used as the classic villains in Korean and
Chinese films. Western films often showed Germans (Nazis) as sadistic, calculated villains for
their role in World War II, so their Asian counterpart and ally, the Japanese, have the dubious
distinction of filling the role for Eastern films. Angela Mao Ying adds a nice feminine touch as
the Chinese heroine and innocuous-looking Ann Winton is the Causcasian heroine who joins
forces with Rhee and Carter Wong. The Japanese are vicious, hunting down all those who
oppose them. Jhoon and his friends fight back but are forced to go into hiding. Eventually
Jhoon is captured and tortured at the Japanese base, but his students and allies arrive to rescue
him. Angela promises a list of Korean patriots for the safe return of Jhoon Rhee. The vile
Japanese accept with confidence, but Angela attacks them and helps Jhoon. Rhee, still chained,
uses his furious Tae Kwon Do kicks to battle the Japanese masters. Not as fancy or fast-paced as
modern day kung-fu film heroes, Jhoon Rhee is a very different style of hero, more subtle,
humble, and without an over-confident air around him. He's style of martial arts and attitude
toward life is simple and he wishes to avoid violence, but will fight back when the cause is
justified.

Why Has Bodhi-Dharma Left for the East
(1989) DramaC-135m   **Korean with English Subtitles**
Catalog #CC1438L   Korea Retail: $69.95
Dir/Scr: Bae Yong-kyun   Dist: Voyager Entertainment
[***]
Korean filmmaker Bae Yong-kyun struggled for a decade to produce his spiritual film. Though
Korea has not achieved the international reputation of filmmaking that Asian nations like Japan,
China, and Hong Kong have achieved, more and more Korean filmmakers have gained
recognition throughout the film community. Recently issued on laserdiscs by the Voyager
Company, Bae's film focuses on the inner spirit of a man and his natural surroundings. The films
takes place in a remote monastery in the serene mountains of Korea. An old Buddhist master
who is nearing death contemplates his life and leads his disciples in a search for inner spiritual
freedom. The film's title is in reference to a Zen koan, an unanswerable riddle that serves as an
aid on the path to enlightenment.

Wicked City
(1987) Japanime: Horror   C-90m Dubbed   Catalog # SPV 90923
Japan   Retail: $19.95
Dir: Yoshiaki Kawajiri   Scr: Kisei Cho   Music: Osamu Shoji

PC: Japan Home Video   Dist: Streamline Pictures
(based on the novel by Hideyuki Kikuchi)
[**1/2]

Japanese horror novel by Kikuchi which was transformed into an erotic, noir-ish film that gained notoriety in animated circles. The Earth exists side by side with a parallel world of demons and shape-changers known as the Black World. The two parallel worlds exists in relative peace with a bonding treaty that is soon to expire and needs to be renegotiated. The conference is to be held by delegates representing both sides. Meanwhile, elite agents must stop the race of supernatural beings who wish to see the treaty fail and take over Japan and the world. The creatures have the power to assume human shape and then morph into vicious demons of amazing proportions. On the human side, a hard-nosed detective arises as the hero while a female with unique laser-red nails assists from the demon side and develops a relationship with her human counterpart. Plenty of nasty creatures try to kill the detective and cast Earth and the Black World into total chaos. The opening scene is one of the most amazing visual combinations of horror, animation, and sexual violence when an agent is attacked by a seductive female who shows more sexual bite than should be shown in public (the same scene looks ridiculous in the live-version). Though the story is fascinating, the scenes of violence and sex may deter sensitive viewers - discretion is advised and children should not be allowed to see the film. Followed by a live action attempt from Hong Kong filmmakers: Wicked City.

Wicked City, The
(1992) Horror/Scifi C-98m Dubbed   R   VA
Catalog #1397   Hong Kong   Retail: $19.98
Dir: Peter Mak Tai Kit   Prod: Tsui Hark
Prod Supervisor: Raymond Lee, Mak Chi Sin   Prod Planning: Bill Kong
PC: Film Workshop Inc.   Dist: Tai Seng Video
Jacky Cheung   Ken Kai
Leon Lai   Taki
Michelle Reis   Windy
Tatsuya Nakadai   Daishu
Roy Cheung   Shudo
Yuen Woo Ping, Carmen Lee
[**]

Wicked City is a prime example of the limitations of live special effects when compared to the boundless energy of animation. The Hong Kong version is a live-action remake of the animated film Wicked City which is based on Youjuu Toshi (Supernatural Beast City), a novel by Kikuchi Hideyuki. The film is masked in blue light to capture a supernatural ambience, while most of the scenes take place in the evening or under rainy conditions. The film attempts to be an ambitious mix of horror, passion, and action under one umbrella with a host of wild special effects good for Asian standards, but sub-standard for American fans of horror, fantasy, and science fiction. Though the effects are similar to fantasy kung-fu films, the contemporary setting and characters seem awkward when compared to the murky, poor-lit creatures who provide conflict. Fantasy kung-fu is a unique Asian genre that seems to garner its own style of effects, but when treading in familiar ground, Wicked City looks pale in comparison to films like "Alien", "Aliens", "Species", and "The Thing".

Two special government agents (Ken and Taki) must track down and destroy aliens imitating humans, known as Reptoids. Similar to John Carpenter's "They Live", the V-series, and "Invasion of the Body Snatchers", the aliens live among us, look just like us, and despise the human race. In their human guise, we trust them, work with them, and sometimes even fall in love with them. But when we discover their existence, it is up to humanity to destroy them. Initially seen as a threat and an evil race bent on taking over the Earth, more compassionate Reptoids emerge into the story. The first is one of the agents who is a half-Reptoid, since his father fell in love with a Reptoid female. The other agent falls in love with a mysterious female Reptoid with laser-red fingernails who saves his life. The two men are caught between their hatred for pure Reptoids while coming to grips with their own inner feelings. When the main Reptoid boss is betrayed by his own son, he attempts to join forces with the human agents who possess psychic powers. The final battle is an outlandish, confusing, and ill-paced sequence of camera tricks, darkly lit stages, and campy special effects. Some films fail due to their look and appearance, while animation often succeeds for the same reason. A proven statement that some films are best left animated.

Wind Named Amnesia, A
(1993) Japanime   C-80m Dubbed/Japanese with English Subtitles   VA
Catalog # USM 1473/USM 1108   Japan Retail: $19.95/$29.95
Dir: Kazuo Yamazaki   Scr: Kazuo Yamazaki, Yoshiaki Kawajiri
Original Story: Hideyuki Kikuchi
Character Design: Satoru Nakamura   Mecha Design: Morifumi Naka
Art Dir: Mutsuo Koseki   Music: Kazz Toyama
PC: Right Stuff Office/Japan Home Video Dist: U.S. Manga Corps
[*1/2]**
An intelligent and well-made post-apocalyptic film that will appeal to fans of science fiction and animation. The film has the feel and look of a classic American science fiction tale and the Japanese animators even chose the United States as the primary setting. For vintage film fans, think of movies like "The Omega Man" and "Day of the Triffids". When a mysterious wind envelops the planet, everyone in society loses their memory and reverts into a complete simpleton. Society is thrown into chaos and primal instincts for survival create a new order. Machines from the previous order are still active and cause a menace to society. One man is fighting to make a difference and with a beautiful, mysterious woman travels across America in search of others and the truth. As they travel together, he recounts his own past events. He was also affected by the amnesia wind, but was discovered by a brilliant young man who was part of a government memory enhancement program. Due to some experiments, his memory was improved and therefore was not affected by the wind. He helps him regain his memory and teaches him how to survive.
Now on his own, the brave hero and the woman travel across the country and encounter exciting adventures with moral implications for humanity. When the woman finally reveals her true identity, she gives her love to him and promises hope for the future.

Windaria
(1986) Japanime   C-95m Dubbed   VA   Catalog # BFV 956   Japan
Retail: $19.95

Dir: Kunohiko Yuyama   Art Dir: Toru Katsumata
Character Design & Animation: Mutsumi Inomata & Kanami Productions
PC: Idol Co. Ltd./Harmony Gold USA Inc.   Dist: Streamline Productions
[***]
A mature story with a somewhat preachy antiwar message and moderate pace. Action and drama unfold in this multilayered love/war story between two kingdoms and the rulers' children. The story is told from the main character's point of view and seen as a flashback story. He is now an old man with a burden of guilt he must clear. His name is Alan and he caused the destruction of his kingdom through his own arrogance and pride. Unfortunately, he is rather two-dimensional character and doesn't really develop throughout the story, since his dramatic transformation from pure good to evil to good again is not created convincingly. On the other hand, the Princess Veronica is an admirable character with a passionate spirit and a strong will, while her counterpart Prince Roland is her lover who must decide between her or his kingdom. Veronica and Roland are tragic lovers from two different kingdoms which vie for control of the land's fresh water system. Saboteurs are sent to destroy the kindgom's dam-locking system to prevent the future control of the water supply. A senseless war erupts and casualties run high on both sides, including the royal lovers. Clean animation worth checking out for fans of mature/tragic stories.

Wing Chun
(1994) Kung-Fu   C-94m Dubbed/Chinese with English Subtitles   VA
Catalog #44603   Hong Kong   Retail: $19.99
Dir: Yuen Wo Ping   Scr: Anthony Wong, Elsa Tang   Prod: Yuen Wo Ping
Ex. Dir: Anthony Wong   DP: Mark Lee   Art Dir: Andy Lee
Associate Prod: Stephen Wong Wai Hum   Costume Designer: Edith Tsui
MAD: Yuen Wo Ping, Yuen Shun Yi, Yen Chi Tan
PC: Wo Ping Films Co. Ltd.   Dist: Tai Seng Video
Michelle Khan, Donnie Yen Chi Tan, Waise Lee Chi Hung, Chui Siu Keung,, Yuen King Tan, Catherie Hung
[***]
By now, the name Michelle Khan will be familiar to fans of kung-fu movies, since her American theatrical debut in Jackie Chan's Supercop. She's no slouch and proves she can keep up with Chan in both martial skills and crazy stunts. Wing Chun capitalizes on her stardom and was recently released by Tai Seng Video alongside Heroic Trio 1 & 2. The historical character of Yim Wing Chun is the female founder of the Wing Chun style of martial arts, a close-quarter style of blocking and counterblocking attacks popularized by Bruce Lee who studied under Wing Chun master Yip Man. The story is a liberal interpretation of the historical events surrounding the creator of Wing Chun. The segment that is left out (based on speculation and legend) is the actual creation of Wing Chun. According to legends, Yim was forced to marry a man, but then offered an escape if she could beat the man in combat. Under the tutelage of a nun, she developed a new form of martial arts to take advantage of her demure size and shorter reach. She was able to beat her suitor and became a great instructor in the world of martial arts. This story takes place afterwards presumably, since she is already a renowned fighter. Though the film uses creative choreography rather than real Wing Chun techniques, Michelle Khan is charming and engaging to watch both as a fighter and as a romantic lead. The story begins with

Yim Wing Chun attending the marriage of her younger sister. Yim is a bit of a rough girl "butch" and dresses like a man and doesn't concern herself with physical romance or dainty appearances. Suddenly during a celebration, a sick man and his daughter arrive from down river and enter the town pursued by bandits. The townspeople fear the bandits and refuse to help, but Yim is rambunctious and defeats all the bandits. The father passes away from his illness and the daughter must sell herself to raise money for a proper funeral (not uncommon in that era). At the same time, a handsome young scholar pursues Yim and any other pretty girls...and the new girl in town is quite gorgeous. He plans to buy her but Yim and her sister convince him to pay out of generosity and Confucian kindness. The gracious girl comes and lives with Yim in their tofu shop. Meanwhile the bandits won't leave the town alone and the leader's brother wants the beautiful girl for himself. They attempt to nab the woman time after time, running into a formulaic circle with the gang succeeding then failing then trying once again. What stands out is Khan's amazing performance and the fast-paced action sequences which also include Waise Lee and Donnie Yen as the suitor interested in Khan.

Wings of Honneamise "The Royal Space Force"
(1987) Japanime: Scifi   C-124m   Dubbed/Japanese with English Subtitles
VA   Catalog # MGV 634797/MGV 635253   Japan Retail: $19.95/$24.95
Dir/Scr: Hiroyuki Yamaga Character Design: Yoshiyuki Sadamoto
Animation Dir: Hideaki Anno, Yuji Moriyama, Fumio Lida, Yoshiyuki Sadamoto
Art Dir: Hiromasa Ogura   Music: Ryuichi Sakamoto
PC: Gainax/Bandai Visual Dist: Manga Entertainment
[***1/2]
A surprisingly mature story about a nation's race to send a man into outer space. Unlike many other Japanese animated stories that fall into the ludicrous and campy, Wings never delves into the childish antics of animation, but stays in focus with its mature story. The animation is top-notch and the characters' actions are realistic with full-blown human problems, frailities, and doubts.
The story starts with a young man recounting his childhood days. As a child he watched planes take off from aircraft carriers and dreamed of becoming a fighter pilot. Growing up, Shiro's grades weren't good enough for the air force, so he joins the fledgling Royal Space Force. At first you wonder how he could make such an elite program. Then you discover the program is a joke, half-heartedly funded by the government and employing screwups and quirky scientists. No one believes it is possible to send someone into space including the young space pilots in the program. Dressed in outlandish, almost Incan/Aztec-style uniforms, the cadets salute a comrade who died in training when his urine bag erupted and short circuited the simulator. The cadets almost seem disinterested and return to their daily lives which include brawls with the real cadets of the air force. Shiro wanders through his misguided life and meets a young woman putting up reform bills. He is taken by the woman's courage and direction in life. He meets her child and becomes a frequent guest at her house. She becomes a dear friend and a strange platonic relationship develops which is almost ruined when Shiro attempts to rape her in a fit of fevered passion. Never expect Japanese stories to be one-dimensional or predictable, but they resume their cautious friendship.
Actions are set into motion by higher officials who decide to use the space program as bait to attract another country into starting a war. Unknowingly to the members of the space program,

the officials leak out the launch date and establish the base near the border. The space pilots and scientists work frantically to succeed, finally receiving the financial and moral support of the government. The training and development portion of the film is reminiscent of major live-action films like"The Right Stuff" and "Apollo 13" but with a slightly off-world appearance, mixing known technology with alien technology. When the time comes near for launch, a full scale war breaks out as tanks and troops pour across the border. The mission is in jeopardy, but instead of aborting, the space team valiantly work together to achieve launch. In a wonderful scene, the rocket explodes to life and both sides watch in awe as mankind finally ventures into outer space. A true testament to human achievement, the new perspective on life reawakens humanity as they discover there is more to life than what was previously known and feared. New avenues, possibilities, and hopes are symbolized through the brave efforts accomplished by the space team's unity and belief in themselves.

The film's rich subtext and parallel to modern society may be missed on initial viewings, and the film was a financial disappointment in Japan. Lacking the scantily clad girls or big mech action sequences, some anime viewers were disappointed with the mature, slow-paced nature of the film. At the time, WOH was the most expensive animated film made (and the first financed by toy giant Bandai) in Japan and opened the door for more mature and experimental themes in the field of anime. The polished animation and multilayered story is one of the finest animated films from Japan and deserves a second glance from fans and critics.

Woman in the Dunes(Suna no Onna)
(1964) DramaB&W-123m   Japanese with English Subtitles   VA
Catalog #CVC 1057 Japan Retail: $29.95

Dir: Hiroshi Teshigahara	**Scr: Kobo Abe**	**Prod: Kiichi Ichikawa, Tadashi Ohono**
DP: Hiroshi Segawa	**Editor: F. Susui**	**Music: Toru Takemitsu**

Dist: Connoisseur Video Collection
(based on the novel Suna no Onna by Abe)

Eiji Okada	**Niki Jumpei**
Kyoko Kishida	**Woman**

Koji Mitsui, Hiroko Ito, Sen Yano, Ginzo Sekigushi, Kiyohiko Ichiha, Tamutsu Tamura, Hiroyuki Nishimo
[****]

A harrowing and profound parable filled with elements of desperation, horror, and passion. An entomologist named Niki Jumpei travels to a desert bordered by the sea. He searches for rare specimens of insects and leisurely reflects upon his past relationships. A kindly, old villager informs him that the last bus to town has left. He invites him to stay at one of the local homes. Niki follows him to a large pit surrounded by walls of sand. He climbs down the rope to the bottom of the pit and enters the modest home and greets the woman (Kishida). She is kind and courtesy, making his stay comfortable.

The next morning, the rope ladder has disappeared and only the woman remains. Niki tries to comprehend the situation, but quickly discovers he is a prisoner. Acting in a manner any sane man would, he tries to escape by holding the woman prisoner, refusing to dig sand, and plotting escape plans. The purpose of the pit is to keep back the flow of sand from eroding and endangering the entire village. Their population has dwindled, so it is necessary for the remaining villagers to recruit (capture) new volunteers. If they don't dig, they don't get any food or water. The images of sand cascading down the inclined slopes and the visual mirages are disturbing and memorable. Like a pathetic insect trapped in a lion ant's pit, Nikki flounders against the wall of sand until he breaks down. He gives into the captors' demands and helps the woman dig sand, while secretly looking for subtle ways to escape. Niki is an intelligent man, but his human desires for companionship and survival take over his logical reasoning and bring out his primal instincts. He becomes obsessed with trying to capture a crow to tie a message around its leg and to build a waterhole. As the months expire, he falls into a pattern of life dictated by his captors. His escape attempts are futile and he falls in love with the woman and his surroundings. One night, he discovers she is pregnant with his child. The villagers come down to help her and leave the ladder. Niki climbs out and walks toward the ocean. He glances at the empty expanse and realizes his life is in the pit. He walks back and descends into the pit, fathering the waterhole he so lovingly created and waiting for his wife's return.

The film was nominated for Best Foreign Film at the 1964 Academy Awards and earned Hiroshi Teshigahara a nomination for Best Director. Also winner of the Grand Jury Prize at the Cannes Film Festival.

The World of Apu
(1959) Drama B&W-103m   Not Rated   Indian with English Subtitles   VA
Catalog #HSV 5268   India
Dir/Scr/Prod: Satyajit Ray DP: Subrata Mitra
Editor: Dulal Dutta Music: Ravi Shankar   Art Dir: Banshi Chandra Gupta
Dist: Video Yesteryear
(based on the novel Aparajito by Bibhutibhusan Bandopadhaya)
Soumitra Chatterjee Apurba Kumar Roy
Sharmila Tagore   Aparna
Shapan Mukerji   Pulu
S. Alke Chakravarty Kajal
[***1/2]
Third and final film in the Apu Trilogy, the best known and critically acclaimed films to come out of India. Pather Panchali (1955) and Aparajito (1956) followed Apu's early childhood and school days, while the final film focuses on an adult Apu. Filmed in black and white, the print I viewed is considerably dated and modest in terms of modern filmmaking. From the opening scenes, Apu is in desperate need of a job, but lacks the qualifications or skills to find work. He is encouraged to pursue his writing career and even sells one of his stories. He still needs money to pay his landlord, so he sneaks into his apartment and quietly plays his flute. His life changes when he meets an old friend and attends a wedding where the groom abandons his bride. Instead of suffering humiliation, Apu helps the young bride by accepting to marry her. Together, the newlywed couple return to Apu's simple apartment in the city, but even his best intentions can not change materialistic necessities. A poignant film which addresses certain social issues and carries a dramatic consciousness that remains evident forty years later. As the endearing story unfolds, be patient with the early look of the film and the faded subtitles.

-Y-

Yamato - See Star Blazers

Yojimbo
(1961) Samurai   B&W-110m   Japanese with English Subtitles   VA
Catalog #6143   Japan Retail: $29.95
Dir: Akiro Kurosawa   Scr: Akira Kurosawa, Ryuzo Kikushima, Hideo Oguni
DP: Kazuo Miyagawa   Music: Masaru Sato
Art Design & Costumes: Yoshiro Muraki
PC: Toho Studios   Dist: Video Yesteryear
Toshiro Mifune   Sanjuro Kuwabatake
Eijiro Tono   Gonji the Sake Seller
Seizaburo Kawazu   Seibei
Isuzu Yamada   Orin
Hiroshi Tachikawa   Yoichiro
Kyu Sazanka   Ushitora
Daisuke Kato   Inokichi
Tatsuya Nakadai   Unosuke
Kamatari Fujiwara   Tazaemon
Takashi Shimura   Tokuemon
Ikio Sawamura   Hansuke
Atsushi Watanabe   Coffin Maker
Yoshio Tsuchiya   Kohei the Farmer
Yoko Tsukasa   Nui
Akira Nishimura   Kuma
Susumu Fujita   Homma
Yosuke Natsuki   Farmer's Son
Jerry Fujio   Roku
[****]

Akira Kurosawa's classic samurai story once again stars Toshiro Mifune as the rogue warrior who stumbles upon a town wrapped up in violence. An inspiration for the Clint Eastwood western "Fistful of Dollars" and the Bruce Willis crime drama "Last Man Standing". Mifune is Yojimbo (means bodyguard), a masterless samurai who enters a provincial town ruled by two warring factions. One side of the town is controlled by the silk merchant, the other side by the sake merhcant, and the rest of the town lives in fear. Mifune casually enters the life of the townspeople and the rival merchants. He discovers the two clans despise each other, but are reluctant to attack since they are equally matched and neither side wants to make the first move. He offers his service to one side and shifts the balance of power, but then when they are winning, he changes sides and manipulates both clan leaders. When Mifune's actions are discovered, he is ambushed, brutally beaten, and imprisoned. The kindly coffin-maker, who befriended Mifune from the beginning, rescues him. In a climatic showdown, Mifune is prepared to destroy the power of both merchants and restore peace and order in the town. Kurosawa crafts an intriguing tale of deceit and greed, breaking with conventional molds of the noble samurai. Mifune's character walks down the grey road of life and his actions are questionable at best. Beautifully crafted and shot, the film provides subtle gestures of humor, drama, and action which represent the samurai (Japan's version of the Old West) films at its best.

Yongkari, Monster of the Deep (Great Monster Yongkari, Monster Yongkari, Dai Koesu Yongkari)
(1967) Monster   C-79m PG   Dubbed   Korea
Dir: Kim Ki Dak   Scr: Suh Yunsung   DP: Kenichi Nakagawa, Inchib Byon
PC: Kuk Dong Film Co.   Dist: Orion Pictures
Oh Young Il, Nam Chung Im, Lee Soom Jai, Kang Moon, Lee Kwang Ho
[*1/2]
You may not recognize the title, but if you're a fan of Godzilla movies you probably saw this early monster film on television. Yongkari is a giant reptile that walks on all fours and is similar in style and content to other Japanese monsters. Trying to popularize on the Godzilla craze, Korean financiers developed a project with a giant creature terrorizing South Korea. I have a mild fondness for the film, since it is the only Korean monster movie I have ever seen. Though indistinguishable from many other monster films to come out of Japan, Yongkari lacks the humor, charisma, and panache that Godzilla possesses and the Korea attempt somehow becomes nothing more than a shallow, mindless clone of the popular Japanese films that predated it. Seoul isn't as impressive as the Tokyo-city sets and the miniature work suffers when compared to current visual effects standards. Still worth a look for monster fans and Koreans will definitely recognize and appreciate the detailed miniatures of their country. Basically Yongkari awakens, goes on a rampage, and seems unstoppable by conventional means. The scientist discover a way to beat Yongkari, and the defeated monster collapses beside a bridge and bleeds to death. Check out the Godzilla and Gamera pictures first and then take a look at this forgotten film.

Yotoden: Chronicle of the Warlord Period - Chapter 1: Break Out
(1987) Japanime   C-41m Japanese with English Subtitles
Catalog # USM 1625 Japan Retail: $19.99
Dir: Osamu Yamazaki   Scr & Original Story: Takeshi Narumi
Prod: Yoshiaki Aihara, Tomoyuki Miyata Ex. Prod: Makoto Hasegawa
Music: Seiji Hano   Character Design: Kenichi Onuki
Monster Design: Junichi Watanabe
English Version - Ex. Prod: John O'Donnell   Prod: Stephanie Shalofsky
Translation: William Flanagan, Yuko Sato
PC: J.C. Staff Dist: U.S. Manga (division of Central Park Media Corporation)
[***]
An enjoyable fantasy that mixes events from Japanese history with fictional accounts of ninjas and demons. Based on true historical events of the 1580's, a warlord named Oda Nobunaga rose to power and attempted to unify Japan under his rule. This is a critical period in Japanese history, since Japan would be unified with the aid of great warlords like Oda Nobunaga, Takeda Shingen, Tokugawa Ieyasu, and Toyotomi Hideyoshi into one nation for all people. In the years before the final unification, the nation is in turmoil and civil conflict. This era is ripe for fiction and produced many great stories of ninja, samurais, and warlords who battled against each other for control.
According to this version, Oda Nobunaga has made a deal with demons to conquer Japan. He is no longer mortal and uses dark magic to win his battles. To consolidate his control, he eliminates his rivals with the help of supernatural creatures. A group of ninjas who survived the initial onslaught band together to fight Oda. The story follows their paths, but the main hero is a

female ninja named Ayanosuke who uses a short sword. She is accompanied by her loyal friend Ryoma, a muscular warrior who uses a halberd, and the moody Sakon who uses a long sword. They take refuge in a ninja fortress where Ayanosuke develops a friendship with the master's daughter Kikyo. A powerful monk attacks the fortress and Ayanosuke must delve deep into her soul to release the powers of the ancient sword of sorcery and save the rebel ninjas. Combining sorcery and traditional martial arts, the film features a fascinating glimpse into Japan's warlord era. The animation will appeal to fans who enjoy a dark, moody, and serious style, while the interesting mix of genre elements and characters are full of exciting possibilites.

Yotoden: Chronicle of the Warlord Period - Chapter 2
(1987) Japanime   C-41m Japanese with English Subtitles
Catalog # USM 1625 Japan Retail: $19.99
Dir: Osamu Yamazaki   Scr & Original Story: Takeshi Narumi
Prod: Yoshiaki Aihara, Tomoyuki Miyata Ex. Prod: Makoto Hasegawa
Music: Seiji Hano   Character Design: Kenichi Onuki
Monster Design: Junichi Watanabe
English Version - Ex. Prod: John O'Donnell   Prod: Stephanie Shalofsky
Translation: William Flanagan, Yuko Sato
PC: J.C. StaffDist: U.S. Manga (division of Central Park Media Corporation)
[***]
The year is 1581 spring, the remaining heroes have banded together and prepare to do battle against Lord Nobunaga's advancing armies. Only Iga province remains and Ayanosuke and Ryoma have found shelter in the mighty ninja fortress of Kashiwabara. Ninja Kayo, from the Wada Clan of the Kogas, saves Ayanosuke and Ryoma from a wicked illusionist. She assures the Iga ninjas that the Koga ninjas have not betrayed them and will prepare for a counterattack. Master Sakon does not believe Kayo and decides to leave the bloody war, discovering treachery along his path. Under Ranmaru's advice, Lord Nobunaga attacks and sends the rebel ninjas back in defeat. Using the powers of the Seven Orobo Ninjas, Nobunaga's realm increases in size and power. Even the mighty Iga ninjas fall to the power of the gun and the trickery of the demons. The heroes learn more about their magical weapons and Yotoden "Legends of the Swords of Sorcery", but their efforts are no match for the mighty armies of Nobunaga. In an act of utter betrayal, Kayo reveals that she is possessed by a gigantic demon. Ryoma and Ayanosuke must battle the monster and free Kayo's tortured soul. Enjoyable sequel to the first film which continues the exploits of three heroes caught in the middle of a bloody war.

Young Master, The
(1980) Kung-Fu   C-86m Chinese with English Subtitles   VA
Catalog #3380   Hong Kong   Retail: $9.95
Dir: Jackie Chan   Scr: Jackie Chan   Prod: Leonard K.C. Ho   Dist: Simitar
Jackie Chan, Yuen Biao, Wei Pei, Li Li-Li, Whong In Sik
[***]
Most of Chan's modern movies are a drastic improvement in budget, style, and effort over his earlier films. Though you may prefer modern action over traditional kung-fu, Young Master is a Chan film that showcases his raw talent and energy. Jackie Chan is Dragon and his best friend is called Tiger. They are both students of a martial arts school that competes in a lion dance

festival. The top student Tiger feigns injury and resigns from the competition, so Chan takes his place and controls the Gold Lion. The Gold Lion consists of two martial artists, Chan controls the ornate head while a fellow student holds the tail. Using the mouth of the lion they attempt to swallow the prize which is placed in a hard to get position. Their rival school enters the Black Lion which is secretly controlled by Tiger. He has betrayed the school for money to help finance his bad habits, including wine and prostitutes. Chan performs brilliantly, but he does not want to injure his friend Tiger and ends up losing the tournament. Eventually, the master discovers the truth and expels Tiger who quickly joins the Black Lion School and enters a life of crime. Chan convinced of his friend's integrity attempts to exonerate him and bring him back to the school. What follows is a treat for Jackie Chan fans as a number of creative routines follow one after the other. In many ways, this early film is better than the big-budget explosive features he currently makes. There are no guns, screeching cars, and exploding buildings to distract from the pure essence of Chan's strength, ability, and charisma. What you see is what you get and Chan performs with a 100 percent energy level. Along the way, a law officer mistakes him for Tiger who is notorious for using a White Fan. A brilliant number of choreographed scenes include the over-sized fan fight, the initial duel between the two lions, a fight with Yuen Biao (the son of the law officer) using benches, comical fights with pipes and swords, and a colorful fight where Chan uses a woman's skirt. Though the budget still maintains a certain modesty, Chan's personal stamp is evident in the direction and writing. There are moments of humor which enchance the story. While searching for his friend Tiger, Chan keeps getting into deeper trouble with more new enemies. A wonderful early effort from a man destined to be a star.

-Z-

ZAITOCHI: THE BLIND SWORDSMAN SERIES (Shintaro Katsu)

In the history of Japanese cinema, only a few screen characters have sparked the viewer's interest and loyalty, producing dozens of sequels and hordes of imitators. Zaitochi (Japanese actor Shintaro Katsu) is a portly, scruffy, unattractive swordmaster who happens to be blind. He travels alone, working as a lowly masseur (a popular job for the blind), and keeps to himself. In his former years when he was young and could see, he mastered the sword, gambled, and vowed never to be pushed around. He possesses these traits and lives by his own tempermental code of honor, but ruefully travels the countryside without a master or home. He carries himself with Zen-like aplomb, but doesn't shirk to any man and finds himself at odds with gangsters and bandits. He is the quintessential handicapped warrior, relying on his other senses like hearing and smelling to defeat his vicious opponents. Fortunately many of his enemies don't bathe and smell awful. His abilities border on the supernatural and require a certain suspension of disbelief. His life is spent in rigorous and brutal training while he enjoys a cup of sake, a bit of gambling, and helping widows and orphans. When trouble crosses his path, he takes no prisoners and gets the job done in a hasty and messy way. He doesn't necessarily seek violence, but his bloody path has created many enemies who want revenge or to test his skills. Though the films are not rated they are inappropriate for younger children. Many of the scenes contain violent sword fights and mature themes. Actor Shintaro Katsu is the embodiment of Zaitoichi and his role is as loved as Sean Connery's James Bond, Basil Rathbone's Sherlock Holmes, or Johnny Weismueller's Tarzan which all demanded new adventures on a regular basis. The serials were extremely popular and followed a familiar pattern, since that was expected of the Zaitochi chambara films. The films will appeal to you as a group or not at all and should best be viewed by people interested in the genre. Kurosawa's style of filmmaking they are not, but they provide plenty of action and excitement in a comic book model. The following is a capsule review of selected Zaitochi films available on video. I am planning on expanding this section with more detail and history, so my father and I have watched every single film again, if you like one, you'll like them all.

Zaitochi: The Blind Swordsman and the Chess Expert
(1965) Samurai   C-87m Japanese with English Subtitles   VA
Catalog #MVP 933   Japan Retail: $19.95
Dir: Kazuo Ikehiro   Dist: Facets Multimedia, Inc.
Shintaro Katsu
[1/2]**
While traveling for the holidays, Zaitochi meets a chess player and the two men play a game or two, becoming friends and admiring each other's skill. They meet a woman who is attacked and injured by gangsters. Zaitochi risks his life and fortune to save the woman. He uses a cane sword which also doubles as a blindman's walking stick.

Zaitochi: The Blind Swordsman and the Fugitives
(1968) Samurai   C-82m Japanese with English Subtitles   VA
Catalog #CE 102   Japan Retail: $19.95
Dir: Kimiyoshi Yasuda   Scr: Kinga Naoi
DP: Kazuo Miyagawa   Editor: Iwao Ohtani Music: Hajime Kaburagi
Art Dir: Shigero Kato
PC: Daiei   Dist: Facets Multimedia, Inc.
Shintaro Katsu, Yumiko Nogawa, Kayo Mikimoto, Kyosuke Machida
[1/2]**
A group of bandits terrorize a local village and Zaitochi must put aside his personal vices and save the people. Underestimated as usual, Zaitochi's lighting fast sword techniques dispatch his enemies in a blink of an eye.

Zaitochi: The Blind Swordsman's Vengeance
(1966) Samurai   C-83m Japanese with English Subtitles   VA   Japan
Dir: Tokuzo Tanaka Scr: Hajime Takaiwa   DP: Kazuo Miyagawa
PC: Daiei   Dist: Facets Multimedia, Inc.
Shintaro Katsu, Shigeru Amachi, Kei Sato, Mayumi Ogawa
[1/2]**
Zaitochi protects a dying man against a group of gangsters who have taken over a quiet village. This doesn't bode well with the gangsters' boss who decides Zaitochi must be eliminated.

Zaitochi: The Life and Opinion of Masseur Ichi
(1962) Samurai   C-96m Japanese with English Subtitles   VA   Japan

Dir: Kenji Misumi   Scr: Minoru Inunzuka   DP: Chishi Makiura
PC: Daiei   Dist: Facets Multimedia, Inc.
Shintaro Katsu, Masayo Mari, Ryuzo Shimada, Gen Mitamura, Shigeru Amachi
[1/2]**
The film that started it all and introduced filmgoers to the rough, portly Zaitochi. Keep in mind that chambara films (sword slashers) are very different from the epic Kurosawa films. Zaitochi is brutal and vulgar in many ways, so don't expect a clean-cut noble film of honorable warriors in shining suits of armor.

Zaitochi: Master Ichi and a Chest of Gold
(1964) Samurai   C-83m Japanese with English Subtitles   VA
Catalog #MVP 934   Japan Retail: $19.95
Dir: Kazuo Ikehiro   Scr: Shozoburo Asai, Akikazu Ota DP: Kazuo Miyagawa
PC: Daiei
Shintaro Katsu, Mikiko Tsubuchi, Machiko Hasegawa, Kenzaburo Joh, Shogo Shimada
[1/2]**
Zaitochi falls into a robbery by a group of bandits and then is framed for the gold robbery. He must clear his name and defeat the evil bandits.

Zaitochi vs. Yojimbo
(1970) Samurai   C-90m Japanese with English Subtitles   VA   Japan
Dir: Kihachi Okamoto   Scr: Kihachi Okatomo, Tetsuro Yoshida
DP: Kazuo Miyagawa   Music: Akira Ifukube   Art Dir: Yoshinobu Nishioka
PC: Daiei   Dist: Facets Multimedia, Inc.

Shintaro Katsu	**Zatoichi**
Toshiro Mifune	**Yojimbo**
Ayako Wakao	**Umeno**
Yonekura Masakene	**Masagoro**
Takizuwa Shu	**Eboshiya Yasuke**
Mori Kishida	**Kuzuryu**
Kanjuro Arashi	**Hyoroku**

[***]
The best in the series, pitting screen legend Toshiro Mifune against Shintaro's Zaitochi. Zaitochi has reached an older age and wishes to settle down in his village, but bandits capture the town. Zaitochi is forced to fight the ronin Yojimbo, from Akira Kurosawa's film Yojimbo. Mifune plays the master samurai with a comic twist as swords blaze and the action heats up.

Zaitochi: Zaitochi's Flashing Sword
(1964) Samurai   C-82m Japanese with English Subtitles   VA
Catalog #CE 105   Japan Retail: $19.95
Dir: Kazuo Ikehiro   Scr: Minoru Inuzuka   DP: Yasukaza Takemura
PC: Daiei   Dist: Facets Multimedia, Inc.
Shintaro Katsu, Mayumi Nagisa, Naoko Kubo, Ryutaro Gami, Yutaka Nakamura
[1/2]**
Caught in the middle of two feuding yakuza gangs, Zaitochi makes enemies when he sides with

boss Tusmugi. The other boss then sends his best men to teach Zaitochi a bloody lesson. Keep in mind that the films are geared toward genre lovers and are dated by today's standards. Still, Zaitochi delivers a straight-forward plot and sword action for die-hard fans.

Zenki: Volume 1-6
(1995) Japanime: Fantasy   C-90m Japanese with English Subtitles   VA
Catalog # SSVS 1007 Japan Retail: $24.95
Dir: Junichi Nishimura   Original Story: Kikuhide Tani, Yoshihiro Kuroiwa
Ex. Prod: Tetsu Ijichi   PC: Studio Dhin   Dist: Software Sculptors
[1/2]**
Episodic supernatural series with the first video volume containing three episodes. In present day Japan, demons and magical powers are just legends and stories told to tourists who visit the ancient shrines and temples. But for a young disciple and her friends, fighting demons is a daily chore. Young Chiaki is the 55th generation of the master monk Enno Ozuno who 1200 years ago locked away the demonic powers of Zenki: The Great Demon Lord. Now evil has returned to Japan and the malevolent god Karma unleashes 108 Seeds of Possession into the human world. Each seed contains demonic powers which corrupt a human soul and turn him/her into a hideous creature. It is up to Chiaki and her friends to stop them with the aid of Zenki's ancient power. When summoned by Chiaki, the muscular Zenki appears hostile and attempts to murder anyone who gets in his ways. His demonic tendecies are kept under control by Chiaki who possesses a magic bracelet of protection. Under her orders, the demon lord Zenki battles the 108 monsters (one or two per episode) and then enjoys eating the tasty seed which gave birth to them. The show's unique humor lies in Chiaki's ability to turn the mighty Zenki into a child-demon. In his tiny form, he's rather harmless, adorable, and provides plenty of plot mischief. Only when he's needed does Chiaki unleash his true demonic powers. Since episodic in nature, each story is a variation of the original premise and will appeal to you based on your initial fascination with the first volume. The violence factor is subdued for a more comedic approach, but still contains elements of supernatural horror and "girls in anime" hijinks. Followed by additional volumes now available.
Episode 1: Zenki: The Demon Lord Stands Before You! I am Zenki, the great and Notorious!
Episode 2: Karma the Malevolent Presenting the Three Masters of Evil!
Episode 3: Chiaki in Trouble Beware the Camera's Gaze
Zenki: Vol. 2 Catalog # SSVS 1008 Japan Retail: $19.95
Episode 4: The Jar of Desires - Operation: Golden Shikigami-cho
Episode 5: The Appetite Fiend - How Many Stars Will a Taste of Zenki Rate?
Zenki is starving
Zenki: Vol. 3 Catalog # SSVS 1009 Japan Retail: $19.95
Episode 6: Teletemptation - The Little Boy Rings Again
Episode 7: The Obsessed Runner - Dash for the Daybreak Finish Line
Zenki: Vol. 4 Catalog # SSVS 1009 Japan Retail: $19.95
Episode 8: The Mummy Inn - Young Girls Gladly Welcome
Episode 9: The Devil in the Basement - Blast Forth Khan! The Spell of Flames
Zenki: Vol. 5 Catalog # SSVS 1010 Japan Retail: $19.95
Episode 10: March of the Hell Hound - Rage Hard, Fuuta
Episode 11: A Voice from the Underworld - Requiem for a Samurai

Zenki: Vol. 6 Catalog # SSVS 1011 Japan Retail: $19.95
Episode 12: The Witch on the Hill Memories - Lost in the Snow
Episode 13: The EMA Struggle Crash - It's a Great Mid-Air Battle

Zen of Sword
(1992) Kung-Fu   C-100m   Chinese with English Subtitles   Catalog #1331
Hong Kong   Retail: $39.99
Dir: Yu Mang San   Scr: Li Man Choi, Leung Kim Ho
Ex. Prod: Wang Ying Shiang, Lui Kwok Wai   Prod: Stephen Shin
DP: Ko Chiu Lam, Wong Po Man, Cheng Siu Keung   Editor: Wong Wing Ming
Associate Prod: Tang Sam   Prod manager: Wan Yat To
Prod Design: Siu Hin Fai, Cheng Siu Keung
Art Dir: Lau Man Hung   Assistant Dir: Jupiter Wong, Cheung Chi Wai
Sound: Tsang King Cheung Costume: Bruce Yu
MAD: Kwok Chun Fung, Tang Tak Wing
PC/Dist: Long Shores Pictures, Ltd./Citimedia Limited
Michelle Reis, Cynthia Khan, Lau Sik Ming, Lee Chi Hung, Lau Suen, Hui Ying Hung, Lau Siu Ming, Kwok Chun Fung
[***]
A fun but frenetic film that features many familiar elements found in other sword-flying kung-fu films. Princess Michelle Reis and her entourage are attacked, forcing her to hide in the wilderness. Her two bodyguards, a fierce male and female warrior, do their best to protect her from deadly monks and assassins. The two bodyguards, also lovers, are separated and the male warrior is captured by the enemy and turned toward the dark side. The female warrior, the fierce and beautiful Cynthia Khan, does her best to stay near the princess and protect her. In a hidden camp, a mighty woman warrior Hui Ying Hung, has chosen a handsome young hero to represent their clan's cause. He wields a mighty sword and must master the difficult techniques. During a nighttime training routine, he slices at straw bodies that swing toward him from above. Then Hui tosses a woman, and she is sliced in half. Horrified by his actions, he wants no part of the bloodshed and walks out on the clan. He can not escape his destiny and the actions of his fellow clansmen open his eyes to the harsh realities of life. He eventually meets the wandering Princess and protects her from deadly assassins. A few fight scenes erupt due to misunderstandings between the main characters, but a passionate relationship forms between the hero and the princess. She is later discovered and rescued by one of her own generals and the male bodyguard who later betray a noble warrior and reveal their true nature. Meanwhile, Hui and her clan are attacked by their enemies and it is then revealed that the hero's target is the princess. He puts aside his compassion and goes after Michelle Reis, fully intent on killing her and avenging his clan. Though Zen's hero doesn't match the charisma of Jet Li in Swordsman, viewers who enjoy flying sword battles will find the film enjoyable. One nice note is the appearance of veteran star Hui, if she looks familiar than you are a true Shaw Brothers connoisseur. Hui was a popular fixture in classic Shaw Brothers kung-fu movies directed by her companion Liu Chia Liang. Her beauty and poise seem timeless, though her actual screen time is minimal and her character is reminiscent of Brigitte Lin.

Zu: Warriors of the Magic Mountain

(1983) Fantasy Kung-Fu   C-94m Chinese with English Subtitles
Catalog #0050   Hong Kong   Retail: $39.99
Dir/Prod: Tsui Hark Dist: Tai Seng Video
Yuen Biao   Ti
Adam Cheng   Ting Yen
Brigitte Lin   Countess
Lau Chung Yan, Randy Man, Judy Ong, Samo Hung
[*1/2]**

Chinese culture is rich with legends and folklore, so it comes as no surprise that many of the modern films from Hong Kong incorporate the wild imaginative nature of mythological fantasy mixed within the bounds of history and traditional martial arts. Director/producer Tsui Hark helped spark the supernatural kung-fu craze with his first fantasy masterpiece. Followed by many other fantasy films from various directors, including Hark, key elements will be found in every rendition. Expect a large dose of lavish costumes, supernatural creatures, flying kung-fu, and a carefree attitude towards the laws of physics and nature. Set in the 10th century, youthful Ti escapes the carnage of a clan war, seeks refuge, and comes under the attack of a fiendish creature. He is saved by Master Ting Yen and joins him on a wild, exciting journey into a world of monsters, demonic possession, magic spells, and plenty of kung-fu. Along the way, the heroes meet the Countess of Ice Fortress, wonderfully played by Lin, who guides the group through their ordeal dealing with possession and poisonous monsters. The film features some bizarre images and plenty of classic elements found in modern-made fantasy kung-fu films like Chinese Ghost Story, Green Snake, Kung Fu Cult Master, and The East is Red (Swordsman III). For those who enjoy traditional kung-fu action, don't worry there's a dose of that too. For example, a funny scene with Yuen and Samo who are trapped in the middle of a major battle in the forest. Each clan is dressed in colorful uniforms, but Yuen and Samo pretend to fight against each other and trick fighters to fight with anyone else besides them. At one point, the enemies look at each other, point to Yuen and Samo, and decide to get the two trouble makers. If you enjoy previous Tsui Hark productions and the fantasy genre, Zu is a wonderful example of Hong Kong's creative imagination and non-Hollywood style of approach to the supernatural.

PART II

ASIAN FILMS FROM AMERICA AND EUROPE

(I've also included a list of films that feature Asian characters or themes, but were produced, financed or filmed outside of Asia.)

American Shaolin: King of the Kickboxers II
(2001) Kung-Fu C-103m English PG-13 VA Catalog #1555 USA
Dir: Lucas Lowe Scr/Prod: Keith W. Strandberg   Ex. Prod: Ng See Yuen
DP: Viking Chiu, Luis Cubilles Editor: Alan Poon   Music: Richard Yuen
MAD: Corey Yuen
Art Direction: John Ting   Prod. Manager: Richard Strickland, Eliza Suen
Prod Supervisor: Bernard Yim   Prod Coordinator: Eva Andrews, Patrick Wu, Derek
                                    Ho
PC: Seasonal Films Dist: Academy Entertainment

Reese Madigan	Drew
Trent Bushy	Trevor Gottitall
Daniel Dae Kim	Gao
Billy Chang	Li
Cliff Lenderman	D.S.
Zhang Shi Yen	San De
Kim Chan	Master Kwan
Alice Zhang Hung	Ashena

[**1/2]
Ng See Yuen continues to introduce Hong Kong style action films with a Western flavor. The story is familiar and the acting is quite limited, but the film has a bit of charm and appeal for genre fans. Rather than straightforward action and revenge, the film offers a comedic and romantic side to the plot. Young American Drew is defeated in a tournament by the ruthless Trevor Gottitall who believes in humiliating his opponents with a Steven Segal-like swagger.

Anna and the King
(1989) Drama/Romance C-147m English VA USA
Dir: Andy Tennant Scr: Steve Meerson, Peter Krikes   Prod: Lawrence Bender, Ed Elbert
Co-Prod: Jon Jashni, G. Mac Brown Ex Prod: Terence Chang
DP: Caleb Deschanel Editor: Roger Bondelli   Music: George Fenton
Prod Design: Luciana Arrighi   PC: Fox 2000 Pictures

Chow Yun Fat	King Mongkut
Jodie Foster	Anna Leonowens

[***1/2]
A beautiful adaptation of Anna Leonowens' true experience as a schoolteacher to the children of King Mongkut of Siam (Thailand). The film bears little resemblance to the musical version, King and I, which is a wonderful treat of songs, sets and costumes. Anna and the King focuses on the drama and tensions that underlie a nation under change and pressure from forces within

and without. Beautifully filmed on exquisite locations, the film is a true visual and sensory gem of majestic sets and costumes. Jodie Foster (her English accent is a bit forced) is a proper choice as the educated, stiff, and resolute English schoolteacher who warms the heart of King Mongkut, dozens of his wives, and his 58-plus children. The history and politics of Southeast Asia in the mid-1800's was a tenuous and complex situation fraught with dangers, but Siam managed to maintain its independence and avoid the colonial oppression that befell its neighbors in Burma, Vietnam, Cambodia, and China. King Mongkut is a man caught on the crossroads of history, one foot stepping forward to reform, equality, and modernization, and another foot caught behind in tradition, superstition, and stubbornness. The widow Anna and her young son Louis befriend the King and his children, slowly bridging the gap between East and West, bonding a unique friendship of love, trust, and understanding. Along the way, Anna fosters one of the King's ladies, Tuptim, who is later punished for her infidelity, helps host a lavish European-style party for British delegates, participates in the Rice Festival and search for the white elephant, and is embroiled in a bitter civil war between the King and his once trusted General Alak. Chow Yun Fat is superb as the charismatic king who tries to be so many virtues to so many people at the sacrifice of his own self.

Best of the Best
(1989) Martial Arts C-95m English   PG-13   VA   Catalog #022604
USA   Retail: $9.99
Dir: Robert Radler   Story: Phillip Rhee, Paul Levine
Prod: Phillip Rhee, Peter E. Strauss
Ex. Prod: Michael Holzman, Frank Giustra
DP: Doug Ryan   Editor: William Hoy Music: Paul Gilman
Art Dir: Maxine Shepard   Prod Design: Kim Rees   Associate Prod: Deborah Scott
Line Prod: Marlon Staggs   Casting Dir: Jim Tarzia   Costume: Cynthia Bergstrom
Makeup/Sp. Fx: Peggy Teague   MAD: Simon Rhee
PC: Taurus Entertainment   Dist: Columbia

Eric Roberts	**Alex Grady**
Phillip Rhee	**Tommy Lee**
Simon Rhee	**Dae Han**
Sally Kirkland	**Catherine Wade**
Christopher Penn	**Travis Brickley**
James Earl Jones	**Coach Couzo**
John P. Ryan	**Jennings**
John Dye	**Virgil Keller**
David Agresta	**Sonny Grasso**
Tom Everett	**Don Peterson**
Louise Fletcher	**Mrs. Grady (Alex's mom)**
Hee Cho Il	**Korean Coach**
Chang Park Kim	**Referee**
Dae Kyu Chang	**Tung Sung Moon**
Ho Sik Pak	**Han Cho**
James Lew	**Sae Jin Kwon**
Ken Hagayama	**Yung Kim**

[***]

The first in a series of martial arts films examining the Korean art of Tae Kwon Do, starring Phillip Rhee who helped produce the series. By far, the first film is the most entertaining and features a talented cast of actors led by Eric Roberts, James Earl Jones, and Phillip Rhee. What sets these movies apart from the myriad of martial arts clones is that they involve the popular Korean style of Tae Kwon Do and numerous Korean characters. Though Korea is a prominent Asian nation, her culture and story are often absent on the large screen. Before Phillip Rhee, the only major Korean star to exhibit Tae Kwon Do was Jhoon Rhee. The story is very straightforward and combines the underdog elements of "Rocky". Unfortunately, instead of mentioning Tae Kwon Do, the style is purposely referred to as Korean Karate, to help layman understand the term. In true sports-fashion, five athletes from all walks of life are chosen to represent the American team. We are given background information on each character, but the main focus is on Roberts and Rhee. Eric Roberts is a single parent who suffered an accident that prematurely ended his martial arts career. Now buffed and healed, he hopes to make a comeback and leaves his son under the protective gaze of his mother. Phillip Rhee is the young prodigy, a world-class fighter who is torn between revenge and honor, ever since his brother was killed in a tournament by Korean champion Dae Han. The five men qualify at a trial competition and then graduate to an elite training facility with James Earl Jones as the head coach and Sally Kirkland as a spiritual/health advisor. A variety of entertaining training scenes are intermixed with personal problems suffered by the two main characters. Another positive aspect of the film is their portrayal of the Korean National Team, the world champions and heavy favorites against the fledgling American team. The Korean training scenes are fascinating and different from the Americans, but true to the core of Korean training philosophy. The finale takes place in Seoul, Korea where the five-man teams match up against each other in well-choreographed fight scenes. The highlight is an amazing fight between real-life brothers Phillip and Simon Rhee who demonstrate the amazing beauty of Tae Kwon Do. A touching end and realistic martial arts also add to the film's shine which is definitely a breath of fresh air for martial arts fans looking for something instead of generic revenge and violence. Though the melodrama is predictable, the scenes are fast-paced and the characters engaging thanks in part to the talented Hollywood actors in their supporting roles.

Best of the Best 2
(1993) Martial Arts C-100m   English   R   VA   Catalog #3380
USA   Retail: $19.95
Dir: Robert Radler   Scr: John Allen Nelson, Max Storm
Prod: Frank Giustra, Phillip Rhee, Deborah Scott, Marlon Staggs
DP: Fred Tammes   Editor: Bert Lovitt, Danny Retz   Music: David Michael Frank
Art Dir: Bill Rea   Prod Design: Steve Brown. Gary Frutkoff, Bill Rea
Set Design: Colin Irwin, Anna Rita Raineri   Costume: Mona May
MAD: Simon Rhee   Dist: Fox Video
Eric Roberts   Alex Grady
Phillip Rhee   Tommy Lee
Christopher Penn   Travis Brickley
Meg Foster   Sue
Wayne Newton   Weldon

Simon Rhee	Dae Han
Edan Gross	Walter Grady
Sonny Landham	James
Ralph Moeller	Brakus

[**]

Phillip Rhee, Eric Roberts, and Chris Penn are back in action, but this time they're partners in a martial arts school outside Las Vegas. Not satisfied with the Miyagi-stint, impetuous Travis Brickley enters illegal fighting tournaments sanctioned by hi-rollers on the Vegas strip. The ultimate champion, a Dolph Lundgren-clone, teaches Brickley a deadly lesson. For some silly reason, Eric Roberts' son is at the illegal fight and becomes a potential witness to the bloody death matches. The hi-rollers decide to go after Roberts' son and anyone else who may squeal on their operation headed by slimy Wayne Newton. After the mob destroys their home, the men escape to the desert and study Native America philosophy. The coolest part in this silly, revenge fest is the visiting Korean National Tae Kwon Do Team (from the first film) who provide Phillip and Eric with some backup and start a fight inside the casino-front for the illegal tournament. Now good friends with the American team, they provide some entertaining support, but only for a brief moment. Eric and Phillip fight their way through the bad guys, but must challenge the muscular fighter in the center ring if they hope to be victorious. The film will entertain for those who enjoy the revenge/fight format, but the sequel lacks the heart and realism of the first film. Followed by a sequel without Eric Roberts, focusing on Phillip Rhee (Best of the Best 3: No Turning Back).

Beyond Rangoon
(1995) DramaC-99m English   R   VA
Catalog #27723   USA   Retail: $19.99 Widescreen Available
Dir: John Boorman   Scr: Alex Lasker, Bill Rubenstein
Prod: John Boorman, Eric Pleskow, Barry Spikings   Ex. Prod: Sean Ryerson
DP: John Seale   Editor: Ron Davis   Music: Hans Zimmer
Prod Design: Anthony Pratt   Costume: Deborah La Gorce Kramer
PC: Pleskow/Spikings Production   Dist: Castle Rock Entertainment

Patricia Arquette	Laura
U Aung Ko	U Aung Ko
Frances McDormand	Andy
Spalding Gray	Jeremy Wytt
Tiara Jacquelina	Desk Clerk
Kuswadinath Bujang	Colonel
Victor Slezak	Mr. Scott
Tiara Jacquelina	San San
Adele Lutz	Aung San Suu Kyi

[***]

August 1988, a young American tourist is travelling through Southeast Asia with her older sister. She is spiritually lost, emotionally troubled, and disoriented with life. When she meets some freedom rights activists in Burma (now Myanamer), she is moved by their charismatic leader, Aung San Suu Kyi (Nobel Peace Prize Winner 1991) and their noble cause. She ends up offending a military colonel and gets trapped in the country without a passport.

The film is based on true historical events of 1988, a turbulent period in Burma's history. Patricia Arquette plays Laura, a young doctor who must begin a spiritual and physical quest for freedom. When separated, her sister (McDormand) urges Laura to go to the American Embassy and leave the country as soon as possible. Of course, we know how helpful bureaucrats are and so does Laura who hops on a cab driven by a dissident ex-professor. The two form a powerful friendship as they travel the country and show the beauties and wonders of Burma. When the political situation becomes extremely volatile, they attempt to make their way out of the country. They meet some friends, but Laura and U Aung Ko are on their own. He is injured at a border check and she must now take control of the situation. Through sheer luck and determination, she is able to find medical supplies to help him and bribe passage on a river boat to the country's border. As the villainous soldiers close in on their position, they join a group of refugees and escape across the border. They suffer through horrible conditions and barely escape with their lives, but the film's portrayal is accurate to historical accounts of brutality. Boorman's visuals are enchanting and his story takes us in one step at a time into an exotic and dangerous world torn from within. Arquette is competent and gives a credible performance, though at times her lucid demeanor is lost within the situation.

Big Brawl, The (Battle Creek Brawl)
(1980) Kung-Fu   C-95m English   R   VA
Catalog #0408   USA   Retail: $39.99
Dir/Scr: Robert Clouse   Prod: Fred Weintraub, Terry Morse
DP: Robert Jessup   Editor: David Garfield, George Grenville Music: Lalo Schifrin
Art Dir/Prod Design: Joe Altadonna   PC: Warner Bros.
Dist: Tai Seng Video/Warner

Jackie Chan	**Jerry**
Jose Ferrer	**Dominici**
Mako	**Herbert**
Kristine de Bell	**Nancy**
Ron Max	**Legetti**
Rosalind Chao	**Mae**
Chao Li Chi	**Kwan**
H.B. Haggerty	**Les Kiss**
Joycelyne Lew	**Miss Wong**

[**1/2]

The creative team that put Bruce Lee on the screen in Enter the Dragon, attempt to do the same with Jackie Chan in the Big Brawl. Unfortunately, American audiences weren't quite ready for the comical/physical martial artist Chan who bore little resemblance to the explosive Bruce Lee. Set in the USA in the depression-laden 1930's, Chan is a typical nice guy who gets involved with the wrong sort of folks. The title refers to a major fight contest which offers a huge cash prize to the winner. A no-holds barred fight similar to the Ultimate Fighting Competitions which are so popular on pay-per-view. Jackie is reluctant to enter the brawl at Battle Creek, but is forced to when gangsters kidnap his brother's fiance and force him to fight. An interesting melding of martial arts and gangster genres with a good deal of humor and a strong cast, but the out of vogue time setting and the mixture of non-martial arts and martial arts choreography lack appeal for die-hard kung-fu fans. Jackie must defeat the opposing mob's powerful fighter Les Kiss in order to win. Jackie's first attempt at breaking into the American market was a good effort and fine for some laughs but failed to catapult his career. Don't expect too much from the fight scenes, but Chan fans will still have a good time.

Big Trouble in Little China
(1986) Fantasy Kung-Fu   C-100m   English   PG-13 VA
Catalog #1502-85   USA   Retail: $19.99 Widescreen Available
Dir: John Carpenter Scr: John Carpenter, Gary Goldman, David Z. Weinstein
Ex. Prod: Paul Monash, Keith Barish   Prod: Larry J. Franco
Music: John Carpenter   Effects: Richard Edlund
PC: Taft/Barish/Monash Production   Dist: Fox Video
Kurt Russell   Jack Burton
Kim Cattrall   Gracie Law
Dennis Dun   Wang Chi
James Hong   Lo Pan
Victor Wong   Egg Shen
Kate Burton   Margo
Suzee Pai   Miao Yin
[***]

American director John Carpenter attempts to capture the magic and lunacy of martial arts/fantasy films in this wild and fun-spirited adventure. Geared toward an American audience, Carpenter focuses on the tale of an American truck driver who gets involved in the magical underworld of San Francisco's Chinatown. Though the film lacks tight cohesion and is speckled by outlandish scenes that don't always meld, the visuals, martial arts scenes, and madcap mayhem make for a wild treat and a unique alternative for fans of the spoofed genres. The fantasy-action-martial arts plot has a mish-mash of various Chinese and American elements that could confuse anyone not familiar with the genre, but the film is definitely a treat so let me guide you through the main points. Kurt Russell is Jack Burton, a tough, All-American trucker, whose Chinese-American friend Wong is picking up his bride at the San Francisco airport. At the airport, she is kidnapped by Chinatown gangsters, Lords of Death, under the rule of billionaire Lo Pan. The girl is sent to a brothel where it is discovered she has green eyes, a rarity in Chinese women. Coincidentally, Lo needs a virgin with green eyes, so that he can become human again and take over the world. Russell and his friend pursue the thugs and end up being caught in a gang war between Lo's Wing Kong and a good clan called the Chang Sing. Things explode in a Chinese standoff with some solid martial arts sequences featuring some of the best fighters in Hollywood. Just when things look good for the Chang Sing, the Three Storms enter the battle. A highlight of the film, the Three Storms are mystical kung-fu fighters (popular in Hong Kong fantasy films) who each possess special powers: Thunder, Lightning, and Rain. Other popular Chinese elements include magic, monsters, spirits, and flying kung-fu. Lo eventually finds two women with green eyes, including the gutsy Kim Cattrall who's never looked cuter. She and Wong's friends are trying to help free the women who have been kidnapped by the Lords of Death. The lunacy gets wilder as the naive Russell can't believe his own eyes when he penetrates the underground palace of Lo Pan. The heroes meet up with a Chinese wizard who aids them in their quest and in climatic fantasy fashion, a team of warriors break into Lo's fortress and defeat his army and save the women. Fast-paced with one-liners that seem adlibbed pop up among wild action scenes and fancy special effects. An interesting point is that Carpenter doesn't relegate his Asian cast to meandering or generic roles. He gives good screen time to both races and often shows the Caucasians as arrogant, bumbling, and useless. Thankfully, Carpenter treats the Asian fantasy elements of the film with passion and authenticity. He never allows the Chinese characters to fall behind Russell and Cattrall, but provides plenty of action and comedy for the entire cast.

Black Eagle
(1988) Martial Arts C-93m English   R   VA   Catalog #65303
USA   Retail: $19.95
Dir: Eric Karson, Robert Gordon Scr: Edward Huebsch, Hal Smith
Prod: Robert Cohn   DP: Henry Freulich   Editor: James Sweeney
Music Dir: Mischa Bakaleinikoff   Art Design: Carl Anderson
Set Design: Louis Diage
(based on the story "The Passing of Black Eagle" by O. Henry)
Jean-Claude Van Damme, Sho Kosugi

William Bishop	**Jason Bond**
Virginia Patton	**Ginny Long**
Gordon Jones	**Benjy Laughton**
James Bell	**Frank Hayden**
Trevor Bardette	**Mike Long**
Will Wright	**Clancy**
Edmund MacDonald	**Si**
Paul E. Burns	**Hank Daniels**
Harry Cheshire	**The General**
Al Ehen	**Chicken**
Ted Mapes	**Sam**
Richard Talmadge	**Mort**

[**]
After the success of Jean-Claude's Bloodsport, Cannon scrambled to release some of his other projects. No Retreat and No Surrender and Black Eagle are both earlier Van Damme features that portray him as a Russian villain. Though the acting and character development is limited, his physical talent is apparent in both films. Black Eagle was originally slated as a Sho Kosugi-starring project with a modest budget. Sho is an American agent on assignment who runs into the Russian killer Van Damme. The two never build any conflict between each other in this pre-Glasnost spy adventure and their fight scenes are poorly conceived and mismatched in technique. Van Damme spends most of his time in straddle splits, throwing knives and impressing his comrades. Meanwhile Sho and his partners run around the city looking for clues. The remainder of the film attempts to salvage the Bond-esque plot which deals with a KGB and CIA attempt to retrieve vital equipment in the sunny, scenic countryside of the Mediterranean. The film is quite forgettable in every aspect.

Black Rain
(1989) Crime Drama C-125m   English   R   VA   Catalog #24171
USA   Retail: $19.95 Widescreen Available

Dir: Ridley Scott   Prod: Stanley R. Jaffe, Sherry Lansing
Scr: Craig Bolotin, Warren Lewis DP: Jan De Bont   Editor: Tom Rolf
Music: Hans Zimmer   Prod Design: Norris Spencer
Costumes: Ellen Mirojnick Dist: Paramount
Michael Douglas   Nick Conklin
Andy Garcia   Charlie Vincent
Ken Takakura   Masahiro Matsumoto
Kate Capshaw   Joyce Kingsley
Yusaku Matsuda   Sato
Tomisaburo Wakayama   Sugai
Shigeru Koyama   Ohashi
Yuya Uchida   Nashida
Miyuki Ono   Miyuki
[**1/2]

Though the top-billed actors are non-Asian, the film primarily settles in Japan and co-stars veteran actor Ken Takakura. The industrial city of Osaka, Japan plays the background for this dark crime drama about a middle-aged American cop breaking the rules in Japan. Michael Douglas and Andy Garcia are two New York City cops who bust a Japanese gangster in their city. They must extradite the criminal back to Japan, sign for his transfer, and come right back to the United States. The airplane lands and they sign for the release of the criminal, but minutes later another officer boards the plane and asks for the same thing. Suddenly, they realize the first group were impostors and that they've screwed up. Douglas, tough and seasoned as usual, decides to help the Japanese police whether they want his help or not. He meets up with an American living in Japan, an attractive hostess played by Kate Capshaw who enlightens him (and the audience) about Japanese culture. Douglas gets some help from the wise Takakura and together they descend into the world of Japanese organized crime. The criminals are also facing their own problems and don't appreciate the constant pressures from Douglas. After a number of high powered chase scenes, Douglas finally gets his man, but at the cost of his partner. A decent action film well crafted by Scott, but lacking the charisma and power seen in Hong Kong crime films.

Bloodsport
(1988) Kung-Fu   C-92m English   R   VA   Catalog #22833
USA   Retail: $14.95
Dir: Newton Arnold   Scr: Sheldon Lettich, Christopher Cosby, Frank Dux
Prod: Mark DiSalle DP: David Worth   Editor: Carl Kress   Music: Paul Hertzog
Prod Design: David Searl   Costume: Wei Sau Ling   Makeup: Tommy Chan, Jenny Chui, Chan Man Fai MAD: Steve Lee Ka Ding   PC/Dist: Cannon Group
Jean-Claude Van Damme   Frank Dux
Roy Chiao   Senzo Tanaka
Bolo Yeung   Chong Li
Donald Gibb   Ray Jackson
Leah Ayres   Janice
Ken Boyle   Col. Cooke
Forrest Whittaker   Rawlins

Norman Burton	Helmer
Michael Paul Chan	Yasuda
Philip Chan	Capt. Chen
Lily Leung	Mrs. Tanaka
Mandy Chan	Janitor

[***]

The film that launched a thousand kicks, punches, and flips, skyrocketing Belgian actor Jean-Claude Van Damme to international fame. Bloodsport was the major debut for Van Damme, "Muscles from Brussels", and helped revitalize a sagging interest in martial arts films. Though Van Damme is non-Asian, the film is an excellent example of an Asian-style kung-fu movie with key parts delegated to Asian actors. The major non-Asian roles are Van Damme, his oafish sidekick Jackson, two bumbling army agents, and the pretty but two-dimensional Leah Ayres. The comedic sidekick, the main villains, the police chief, the master, and the majority of the cast are Asian actors. The story begins with a wonderful training montage of different styles of martial arts and their practitioners. The fighters are preparing for the Kumite, an illegal full-contact tournament in Hong Kong sponsored by the Triads. The most impressive is Bolo, a massive Korean martial artist who destroys blocks of ice with his bare hands. Army officer Jean-Claude also attends the tournament, but must go AWOL to do so and is pursued throughout the film by a comedic duo of US Agents. Initially billed as the true biography of Frank Dux for publicity reasons which was later rescinded, Van Damme portrays Dux, the first American to win the Kumite. As a young delinquent, Dux is introduced to the world of martial arts to provide focus and discipline in his life. In a wonderful series of training scenes, he learns from a Japanese master called Tanaka who lost his own son at the Kumite. Dux vows to his dying master that he will win the coveted sword prize. His opposition is tough and features fighters from around the world. He manages to become friends with Jackson - a street fighter from America, a Hong Kong guide, and a beautiful undercover reporter. When Bolo decides to squash Jackson's head, Dux promises to defeat the him. Meanwhile, the pretty blonde reporter sleeps her way into the Kumite and tries to stop Dux from getting hurt. The film's highlights come in the well-choreographed and tense fight scenes which place this movie as one of the most popular American-martial arts movie of recent time. Jean-Claude's grace, fluidity, and flexibility are perfect for the screen, and his body is a piece of art in motion. Similar to Bruce Lee's grace in many ways, Bloodsport capitalizes on Damme's skills and the versatility of the martial arts world. A fast-paced and extremely entertaining film for genre lovers.

Bridge on the River Kwai, The
UK (1957): War   C-161m   English   VA   Catalog #65410
USA   Retail: $19.95   Widescreen Available
Dir: David Lean   Scr: Pierre Boulle, Michael Wilson (uncredited), Carl Foreman (also uncredited, both men were blacklisted during the McCarthy hearings)
Prod: Sam Spiegel   (based on the novel by Boulle)
DP: Jack Hildyard   Editor: Peter Taylor   Music: Malcolm Arnold
Dist: Columbia/Tri Star Home Video
William Holden	Shears
Alec Guinness	Col. Nicholson
Jack Hawkins	Maj. Warden

Sessue Hayakawa	Col. Saito
James Donald	Maj. Clipton
Geoffrey Horne	Lt. Joyce
Andre Morell	Col. Green
Peter Williams	Capt. Reeves
John Boxer	Maj. Hughes
Percy Herbert	Grogan
Harold Goodwin	Baker
Ann Sears	Nurse
Henry Okawa	Capt. Kanematsu
K. Katsumoto	Lt. Miura

M.R.B. Chakrabandhu - Yai
Vilaiwan Seeboonreaung, Ngamta Suphaphongs, Javanart Punynchoti, Kannikar Wowklee
[****]

When most people recall World War II, two enemies come to mind: Hitler's German Nazis and Prime Minister Tojo's Imperial Japan. During Japan's quick strike into Allied territories in the Pacific, thousands of British, American, and Australian troops were captured and sent to prison camps. Though POW (prisoner of war) movies are in abundance, none have matched the brilliance of The Bridge on the River Kwai. One of the finest films ever made, the true enemy to the British soldiers aren't the Japanese, but their own commander, brilliantly played by Sir Alex Guinness. Force marched to a jungle prison camp in the heart of Southeast Asian, the British officers and enlisted men are ordered to work side by side and build a bridge over the River Kwai to help transport Japanese supplies to Burma. The crusty Colonel Nicholson refuses to let his officer work, quotes the Geneva Convention rules, and plays a psychological chess game with the Japanese commander Saito. In due time, Nicholson wins out and goes about building the bridge. Instead of sabotaging the Japanese efforts, Nicholson decides the British prisoners need discipline and an objective in life. In a wonderful transition, Nicholson and his men oversee the project and give orders to the Japanese soldiers and engineers. Colonel Saito is amazed at the turn of events and suffers from a loss of face (shame) in front of the Allied prisoners which is only offset by his orders to complete the bridge on time. An American soldier (Holden) escapes from the prison and makes it back to an Allied base where he teams up with a commando unit planning to destroy the bridge. Reluctantly, Holden is recruited and the team enter enemy territory and discover a magnificent bridge standing over the River Kwai. Ironically, Colonel Nicholson build a better bridge than the Japanese had planned on, rationalizing his judgment for future generations. The end is both startling and revealing in its testament to human nature and the madness of war. Hayakawa's performance as the camp commander is powerful, showing the Japanese cruelty toward Allied prisoners, but also showing his sense of teamwork and admiration for Nicholson. The film went on to win numerous awards, including the Academy Award for best film, best actor, and nominated for best supporting actor (Hayakawa). Few films match The Bridge on the River Kwai's intense drama and poignant story. Every aspect of the film is a true marvel to filmmaking.

Bruce Lee: Curse of the Dragon   (The Curse of the Dragon)
(1993) Documentary C-90m English   VA   Catalog #12960
USA   Retail: $34.95

Dir: Fred Weintraub, Tom Kuhn   Scr: Davis Miller
Ex. Prod: Bob Wall   Prod: Tom Kuhn, Fred Weintraub
DP: John Axelson   Supervising Editor: Ronald L. Silveira
Music: David Wheatley, Fred Weintraub
PC: Time Warner Entertainment   Dist: Warner Home Video
Narrated by George Takei
Interviews: Chuck Norris, James Coburn, Dan Inosanto, Kareem Abdul-Jabar
[***]
From what I've seen, this is probably the best documentary on the life of screen legend Bruce
Lee. The entire documentary is collected from actual testimonies and interviews of people who
knew Bruce Lee. A number of scenes from his films are shown as well as rare footage of his
childhood acting career. The only speculation comes towards the end, discussing Bruce Lee's
mysterious death at 32, but the information is handled carefully and offered as possible
suggestions not definitive fact. Chronicling his life from beginning to end, the documentary also
spends some time on the tragic death of Brandon Lee, Bruce's son, who was shot while filming
the Crow. Both men never lived to realize their potential and Brandon has no surviving
offsprings to continue the Lee legacy. If you have any fascination in martial arts films or screen
legends, the documentary is an excellent investment of time and will offer insight while viewing
Lee's films.

The Bushido Blade	(The Bloody Bushido Blade)				
(1979) Samurai	C-104	English	R	VA	USA
Dir: Tom Kotani	Scr: William Overgard	Prod: Arthur Rankin Jr.			
DP: Shoji Ueda	Editor: Yoshitami Huroiwa Music: Maury Laws				
Richard Boone	Commodore Matthew Perry				
Sonny Chiba	Prince Edo				
Toshiro Mifune	Shogun's Commander				

Frank Converse, Laura Gemser, James Earl Jones, Mako, Timothy Murphy, Mike Starr,
Tetsuro Tamba, Mayumi Atano
[**1/2]
A decent, but dated attempt which should be viewed with caution and a grain of salt due to its
fictionalization of a significant historical events. In 1853, Commodore Perry arrived in Japan
with the dreaded "Black Ships" and used gunboat diplomacy to land in Japan, altering the destiny
of an entire nation. Commodore Perry is sent by U.S. President Franklin Pierce to establish trade
relations with Japan and open up a number of port cities. The Tokugawa government is not keen
on the idea of foreign visitors, but can do little against Western weaponry. Problems arise when
the pivotal negotiations of a treaty hinge on the retrieval of a treasured samurai sword which
must be returned at all costs. To save honor, Boone must send a party of his men armed with
rifles to battle the warriors who took the sword. They are part of a Japanese faction which hopes
to sabotage the treaty and push out the foreign devils. A number of action scenes are followed
with cultural gap scenes, the typical ignorant Westerners in a strange land scenario. Boone's last
film performance. Screen action star of "Street Fighter", Sonny Chiba plays Prince Edo, and
legendary star Mifune (who appeared in many American films dealing with Japan) plays the
Shogun's Commander and adds some force to the film's charisma.

Captive Hearts
(1987) DramaC-97m English   PG   VA   Catalog #4741   USA
Dir: Paul Almond   Scr: Patrick N. Morita, John A. Kuri
Prod: John A. Kuri   Ex. Prod: Milton Goldstein
DP: Thomas Vamos   Editor: Yuri J. Luhovy   Music: Osamu Kitajima
PC: Kurissama Production   Dist: CBS/Fox Video
(based on "The Hawk" by Sargon Tamimi)

Noriyuki Morita	Fukushima
Chris Makepeace	Robert
Mari Sato	Miyoko
Michael Sarrazin	Sergeant McManus
Seth Sakai	Takayama
Dennis Akiyama	Masato
Sho Togo	Military Officer
Shin Sugino	Senior Officer
Robert Ito	Guard

[***]

A heartwarming story about an American airman and a beautiful Japanese girl who fall in love during World War II. While on a bombing raid over northern Japan in 1944, an American plane is shot down and two airmen parachute to safety. They land in a snow-covered forest and are discovered by some Japanese villagers. They are almost executed, but saved by the village leader Fukushima. The American prisoners are bound and escorted to a remote village until a military patrol can arrive and take them away. Because of the time period and the remote locale, the villagers are surprised by the Caucasian men and glance at them with curiosity and suspicion. Slowly, the Japanese learn more about the Americans who in return learn more about their Japanese captives. The racist Sergeant McManus hates his captives and attempts an escape. The two airmen knock out the guard and kidnap the lovely Miyoko, taking her along as a prisoner and sex slave. Robert refuses to go any further and the two men fight. Later the injured Robert awakens in Fukushima's home. The village leader is thankful and bonds with the young man, taking him into his own home and protecting him from the Japanese patrols. Fukushima and Miyoko both speak English, spending a great deal of time teaching Robert the ways of the Japanese. He is young and impressionable, eager to learn and easy to forget the war. When Robert falls in love with Miyoko, he dishonors the family name and is punished by Fukushima. It is decided he leave the village, but the jealous Takayama has other plans for the young airman. The film's treatment is realistic and touching, but simple and straightforward. Don't expect a big budget drama or anything along the lines of spectacular effects, but the fine performances are down to Earth and moving. Special credit to Morita's solid performance and Mari Soto's English debut.

Challenge, The
(1982) Action C-108m   English   R   VA   Catalog #33405   USA   Retail: $19.95
Dir: John Frankenheimer   Scr: John Sayles, Richard Maxwell
Prod: Ron Beckman, Robert L. Rosen   DP: Kozo Okazaki   Editor: John W. Wheeler
Music: Jerry Goldsmith   Prod Design: Yoshiyuki Ishida   Dist: CBS/Fox Video

Scott Glenn	Rick
Toshiro Mifune	Yoshida
Donna Kei Benz	Akiko
Atsuo Nakamura	Hideo
Calvin Jung	Ando
Clyde Kusatsu	Go

Calvin Young, Yoshio Inaba, Seiji Miyaguchi, Miiko Taka
[**1/2]

An American in Japan story. Scott Glenn is an American visiting Japan who gets caught between a rivalry between two brothers over a priceless samurai sword. Toshiro Mifune plays the good brother who lives a traditional life and believes the family sword is sacred. His brother is the rich, tycoon type who lives in a modern mansion and demands that everything should be his. In true East meets West fashion, Glenn is at first rude and unhelpful, but later learns the ways of the samurai and helps Toshiro regain the sword and defeat his evil brother. Though a talented cast and crew are behind the film, the story never evolves deeply beyond the standard action fare. The locales and fight scenes are good and Glenn is believable as the ugly American who learns the Japanese way.

China Girl
(1987) Romance C-90m English R VA USA
Dir: Abel Ferrara Scr: Nicholas St. John Prod: Mitchell Cannold, Nichael Nozik
DP: Bojan Bazelli Editor: Anthony Redman Music: Joe Delia
Prod Design: Dan Leigh Set Design: Leslie Rollins Costume: Richard Hornung
Dist: Vestron Video

Richard Panebianco	Tony Monte
James Russo	Albert Alby Monte
Sari Chang	Tyan Hwa
Joey Chin	Tsu Shin
James Hong	Gung Tu
Russell Wong	Yung Gan
David Caruso	Johnny Mercury
Philip Ahn	Dr. Young
Lynn Bari	Capt. Fit

[**1/2]

East falls in love with West in this Romeo & Juliet (West Side Story) inspired tale of a young Italian-American man and a Chinese-American woman. To complicate matters, a violent gang war erupts between the Chinese and Italians over the streets of New York City. As is the case in tragic romances, Panebianco's Italian friends try to dissuade his feelings, while Chang's family and friends also try to ruin her relationship with the handsome young Caucasian. The film features a familiar story with some nice performances, and energetic direction from Ferrara. Though it does seem that Italians (best lovers?) are the most popular ethnic group to be paired in interracial relationships.

City of Joy
(1992) Drama C-134m English PG-13 VA Catalog #26922 USA Retail:

$19.95 Widescreen Available
Dir: Roland Jaffe   Scr: Mark Medoff   Prod: Jake Eberts, Roland Joffe
DP: Peter Biziou   Editor: Gerry Hambling   Music: Ennio Morricone
Prod Design: Roy Walker   Art Design: Asoke Bose
Set Design: Rosalind Shingleton   Costume: Judy Moorcroft
Dist: Columbia
(from the novel by Dominique Lapierre)

Patrick Swayze	Dr. Max Lowe
Pauline Collins	Joan Bethel
Om Puri	Hasari Pal
Shabana Azmi	Kamla Pal
Art Malik	Ashoka
Ayesha Dharker	Amrita Pal
Santu Chowdury	Shambu Pal
Imran Badsah Khan	Manooj Pal
Nabil Shaban	Anouar
Debtosh Ghosh	Ram Chander
Suneeta Sengupta	Poomina
Mansi Upadhyay	Meeta
Shyamanand Jalan	GodfatherGhatak
Shyamal Sengupta	Gangooly
Masood Akhtar	Rassoul
Loveleen Mishra	Shanta
Pavan Malhotra	Ashish
Anashua Mujumdar	Selima

[***]

Though the film has been criticized for its saintly view of Calcutta and Swayze's offhanded performance, I recommend the film for its fascinating glance into the second most populated nation in the world and for the fine performances of Pauline Collins, Om Puri, and the entire Indian cast. Not enough American films have attempted to capture the wonders and sorrows of the Indian people and their rich culture. Swayze is an American doctor who loses faith in life after losing a patient. He travels to the far reaches of India as a way of escaping his western confines, but runs into trouble when a group of thugs beat him and rob him. He loses his money, his watch, and his plane ticket. He is helped by a poor India farmer who with his family has moved to Calcutta in search of a better life. They are penniless after being swindled out of their money. Hasari Pal's family and life are the film's second focus and should be given special attention for their wonderful performances. Swayze receives medical care from a kindly woman (Collins) who runs a medical center in a rural area of Calcutta. The area is one of the poorest in India and humans live like animals under horrible conditions. She begs Swayze to offer his medical services, but he refuses and leaves for his hotel. Unable to leave the country immediately, he feels helpless and begins a spiritual reawakening as his friendship with Collins and Hasari develops. Hasari eventually receives a job as a rickshaw puller for a corrupt businessman. Problems arise when the workers demand better conditions, but are met by corruption, hostility, and retribution which includes a horrible scene against a beautiful Indian girl. They take away Hasari's rickshaw and threaten his life. With the help of others, Hasari builds his own rickshaw and struggles to survive on the cruel streets of Calcutta. Swayze's transformation is predictable, but his viewpoint allows us a wonderful eye into India society, a country with a rich culture and ancient tradition that suffers from extreme poverty, social turmoil, and old traditions conflicting with new.

Close to Eden
(1992) DramaC-106m   Russian with English Subtitles   PG
Catalog #15181   Russia
Dir: Nikita Mikhalkov   Scr: Rustam Ibragimbekov, Nikita Mikhalkov
Prod: Michel Seydoux   DP: Villenn Kaluta   Editor: Joelle Hache
Music: Eduard Artemyev   Prod Design: Aleksei Levtchenko   Costume: Irina Guinno
Dist: Miramax
Badema, Baoyinhexige, Vladimir Gostyukhin, Nikita Mikhalkov
[**1/2]
During its existence, the Soviet Union stretched across two continents and included dozens of ethnic groups. Most people visualize Slavic races from Europe when asked about the Soviet Union, and films often focus on Moscow, the Ukraine, the Baltic States, and St. Petersburg. However, the Soviet Union extended into Asia and included citizens of Asian races, such as Mongolians, Koreans, and Chinese. Hoping to expand cultural awareness, Russian filmmakers create their own West meets East film, focusing on Mongolian characters and their traditions.
Though filmed by a Russian crew, Close to Eden focuses on the life of a Mongolian man and his family living in the outskirts of China. The nomadic group of Mongolians are a proud and rare breed whose ancestors dominated much of the Asian plain. The great leader Genghis Khan led his Mongol warriors on a road to victory, conquering most of Asian and regions of Europe. Now the Mongols have migrated to regions of China and the former Soviet Union and live as forgotten minorities. We glimpse into their simple rural life, a land without roads, telephone pools, or automobiles. The main character Gombo is the father of his family and lives in the tradition of his forefathers and their forefathers. Living off the vast steppes, they travel by horse, cook meals from freshly slaughtered animals, and take care of themselves through hard work and perseverance without the luxuries of modern society. One day, a truck (symbol for modern society) from Russia passes through the vast countryside and crashes into a riverbed. The Russian driver named Sergei is in desperate need of help and finds it in the kind Gombo. Sergei enters Gombo's world and returns the favor by taking Gombo to a Chinese city. After dropping off his truck shipment, Sergei and Gombo enjoy the night life and intermingle with some fringe characters that represent the people who have modernized and integrated into society. Here Gombo enters the civilized world of roads, cars, televisions, condoms, and vices. Sergei becomes intoxicated and runs into some trouble, but Gombo is able to help his friend once more. Gombo decides to bring back two things from the modern world, but he must work up courage and conviction to go against traditional beliefs. On his way back home, he experiences a stunning illusion that involves a trip back into time when the Mongolians were a master race that ruled the steppes on horseback. His wife and friends accuse him of being a foreigner and lash out against him. Soon the image ends and the confused Gombo returns to his home with a new perspective on life. Without misleading you, Close to Eden is a slice of life that offers a brief portrait into another time and culture. A film that offers you a visa into a remote part of the world, but doesn't necessarily reveal too much to the viewer. The film is small, caring, and

fascinating, but high drama is not a part of the formula and much of the characters' motivations and developments are left half formulated. In other words, there's not much going on and the film's pace is methodically slow. If the culture or region interest you, the film is worth watching. Otherwise the film doesn't create much tension or build dramatic characters who endure serious conflicts or moral decisions.

Come See the Paradise
(1990) Drama/Romance   C-138m   English   R   VA   Catalog #67752
USA   Retail: $19.95
Dir/Scr: Alan Parker   Prod: Robert F. Colesberry
DP: Michael Seresin Editor: Gerry Hambling   Music: Randy Edelman
Art Dir: John Willett   Prod Design: Geoffrey Kirkland, John J. Smith
Set Design: Jim Erickson, Stephen Traxler   Costume: Molly Maginnis
Stunts: John Robotham   Dist: CBS/Fox Video
Dennis Quaid Jack McGurn
Tamlyn Tomita   Lily Kawamura
Sab Shimono   Mr. Kawamura
Shizuko Hoshi   Mrs. Kawamura
Stan Egi   Charlie Kawamura
Ronald Yamamoto   Harry Kawamura
Akemi Nishino, Pruitt Taylor Vince, Naomi Nakano, Brady Tsurutani
[***]
Hollywood attempts to portray the humiliating and wrongful persecution of Japanese-Americans citizens during World War II. After the bombing of Pearl Harbor, President Roosevelt issued a law ordering all Japanese-Americans on the West Coast to be relocated to camps in the Midwest under suspicion of sedition and treason.   This action was enforced by Congress and not questioned by most of the citizens of the United States, though the circumstances were similar to the deportation of Jews in Hitler-occupied Europe.   Held under armed guard, Japanese-Americans lost their homes and jobs, but peacefully obeyed the legal edict and relocated to the spartan detention camps. Before the war, a handsome Caucasian (Dennis Quaid) falls in love with the Japanese-American daughter of a man who owns a local movie theater.   Their relationship develops under the racist scrutiny of the time, but their passion and love for each other are strong and lead to marriage. Then World War II breaks out and Quaid must join the military while his wife and daughter are deported to the camp with her entire family. Events are shown from within the camp, as young Japanese-Americans question their imprisonment and express their bitterness. However, Quaid is on the outside and Tomita is on the inside and the film fails to focus itself and deliver a solid message, vacillating between two morals: interracial marriage and unjust deportation. A bitter love story about racism and injustice which explores the historical issues from a superficial level. This is a topic that still deserves Hollywood's attention, and should focus more on the Japanese-American plight, instead of a candy-coated interracial romance.

Deadliest Art, The: The Best of the Martial Arts Films
(1992) Kung-Fu Documentary   C-90m English   VA
Catalog #5583   USA   Retail: $24.95 Widescreen Available

Dir/Scr: Sandra Weintraub Ex. Prod: Raymond Chow Prod: Fred Weintraub
Associate Prod: David Chan, Marlene Pivnick
PC: Golden Harvest Dist: Fox Video
Narrated by John Saxon
Jackie Chan, Samo Hung, Yuen Biao, Sho Kosugi, Bruce Lee, Angela Mao Ying, Cynthia
Rothrock, Jean-Claude Van Damme
[***]
An entertaining documentary on modern kung-fu/action films from Hong Kong. This is
available on video and laserdisc and is a must see for anyone interested in martial arts movies.
Many of the scenes shown are some of the best fight scenes filmed in the 1980's, including a
number of rare highlights from difficult to find Jackie Chan films. The documentary also
focuses on the films of Bruce Lee, Cynthia Rothrock, Samo Hung, Yuen Biao, Richard Norton,
Van Damme, and many other recent stars. The film centers on modern kung-fu films and avoids
any historical overview, omitting the popular Shaw Brothers films and earlier costume kung-fu
epics. The compilation of clips are entertaining and diverse, featuring plenty of classic moments
from the big screen. The various clips are interspersed with interviews of the stars of Hong
Kong cinema.

Dim Sum "A Little Bit of Heart"
(1985) DramaC-88m English   PG   VA   USA
Dir: Wayne Wang   Scr: Terrel Seltzer
Prod: Tom Sternberg, Wayne Wang, Danny Yung
DP: Michael Chin   Editor: David Lindblom, Raplh Wikke   Music: Todd Boekelheide
Prod Design: Lydia Tanji   Set Design: Danny Yung   Costume/Makeup: Lydia Tanji
Dist: Orion
Laureen Chew, Kim Chew, Victor Wong, Cora Miao, Joan Chen
[***]
The film is best described as a pleasant slice of life, following the times of Chinese-Americans
struggling to make a better life in San Francisco's Chinatown. A number of the characters have
romantic problems which lead to the main conflicts in the film, but the primary focus is
generational differences between a mother and her daughter. Sweet and simple, a heartwarming
film that helped solidify Wang's directorial talents as a prominent Asian-American filmmaker.

Double Impact
(1991) Martial Arts C-118m   English   R   VA   USA   Retail: $19.95
Dir: Sheldon Lettich Scr: Sheldon Lettich, Jean-Claude Van Damme
Prod: Ashok Amritraj, Jean-Claude Van Damme
Ex. Prod: Moshe Diamant, Charles Layton
DP: Richard Kline   Editor: Mark Conte Music: Arthur Kempel
Prod Design: John Jay Moore   Set Design: Suzette Sheets
Costume: Joseph Porro, Karyn Wagner   MAD: Vic Armstrong, John Cheung
Dist: Columbia
Jean-Claude Van Damme   Chad/Alex
Cory Everson   Kara
Bolo Yeung   Moon

Geoffrey Lewis	**Frank Avery**
Alan Scarfe	**Nigel Griffith**
Alonna Shaw	**Danielle Wilde**
Eugene Choy	**Mr. Chen**

[**1/2]

Van Damme is back in Hong Kong and ready for a re-match with his old nemesis Bolo from Bloodsport. The film falls way short of the mark, but is enjoyable for its exotic locale, action sequences, and the appearance of two Van Dammes. Twin brothers (Van Damme) are separated at birth when an evil businessman kills their wealthy parents. The loyal bodyguard manages to fight off the assassins, but can only save one son. The other son is left at an orphanage and raised by nuns. The bodyguard raises Van Damme #1 in American and treats him to the better things of life. In other words, he's the tender, suave, girlie-man Van Damme while his brother in the nun's orphanage grows up as the tough, rough, macho-man. When the time comes, the guardian and Van Damme #1 go to Hong Kong and tells Van Damme #2 about his past. Van Damme #2 doesn't believe a word and continues his illegal life of smuggling and almost gets caught by the police. For some reason, a beautiful and intelligent woman is Van Damme #2's girlfriend and investigates her boss, discovering he's a criminal and behind the assassination of the Van Damme's parents. The two brothers at first dislike each other, but must put aside their differences and work together to avenge their parents. Plenty of fight scenes, multiplied by two, with a host of vicious killers and nice locale shots of Hong Kong spice up the film. A treat for people who enjoy Van Damme.

Dragon: The Bruce Lee Story
(1993) Biography/Drama/Kung-Fu C-119m   English   PG   VA   Catalog   #
        USA   Retail: $19.95
Dir: Rob Cohen   Scr: Edward Khmara, John Raffo, Rob Cohen
Prod: Raffaella De Laurentiis, Charles Wang
DP: David Eggby   Editor: Peter Amundson   Music: Randy Edelman
Art Dir: Ted Berner   Prod Design: Robert Ziembicki
Set Designer: Dayna Lee   Costumes: Carol Ramsey
PC/Dist: Universal/MCA
(based on the book "Bruce Lee: The Man Only I Knew" by Linda Lee Cadwell)

Jason Scott Lee	**Bruce Lee**
Lauren Holly	**Linda Lee**
Robert J. Wagner	**Bill Krieger**
Michael Learned	**Vivian Emery**
Nancy Kwan	**Gussie Yang**
Kay Tong Lim	**Philip Tan**
Ric Young	**Bruce's Father**
Luoyong Wang	**Yip Man**
Sterling Macer	**Jerome Sprout**
Sven-Ole Thorsen	**The Demon**
John Cheung	**Johnny Sun**
Ong Soo Han	**Luke Sun**
Eric Bruskotter	**Joe Henderson**

Aki Aleong	Principal Elder
Chao-Li Chi	Elder
Iain M. Parker	Brandon Lee
Sam Hau	Young Bruce
Michelle Tennant	Shannon
Clyde Kusatsu	History Teacher
Alicia Tao	April
Kong Kwok Keung	Mr. Ho
Johnny Cheung	Cook
Anthony Carpio	Cook
Chan Tat Kwong	Cook
John Lacy	Nunnemacher
Harry Stanback	Benny Sayles
Michael Cudlitz	Tad Overton
Forry Smith	Green Hornet
Van Williams	Green Hornet Director
Paul Raci	Bad Guy
Ed Parker, Jr.	Ed Parker
Shannon Lee	Party Singer
Lala Sloatman	Sherry Schnell
Fu Suk Han	Cha Cha Dancer
Nick Brandon	Boswain
Lau Pak Lam	"Big Boss" Director
Rob Cohen	"Enter the Dragon" Director

[***1/2]

The legend of Bruce Lee remains alive in Hollywood through the wonderful efforts of director Cohen and star Jason Scott Lee. Cohen creates a film that is both enjoyable as a biographical drama and a martial arts action film. The numerous fight scenes are choreographed with the same intensity and excitement found in Hong Kong action films, but never delve into the realm of camp or fantasy. No relation to Bruce Lee, Jason Scott brings a sense of tenderness, humor, and down-to-earth compassion in his screen portrayal. A talented actor whose physical prowess was well suited to portray the strength and speed of the martial arts legend. Ironically Jason Scott was not a martial artist in real life, but required months of intense training to complete the kung-fu action scenes. He manages to succeed on all accounts, but has avoided typecasting and has not appeared in any other kung-fu films.

This is the quintessential biodrama of Bruce Lee, focusing on his real life and less on his screen life. Upon first viewing the film, I was surprised at how little the film focused on his professional career and the mysteries surrounding his death. Practically every biodrama before had followed this treatment, but then the film's message became evident that it is more important to remember how a man lived rather than how he died. This is not a story so much about Bruce Lee the superstar, but Bruce Lee the man, seen through the eyes of the woman who loved him and who he loved dearly. The film's story is taken from the autobiographical writings of Lee's wife, Linda Lee Cadwell, who is played charmingly by Holly. In standard biodrama fashion, we are told Lee's life from his birth until his climatic rise to fame in Enter the Dragon (Lee died after he completed the picture). Every major step in his life comes into the picture: his discovery, his first kung-fu school, his marriage, his first child, and so on. Born in the United States, Lee returned to Hong Kong with his father, a travelling actor. Lee's early life of acting is left unexplored, but his training in kung-fu is portrayed with Yip Man. Cohen deftly captures the excitement, speed, and power of Asian martial arts which will appeal on all levels of appreciation. The scenes have a mild element of superhuman power often seen in Hong Kong productions, but becomes believable in the hands of Jason Scott Lee who, after all, is portraying the legendary Bruce Lee. If Bruce Lee couldn't do those stunts who could? Also because of the time period, a portion of the film explores racial attitudes. The interracial marriage of Bruce and Linda was not a common sight in the sixties and presented plenty of problems for the young couple. Cohen also adds a supernatural twist to the film with the addition of a mysterious spirit warrior who is hunting after Bruce Lee's spirit. To hide from the spirit, Bruce's father uses all types of charms and tricks which Bruce later uses to save his own son Brandon. What can easily be dismissed as theatrics takes on an ominous note, since Brandon Lee was fatally shot and killed on the set of a movie. Certain creative liberties are taken in the film's portrayal of Bruce Lee's life and should not be viewed as a definitive biography, but rather a portrayal of what the man was like and how he lived his life. Overall, the film is a wonderful example of a film that works on a dramatic/romantic level as well as an action/kung-fu level. Watch it for entertainment or enlightenment, and also check out the Bruce Lee documentary Curse of the Dragon. Some of the great kung-fu highlights include: Lee's fight in a dance hall against some rowdy sailors, Lee's fight against the jealous cooks, Lee's two fights against Johnny Sun and the amazing fight against his brother Luke, and the battle against the spirit warrior.

Empire of the Sun
(1987) Historical Drama   C-153m   English   PG   VA   Catalog #11753
USA   Retail: $19.95 Widescreen Available
Dir: Steven Spielberg   Scr: Tom Stoppard   Ex. Prod: Robert Shapiro
Prod: Steven Spielberg, Kathleen Kennedy, Frank Marshall
DP: Allen Daviau   Editor: Michael Kahn   Music: John Williams
Art Dir/Prod Design: Charles Bishop, Norman Dorme, Maurice Fowler, Fred Hole
Set Design: Harry Cordwell, Michael D. Ford   Costume: Bob Ringwood
Makeup: Paul Engelen   Sp. Fx: Ye Mao Gen (ILM) Stunts: Vic Armstrong
PC: Warner Bros. Inc./Amblin Entertainment   Dist: Warner Home Video
(based on the novel by J.G. Ballard)
Christian Bale   Jim Graham
John Malkovich   Basie
Nigel Havers   Dr. Rawlins
Joe Pantoliano   Frank Demerest
Robert Stephens   Mr. Lockwood
Leslie Phillips   Maxton
Burt Kwouk   Mr. Chen
Miranda Richardson Mrs. Victor
Ben Stiller   Dainty
Rupert Frazer   Jim's Father
Emily Richard   Jim's Mother
Masato Ibu   Sgt. Nagata

[****]
Steven Spielberg won an Academy Award for Best Director for his dramatic historical film, Schindler's List. But before Schindler's List, Spielberg created other historical dramas that also deserve attention and praise. The Color Purple is one and Empire of the Sun in another. Empire of the Sun is set in China during the Japanese occupation of World War II. Simply, it follows the tale of a young boy who grows up in a prison camp. Based on J.G. Ballard's bestelling novel about his true exploits, Bale is the youthful Jim Graham (shades of Ballard's youth) who lives in an idyllic world of Rolls-Royces and tea parties in the British occupied territory of Shanghai. Japan has been at war with China for years, but maintains a safe distance from the western powers. The rich are brutally portrayed as pampered, arrogant aristocrats who don't care for the suffering Chinese, but situations change when on the eve of Pearl Harbor, Japan launches a massive surprise attack throughout the Pacific Rim. In a matter of months, Japan gobbles up large portions of territory forcing the British to retreat. In the confusion, Bale is separated from his parents with nothing but the clothes on his back. Bale does an incredible acting job, portraying the lost Jim who must learn to fend for himself and survive in war-torn Asia. He befriends a wily American, John Malkovich, and they are sent to a Japanese prison camp for foreigners. The film's pace changes and Bale grows up in prison, running errands for Malkovich's prison organization. There is too much to cover in the extent of emotion, detail, and character interaction, but the heart of the film is Bale's Jim and his experiences throughout the war from beginning to end. The film is a marvelous historical achievement especially for Bale's brilliant performance as a naive child into a mature, seasoned young adult. Bale is in almost every scene and performs with a detached sense of loss as his childhood is stolen away from him. In a moving scene, he cries and reveals that he has forgotten what his mother looks like. A majority of the film takes place in the Japanese prison camp where life becomes a routine chore of staying fit and alive. What some may mistake for a slow pace is the representation of tedium spent from years of doing the same task over and over. Simple things like winning marbles, getting a pair of old boots, and cutting out a picture from a magazine are the greatest joys in life. The stoic Japanese are seen as honorable and cruel, living in a world of rigid traditional customs, but showing a glimmer of compassion. Eventually as history follows its course, Bale is freed from prison and reunited with his parents. At times, Spielberg could have delved more into Malkovich exploits after their release or the relationship between Bale and his Japanese friend, but Spielberg remains faithful to Ballard's book and focuses on the boy's life and not the precepts of Hollywood filmmaking.

Enter the Ninja - See under Ninjamania

Farewell to the King
(1989) Drama/War C-114m   English   PG-13   VA   USA
Dir/Scr: John Milius Prod: Andre Morgan, Albert S. Ruddy
DP: Dean Semler   Editor: Anne V. Coates, Timothy O'Meara
Music: Basil Poledouris   Art Dir/Prod Design: Bernard Hides
Set Design: Virginia Bieneman   Choreography: Anne Semler
Costume: David Rowe   Makeup: Jose Perez Sp. Fx: Dewey Gene Grigg
Stunts: Terry Leonard   PC/Dist: Orion
Nick Nolte   Learoyd

Nigel Havers	Botanist
Frank McRae	Tenga
Gerry Lopez	Gwai
Marilyn Tokuda	Yoo
Choy Chang Wing	Lian
James Fox	Ferguson
Aki Aleong	Colonel Mitamura

[**1/2]

A rather pretentious film based on Pierre Schoendoerffer's novel "L'Adieu Au Roi". Nick Nolte is an American aviator who crashes on a remote island in Bornea, Pacific Ocean. He is discovered by the natives and because of his unique Aryan features is revered as a god. His life is spared, so Nolte decides to remain on the idyllic island. He takes a beautiful mate and becomes the village's leader. Then the real world encroaches on his tropic paradise and threatens the life of the natives. World War II is still raging and the Japanese and British battle over the island's strategic position. Havers and his fellow soldiers try to convince Nolte to help their fight against the Japanese. Nolte is hesitant and refuses to get involved, but eventually must to save the lives of his people. In the background, a mysterious Japanese commander on a white horse represents a spiritual enemy that causes problems for the British. The Japanese retaliate against the natives and Nolte must hide his villagers, while helping the British free his island of occupation. Nolte's portrayal of Learoyd is curious at best, his transformation from civilized man to native has moments of interest. The film though slips back and forth from a war drama to a psychological film dealing with Learoyd and does not provide solid entertainment for viewers looking for pure drama or pure action.

Flower Drum Song
(1961) Musical   C-133m   English   G   VA
Catalog #80198   USA   Retail: $19.99 Widescreen Available
Dir: Henry Koster   Scr: Joseph Fields   Prod: Ross Hunter
DP: Russell Metty   Editor: Miton Carruth
Music: Richard Rodgers Lyrics: Oscar Hammerstein
Art Dir/Prod Design: Alexander Golitzen Choreography: Hermes Pan
Costume: Irene Sharaff   PC/Dist: Universal Pictures Company

Nancy Kwan	Linda Low
Miyoshi Umeki	Mei Li
James Shigeta	Wang Ta
Jack Soo	Sammy Fong
Juanita Hall	Madame Liang
Benson Fong	Wang Chi Yang
James Hong	Headwaiter

Spencer Chan, Jon Fong, Robert Kino, Virginia Lee, Reiko Sato, Arthur Song, Kam Tong
[***]

You may be surprised to discover a musical listed, but Flower Drum Song is a unique film that deserves praise for its clever premise. In my experience, musicals are not a very popular format for Asian filmmakers and difficult to appreciate due to cultural and linguistic barriers. Surprisingly, Hollywood decided to make a musical with an all-Asian cast set in Chinatown.

Though ambitious in scope and acquiring a talented cast of Asian-American actors, the film suffers from a number of problems and does not equate with the other Rodgers and Hammerstein musicals: Sound of Music, Oklahoma, King and I. Still there's enough charm in the sets, costumes, music, and cast to appeal to viewers looking for light-hearted romance and humor with an English-speaking cast.

The story is a fairly simple romance dealing with two sets of Chinese couples. Miyoshi Umeki is a young girl from China who arrives in Chinatown, San Francisco to marry Americanized Jack Soo. The problems start when Jack turns out to be an older, wilder nightclub owner who has sights set on sexy dancer Nancy Kwan. Nancy annoyed at Jack's womanizing and lack of commitment goes after the clean-cut affluent James Shigeta. While staying at Shigeta's house, Miyoshi also falls in love with him, but he is hooked on Nancy's charms. In the end everything works out blissfully with the properly matched couples. Though the ingredients seem in place for a great musical, promising exotic locales and customs, the fault lies in a pedestrian score that lacks the showstopping power of past Rodgers and Hammerstein songs. Unfortunately, Asian actors were never in demand for musical roles, so the film hired recognizable Asian stars whose backgrounds were not in musicals and appear miscasted. Though their performances are admirable and the dancing routines cute, the singing performances will most likely be forgotten and remembered only for their novelty. A few nice highlights include the sexy Nancy Kwan routine "I Like Being A Girl" and Miyoshi's sweet "A Hundred Million Miracles" song.

Gandhi
(1982) DramaC-188m   English   PG   VA
Catalog #23552   USA   Retail: $29.95 Widescreen Available
Dir: Richard Attenborough Scr: John Briley   Prod: Richard Attenborough
DP: Billy Williams, Ronnie Taylor Editor: John Bloom
Music: Ravi Shankar, George Fenton
Prod Design: Stuart Craig
Art Design: Robert Laing, Ram Yedekar, Norman Dorme
Set Design: Michael Seirton Sp. Fx: David Hathaway
Costumes: John Mollo, Bhanu Athaiya   Dist: Columbia
Ben Kingsley   Mahatma Gandhi
Candice Bergen   Margaret Bourke-White
Edward Fox   Gen. Dyer
John Gielgud Lord Irwin
Trevor Howard   Judge Broomfield
John Mills   The Viceroy
Martin Sheen Walker
Rohini Hattangandy Kasturba Ghandi
Ian Charleson   Charlie Andrews
Athol Fugard   Gen. Smuts
Saeed Jaffrey   Sardar Patel
Geraldine James   Mirabehn
Alyque Padamsee   Mohammed Ali Jinnah
Amrish Puri   Khan
Roshan Seth   Pandit Nehru

Ian Bannen	Sr. Police Officer
Michael Bryant	Principal Secretary
John Clements	Advocate General
Richard Griffiths	Collins
Nigel Hawthorne	Kinnoch
Bernard Hepton	GOC
Michael Hordern	Sir George Hodge
Peter Harlowe	Lord Mountbatten
Jane Myerson	Lady Mountbatten
Shreeram Lagoo	Prof. Gokhale
Om Puri	Nahari
Virendra Razdan	Maulana Azad
Richard Vernon	Sir Edward Gait
Harsh Nayyar	Nathuram Godse
Prabhakar Patankar	Prakash
Vijay Kahsyap	Apte
Nigam Prakash	Karkare
Supriya Pathak	Manu
Neena Gupta	Abha
Shane Rimmer	Commentator
Anang Desai	J.B. Kripalani
Alok Nath	Tyeb Mohammed
Dean Gaspar	Singh
David Gant	Daniels
Daniel Day-Lewis	Colin
Avis Bunnage	His Mother
Sunila Pradhan	Mrs. Motilal Nehru
Manohar Pitale	Shukla
Ernest Clark	Lord Hunter
Pankaj Mohan	Mahadev Desai
Bernard Horsfall	Gen. Edgar
Daleep Tahil	Zia

[****]

On April 19, 1950, a lone assassin walked up to a frail man and shot him in the chest. The next day, a sixth of the world's population mourned the death of a spiritual leader who freed their country from Imperial British rule. This is the story of Gandhi, a spiritual leader and activist who used peaceful methods to end British control over his homeland. Along the way, he made enemies with powerful people, but his fragile appearance, gentle demeanor, and kind attitude toward all people own over millions of followers and ushered in an era of passive resistance. Few men in history are as well known, admired, and emulated as Mahatma Gandhi. This film brilliantly portrays the life and death of India's greatest leader, a man who fought against injustice in a country that was ruled by foreigners. His entire life is traced with a good deal of emphasis placed on his young adult life as a respected professional in the British Empire. Moving scenes are showcased through the film's long running time, but the drama of the story never falters or bogs down into overblown theatrics. Much credit must be given to Ben

Kingsley's stellar performance in what brings the film to awe and critical acclaim. The film is epic in scope and traces decades of one character's life over three hours of screen time, similar to the Chinese epic The Last Emperor which also won critical acclaim at the Academy Awards. The film is based on history and actual characters. One of the most recognized films about Indian and a perfect historical/biographical film.

Ghostwarrior
(1986) Action C-86m English   VA   USA
Dir: Larry Carroll   Prod: Albert Band, Charles Band   DP: Mac Ahlberg
Editor: Brad Arensman   Dist: Empire Pictures
John Calvin, Hiroshi Fujioka, Janet Julian, Andy Wood
[**]
The opening of the film is very reminiscent of classic Japanese samurai films. The good samurai (Fujioka) must battle an evil samurai and save the damsel in distress. While battling atop a snowy ravine, Fujioka falls into a stream of ice and is perfectly frozen. He is later thawed in modern day times and makes his way to America. He finds himself walking the city streets and manages to fight off some thugs, thanks to his samurai sword. In no time, police and scientists are after the "time" traveller, but will he be able to survive life in the 20th century. A hokey premise that stretches the east meets west plot to its limits. Low production value and forgettable characters, often shown late night on television.

The Good Earth
(1937) DramaC-138m   English   VA
Catalog #26109   USA   Retail: $19.95
Dir: Sidney FranklinScr: Talbot Jennings, Tess Slesinger, Claudine West, Frances Marion (uncredited)   Prod: Irving G. Thalberg, Albert Lewin
DP: Karl Freund   Editor: Basil Wrangell   DP: Karl Freund
Music: Herbert Stothart   Art Design: Cedric Gibbons, Harry Oliver, Arnold Gillespie
Set Designer: Edwin B. Willis   Costumes: Dolly Tree   Dist: MGM
(based on the novel by Pearl S. Buck)

Paul Muni	Wang Lung
Luise Rainer	O-Lan
Walter Connolly	Uncle
Tilly Losch	Lotus
Charley Grapewin	Old Father
Jessie Ralph	Cuckoo
Soo Yong	Aunt
Keye Luke	Elder Son
Roland Got	Younger Son
Ching Wah Lee	Ching
Harold Huber	Cousin
Olaf Hytten	Grain Merchant
William Law	Gateman
Mary Wong	Little Bride
Lotus Liu	Voice of Lotus

Soo Young	Old Mistress Aunt
Charles Middleton	Banker
Suzanna Kim	Little Fool
Caroline Chew	Dancer
Chester Gan	Singer in Teahouse
Miki Morita	House Guest of Wang
Philip Ahn	Captain
Sammee Tong	Chinaman
Richard Loo	Farmer/Rabble Rouser/Peach Seller

[***]

Desperately in need of a modern remake with real Asian actors in the place of Muni and Rainer who are made to look like Chinese peasants. Still, the film holds up amazingly well due to the strong story and fine performances of the cast. The Good Earth is the dramatic tale of a husband and wife who suffer and prosper in the countryside of China. The classic film is based on the astounding novel by Nobel Prize winner Pearl S. Buck who spent a considerable time in China. The story catches the flavor and the hardship of peasant life and the injustices of male dominance over female rights long before Fifth Generation filmmakers created their masterpieces with Gong Li. O-Lan is a strong woman who is neither too pretty nor too bright. She marries a simple farmer Wang Lung and raise a family in the countryside. Together they go through hardship, surviving against locust swarms and bitter seasons, to survive and prosper in life. O-Lan is like a pillar of strength, always by Wang's side. The film differs slightly from the book, but in both cases O-Lan is taken for granted by her husband. A wonderful story and a fine film for its era, but the age of the film and non-Asian performances dispel much of the illusion. Read the book first, and maybe in the near future a new film version will be produced.

Great Wall, A
(1986) DramaC-103m   English   PG   VA   USA
Dir: Peter Wang   Scr: Peter Wang, Shirley Sun   Prod: Shirley Sun
DP: Peter Stein, Robert Primes   Editor: Graham Weinbren
Music: David Liang, Ge Ganru   Dist: Facets Multimedia, Inc.

Peter Wang	Leo Fang
Sharon Iwai	Grace Fang
Kelvin Han Yee	Paul Fang
Li Qinqin	Lili Chao
Hy Xiaoguang	Mr. Chao
Shen Guanglan	Mrs. Chao
Wang Xiao	Liu Yida
Xiu Jian	Yu
Ran Zhijuan	Jan
Han Tan	Old Liu
Jeannette Pavini	Linda
Howard Friedberg	Neil Mahoney
Bill Neilson	Mr. Wilson
Teresa Roberts	Kathy

[***]

A clever, familiar tale about culture clash between immigrants who return to their native homeland. A Chinese-America family decides to travel back to China and visit their old relatives and friends. Of course, their children are obviously Americanized and bring with them their horrible American traits of fast cars, greasy food, and rock and roll. The oldest son who hangs with Caucasian girls and loves table tennis manages to make some headway as he plays his way to new friendships. East meets west mentality from within, capturing the nuances of human nature between Chinese and Chinese-American folks. A sweet little film that will seem all too familiar for anyone who has foreign relatives.

Gung Ho
(1986): Comedy   C-111m   English   PG-13 Catalog #1751   USA
Retail: $14.95
Dir: Ron Howard   Scr: Lowell Ganz, Babaloo Mandel
Prod: Tony Ganz, Deborah Blum
DP: Don Peterman   Editor: Daniel Hanley, Michael Hill   Music: Thomas Newman
Prod Design: James Schoppe   Art Design: Jack G. Taylor Jr.
PC/Dist: Paramount

Michael Keaton	**Hunt Stevenson**
Gedde Watanabe	**Kazihiro**
George Wendt	**Buster**
Mimi Rogers	**Audrey**
John Turturro	**Willie**
Soh Yamamura	**Sakamoto**
Sab Shimono	**Saito**
Rick Overton	**Googie**
Clint Howard	**Paul**
Jihmi Kennedy	**Junior**
Michelle Johnson	**Heather**
Rodney Kageyama	**Ito**
Rance Howard	**Mayor Zwart**

[1/2]**

Animosity towards Japanese automobile firms reached a fevered pitch in the 1980's when an Asian-American was killed in Detroit for just being Asian. Ironically he wasn't even Japanese and his death survived no purpose except to remind people the dangers of blind hostility. Perhaps to quell hostilities, Hollywood director and veteran star, Ron Howard, set to work in filming a movie about a town's dependency on a Japanese automaker to keep their American way of life alive. Using comedy as a device to ease tensions and explain away ignorant differences, Gung Ho portrays both sides of the story. On the American side is Michael Keaton, an honest Joe, who wants to appease both sides and keep his own job in tact. He flies to Japan and convinces the executives to open an auto factory in his hometown of Hadleyville. The Japanese arrive in force led by Gedde Watanabe, a thin by the book Japanese middle manager. He brings along his traditional Japanese family and worries about his precarious position in trying to open a Japanese auto factory in America. Plenty of skeptics, including co-manager Saito, believe the idea is foolhardy. Watanabe is in charge of bringing the US plant up to Japanese specifications and turning the "lazy" Americans into hard-working employees modeled after Japanese work ethics. George Wendt and the good old boys aren't too happy with the changes and blame Keaton for their problems. In a few weeks, the Japanese executives plan to make an inspection of the factory and decide on its permanent fate. All hell breaks loose as both sides refuse to budge on issues while Keaton gets stuck in the middle. Plenty of east meets west humor abound as both sides try to get their point across. Luckily, Keaton and Watanabe work out their personal differences and help stop the protesting between the American laborers and the Japanese managers, rushing to fulfill their quota and prove people can work together. Not a great comedy, but filled with heart and humor.

Heaven & Earth
(1993) DramaC-142m   English   R   VA   Catalog #12983   USA   Retail: $19.99 Widescreen Available
Dir/Scr: Oliver Stone   Prod: Oliver Stone, Arnon Milchan, Robert Kline, A. Kitman Ho   DP: Robert Richardson   Editor: David Brenner, Sally Menke
Music: Kitaro   Prod Design: Victor Kempster
Art Design: Stephen Spence, Leslie Tomkins, Chaiyan "Lek" Chunsuttiwat, Woods Mackintosh   Set Design: Ted Glass, Merideth Boswell, Jack G. Taylor Jr.
Technical advisor: Dale Dye   Costume: Ha Nguyen
PC/Dist: Warner Bros.
(from the autobiographies "When Heaven and Earth Changed Places" by Le Ly Hayslip and Jay Wurts, and "Child of War, Woman of Peace" by Le Ly and James Hayslip)

Tommy Lee Jones	Steve Butler
Haing S. Ngor	Papa
Joan Chen	Mama
Hiep Thi Le	Le Ly Hayslip
Dustin Nguyen	Sau
Michael Paul Chan	Interrogator
Vivian Wu	Madame Lien
Long Nguyen	Anh
Robert Burke	GI Paul
Tim Guinee	Young Sergeant
Timothy Carhart	Big Mike
Dale Dye	Larry
Conchata Ferrell	Bernice
Debbie Reynolds	Eugenia
Annie McEnroe	1st Dinner Guest
Marianne Muellerleile	2nd Dinner Guest
Marshall Bell	3rd Dinner Guest
Le Ly Hayslip	Jewelry Broker
Bussaro Sanruck	Le Ly Age_5
Supak Pititam	Buddhist Monk
Thuan K. Nguyen	Uncle Luc
Lan Nguyen	Calderon Ba
Thuan Le	Kim
Mai Le Ho	Hai

Vinh Dang	Bon
Khiem Thai	Brother in Law
Liem Whatley	Viet Cong Captain
Michelle Vynh Le	Viet Cong Cadre Woman
Tuan Tran	Rapist
Aron Starrat	Helicopter Soldier
Peter Duong	Republican Colonel
Hieu Van Vu	Teacher
Phil Neilson	Marine in Helicopter
Michael Lee	Ky La Wizard
Thanh Vo	Grenade Girl
George Roarke	US Advisor
Dave Cooper	Bald Onlooker
Irene Ng	1st Torture Girl
Thuc-Hanh Tran	2nd Torture Girl
Vu Anh Phan	Snakeman
Mai Le	Steward
Term Saefam	Herbalist
Tran Huy	Danang Cop
Yeun Yong Dumda	Jimmy Age_1
Kevin Gallagher	Tall Marine
Brian Helmick	Short Marine
Catherine Ai	Bar Girl
Somsak Hormsombat	Siclo Driver
Nuttikit	Jimmy Age 3
Don Ho Jr.	Tommy Age_2
Phuong Huu Le	Jimmy Age 6

[***1/2]

"This film is based on the true life story of
Phung Thi Le Ly Hayslip, from Ky La, a rice-
farming village in Central Vietnam. It is the early
1950's and Ky La has been under the domination of
France for nearly seventy years as part of the country's
vast Indochinese colonial empire.
The French rulers are far away in Saigon, Hanoi, or Paris,
but in Ky La, life goes on as it has for a thousand years,
protected by Father Heaven, Ong Troi, and Mother Earth,
Me Dat.
Between Heaven and Earth--Troi va Dat--are the people,
striving to bring forth the harvest and follow
Lord Buddha's teachings."

Opening Card

The opening statement explains the setting and meaning of the film which is the third installment of Oliver Stone's Vietnam trilogy, following "Platoon" and "Born on the Fourth of July". The story focuses on the life of a Vietnamese woman who marries an American officer. Her life unfolds from a brutal past until she moves to America where problems persist with an abusive husband, portrayed by Tommy Lee Jones. Eventually she is westernized and finds her own spiritual awakening. That's the short synopsis, underneath the interracial relationship is a much richer story about innocence, betrayal, and the events that changed the lives of millions of Vietnamese.

Keep in mind Heaven and Earth is based on a true story and the relevance of Le Ly's life strikes a haunting cord for many immigrants, including my own family heritage. My parents lived under similar harsh conditions during the Japanese occupation of World War II. They then struggled to stay alive during the Korean War, and eventually travelled to America, prospered, and gave birth to Asian-American children.

In many ways, Heaven and Earth is the Vietnamese version of Gone with the Wind. Both films deal with a woman who desperately struggles to survive a vicious civil war and maintain their sanity. They are strong, resourceful women who care for their families and never falter under adversity. They persevere and meet men who take them away from their hard lives, but then encounter domestic problems that result in separation. I do not compare the artistic merit or caliber of the two films, but comment on the strong similarity of the two stories. There is much to discover in Le Ly's life and the film is a heart-wrenching story that does not shy away from the brutality of warfare. Told through voice-over narration, Le is a simple Vietnamese girls who lives with her family in a peasant village. Her life changes when the Vietnam War erupts and her village is caught in the middle, facing hostilities from both sides. Through a whirlwind of circumstances, Le is no longer a sweet virgin and suffers from the abuses of men in society. She meets a rugged American soldier who marries her and takes her to American when Saigon falls to the communists. The contrast between her Vietnemese life and her new American life is shocking and poignant, but Le devotes her efforts and prospers in American society which causes a rift in her marital relationship. After her marriage ends, she then spends time in her own spiritual reawakening and returns to her village in Vietnam, escorted by her three healthy sons. Time heals certain wounds, but she discovers the deep wounds of her past can never completely heal without a few scars. Her parents are brilliantly portrayed by veteran Asian stars, Haing S. Ngor and Joan Chen.

Hiroshima Maiden
(1988) DramaC-58m English   USA
Dir: Joan Darling   Dist: Public Media Video/Hemdale Home Entertainment
Tamalyn Tomita, Susan Blakely, Richard Masur
[***]
It wasn't a theatrically released film, but a television special made for PBS as part of the "Wonderworks" family series. Based on true excerpts of Japanese children sent to American for reconstructive surgery to remove tissue damage done by the atomic bomb. The show deals with a young boy whose American family has taken in Tamalyn Tomita. She is a beautiful, kind fragile girl whose only crime is that she is Japanese and suffers horrible radiation scars. At first the boy is angered toward her, blaming her for Pearl Harbor and calling her a yellow "Jap" or a "Nip". But as time passes, he discovers the true inner beauty within her and even fights to protect her honor against his school friends who now call him a "Jap" or a "Nip" lover. Misguided children are a dangerous and vicious group, breeding hatred and ignorance which will

flourish into their adult lives if unchecked. Hopefully films like this will help enlighten young people. I'm not naive to racial harassment and some of the comments said by the children about Tomita strike a sensitive core in all minority groups. A small-budget, simple film with a heartwarming message about racism and ignorance.

House Where Evil Dwells
(1982) Horror   C-88m English   VA   USA
Dir: Kevin Connor   Scr: Robert Suhosky Prod: Martin B. Cohen
DP: Jacques Haitkin Editor: Barry Peters Music: Ken Thorne
Art Dir: Yoshikazu Sano   PC/Dist: MGM/UA

Edward Albert Jr.	**Ted**
Susan George	**Laura**
Doug McClure	**Alex**
Amy Barrett	**Amy**
Mako Hattori	**Otami**
Toshiyuki Sasaki	**Shugoro**
Toshiya Maruyama	

[*1/2]
American attempt at Japanese horror doesn't hit the mark and suffers from a poorly conceived script and mediocre performances. An American couple move into a beautiful house in Japan. Of course, they get the house at a great deal because no sane Japanese couple would move into a cursed house. Odd things start to happen, including an attack by creepy killer crabs. Still the couple try to rationalize everything and remain until they're all slaughtered. Many centuries earlier a tragic fate befell on the original occupants of the house. A Japanese samurai caught his wife having and affair with his friend. The ordeal led to bloodshed for the trio whose evil spirits possess the modern day couple and their good friend. At the end, the ghosts who had possessed the bodies depart the corpses, giggling with devilish delight. Looks like only the dead will appreciate this film.

Hunted, The
(1994) Action C-110m   English   R   VA
Catalog #67263   USA   Retail: $19.95 Widescreen Available
Dir/Scr: Jonathan F. Lawton   Prod: John Davis, Gary W. Goldstein
Ex. Prod: William Fay
DP: Jack Conroy   Editor: Robert A. Ferretti, Eric Strand   Music: Motofumi Yamaguchi
Prod Design: Phil Dagort   MAD: Tom Muzila   Costume: Rita Riggs
PC: Davis Entertainment Company   Dist: Universal Pictures

Christopher Lambert	**Paul Racine**
John Lone	**Kinjo**
Joan Chen	**Kirina**
Yoshio Harada	**Takeda**
Yoko Shimada	**Mieko**
Maria Natsuki	**Junko**
Tak Kubota	**Oshima**

Masumi Okada	Lt. Wadakura
Tatsuya Irie	Hiryu
James Saito	Nemura
[***]	

"One who is a samurai must before all things
keep constantly in mind, by day & by night...
the fact that he has to die."   Daidoji Yuzan
16th Century

Though the film didn't get much notice, except for negative criticism, the story is a modern reworking of the chambara (sword/samurai/ninja) action films of earlier decades. Unfortunately, the film's weakness is its main star whom without the film would not have been made. Christopher Lambert is an American businessman who meets an exotic woman in Japan and goes to her hotel room for an evening of passion. Joan Chen is the woman and she knows she has been marked for assassination after leaving her wealthy lover. She decides to spend her last night in torrid sex with a stranger. Not a bad way to go, but then ninjas break in and ruin everything. Chen accepts her fate, but Lambert fights back and manages to catch a glimpse of the ninja leader, John Lone. Lambert survives and goes to the hospital under police custody. A Japanese woman, the wife of a kendo master, decides to aid Lambert. Now this is where the film definitely shines and would have been better if the story focused on the Japanese characters rather than follow a subdued and familiar course with Lambert as the Westerner who learns the ways of the East and triumphs. The kendo master (kendo is a form of martial arts using bamboo swords and protective equipment, similar to European fencing) has a long rivalry against Lone's ninja clan and takes a personal interest in Lambert. His own desires for revenge lead him to use Lambert as bait, blinding him to the growing number of dead. The ninjas use their stealth and skills to infiltrate the hospital and kill a squad of police officers, then they move onto a spectacular battle on the Shinkansen express (bullet train), and finally infiltrate an island of kendo masters. But Lambert is the star, so the film falls back on his interaction with an elderly swordmaker and his constant guilt-ridden flashbacks of Chen. In the end, he must battle it out with Lone during a stormy night in an open courtyard. I don't make claims that this is a great film and in many ways if you dislike Lambert's past performances the overall quality of the film will suffer. What I do admire are a number of the action scenes and the strong portrayal of the Japanese characters featured in the film.

Indochine
(1992) Romance   C-156m   French with English Subtitles   PG-13   VA
**   Catalog #27233   FranceRetail: $19.99 Widescreen Available**
Dir: Regis Wargnier Scr: Erik Orsenna, Louis Gardel, Catherine Cohen, Régis Wargnier
Prod: Eric Heumann, Jean Labadie   DP: François Catonne
Editor: Genevieve Winding   Music: Patrick Doyle
Costumes: Gabriella Pescucci, Pierre-Yves Gayraud
Sets: Jacques Bufnoir
PC: Paradis Films et La Generale D'Images
Dist: Columbia Tristar Home Video
Catherine Deneuve   Eliane
Vincent Perez   Jean-Baptiste

Linh Dan Pham	Camille
Jean Yanne	Guy
Dominique Blanc	Yvette
Henri Marteau	Emile
Carlo Brandt	Castellani
Gerard Lartigau	The Admiral
Hubert Saint-Macary	Raymond
Andrzej Seweryn	Hebrard
Mai Chau	Shen
Alain Fromager	Dominique
Chu Hung	Mari De Sao
Jean-Baptiste Huynh	Etienne Adult
Thibault DeMontalembert	Charles-Henri
Eric Nguyen	Tanh
Trinh Van Thinh	Minh
Tien Tho	Xuy
Thi Hoe Tranh Huu Trieu	Madame Minh Tam
Nguyen Lan Trung	Kim
Nhu Quynh	Sao

[***]

A beautiful film with exceptional cinematography shot on location in Vietnam. The film has a melodramatic overtone and meanders at time, but the overall result is quite enchanting especially with Catherine Denueve's ageless beauty guiding the way. The film represents the romanticized era of Colonial rule and European dominance in Southeast Asian. Denueve portrays a wealthy woman, Elaine, who lives a life of elegance from the 1930's to the rise of communism in the 1950's in what was then called Indochine. The focus of the story is Denueve's attitude as the world she knows so well changes around her and effects the people she knows. A key character is her adopted daughter, played by Linh Dan Pham. Linh is a native Asian raised in the opulence and education of Western ideas. She is caught up in a whirlwind romance with a dashing officer which leads to tragedy and betrayal. The officer loses his life and poor Linh is trapped in enemy territory. Denueve does her best to find her daughter, but when they are reunited a new climate has swept past them and changes their relationship forever. Winner of the Academy Award for Best Foreign film 1992.

Joy Luck Club, The
(1993) DramaC-136m   English & Chinese with English Subtitles R   VA
Catalog # 2291 AS   USA   Retail: $39.99 Widescreen Available
Dir: Wayne Wang   Scr: Amy Tan, Ronald Bass
Prod: Wayne Wang, Amy Tan, Ronald Bass, Patrick Markey
DP: Amir Mokri   Editor: Maysie Hoy   Music: Rachel Portman
Prod Design: Donald Graham Burt
Art Design: Diana Kunce, Kwan Kit "Eddy" Kwok, Jian Jun Li
Set Design: Jim Poynter   Choreography: Michael Smuin
Costumes: Lydia Tanji, Shu Lan Ding   Ex. Prod: Oliver Stone, Janet Yang
PC: Oliver Stone Production   Dist: Hollywood Pictures

(Based on the book by Amy Tan)

Kieu Chinh	Suyuan
Tsai Chin	Lindo
France Nuyen	Ying Ying
Lisa Lu	An Mei
Ming Na Wen	June
Tamalyn Tomita	Waverly
Lauren Tom	Lena
Rosalind Chao	Rose
Chao-Li Chi	June's Father
Melanie Chang	June_Age 9
Victor Wong	Old Chong
Christopher Rich	Rich
Nicholas Guest	Hairdresser
Russell Wong	Lin Xiao
Michael Paul Chan	Harold
Philip Moon	Ken
Vivian Wu	An Mei's Mother
Andrew McCarthy	Ted
Tian Ming-Wu	Wu Tsing
Lisa Connolly	Singing Girl
Vu Mai	Waverly_Age 6-9
Ying Wu	Lindo_Age 4
Mei Juan-Xi	Lindo's Mother
Guo-Rong Chen	Huang Tai-Tai
Hsu Ying-Li	Matchmaker
Irene Ng	Lindo_Age 15
Qugen Cao	Lindo's Father
Anle Wang	Lindo's Brother
Yan Lu	Lindo's 2nd Brother
Boffeng Liang	Pedicab Driver
William Gong	Tyan Yu
Diana C. Weng	Lindo's Servant
Yuan-Ho C. Koo	Matchmaker's Friend
Zhi Xiang-Xia	Huang Tai-Tai Servant
Dan Yi	Servant's Boyfriend
Kim Chew	Mrs. Chew
Jason Yee	Waverly's Brother
Ya Shan-Wu	Lindo's Husband
Samantha Haw	Shoshana
Yu Fei-Hong	Ying Ying_Age 16-25
Grace Chang	Lin-Xiao's Opera Singer
Melissa Tan	Jennifer
Yi Ding	An Mei_Age 9
Emmy Yu	An Mei_Age 4

Lucille Soong	**Popo**
You Ming-Chong	**An Mei's Uncle**
Fen Tian	**1st Auntie**
Lena Zhou	**2nd Auntie**
Jeanie Lee Wu	**3rd Auntie**
Jack Ford	**Mr. Jordan**
Diane Baker	**Mrs. Jordan**
Elizabeth Sung	**2nd Wife**
Eva Shen	**An Mei's Nanny**
Sheng Yu Ma	**Suyuan's 1st Twin Daughter**
Sheng Wei Ma	**Suyuan's 2nd Twin Daughter**

[****]

The old woman remembered a swan she had bought many years ago in Shanghai for a foolish sum. "This bird," boasted the market vendor, "was once a duck that stretched its neck in hopes of becoming a goose, and now look! It is too beautiful to eat." Then the woman and the swan sailed across an ocean many thousands of li wide, stretching their necks toward America. On her journey, she cooed to the swan, "In America I will have a daughter just like me. But over there, nobody will say her worth is measured by the loudness of her husband's belch. Over there,

nobody will look down on her ...because I will make her speak only perfect American English. And over there, she will always be too full to swallow any sorrow. She will know my meaning because I will give her this swan, a creature that became more than what was hoped for." But when she arrived in the new country, the immigration officials pulled the swan away from her, leaving the woman fluttering her arms and with only one swan feather for a memory. For a long time now, the woman had wanted to give her daughter the single swan feather and tell her, "This feather may look worthless but it comes from afar and carries with it all my good attentions."

Opening of "The Joy Luck Club"

Based on the bestselling novel by Amy Tan, The Joy Luck Club is a beautiful tale of four Chinese mothers and their Chinese-American daughters, tracing the lives of three generations of women.

The first generation represents the oppressed women of China who were traditionally given little power in the male-dominated society. The second generation follows the women who break away from traditional views and leave China for a new life (the quote reflects their struggle), these represent the transitional woman who were pioneers but maintained a traditional belief. And the third generation is the modern Chinese-American women, the women who stands equal with males but are somewhat spoiled by the excess of success and fail to realize the struggles their mothers went through.

The opening passage is slowly recited over the opening credits by Ming Na Wen, the lovely actress who plays the principal character. The story is structured within a framework of past narrations from a group of women. Ming Na Wen is Jun, a young Chinese-American women whose mother recently passed away. When it is discovered that Jun has two long lost twin sisters, it is decided she go to China and reunite with them. A farewell party is held at her house and is the catalyst for the film as friends and family come to celebrate and reflect on their past hardships. Her mother's best friends are a group of women who gather to play mah jongg, calling themselves the Joy Luck Club.

The main frame of the story takes place at the celebration where all the characters have gathered, including a cameo by author Amy Tan. One by one, Jun, her friends, and their mothers reveal the sacrifices they made for love and family. Some are sad, some are humorous, but each story is universally touching, covering the spectrum of human relationships. The young women narrate their stories in perfect English, their mothers speak in broken (but completely understandable) English, while their mothers speak in Chinese. The first flashback is Jun as a young girl and her conflicts with her mother. Jun always felt like a failure, since she never excelled in school, work, piano, or marriage. The second flashback falls on Waverly and her mother Lindo who is not happy with her new Caucasian son-in-law. Lindo suffered when she was given away as a bride through a pre-arranged marriage at fifteen. She is unhappy with her overweight and very childish husband. Waverly recounts her conflicts with her demanding mother who is not happy with anything she does in life. The next segment moves to Lauren Tom and her mother. Lauren is in a horrible marriage with a self-centered, arrogant man while her mother suffered a similar instance with her brutal ex-husband Russell Wong. The fourth is Rosalind Chao and her mother. Rosalyn marries handsome, successful Andrew McCarthy, but problems arise when he starts an adulterous relationship that leads to divorce. Her mother's story is the death of her own mother when she is raped and forced to be a concubine in a nefarious man's mansion.

The vignettes seamlessly slide from one woman to another in a series of flashbacks that begin with Jun and end with her trip to China where she is reunited with her two sisters. Since the characters are long time friends, characters overlap within the flashbacks and stories are seen from the eyes of the women at all stages of life. The film is a well-crafted adaptation of the novel which is also highly recommended. The nuances and depth of the story go well beyond the details mentioned in the review. This is one of the best dramatic Asian films ever made and highlights a pool of great Asian talent available in Hollywood. The list of actors read like a whose who of Asian-American talent and everyone adds strong performances in this universal story of love and sacrifice. Don't be scared away by rumors of it being a women's film or a tearjerker, I will not deny that the focus is from the female point of view and the theme covers tragedy and passion, but the direction, beautiful appearance of the film, and moving characters are a powerful statement to human life and relationships. The story is rich and visually detailed, incorporating pure Asian values mixed with Asian-Americanized values. A wonderful testament to the difficulties of growing up in a multicultural background, but also pointing out the strengths and bounties of such a lifestyle. Hopefully the film will be followed by other Asian-American productions, including Amy Tan's other bestsellers "The Kitchen God's Wife" and "The Hundred Secret Senses".

***Rudyard Kipling's* The Jungle Book**
(1994) Adventure   C-111m   English   PG   VA   Catalog #4604
USA   Retail: $24.95

Dir: Stephen Sommers   Scr: Stephen Sommers, Ronald Yanover, Mark G. Geldman
Prod: Edward S. Feldman, Sharad Patel   DP: Juan Ruiz-Anchia
Editor: Robert Ducsay   Music: Basil Poledouris   Prod Design: Allan Cameron
Art Design: Steve Spence, Nitir Desai   Set Design: Crispian Sallis
Sp Fx: Peter Montgomery, Chris Evans   Stunts: David Ellis, Tim Davison
Makeup: Cindy Williams, Mustaque Ashrafi, Noriko Watanabe
Costumes: John Mollo   PC/Dist: Disney
(From a story by Ronald Yanover and Geldman based on the novel by Rudyard Kipling)

Jason Scott Lee	Mowgli
Cary Elwes	Boone
Lena Headey	Kitty
Sam Neill	Colonel Brydon
John Cleese	Dr. Plumford
Jason Flemyng	Wilkins
Stefan Kalipha	Buldeo
Ron Donachie	Harley
Anirudh Agrawal	Tabaqui
Faran Tahir	Nathoo
Sean Naegeli	Mowgli_Age 5
Joanna Wolff	Kitty_Age 5
Liza Walker	Alice
Rachel Robertson	Rose
Natalie Morse	Margaret
Gerry Crampton	Sgt. Major
Amrik Gill	Butler
Rick Glassey	Sgt. Claibourne

[***]

Exciting and well-made live-action adaptation of "The Jungle Book" with Lee portraying an adult Mowgli. The setting is India at the turn of the century under British occupation. Mowgli saves the life of the beautiful Kitty, the daughter of the British Commander, Major Brydon. Mowgli sneaks into the British headquarters to see her again which infuriates her white suitor, Captain Boone. He distrusts the native and attempts to kill Mowgli. But when Boone discovers there is a long lost treasure in the jungle, he forces Mowgli to lead him there and takes Kitty and Brydon as prisoners.

The film features the lovable animals (real one) like Grey Brother the wolf, Baloo the bear, Bagheera the panther, and King Louie the orangutan in non-speaking, but helpful roles similar to the early Tarzan films. Lee gives a likeable performance in this exotic adventure with beautiful locales filmed on location in India. The tone of the story is geared toward children, but the final sequence inside the lost palace may frighten young children. Still a worthwhile adventure film for the entire family.

Also available is the animated Disney classic The Jungle Book (1967) directed by Wolfgang Reitherman. Recently Disney has remade many of its animated classics into live-action films, including "That Darn Cat" and "101 Dalmatians". The animated film is about an orphan boy, Mowgli, raised in the jungles of India by a pack of wolves. His adventures are broken into a series of musical scenes with a variety of vivacious animal characters. King Louie is the leader of the orangutans who wants to learn the secret of man's fire. Kaa is a slithering python who wants to get the squeeze on Mowgli. The Colonel is a pompous British elephant with his own regime. Baloo is a lovable bear without a care in life. Bagheera is the panther who looks after Mowgli. Shereeh Khan is the evil tiger bent on destroying Mowgli. The film was the last animated feature to be supervised by Walt Disney.

Karate Kid, The
(1984) KarateC-126 min   English   PG   VA   Catalog #60406   USA   Retail: $14.99
Dir: John G. Avildsen   Scr: Robert Mark Kamen   Prod: Jerry Weintraub
Editor: Bud Smith, Walt Mulconery, John G. Avildsen
DP: James Crabe   Music: Bill Conti   Production Designer: William J. Cassidy
Set Design: John Anderson Sp Fx: Frank Toro
Choreography: Pat E. Johnson   Costumes: Richard Bruno, Aida Swenson
Dist: Columbia

Ralph Macchio	Daniel
Noriyuki "Pat" Morita	Miyagi
Elisabeth Shue	Ali
Martin Kove	Kreese
Randee Heller	Lucille
William Zabka	Johnny
Ron Thomas	Bobby
Rob Garrison	Tommy
Chad McQueen	Dutch
Tony O'Dell	Jimmy
Israel Juarbe	Freddy
William H. Bassett	Mr. Mills
Larry B. Scott	Jerry
Juli Fields	Susan
Dana Andersen	Barbara
Frank Burt Avalon	Chucky
Jeff Fishman	Billy
Ken Daly	Chris
Tom Fridley	Alan
Pat E. Johnson	Referee
Bruce Malmuth	Ring Announcer
Darryl Vidal	Karate Semifinalist
Frances Bay	Woman with Dog
Christopher Kriesa	Official
Bernard Kuby	Mr. Harris
Joan Lemmo	Restaurant Manager
Helen Siff	Cashier
Molly Basler	Cheerleading Coach
Larry Drake	Yahoo
Brian Davis	Boy in Bathroom

David DeLange	Waiter
Erik Felix	Karate Student
Peter Jason	Soccer Coach
Sam Scarber	Referees
William Norren	Doctor
Scott Strader	Eddie

[****]

It took Hollywood a long time to finally make a martial arts film that focused on characters and story rather than the amount of kicks and broken bones. The Karate Kid is an excellent film that highlights the values and principles of martial arts in a positive and realistic manner. Young Danny (Macchio) is a teenager from New Jersey who moves to California with his single mom. He tries to fit in on the west coast, but problems escalate when he falls for a cute girl who is the ex-girlfriend of the leader of the Cobra-Kai, a gang of high school seniors enrolled in a Combat Karate School under the supervision of ex-Marine Kove.

During an evening beach party, Johnny and his thugs harass Ali and her friends. Danny is not one to back down, but his brave actions are no match for the vicious black belt. His friends desert him and even Ali tries to avoid trouble by staying away from Danny. He attempts to learn martial arts with a book and pursues his relationship with Shue. After a Halloween party, Johnny and his Cobra-Kai students corner him and beat him brutally. Miyagi, the maintenance worker for Danny's apartment complex, comes to his rescue. Danny is rescued and starts a life-long friendship with the Japanese-American Miyagi who is a grandmaster in Okinawan Karate. Miyagi is a pacifist and tries to end the childish feud between the students. He and Danny travel to the Cobra-Kai school where they discover the master is even more ruthless and arrogant than his students. Miyagi offers a challenge to Kove, takes Danny as his student, and prepares him for a Karate tournament. The film uses clever training sequences not merely as a way to beat up people, but to develop the friendship between Miyagi and Danny. The characters grow in the film; they're real people with dreams, fears, and goals like anyone else. Danny and Ali develop a wonderful relationship with Miyagi and Danny's mother providing support and guidance. The day of the tournament arrives and Danny (first time) must fight his way to the finals and defeat defending champ Johnny. Danny wants to be respected and happy in life, his goals for learning martial arts aren't to kill and injure for revenge. Those violent actions are brilliantly played by Kove, an example of a misguided teacher. An old saying: There are never bad students, just bad teachers. The film is full of Miyagi witticisms on life and Morita's performance is Academy-level caliber, garnering him a Best Supporting Actor Nomination. The entire film is well produced and skillfully combines martial arts with drama into a first-class film.

Karate Kid, The: Part 2
(1986) KarateC-113m   English   PG   VA
Catalog #60717   USA   Retail: $14.99
Dir: John G. Avildsen   Scr: Robert Mark Kamen   Music: Bill Conti
Prod: Jerry Weintraub   DP: James Crabe
Editor: David Garfield, Jane Kurson, John G. Avildsen
Music: Bill Conti   Prod Design: William J. Cassidy
Art Design: William F. Matthews   Set Design: Lee Poll
Technical advisor: Yasukasu Takushi, Zenko Heshiki

Sp Fx: Dennis Dion   Makeup: James Kail, John Elliott
Choreography: Paul De Rolf, Nobuko Miyamoto, Jose De Vega, Pat E. Johnson
Costumes: Mary Malin   PC/Dist: Columbia Tristar Pictures
(based on characters created by Kamen)

Ralph Macchio	Daniel
Noriyuki "Pat" Morita	Miyagi
Nobu McCarthy	Yukie
Danny Kamekona	Sato
Yuji Okumoto	Chozen
Tamlyn Tomita	Kumiko
Pat E. Johnson	Referee
Bruce Malmuth	Announcer
Eddie Smith	Bystander
Martin Kove	Kreese
William Zabka	Johnny
Chad McQueen	Dutch
Tony O'Dell	Jimmy
Ron Thomas	Bobby
Rob Garrison	Tommy
Will Hunt	Postman
Evan Malmuth	Cab Driver
Joey Miyashima	Toshio
Raymond Ma	Cab Driver in Okinawa
George O'Hanlon Jr.	Soldier
Charlie Tanimoto	Miyagi's Father
Tsuruko Ohye	Village Woman
Arsenio Trinidad	Ichiro
Marc Hayashi	Taro
Robert Fernandez	Watchman
Natalie N. Hashimoto	Kumiko's Street Friend
Diana Mar	Girl in Video Store
Bradd Wong	Boy on Street
Wes Chong	Sato's Houseman
Traci Toguchi	Bell Ringer

[***1/2]

Excellent sequel to The Karate Kid and the second film in The Karate Kid Trilogy which follow the exploits of a New Jersey boy who befriends a wise old Japanese-American master of Okinawan Karate. The prequel is excellent and should be viewed first, but does not include as many Asian references. The second film uses an entirely Asian cast (except Macchio) and moves the locale from California to Okinawa, Japan. Also followed by a weak and forgettable third film Karate Kid 3 which returns the characters to California and tries to recapture elements from the first film.

The stakes are much higher when Danny and Miyagi travel to Okinawa to pay respects to Miyagi's dying father and confront an old rival who demands to battle Miyagi to the death.

The original film cleverly segues into the sequel, showing the results of Danny's victory at the martial arts tournament. The arrogant sensei (Kove) from the Cobra-Kai Karate Academy is accosting his students for their failure in losing to Danny. Miyagi slowly walks up to the sensei and uses an arm lock to throw him aside. Silently, Miyagi stands still as the sensei assumes a fighting stance. Miyagi avoids the punches and manages to cripple his opponent without lifting a finger. In what seems brutal retaliation, Miyagi prepares to deliver a death blow to Kove, but at the last moment humiliates him by honking his nose.

As the school year ends and the summer starts, Danny and his girlfriend break up. Then Miyagi receives a letter from Japan informing him his father is dying. Danny uses his college money and follows Miyagi to Okinawa, an island south of Japan. As the story goes, Miyagi left Japan when he was a young man because of a rivalry between him and his best friend Sato over the love of a woman. Sato challenged him to a fight, but Miyagi decided to leave, and the woman never forgave Sato who has carried the grudge for decades. Now Sato is a wealthy businessman and a grandmaster in Okinawan Karate. His opulent home rests along a beach and in the backyard is a huge block of wood which he attempts to split in half, but fails.

Miyagi's dying father tries to reconcile the difference between his student and son, but with his death ends any possibility of a truce. Sato uses terrorist tactics to force Miyagi to fight and uses his students to harass Danny and a beautiful Japanese girl (Tomita) who falls in love with Danny. When Miyagi's old village is threatened to be destroyed, he gives in and challenges Sato with the village's fate as the prize.

On the day of the match, a violent storm erupts across the island. The villagers rush to a shelter and Sato's top student claims a massive log crushed and killed Sato. Miyagi and Danny refuse to believe Sato is dead and risk their lives to search for him. In the pouring rain and wind, Miyagi finds Sato trapped under a massive, unmovable log. As the rain crashes down, Miyagi positions himself above Sato. Danny is confused, since it seems Miyagi is preparing to kill Sato and end the feud. In an instant, Miyagi strikes down and breaks the massive log, saving the bewildered Sato. The two men reconcile their differences and rush back to the shelter where they discover a girl is trapped on a warning tower. Sato orders his student to rescue the child, but he refuses and cowers in the back. Danny and Tomita rescue the child. Sato curses his student who then runs away into the mad storm.

Days later, the villagers gather for a traditional festival of dance and celebration, but Sato's top student attacks and attempts to kill Tomita and Danny. Using the symbol of a toy drum, expressing equilibrium and balance, Danny defeats him and saves Tomita. Sato expresses shame for his misguided student and his own blind hatred. Promising to keep in touch, Danny and Miyagi return to California while Sato rebuilds the damaged village. Though the story showcases Danny and Tomita in a number of romantic scenes, the true beauty of the story lies within Miyagi and Sato's friendship and hatred for each other over the woman they both loved. A number of Japanese customs are introduced and the martial arts scenes provide insight into the true art of karate, while still providing entertainment. The performances are strong overall and Tomita's beauty shines in her first major Hollywood role. One of the finest American-made films depicting Asians and the principles of martial arts: cruel masters create cruel students, never use martial arts for personal gain, use martial arts to protect the weak and innocent, and never let anger or vengeance guide you to the path of self-destruction.

Karate Kid, The: Part 3
(1989) KarateC-111m   PG   English   VA

Dir: John G. Avildsen   Scr: Robert Mark Kamen   Prod: Jerry Weintraub
Music: Bill Conti   Dist: Columbia

Ralph Macchio	Daniel
Noriyuki "Pat" Morita	Mr. Miyagi
Robyn Elaine Lively	Jessica
Thomas Ian Griffith	Terry
Sean Kanan	Mike Barnes
Jonathan Avildsen	Snake
Christopher Paul Ford	Dennis
Randee Heller	Lucille
Martin Kove	Kreese

[**]

I confess - I loved the first two films and eagerly awaited the third installment. Catching Morita on a late night talkshow, I watched a clip from the upcoming movie. It was wonderful and my expectations ran high. Sadly, the clip was the only good part of the film. The story took a serious nose dive in the third part of the trilogy. The cast is back, but the film blatantly steals from the first two films and lacks the originality of incorporating martial arts philosophy with real life conflicts. The film's heart should be based on the bond between Miyagi and Danny which is blatantly thrown out for plot contrivances. Macchio, appearing bloated and apathetic, hopes to defend his karate title from the first film. Miyagi refuses to teach Danny, so he goes and learns from a martial artist who is blatantly the villain. For reasons unknown, the villain, a friend of Kreese (villain from the first film), decides to invest his time and money to rebuild the Karate School and set up an elaborate revenge scheme. A multimillionaire involved in chemical waste, he owes his life to Kreese for saving him in Vietnam. It's good to see that full-grown adults who were war heroes in Vietnam and filthy rich have nothing better to do in their life except to terrorize poor teenagers. Their plot includes the tournament, so they hire a young martial arts fighter. Danny is terrorized day and night by karate thugs who demand he fight in the tournament or they'll kill him and his cute new girlfriend. Of course, the police are never seen nor are there any intelligent onlookers. Finally in a predictable series of sequences, Danny and Miyagi rejoin, train for the tournament, and win. As a symbol for the film's heart, much of the plot involves a bonsai tree growing alongside a precarious cliff. The only highlight in the film is Miyagi's scene in which he rescues Danny and fights the trio of villains. He defeats the arrogant men, bows politely, and imitates Bruce Lee's trademark gesture.

Karate Kid, The: Part 4   **(The Next Karate Kid)**
(1994) KarateC-104m   **PG**   **VA**   **Catalog #73253**   **USA**   **Retail: $19.95**
Dir: Christopher Cain   **Scr: Mark Lee**   **Prod: R.J. Louis, Jerry Weintraub**
DP: Laszlo Kovacs **Editor: Christopher Greenbury**   **Music: Bill Conti**
Prod Design: R.J. Louis, Walter Paul Martishius Set Design: Tracy A. Doyle
Costume: Carole James   **Dist: Columbia**
Noriyuki "Pat" Morita, Hilary Swank, Michael Ironside, Constance Towers, Chris Conrad, Joy Todd
[**]

Hollywood sequels are notorious for digging a once-good idea deep into the grave. Adding insult to injury, newcomer Swank plays Julie Pierce, the Next Karate Kid, replacing the aged

Macchio. The film attempts to recycle old material but with a young, feisty female character. Morita returns in the film and still teaches martial arts to troubled young people. He takes Julie, the daughter of a war buddy who saved his life, to a Japanese monastery in California where she learns to calm her inner hostility and learn the way of zen. Since Miyagi is now dealing with a girl, it's not all martial arts, so he teaches Julie to waltz and act like a woman. Of course, bad guy Ironside and his martial arts goons are not going to leave anyone alone. In a disappointing climax, the heroes meet the villains for a wharfside fight and through quick editing win the battle. The purity and beauty of the martial arts have once again been marred by a film that stresses over-the-top violence and generic action. Though Swank does her best, this film is nothing more than a water-downed, direct-to-video actioner similar to films starring Cynthia Rothrock, Don Wilson, and Bolo Yeung.

Kickboxer
(1989) Martial Arts C-105m   R   English   VA   USA
Dir: Mark DiSalle   Scr: Glenn Bruce, Jean-Claude Van Damme   Prod: Mark DiSalle
DP: Jon Kranhouse Editor: Wayne Wahrman   Music: Paul Hertzog
Art Dir: Chunsuttiwat Chaiyan, Sita Yeung   Prod Design: Shay Austin
Makeup: Toomy Chan, Earl Ellis Sp. Fx: Tuffy Lau, Tommy Chan, Lennart Bang
MAD: Jean-Claude Van Damme   Stunts: John Cheung
PC: Cannon   Dist: HBO/Warner

Jean-Claude Van Damme	**Kurt Sloane**
Denis Alexio	**Eric Sloane**
Dennis Chan	**Xian Chow**
Tong Po	**Tong Po**
Haskell Anderson	**Winston Taylor**
Rochelle Ashana	**Mylee**
Richard Foo	**Tao Liu**

[**]
After the success of Bloodsport, a number of martial arts films were launched to capitalize on Jean-Claude's amazing talents as a flexible, powerful, and dynamic fighter. Van Damme travels to Thailand with his brother, a cocky American kickboxer. He is set to battle a human monster called Tong Po, a muscular Thai kickboxer with a brutish face only a mother could love. It comes as no surprise that Van Damme's brother is swiftly and brutally beaten up, initiating the over-worn train/revenge plot. Now relegated to a wheelchair, the duo plan to return to America, but Van Damme comes into contact with a wise Thai master of kickboxing and some friendly natives. The Thai elder is small and innocuous looking, but amazes the ignorant Van Damme with a series of lighting quick kicks. They become friends and begin a rigorous training procedure, beating up locals in a bar as a means of practice. After a long series of training scenes, Van Damme challenges Tong Po to a kickboxing match with gloves covered with glue and broken glass. Tong Po's mobster pals kidnap Van Damme's brother and forces him to lose the fight. Van Damme is beaten to a bloody pulp, but at the last second turns into a super-fighter when he spots his rescued brother. Thanks to his Thai master and an ex-patriot Rambo-clone, the good guys win and the bad guys lose. Standard series of fight scenes and contrived plot, enhanced by Van Damme's charisma.

Killing Fields, The
(1984) DramaC-142m   English   R   VA   Catalog #11419   USA
Retail: $19.99 Widescreen Available
Dir: Roland Joffe   Scr: Bruce Robinson Prod: David Puttnam
DP: Chris Menges   Music: Mike Oldfield   Editor: Jim Clark
Prod Design: Roy Walker   Art Design: Roger Murray Leach, Steve Spence
Set Design: Tessa Davies   Special effects: Fred Cramer   Stunts: Terry Forrestal
Makeup: Tommie Manderson   Costumes: Judy Moorcroft Dist: Warner Home Video
(based on the magazine article The Death and Life of Dith Pran by Sydney Schanberg)

Sam Waterston	Sydney Schanberg
Dr. Haing S. Ngor	Dith Pran
John Malkovich	Al Rockoff
Julian Sands	Jon Swain
Craig T. Nelson	Military Attache
Spalding Gray	US Consul
Bill Paterson	Dr. Macentire
Athol Fugard	Dr. Sundesval
Graham Kennedy	Dougal
Katherine Krapum Chey	Ser Moeun
Oliver Pierpaoli	Titonel
Edward Entero Chey	Sarun
Tom Bird	US Military Advisor
Monirak Sisowath	Phat
Ira Wheeler	Ambassador Wade
David Henry	France
Patrick Malahide	Morgan
Nell Campbell	Beth
Joan Harris	TV Interviewer
Joanna Merlin	Schanberg's Sister
Jay Barney	Schanberg's Father
Mark Long	Noaks
Sayo Inaba	Mrs. Noaks
Mow Leng	Sirik Matak
Chinsaure Sar	Arresting Officer
Hout Ming Tran	KR Cadre
Thach Suon	Sahn
Neevy Pal	Rosa

[****]

A powerful true-life drama about the brutal massacres in Cambodia by the Khmer Rouge. Special attention must be given to the amazing performance of Haing S. Ngor who actually was a true life Cambodian survivor, only later to be murdered in Los Angeles. Sam Waterston is reporter Sydney Schanberg while Dr. Haing S. Ngor is Dith Pran, Schanberg's translator and guide. The two men are in Cambodia before its tragic fall and seek refuge at the British Embassy. The two men share a life threatening situation and become good friends. When the country is evacuated, the men get separated and Schanberg returns to America while Pran is captured and sent to a prison camp. The film follows Pran's amazing ordeal as he manages to survive from day to day under a tyrannical regiment.

The Killing Fields refer to the horrendous massacres which left thousands of dead bodies bleeding in open fields. Back in America, Schanberg tries desperately to find Pran and get his country politically involved with little success. Pran avoids death, manages to escape, and eludes his captors. Pran's only hope is to travel through miles of enemy territory and find safe haven. Living in a modern country with a relatively peaceful environment, it is easy to become complacent in society and accept the fact that the world has achieved stability in the 20th century. Films like The Killing Field are a rude awakening to the folly of such beliefs and prove that injustice and brutality continue throughout the modern world. Keep in mind the film is based on a true story and that the actual carnage was toned down for viewers. The actually death count will never be verified, but millions lost their lives in the violent struggle.

King and I, The
(1956) Musical   C-133m   English   VA   Catalog #1004   USA
Retail: $19.99 Widescreen Available
Dir: Walter Lang   Scr: Ernest Lehman Prod: Charles Brackett
DP: Leon Shamroy   Editor: Robert Simpson   Music Dir: Alfred Newman
Music: Richard Rodgers   Lyricist: Oscar Hammerstein II
Art Design: Lyle Wheeler, John DeCuir   Set Design: Walter M. Scott, Paul S. Fox
Dance Choreography: Jerome Robbins   Costumes: Irene Sharaff
Dist: Fox Home Video
(based on the musical by Oscar Hammerstein II and Richard Rodgers, from the book Anna and the King of Siam by Margaret Landon)

Deborah Kerr	**Anna Leonowens**
Yul Brynner	**The King**
Rita Moreno	**Tuptim**
Martin Benson	**Kralahome**
Terry Saunders	**Lady Thiang**
Rex Thompson	**Louis Leonowens**
Carlos Rivas	**Lun Tha**
Patrick Adiarte	**Prince Chulalongkorn**
Alan Mowbray	**British Ambassador**
Geoffrey Toone	**Ramsay**
Yuriko	**Eliza**
Marion Jim	**Simon Legree**
Robert Banas	**Keeper of the Dogs**
Dusty Worrall	**Uncle Thomas**
Gemze de Lappe	**Specialty Dancer**
Michiko Iseri	**Angel in Ballet**
Charles Irwin	**Ship's Captain**
Leonard Strong	**Interpreter**
Irene James	**Siamese Girl**
Jadin Wong	**Amazons**
Jean Wong	

FujiWeaver Levy	Whipping Guards
William Yip	High Priest
Eddie Luke	Messenger
Josephine Smith	Guest at Palace
Jocelyn New	Princess Ying Yoowalak

[****]

One of the longest running Broadway shows with a star-making performance from Yul Brynner was brought to the glorious film screen. Based on "Anna and the King of Siam", the King and I is a classic romantic musical dealing with East meets West mentality. In the film, the East is represented by Siam (now known as Thailand) while the West is England. A British school teacher, Anna, accepts a position at the royal palace to tutor the King's many children. She is a widow and brings along her only son. Since the time period is the early turn of the century, Anna's ways of dress and culture are completely foreign to the King's children and his many wives. The King is content to teach his children the knowledge of the West, but when his own actions dealing with women and policies are contradicted by Anna, he is torn by conflicting thoughts on what is right and wrong. Gradually, the King learns to respect Anna's opinions and discovers a true passion for the woman. Her departure leaves him heart-broken and eventually he passes away and leaves the mantel of the throne to his eldest son who promises to bring western reform. The film is full of electrifying musical numbers, both romantic and cheerful while the entire cast gives a first-class performance. Highpoints include Anna and the children singing and dancing to "Getting to Know You", the Uncle Tom's Cabin ballet with its surreal imagery and blend of East/West dancing, the showstopping "Shall We Dance" with Kerr and Brynner embraced in an empty ballroom, and the romantic solos sung by the lonely women. Arguably, Yul Brynner's best role on film and one of the finest film adaptations from Rodgers and Hammerstein. While accuracy in Siamese (Thai) culture may have been shuffled for poetic license, the visual beauty of the sets and the grandeur of the costumes are rich and delightful. Under the King's broad-minded guidance, the real Siam (Thailand) remained an independent, free of foreign influence, country. Currently, the Broadway stage version has been revived to glorious reviews.

Kinjite: Forbidden Subjects
(1989) DramaC-97m English   R   VA   USA
Dir: J. Lee Thompson   Scr: Harold Nebenzal   Prod: Pancho Kohner
Dist: MGM/Cannon Video

Charles Bronson	Lieutenant Crowe
Perry Lopez	Eddie Rios
Juan Fernandez	Duke
Amy Hathaway	Rita Crowe
Peggy Lipton	Kathleen Crowe
James Pax	Hiroshi Hada
Kumiko Hayakawa	Fumiko Hada

Bill McKinney, Richard Egan Jr., Sy Richardson, Alex Hyde-White
[**]

A sordid, decadent and misguided film about child prostitution. The urban crime thriller stars Bronson in his veteran tough guy role as a senior cop. Detective Crowe despises scummy pimp

Fernandez who specializes in turning teenage girls to prostitution. A typical Japanese (in Hollywood terms: conservative, hard-working, tight-lipped) family moves to Los Angeles. Mr. Hada and his family maintain their traditional ways which include a sexist attitude toward women. One of Hada's Japanese friends tells a story about a crowded subway car where a woman was groped by a man. She didn't want to make a scene, so she accepts the harassment and doesn't cry out for help. Mr. Hada, while intoxicated, attempts to fondle an American teenage girl who does yell out. She happens to be the daughter of Bronson who uses the attack as a reason to accost Japanese citizens and roar like a racist idiot. In what is suppose to be poetic irony, Hada's daughter is kidnapped and sold into prostitution. We watch as she is drugged and taken from one client to the next which includes a rich older woman who is fond of schoolgirls because of her repressed childhood in an all girls' school. Meanwhile Bronson cracks down on Fernandez and ends the prostitution ring. Fumiko is rescued by Bronson, but she can not cope with the shame, addiction, and past, so she commits suicide. In what is suppose to be a touching scene, but appears degrading, Hada thanks Bronson for his help and then meets his daughter (around the same age as Fumiko) who he fondled earlier in the film. Moral statements fail to impact the viewer and the serious nature of the film does not translate well into entertainment. A feeble attempt to expose child prostitution and chastise Japanese male behavior.

Kung Fu
(1972) Kung-Fu   C-75m English   VA
Catalog #11383   USA   Retail: $19.95
Dir: Jerry Thorpe   Scr: Ed Spielman, Howard Friedlander   Prod: Alex Beaton
Editor: John C. Horger, David Rawlins   Music: Jim Helms
Prod Design: Jack SenterTechnical Advisor: David Chow
Dist: Warner Bros. TV
David Carradine, Keye Luke, Barry Sullivan, Keith Carradine, Philip Ahn
Wayne Maunder, Albert Salmi, Benson Fong, Richard Loo, Victor Sen Yung
[***]
Even before Bruce Lee ignited the American screens, Hollywood realized martial arts story could have a place on American television. David Carradine (Bruce Lee was considered too risky because of his Asian background) was chosen to play the main role and the story was touted as a Western with East influences. Carradine underwent a makeup process to appear more Asian and spoke with a soft, slow tone. As a young boy in China, Caine (Carradine) stands in the pouring rain, hoping to become a disciple of Shaolin Temple. He is accepted and trains under the guidance of a blind monk (Luke). His adult adventures are spent in the old west of American.
The pilot film started off the popular series which then capitalised on the kung-fu craze in America ushered in by Bruce Lee. Ironically, Lee was past up for the role and non-Asian actor Carradine was chosen to portray Kwai Chang Caine, the half-Chinese, half-American martial arts expert. This is the best in the series, since it spends the most time dealing with the internal workings of the Shaolin Temple. Most of the stories were very routine following the formula of Caine entering a new town, refusing to fight, but then forced to fight for justice of the weak or prove his innocence. Keye Luke plays the memorable blind master Po who reappeared in every episode as a flashback mentor. The story shows Caine's past as a young half-breed orphaned and forced to seek refuge at Shaolin Temple. He is refused admittance, but doesn't leave and stands

for days in the pouring rain. His dedication is finally accepted and he grows up to be a Shaolin master nicknamed grasshopper by his favorite mentor Po. When Po is murdered in the street by the royal nephew, Caine lashes out and kills him. He becomes a wanted man and escapes to the United States where he works as a railroad worker. Wherever he goes, he brings along a sense of justice and his views on Eastern philosophy are full of flashback memories from his peaceful days at the temple. The film melds the genres of the western and martial arts into a realistic treatment of a Shaolin monk in the old west. He suffers racism and self-doubts, while never allowed to rest from Manchurian assassins, but searches endlessly for a long lost brother. Don't compare this to a Hong Kong Shaolin film, but consider it along the lines of an alternative western.

Kung Fu: The Movie
(1986) Kung-Fu   C-100 min   English   VA   USA
Dir: Richard Lang   Music: Lalo Schifrin Dist: Warner
David Carradine, Brandon Lee, Kerri Keane, Mako, William Lucking, Luke Askew, Benson Fong, Keye Luke, Martin Landau
[1/2]**
Kung Fu: The Television Series was enjoyable for many reasons. It capitalized on the popular westerns of the early decades and also featured Shaolin Temple and kung-fu, a topic popular in Chinese films but rarely mentioned in Hollywood productions. After the series was cancelled, attempts were made to bring back the show with David Carradine. This movie was produced to guage the interest of the genre/show and also starred Brandon Lee, son of Bruce Lee. The new series never appeared, probably due to the death of the westerns, but years later the series was up-dated to modern day and given a cop/kung-fu angle which capitalized on the Jackie Chan craze. The new series caught on and currently airs on television with David Carradine playing the grandson of Caine while his Caucasian son plays a cop.

The followup to the original Kung-Fu Series continues the further exploits of Kwai Chang Caine, a half-Chinese, half-American Shaolin master in the old west. The plot is routine and episodic, providing some interest to fans of the series. Caine arrives in town and gets a job with local Chinese workers. He minds his own business, but gets involved and accused in the murder of an honorable white man who preached the word of God. Not only are the white men after him, but a Chinese nobleman (Mako) arrives in America to take vengeance for the death of his son. He has brainwashed Caine's own son (Lee) into a deadly killing machine. Caine joins with the dead man's wife and the two discover that her father-in-law ordered the murder of his own son. He is using the funeral crates of dead Chinese workers to ship opium to China and gold back into the United States. The local sheriff and marshall are not to be trusted, so Caine breaks out of prison and solves the crime.

The most interesting aspect is the appearance of Brandon Lee who plays a pivotal character in the film. Initially Brandon avoided kung-fu roles, not wanting to be compared to his father. He falsely befriends Caine, since he is under the spell of the Manchurian warlord played by Mako. The film hints at Lee being the new lead for Kung-Fu, but sadly this never materialized. The two men battle in the final scene, but the martial arts choreography is well below Hong Kong standards and quite laughable with its snail's pace, constant camera changes, and lack of imagination. Don't worry if you can't remember the original series, the film contains plenty of flashbacks from the series to refresh your memory.

Lover, The
(1992) Romance   C-110m   Subtitled   R   VA
Catalog # 903183   FranceRetail: $19.99
Dir: Jean-Jacques Annaud Scr: Jean-Jacques Annaud, Gerard Brach
Prod: Claude Berri, Paul Rassam DP: Robert Fraisse
Editor: Noelle Boisson   Music: Gabriel Yared   Prod Design: Thanh At Hoang
Art Design: Olivier Rudot Set Design: Sophie Martel Costume: Yvonne   Sassinot DeNesle
Dist: MGM/UA Home Video
(from the novel by Marguerite Duras)

Jane March	Young Marguerite Duras
Tony Leung	Chinese Lover
Frederique Meininger	Mother
Arnaud Giovaninetti	Elder Brother
Melvil Poupaud	Younger Brother
Lisa Faulkner	Helene Lagonelle
Xiem Mang	Chinese Man's Father
Philippe LeDem	French Teacher
Ann Schaufuss	Anne-Marie Stretter
Quach Van An	Driver
Tania Torrens	Principal
Raymonde Heudeline	Writer
Yvonne Wingerter	Writer
Do Minh Vien	Young Boy
Helene Patarot	Assistant Mistress
Jeanne Moreau	Voice of Marguerite Duras

[**1/2]
A romantic-period piece set during the French colonization of Vietnam. March is a young schoolgirl who is blooming sexually and in search of some excitement. She discovers a mature man on a steamer and meets with him again to start a torrid affair. The art film borders on tedium as young girl-older man fantasies are enacted with the frail, but lovely March. We discover the young French girl's family fortunes have fallen, so her affair with the rich Chinese merchant's son is dubious and ponderous. The film is beautifully shot and the time period is nicely recreated, but March's appearance is more noted for her steamy sex scenes and not for her acting or the film's plot.

M. Butterfly
(1993) Romance   C-110m   English   R   VA
Catalog #27539   USA   Retail: $19.95 Widescreen Available
Dir: David Cronenberg   Scr: David Henry Hwang   Prod:Gabriella Martinelli
DP: Peter Suschitzky   Editor: Ronald Sanders   Music: Howard Shore
Prod Design: Carol Spier   Art Design: James McAteer
Set Design: Elinor Rose Galbraith Costumes: Denise Cronenberg
Dist: Warner

(based on the play by D. H. Hwang)

Jeremy Irons	Rene Gallimard
John Lone	Song Liling
Barbara Sukowa	Jeanne Gallimard
Ian Richardson	Ambassador Toulon
Annabel Leventon	Frau Baden
Shizuko Hoshi	Comrade Chin
Richard McMillan	Embassy Colleague
Vernon Dobtcheff	Agent Etancelin
David Hemblen	1st Intelligent Officer
Damir Andrei	2nd Intelligent Officer
Anthony Parr	3rd Intelligent Officer
Margaret Ma	Song's Maid
Tristram Jellinek	Defense Attorney
Philip McGough	Prosecution Attorney
David Neal	Judge
Sean Hewitt	Ambassador's Aide
Peter Messaline	Diplomat at Party
Barbara Chilcott	Critic at Garden Party
George Jonas	Mall Trustee
Carl Zvonkin	Surveillance Technician
Viktor Fulop	Marshal
Cadman Chui	Accordian Player
Carly Wong	Red Guard Dancers

[**]

Let me begin by saying that the subject material did not bother me. I was actually intrigued by the premise, having heard good things about the stage production and also being an avid admirer of "Madame Butterfly" and "The Crying Game". Instead of finding a film charged with sexual tension and deception, I was disturbed by the mundane nature of the film. Irons character is two-dimensional and his lustful desire for Butterfly never comes across with conviction. Perhaps the fault lies in the casting of John Lone, a handsome distinguished actor who has appeared in numerous films. In "The Crying Game", we are pulled into the illusion of seeing a man as a woman. No such thing happens with Lone who appears masculine from scene one. His popularity and presence in films is too strong to negate his natural masculinity. It would be like casting Harrison Ford as a woman in love with Clint Eastwood.

If you can get by the illusion, the story is based on the true exploits of Rene Gallimard, a French diplomat in China 1964. He's married and has plenty of beautiful women to choose from, but is captivated by Lone's performance of Madame Butterfly. From there he follows her/him and carries on a passionate love affair, though he is never allowed to see her with her clothes off. Their relationship develops, but the momentum and passion are not evident. Gallimard receives a promotion and uses his expertise to gauge China's reaction to the Vietnam Conflict. The film then reveals Lone's duplicity and his role as a spy collecting information from Gallimard. As their relationship intensifies, Gallimard demands more of a commitment from Lone. He wants to see her naked, but she uses her shyness and embarrassment in having a paltry body when compared to Western women (should Asian women take offense to this fact?) Gallimard's life starts to break down and his own status in the French government is threatened. Lone convinces Gallimard that she is pregnant and must return to her village to give birth to their son. No blood tests are necessary, so Gallimard accepts the fact that the baby is his own child. He is then demoted and sent to Paris, working as a government courier. Butterfly follows him to France and convinces him that their son is held by the Chinese government and will be killed unless they provide critical documents. He will do anything for his lovely Butterfly and becomes a spy for China.

In routine fashion, a scandal breaks out and both men are tried for treason in a standard court scene. They share an uneasy ride in the police wagon where Lone undresses and attempts to seduce Gallimard for the last time. Unable to live with his shame and loss, Gallimard dresses like Madame Butterfly and re-enacts the end of the play with the same devotion. Lone is arrested and extradited. I enjoyed the parallelistic references to Puccini's Madame Butterfly, a classic Italian Opera which I have always loved. Moments of the dialogue are particularly poignant and the film attempts to capture a lost age and time of French arrogance.

Midway
(1976) War   C-132m   English   PG   VA
Catalog #87160   USA   Retail: $19.95
Dir: Jack Smight   Scr: Donald S. Sanford   Prod: Walter Mirsch
DP: Harry Stradling, Jr.   Editor: Robert Swink, Frank J. Urioste
Music: John Williams   Art Dir: Walter Tyler   Set Design: John M. Dwyer
Sp. Fx: Jack McMasters   Dist: MCA/Universal Home Video

Charlton Heston	Matt Garth
Henry Fonda	Chester W. Nimitz
James Coburn	Vinton Maddox
Glenn Ford	Raymond A. Spruance
Hal Holbrook	Joseph Rochefort
Robert Mitchum	William F. Halsey
Cliff Robertson	Carl Jessop
Toshiro Mifune	Isoroku Yamamoto
Robert Wagner	Ernest L. Blake
Edward Albert	Tom Garth

Robert Webber, Ed Nelson, James Shigeta, Monte Markham, Christopher George, Glenn Corbett, Tom Selleck, Robert Ito, Pat Morita, Dabney Coleman, Erik Estrada, Sab Shimono, Clyde Kusatsu
[***]

"This is the way it a was--
The story of the battle that was the
turning point of the war in the pacific,
told wherever possible with actual film
shot during combat. It exemplifies the
combination of planning, courage, error
and pure chance by which great events
are often decided."

                                    Opening Card

Melodramatic war drama which recounts the great naval battle of Midway. Pure history buffs may find fault with the characterization and silly love story, while romance buffs may be dissuaded by the abundance of war footage. A film with a narrow and limited appeal, which definitely grows tiresome with age. Still the film features a blockbuster cast and an interesting insight into one of the most important naval conflicts of World War II. To refresh your history, the Japanese Imperial Navy bombed Pearl Harbor and continued to expand into the Pacific. The Japanese seemed impossible to stop and launched a massive attack against the island of Midway. The United States, through sheer luck and brilliance, managed to stop a superior fleet and halt Japan's expansion once and for all. Noted as the turning point in the Pacific War, Japan would never recover from the massive loss of their four heavy carriers, hundreds of aircraft, and thousands of lost lives. This is the story of the men who were involved in the conflict.

Mortal Kombat
(1995) Martial Arts/Fantasy   C-101m   English   PG-13   VA
Catalog #67546   USA   Retail: $19.95 Widescreen Available
Dir: Paul Anderson   Prod: Lawrence Kasanoff
DP: John R. Leonetti   Editor: Martin Hunter   Music: George S. Clinton
Music Dir: Steve Nelson   Sp. Fx: Alec Gillis, Tom Woodruff Jr.
Costume: Ha Nguyen   Dist: New Line Cinema
Christopher Lambert   Lord Rayden
Robin Shou   Liu Kang
Linden Ashby   Johnny Cage
Cary-Hiroyuki Tagawa   Shang Tsung
Bridgette Wilson   Sonya Blade
Talisa Soto   Princess Kitana
Trevor Goddard   Kano
[***]

Perhaps not the perfect example of an Asian film, but this American-released martial arts film is unique for capturing fantasy elements and allowing the main star and villain to be portrayed by Asian actors. The climatic hero is the Chinese Lou Kang rather than American Johnny Blade. Based on the popular Williams Arcade Game, Mortal Kombat combines fantasy, martial arts, and mayhem in a film that breaks away from the childhood image of its predecessor (Street Fighter: The Movie). Technically, Mortal Kombat features a dizzying array of Hollywood-level special effects and plenty of impressive sets and costumes. On par with the imagination of Hong Kong fantasy films, Mortal Kombat is the story of an eternal tournament that takes place between the greatest fighters on Earth and the Outworld, an outer dimensional realm ruled by an evil tyrant. Whichever side wins the tournament will decide the fate of the Earth. Helping the humans is the ancient god Lord Rayden (Asian god of thunder and lightning) who guards over the brave fighters and makes sure the rules are fair for both sides. His three favorite contestants are Lou Kang, a martial artist whose brother was killed by Shang, Johnny Cage, a cocky American actor, and Sonya, the beautiful blonde crime fighter. They each have their own reasons for fighting in the tournament, but realize their actions will effect the fate of the world. They battle Shang's bare-chested minions including the multi-armed monster Goro. Shang attempts to escape back into his own realm with Sonya (sexy window dressing), so Johnny and Lou follow him and do battle in a dark, mysterious, war-torn planet. Plenty of spectacular martial arts sequences and Hollywood-level visual effects will appeal to young fans who enjoy action/fantasy. The acting is pedestrian at times and the story is not totally solidified, but more an excuse to string along some fight scenes. Christopher Lambert is the top-billed actor, but doesn't fight, staying on the sidelines as a mentor and observer. Followed by a sequel which continues the events of the first film.

Mr. Baseball
(1992) Comedy **C-109m** **English** **PG-13** **VA** **Catalog #81231**
USA Retail: $19.95
Dir: Fred Schepisi Scr: Gary Ross, Kevin Wade, Monte Merrick **Music: Dave Grusin**
Prod: Fred Schepisi, Doug Claybourne, Robert Newmyer
(from the story by Theo Pelletier and John Junkerman)
DP: Ian Baker Editor: Peter Honess Music: Jerry Goldsmith
Prod Design: Ted Haworth Costumes: Bruce Finlayson
Dist: MCA/Universal Home Video

Tom Selleck	Jack Elliot
Ken Takakura	Uchiyama
Aya Takanashi	Hiroko Uchiyama
Dennis Haysbert	Max "Hammer" Dubois
Toshi Shioya	Yoji Nishimura
Kohsuke Toyohara	Toshi Yamashita
Toshizo Fujiwara	Ryoh Mukai
Mak Takano	Shinji Igarashi
Kenji Morinaga	Hiroshi Kurosawa
Joh Nishimura	Tomohiko Ohmae
Norihide Goto	Issei Itoi
Kensuke Toita	Akito Yagi
Naoki Fujii	Takuya Nishikawa
Takanobu Hozumi	Hiroshi Nakamura
Leon Lee	Lyle Massey
Jun Hamamura	Hiroko's Grandfather
Mineko Yorozuyo	Hiroko's Grandmother
Shoji Ohoki	Coach Hori
Tomoko Fujita	Hiroko's Assistant
Kinzoh Sakura	1st Umpire
Ikuko Saitoh	Morita San
Hikari Takano	Commercial Director
Tim McCarver	Himself
Sean McDonough	Himself

Makoto Kuno, Michiyo Washizukan, Shinsuke Aoki, Rinzoh Suzuki, Shintaro Mizushima, Nobuyuki Kariya, Satoshi Jinbo, Masanao Matsuzaki, Shotaro Kusumi, Katsushi Yamaguchi Kobayashi, Hiro Nagae, Yoshimi Imai, Cin Chi Cheng, Makoto Kaketa, Kazukuni Mutoh
[**1/2]
Tom Selleck is a washed-up pro baseball player who can't get a single major league team to sign

him up. So his agent convinces him to go to Japan and play on the Chunichi Dragons. Reluctant at first, the arrogant Selleck accepts and imagines himself the prima donna of the field. When his arrogant antics don't go well with strict coach Ken Takakura it is up to the sexy PR agent to placate things. Funny thing, but she turns out to be the daughter of coach Takakura. It takes time, but Selleck adopts to the Japanese way and becomes a true trooper. He trains hard with his teammates and friendships are established which help the Dragons do well in competition. There's only one other American player on the team who helps Selleck through his transition, so there's plenty of humor based on language and cultural gaps. Typical East meets West plot, but appealing for Selleck fans and viewers who enjoy light-hearted baseball films. In Japan, baseball is an amazingly popular sport and many American athletes have played in the Japanese leagues. Tides have turned and now teams like the LA Dodgers feature Hideo Nomo (Japan) and Chan Ho Park (Korean) and the NY Yankees have Hideki Irabu (Japan). Perhaps in the future, Japan and the United States will even compete against each other at the World Series.

NINJAMANIA: (The Silent Assassins from Japan)

Ninjas were feudal assassins hired by powerful lords to kill their rivals, scout enemy territories, steal valuable assets, and provide intelligence information. Historical spies who were trained from childhood and never left the service. During the 1980's, a decade after kung-fu movies leapt onto the screen, ninjas provided martial arts entertainment with a diabolic twist. In an attempt to capitalize on western fascination with the subject, hundreds of films were released, specials aired on television, books popped up in stores, and even network television aired a show called The Master, starring Sho Kosugi as an evil ninja pursuing renegade good ninja Lee Van Cleef. What follows is a list of some of the movies that are available, but sadly the majority of the lot were low-exploitation films made to capitalize on violence and sex. With a few exceptions, treat this as a list of films to avoid. Most titles are weak films that capitalized on the ninja name, but including characters who wore black costumes and mask, while carrying swords and throwing shurikens. Best to avoid the following stinkers: Ninja Academy, Ninja American Warrior, Ninja Brothers of Blood, Ninja Checkmate, Ninja Commandments, Ninja Condors, Ninja Connection, Ninja Death Squad, Ninja Exterminators, Ninja Massacre, Ninja Nightmare, Ninja of the Magnificence, Ninja Operation: Licensed to Terminate, Ninja Phantom Heroes, Ninja Pirates, Ninja Powerforce, Ninja Showdown, Ninja Strike Force, Ninja Supremo, Ninja Sword of Death, Ninja Turf, Ninja vs Ninja, Ninja vs. Shaolin, Ninja's Extreme Weapons.

Enter the Ninja
(1981) Martial Arts C-99m English   R   VA   USA
Dir: Menahem Golan   Scr: Judd Bernard, Dick Desmond, Menahem Golan
Prod: Judd Bernard, Patricia Casey, Yoram Globus
DP: David Gurfinkel Editor: Mark Goldblatt
Music: W. Michael Lewis, Laurin Rinder Stunts: Mike Stone
PC: Cannon   Dist: MGM
Franco Nero   Cole
Sho Kosugi   Hasegawa

Susan George	Mary-Ann Landers
Christopher George	Charles Venarius
Alex Courtney	Frank Landers
Will Hare	Dollars
Zachi Noy	The Hook
Dale Ishimoto	Komori

[**]

The film that kickstarted the Ninjamania craze and made Sho Kosugi the official spokesninja of America. Nero is an American ninja who trained in Japan. He excelled and was the best student in the school which infuriated rival Sho Kosugi. Many years later, Nero is travelling the world and visits his old army buddy in the Philippines. He and his lovely wife own a nice ranch in the remote jungles, but a local land baron wants the property for his own purposes and will stop at nothing to get it. As usual, common sense eludes the couple, as they decide to stay and battle to keep their home. Their workers are terrorized, the wife is accosted, and life in general is horrible until Nero shows up and starts to put things right. This encourages Christopher to keep fighting, but his wife wants the violence to end. She is pushed away by him, so she seeks comfort from Nero's hairy arms. When it is discovered Nero is a ninja, the bad guys send for their own ninja from Japan who happens to be old-time rival Sho Kosugi. The film features a number of standard action scenes which are highlighted by vicious ways of assassinating your opponent. The film used a double for Nero's white ninja who easily terminates the hired thugs and assassins, meeting Sho Kosugi in an abandoned arena for the final conflict. Audiences were fascinated with the ninjas amazing abilities, stealth-like skills, and deadly detachment, creating a renewed passion in Asian action films. Hundreds of ninja-type films were made afterwards, the majority falling in a category worse than this film. The overall appeal is the male adrenaline rush when viewing a single hero (armed only with a sword) standing against dozens of enemies while protecting a beautiful, scantily clad woman. The sequel was to feature the martial arts star who played Nero's white ninja (Mike Stone), but he was replaced by Kosugi who then rocketed to fame and appeared in a number of ninja sequels.

Nine Deaths of the Ninja
(1985) Martial Arts C-93m English   VA   USA
Dir/Scr: Emmett Alston   Dist: Media Home Entertainment
Sho Kosugi, Brent Huff, Emelia Lesniak, Regina Richardson, Kane Kosugi, Shane Kosugi
[*]

Sho Kosugi's career reaches an all-time low as this horrible and insulting film foreshadows the death of ninjamania in America. Sho Kosugi reprises his role as a stoic, lethal ninja who travels with his two kids who are also nunchaku-yielding, star-chucking ninjas. Their tour group is hijacked by a scrawny, bizarre villain who epitomizes the worst caricatures of villains in any film. The rest of the film ridiculously involves women warriors and a commando team sent to rescue the tourists.

Ninja III: The Domination
(1984) Martial Arts C-95m English   VA   USA
Dir: Sam Firstenberg   Scr: James R. Silke
Prod: Menahem Golan, Yoram Globus   DP: Hanania Baer

Editor: Michael J. Duthie   Music: Udi Harpaz, Misha Segal, Arthur Kempel
Art Design: Elliott Ellentuck   Set Design: Dian Perryman
Stunts: Steve Lambert   MAD: Sho Kosugi
Costumes: Nancy Cone   Dist: MGM

Sho Kosugi	Yamada
Lucinda Dickey	Christie
Jordan Bennett	Secord
David Chung	Black Ninja
Dale Ishimoto	Okuda
James Hong	Miyashima
Bob Craig	Netherland
Pamela Ness	Alana
Roy Padilla	Winslow
Moe Mosley	Pickwick
John La Motta	Case
Ron Foster	Jimenez
Alan Amiel	Black Ninja Double
Steve Lambert	Pilot
Earl Smith	Jefferson
Carver Barnes	Nicholson
Karen Petty	Tracy
Randy Mulkey	Thug
James Maher	Frankel
Judy Starr	Doctor
Cheryl Van Cleve	Stacy
Suzanne Collins	Patty
Rosemary Ono	Megumi
Janet Marie Heil	Lucy
Charly Harroway	Chang
John Perryman	Tom
Chris Micelli	Pulley
Lem Cook	Helicopter Pilot
Howard Dean	Policeman
Tom Catronova	Sgt. Cone

[**]

After the entertaining Revenge of the Ninja, executives in Hollywood decided to do something completely asinine and remove all the agreeable elements from the prequel and create Ninja III: The Domination. The whole premise of the story revolves around a deadly ninja who possesses the nubile body of a woman and uses her as a sexy assassin. In an exciting opening scene which is never explained, an elite ninja in camouflage pops up in sunny California. He assassinates his target and has the entire police force after him. One by one, the ninja slaughters a host of police officers (Terminator-like) and their bullets seem to be useless. Eventually, the ninja goes down and the surviving officers sign in relief.

Christie is a free-spirited eighties girl who happens to work for a phone company and enjoys aerobics, but nudity doesn't play a prominent role. At night, the dead ninja's spirit possesses her and makes her dress like a ninja. She hunts down the surviving officers who were involved in the attack. One of the officers unknowingly develops a relationship with Christie. Finally from Japan, wearing an eye-patch, Kosugi attempts to save the girl and the film. His arrival is to late and he must battle her and unleash the evil ninja's spirit. The officer/boyfriend looks on in disbelief (so do we) as Kosugi battles the evil ninja.

Ninja Wars
(1985) Martial Arts C-95m Dubbed   VA   Catalog # MN7748
Japan   Retail: $9.99
Jackie Chan   Dist: Prism Entertainment
[*]
A convoluted and disappointing film that includes a cameo from Jackie Chan. Unfortunately this movie tends to be a popular title carried by mainstream video stores, but best to stay away from it. The film is very heavy into the fantasy/mysticism elements. A rogue ninja must battle five other ninja assassins and an evil sorcerer who has kidnapped his girlfriend. Scenes rage quickly as the ninja brutally dispatches his enemies in the Feudal Period of Japan. My memories of this film are quite disappointing and insulting.

Pray for Death
(1985) Martial Arts C-93m English   R   VA   USA
Dir: Gordon Hessler   Scr: James Booth   Prod: Don Van Atta
DP: Roy H. Wagner   Editor: Bill Butler, Steve Butler   Music: Thomas Chase
Dist: USA Home Video
Sho Kosugi, Kane Kosugi, Shane Kosugi, James Booth, Donna Kei Benz, Robert Ito
[*]
Pray for the end would be a more apt title. Another poor effort from Sho Kosugi who has locked himself into an endless stream of ill-conceived Ninja films. He is a simple family man with two kids. He gets involved with a ruthless criminal who murders his wife and threatens his children. When his family is harassed, he puts on a ninja suit with a metal face mask and kills everyone, including the plot.

Revenge of the Ninja
(1983) Ninja C-90m English   R   VA
Catalog #M800329   USA   Retail: $19.95
Dir: Sam Firstenberg   Scr: James R. Silke   Prod: Yoram Globus, Menahem Golan
DP: David Gurfinkel Editor: Michael J. Duthie, Mark Helfrich
Music: Rob Walsh   Art Dir: Paul Staheli Prod Design: Ivo Cristante
Set Design: Dian Perryman MAD: Sho Kosugi   Sp. Fx: Joe Quinlivan
Stunts: Steve Lambert   PC: Cannon   Dist: MGM

Sho Kosugi	**Cho Osaki**
Arthur Roberts	**Braden**
Keith Vitali	**Dave Hatcher**
Virgil Frye	**Lt. Dime**
Ashley Ferrare	**Grandmother Osaki**
Kane Kosugi	**Kane Osaki**

John Lamotta   Joe
Mario Gallo   Caifano
Grace Oshita, Melvin C. Hampton, Don Shanks, Toru Tanaka, Jack North, Alan Amiel
[***]
The best ninja film of the group (maybe that's not saying a lot) is also my personal Kosugi favorite. Kosugi is the sole star of the film and plays a good family man who happens to be a ninja master. Martial arts actor Kosugi was instrumental in ushering in the Ninja-craze of the 1980's and his popularity was brief but intense. American audiences were tired of Bruce Lee clones and were not yet fully exposed to Jackie Chan's physical charisma. Sonny Chiba was a little too sloppy and brutal for the kids. Then came along a tranquil-looking Japanese man in his middle ages. Not looking overly muscular like Jean-Claude Van Damme or as imposing as Steven Seagal, the humble Kosugi would don a black mask and became the deadliest killer on screen. Initially the villain in Enter the Ninja, Kosugi lobbied hard to become the lead in the next movie. Gambling on Asian stars were still risky, but the green light was given and instead the villain was Caucasian. Kosugi's stoic mannerism and rough English added believability to his character and the introduction of his ninja son also adds a bit of fun.
In rural Japan, Kosugi's entire family is attacked by evil ninjas. Only his son and mother survive the brutal onslaught. His Caucasian friend and business partner convinces him to come to America and open up a Japanese art shop. In reality, the American partner is an evil ninja who is using his shop as a drug front. The store does well, but one day a shipment of statues are being stolen. Sho beats up the thugs and chases down their getaway van. His friend Braden is carrying on a personal war agains the mafia and plans to infiltrate their headquarters and take out the boss. Kosugi and his police detective pal also go after the evil ninja and the mobsters. Meanwhile, Kosugi's grandmother, son, and sexy girlfriend have problems of their own. When the truth of Braden's betrayal comes out, the two ninjas battle on top of the mafia's skyscraper, using every ninja trick in the book and then some. The formula and a number of generic characters may slow the film down, but Kosugi's prowess and the unique look and style of ninjutsu cuts this film about the rest in the group. Plenty of decent fight scenes, exotic weapons, and a high body count will appeal to action/ninja fans. Followed by a number of horrible sequels that relegated Sho Kosugi to substandard role and helped kill the ninjamania craze.

~End of Ninjamania Section~

None But the Brave
(1965) War Drama   C-105m   English   VA
Catalog #25061   USA   Retail: $29.95
Dir: Frank Sinatra   Scr: John Twist, Katsuya Suzaki   Prod: Frank Sinatra
Ex. Prod: Howard W. Koch   Associate Prod: William Daniels
DP: Harold Lipstein Editor: Sam O'Steen Music: John Williams
Art Design: LeRoy Deane, Haruyoski Oshita   Set Design: George James Hopkins
Sp. Fx: Eiji Tsuburaya   Dist: Warner
(based on a story by Kikumaru Okuda)
Frank Sinatra   Chief Pharmacist's Mate Maloney
Clint Walker   Capt. Dennis Bourke
Tommy Sands   2nd Lt. Blair

Brad Dexter	Sgt. Bleeker
Tony Bill	Air Crewman Keller
Tatsuya Mihashi	Lt. Kuroki
Takeshi Kato	Sgt. Tamura
Sammy Jackson	Cpl. Craddock
Dick Bakalyan	Cpl. Ruffino
Rafer Johnson	Pvt. Johnson
Jimmy Griffin	Pvt. Dexter
Christopher Dark	Pvt. Searcy
Don Dorrell	Pvt. Hoxie
Phillip Crosby	Pvt. Magee
John Howard Young	Pvt. Waller
Roger Ewing	Pvt. Swensholm
Homare Suguro	Lance Cpl. Hirano
Kenji Sahara	Cpl. Fujimoto
Masahiko Tanimura	Lead Pvt. Ando
Hisao Dazai	Pvt. Tokumaru
Susumu Kurobe	Pvt. Goro
Takashi Inagaki	Pvt. Ishii
Kenichi Hata	Pvt. Sato
Toru Ibuki	Pvt. Arikawa
Ryucho Shunputei	Pvt. Okuda

[***]

Frank Sinatra's directorial debut has been met with criticism, but the film's attempt at treating racism and World War II from a different angle is refreshing and intriguing. A group of U.S. marines are marooned when their transport plane crashes on a remote island in the Pacific Ocean. At first, the soldiers believe the island is deserted and decide to wait for an inevitable rescue. In reality, a squad of Japanese soldiers are stationed on the island and have also been cut off from their country. Conflicts arise when the two groups battle each other, but since both sides are marooned on the island and need each other for survival, they come to a loose truce. The Japanese control the only fresh water source while the Americans have a doctor (Sinatra) and medical supplies. Hatred gives way to teamwork when a hurricane nearly destroys both camps, which then leads to friendship. Life becomes pleasant and many of the soldiers become friends, including the Japanese and American commander. When the American soldiers manage to get their radio working and the outside world is contacted, hostilities rematerialize and end the truce. Captain Bourke begs the proud Japanese soldiers to surrender when an American warships appears. The noble captain even considers leaving the island and forgoing any mention of the Japanese soldiers to his superior, since the island is of little strategic significance. The Japanese soldiers, honor bound to their emperor, refuse surrender, disappear into the jungle, and prepare for war. As the American soldiers prepare to leave the island, a brutal and costly battle erupts on the beachfront. A touching testament to the futility and stupidity of war.

In most World War II films, the Japanese are portrayed as emotionless killers dedicated to one cause. In the film we get to see various aspects of the characters and any lack of direction is favorably balanced by its genuine portrayal of Japanese and American characters who share similar hopes, fears, dreams, and lives.

The Perfect Weapon
(1991) Martial Arts C-112m   English   R   VA
Catalog #25627   USA   Retail: $19.95
Dir: Mark DiSalle   Scr: David C. Wilson   Prod: Mark DiSalle, Pierre David
Ex. Prod: Ralph Winter   DP: Russell Carpenter   Editor: Wayne Wahrman
Music: Gary Chang   Prod Design: Curtis A. Schnell
Line Prod: Martin Hornstein   Costume: Joseph Porro
PC: DiSalle/David Production   Dist: Paramount Pictures

Jeff Speakman	Jeff
John Dye	Adam
Mako	Kim Kwan
James Hong	Yung
Mariska Hargitay	Jennifer
Dante Basco	Jimmy Ho
Seth Sakai	Master Lo
Professor Toru Tanaka	Tanaka
Clyde Kusatsu	Detective Wong
Cary-Hiroyuki Tagawa	Kai

[**]

Another American entry into the world of martial arts, spiced up with the usual Westerner in the East plot. A cut below the Jean-Claude Van Damme/Steven Seagal films, newcomer Jeff Speakman is Jeff, a master of kempo karate. Jeff's a rebellious young man who never got along with his hard-nosed cop/father or his conscientious younger brother. In a flashback, we learn Jeff's mother died and he becomes a rebellious teenager. Jeff's father looks to wise Kim for some help and the Korean friend recommends martial arts as a way to gain discipline and strength. In a clever montage, Jeff rises up the ranks until he becomes a black belt master. Now a construction worker, he returns to visit his friend Kim (Mako) who is having problems with the Korean mob in Los Angeles' Koreatown. Jeff kicks some ass with his fast-paced, highly edited style of kempo. When Mako is killed by Tanaka, Jeff enters the seedy underworld of Koreatown bent on finding the real killer. He meets a crime boss (Hong) who gives him some information on a Korean godfather. Jeff breaks into the godfather's high rise, passing the security forces without breaking a sweat and hitching a ride on the glass elevator to the penthouse. Jeff attacks the godfather and his family, but discovers he was set up by James Hong when teenage-friend Jimmy explains the truth. Teaming up with the Korean godfather and Jeff's kid brother who is a cop, Jeff goes after Hong and his mountainous hitman Tanaka. Jeff's screen debut is inauspicious, but the film offers some decent fight scenes and is noted for its use of Koreans as the major Asian force.

Protector, The
(1985) Action C-94m English   R   VA
Catalog #21646   USA   Retail: $19.95
Dir/Scr: James Glickenhaus Prod: David Chan   Ex. Prod: Raymond Chow
DP: Mark Irwin, Harry Stradling Editor: Evan Lottman   Music: Ken Thorne
Art Dir/Prod Design: William F. de Seta   Sound Editor: Skip Lievsay

Costume: Michele Mao   Stunts: Alan R. Gibbs   Dist: Warner

Jackie Chan	Billy Wong
Danny Aiello	Danny Garoni
Roy Chiao	Mr. Ko
Bill Wallace	Benny Garucci
Saun Ellis	Laura Shapiro
Kim Bass	Stan Jones
Richard Clarke	Whitehead

[**1/2]

Jackie Chan tried to capture the heart of American audiences with The Big Brawl and Cannonball Run. He didn't succeed, so it was thought a film along the lines of a crime drama would do better. The idea was good (Police Story, Supercop), but sadly the film was a disappointment even for dedicated Chan fans. Filming under the constraints of the Hollywood style, Chan was not allowed to do major stunts and his character lacks humor and humility. Figuring Chan needed some box office help, he was paired with wiseguy Danny Aiello (of all people). Rehashing the buddy cop formula, Chan and Aiello are part of New York City's finest. They follow a major drug operation linked to a woman's kidnapping to the heart of Hong Kong. There Chan discovers the rich industrialist Roy Chiao is the head of the drug operation and behind the kidnapping of the wealthy businessman's daughter. Chan and Aiello spend time visiting brothels, arguing with each other, fighting off assassins, quarreling with the Hong Kong chief of police, and getting help from the locals. None of the supporting characters are allowed to develop, but appear as caricatures to move along the hackneyed plot. Chan and his pretty helper visit a Chinese fortune teller who provides them with enough clues. Chan, Aiello, and an ex-Navy SEAL (they're always around when you need them) break into Chiao's warehouse, blow up the drug facility, and rescue the damsel in distress. When they do chase down the main villains, Chan must fight Bill "Superfoot" Wallace (a real life Karate champion) and rescue his tied up partner. Chan's fight is pale in comparison to his Hong Kong films, but manages to get the job done and chase after Chiao. The battle moves out of the warehouse and into the construction yard where Chan battles a muscular Chinese henchman on top of a swinging girder high above the yard. Chiao manages to reach a helicopter, but Chan and Aiello stop him. They return to NYC and receive a hero's welcome, but the movie goers were less appreciative. Though disappointing, Chan does try his best and there are moments of excitement in this slick-looking action film from Hollywood.

Red Sun
(1971) Samurai/Western   C-115m   English   PG   VA
Catalog #40080   France/Italy/Spain   Retail: $19.95
Dir: Terence Young Scr: William Roberts   Prod: Ted Richmond
DP: Henri Alekan   Editor: Johnny Dwyre   Music: Maurice Jarre
Art Dir: Enrique Alarcon Set Design: Rafael Salazar Costume: Tony Pulo
Makeup: Alberto de Rossi Sp. Fx: Karl Baumgartner
PC: National General   Dist: Video Gems

Toshiro Mifune	Kuroda
Charles Bronson	Link
Alain Delon	Gauche

Ursula Andress Cristina
Capucine   Pepita
Georges Lycan, Antonio Margheriti, Jose Nieto, Julio Pena
[**]
Another early attempt at East meets West genres, but time has not boded well for this film which seems ponderous and stereotypically portrayed. Though it still has moments of excitement, especially when Mifune slices up some cowboys and Indians. Westerns were a popular genre in early Hollywood and many Asian filmmakers grew up on John Wayne, Audie Murphy, and Gary Cooper. In return, a number of attempts were made to capture Asian techniques and western lore into one film. Kung-fu expert Lo Lieh once teamed up with gunfighter Lee Van Cleef and Samo Hung, Cynthia Rothrock, and Richard Norton also had fun in Shanghai Express. Though the most often seen genre mixer is Red Sun, starring some of the hottest stars of that era: Mifune, Bronson, and Andress.

In the old west, the emperor of Japan sends a special convoy to deliver gifts and establish peace with America. While on board a train bound to Washington DC, a group of bandits rob the train and steal everything, including a priceless sword. One of the samurai warriors draws his sword and tries to prevent the theft but is gunned down. Bronson, part of the group, is betrayed by the leader and left behind. He unwillingly teams up with Mifune and the two go after the sword and the bandit leader. At first, Bronson attempts to escape and ends up confronting Mifune. Soon the two warriors learn to appreciate each other, depend on each other, and become good friends. They combine their unique talents and go after the bandits, battling them and deadly Commanches to the death. Bronson retrieves the bejeweled sword and leaves it in a safe place for the authorities to find. The film features some nice performances and an interesting bit of chemistry between Bronson's cowboy and Mifune's samurai, two men who know how to play their parts straight and clear.

Rising Sun
(1993) Crime Drama C-129m English R VA
Catalog #8520 USA Retail: $19.95 Widescreen Available
Dir: Philip Kaufman Scr: Michael Backes, Michael Crichton, Philip Kaufman
Prod: Peter Kaufman DP: Michael Chapman
Editor: Stephen A. Rotter, William S. Scharf Music: Toru Takemitsu
Prod Design: Dean Tavoularis Art Design: Angelo Graham
Set Design: Gary Fettis, Peter Kelly, Robert Goldstein
Sp. Fx: Larry L. Fuentes Costumes: Jacqueline West
Dist: CBS/Fox Video
(from the original screenplay based on the novel by Michael Crichton)
Sean Connery   John Connor
Wesley Snipes   Web Smith
Harvey Keitel   Lt. Tom Graham
Cary-Hiroyuki Tagawa Eddie Sakamura
Kevin Anderson   Bob Richmond
Mako   Yoshida-San
Ray Wise   Senator John Morton
Stan Egi   Ishihara

Stan Shaw	Phillips
Tia Carrere	Jingo Asakuma
Steve Buscemi	Willy "The Weasel" Wilhelm
Tatjana Patitz	Cheryl Lynn Austin
Peter Crombie	Greg
Sam Lloyd	Rick
Alexandra Powers	Julia
Daniel von Bargen	Chief Olson - Interrogator
Lauren Robinson	Zelly
Amy Hill	Hsieh
Tom Dahlgren	Jim Donaldson
Clyde Kusatsu	Tanaka
Michael Chapman	Fred Hoffman

[**1/2]
Standard action-drama from mass-market novelist Michael Crichton. The novel was originally criticized for anti-Japanese implications, dealing with political and business corruption, deceit, and espionage. Many of the harsh racial elements were deliberately taken out of the film which becomes a straight-forward buddy-cops film. Sean Connery and Wesley Snipes are police detectives teamed together to solve the mysterious death of a beautiful woman at a Japanese corporation. The only lead is a security camera tape that shows the sexy blonde engaged in rough sex with a mysterious man. Wesley plays the insensitive, ugly American while Connery is the Nipponophile who is a master of Japanese culture and speaks Japanese with a Scottish brogue. They infiltrate the company's hierarchy and come in conflict with the powerful Japanese businessmen led by the ever-ruthless Tagawa. The two men follow a trail of clues and use Crichton's trademark hi-tech skills to discover the real killer. The beautiful Carrere is a half-Asian computer wiz who aids the group.

Sayonara
(1957) Romance   C-147m   English   VA   Catalog #69014
USA   Retail: $19.95 Widescreen Available
Dir: Joshua Logan   Scr: Paul Osborn
Prod: William Goetz DP: Ellsworth Fredricks
Editor: Arthur Schmidt, Philip W. Anderson   Music: Franz Waxman
Art Design: Ted Haworth   Set Design: Robert Priestley
Choreography: LeRoy Prinz   Costume: Norma Koch   Dist: CBS/Fox Video
(based on the novel by James A. Michener)

Marlon Brando	Maj. Lloyd Gruver
Ricardo Montalban	Nakamura
Red Buttons	Joe Kelly
Patricia Owens	Eileen Webster
Martha Scott	Mrs. Webster
James Garner	Capt. Mike Bailey
Miiko Taka	Hana-ogi
Miyoshi Umeki	Katsumi
Kent Smith	Gen. Webster

Douglas Watson	Col. Craford
Reiko Kuba	Fumiko-san
Soo Young	Teruko-san
Harlan Warde	Consul

Shochiku Kagekidan Girls Revue
[***1/2]

Marlon Brando is a dashing officer in the United States Army assigned to a Japanese post during the Korean War. His future father-in-law, a three-star general, plays a part in his career placement which plants doubts in Brando's intended marriage to sweetheart Patricia Owens. While in Japan, he is attracted to a beautiful Asian dancer/actress and pursues the relationship against the recommendations of others. Meanwhile, his close friend (Buttons) falls in love with a sweat Japanese girl (Umeki). He breaks official policies to marry her and endangers his career. Even Brando tries to debate the pros and cons of interracial marriage with his friend, but his frequent visits to their humble home prove their love is stronger than racist bureaucratic mentality. When Buttons receives transfer orders, Brando tries to help his friend and get Umeki a visa. The officials believe good old American cooking and white women will end Buttons Asian folly. The film's takes a tragic turn as Buttons and Umeki struggle to stay together. Their devoted love causes Brando to awaken to the misguided views of the American men and women who he once thought of as friends.

Filmed in the 1950's only a scant few years after the Korean War and World War II in the Pacific, the film's heartbreaking story reflects a true-life situation. Many American soldiers fell in love with Asian women, hoping to bring back their brides to America. In the light of discrimination, many women suffered hardship from racist Americans and also Asians who viewed them as traitors. Women were abandoned by returning soldiers, orphaning many children, and causing great sorrow and hardship.

Faced with a McCarthy-era mentality, the film brings to light the foolish bigotry and racism that still persists today among certain people.

Based on the novel by James Michner. The film was nominated for numerous Academy Awards, including its brilliant performances by Buttons (Best Supporting Actor) and Umeki (Best Supporting Actress) who both took home Oscars. Umeki was the first Asian to win an Academy Award in acting.

Shogun

(1980) Samurai	C-125 m	English/Japanese with English Subtitles	VA
Catalog #22989	USA	Retail: $29.95	
Dir: Jerry London	Music: Maurice Jarre	Prod Design:	
PC: Paramount TV/NBC	Dist: Ingram International/Paramount		
Richard Chamberlain	John Blackthorne		
Toshiro Mifune	Toranaga		
Yoko Shimada	Mariko		

Frankie Sakai, Yuri Meguro, John Rhys-Davies, Michael Hordern
Narrated by Orson Welles
(based on the novel by James Clavell)
[***]

The epic television miniseries based on the James Clavell novel was re-edited and released on a single video tape. I prefer the full-length miniseries which allows for deeper exploration into the characters and a more thorough look into Japanese society and culture. For an in-depth look into Japanese customs of the 16th century, there is no better film for the American viewer. The film which takes place completely in Japan is full of references and classic characters such as ninjas, samurais, and the shogun. I stress if possible, try to view the entire miniseries (550 minutes) instead of the truncated film which cuts many of the fascinating characters and hastens the overall mood of the film. The complete saga is quite ambitious and receives a much higher rating that the short version.

John Blackthorne is a charismatic pilot (navigator) for an English warship that goes down off the coast of Japan. On the behalf of the British navy, his crew is searching for a safe passage route from England to Asia. They are caught in a violent storm and nearly perish, but their ship remains in tact. He and a few surviving crewmates are rescued by the local Japanese lord and arrested. At first, they are treated like barbarians and suffer drastic cultural shock. Slowly, Blackthorine adapts to Japanese customs, takes the name Anjin-san, and falls in love with his beautiful translator, Mariko. Thus begins an incredible journey into Japan's history which eventually leads to friendship with the Shogun, played by Mifune. Along the way, he becomes a samurai, learns Japanese, duels ninjas, and confronts the Portuguese delegates who want Japan for themselves. Hoping to stay true to the novel, Shogun features dramatic scenes of violence, prosecution, and a good amount of Japanese with English subtitles.

Showdown in Little Tokyo
(1991) Kung-Fu   C-78m English   R   VA
Catalog #25944   USA   Retail: $19.95
Dir: Mark L. Lester Scr: Caliope Brattlestreet   Prod: Martin E, Caan, Mark L. Lester
DP: Mark Irwin   Editor: Michael Eliot   Music: David Michael Frank
Prod Design: John C. Broderick, Craig Stearns   Set Design: Ellen Totleben
Costume: Robyn Smith   Stunts: Terry J. Leonard
Dist: Warner
Brandon Lee   Johnny Murata
Dolph Lundgren   Chris Kenner
Tia Carrere   Minako Okeya
Cary-Hiroyuki Tagawa   Yoshida
Reid Asato   Muta
Philip Tan   Tanaka
[**]

A somewhat forgettable, but fun movie with mixed results, so tread cautiously and decide how much you enjoy watching Brandon Lee and Dolph Lundrgen. Not to sound biased, but American martial arts films rarely match up to the speed, energy, and excitement of Asian kung-fu films. Classic East meets West, but with a unique twist when the roles are reversed. Asian-American Brandon and Dolph are both martial arts experts who happen to be cops teamed together to battle the Yakuza (Japan's mob) led by perennial villain Tagawa. Lee is an Asian who loves hot dogs, rock and roll, and the American way of life while non-Asian Lundgren is a Zen master who speaks Japanese and follows the code of Bushido based on his long expertise in Asian culture. The two don't see eye to eye, but end up fighting their way to victory and sharing some philosophy along the way. Their styles are different and the two cops bicker as much as they fight, but in a fun-spirited way. They try to impress each other with their respective fighting styles, but Brandon (cocky American) enjoys showing off with a more energetic and acrobatic style. How's that, he gloats. Dolph asks when he started training. Brandon proudly replies, since I was a kid. Dolph coldly replies, you should have started younger, and dismisses the whining Brandon. They eventually follow their leads and infiltrate the enemy stronghold and battle from one room to another, dispatching sword-wielding assassins from every corner. The two heroes trap the Yakuza boss and deliver his just award. A Hollywood action/martial arts film that looks like a romp in kindergarten when compared to the dark, nihilistic, and bloody Triad films from Hong Kong.

Snow Falling on Cedars
(1997) Drama/Romance C-128m English
PG-13 VA   USA
Dir: Scott Hicks   Scr: Ron Bass, Scott Hicks
Ex. Prod: Carol Baum, Lloyd A. Silverman
Prod: Kathleen Kennedy, Frank Marshall, Harry J. Ufland, Ron Bass
DP: Robert Richardson   Editor: Hank Corwin
Music: James Newton Howard
Production Design: Jeannine Claudia Oppewall   Art Direction: Doug Byggdin
Set Decoration: Jim Erickson   Costume Design: Renee Ehrlich Kalfus
PC: Universal Pictures, The Kennedy & Marshall Company   Dist: Universal Pictures

Ethan Hawke	**Ishmael Chambers**
Youki Kudoh	**Hatsue Miyamoto**
Reeve Carney	**Young Ishmael Chambers**
Ann Suzuki	**Young Hatsue Imada**
Rick Yune	**Kazuo Miyamoto**
Max von Sydow	**Nels Gudmundsson**
James Rebhorn	**Alvin Hooks**
James Cromwell	**Judge Fielding**
Richard Jenkins	**Sheriff Art Moran**
Arija Bareikis	**Susan Marie Heine**
Eric Thal	**Carl Heine Jr.**
Celia Weston	**Etta Heine**
Daniel von Bargen	**Carl Heine**
Akira Takayama	**Hisao Imada**
Ako	**Fujiko Imada**
Cary-Hiroyuki Tagawa	**Zenhichi Miyamoto**
Zak Orth	**Deputy Abel Martinson**
Max Wright	**Horace Whaley**
Sam Shepard	**Arthur Chambers**
Caroline Kava	**Helen Chambers**
Jan Rubes	**Ole Jurgensen**
Sheila Moore	**Liesel Jurgensen**
Zeljko Ivanek	**Dr. Whitman**
Seiji Inouye	**Young Kazuo Miyamoto**

Saemi Nakamura	Sumiko Imada
Mika Fujii	Yukiko Imada
Dwight McFee	Bus Driver
Bill Harper	Levant
Reng Jiang Xi	Nagaishi
Myles Ferguson	German Soldier
Noah Heney	Ship's Doctor
John Destrey	Bailiff
A. Arthur Takemoto	Buddhist Priest
Ken Takemoto	Monk

[***]

An enchanting story set right after World War II in the scenic community of San Piedro Island in Washington State, based on the novel by David Guterson. A murder mystery laced with post-war anti-Japanese sentiments and interracial love focus on a fictional town and its characters. Well made but rather forgetful and formulaic, the film features Ethan Hawk as the town's newspaper editor who defends Kazuo, a Japanese American accused of killing Carl Heine, a local fisherman. Of course both main charcaters are honorable war veterans that fought for the United States and both men are in love with the same woman. A love triangle with plenty of stereotypical characters in the background that support or dissuade the main plot themes. Friendship and relationships are tested before and after the war, while bitterness, regret, and prejudice are complexly examined and revealed. The film was nominated for an Academy Award for Best Cinematography and features a beautiful portrayal of the northwest scenery and small town life. If you can figure out the ending of the film through the initial summary, you are correct.

Tai-Pan
(1986) Historical Drama   C-130m   English   R   VA   USA
Dir: Daryl Duke   Scr: John Briley   Prod: Raffaella de Laurentiis
DP: Jack Cardiff   Editor: Antony Gibbs   Music: Maurice Jarre
Art Dir/Prod Design: Pier Luigi Basile, Benjamin Fernandez
Set Design: Giorgio Desideri   Makeup: Giannetto de Rossi
Sp. Fx: Kit West   Stunts: Vic Armstrong
PC: DEG   Dist: Vestron Video

Bryan Brown	Dirk Struan
Joan Chen	May-May
Bill Leadbitter	Gorth
Bert Remsen	Tillman
John Stanton	Brock
Kyra Sedgwick	Tess
Tim Guinee	Culum
Russell Wong	Gordon
Janine Turner	Shevaun

[**]

Based on the brilliant novel by James Clavell, Tai-Pan is a romantic adventure that mixes intrigue, interracial love, political power, and historical drama. A great admirer of the novel (lengthy), I found difficulty in accepting Brown as the title character. The film fails to capture the vast nuances and intrigues placed down in the text of a European robber baron who travels to 19th Century China. A Tai-Pan is a powerful leader, a shrewd businessman who commands wealth, influence, and respect. Bryan Brown is such a man and has built an empire in Hong Kong. He is a Scottish trader who appears to be a regular businessman, but his secret life is that of a ruthless, powerful godfather of Chinese trade. The film follows his exploits and his love for a Chinese woman, Joan Chen. His enemies are more than eager to see him fall from power. Treachery and betrayal lie behind every corner, but the Tai-Pan is a resourceful man who meets each challenge head on. Tai-Pan's film production company was the first major company to film in mainland China. The book is followed by a literary sequel, The Noble House.

Tarzan's Three Challenges
(1963) Adventure   C-92m English   Not Rated   USA
Dir: Robert Day   Scr: Berne Giler, Robert Day   Prod: Sy Weintraub
DP: Ted Scaife   Editor: Fred Burnley   Music: Joseph Horovitz
Music Dir: Marcus Dods   Prod Design: Wilfred Shingleton
Sp. Fxs: Cliff Richardson, Roy Whybrow Makeup: Freddie Williamson
PC/Dist: Fox
(based on the characters created by Edgar Rice Burroughs)

Jock Mahoney	Tarzan
Woody Strode	Khan/Tarim
Tsuruko Kobayashi	Cho-San
Earl Cameron	Mang
Salah Jamal	Hani
Anthony Chinn	Tor
Robert Hu	Nari
Christopher Carlos	Sechung
Ricky Der	Kashi
Hungry the Elephant	

[**1/2]

Tarzan, the great white warrior from Africa, takes a trip to exotic Thailand and befriends the rightful heir to the throne. Though Tarzan spends most of his time in Africa, he occasionally earns frequent flyer mileage by visiting the United States and Asia. A young boy named Cho-San is the chosen spiritual/political leader of Thailand, but his muscular uncle Khan has visions of the throne for him and his son. He decides to eliminate the adorable Cho-San and anyone who gets in his way. Unfortunately for Khan, Tarzan is in Thailand and uses his athletic prowess to defeat the rifle-wielding assassins. Cho-San makes it to the coronation ceremony and passes the three tests, but Khan challenges him to an ancient ceremonial duel. Tarzan accepts in Cho-San's place and prepares for the gruelling competition. The two nearly-naked men are strapped together at the wrists and must run to the palace and battle over a mesh net suspended over boiling tubs of oil. One slip means the end of your life and the fate of Thailand. Along the way Tarzan meets an attractive Thai woman, a noble Thai leader, and an adorable little elephant named Hungry. In today's spectrum of muscle-bound actors, Mahoney is competent but has the look of a middle-aged yachtsman instead of a fierce jungle warrior. Completely shot in Thailand with some nice scenic locales and background costumes. The film is dated and doesn't carry much in the way of impressive action, but will appeal to people who enjoy light-weight adventure tales and a predictable premise.

Teenage Mutant Ninja Turtles 3
(1993) Fantasy   C-95m English   PG   VA
Catalog #27428   USA   Retail: $19.95
Dir/Scr: Stuart Gillard   Prod: David Chan, Dale Chan, Raymond Chow, Kim Dawson
DP: David Gurfinkel Editor: William D. Gordean, James Symons
Music: John Du Prez   Art Dir/Prod Design: Mayne Schuyler Berke
Set Design: Ronald R. Reiss Dist: New Line Cinema/Columbia
Elias Koteas   Casey Jones/Whit Whitley
Paige Turco   April O'Neal
Stuart Wilson   Dirk Walker
Sab Shimono   Lord Norinaga
Vivian Wu   Mitsu
[**]

A blend of martial arts, comedy, far-fetched fantasy, and slapstick lunacy, the teenage mutant ninja turtles are a quartet of crime fighting turtles who can talk, eat pizza, and perform ninjutsu. Based on a popular comic book, the turtle phenomenon swept the nation with a massive media/product blitz. The first film is the best in the series and features some fine Asian-style martial arts and should be viewed first. I've included the third film for review, because of its prominent use of Asian characters and settings.

Not surprisingly, in every American-made series dealing with martial arts, there is always one film which includes a trek to the ancient land of Asia (the home of martial arts). Karate Kid 2's trip was to Okinawa, Three Ninjas Kick Back went back to Japan, and even the Bad News Bears (it's a sport) played against a Japanese baseball team.

The four shellheads, Donatello, Leonardo, Michelangelo, and Raphael, are back for their last outing and travel to 17th century Japan to rescue reporter April O'Neal, the turtles long-time guardian and friend. Along the way, they have east meets west clashes with the local Japanese villagers. They help a Japanese woman (Wu) against an evil samurai lord and English pirates. Plenty of traditional style weapons and armor from the samurai era meet the modern day hijinks of the irreverent turtles. Mindless fun and mayhem geared toward kids rather than adults, but somewhat appealing for fans who enjoyed the first two films (TMNT: The Movie [***], TMNT2 [**]).

They Call Me Bruce?   (A Fistful of Chopsticks)
(1982) Comedy   C-88m English   PG   USA
Dir: Elliot Hong   Scr: Tim Clawson   Prod: Elliot Hong
DP: Robert Primes   Music: Tommy Vig   Prod Design: Ivi Cristante
PC: Artists Releasing Corp. Dist: Vestron Video
Johnny Yune   Bruce
Margaux Hemingway   Karmen
Pam Huntington   Anita
Ralph Mauro   Freddy
Martin Azarow   Big Al

[**]
Do you remember this film? Some of the scenes and lines are quite memorable, including Yune's likeable performance as a bumbling simpleton who looks like Bruce Lee. He gets into plenty of trouble with local thugs and must talk his way out of the situation without fighting.

They Still Call Me Bruce?
(1986) Comedy   C-91m English   PG   USA
Dir/Scr/Prod: Johnny Yune, James Orr   DP: Michael R. Delahoussaye
Editor: Roy Watts   Music: Morton Stevens   Art Dir: Jeff McManus
PC: Sharpiro Entettainment   Dist: New World Entertainment
Johnny Yune   Bruce Won
Robert Guillaume   V.A. Officer
David Mendenhall   Orphan
Pat Paulsen   Psychiatrist
Joey Travolta   Joey
Donald Gibb, James Orr, Bethany Wright
[*1/2]
For a short period in time, Johnny Yune was a recognizable and popular comedian appearing as a guest on Love Boat, MASH, and other popular shows of the early decade. His deadpan delivery and deprecating humor was light-heartened and charming in a harmless sort of way. His second venture into film meets with little results as Yune tries to capitalize on the popularity of his goofy, but wimpy persona. Yune searches for the man who saved his life as a child and comes across a chance to do the same for an orphan. He joins the boy and the community, hoping to make it a better place.

Thousand Pieces of Gold
(1991) DramaC-105m   English   PG-13   USA
Dir/Prod: Nancy Kelly   Scr: Anne Makepeace   Prod: Sarah   Green,   Sidney
Kantor, Nancy Kelly, Lindsay Law, Rachel Lyon, John Sham, Kenji Yamamoto
DP: Bobby Bukowski   Editor: Kenji Yamamoto   Music: Gary Remal Malking
Prod Design: Dan Bishop   Set Design: Dianna Treas   Costume: Lydia Tanji
PC: Greycat   Dist: Hemdale Home Video/Ingram International Films
Rosalind Chao   Lalu Nathoy/Polly Bemis
Chris Cooper   Charlie
Michael Paul Chan Hong King
Dennis Dun   Li Po/Jim
Jimmie F. Skaggs   Jonas
Will Oldham   Miles
Evan Kim   Shun Lee
Kim Chan   Li Ping
Mary Lee   Li Yuan
Jianli Zhang   Chen
[***]
A touching period-piece about a young Chinese woman who learns the harsh reality of life when she is sold into servitude in America. Rosalind Chao is a beautiful Chinese woman who dreams

of going to America to find work and a new life. Her poor parents sell her to a marriage broker who finds wives for Chinese men working in the United States. Unfortunately, they are deceived and she is sold as a prostitute, basically indenturing her to a slave like status. She is placed in a small encampment of miners in Idaho, mostly of European descent. Her lack of English and pretty face bring out the worst in the local miners. The shop owner who bought her forces her to submit, but Lalu is tough-spirited and fights back. She is accosted and propositioned constantly. A kind American man (Dun) takes pity on her and buys her out of her slavery contract. At first she distrusts his intentions and treads cautiously around him. A hardworking Chinese miner (Chan) is interested in marrying her but when he discovers her living with Dun, he jumps to conclusions, curses her, and abandons the crying woman. Not able to go back to China, she works at a laundry and struggles to support herself. Slowly, she learns more about Dun, realizing there's more to the man than his skin color. The two fall in love and slowly develop a trusting relationship. Based on a true story and similar to Kayo Hatta's Picture Bride. Chao is the standout, giving a strong and moving performance. It's unfortunate that more films have not featured this talented actress.

Three Ninjas Kick Back
(1994) Family/Comedy/Martial Arts   C-99m English   PG   VA
Catalog #27607   USA   Retail: $19.95
Dir: Charles Kanganis   Scr: Mark Saltzman   Prod: Yoram Ben-Ami, Martha Chang, James Kang, Arthur Leeds, Simon Sheen
DP: Christopher Faloona, Nobuhito Noda Editor: Jeffrey Reiner, David Rennie
Music: Rick Marvin   Art Dir: Scott Meehan
Prod Design: Greg Martin, Hiroyuki Takatsu   Set Design: Karin Mcgaughey
Costume: Miye Matsumoto, Takeshi Yamazaki
Dist: Columbia

Victor Wong	Grandpa
Max Elliott Slade	Colt
Sean Fox	Rocky
Evan Bonifant	Tum Tum
Caroline Junko King	Miyo
Dustin Nguyen	Glam
Sab Shimono	Koga

Margarita Franco, Jason Schombing, Alan McRae, Angelo Tiffe, Joey Travolta
[**1/2]
Juvenile, slapstick fun for children who want to grow up to be ninjas. Sequel to the popular "3 Ninjas" and followed by "3 Ninjas Knuckle Up", the second film replaces the American setting with an adventurous trip to Japan. In almost every American series dealing with martial arts, the American practitioners return to the country where the style was created. So the three cute ninja brothers pack up and arrive in Japan, escorting a very special short sword. The bad guys led by ex-21 Jump Street star Dustin Nguyen and a bunch of surfing losers are ordered to get the sword, but manage to get into more trouble on their own.
The brothers journey to a martial arts tournament held at a remote monastery. There they witness some impressive ninjutsu and marvel at a fighting champion who turns out to be a girl. The three ninjas must protect the sword while keeping it out of the hands of the villains. They

befriend the cute ninja girl and the four combine their martial arts and comic timing to make fools out of any opponent. In the end, all works out well. The film's whole atmosphere is light-hearted and fun without any offensive scenes of violence. Interestingly, the music in the film's background is not Japanese, but a Korean rap song. A good way to keep your children occupied for an hour or two while you do something better.

Tokyo Pop
(1988) Romantic Comedy   C-99m English & Subtitled R   VA
USA   Retail: $19.95
Dir: Fran Rubel Kazui   Scr: Lynn Grossman, Fran Rubel Kazui
Prod: Kaz Kuzui, Joel Tuber   DP: James Hayman
Editor: Camilla Toniolo   Music: Alan Brewer   Dist: Warner
(based on a story by Fran Rubel Kazui)

Carrie Hamilton	Wendy Reed
Yutaka Tadokoro	Hiro Yamaguchi
Taiji Tonoyama	Grandfather
Tetsuro Tamba	Dota
Masumi Harukawa	Mother
Toki Shiozawa	Mama-san
Hiroshi Mikami	Seki
Miker Cerveris	Mike
Gina Belafonte	Holly
Daisuke Oyama	Yoji
Hiroshi Kobayashi	Kaz
Hiroshi Sugita	Taro
Satoshi KanaiShun	

[**1/2]

A sweet and cute little film that captures the essence of a naive American girl living in Japan. Young Carrie Hamilton is an American girl who tires of her aimless life in the United States. She decides to pack her bags and look for opportunities in Japan. She is a singer and tries to get a job, but most Japanese look at her with novelty. Luckily Carrie hooks up with a Japanese musician who asks her to join the band. At first, there's friction and a cultural barrier, but the two find a meeting point and fall for each other. Light-weight comedy with a fish out of water appeal and other similar elements that popularized the romantic comedies of the 1980's. Carrie Hamilton is the daughter of comedic genius Carol Burnett and makes a positive debut.

World of Suzie Wong, The
(1960) Romance   C-129m   English   VA
Catalog #23367   USA   Retail: $19.95
Dir: Richard Quine   Scr: John Patrick   Prod: Ray Stark
DP: Geoffrey Unsworth   Editor: Bert Bates   Music: George Duning
Art Design: John Box   Dist: Paramount
(based on the novel by Richard Mason and the play by Paul Osborn)

William Holden	Robert Lomax
Nancy Kwan	Suzie Wong

Sylvia Syms	Kay O'Neill
Michael Wilding	Ben
Laurence Naismith	Mr. O'Neill
Jacqui Chan	Gwenny Lee
Andy Ho	Ah Tong
Bernard Cribbins	Otis
Yvonne Shima	Minnie Ho
Lier Hwang	Wednesday Lu
Robert Lee	Barman
Ronald Eng	Waiter
Calvin Hsai	Suzie's Baby

[**1/2]

Young, frail Asian beauty Nancy Kwan is a naive prostitute (though a saintly Hollywood one, thanks to the era) who leads a very carefree life on the streets of Hong Kong. She meets an American artist who is kind to her and tries to help her. Interested in him, Kwan lies about her profession and background, hoping to impress the dashing gentleman. At first Holden has no romantic interest in Kwan, and his dealings with her causes insufferable complications in his own personal life. Frustrated he becomes antagonistic, but eventually falls in love with the Asian woman especially after a flood nearly kills her and destroys her village (an elaborate film set). The soap opera-ish format wavers between serious drama and romantic comedy never finding sure footing. The film is interesting for its then rare shoots of actual Hong Kong locales and Nancy Kwan's charming performance. The popular Westerner in the far east plot and the aspects of interracial relationships are explored. Interestingly, when interracial films are produced by non-Asians the woman is Asian while Asian productions often feature a non-Asian woman with an Asian man. Not a rule, but definitely a fact of life that men make the films, and each society has a fascination and desire for women of another race. The grass is always greener on the other side of the Pacific Ocean.

The Yakuza   (Brotherhood of the Yakuza)
(1975) Action C-112m   English   R   VA
Catalog #25587   USA   Retail: $19.95 Widescreen Available
Dir/Prod: Sydney Pollack   Scr: Paul Schrader, Robert Towne
DP: Okazaki Kozo, Duke Callaghan
Editor: Fredric Steinkamp, Thomas Stanford, Don Guidice
Music: Dave Grusin Prod Design: Stephen Grimes   Art Design: Ishida Yoshiyuki
Sp Fx: Richard Parker, Kasai Tomoo   Makeup: Gary Morris
Costume: Dorothy Jeakinsr   Dist: Warner
(based on a story by Leonard Schrader)

Robert Mitchum	Harry Kilmer
Ken Takakura	Tanaka Ken
Brian Keith	George Tanner
Herb Edelman	Oliver Wheat
Richard Jordan	Dusty
Kishi Keiko	Tanaka Eiko
Okada Eiji	Tono Toshiro

James Shigeta	Goro
Kyosuke Mashida	Kato Jiro
Christina Kokubo	Hanako
Go Eiji	Spider
M. Hisaka	Boy Friend
Akiyama	Tono's Bodyguard
Harada	Goro's Doorman

[**1/2]

Sadly, veteran actor Robert Mitchum passed away shortly before I wrote this review. He truly was a marvelous screen presence with dozens of memorable roles and an equally fascinating personal life. I can't say this is one of his most notable films, but his presence does assist this dated-action piece. A chiselled, aged Mitchum is Harry Kilmer, a tough ex-GI experienced in the ways of Asian culture. He gets a call from an old army buddy who desperately needs his help. Gathering his life together, Mitchum accepts and returns to Japan after his long hiatus in the United States. His mission is to rescue buddy Keith's kidnapped daughter before something horrible happens to her. He gets more than he bargained for from the Yakuza mob, but manages to get some much needed help from a past Japanese acquaintance. Standard action fare with the Western in the East plot, spiced up with Hollywood action, locale shooting, and character chemistry. Mitchum and Takakura are fine in this suspenseful action film which suffers from time and the newer mob/action films from Hong Kong directors. Originally shown at 123 minutes, but edited down in various versions.

Year of the Dragon
(1985) Action C-136m   English   R   VA
Catalog #21557   USA   Retail: $19.95 Widescreen Available
Dir: Michael Cimino Scr: Michael Cimino, Oliver Stone
Prod: Dino De Laurentiis   DP: Alex Thomson   Editor: Françoise Bonnot
Music: David Mansfield   Prod Design: Wolf Kroeger
Set Design: Robert Drumheller, Randy Ostrow, Gretchen Rau, Richard Kane
Art Design: Vicki Paul   Costume: Marietta Ciriello   Dist: MGM
(based on the novel by Robert Daley)

Mickey Rourke	Stanley White
John Lone	Joey Tai
Ariane	Tracy Tzu
Leonard Termo	Angelo Rizzo
Raymond J. Barry	Louis Bukowski
Caroline Kava	Connie White
Eddie Jones	William McKenna
Joey Chin	Ronnie Chang
Victor Wong	Harry Yung
K. Dock Yip	Milton Bin
Jimmy Sun	Elders
Daniel Davin	Francis Kearney
Mark Hammer	Commissioner
Dennis Dun	Herbert Kwong

Jack Kehler	Alan Perez
Steven Chen	Tony Ho
Paul Scaglione	Teddy Tedesco
Joseph Bonaventura	Lagnese
Jilly Rizzo	Schiro
Tisa Chang	Nuns
Gerald Orange	Bear Siku
Fan Mui Sang	White Powder Ma
Yukio Yamamoto	Ban Sung
Doreen Chan	Red Hair
Harry Yip	Old General
Dermot McNamara	Scappy Peck
Vallo Benjamin	DEA Man
Myra Chen	Shanghai Palace Singer
Johnny Shia	Chia
James Scales	Connie's Assassin
Ming C. Lee	Jackie Wong
Kader Ma	Jackie Wong's Assassin
Paul Lee	Jackie Wong's Son
Manny Fung	Jackie Wong's 2nd Son
Emily Woo	Mrs. Wong
Roza Ng	Laura Wong Tai
Gloria Au	Joey Tai's Daughter
Jadin Wong	Mrs. Harry Yung
Lin Ngan Ng	Chinese Widow
Janice Wong	Tina
Cecelia Pei	Harry Yung's Secretary
Quan Eng	Mortician

[**1/2]

Mickey Rourke (remember him) is a jaded police chief who decides to launch his own personal war against the Triads of Chinatown, New York. A violent Triad-internal war has erupted and the mayor demands results to quell the negative media coverage. Rourke comes into direct conflict with the charismatic gangster boss (Lone) who has his own plans of taking over the city. Rourke starts a romantic relationship with a bright Chinese-American woman and must explore his own hostilities and racism that motivate his hatred. The action gets tense as gangsters battle each other and the police. A beautifully shot film from veteran director Cimino who attempts to uncover the corruption and violence of New York City's Chinatown. Rourke's character gets ugly at times, revealing his own weakness and prejudice. Lone is superior as the suave, upscale crime boss who shakes hands with politicians while ordering the assassination of his rivals. In film after film, Lone's characters are convincing and charismatic but his acting talents are never given the praise it deserves.

You Only Live Twice
(1967) Action C-125m   English   PG   VA
Catalog #23735   USA   Retail: $19.95 Widescreen Available

Dir: Lewis Gilbert   Scr: Roald Dahl, Harold Jack Bloom
Prod: Albert R. Broccoli, Harry Saltzman

DP: Freddie Young	Editor: Peter Hunt	Music: John Barry
Prod Design: Ken Adam	Art Design: Harry Pottle	Set Design: David Ffolkes
Sp. Fx: John Stears	Makeup: Basil Newall, Paul Rabiger	

Costumes: Eileen Sullivan
(based on the novel by Ian Fleming)
Dist: MGM/UA

Sean Connery	James Bond
Akiko Wakabayashi	Aki
Donald Pleasence	Ernst Stavro Blofeld
Tetsuro Tamba	Tiger Tanaka
Mie Hama	Kissy Suzuki
Teru Shimada	Osato
Karin Dor	Helga Brandt
Lois Maxwell	Miss Moneypenny
Desmond Llewelyn	"Q"
Charles Gray	Henderson
Tsai Chin	Chinese Girl
Bernard Lee	"M"
Burt Kwouk	SPECTRE No. 3
Michael Chow	SPECTRE No. 4

[***]

The only Bond film to feature Asian main characters in a completely Asian setting. The film was shot primarily in Japan (China and Southeast Asia were the sites for The Man with the Golden Gun, but Asian characters did not play a prominent role). Sean Connery is British Secret Service Agent 007, license to kill. One of my personal favorites, You Only Live Twice was the fifth 007 film in a continuing series of spy adventures, and due to the difficulties of filming and the pressure of stardom, Sean Connery vowed it would be his last.

Though not the best in the series, You Only Live Twice includes a number of interesting characters and spectacular action scenes that hold its own. The outlandish plot deals with SPECTRE, a global criminal network led by a bald, would-be dictator named Ernst Stavro Blofeld. SPECTRE uses a secret launching base in Japan to steal manned spaceships from the United States and the USSR. Both countries blame the other of sabotage and war seems imminent in this cold war adventure. Under orders from the British government, Bond is sent to investigate the situation and to stop SPECTRE's diabolical plan. As only Bond can, he seduces women, gathers clues, and kills all his opponents before destroying the enemy spaceship and saving the world.

Opting for a primarily Asian cast and backdrop was something unique for the Bond series, which has not been repeated since. The film did not relegate Asian characters into minor stereotypical roles, but instead featured fully developed and proudly portrayed villains, heroines, and heroes. Bond's main ally is Japanese Secret Service Chief Tiger Tanaka well played by Testuro Tamba. Tanaka is bright, suave and confident, an equal to James Bond in many respects. Though chief of Japanese Intelligence, he is a hands on agent who joins the fray and fights side by side with Bond. The evil front man for SPECTRE is Osato, a rich Japanese businessman under the thumb of Blofeld. His beautiful assistant is played by Karin Dor, a German actress.

And of course, what would a Bond film be without its women. You Only Live Twice features three lovely Asian women in the film. Ling plays the Chinese actress in the teaser who gets to seduce and assassinate Bond. On the side of good, Agents Aki and Kissy are women of intelligence, beauty and resourcefulness. They work for Tiger Tanaka and are highly trained agents, beautiful but deadly. No other Bond film has ever featured an Asian actress as the main love interest. In one of the more ludicrous scenes to applaud, Connery undergoes cosmetic surgery to look like a Japanese villager. No amount of makeup will ever make Connery look Japanese, but suspend your disbelief as he marries agent Kissy and goes undercover in a remote fishing village. Bond is captured by Blofeld and enters his massive underground fortress, a truly impressive set. As the clock counts down, Blofeld plans to start World War III and only Bond and his allies can save the world.

A number of other Asian characters are portrayed including Kissy's Japanese village and Tanaka's 100-man Ninja army that storms the volcano base at the climatic end. Though dated, the film features plenty of on site locations including Japan's metropolitan cities and its island countryside. A classic bond film that takes advantage of the popular ninja/samurai themes from classic Japanese films, reworking them into a modern action film.

THANK YOU
DOMO ARIGATO GOZAIMASU
KAM SA HAMNIDA
SYEN SYEN NI

APPENDICES

Appendix I (Genre/Country Picks)

Appendix II (All-Time Favorites)

Appendix III (Who's Who in Asian Cinema)

Appendix IV (Filmography)

Appendix V (Distributors & Retail Outlets)

Appendix VI (Conventions & Internet Sources)

Appendix VII (Glossary)

Appendix VIII (Bibliography)

Name Index

Appendix I (Genre/Country Picks)

Genre fans are a common breed of film lover. People who prefer to watch a particular style of film, often regardless of critical merit to achieve a level of satisfaction and entertainment. They're devoted to a particular genre to a passionate degree and eagerly seek out any and all films within a specific genre.There's a key element that strengthens the appeal and eclipses other standard elements of the filmmaking. I should know, I'm a huge genre fan myself and will automatically rent any martial arts or monster film regardless of who stars, directs, or produces. Perhaps you love only anime, kung-fu, girls with guns, or Godzilla movies, well then you're in luck. The following is a list of Asian films categorized purely by genre and country of origin/setting. For those who are genre fans exclusively, I have included additional films not reviewed in the book. Have fun and enjoy a movie tonight.

Chinese Historical Dramas
The Blue Kite
The Emperor and The Assassin
Farewell, My Concubine
The Go Masters
Ju Dou
The Last Emperor
Life on a String
Peking Opera Blues
Raise the Red Lantern
Red Dust
Red Sorghum
Shanghai Triad
The Silk Road
The Story of Qiu Ju
Tempest Moon
To Live

Hong Kong Action (May Combine Comedy, Sex, and who knows what else.)
Aces Go Places 1
Aces Go Places 2
Aces Go Places 3
Aces Go Places 4
Aces Go Places 5
An Eye for an Eye
Angel
Angel 2
Angel 3
Angel Mission
Angel of Vengeance
Angel or Whore

Angel Terminators
Angel Terminators 2
Angel, The
Armour of the Gods
Armour of the Gods 2: "Operation Condor"
Arrest the Restless
Beauty Inspectors
Best Friend of the Cop
Best of the Best
Better Tomorrow 2, A
Better Tomorrow 3, A
Better Tomorrow, A
Big Brawl
Big Heat, The
Big Score
Black Cat
Black Cat 2
Black Morning Glory, The
Black Panther
Black Panther Warriors
Blood Money
Bloody Fight, A
Bloody Morning
Bodyguard from Beijing, The
Bogus Cops
Bullet for Hire
Bullet in the Head
Case of the Cold Fish
Casino Raiders
Casino Raiders 2
Casino Tycoon
Chaos by Design

Cheetah on Fire
Cherry Blossoms
Chez'n Ham
China Girls
China White
Chinatown Kid
City Cops
City Hunter
City Kids
City on Fire
City War
Code of Honour
Cop Image
Countdown in Kung Fu
Crime Story
Crossings
Crucifixion, The
Crying Freeman
Crystal Fortune Run
Crystal Hunter
Day Without Policeman, A
Days of Being Wild
Days of Tomorrow
Deadly Deal
Deadly Dream Woman
Demon Fighter
Descendant of the Sun
Devil's Sorcery
Devil's Vendetta
Diary of a Big Man
Dignified Killers
Doctor Lamb
Doctor Vampire
Doctor's Heart
Don't Give a Damn
Don't Play with Fire
Don't Stop My Crazy Love for You
Dragon Forever
Dreadnought
Dust in the Wind
Dynamo
Eastern Condors
Executioner, The
Fantasy Mission Force
Fatal Game, The

Fatal Recall
Fatal Termination
Father and Son
Fearless Match
Fight Back to School
Fight Back to School 2
Fight Back to School 3
Fight for Survival
Figures from Earth
Final Judgement, The
Final Justice
Final Test, The
First Mission
First Shot
First Time is the Last Time
Fists of Fury 1991
Fists of Fury 1991 Part 2
Forbidden Arsenal
Force of the Dragon
Fortune Code
Full Contact
Full Moon in New York
Full Throttle
Future Cops
Game of Death
God of Gamblers
God of Gamblers 2
God of Gamblers 3
Gold Hunter
Golden Queens Commando
Goodbye Hero
Guardian Angel
Gun and Roses
Gun of Dragon
Gunmen
Guns & Roses
Hapkido
Hard Boiled
Hard Way to Die, A
Haunted Cop 2
Head Hunter, The
Heart Against Heart
Heart of a Killer
Her Fatal Ways
Her Fatal Ways 2

Her Fatal Ways 3
Her Fatal Ways 4
Her Judgement Day
Her Vengeance
Hero
Hero of Hong Kong
Heroic Trio
Heroic Trio 2: Executioners
Hidden Desire
Hidden Fortress, The
High Risk
Highway
Hong Kong Godfather
Hong Kong Playboys
Hot Blood
In the Line of Duty
In the Line of Duty 2
In the Line of Duty 3
In the Line of Duty 4
In the Line of Duty 5
Incorruptible
Incorruptible, The
Incredibly Strange Films
Inspector Wears Skirts
Inspector Wears Skirts 2
Inspector Wears Skirts 3
Inspector Wears Skirts 4
Killer, The
My Father is a Hero 2
My Lucky Stars
Midnight Angel
Naked Killer
Peace Hotel
Police Story
Police Story 2
Project A
Project A 2
Protector, The
The Rapist
Return of the Dragon
Return of a Killer
Ring of Death
Rumble in the Bronx
She Shoots Straight
Supercop

Superpower
Thunderbolt
Twinkle, Twinkle Lucky Stars
Velvet Gloves
When Tae Kwon Do Strikes
Wicked City
Wong vs. Wong

Hong Kong "Girls with Guns"
Angel (Iron Angels)
Angel 2 (Iron Angels 2)
Angel 3 (aka Iron Angels 3)
Angel Enforcers
Angel Hunter
Angel's Project
Angel of Vengeance
Angel Terminators
Angel Terminators 2
Angel's Mission (Kicking Buddha)
Avenging Quartet
Beauty Inspector (Beauty Investigator)
Black Cat
Black Morning Glory, The
Bogus Cops
A Book of Heroes
Boys Are Easy
Brave Young Girls
Braveful Police
Burning Ambition
Bury Me High
City Cops
Combat at Heaven Gate
Crystal Hunt
Devil Hunters
Dignified Killers
The Direct Line
Dreaming the Reality
Fantasy Mission Force
Fatal Chase
Fatal Termination
Forbidden Arsenal
Golden Queen's Commando (aka Commando Amazon / Amazon Commando)
Guardian Angel
Heroic Trio

Heroic Trio 2: Executioners
I Love Maria (Roboforce)
In the Line of Duty (Royal Warriors)
In the Line of Duty 2: Middleman
In the Line of Duty 3 (Force of the Dragon, Yes Madam 2)
In the Line of Duty 4
In the Line of Duty 5
Inspector Wears Skirts 1 (aka Top Squad)
Kick Boxer's Tears
Killer Angels
Lady Super Cop
Lethal Panther
Lethal Panther 2
License to Steal
Lucky Seven 2
Madam City Hunter
Magnificent Warriors
Midnight Angel
Mission of Justice
Naked Killer
The Nocturnal Demon
On Parole
Outlaw Brothers
Passionate Killing in the Dream
Pink Force Commando
Police Story 3: Supercop
Princess Madam (Under Police Protection)
Queen's High
Raped by an Angel (Naked Killer 2)
Righting Wrongs (Above the Law)
Righting Wrongs 2: Blonde Fury / Lady Reporter (Above the Law 2)
Robotrix
Satin Steel
Sea Wolves
She Shoots Straight
Story of a Gun
Police Story 4: Project S (Once a Cop)
Tiger Cage 2.
Ultracop 2000
Way of the Lady Boxers (aka Madam the Great)
Wonder 7
Yes Madam '92: A Serious Shock

Yes Madam!

India
Aparajito
The Bandit Queen
The Big City
City of Joy
The Deceivers
Distant Thunder
An Enemy of the People
Gandhi
The Home and the World
The Householder
Kama Sutra
Mississippi Masala
Oather Panchali
The River
Salaam Bombay!
Shakespeare Wallah
Shalimar
Two Daughters
World of Apu

Japanese Animation "Anime"
8th Man After
AD Police
Adventure Kid
Ai City
Akai Hayate
Akira
Ambassador Manga
Angel of Darkness
Arcadia of My Youth
Area 88
Ariel
Armitage
Armored Trooper Votoms
Art of Fighting
Astro Boy
Babel II
Baoh
Barefoot Gen
Battle Angel
Battle Royal High School
Battle Skipper

Big Wars
Black M-66
Blue Seed
Blue Sonnet
Blue Submarine 6
Bubblegum Crash
Bubblegum Crisis
Burn Up!
Countdown
Crying Freeman
Crystal Triangle
Curse of the Undead - Yoma
Cutey Honey
Cyber City Oedo 808
Cybernetics Guardian
Cyborg 009
Dagger of Kamui
Dallos
Dancougar
Dangaio
Darkside Blues
Demon Beast Invasion
Demon City Shinjuku
Devil Hunter Yoko
Devilman
Dirty Pair Films
Dirty Pair: Affair at Nolandia
Dog Soldier
Dominion Tank Police
Doomed Megalopolis
El Hazard
The Elven Bride
End of Summer
Explorer Woman Ray
F 3
Fatal Fury: The Motion Picture
Fire Tripper
Fist of the North Star
Galaxy Express 999
Gall Force
Gatchaman
Genesis Survivor Gaiarth
Genocyber
Ghost in the Shell
Giant Robo

The Girl from Phantasia
Godmars
Golden Boy
Golgo 13: The Professional
GoShogun: The Time Etranger
Grandizer
Grappler Baki
Grave of the Fireflies
Green Legend Ran
Gunbuster
Gundam Series
Gunsmith Cats
Guy: Awakening of the Devil
Guyver, The
The Hakkenden
Harmageddon
Heroic Legend of Arislan
Homeroom Affairs
The Humanoid
Hyper Doll
Iczer
Iria: Zeiram the Animation
Judge
Junk Boy
Kabuto
Kekko Kamen
Keroppi
Kiki's Delivery Service
Kimagure Orange Road
Kishin Corps
Kizuna
Lain
Laughing Target
Lensman
Lily CAT
Luna Varga
M.D. Geist
M.D. Geist II
Macross
Macross II
Madox-01
Maris the Chojo
MD Geist
Mermaid Forest
Mermaid's Flesh

Mermaid's Scar
Metal Fighters Miku
Metal Skin Panic Maddox-01
Moldiver
Monster City
My My Mai
My Neighbor Totoro
Neon Genesis Evangelion
Ninja Scroll
Odin: Photon Space Sailer Starlight
Oh My Goddess!
Orguss
Otaku no Video
Oulanders
Outlanders
Pat Labor
Peacock King
Planet Busters
Plastic Little
Private Psycho Lessons
Professional: Golgo 13
Project A-ko
Project A-ko 2
Project A-ko 3
Project A-ko 4
Project A-ko: Blue & Grey
Ramna 1/2
Record of Lodoss Wars
Riding Bean
Robot Carnival
Roots Search
Roujin Z
Silent Mobius
Slayers
Sohryuden: Legend of the Dragon Kings
Sol Bianca
Street Fighter 2: Animated Movie
Suikoden
Tenchi Muyo in Love: The Movie
Tenchi Muyo: TV Series
They Were 11
Tobor, The 8th Man
Twilight of the Cockroaches
U-Jin Brand
Ultimate Teacher

Urotsukidoji
Urusei Yatsura: Moive 1-6
Valley of the Wind
Vampire Hunter D
Vampire Princess Miyu
Venus Wars
Visionary by U-Jin
Wandering Kid, The: Urotsukidoji
Wanna Be's
Warriors of the Wind
Wicked City
A Wind Named Amnesia
Windaria
Wings of Hommensaise
Yamato Series
Yotoden
Zenki: Great Demon Lord
Zillion

Japanese Monsters (unless noted)
Frankenstein Conquers the World
Gamera Guardian of the Universe
Gamera vs Barugon
Gamera vs Gaos
Gamera vs Guiron
Gamera vs Jiger
Gamera vs Viras
Gamera vs Zigra
Gamera, The Invincible
Godzilla 1985
Godzilla Destory All Monsters
Godzilla King of Monsters
Godzilla vs Biollante
Godzilla vs Cosmic Monster
Godzilla vs Destroyer
Godzilla vs Gigan
Godzilla vs King Ghidorah
Godzilla vs Mechagodzilla
Godzilla vs Megalon
Godzilla vs Monster Zero
Godzilla vs Queen Mothra
Godzilla vs Sea Monster
Godzilla vs Smog Monster
Godzilla vs Space Godzilla
Godzilla vs Thing

Godzilla's Revenge
Godzilla's Terror of Mechagodzilla
Godzilla, Son of
Green Slime
Gunhed (robots)
Guyver
Infra-Man (Hong Kong)
King Kong Escapes
King Kong vs Godzilla
Rodan
Tetsuo: The Iron Man
War of the Gargatuans
Wicked City (Hong Kong)
Yongkari, Monster of the Deep (Korea)

Japanese Samurai
Buraikan
The Bushido Blade
Gate of Hell
Gonzo the Spearman
Eijanaika
47 Ronin, Part 1 & 2
Goyokin
Hara-Kiri
Heaven and Earth
Hidden Fortress
Lightning Swords of Death
Ran
Rashomon
Rebellion
Red Beard
Samurai Assassin
Samurai Spy
Samurai Trilogy
Samurai Wolf
Sanjuro
Sansho the Bailiff
Secret of the Urn
Seven Samurai
Shogun Assassin
Sword of the Beast
Three Outlaw Samurai
Yojimbo
Zaitochi Series

Korea
301, 302
Why Has Bodhi-Dharma Left for the East
Yongkari, Monster of the Deep

Kung-Fu "chop-socky" (Fantasy, Traditional, and Action)
18 Bronzemen
3 Evil Masters
36 Crazy Fists
4 Assassins
7 Blows of the Dragon
Above the Law (Aikido)
Against the Drunken Cat Paws
All Men are Brothers
Angel 2
Angel on Fire
Armour of God
Armour of God 2
Ashes of Time
Avenging Eagles
Avenging Quartet
Bare-footed Kid, The
Best of the Best 1, 2, 3 (Tae Kwon Do)
Big Brawl
Big Trouble in Little China
BL: Curse of the Dragon
BL: His Last Days, His Last Nights
Blade of Fury
Bloodsport
Bodyguard from Beijing
Born Invincible
Bride with White Hair 2, The
Bride with White Hair, The
Bruce Le's Greatest Revenge
Bruce Lee Fights Back from the Grave
Bruce Lee's Ways of Kung Fu
Bruce Li in New Guinea
Bruce Li the Invincible
Bruce the Superhero
Bruce's Deadly Fingers
Bruce's Fists of Vengeance
Challenge of the Masters
Challenge of the Ninja
Chinatown Kid

Chinese Boxer
Chinese Connection
Chinese Connection 2
Chinese Ghost Story
Chinese Ghost Story 2
Chinese Ghost Story 3
Cinema of Vengeance
Circus Kids
City Hunter
Comet Butterfly and Sword
Crime Story
Crouching Tiger, Hidden Dragon
Deadful Melody
Deadliest Art
Deadly Dream Woman
Deadly Mantis
Death Chamber
Defender, The
Dirty Ho
Doctor Wai
Double Impact
Dragon Chronicles
Dragon Fist
Dragon Inn
Dragon Lord
Dragon, the Hero
Dragons Forever
Drunken Master
Drunken Master 2
Drunken Master 3
Duel of Iron Fists
Duel of the 2 Masters
Duel to the Death
Dynamo
Eagle Shadow Fist
Eagle Shooting Heroes
Eight Diagram Pole Fighter
Enter the Dragon
Enter the Panther
Enter Three Dragons
Executioners of Death
Fantasy Mission Force
Fearless Hyena
Fearless Hyena 2
Fight to the Death

Fighting Duel of Death
Fire Dragon
First Mission (Heart of the Dragon)
First Option
First Strike
Fist of Fear, Touch of Death
Fists of Chan
Fists of Dragon
Fists of Fury
Fists of Fury 2
Fists of Legend
Fists of the White Lotus
Five Deadly Venoms
Five Fingers of Death
Five Masters of Death
Flirting Scholar
Flying Dagger
Flying Guillotine
Fong Sai Yuk
Fong Sai Yuk 2
Forbidden Arsenal
Four Shaolin Challengers
Game of Death
Game of Death 2
Green Snake
Half a Loaf of Kung-fu
Hapkido
Heroes of Shaolin
Heroic Trio
Heroic Trio 2
High Risk
Incredible Master Beggars
Infra-man
Instant Kung-Fu Man
Instructors of Death (Martial Club)
Iron Monkey
Iron Monkey 2
Island on Fire
Jade Claw
Just Heroes
Kid from Tibet
Kid with the Golden Arm
Killer from Shantung
Killer Meteors
Killer of Snake, Fox of Shaolin

King Boxer
King of Beggars
Kung Fu Arts
Kung-Fu
Kung-fu Massacre
Kung-fu Avengers
Kung-Fu Commandoes
Kung-Fu Cult Master
Kung-fu Rebels
Kung-fu Warlords
Kung-Fu: The Movie
Last Hurray for Chivalry
Legacy of Rage
Legend of the 7 Golden Vampires
Legend of the Liquid Sword
Legendary Weapons of Kung-fu
Lethal Lady
Mad Monk
Mad Monkey Kung-Fu
Magic Crane
Magnificent Bodyguards
Magnificient Warriors
Martial Arts Master Wong Fey Hung
Marvellous Fists
Master Killer
Master of Disaster
Master with Cracked Fingers
Master Wong vs Master Wong
Master, The
Mortal Combat
Mortal Kombat
My Father is a Hero
My Lucky Stars
My Young Auntie
Naked Killer
Naked Killer 2: Raped by Angel
New Fist of Fury
New Legend of Shaolin
New One-Armed Swordsman
No Retreat, No Surrender
Once Upon a Time a Hero in China
Once Upon a Time in China
Once Upon a Time in China 2
Once Upon a Time in China 3
Once Upon a Time in China 4

Once Upon a Time in China 5
Once Upon a Time in China 6
One-Armed Swordsman
Operation Scorpio
Peace Hotel
Pole Master
Police Story
Police Story 2
Police Story 3: Supercop
Police Story 4
Project A
Project A 2
Protector
Real Bruce Lee. The
Return of the Dragon
Return of the Master Killer
Rumble in the Bronx
Sam the Iron Bridge
Savage 5
Secret Rivals
Shanghai Express
Shanghai Noon
Shaolin Deadly Kicks
Shaolin Handlock
Shaolin Invincible
Shaolin Kung-fu Kids
Shaolin Martial Arts
Shaolin Plot
Shaolin Temple
Shaolin Temple 2
Shaolin Temple 3
Shaolin Traitor
Shaolin Wooden Men
Skinny Tiger and Fatty Dragon
Slaughter in San Francisco
Snake and Crane Arts of Shaolin
Snake in the Eagles Shadow
Spearman of Death
Spirits of Bruce Lee
Spiritual Kung-fu
Streets of Hong Kong
Super Dragon's Dynamo
Super Ninjas
Superpower
Sword of Many Loves

Sword Stained with Royal Blood
Swordsman
Swordsman 2
Swordsman 3
Sworn Brothers
Tai Chi 2
Tai Chi Master
Ten Tigers of Kwantung
Three Avengers
Thunderbolt
To Kill with Intrigue
Twin Dragons
Twin Warriors
Twinkle Twinkle Little Stars
Two Shaolin Kids in Hong Kong
Unbeatable Dragon
Warrior from Shaolin
Warrior's Tragedy
Warrior's Tragedy 2
Wheels on Meals
When TaeKwonDo Strikes
Wing Chun
Wonder Seven
Young Dragon
Young Master

Ninja Films
Ninja vs. Shaolin
Ninja's Extreme Weapons
Ninja Wars
Nine Deaths of the Ninja
Pray for Death
Revenge of the Ninja
Shogun's Ninja
Yotoden (Japanime)

American Ninja
Dagger of Kamui (Japanime)
Enter the Ninja
Ninja III the Domination
Ninja Academy
Ninja American Warrior
Ninja Brothers of Blood
Ninja Checkmate
Ninja Commandments
Ninja Condors
Ninja Connection
Ninja Death Squad
Ninja Exterminators
Ninja Massacre
Ninja Nightmare
Ninja of the Magnificence
Ninja Operation: Licensed to Terminate
Ninja Phantom Heroes
Ninja Pirates
Ninja Powerforce
Ninja Scroll (Japanime)
Ninja Showdown
Ninja Strike Force
Ninja Supremo
Ninja Sword of Death
Ninja Turf,
Ninja vs Ninja

APPENDIX II
ALL-TIME FILM FAVORITES -

I'm sure at some point in time, every film critic is asked which movies/actors/directors make it to their coveted list of top favorites. It's amusing to make your own list and to compare, especially if you've seen a number of films, and over the years, I have updated and reassessed my list often asking why did I choose that film. So let's see how many films you may have chosen as your favorites and please use the list for recommendations. This is not a definitive list of the greatest films of all time, but rather a personal list of favorites I have enjoyed over the course of time for personal reasons of entertainment, no films past 2000 are listed in this volume. To limit myself, each list contains twelve entries. These aren't the only Asian films that I own and love, but these represent the films I would definitely possess and view again. The films are not ranked in any particular order.

JAPANIMATION
1 Record of Lodoss War
2 Akira
3 Project A-Ko
4 Star Blazers (Yamato)
5 Silent Moebius
6 Kimigure Orange Road
7 Gunbuster
8 Dangaio
9 Princess Mononoke
10 Ranma 1/2
11 My Neighbor Totoro
12 Grave of the Fireflies

TRADITIONAL KUNG-FU
1 Master Killer
2 Avenging Eagles
3 Legendary Weapons of Kung-Fu
4 Fist of Legend
5 The Five Deadly Venoms
6 Tai Chi Master
7 Drunken Master II
8 Challenge of the Ninja
9 Crouching Tiger, Hidden Dragon
10 Fong Sai Yuk
11 Iron Monkey
12 Once Upon A Time in China 1-6

DRAMA/ROMANCE
1 Stray Dog
2 High and Low
3 Tokyo Story
4 Early Summer
5 Eat Drink Man Woman
6 Hu-Du-Men
7 Iron & Silk
8 The Joy Luck Club
9 The Wedding Banquet
10 Salaam Bombay
11 Ikuru/To Live
12 Picture Bride

HISTORICAL/EPIC
1 Seven Samurai
2 Yojimbo
3 The Last Emperor
4 Rashomon
5 To Live
6 Raise the Red Lantern
7 Samurai Trilogy
8 Kama Sutra
9 Farewell My Concubine
10 The Killing Fields
11 Gandhi
12 The Hidden Fortress

ACTION/MODERN MARTIAL ARTS
1 The Killer
2 Hard-Boiled
3 A Better Tomorrow
4 Enter the Dragon
5 Police Story
6 Dragons Forever
7 Full Contact
8 Bullet in the Head
9 Dragon: The Bruce Lee Story
10 Bloodsport
11 Supercop
12 Rumble in the Bronx

COMEDY/QUIRKY/HORROR/MISC.

1 Tampopo
2 Zen of Sword
3 Funeral
4 Chinese Ghost Story
5 Swordsman II
6 Godzilla Series
7 The Bride with White Hair
8 Kwaidan
9 Heroic Trio
10 Chinese Ghost Story
11 King and I
12 Naked Killer

ACTRESS (There's so many I love, it was difficult to choose only twelve.)

1 Maggie Cheung
2 Tamalyn Tomita
3 Michelle Yeoh
4 Joan Chen
5 Joey Wong
6 Vivian Wu
7 Cynthia Khan
8 Brigitte Lin
9 Angela Mao Ying
10 Hui Ying Hung
11 Gong Li
12 Chingmy Yau

ACTOR

1 Bruce Lee
2 Ti Lung
3 Chow Yun Fat
4 Jackie Chan
5 Jet Li
6 Gordon Liu (Lau Kar Fai)
7 Samo Hung
8 Simon Yam
9 Chen Kuan Tai
10 Toshiro Mifune
11 Takashi Shimura
12 John Lone

DIRECTOR

1 John Woo
2 Akira Kurosawa
3 Liu Chia Liang
4 Chang Cheh
5 Tsui Hark
6 Ringo Lam
7 Juzo Itami
8 Ang Lee
9 Yasujiro Ozu
10 Chen Kaige
11 Zhang Yimou
12 Samo Hung

WEAPONS

1 Staff
2 Samurai Sword
3 Three-Sectional Staff
4 Nunchaku
5 Tai Chi Sword
6 Hook Sword
7 Shurikens
8 Whip Chain
9 Spear
10 Sai
11 Bench
12 Chopsticks

MARTIAL ARTS TECHNIQUES

1 Wing Chun
2 Ninjutsu
3 Tiger
4 Aikido
5 Hapkido
6 Tae Kwon Do
7 Crane
8 Judo
9 Shotokan Karate
10 Tai Chi
11 Jeet Kune Do
12 Shaolin Style

CITIES

1 Hong Kong
2 Tokyo
3 Seoul
4 Beijing
5 Shanghai
6 Osaka
7 Kyoto
8 Bangkok
9 Taipei
10 Manila
11 Singapore
12 Kuala Lumpur

APPENDIX III
~WHO'S WHO: ASIAN GALLERY~

It's difficult to gain respect for movies when you can't even remember, let alone pronounce, or recognize the names of actors, actresses, and filmmakers who are an important part of the film's production. Just like in America, Asian fans adore their favorite stars and directors, seeking out their films both early and new. You start to form bonds and personal relations with the characters portrayed by them on screen. Fans clubs form, and magazines and websites are dedicated to their careers. Ever since I started watching Asian films, I've come to admire many new stars and directors, and I hope you also discover a favorite or two. So here's a list of names and a brief description for the biggest Asian and Asian-American talents.

Tia Carrerre - Tall, beautiful actress of mixed Asian heritage who has appeared in a number of Hollywood pictures. Brought to prominence and best known for her role as Wayne's (Mike Meyers) girlfriend in the Wayne's World films. Her exotic beauty and athletic stature has allowed her to enjoy roles outside the classic Asian female. She has appeared with superstars like Arnold Schwarzeneggar in True Lies and Sean Connery in Rising Sun.

Jackie Chan - Currently, Chan is the biggest star to come out of Asia and is quickly becoming a household name in America with the recent releases of Rumble in the Bronx, Supercop, First Strike, and Operation Condor. Known by martial arts fans for decades, Chan never captured mainstream America recognition in early attempts such as The Big Brawl, Cannonball Run, and The Protector. As a child, Chan entered a rigorous training program in Chinese opera and acrobatics, meeting fellow students Hung and Yuen Biao. His early career in Hong Kong was full of generic, poorly conceived kung-fu movies that capitalized on the Bruce Lee/kung-fu craze. Chan struggled many years to become the new Bruce Lee, but finally decided to go down his own path and create an exciting cross genre of comedy kung-fu films which paid homage to Hollywood idols Harold Lloyd and Buster Keaton. As Chan's films gained popularity in Asia, his roles became more significant and he was able to take more control of directing, writing, and choreographing his films. His early American attempts at stardom were difficult since filmmakers tried to westernize him rather than re-create his unique own screen charisma. Though popular among action fans with dozens of films under his belt, he stills lack the overall recognition and stardom garnered by Bruce Lee. Outside of America, the story is quite different where Chan is the ultimate film superstar. Only time will tell if Chan's career push in the United States is as successful. Riding high on recent success, Chan has appeared in American commercials, specials, and upcoming films. The year 2000 saw the premiere of the Jackie Chan cartoon for children.

David Chiang - Popular martial arts star of the 70's, usually teamed with Ti Lung or Chen Kuan Tai and directed by Chang Cheh. Chiang's physique was smaller and thinner compared to most of his co-stars. Capitalizing on his wily charm, David would play the rogue or con-artist with a good heart deep inside. During the martial arts craze of the 70's and 80's, Chiang was a major star at Shaw Brothers and became one of the most recognizable Asian actors in America. He even appeared in the Hammer/Shaw Brothers crossover film, Legends of the Golden Vampire with Peter Cushing. After he left Shaw Brothers his popularity diminished quickly and he has stepped out of the current limelight. He is still recognized by Americans kung-fu fans due to his prolific status, having appearing in dozens of kung-fu classics: Savage Five, Shaolin Mantis, 7

Blows of the Dragon, Duel of the Iron Fists, Killer from Shantung, Shaolin Handlock.

Rosalyn Chao - Chinese-American actress popular for her role as Keiko O'Brien in Star Trek: The Next Generation and Deep Space Nine, and her film role in The Joy Luck Club. She has appeared in dozens of movies and television shows. Smart, intuitive looking woman who adds emotional depth to various roles.

Chang Cheh - Before there was John Woo, there was Chang. Actually Woo and many prominent directors studied filmmaking under Chang. A prominent action director for Shaw Brothers, he created some of the best known kung-fu movies in America. His popular themes of revenge and brotherhood have appeared in countless films and starred a great group of actors, lovingly known as the Chang Gang. The first wave included stars like David Chiang, Ti Lung, and Alexander Fu Sheng and the second gang included muscular Lo Meng, Sun Chen, Kuo Chui in movies like 5 Deadly Venoms, Mortal Combat, The Unbeatable Dragon, Kid with the Golden Arm, and Spearmen of Death. His status in Hong Kong filmmaking is legendary as an entertainer and a teacher.

Joan Chen - Joan is one of the most recognized Asian actresses working in English-speaking films. Having appeared in epics like The Last Emperor and action films like The Hunted, she shows no qualms about experimenting with roles. Elegant, beautiful, and charismatic, her talents cross over into numerous genres and her career is still quite active.

Chen Kuan Tai - The definitive Shaw Brothers actor who appeared in numerous films during the heyday of Shaws power. Unlike many actors who learned martial arts, Chen was already an accomplished martial artist, having studied since eight in monkey style and winning in competitive circles. Versatile character actor, Chen's portrayal of a hero or villain always contained a certain sense of nobility and strength. He's appearance can make even the weakest films into a classic.

Kent Cheng - Rotund, overweight actor who appears in many popular films as the likeable over-weight guy/cop. Kent has played villains, but even then there is a kindness about his character and you can never really hate the guy.

Christy Cheung - Attractive leading lady who appears in a number of versatile roles. While representing Montreal, she was discovered in the TVB Miss Chinese International Pageant 1993.

Jacky Cheung - Boyish charm and good looks, Jacky has turned himself from Hong Kong's premiere singer into a top-notch actor of Hong Kong films. His wild antics are unforgettable as he glides through flying kung-fu fantasies. He has also expanded his roles into other genres, see Bullet in the Head. Part of the Four Golden Kings (singer turned actor), he's in good company with Andy Lau, Leon Lai, and Aaron Kwok.

Leslie Cheung - Born in 1956, Hong Kong, and educated in England. Handsome, slender actor who has appeared in some of Asian's best known productions. Besides appearing in comedy/action films, Cheung has starred in dramatic epics opposite Gong Li - Temptress Moon, Farewell My Concubine. As with many, he started as a popular singer before moving into film. In 1990, he retired completely from music to concentrate on his film career. On July 1995, he re-entered the music arena with an album featuring songs from his films.

Maggie Cheung - Popularly known as May, Jackie Chan's girlfriend in the Police Story movies, Maggie has appeared in a variety of roles as the nice-girl next door roles, but got a big image boost from The Heroic Trio as a hot vixen fighter. One of the best known and best loved actresses, Cheung has crossed over into action, fantasy, comedy, and drama with much ease. Incredibly adorable and charismatic, she is one of Hong Kong's premiere talents.

Billy Chong - Athletic and charismatic actor who appeared in a number of short-lived kung-fu films that were released in the United States. His best known are Jade Claw and Superpower, entertaining films with well-choreographed fight scenes.

Raymond Chow - Mega-producer and director for many of the hottest Hong Kong films, including the films of Bruce Lee and Jackie Chan. Originally an executive at Shaw Brothers, he left and formed his own rival company, Golden Harvest, which gave Shaw plenty of competition. Unafraid to take chances, Chow has collaborated on many ventures with other studios and countries to create a powerful force in the film industry.

Stephen Chow - Popular actor for his comedic roles spoofing every genre. Starting off in television, Chow got a lucky break starring in a parody of God of Gamblers. His boyish charm and physical talent led to a number of spoof films which would capitilize on the trendy Hong Kong film of the year. His career is now cemented into success and fans eagerly await any new release. Since comedy is difficult to translate, Chow's films are not popular in the USA.

Chow Yun-Fat - The Toshiro Mifune of Hong Kong. Millions of fans, Asian and America, already know and love the cool, noble, and suave actor. If you don't know him, just wait and see as his career explodes into Hollywood's mainstream. The star of a number of high profile John Woo films, including the immortal The Killer and Hard-Boiled. Chow started doing television comedies and dramas, before branching off into a brief singing career and then finding gold as a tough, heart-of-gold action star with Woo and Ringo Lam. A superstar in Asia, Chow is prolific and many of his films are available in America. He has moved stateside and appeared in a number of high profile films, including Anna and the King with Jodie Foster, The Corruptor with Mark Walhberg, and The Replacement Killers with Mira Sorvino. His latest film Crouching Tiger, Hidden Dragon with Michelle Yeoh promises to be a huge critical and financial success.

Sonny Chiba - A favorite of Quentin Tarantino and other hard core karate fans. Chiba was billed as a one-man killing machine. Big, bad, and ugly! He broke bones and split skulls. Later he slowed down and took behind the camera chores and supporting roles in more traditional films. He is best known for a string of Street Fighter films and other Japanese-made action flicks that became popular after the death of Bruce Lee.

Mona Fong - Powerful producer at Shaw Brothers who oversaw most of the production on the best known kung-fu films to be released. Her relationship with Shaw and her jealousy toward other actresses, restricted the roles of women in the early Shaw Brothers films until Liu Chia Liang introduced his ingenue, Hui Yin Hung.

Alexander Fu Sheng - Similar in style/appearance to Jackie Chan, Alexander seemed the heir apparent to the Bruce Lee throne, but was tragically killed in an auto accident. He still left a legacy of popular films and millions of fans. His combination of boyish good looks, humor, and physical prowess will be missed.

Inoshiro Honda - The King of Japanese monster movies. Honda has directed the best and worst of Japan's favorite Godzilla films.

Sibelle Hu - Attractive actress and a favorite of Hong Kong comedy/action films.

Kara Hui Yin Hung (Wei Yin Huang) - Slender, attractive actress known for her kung-fu movies and relationship with director Liu Chia Liang. She appeared in a number of his films and was an international star, but most of her films are locked away in the Shaw Brothers vault. Check her out in My Young Auntie, Fists of the White Lotus, and Legendary Weapons of Kung-fu. Amazingly Kara's still going strong, appearing in modern films, looking as beautiful and athletic as ever. Check her out in Zen of Sword.

Samo Hung (Sammo Hung) - Portly, but quick and powerful fighter who has created a name for himself in directing as well as acting. Part of the trinity with Jackie Chan and Yuen Biao, he is the oldest of the trio and commonly known as "Big Brother". Hung's films are often laced with comedy, but his martial arts epics are wonderful. A multi-talented star who is a modern version of director/actor/choreographer Liu Chia Liang. In 1994, he married Australian/Hong Kong star Joyce Godenzi who appeared in Hung's Eastern Condors. Samo then moved his energies to the United States and started work on the enjoyable cop/buddy television series, Martial Law.

Juzo Itami   - Popular Japanese director of contemporary satires who began his career as an actor. Made international waves with The Funeral and Tampopo, starring his wife. Sadly, he committed suicide due to a possible scandal situation. His death occurred around the same time as Akira Kurosawa and Toshiro Mifune which truly saddened admirers of Japanese cinema.

Cynthia Khan (Yeung Lai-Ching) - Attractive, tough heroine of numerous action movies. Best known for her work "In the Line of Duty" series. Khan filled the vacuum of female action stars when Michelle Khan got married and retired and Cynthia Rothrock moved to make American films. Her name is an amalgamation of the two heroines. At first, Cynthia Khan appeared in low-budget action films that capitalized on her looks and flexibility. Gradually, she has appeared in better films, proving her worth as an actor who is both beautiful and tough. She has plenty of "Girl with Guns" roles, but also check out her wonderful period-pieces, Blade of Fury and Zen of Sword.

Nancy Kwan - Beautiful actress with stunning eyes who starred in numerous American films. For many years, Kwan was the premiere Asian-American actress, appearing opposite Asian and non-Asian leading males. Her beauty is evident today and she occasionally appears in films, like Dragon: The Bruce Lee Story.

Sho Kosugi   - Japanese actor famous for his portrayal as a Ninja in movies and television. His fame was mostly in the 1980's during Ninjamania. Later on his films included his two sons and a television series known as The Master with Lee Van Cleef.

Akira Kurosawa - Japan's greatest director, a living legend among the film community. Born on March 23, 1910 at Omori, Tokyo, Japan, he studied at Doshusha School of Western Painting and worked under the influences of Imperial Japan. Best known for his highly admired and recognized historical samurai films starring Toshiro Mifune. Kurosawa delved deeply into the Post-War chaos of Japan and his own life to create memorable characters who often met adversity and self-doubt. Producing films with Asian and Western influences, Kurosawa is a modern director that transcends cultural boundaries. Ironically, Kurosawa has seen some disfavor in Japan and his films are not always guaranteed box-office successes. Kurosawa is admired as the greatest Asian filmmaker and is a world-class film legend on the same plateau as Alfred Hitchcock and Martin Scorsese.

Rosamund Kwan (Kwan Chi-Lam) - Cute, doe-eyed beauty who appears in numerous films, including opposite Jet Li and Jackie Chan. Rosamund's beauty matches her first name and she is often seen as the innocent or pure.

Ringo Lam - Started in Hong Kong television in the seventies where he met Chow Yun Fat. Lam studied film at York University in Toronto, Canada and returned to make films in Hong Kong. Received a big boost with City on Fire which won him the 1987 Best Director HK Film Award. Since then Lam has been a premiere director of Hong Kong action/crime films, starring Chow and many other top-name performers. He followed Woo's move and made the Hollywood action film, once again starring Jean Claude Van Damme, Maximum Risk.

Andy Lau - Handsome and prolific leading actor/singer who has appeared in a variety of popular roles. The most successful of the Four Golden Kings, see Jacky Cheung.

Ang Lee - Prominent director who won critical acclaim for Hollywood's Sense & Sensibility, starring Hugh Grant and Emma Thompson. His strength seems to be in life stories, creating vivid characters who share the same dreams and frailties we recognize in ourselves. Many of his stories deal with family problems: father-son, husband-wife, etc. Due to the strength and humor of his films the Wedding Banquet and Eat Drink Man Woman, he was chosen to direct the Jane Austen film Sense & Sensibility which was nominated for an Academy Award in various categories, but was snubbed for best director nomination. Undaunted, Ang Lee has continued in the Hollywood jungles, directing films like the Ice Storm, Riding with the Devil, and the highly lauded Crouching Tiger, Hidden Dragon, a martial arts epic which has given the critics something to finally admire.

Brandon Lee - Son of legend Bruce Lee. Brandon started off on a film career, but focused more on adapting his acting skills rather than honing his martial arts. An accomplished actor, he appeared in numerous Asian and American-made films. Sadly, he was killed in a film accident on the set of the Crow. He never married or had any children, ending the amazing Lee Dynasty.

Bruce Lee - Born Lee Yeun Kam on November 27, 1941, San Francisco, CA and later died of a cerebral edema triggered by a chemical reaction to a painkiller in July 20, 1973, Hong Kong. Lee's father, an actor, raised Lee in Hong Kong where he learned Wing Chun and appeared in a number of early films. He returned to the United States and attended the University of Washington for philosophy. Lee started a kung-fu school, teaching his famous Jeet Kune Do to many high-profile people. His attempts to break into television (The Green Hornet) and films (Marlowe) proved disappointing, so he travelled to Hong Kong and the rest is history. A national poll proved that Bruce Lee is still the best-known and most popular Asian star in American and perhaps the world. His image still appears on books, magazines, and specials. Only a few stars like James Dean, let alone an Asian actor, has reached a worldwide audience in such a short career period. Dying at only 32 years old, he left only four completed films which catapulted him into a screen legend.

Danny Lee - Innocuous looking actor best known for his noble cop role in The Killer opposite Chow Yun Fat. Seems to have been typecast as the cop, but has independently sought different roles and more control over his productions. Ironically, his father is a prominent police officer in Hong Kong.

Jason Scott Lee - Achieved fame by portraying Bruce Lee in Dragon: The Bruce Lee Story. A fine actor of Hawaiian descent, Lee went on to appear in a number of films, playing a variety of racial roles: Alaskan, Indian, and Asians. His excellent physique and acting talents have always added to his screen charisma.

Moon Lee - Actress best known for her roles in the "Girls with Guns" Angel films where she usually plays the cute, supercop after Japanese villain Yukari Oshima.

Jade Leung - Made her debut in Black Cat, providing screen intensity and ferocity against any opponent. Look for the rising star in other action films as well.

Tony Leung Kar Fai - Handsome lead actor who appears in many dashing roles. Don't get him confused with other Leungs who are also named Tony.

Bruce Li (Ho Chung Tao) - Charismatic Bruce Lee clone who appeared in dozens of films and did quite well for himself, standing out from other clones. The most popular of the clones, Li performed admirably in other films that experimented with his own style and screen presence.

Gong Li - Born December 31, 1965 at Shenyang, Liaoning Province, China. She entered the Central Drama Academy in Beijing and two years later met Zhang Yimou while auditioning for Red Sorghum which started her career. Beautiful, strong-willed Chinese actress who has made a string of remarkable dramas and romances under the direction of China's "Fifth Generation" of filmmakers. Her subtle, non-powering beauty, strength of character, and superb acting has put her on the forefront of Asian performers. She is now actively sought after by Hollywood. Her off-screen romance ended with Zhang ended in 1995.

Jet Li (Li Lian Jie) - Known in China as Li Lian Jie, Jet Li is one of the hottest stars in Asia and on the threshold of toppling Jackie Chan as the King of Martial Arts Movies. Appearing in period pieces as well as modern action pictures, the mainland Chinese actor has spent considerable time perfecting his martial arts and acting ability. Filled with charm, boyish good lucks and incredible body movement, nothing seems to be able to stop Jet Li's worldwide success. Like many of his fellow Asian actors, Jet Li has come to Hollywood appearing with Mel Gibson in Lethal Weapon 4 and Aaliyah in Rome Must Die. Upcoming projects may include Matrix 2 and the role of Bruce Lee's Kato in the Green Hornet with Mark Wahlberg.

Lo Lieh - You may not recognize him without the white wig and beard, but he is one of the most prominent villains in Chinese kung-fu movies. The star of Five Fingers of Death, Lo quickly went on to play elderly villains in a number of Shaw Brothers classics. He later went on to direct and write.

Brigitte Lin - Attractive female lead in a number of movies, moving from mediocre roles to the quintessential fantasy warrior. Unfortunate for fans, in 1994 she married and retired from working in the film industry. Don't fret she has dozens of great films available for rent and purchase. Try, The Bride with White Hair, Deadful Melody, Swordsman III, and Police Story.

Liu Chiang Liang (Lau Kar Leung) - The godfather of martial arts/action films, Liu can do it all: actor, director, choreographer, you name it, he's done it, and done it well. Short and compact with a rough face, Liu started off in a number of roles, before developing his career into a prominent director. His unique films altered the way kung-fu movies were made and often starred his step-brother Gordon Liu. His legacy has created some of the best known films in American and are definitely worth seeing. He is still active on and off the screen. See his filmography and treat it like a list of recommendations.

Gordon Liu (Liu Chia Hui or Lau Kar Fai) - Liu Chia Hui better known as the Master Killer. One of the most recognized stars in Asia and America, especially since he's bald. The adopted brother of famed director Liu Chia Liang and Liu Chia Yung. Gordon has appeared in some of the best martial arts films ever made and his boyish charisma, noble stature, and kung-fu prowess have made him an international superstar. At one point in time, he was the second biggest box-office draw in Asia, next to Jackie Chan.

Ti Lung - Venerable actor Ti Lung has kept busy throughout every decade of Hong Kong films. He represents nobility and strength. His charisma has never gone out of vogue, making him the Clint Eastwood/Sean Connery of Hong Kong films. Tall and muscular, Ti has appeared in dozens of classic kung-fu films and then made the transition into Triad action films, such as John Woo's A Better Tomorrow.

John Liu - Though not popular anymore, you can never forget a John Liu film. Billed as the incredible kicker, his leg work is phenomenal and the highlight of all his kung-fu films.

Mako - Goofy, fun spirited character actor who starred opposite Arnold Schwarzeneggar in both

Conan films as the eager wizard. Mako has also had a long career in Hollywood, but mostly in restricted roles.

Angela Mao Ying - Not as well known by current standards, but was once known as the Queen of Martial Arts in the 70's. Popular for her excellent flexibility and speed in Korean kicking-styles, she has appeared with Bruce Lee in Enter the Dragon, Carter Wong in Hapkido and Jhoon Rhee in When Tae Kwon Do Strikes. Having started in Chinese Opera, Mao began acting at the age of four and was lucky enough to sign a five-year contract with Raymond Chow at age 19. she quickly went on to become a box office success, performing her fighting skills with a serious, no-nonsense bravado. In a field where men dominated, Angela stood out with the best of them.

Toshiro Mifune - One of the greatest actors to come out of Japan. Mifune is the star of such famous Kurosawa films as The Seven Samurai, Sanjuro, Yojimbo, and Roshomon. The two bonded and made numerous films in a tightly-knit relationship similar to John Ford-John Wayne and Martin Scorsese-Robert DeNiro. Mifune's fame helped him to discover a career in the United States, but most of his roles were stereotypical: Japanese Naval officer, samurai, etc.

Ming Na-Wen - Once voted as People's Top 50 Most beautiful people, Na-Wen made waves as the main character in The Joy Luck Club. Attractive, intelligent, and talented, she has entered into a successful television career, appearing on shows like All-American Girl, ER, and The Single Guy.

Nobuko Miyamoto - Comely Japanese actress who appears in numerous films directed by husband Juzo Itami. Pleasant and warm-looking, her human gestures mix with subtle humor.

Noriyuki "Pat" Morita - One of the best loved and known Asian-American actors, popular for his mentor role in all four Karate Kid films and the wisecracking cook/owner of Arnold's restaurant on Happy Days. Morita is a veteran of the Hollywood screen, appearing in dozens of films. Most of his roles have been relayed to stereotypical minor parts where Asian characters are needed, but with the Karate Kid fame and receiving an Academy Award nomination for his role, he has branched off into writing and starring in more films, such as Captive Hearts. Still acting, you can regularly spot him on television.

Anita Mui   - Thin, long-faced actress of various roles. Though attractive, her unique features able her to play a geeky spinster or a sultry seductress.

Soon Taek Oh - Popular character actor of American films, usually in memorable but minor roles. Though of Korean descent, Soon has played all types of Asian roles. He has appeared in numerous films with the biggest stars in Hollywood for many decades. You might recognize him in The Man with the Golden Gun with Roger Moore or The Final Countdown with Kirk Douglas.

Yukari Oshima - Japanese female action star popular in Hong Kong films. One of the bad "Girls with Guns" actress, appearing opposite Cynthia Khan or Moon Lee. Her popularity in the Philippines prompted her to open a production company in the country where she is known as Cynthia Luster.

Yasujiro Ozu - Critically renowned director of Japanese dramas. Ozu set many new standards and has an endearing effect on many filmmakers who studied his style.

Jhoon Rhee   - Father of American Tae Kwon Do, Jhoon Rhee started a popular chain of martial arts schools in the Washington DC area with a few senators as students. He branched off into films, books, and equipment.

Henry Sanada - A protege of Sonny Chiba's, Henry is a lithe, athletic performer who appeared in a number of action films from Japan.

Shaw Brothers - the premiere filmmakers of Hong Kong. Run Run Shaw and Runme Shaw transformed their father's fortune into a major film power during the post World War II era. At their peak of power, they claimed the largest film studios in the world with thousands of employees and a wardrobe department that included costumes from every dynasty in China. The major studio of Asia, almost every major director or actor has seen some work at their studios. In the heyday of their success, hundreds of films were produced and distributed around the world. Sadly, the film branch of the studio so rising costs, competition, and television as a reason to close down major productions. No longer a player in the film industry, the film archives have been closed for commercial release. Hopefully, this will not be permanent and the Shaws will once again be a leader in the film industry.

Rumiko Takahashi - a leading creative force in the world of Japanime and mangas (comics). Her style of blending romance, humor, and the supernatural/wild have provided countless incarnations into popular stories that have been transformed into animation.

George Takei - Few other Asians are as well known or remembered as George Takei. His thirty year role as the helmsman of the Enterprise has given him legendary status as Star Trek's affable Mr. Hikaru Sulu. Takei has appeared in many other films and television shows and his charismatic voice has also been heard as narration and on audio books.

Tamalyn Tomita - Hauntingly beautiful and serene actress, popularly known from her early role in The Karate Kid II and later in The Joy Luck Club. Of Japanese heritage, the beautiful Tomita is a wonderful choice for woman of emotion, intelligence, and tenderness.

Stanley Tong - Popular Hong Kong director and ex-stuntman who has collaborated with Jackie Chan on a number of films. He has also made the move to Hollywood and will direct Mr. Magoo starring Leslie Nielsen.

Tsui Hark - The Steven Spielberg of Asia. Brilliant Chinese filmmaker who writes, directs, and produces many of his projects, including the kung-fu epics with Jet Li. Hark has been a constant driving force in re-inventing and modernizing the Hong Kong film industry. His re-invention of the classic Wong series ushered in a new wave of popularity for traditional kung-fu films.

Miyoshi Umeki - delicate Japanese actress who has appeared in a number of high profile films in America. She is the first Asian to win an Academy Award for acting (Best Supporting Actress in Sayonara).

Wang Lung Wei - The Jack Palance/Christopher Lee of kung-fu movies. A classic Shaw Brothers villain who appeared in numerous films as the leader or the main henchman of the ruthless villains. Sporting a thin moustache and black hair, Wang's abilities rival the best of the heroes he terrorized. He has fought opposite Ti Lung, David Chiang, Jackie Chan, and Gordon Liu.

Garrett Wang - Up-and-coming actor who has appeared in a number of roles. He is now a regular cast member of Star Trek: Voyager, portraying the bright, energetic Ensign Harry Kim of Korean descent.

Wayne Wang - One of American's most talented Asian-American filmmakers. Born in Hong Kong, Wayne studied film, TV, photography, and painting at the College of Arts and Crafts, Oakland, CA. He returned to his homeland and started to work on television and films, before returning to America and scraping $22,000 to film the low-budget Chan is Missing. This led to critical success and many more independent films dealing with Chinese-American issues about the family, love, and culture. Delving into non-Asian Slamdance proved a mistake, but Wang eventually hit box office success with The Joy Luck Club.

Lo Wei - Prolific producer/director and a key player in Hong Kong's film world. Starting at Shaw Brothers, Lo joined Raymond Chow at his new company Golden Harvest. Lo's first break was to direct newcomer Bruce Lee in Fists of Fury and the Chinese Connection. Later Lee and Lo came to a disagreement on who deserved credit for the films' success. In 1975, Lo left Golden Harvest and started his own production company, discovering Jackie Chan. His string of "chop-socky" films were hardly on the level of Shaw Brothers and Golden Harvest, best forgotten. His financial power waned, but he still produces films in collaboration with other talented directors/actors.

Carter Wong - Muscular Asian kung-fu star who grunts a lot and has appeared in American films as well as Asian kung-fu movies. Best known as Thunder in Big Trouble in Little China. Wong is a respectable fighter, but his screen presence has failed to capture international success, mainly due to the poor quality of his Hong Kong films.

Wong Jing - Best described as the John Carpenter of Hong Kong, Wong is incredibly prolific and has a loyal base of fans. His direction though wavers from more serious films to more campy films involving fantasy/horror elements. You're never too sure what kind of quality Wong will hit, but his films attract the biggest stars and are fun for the most part.

Russell Wong - Handsome, dashing leading man of Chinese heritage. Appeared in numerous films like The Joy Luck Club. Russell was the star of the television series The Vanishing Son, created by Rob Cohen, the director of Dragon: The Bruce Lee Story.

Victor Wong - Veteran Asian-American actor of dozens of familiar films, his heavy-eyelids and wizened appearance are instantly recognizable. Appeared in many of Wayne Wang's films, but also a popular character actor in Hollywood.

John Woo - Born in 1948, Canton, Guangdong province, South China, Woo was the first Asian to direct a major Hollywood film. His status in Asian filmmaking is undeniably as he helped popularize the Triad/crime genre within Asia and America. Bet known among modern fans of Hong Kong films, Woo's trademark use of slow-motion, male bonding, loyalty, chastisement, and intense violence are much imitated and praised. As a Hong Kong director/writer, he reached international fame with his stylized gangster films like The Killer, Hard-Boiled, and A Better Tomorrow. His films are successful and have given critics plenty to debate about. Lulled by Hollywood, he is directing American action films with stars like John Travolta, Christian Slater, Nicholas Cage, and Jean Claude Van Damme.

Xie Miao - Child actor known for his amazing kung-fu stunts with Jet Li. Small, rugged, and full of energy. One of the rising stars in Hong Kong cinema.

Xiong Xin-Xin - Rising star in Hong Kong cinema. Powerful and intense martial artist, best known for his striking role as Clubfoot in the Once Upon a Time in China 3-6.

Simon Yam - Hardest working actor in Hong Kong, Simon has appeared in many of Hong Kong's most recent films, ranging from big-budget action to melodramatic romances to sleazy comedies. A popular actor, Simon's versatility has given life to memorable villains and heroes in all genres of film.

Chingmy Yau - Incredibly attractive, minx like star who uses her wily smile and charm to seduce anyone from kings to beggars to women. Chingmy is one of the most popular stars in Asia, mixing the seductiveness of Demi Moore with the charm of Meg Ryan into one package. She can fight, dance, and do anything else. Her talents are used from traditional kung-fu to modern action to romantic comedy films.

Donnie Yen (Donnie Yan) - Popular stoic actor who appears as second fiddle in numerous movies, but has really shined in his solo efforts as well. Definitely part of the new breed of emerging stars. Highlights include battling Jet Li in Once Upon A Time In China 2, pursuing Michelle Khan in Wing Chun, and portraying Wong Fei Hung's father in Iron Monkey.

Michelle Yeoh (Michelle Khan) - The hottest Hong Kong female star is about to get an international boost with her appearance in the latest James Bond film, Tomorrow Never Dies, co-starring Pierce Brosnan and Terri Hatcher. Co-starring in the American-released Supercop with Jackie Chan, Michelle has proved her commercial value and fighting prowess. Originally a Miss Malaysia with a Chinese background, she branched off into a modelling/acting career. Though her background was in ballet, not kung-fu, her added agility, grace, and flexibility allowed her to instantly learn the intricate moves and quickly rise in the ranks of action stars. In 1986, she made a string of popular films for Dickson Poon's D&B Productions and soon after married the Hong Kong tycoon. She retired due to her marriage with Poon, but after her marriage disintegrated, she returned to the big screen and re-debuted in Supercop (1993). Since then, her career has skyrocketed with roles opposite Hong Kong's hottest stars: Jet Li and Yuen Biao (Tai Chi Master), Maggie Cheung and Anita Mui (Heroic Trio 1, 2), and Donnie Yen (Wing Chun). Fluent in English, Michelle has toured the United States to publicize her new films and with the help of Tai Seng Video Marketing, a number of her films have been released on video and shown on television in dubbed English. Michelle must also be applauded for her wonderful appearance opposite Pierce Brosnan in the James Bond film Tomorrow Never Dies. Her fluent English and Chinese has entitled her to be in great demand both in America and Asia.

Bolo Yeung - To know Bolo Yeung is to have seen Enter the Dragon or Bloodsport. His massive body and deadly scowl will not soon be forgotten. Originally a character villain, Bolo has gained international recognition for his memorable roles and has expanded to more heroic roles in the lead position. A bodybuilder and winner of numerous Mr. Hong Kong titles, Bolo (stage name) has appeared in countless numbers of films in a career that spans decades.

Yuen Biao - The youngest of the super-action trinity: Samo Hung, Jackie Chan, and Yuen Biao. The trio trained together for many years and starred in some memorable films, later breaking off into separate careers. Yuen Biao is the thin fighter, using flexibility and speed. He has a successful career, appearing in a number of traditional kung-fu movies with stars like Jet Li. Since he is younger, many of his earlier roles involved teenage hijinks and a sense of naiveness.

Johnny Yune - Korean comedian popular for his appearance on television and variety shows, including guests spots on The Love Boat and The Don Rickle special Even though a black belt in Tae Kwon Do, Yune would play comedic role making himself the buffoon who didn't know martial arts, They Call Me Bruce. Johnny is still enjoying success in South Korea.

Zhao Wen Zhou - Rising Hong Kong star who has appeared in a number of high-profile starring roles. Best known for taking over Jet Li's role as Wong Fei Hung in the Once Upon a Time in China 4 & 5. A noble actor trained in martial arts, he has appeared as villains and heroes.

APPENDIX IV
- FILMOGRAPHY OF ACTORS, ACTRESSES, AND FILMMAKERS

The Asian and Asian-American talent in front and behind the camera with a listing of their major films. All names are listed in alphabetical order based on family name. If an English surname is given, it will be listed after the Asian family name and Asian surname. Films will be listed in chronological order by year of production. Hong Kong based film stars will be listed in alphabetical order (years may be incorrect or not given).
Next to the name you will find alternative names, their birthyear, occupation, heritage, and Chinese pronunciation (when available). If he/she performs more than one role in the production of the film look for a plus (+director), if they had an alternative function to their occupation, look for a title without the plus. Example: "Dir Prod" equals only director and producer of the film.

Carrere, Tia (1968 -   )
Actress   Chinese/Spanish/Filipino
1987   Zombie Nightmare
1988   Aloha Summer
1989   The Road Raiders
1990   Fatal Mission
1990   Instant Karma +song performer
1991   Harley Davidson and the Marlboro Man
1991   Showdown in Little Tokyo
1992   Little Sister
1992   Wayne's World
1993   Batman: Mask of the Phantasm song vocals
1993   Rising Sun
1993   Wayne's World 2
1994   Quick
1994   Treacherous
1994   True Lies
1995   Jury Duty
1997   Kull

Chan Fan-Kei, Frankie   Actor
**   Chinese**
Cantonese: Chan Fan Kei
Mandarin: Chen2 Xun1 Ji1
   Armour of God 2: Operation Condor (1991) Dir
   Burning Ambition (1989) +Dir Prod
   Carry on Pickpocket
   Come Fly the Dragon (1992) +Action
   Dream of Desire

Everlasting Rhapsody
Fortune Code (1989) Cameo
Fun and Fury (1992) +Dir
Good, the Bad, and the Beauty, The (1990) +Dir
Just for Fun (1985) Dir
Oh! Yes Sir! (1994) +Dir
Outlaw Brothers (1988) +Dir Writer
Prodigal Son (1983)
Read Lips
Silent Romance
Sweet Surrender
Thunderbolt (1995) Action
Tragic Commitment (1995) Dir
Unforgettable Fantasy
Warrior's Tragedy, A (1993) +Dir
Wrath of Silence (1994) Dir Writer

Chan Car-Seung, Gordon
Director   Chinese
Cantonese: Chan Ga Seung
Mandarin: Chen2 Jia1 Shang4
   Bodyguard from Beijing, The (1994) Writer
   Brief Encounter in Tokyo
   Dream Lover (1995) Prod
   Fight Back to School (1991)
   Fight Back to School II (1992)
   Final Option, The (1994) +Writer
   Fist of Legend (1994) +Writer
   Game Kids (1992) +Writer
   Inspector Pink Dragon

King of Beggars (1993)
Long and Winding Road (1994) +Writer
Royal Tramp (1992)
Royal Tramp II (1992)
Thunderbolt (1995)
Tom, Dick, and Hairy (1993) Prod
Yuppie Fantasia, The

Chan, Jackie (Sing Lung)   (1954 -   )
Actor   Chinese
Cantonese: Sing Lung
Mandarin: Cheng2 Long2

36 Crazy Fists, The (1977) Dir Action
An   Alan   Smithee   Film: Burn,
Hollywood, Burn (1997)
Armour of God (1986) + Dir Writer
Armour of God 2: Operation Condor
(1991) + Dir Writer
Best of the Martial Arts Films, The
(1990)
Big Brawl, The (1980 U.S.A.)
Cannonball Run (1981)
Cannonball Run II (1984)
Cinema of Vengeance (1994 UK)
City Hunter (1992)
Countdown in Kung Fu (1975)
Crime Story (1993)
Dragon Fist (1978)
Dragon Lord (1982) + Dir Writer Prod
Dragons Forever (1987)
Drunken Fist Boxing Cameo
Drunken Master (1979) + Writer
Drunken Master II (1994)
Eagle Shadow Fist (1977)
Enchanting Night (197?) Prod
Enter the Dragon (1973 USA) Cameo
Fantasy Mission Force (1979)
Fearless Hyena, The (1979) +Dir Writer
Fearless Hyena Part II, The (1980)
First Mission, The (1982)
Gold Hunter Prod
Gorgeous (1999)
Half a Loaf of Kung Fu (1977)
Wheels on Meals (1984)
Who am I? (1998)

Highway
Incredibly Strange Picture Show: Jackie
Chan
Inspectors Wear Skirts (1988) Prod
Inspectors Wear Skirts 2 Prod
Island of Fire (1990)
Jackie Chan: My Story (1997)
Jackie Chan Stunts
Karate Bomber (197?)
Killer Meteors (1977)
Kung Fu Girl (1983) Cameo
Magnificent Bodyguards (1978)
Marvellous Fists (1982)
Master with Cracked Fingers (1971)
Miracles: The Canton Godfather (1989)
+Dir
Mr. Nice Guy (1997)
My Lucky Stars (1985)
Naughty Boys Prod
New Fist of Fury (1976)
Ninja Wars (1985) Cameo
Once a Cop (1993) Cameo
Police Story (1985) +Dir Writer
Police Story Part 2 (1988) +Dir Writer
Police Story 3: Supercop (1992)
Police Story 4 (1996) cameo
Project A (1983) +Dir Writer
Project A, Part II (1987) +Dir Writer
Protector, The (1985 U.S.A.)
Read Lips Prod
Rough, The Prod
Rumble in the Bronx (1995)
Rush Hour (1998)
Shanghai Noon (1999)
Shaolin Wooden Men (1976)
Snake and Crane Arts of Shaolin (1977)
Snake in Eagle's Shadow (1978) +Writer
Spiritual Kung Fu (1978)
Thunderbolt (1995) +Action
To Kill with Intrigue (1977)
Twin Dragons, The (1992)
Twinkle Twinkle Lucky Stars (1985)
Two in a Black Belt (1984) Cameo
Winners and Sinners (1983)
Young Master, The (1980) +Dir Writer

Chang Cheh   Director
Chinese

7 Blows of the Dragon (1972)
7 Soldiers of Kung Fu (197?)
Assassin
Assassins
Attack of the God of Joy (1983)
Blood Brothers (1973)
Boxer From Shantung (1972)
Brave Archer (1978)
Brave Archer 2
Brave Archer 3 (1979)
Chinatown Kid (1977)
Crippled Avengers (1978)
Daredevils of Kung Fu
Deadly Duo (197?)
Death Chambers
Destroyers
Five Deadly Venoms (1978)
Five Shaolin Masters (1975)
Girl With the Thunderbolt Kick, The (1968)
Heroic Ones (1970?)
House of Traps (1981)
Invincible Kung Fu Brothers
Just Heroes (1987) Prod
Kid With the Golden Arm, The (1978)
Killer Army
Masked Avengers (1981)
Men from the Monastery (1974)
New One-Armed Swordsman (1972)
Nine Demons (1984)
One-Armed Swordsman (1967)
One-Armed Swordsman Returns (1969)
Savage 5 (1979?)
Shaolin Martial Arts (1974)
Spearmen of Death (1980)
Street Gangs of Hong Kong
Super Ninjas (1982)
Sword and the Lute
Ten Tigers of Kwangtung (1979)
Unbeatable Dragon
Vengeance (1970)

Chen, Joan   (1961 -   )
Actress   Chinese

1976   Youth
1978   Little Flower
1979   Overseas
1980   The Awakening
1981   Peking Encounter
1984   Dim Sum: A Little Bit of Heart
1986   Tai-Pan
1987   The Last Emperor
1987   The Night Stalker
1988   Dim Sum Take-Outs
1990   The Blood of Heroes/Salute of the Jugger
1991   Deadlock
1992   Turtle Beach
1993   Golden Gate
1993   Heaven & Earth
1993   You Seng/Temptation of a Monk
1994   On Deadly Ground
1994   Red Rose, White Rose
1995   The Hunted
1995   Judge Dredd

Chen Kaige   (1952 -   )
Director   Chinese

1984   Yellow Earth/Huang Tudi
1986   The Big Parade/Da Yuebing
1987   The Last Emperor   performer
1988   King   of   Children/Haizi   Wang   +screenwriter
1991   Life on a String/Bian Zhou Bian Chang screenplay
1993   Farewell, My Concubine
1996   Tempest Moon

1999   The Emperor and the Assassin

Chen Kuan-Tai   **Actor**
        Chinese
Cantonese: Chan Goon Taai
Mandarin: Chen2 Guan4 Tai4
    Big Boss of Shanghai (1979) + Dir
    Black Magic With Buddha (1983)
    Blood Brothers (1973)
    Boxer From Shantung (1972)
    Crippled Avengers (1978)
    Deadly Duo (197?)
    Dirty Trick
    Eagle's Claw (1978) Dir
    Executioners From Shaolin (1977)
    Flying Guillotine (197?)
    Fortune Code (1989) Cameo
    I Will Finally Knock You Down, Dad
    Iron Monkey, The (1977) + Dir
    Just Heroes (1987)
    Kung Fu Hellcats
    Savage 5 (1979?)
    Three Evil Masters
    Tigers, The (1991)
    Warrior of Steel

Cheng Siu-Chow, Adam   Actor
        Chinese
Cantonese: Jeng Siu Chau
Mandarin: Zheng4 Shao3 Qiu1
    Cat Versus Rat (1982)
    Drunken Master III (1994)
    Eight Hilarious Gods, The (1994)
    Fantasy Mission Force (1979)
    Fong Sai Yuk (1993)
    Fong Sai Yuk II (1993)
    Frigidity
    Gunmen (1988)
    Heaven Sword and Dragon Sabre
    Last Night's Light
    Moon and Stars
    New Legend of Shaolin, The (1994)
    Painted Skin (1992)
    Path of Glory

    Profile of Pleasure (1987)
    Sap Sup Bup Dub
    Seven Warriors
    Shaolin and Wu Tang
    Shaolin Popey 2: Messy Temple (1994
Taiwan)
    Sword, The (1980)
    Zu: Warriors of the Magic Mountain
(1983)

Cheng Juk-Si, Kent (Cheng Chuen Yan)
        Actor Chinese
Cantonese: Jeng Jak Si
Mandarin: Zheng4 Ze2 Shi4
    Accident, The
    Ancient Chinese Whorehouse (1994)
    Beginner's Luck (1994) +Writer Prod
    Beloved Daddy
    Bloody Brothers (1994)
    Bodyguard from Beijing, The (1994)
    Bomb Lover (1995)
    Cohabitation (1994)
    Cop Busters
    Crime Story (1993)
    Diary of a Big Man (7/1988)
    Doctor Lamb (1992)
    Dragon in Jail (1990) Dir
    Dragon, the Odds, The (197?) Cameo
    Easy Money (1987)
    Family Day   +Writer
    Fat Cat (1988)
    Fortune Code (1989) +Dir
    From the Great Beyond
    Fun and Fury (1992)
    Ghost Legend
    Give Me Back
    Gods Must Be Funny in China, The
(1994)
    Good, the Bad, and the Beauty, The
(1990)
    Heaven Can't Wait (1995)
    Hero of Hong Kong 1949
    Hong Kong Graffiti (1995) Cameo
    Kidnap of Wong Chak Fai, The (1993)

Kung Fu Scholar, The (1994) Cameo
Let's Go Slam Dunk (1994)
Lethal Contact   +Dir
Lifeline Express
Lord of East China Sea (1993)
Lord of East China Sea 2 (1993)
Lucky Encounter
Man from Vietnam, The
Man of the Times (1993)
Mermaid Got Married (1994)
Mission to Kill
Most Wanted, The (1994)
Mr. Smart
Mr. Sunshine (1990)
Oh! My Cops
Once Upon a Time in China (1990)
Once Upon a Time in China 5 (1994)
Powerful Four (1991)
Roof With a View (1990) Cameo
Run and Kill (1993)
S.D.U. - Mission in Mission (1994)
Sentenced to Hang
Sex and Zen (1989)
Spiritual Trinity Prod
Spooky Family, The
Sweet & Sour Cops, The
Sweet & Sour Cops II, The
Those Were the Days... (1995)
To Be Number One (1991)
Turning Point, The
Vampire Buster
Vampire's Breakfast
Vendetta (1992)
Why Me? (10/1985)   +Dir
Wonder Seven (1994)
You're My Destiny (1987) Cameo

Cheng Man-Ar, Olivia
Actress   Chinese
Cantonese: Jeng Man Nga
Mandarin: Zheng4 Wen2 Ya3
    Blue Lightning
    Dragon Force (1982)
    Family Affair, A (1984)
    My Dear Son (1989)

Legend of the Brothers (1991)
How to be a Billionaire
Killer's Blues, A
Missed Date, The (5/1986)
Shanghai Express (1986)
Till Death Do We Scare
United We Stand
Why Me? (10/1985)
Wild Ones, The
Winner Takes All

Cheung Hok Yau, Jacky   (7/10/1961-
**   )   Actor Chinese**
Cantonese: Jeung Hok Yau
Mandarin: Zhang1 Xue2 You3
    As Tears Go By (1988)
    Ashes of Time (1994)
    Banquet, The (1991)
    Best Friend of the Cops
    Best of the Best (1992)
    Boys Are Easy (1993)
    Bullet for Hire (1991)
    Bullet in the Head (1990)
    Chinese Ghost Story Part II, A (1990)
    Chinese Ghost Story Part III, A (1991)
    Chinese Legend, A (1991)
    Couples, Couples, Couples
    Curry and Pepper (1990)
    Days of Being Dumb, The (1992)
    Days of Being Wild (1990)
    Deadly Dream Woman (1992)
    Demoness from Thousand Year
    Double Fixation
    Eagle Shooting Heroes, The (1993)
    Eight Happiness, The (2/1988)
    Enigma of Love (1993)
    Flying Dagger (1993)
    Future Cops (1993)
    Haunted Cop Shop (1987) Cameo
    Haunted Cop Shop II (1988)
    High Risk (1995)
    Love on Delivery (1994) Cameo
    Miracles: The Canton Godfather (1989)
Cameo
    My Dream is Yours

No More Love, No More Death (1993)
Nobles
Off Track (1990)
Once Upon a Time in China (1990)
Perfect Match 1991, The (1991)
Point of No Return (1991)
Pom Pom & Hot Hot (1992)
Private Eye Blues (1994)
Raid, The (1991)
Seven Warriors
Slickers vs. Killers (1991)
Soul (1986)
Swordsman (1990)
Tiger Cage (1988)
To Live and Die in Tsimshatsui (1994)
True Love (1992)
Vampire Buster
Where's Officer Tuba (1988)
Wicked City, The (1992)
Will of Iron (1991)
With or Without You (1991?)

Cheung Kwok Wing, Leslie (1956-   )
Actor   Chinese
Cantonese: Jeung Gwok Wing
Mandarin: Zhang1 Guo2 Rong2
Aces Go Places 5: The Terracotta Hit (1989)
All's Well, Ends Well (1992)
All's Well, Ends Well Too (1993)
Arrest the Restless (1992)
Ashes of Time (1994)
Banquet, The (1991)
Better Tomorrow, A (8/1986)
Better Tomorrow II, A (12/1987)
Bride with White Hair, The (1993)
Bride with White Hair 2, The (1993)
Chinese Feast, The (1995)
Chinese Ghost Story, A (1987)
Chinese Ghost Story Part II, A (1990)
Crazy Romance (1982)
Days of Being Wild (1990)
Double Decker (1984)
Enigma of Love (1993)
Executioners (1993)

Drummer, The (1980)
Eagle Shooting Heroes, The (1993)
Erotic Dream of the Red Chamber
Farewell, My Concubine (1993)
Fatal Love (1988)
Fate (1984)
For Your Heart Only (1985)
He is a Woman, She is a Man (1994)
Intellectual Trio (1984?)
It's a Wonderful Life (1994)
Last Song in Paris (1982)
Long and Winding Road (1994)
Merry Christmas (1984) Cameo
Nomad (1982)
On Trial (1980)
Once a Thief (2/1991)
Over the Rainbow Under the Skirt (1994)
Cameo
Phantom Lover (1995)
Rouge (1987)
Temptress Moon (1997)

Cheung Man Yuk, Maggie   (9/20/1964-
)   Actress
Chinese
Cantonese: Jeung Maan Yuk
Mandarin: Zhang1 Man4 Yu4
Actress (1992)
Alan and Eric - Between Hello and Goodbye (1991)
All's Well, Ends Well (1992)
As Tears Go By (1988)
Ashes of Time (1994)
Bachelor's Swan Song (1989)
Banquet, The (1991)
Bare-Footed Kid, The (1993)
Boys Are Easy (1993)
Call Girl '88 (1988)
Days of Being Wild (1990)
Doubles Cause Troubles (1989)
Dragon from Russia (1990)
Eagle Shooting Heroes, The (1993)

Farewell China (1990)
Fat Cat (1988)

Fate (1984)
First Shot (1993)
Fishy Story, A (1989)
Flying Dagger (1993)
Frog Prince, The (1984)
Full Moon in New York (1990)
Game They Call Sex, The (1987)
Green Snake (1993)
Happy Fat New Year (1988)
Happy Ghost 3 (1986)
Heart Against Hearts (1991) Cameo
Heart into Hearts (1990)
Heartbeat 100 (1987)
Hearts No Flowers (1989)
Heavenly Fate (1987)
Heroic Trio, The (1992)
Holy Weapon (1993)
Iceman Cometh (1989)
In Between (1/1994)
In Between Love (1989)
It's a Drink, It's a Bomb (1985)
Last Romance (1988)
Little Cop
Love Army (1988)
Lovelorn Expert, The
Mad Monk (1993)
Millionaire Cop (1993)
Modern Cinderella (1985)
Moon Warriors (1992)
My Dear Son (1989)
New Dragon Inn (1992)
North and South Mamas (1988)
Paper Marriage (1988)
Perfect Match 1991, The (1991)
Police Story (1985)
Police Story Part 2 (1988)
Police Story 3: Supercop (1992)
Project A, Part II (1987)
Red Dust (1990)
Romancing Star, The (6/1987)
Rose (1992)
Seventh Curse, The (10/1986)
Holy Weapon (1993)
It's Now or Never (1992)
King of Beggars (1993)

Soldier of Love (1988)
Song of the Exile (1989)
Story of Rose, The (2/1986)
Sun, Moon, and Star (1988)
Today's Hero (1991)
Too Happy for Words (1992)
True Love (1992)
Twin Dragons, The (1992)
What a Hero (1992)
Will of Iron (1991)
You're My Destiny (1987) Cameo

Cheung Man   Actress
Chinese
Cantonese: Jeung Man
Mandarin: Zhang1 Min3
All for the Winner (1990)
Bet on Fire
Buddhist Spell, The
Call Girl '92 (1992)
Cheetah on Fire (1992)
Chinese Legend, A (1991)
Crystal Fortune Run (1994)
Dances with the Dragon
Deadly Dream Woman (1992)
Devil's Vendetta (1991)
Dragon Killer (1995)
Dream Lover (1995) Prod
Dream of Desire
Faithfully Yours
Fight Back to School (1991)
Fight Back to School II (1992)
Fight Back to School III (1993)
Flying Dagger (1993)
God of Gamblers (12/1989)
God of Gamblers II (1989)
God of Gamblers III: Back to Shanghai (1991) Cameo
God of Gamblers' Return (12/1994) Cameo
Hail the Judge (1994)
Handsome Siblings (1992)
Kung Fu Cult Master, The (1993)
Last Hero in China, The (1993)
Lee Rock I

Lee Rock II
Lee Rock III
Legend of the Liquid Sword (1993)
Cameo
My Neighbors are Phantoms
Rhythm of Destiny (1992)
Romancing Star III, The
Romantic Dream (1995)
Royal Tramp (1992)
Royal Tramp II (1992)
Semi-Gods and Semi-Devils (1994)
Story of Kennedy Town
Sword of Many Loves, The (1992)
Sword Stained With Royal Blood (1993)
Swordsman (1990)
Ten Brothers (1995)
Tiger Cage 3 (1991)
To Miss with Love (8/1992)
Tricky Gambler
Truant Heroes
Underground Judgement (1994)
Vendetta (1992)

Chiang, David (Keung Dai-Wai)
Actor   Chinese
Cantonese: Geung Daai Wai
Mandarin: Jiang1 Da4 Wei4
7 Blows of the Dragon (1972)
7 Soldiers of Kung Fu (197?)
Adventurers, The (1995)
Angel (1986)
Assassinators
Blood Brothers (1973)
Deadly Duo (197?)
Deadly Mantis (1978)
Death Chambers
Duel of Fists
Duel of Iron Fists
Five Shaolin Masters (1975)
Funny Soldier
Heroic Ones (1970?)
All Mighty Gambler
Challenge to Devil Area
Come from China
Crazy Shaolin Disciples

Just Heroes (1987)
Legend of the 7 Golden Vampires
Legend of the Owl, The
Mother of a Different Kind (1995) Dir
My Dear Son (1989) Dir
New One-Armed Swordsman (1972)
Once Upon a Time in China 2 (1991)
One Armed Swordsmen, The +Dir
Return of the Deadly Blade
Savage 5 (1979?)
Slice of Death
Tiger on Beat (3/1988)
Till Death Do We Scare
Twin Dragons, The (1992)
Vengeance (1970)
What Price Survival (1994)
Where's Officer Tuba (1988)
Will of Iron (1991) Dir
Wrong Couples, The (1987) Dir

Chiang Sheng   Actor
Chinese
Brave Archer 3 (1979)
Crippled Avengers (1978)
Daredevils of Kung Fu
Destroyers
Five Deadly Venoms (1978)
House of Traps (1981)
Kid With the Golden Arm, The (1978)
Killer Army
Masked Avengers (1981)
Ninja's Deadly Trap
Ode to Gallantry
Spearmen of Death (1980)
Ten Tigers of Kwangtung (1979)
Unbeatable Dragon

Chin Siu-Ho Actor   Chinese
Cantonese: Chin Siu Ho
Mandarin: Qian2 Xiao3 Hao2

Dead Target
Don't Give a Damn (1995)
Edge of Darkness
Fist of Legend (1994)

Fortune Hunters
Four Dragons
Fumbling Cops
Ghosts Galore
Happy Together 1993 (1993?)
Hero Dream (1993)
I Will Finally Knock You Down, Dad
Into the Fire
Masked Avengers (1981)
Mr. Vampire (1984)
Mr. Vampire 4 (1987)
Mr. Vampire 1992 (1992)
New Kids in Town
New Mr. Vampire
One Eyebrow Priest
Righting Wrongs 2: Blonde Fury (1987)
Seventh Curse, The (10/1986)
Tai Chi Master (1993)
Ten Tigers of Kwangtung (1979)
Two Champions of Shaolin
Ultimate Vampire (1987)
Vengeance of the Six Dragon, The
Visa to Hell

Ching Siu Tung   Director
Chinese
Cantonese: Ching Siu Dung
Mandarin: Cheng2 Xiao3 Dong1
Better Tomorrow II, A (12/1987) Action
Butterfly and Sword (1993) Action
Casino Raiders II Action
Chinese Ghost Story, A (1987)
Chinese Ghost Story Part II, A (1990)
Chinese Ghost Story Part III, A (1991)
Chinese Odyssey Part One - Pandora's Box, A (1995) Action
Chinese Odyssey Part Two - Cinderella, A (1995) Action
City Hunter (1992) Action
Duel to the Death (1982)
Romance of the Vampires (1994)
Tough Beauty and the Sloppy Slop (1995)

Chow Sing-Chi, Stephen   Actor

Executioners (1993) +Prod
Flying Dagger (1993) +Action
Heroic Trio, The (1992) Action Prod
Holy Weapon (1993) Action
I Love Maria (1988) Action
Justice, My Foot (1992) Action
Killer, The (7/1989) Action
Mad Monk (1993)
Moon Warriors (1992) Action
New Dragon Inn (1992) Action
Once Upon a Time in China (1990) Action
Peking Opera Blues (1986) Action
Raid, The (1991) Actor Dir
Scripture with No Words, The (1996)
Son on the Run (1991) Action
Swordsman (1990)
Swordsman II (1991)
Swordsman 3: East is Red (1993)
Terracotta Warrior, The (1989)
Witch from Nepal (2/1986)
Wonder Seven (1994)

Chow Bei-Lei, Billy   Actor
Chinese
Cantonese: Jau Bei Lei
Mandarin: Zhou1 Bi3 Li4
Dragons Forever (1987)
Escape from the Brothel (1992)
Fist of Legend (1994)
Gambling Baron (1994)
High Risk (1995)
Horrible High Heels (1996)
In the Line of Duty 2: Middleman (1987)
Kick Boxer's Tears (1992)
Magic Cop (1989)
Miracles: The Canton Godfather (1989)
Pedicab Driver (1989)
Righting Wrongs 2: Blonde Fury (1987)
Robotrix (1991)
Chinese
Cantonese: Jau Sing Chi
Mandarin: Zhou1 Xing1 Chi2
All for the Winner (1990)
All's Well, Ends Well (1992)

Banquet, The (1991)

Chinese Odyssey Part One - Pandora's Box, A (1995)

Chinese Odyssey Part Two - Cinderella, A (1995)

Crazy Safari (1991)

Curry and Pepper (1990)

Dragon Fight (1988)

Faithfully Yours

Fight Back to School (1991)

Fight Back to School II (1992)

Fight Back to School III (1993)

Final Justice

Fist of Fury 1991 (1991)

Flirting Scholar (1993)

From Beijing with Love (1994) +Dir Writer

God of Gamblers II (1989)

God of Gamblers III: Back to Shanghai (1991)

Hail the Judge (1994)

He Who Chases After the Wind

Just Heroes (1987)

Justice, My Foot (1992)

King of Beggars (1993)

Legend of the Dragon (1990)

Look Out, Officer!

Love is Love

Love on Delivery (1994)

Lung Fung Restaurant

Mad Monk (1993)

Magnificent Scoundrels (1991)

My Hero

My Hero 2 (1993) Cameo

Out of the Dark (1995)

Royal Tramp (1992)

Royal Tramp II (1992)

Sixty Million Dollar Man (1995)

Sleazy Dizzy

All About Ah Long (3/1989)

Anna and the King (1999)

Autumn's Tale, An (7/1987)

Better Tomorrow, A (8/1986)

Better Tomorrow II, A (12/1987)

Better Tomorrow III: Love and Death in

Thunder Cops

Thunder Cops 2 (1989)

Top Bet Cameo

Triad Story

Tricky Brains (1991)

Unmatchable Match, The (1989)

When Fortune Smiles

**Chow Wai-Man, Vivian   (11/20/1967-
)   Actress   Chinese**
Cantonese: Jau Wai Man
Mandarin: Zhou1 Hui4 Min3

Angel Hunter (1991)

Arrest the Restless (1992)

Devil's Vendetta (1991)

Family Affairs (1994)

Fruit Punch (1992)

Fun and Fury (1992)

Girls Without Tomorrow (1992)

Goodbye Hero

Happy Together (1989)

Heart Against Hearts (1991)

Heart into Hearts (1990)

Heart to Hearts (1988)

Kung Fu Scholar, The (1994)

No Regret, No Return (1993)

Path of Glory

Perfect Match 1991, The (1991)

Summer Lovers (1992)

To Love Ferrari (1994)

Tom, Dick, and Hairy (1993) Cameo

Unmatchable Match, The (1989)

**Chow Yun-Fat, Donald   (5/181955 -
)   Actor   Chinese**
Cantonese: Jau Yun Faat
Mandarin: Zhou1 Run4 Fa1

100 Ways to Murder Your Wife (6/1986)

Saigon, A (10/1989)

Blacklist (1986)

Blood Money (3/1983)

Bund, The (1/1983)

Bund Part II, The (1/1983)

Cherry Blossoms (9/1988)

City on Fire (2/1987)
City War (12/1988)
Code of Honour (3/1987) [Cameo]
Corruptor, The (1999)
Crouching Tiger, Hidden Dragon (2000)
Diary of a Big Man (7/1988)
Dream Lovers (4/1986)
Eight Happiness, The (2/1988)
Executioner, The (3/1981)
Flaming Brothers (7/1987)
Fractured Follies (7/1988)
Full Contact (7/1992)
Fun, the Luck, and the Tycoon, The (1/1990)
God of Gamblers (12/1989)
God of Gamblers' Return (12/1994)
Goodbye, Hero (10/1988)
Greatest Lover, The (7/1988)
Hard Boiled (4/1992)
Head Hunter, The (3/1983)
Hearty Response, A (10/1986)
Heroic Cops
Hong Kong 1941 (11/1984)
Hot Blood (9/1977)
Hunter, the Butterfly, and the Crocodile, The (11/1976)
Joy to the World (6/1980)
Killer, The (7/1989)
Last Affair, The (12/1983)
Learned Bride Thrice Fools Bridegroom (4/1976)
Love in a Fallen City (8/1984)
Love Unto Waste (8/1986)
Lunatics, The (6/1986)
Massage Girls (9/1976)
Miss O (4/1978)
Missed Date, The (5/1986)
Now You See Love, Now You Don't Killer, The (7/1989)
Once a Thief (2/1991)
Raid, The (1991)
To Be Number One (1991)

Chung, Cherie (Chong Chu Hung)
Actress   Chinese

(2/1992)
Occupant, The (9/1984)
Once a Thief (2/1991)
Peace Hotel (4/1995)
Pembunuhan Pursuit
Police Sir (9/1980)
Postman Strikes Back (6/1982)
Prison on Fire (11/1987)
Prison on Fire 2 (6/1991)
Reincarnation, The (3/1976)
Replacement Killers, The (1998)
Rich and Famous (5/1987)
Romancing Star, The (6/1987)
Scared Stiff (3/1987)
See-Bar (1/1980)
Seventh Curse, The (10/1986)
Spiritual Love (9/1987)
Story of Rose, The (2/1986)
Story of Woo Viet, The (4/1981)
Their Private Lives (1/1978)
Tiger on Beat (3/1988)
Tragic Hero (2/1987)
Treasure Hunt (2/1994)
Triads - The Inside Story (8/1989)
Why Me? (10/1985)
Wild Search (6/1989)
Witch from Nepal (2/1986)
Women (6/1985)
You Will I Will (11/1986)

Chu Kong, Paul   Actor
**   Chinese**
Cantonese: Jue Gong
Mandarin: Zhu1 Jiang1
Big Heat, The (1988)
Dances with the Dragon Cameo
Fong Sai Yuk (1993)

Cantonese: Jung Choh Hung
Mandarin: Zhong1 Chu3 Hong2
18 Times
Autumn's Tale, An (7/1987)
Banana Cop (1984)
Bet on Fire
Carry On Hotel (1988)

Chaos by Design
Cherie (1984)
Couples, Couples, Couples
Dead and the Deadly, The (1982)
Descendant of the Sun
Diary of a Small Man
Double Fixation
Eclipse
Eight Happiness, The (2/1988)
Fatal Love (1988)
Frog Prince, The (1984)
Golden Swallow (10/1988)
Good, the Bad, and the Beauty, The (1990?)
Goodbye Darling
Happy Ding Dong
Happy Together (1989)
Heaven Can Wait
Hong Kong Playboys
Last Romance (1988)
Mr. Mistress
My Darling Genie
Once a Thief (2/1991)
One Husband Too Many
Peking Opera Blues (1986)
Postman Strikes Back (6/1982)
Spiritual Love (9/1987)
Stars & Roses (1990)
Story of Woo Viet, The (4/1981)
Sun, Moon, and Star (1988)
Walk on Fire
Wild Search (6/1989)
Women (6/1985)
Yuppie Fantasia, The
Zodiac Killers

Master of Disaster (1982)
Men from the Monastery (1974)
Shaolin Martial Arts (1974)
Ten Tigers of Kwangtung (1979)

Honda Inoshiro   (1911 - 1993)
Director   Japanese
1949   Stray Dog   assistant dir
1955   Half-Human

Cheung Lai-Tai, Christy
Actress   Chinese/Vietnamese
Cantonese: Jung Lai Tai
Mandarin: Zhong1 Li4 Ti2
Bodyguard from Beijing, The (1994)
Bride with White Hair 2, The (1993)
Faithfully Yours 1995 (1995)
Hail the Judge (1994)
Heaven Can't Wait (1995) Cameo
I Wanna Be Your Man (1994)
Love on Delivery (1994)
Mack the Knife (1995)
Man Wanted (1995)
Mermaid Got Married (1994)
Modern Romance (1994)
Passion 1995 (1995)
Perfect Exchange, The (1993)
Red Wolf, The (1995)
Sting 2, The
Whatever You Want (1994)

Fu Sheng,   Alexander   Actor
**   Chinese**
Brave Archer (1978)
Brave Archer 2
Brave Archer 3 (1979)
Brave Archer 4 (1979)
Cat Versus Rat (1982)
Chinatown Kid (1977)
Death Chambers
Eight Diagram Pole Fighter (1983)
Five Shaolin Masters (1975)
Hong Kong Playboys
Invincible Kung Fu Brothers
Invincible One
Legendary Weapons of China (1982)
1956   Godzilla, King of the Monsters
1957   Rodan
1958   The H-Man
1959   The Mysterians
1962   Mothra
1963   King Kong vs. Godzilla
1963   Matango - Fungus of Terror
1964   Artagon
1965   Ghidrah, The Three-Headed Monster

1966 The War of the Gargantuas
1968 Destroy All Monsters!
1969 Godzilla's Revenge
1969 Latitude Zero
1985 Ran   direction counsellor
1990 Akira   Kurosawa's   Dreame
      creative consultant

Hu Hui Chung, Sibelle
Actress   Chinese
Cantonese: Woo Wai Jung
Mandarin: Hu2 Hui4 Zhong1
Angel Mission (1993)
Angel Terminators 2 (1993)
Bury Me High (1990)
China Heat
City of Sadness, A
Combat at Heaven Gate
Crazy Spirit
Crystal Hunt (1991)
Cute Little Fellow, The
Devil Hunters (1989)
Dragon Fighter (198?)
Dreaming the Reality (1991)
Drugs Area
Fighting Fist
Fire Phoenix
Flying Rainbow, The
Fong Sai Yuk (1993)
Ghost of the Fox
Inspectors Wear Skirts (1988)
Inspectors Wear Skirts 2
Lethal Contact
Lethal Panther (1990)
Inspectors Wear Skirts 2
Inspectors Wear Skirts 4 (1992)
Legend of the Drunken Tiger
Legendary Weapons of China (1982)
Mad Monkey Kung Fu (1979)
Madame City Hunter (1992)
Martial Club (1981)
Mega Force from Highland
My Young Auntie (1981)
Naughty Boys
Never Say Regret

Love on the Big Country
Magic Amethyst, The
Mighty Gambler, The (1992)
Mr. Vampire 2 (1985)
My Lucky Stars (1985)
Queen of Gamble
Raid on Royal Casino Marine (1990)
Roar of the Vietnamese, The
Seventh Curse, The (10/1986)
Sleazy Dizzy
To Spy with Love
Twinkle Twinkle Lucky Stars (1985)
Way of the Lady Boxers (1992)

Hui Ying-Hung, Kara
Actress   Chinese
Cantonese: Wai Ying Hung
Mandarin: Hui4 Ying1 Hong2
Angel Terminators (1990)
Behind the Curtain
Brave Archer (1978)
Brave Archer 2
Brave Archer 3 (1979)
Brave Archer 4 (1979)
Brave Young Girls (1988)
Braveful Police (1990)
Burning Ambition (1989)
Dirty Ho (1979)
Double Decker (1984)
Eight Diagram Pole Fighter (1983)
Fists of the White Lotus (1980)
Ghost Treats People
Happy-Go-Lucky
Inspectors Wear Skirts (1988)
On Parole
Out Bound Killing
Queen of Gambler
Raid on Royal Casino Marine (1990)
Real Me
Stage Door Johnny
Tattoo Girl
That's Money
Vengeance of the Six Dragon, The
Vengeance, The
Visa to Hell

Widow Warriors (1989)
Zen of Sword (1992)

Hung Kam Bo, Samo (Sammo Hung)
Actor (noted director also)
Chinese   Cantonese: Hung
Gam Bo
Mandarin: Hong2 Jin1 Bao3
Ashes of Time (1994) Action
Banquet, The (1991)
Best of the Martial Arts Films, The (1990)
Blade of Fury (1993) +Dir
Broken Oath (1977)
By Hook or by Crook
Carry on Pickpocket +Dir
Cinema of Vengeance (1994 UK)
Close Encounters of the Spooky Kind (1980) +Dir
Close Encounters of the Spooky Kind 2 (1989) +Dir
Countdown in Kung Fu (1975) Actor Action
Daddy, Father and Papa (1991)
Dead and the Deadly, The (1982)
Don't Give a Damn (1995) +Dir Prod
Dragon, the Odds, The (197?) Cameo
Dragons Forever (1987) +Dir
Dreadnought (1981)
Eagle Shooting Heroes, The (1993) Action
Eastern Condors (1986) +Dir
Eight Taels of Gold (1990)
Shanghai Express (1986) +Dir
Shanghai, Shanghai (1990)
Shaolin Plot
She Shoots Straight (1990)
Skinny Tiger and Fatty Dragon (1990)
Skyhawk
Slickers vs. Killers (1991) +Dir Prod
Somebody Up There Likes Me (1996)
Spooky Spooky (1986) +Dir
Tantana, the
Thunderbolt (1995) Action
To Err is Human

Enter the Fat Dragon (197?) +Dir
First Mission, The (1982) +Dir
Fortune Code (1989)
Game of Death (1979 USA)
Ghost Punting (1991)
Incredible Kung-Fu Master, The
Iron Fisted Monk +Dir
Island of Fire (1990)
It's a Drink, It's a Bomb (1985) Prod
Knockabout (1979?) +Dir
Kung Fu Cult Master, The (1993) +Action
Last Eunuch in China (1988)
Lethal Lady (1990) +Prod
Lover's Tear (1991) +Prod
Lucky Stars
Lucky Stars Go Places
Magnificent Butcher
Man from Hong Kong, The (1975 USA)
Moon Warriors (1992) Dir
Mr. Vampire 3 Prod Cameo
My Flying Wife (1991)
My Lucky Stars (1985) +Dir
Operation Scorpio (1991) Prod
Painted Faces (1988)
Painted Skin (1992)
Pantyhose Hero (1990)
Paper Marriage (1988)
Pedicab Driver (1989) +Dir Prod
Prodigal Son (1983) +Dir
Project A (1983)
Righting Wrongs 2: Blonde Fury (1987) Prod
Touch and Go (1991)
Twinkle Twinkle Lucky Stars (1985) +Dir
Valiant Ones (1974)
Victim, The (1980) +Dir
Warriors Two (1978) +Dir
Wheels on Meals (1984) +Dir
Where's Officer Tuba (1988) +Prod
Winner Take All
Winners and Sinners (1983) +Dir
Yes Madam! (1985) +Prod
Zu: Warriors of the Magic Mountain

(1983)

Itami Juzo (Yoshihiro Ikeuchi)   (1933 -1997)
Actor (later Director)   Japanese
1960   The Big Wave
1963   55 Days at Peking
1965   Lord Jim
1967   Nihon Shunka-Ko
1975   I am a Cat
1979   Collections Privees
1980   Mo Hoozue wa Tsukanai
1983   The Politician
1984   The Family Game
1984   The Funeral/Ososhiki   director, screenwriter
1984   Kusameikyu
1985   MacArthur's Children
1985   The Makioka Sisters
1986   Tampopo   producer, director
1987   A Taxing Woman/Marusa no Onna   director, screenwriter
1988   Sweet Home   executive producer
1988   A Taxing Woman's Return/Marusa no Onna II   director, screenwriter
1990   A-Ge-Man   producer, director, screenwriter
1992   The Gangster's Moll/Mimbo no Onna   director, screenplay
1992   Minbo: Anti-Extortion   Woman

Kurosawa started as a talented assistant director and editor. He also went on to write a number of screenplays that were made into films under different directors.
1943   Judo Saga +screenwriter, editor
1944   The Most Beautiful   +screenwriter, story
1945   Judo Saga II   +screenwriter
1945   The Men Who Tread on the Tiger's Tail   +screenwriter
1946   Asu O Tsukuru Hitobito
1946   No   Regrets   for   Our   Youth +screenwriter
1947   Subarashiki Nichiyobi+screenwriter
1947   Yottsu   no   Koi   no   Monogatari

director

Khan,   Cynthia   (Yeung   Lai   Ching)
Actress   Chinese
Cantonese: Yeung Lai Ching
Mandarin: Yang2 Li4 Qing1
    Angel on Fire
    Avenging Quartet (1992)
    Blade of Fury (1993)
    Deadend of Besiegers (1992)
    Forbidden Arsenal (1991)
    In the Line of Duty 2: Middleman (1987)
    In the Line of Duty 3 (1988)
    In the Line of Duty 4: Witness (1989)
    Inspectors Wear Skirts 4 (1992)
    It's Now or Never (1992)
    Madame City Hunter (1992)
    Pink Bomb
    Queen's High (1991)
    Sea Wolves (1990)
    Thirteen Cold-Blooded Eagles (1992)
    Tiger Cage 2 (1990) Cameo
    Tough   Beauty   and   the   Sloppy   Slop (1995)   Transmigration Romance (1991)
    Ultimate Revenge (1995)
    Yes Madam '92: A Serious Shock (1992)
    Zen of Sword (1992)

Kurosawa Akira   (1910   -9/5/1998)
Director/Writer   Japanese
    screenwriter_   "Hatuskoi"/"First Love"
1948   Drunken Angel   +screenwriter
1949   The   Quiet   Duel +co-screenwriter
1949   Stray Dog   +screenwriter
1950   Rashomon   +screenwriter
1950   Shuban   +screenwriter, story
1951   The Idiot   +screenwriter
1952   Ikiru/To Live +screenwriter
1954   The Seven Samurai   +story, editor
1955   Record   of   a   Living   Being +screenwriter, story
1957   The Lower Depths   +producer, screenwriter

1957 Throne of Blood +producer, screenwriter, editor
1958 The Hidden Fortress +producer, story
1960 The Bad Sleep Well/Warui Yatsu Hodo Yoku Nemuru +producer, story
1961 Yojimbo/The Bodyguard +story
1962 High and Low +screenwriter
1962 Sanjuro +screenwriter, editor
1963 The Directors performer
1965 Red Beard +screenwriter
1965 Sugata Sanshiro screenwriter
1970 Dodes'ka Den +producer
1972 75 Years of Cinema Museum performer
1975 Dersu Uzala +screenwriter
1980 Kagemusha (The Shadow Warrior) +producer, screenwriter, co-executive prod
1985 Ran +screenwriter, editor
1985 Runaway Train from screenplay
1990 Dreams +screenwriter
1991 Rhapsody in August +screenplay
1993 Madadayo +screenplay

Kwan, Nancy (1939 -)
Actress Chinese
1960 The World of Suzie Wong
1961 Flower Drum Song
1962 The Main Attraction
Bite of Love, A (1990)
Blade of Fury (1993)
Brief Encounter in Tokyo
Casino Raiders
Challenge of Chasing Girls
Eight Hilarious Gods, The (1994)
End of the Road (1993)
Frog Prince, The (1984)
Game Kids (1992)
Ghost Fever
Gigolo and Whore II
Great Conqueror's Concubine, The (1994)
Head Hunter, The (3/1983)

1963 Tamahine
1964 Fate is the Hunter
1964 Honeymoon Hotel
1965 The Wild Affair
1966 Arrivederci, Baby!
1966 The Corrupt Ones
1966 Lt. Robin Crusoe, USN
1968 Hawaii Five-O
1968 Nobody's Perfect
1969 Girl Who Knew Too Much
1969 The Wrecking Crew
1970 The McMasters
1970 That Lady From Peking
1973 Wonder Women
1975 Supercock
1978 Night Creature/Out of the Darkness
1979 Fragrant Harbor
1983 The Last Ninja
1990 Babies
1990 Miracle Landing
1993 Dragon: The Bruce Lee Story

Kwan Ji Lam, Rosamund (9/24/1962-) Actress Chinese
Cantonese: Gwaan Ji Lam
Mandarin: Guan1 Zhi1 Lin2
Adventurers, The (1995)
All's Well, Ends Well Too (1993)
Armour of God (1986)
Assassin, The (1993)
Banquet, The (1991)
Heart Against Hearts (1991) Cameo
Heart to Hearts (1988)
Her Beautiful Life Lies
Inspector Pink Dragon
Last Duel, The
Long and Winding Road (1994)
Love Among the Triad (1993)
Love is a Fairy Tale (1993)
Magic Crane, The (1993)
No More Love, No More Death (1993)
Once Upon a Time in China (1990)
Once Upon a Time in China 2 (1991)
Once Upon a Time in China 3 (1992)
Once Upon a Time in China 5 (1994)

Once Upon a Time in China 6 (1997)
Pretty Ghost
Project A, Part II (1987)
Proud and Confident
Return to Action
Saviour of the Soul II (1992)
Scripture with No Words, The (1996)
Shanghai Express (1986)
Sting, The
Swordsman (1990)
Swordsman II (1991)
This Thing Called Love (1991)
Three Against the World
Tiger Cage 2 (1990)
Touch of Evil, A (1995)
Tricky Brains (1991)
Twinkle Twinkle Lucky Stars (1985)
Undeclared War (1992)
Vengeance is Mine (1992)
What a Small World
With or Without You (1991?)

Kwok Fu Shing, Aaron
(10/26/1965-)   Actor Chinese
Cantonese: Gwok Foo Sing
Mandarin: Guo1 Fu4 Cheng2
Banquet, The (1991)
Bare-Footed Kid, The (1993)
Big Heat, The (1988)
Close Escape (1989)
Mandarin: Guo1 Zhen4 Feng1
Big Heat, The (1988)
Chinatown Kid (1977)
Crippled Avengers (1978)
Daredevils of Kung Fu
Destroyers
Five Deadly Venoms (1978)
Hard Boiled (4/1992) +Action
Holy Flame of the Martial World
House of Traps (1981)
Kid With the Golden Arm, The (1978)
Killer Army
Masked Avengers (1981)
Ninja's Deadly Trap
Ode to Gallantry

Future Cops (1993)
Game Kids (1992)
Gangs '92 (1992)
Kung Fu Scholar, The (1994)
Lee Rock II
Legend of the Liquid Sword (1993)
Love is a Fairy Tale (1993)
Millionaire Cop (1993)
Moment of Romance 2, A (1993)
Queen of Gamble
Rhythm of Destiny (1992)
Saviour of the Soul (1991)
Shootout, The
Somebody Up There Likes Me (1996)
Truant Heroes
Whatever Will Be, Will Be (1995)

Kwok Ai Ming, Amy
Actress   Chinese
Cantonese: Gwok Oi Ming
Mandarin: Guo1 Ai3 Ming2
Fong Sai Yuk II (1993)
Gleam of Hope, A (1994)
Let's Go Slam Dunk (1994)
Other Side of Romance, The (1994)

Kwok Chun-Fung, Philip   (Kuo Chui)
Actor   Chinese
Cantonese: Gwok Jan Fung

Phantom Lover (1995) Cameo
Spearmen of Death (1980)
Story of Ricky (1991)
Ten Tigers of Kwangtung (1979)
Treasure Hunt (2/1994) +Action
Two Shaolin Kids in Hong Kong (1994)
+Action
Unbeatable Dragon
Zen of Sword (1992) +Action

Lai Ming, Leon   (12/11/1966-)
Actor   Chinese
Cantonese: Lai Ming
Mandarin: Li2 Ming2
Banquet, The (1991)

City Hunter (1992)
Fallen Angels (1995)
Fruit Punch (1992)
Fun and Fury (1992)
Gun N' Rose (1992)
Hearts No Flowers (1989)
Love and the City (1994)
Magic Touch, The (1992)
Run (1994)
Shogun & Little Kitchen (1992)
Sword of Many Loves, The (1992)
Wicked City, The (1992)
With or Without You (1991?)
Without a Promised Land

Lau Ka-Ling, Carina
Actress   Chinese
Cantonese: Lau Ga Ling
Mandarin: Liu2 Jia1 Ling2
    Actress (1992)
    Ashes of Time (1994)
    C'est la Vie, Mon Cherie (1993)
    City Warriors (1991)
    Days of Being Wild (1990)
    Deadful Melody (1994)
    Eagle Shooting Heroes, The (1993)
    Four Lovers (1988)
    Gigolo and Whore (1994)
    Shadow Cop
    She Shoots Straight (1990)
    Tragic Hero (2/1987)

Lam Ling-Tung, Ringo
Director   Chinese
Cantonese: Lam Ling Dung
Mandarin: Lin2 Ling3 Dong1
    Aces Go Places 4 (1986)
    Adventurers, The (1995)
    Burning Paradise (1994)
    City on Fire (2/1987)
    Cupid One (1985) +Writer
    Esprit D'Amour (1983)
    Full Contact (7/1992) +Prod
    Other Side of Gentleman, The (1984)
    Prison on Fire (11/1987)

Girls Without Tomorrow (1992)
He Ain't Heavy, He's My Father (1993)
He is a Woman, She is a Man (1994)
Heart to Hearts (1988) Cameo
Her Beautiful Life Lies
Holy Weapon (1993)
I'm Sorry (1988)
Lady Super Cop (1993)
Lethal Panther 2 (1993)
Lord of East China Sea (1993)
Lord of East China Sea 2 (1993)
Lover of the Swindler (1993)
Lucky Guys
My American Grandson (1991 China)
Naughty Boys
Night Rider, The (1992)
No More Love, No More Death (1993)
Now You See Love, Now You Don't (2/1992)
Private Eyes 7 1/2
Profile of Pleasure (1987)
Project A, Part II (1987)
Return of the Lucky Star
Rich and Famous (5/1987)
Romancing Star II, The
Roof With a View (1990) Cameo
Rose, Rose I Love You (1993)
Saviour of the Soul (1991)
Prison on Fire 2 (6/1991)
Rebel from China Writer Prod
School on Fire
Touch and Go (1991)
Twin Dragons, The (1992) +Cameo
Undeclared War (1992)
Wild Search (6/1989)

Lau Tak Hwa, Andy   (9/27/61)
**   Actor   Chinese**
Cantonese: Lau Dak Wa
Mandarin: Liu2 De2 Hua2
    Adventurers, The (1995)
    As Tears Go By (1988)
    Banquet, The (1991)
    Bloody Brotherhood
    Boat People (1982)

Casino Raiders
Casino Raiders II
Casino Tycoon (1992)
Casino Tycoon II (1992)
City Kids 1989 (1989)
Come Fly the Dragon (1992)
Crazy Companies, The
Crazy Companies II, The
Crocodile Hunter
Dances with the Dragon
Days of Being Wild (1990)
Days of Tomorrow (1993)
Deadly Sin, The
Dragon in Jail (1990)
Drunken Master II (1994)
Drunken Master III (1994)
Everlasting Love (1983)
First Time is the Last Time (1988)
Fortune Code (1989)
Full Throttle (1995)
Future Cops (1993)
Game Kids (1992)
Gangland Odyssey
God of Gamblers (12/1989)
God of Gamblers II (1989)
Gun N' Rose (1992)
Rich and Famous (5/1987)
Romancing Star II, The
Romancing Star III, The
Runaway
Saviour of the Soul (1991)
Saviour of the Soul II (1992)
Stars & Roses (1990)
Sting, The
Sting 2, The
Sworn Brothers
Taste of Killing and Romance, A (1994)
Three Against the World
Three Swordsmen, The (1994)
Tian Di (1994)
Tigers, The (1991)
Tragic Hero (2/1987)
Tricky Brains (1991)
Truth, The (1988)
Truth - Final Episode, The

Handsome Siblings (1992)
Home Too Far, A
Hong Kong Godfather (1991)
In the Blood (1987)
Island of Fire (1990)
Kawashima Yoshiko (1990)
Kung Fu vs. Acrobatic (1991)
Last Blood, The (1990)
Last Eunuch in China (1988)
Lee Rock I
Lee Rock II
Lee Rock III
Little Cop
Long Arm of the Law III
Lucky Stars Go Places
Magic Crystal (1987)
Moment of Romance, A (1990)
Moon Warriors (1992)
My Lucky Stars (1985)
News Attack
No Risk, No Gain
Once Upon a Rainbow (1982)
Perfect Exchange, The (1993)
Perfect Match
Proud and Confident
Return Engagement (1990)
Twinkle Twinkle Lucky Stars (1985)
Unwritten Law, The
Walk on Fire
What a Hero (1992)
What a Wonderful World (1996)
Zodiac Killers

Lau Ching Wan   Actor
        Chinese
Cantonese: Lau Ching Wan
Mandarin: Liu2 Qing1 Yun2
All Men Are Brothers - Blood of the Leopard (1992)
Angel Hunter (1991)
Beginner's Luck (1994)
Bomb Disposal Officer: Baby Bomb (1994)
C'est la Vie, Mon Cherie (1993)
Don't Shoot Me, I'm Just a Violinist

(1994)
 Executioners (1993)
 Fallen Angels (1995) Prod
 Golden Girls, The (1995)
 Happy Hour (1995)
 Happy Massage Girls, The
 Hello! Who Is It?! (1994)
 I Wanna Be Your Man (1994)
 I've Got You, Babe (1994)
 It's a Wonderful Life (1994)
 Live Hard
 Loving You (1995)
 Mack the Knife (1995)
 Most Wanted, The (1994)
 Mother of a Different Kind (1995)
 New Tenant (1995) Cameo
 Oh! My Three Guys (1994)
 Once in a Lifetime (1995)
 Only Fools Fall in Love (1995)
 Pink Bomb
 Police Story Part 2 (1988) Cameo
 Return to a Better Tomorrow (1994)
 Roar of the Vietnamese, The
 Romantic Dream (1995)
 Sea Root (1995)
 School on Fire
 Story of My Son, The
 Tian Di (1994)
 What Price Survival (1994)
 Zu: Warriors of the Magic Mountain
(1983)

Lee Ang   (1954 -   )
Director   Chinese
1982 East to West   sound
1983 Dim Lake
1985 Fine Line
1992 Pushing Hands   +producer,
screenplay
1993 The   Wedding   Banquet
        +producer, screenplay
1994 Eat   Drink   Man   Woman
        +screenplay
1995 Sense and Sensibility

Shanghai Fever (1994)
 Shootout, The
 Silent Love
 Tears and Triumph (1994)
 Third Full Moon, The (1994)
 Thou Shalt Not Swear (1993)
 Tragic Fantasy: Tiger of Wanchai (1994)
 Tricky Business (1995)
 World of Treasure (1995) Cameo

Lau Chung-Yun, Damian   Actor
**   Chinese**
Cantonese: Lau Chung Yan
Mandarin: Liu2 Song1 Ren2
 Duel to the Death (1982)
 Executioners (1993)
 Heroic Trio, The (1992)
 Holy Weapon (1993)
 Last Hurrah for Chivalry (1978)
 Magic Crane, The (1993)
 Murder (1993)
 My Father is a Hero (1995)
 New Legend of Shaolin, The (1994)
 Royal Tramp II (1992)

Lee, Brandon   (1965 - 1993) Actor
**   Chinese/Mix**
1986 Kung Fu: The Movie
1986 Legacy of Rage
1989 Laser Mission
1991 Showdown in Little Tokyo
1992 Rapid Fire
1994 The Crow

Lee Jun Fan, Bruce (1941 - 1973) Actor
**   Chinese**
Cantonese: Lei Siu Lung
Mandarin: Li3 Xiao3 Long2
        Best of the Martial Arts Films, The
(1990)
        Big Boss, The/Fist of Fury (1971)
        Cinema of Vengeance (1994 UK)
        Circle   of   Iron/The   SsilentFlute
(1979) story
        Enter   the   Dragon   (1973   USA)

+Action

Fist of Fury/The Chinese Connection (1972)

Game of Death (1979 USA)

Marlowe   +stunts

Return of the Dragon/Way of the Dragon (1973) +Dir, screenplay

Shaolin Kid

The Wrecking Crew   +technical adviser (karate)

Lee Yuen-Ba, Conan   Actor
    Chinese
Cantonese: Lei Yuen Ba
Mandarin: Li3 Yuan2 Ba4

Aces Go Places 5: The Terracotta Hit (1989)

Big Trouble in Little China (1986 [US])

Cyprus Tigers, The

Dragon Killer (1995)

Fury in Red

Golden Queen's Commando (1984)

King of the Sea (1994)

Ninja in the Dragon Den

Scheming Wonders (1991)

Code of Honour (3/1987)

Cop of the Town

Criminal Hunter

Doctor Lamb (1992) +Dir

Don't Stop My Crazy Love for You (1993)

Executioner, The (3/1981)

Fearless Match (1994)

Final Justice

Great Cheat, The

Hard Boiled (4/1992)

Heroic Cops

Infra-Man

Just Heroes (1987)

Killer, The (7/1989)

Law Enforcer

Law with Two Phases (1984)

Legend of the Dragon (1990) Dir Prod

Love is a Fairy Tale (1993) Prod

Love to Kill (1993)

Tiger on Beat (3/1988)

Tiger on Beat II (1990)

Lee Shiu Shian, Danny   (Lee Sau-Yin)
    Actor
    Chinese
Cantonese: Lei Sau Yin
Mandarin: Li3 Xiu1 Xian2

Aces Go Places 5: The Terracotta Hit (1989) Cameo

Against All

Asian Connection (1995) +Prod

Assassinators

Awakening (1994)

Behind the Storm

Big Boss

Big Score, The

Blue Lightning

Brotherhood

Bruce Lee: His Last Days, His Last Nights (1975)

Case of the Cold Fish, The (1995) +Prod

City Cop (1995) +Prod

City on Fire (2/1987)

Mighty Peking Man

Night Rider, The (1992) +Writer Prod

No Compromise

No Way Back

Organised Crime and Triad Bureau (1994) +Prod

Parking Service

Powerful Four (1991)

Red Shield (1992) +Prod

Rhythm of Destiny (1992)

Rich and Famous (5/1987)

Road Warriors +Dir

Run and Kill (1993)

Savage 5 (1979?)

Stunning Gambling, The

Sword Stained With Royal Blood (1993)

Takes Two to Mingle

Tattoo, The

Thank You Sir

Tiger on Beat II (1990)

Tragic Hero (2/1987)
Twist (1995) +Dir
Undeclared War (1992)
Untold Story, The (1993)

**Lee, Jason Scott (1966 -) Actor
Chinese/Hawaiian**
1987 Born in East L.A.
1989 Back to the Future Part II
1990 Vestige of Honor
1990 The Lookalike
1991 Ghoulies 3: Ghoulies Go to College
1993 Dragon: The Bruce Lee Story
1993 Map of the Human Heart
1994 Rapa Nui
1994 Rudyard Kipling's The Jungle Book
1998 Soldier
1999 Tale of the Mummy (TV)
2000 Arabian Nights (TV)

**Lee Li-Li, Lily Actress
Chinese
Cantonese: Lei Lei Lei
Mandarin: Li3 Li4 Li4**
Forbidden Arsenal (1991)
Girls Unbutton (1994)
Gun N' Rose (1992)
Happy Ghost (1984)
Happy Ghost 4 (1989) Cameo
Happy Together 1993 (1993?)
Highway Man (1995)
Isle of Fantasy, The (1985)
It's a Mad Mad Mad World II
It's a Mad Mad Mad World III
It's a Mad Mad Mad World Too (1992)
Jail House Eros
Kiss Me Goodbye (1986)
Legend of the Liquid Sword (1993)
Merry Christmas (1984)
Mr. Vampire 4 (1987)
Musical Vampire, The
Off Track (1990)
Pink Bomb
Pom Pom & Hot Hot (1992)
Porky's Meatballs (1986)

Asian Cops - High Voltage (1995)
Circus Kids (1994)
Oh! Yes Sir! (1994)
Once in a Lifetime (1995)
Passion Unbounded (1995)
Secret Lover (1995)
Step to Heaven, A (1995)
Wai's Romance (1994)

**Lee Lai-Chun, Loletta
Actress Chinese
Cantonese: Lei Lai Jan
Mandarin: Li3 Li4 Zhen1**
Angel of the Road
Before Dawn
Bless this House
Chicken a la Queen (1990)
Crazy Game
Crazy Love (1993)
Devoted to You
Everlasting Love (1983)
Final Victory
For Your Heart Only (1985)

Remains of a Woman (1993)
Saga of the Phoenix (1990)
Shanghai 1920 (1991)
Shanghai Blues (1984)
Spirit of Love
Student Union
Summer Lovers (1992)
Sweet Peach (1994)
Tricky Business (1995) Writer
Why Wild Girls (1994)
Young Wisely I
Young Wisely II

**Lee Choi-Fung, Moon
Actress Chinese
Cantonese: Lei Choi Fung
Mandarin: Li3 Sai4 Feng4**
Angel (1986)
Angel 2 (1988)
Angel 3 (1989)
Angel Force

Angel Mission (1993)
Angel Terminators 2 (1993)
Avenging Quartet (1992)
Beauty Inspectors (1992)
Big Deal, The
Bury Me High (1990)
Cascading Feeling
Devil Hunters (1989)
Dreaming the Reality (1991)
Fatal Termination (1988)
Inspectors Wear Skirts 4 (1992)
Kick Boxer's Tears (1992)
Killer Angels (1989)
Long Arm of the Law III
Mission Kill
Mission of Justice (1992)
Mr. Vampire (1984)
Mr. Vampire 2 (1985)
New Kids in Town
Nocturnal Demon (1991)
Princess Madam (1990)
Protector, The (1985 U.S.A.)
Diary of a Big Man (7/1988)
Direct Line, The
Fatal Chase (1992)
First Shot (1993)
Forbidden Arsenal (1991)
Gunmen (1988)
He Ain't Heavy, He's My Father (1993)
Her Fatal Ways 2
His Way, Her Way, Their Ways
Incorruptable, The (1993)
Inspector Pink Dragon
Lady Super Cop (1993)
Misty
Mountain Warriors (1990)
Pink Bomb
Powerful Four (1991)
Red Zone (1995)
Roar of the Vietnamese, The
Royal Scoundrel
Shadow Cop
Song of the Exile (1989)
Spy Games (1988)
Stage Door Johnny

Revenge of Angel
Secret Police (1994?)
To Sir with Trouble
Twinkle Twinkle Lucky Stars (1985) Cameo
Yes Madam '92: A Serious Shock (1992)

Lee Chi-Hung, Waise   Actor
**   Chinese**
Cantonese: Lei Ji Hung
Mandarin: Li3 Zi3 Xiong2
Actress (1992)
Angel on Fire
Angel the Kickboxer
Avenging Quartet (1992)
Better Tomorrow, A (8/1986)
Big Heat, The (1988)
Black Morning Glory, The (1993)
Blood Stained Tradewinds
Bullet in the Head (1990)
Cat, The
Chinese Ghost Story Part II, A (1990)
Story of Kennedy Town
Swordsman II (1991)
Taste of Killing and Romance, A (1994)
Thirteen Cold-Blooded Eagles (1992)
To Be Number One (1991)
Tough Beauty and the Sloppy Slop (1995)
Tricky Brains (1991)
Underground Judgement (1994)
Wing Chun (1994)
Yes Madam '92: A Serious Shock (1992)
Zen of Sword (1992)

Leung Ching, Jade   Actress
**   Chinese**
Cantonese: Leung Jing
Mandarin: Liang2 Cheng1
Black Cat (1991)
Black Cat 2 (1992)
Enemy Shadow (1995)
Fox Hunter (1995)
Green Hat (1995)
Satin Steel (1994)

Spider Woman (1995)

Leung Chiu Wai, Tony   **Actor**
   Chinese
Cantonese: Leung Chiu Wai
Mandarin: Liang2 Chao2 Wei3
   Always Be the Winners (1994)
   Ashes of Time (1994)
   Blind Romance (1996)
   Bullet in the Head (1990)
   Butterfly and Sword (1993)
   Chinese Ghost Story Part III, A (1991)
   Chung King Express (1994)
   Come Fly the Dragon (1992)
   Days of Being Dumb, The (1992)
   Days of Being Wild (1990)
   Eagle Shooting Heroes, The (1993)
   End of the Road (1993)
   Fantasy Romance (1993)
   Great Pretenders (1991)
   Three Summers
   Tigers, The (1991)
   Tom, Dick, and Hairy (1993)
   Two of a Kind (1993)
   Young Cops

Leung Kar Fai, Tony   **Actor**
   Chinese
Cantonese: Leung Ga Fai
Mandarin: Liang2 Jia1 Hui1
   92 Legendary La Rose Noire (1992)
   Actress (1992)
   All Men Are Brothers - Blood of the
Leopard (1992)
   Always Be the Winners (1994)
   Ashes of Time (1994)
   Au Revoir Mon Amour (1991)
   Banquet, The (1991)
   Better Tomorrow III: Love and Death in
Saigon, A (10/1989)
   Black Panther Warriors, The (1993)
   Blue Lightning
   Boys Are Easy (1993)
   Burning of the Imperial Palace (1983)
   Cherie (1984)

Happy-Go-Lucky
Hard Boiled (4/1992)
He Ain't Heavy, He's My Father (1993)
Heaven Can't Wait (1995)
Hero from Beyond the End of Time
(1993)
I Love Maria (1988)
Love Unto Waste (8/1986)
Lucky Encounter
Lunatics, The (6/1986)
Mack the Knife (1995)
Mad Mad 83
Magic Crane, The (1993)
My Heart Is That Eternal Rose (1987)
New Heaven Sword and Dragon Sabre,
The
   People's Hero (1987)
   Returning, The (1994)
   Seven Warriors
   Son of the Beach
   Christ of Nanjing, The (1995)
   Dream Lover (1995)
   Eagle Shooting Heroes, The (1993)
   Farewell China (1990)
   Flying Dagger (1993)
   Ghost Lantern (1993)
   God of Gamblers' Return (12/1994)
   Gunmen (1988)
   He Ain't Heavy, He's My Father (1993)
   He and She (1994)
   Her Fatal Ways (1990)
   I Will Wait for You (1994)
   Island of Fire (1990)
   It's a Wonderful Life (1994)
   King of Chess (1988) +Writer
   Lady in Black (1986)
   Laser Man (1986)
   Long and Winding Road (1994)
   Lover of the Last Empress (1995)
   Lover of the Swindler (1993)
   Lover's Lover (1994)
   Lover, The (1991 France)
   Misty
   New Dragon Inn (1992)
   Once Upon a Time a Hero in China

(1992)
People's Hero (1987)
Perfect Exchange, The (1993)
Pretty Ghost
Prison on Fire (11/1987)
Queen's Bench III
Raid, The (1991)
Red and Black (1991)
Roof With a View (1990)
Rose, Rose I Love You (1993)
Royal Scoundrel
Sentenced to Hang
She Shoots Straight (1990)
Sting 2, The
This Thing Called Love (1991)
To Catch a Thief
To Live and Die in Tsimshatsui (1994)
Tom, Dick, and Hairy (1993)
Red Field (1987 China)
Red Sorghum (1987 China)
Semi-Gods and Semi-Devils (1994)
Shanghai Triad (1995 China)
Story of Qiu Ju, The (1991 China)
Terracotta Warrior, The (1989)
To Live (1994 China)

Li Lian Jie, Jet **Actor**
Chinese
Cantonese: Lei Lin Git
Mandarin: Li3 Lian2 Jie2
Abbot Hai Teng of Shaolin
Black Mask
Bodyguard from Beijing, The (1994)
+Prod
Born to Defence (1986?) +Dir
Dragon Fight (1988)
Dragons of the Orient
Fist of Legend (1994)
Fong Sai Yuk (1993)
Fong Sai Yuk II (1993)
High Risk (1995)
Kung Fu Cult Master, The (1993)
Last Hero in China, The (1993)
Lethal Weapon IV (1998)
Li Lian Jie's Shaolin Kung Fu (1994)

Touch of Evil, A (1995)

Li Gong **(12/31/1965-)**
Actress **Chinese**
Cantonese: Gung Lei
Mandarin: Gong3 Li4
Banquet, The (1991)
Daughter of the Nile (199?)
Farewell, My Concubine (1993)
Flirting Scholar (1993)
God of Gamblers III: Back to Shanghai
(1991)
Great Conqueror's Concubine, The
(1994)
Ju Dou (1990 China)
Mary from Beijing (1992)
Peintre, La (1993 China)
Raise the Red Lantern (1991 China)
Martial Arts of Shaolin (1986)
Master, The (1989)
My Father is a Hero (1995)
New Legend of Shaolin, The (1994)
+Prod
Once Upon a Time in China (1990)
Once Upon a Time in China 2 (1991)
Once Upon a Time in China 3 (1992)
Once Upon a Time in China 6 (1997)
Romeo Must Die (2000)
Scripture with No Words, The (1996)
Shaolin Temple (1982)
Shaolin Temple 2: Kids from Shaolin
(1983)
Swordsman II (1991)
Tai Chi Master (1993)

Li Chi, Nina **Actress**
Chinese
Cantonese: Lei Ji
Mandarin: Li4 Zhi4
Aces Go Places 5: The Terracotta Hit
(1989)
Amnesty Decree
Chinese Ghost Story Part III, A (1991)
Criminal Hunter
Dragon Fight (1988)

Dragon from Russia (1990)
Four Lovers (1988)
Fractured Follies (7/1988)
Fun, the Luck, and the Tycoon, The (1/1990)
Greatest Lover, The (7/1988)
Guests in the House
Kid from Tibet, A (1991)
Legend of the Brothers (1991)
Lover's Tear (1991)
Miracle 90 Days
Mr. Mistress
Pedicab Driver (1989)
Perfect Girls
Profile of Pleasure (1987)
Seven Years Itch (1987)
Stone Age Warriors (1990)
Tiger on Beat (3/1988)
Demon Fighter, The (198?)
Different Love
Dream Lovers (4/1986)
Eagle Shooting Heroes, The (1993)
Fantasy Mission Force (1979)
Fire Dragon (1994)
Forever My Love
Ghost in the Mirror (1974)
Girl Friend
Golden Queen's Commando (1984)
Handsome Siblings (1992)
He Loved Once Too Many
Lady in Black (1986)
Lily Under the Muzzle, The
Love Affairs
Love Massacre
Love of the White Snake (197?)
Magnificent 72
Misty Drizzle
New Dragon Inn (1992)
Orchid in the Rain
Other Side of Gentleman, The (1984)
Peach Blossom Land, The (1991)
Peking Opera Blues (1986)
Phoenix the Raider (1985)
Pink Force Commando (1984)
Police Story (1985)

To Spy with Love
Twin Dragons, The (1992)
What a Small World

Lin Ching-Hsia, Brigitte (Venus Lin)
Actress   Chinese
Cantonese: Lam Ching Ha
Mandarin: Lin2 Qing1 Xia2
800 Heroes, The
All the Wrong Spies (1983)
Ashes of Time (1994)
Black Panther Warriors, The (1993)
Boys Are Easy (1993)
Bride with White Hair, The (1993)
Bride with White Hair 2, The (1993)
Chung King Express (1994)
Deadful Melody (1994)

Poor Chasers
Portrait of Lin Ching Hsia, A (1991)
Red Dust (1990)
Royal Tramp (1992) Cameo
Royal Tramp II (1992)
Run Lover Run
Semi-Gods and Semi-Devils (1994)
Starry is the Night (1988)
Swordsman II (1991)
Swordsman 3: East is Red (1993)
There's No Place Like Home
Thirty Million Rush, The (1985?)
Three Swordsmen, The (1994)
True Colours (1986)   Victims of the Assassin (198?)
Web of Deception (1989)
White Crane Woman
Wild Goose on the Wing, The
Yesterday, Today, Tomorrow
Zu: Warriors of the Magic Mountain (1983)

Liu Chia-Hui, Gordon (Lau Kar Fai)
Actor   Chinese
Cantonese: Lau Ga Fai
Mandarin: Liu2 Jia1 Hui1
Avenging Trio

Bloody Fight, A
Cat Versus Rat (1982)
Challenge of the Masters (1976)
Challenge of the Ninja (1979)
Cheetah on Fire (1992)
Cinema of Vengeance (1994 UK)
Crazy Shaolin Disciples
Cry Killer
Crystal Hunt (1991)
Dirty Ho (1979)
Disciples of the 36th Chamber
Drunken Master III (1994)
Eight Diagram Pole Fighter (1983)
Executioners From Shaolin (1977) +Dir
Fiery Family, A
Fire of Love
Shaolin Martial Arts (1974)
Story of the Gun, The
Tiger on Beat (3/1988)
Treasure Hunt (2/1994)
Two Shaolin Kids in Hong Kong (1994)
Warrior from Shaolin

Liu Chia-Liang (Lau Kar Leung)
Director   Chinese
Cantonese: Lau Ga Leung
Mandarin: Liu2 Jia1 Liang2
Aces Go Places 5: The Terracotta Hit (1989)
Bare-Footed Kid, The (1993) Action
Bloody Fight, A Actor
Cat Versus Rat (1982)
Challenge of the Masters (1976) +Actor
Challenge of the Ninja (1979)
Cinema of Vengeance (1994 UK) Actor
Deadly Mantis (1978)
Dirty Ho (1979)
Disciples of the 36th Chamber
Dragon Family
Drunken Master II (1994) +Action Cameo
Drunken Master III (1994) +Actor
Eight Diagram Pole Fighter (1983) +Actor
Girl With the Thunderbolt Kick, The

Fists of the White Lotus (1980)
Flirting Scholar (1993)
Fortune Code (1989) Cameo
Fury of a Tiger
Ghost Ballroom
Killer Angels (1989)
Kung Fu Scholar, The (1994)
Last Hero in China, The (1993)
Legendary Weapons of China (1982)
Martial Club (1981)
Master Killer, The (1978)
Master of Disaster (1982)
Passionate Killing in the Dream (1992)
Peacock King (1987)
Return of Master Killer (1980)
Shaolin and Wu Tang
(1968) Action
Killer Angels (1989) Actor
Legendary Weapons of China (1982) +Actor
Mad Monkey Kung Fu (1979) +Actor
Martial Arts of Shaolin (1986) +Actor
Martial Club (1981)
Master Killer, The (1978)
My Young Auntie (1981) +Actor
New Kids in Town Actor
Operation Scorpio (1991) Actor
Pedicab Driver (1989) Actor
Return of Master Killer (1980)
Shaolin Martial Arts (1974) Action
Spiritual Boxer (1975)
Spiritual Boxer II (1979)
Street Gangs of Hong Kong Action
Thirty Million Rush, The (1985?) Actor
Tiger on Beat (3/1988)
Tiger on Beat II (1990)
Twin Dragons, The (1992) Cameo

Liu Chia-Yung (Lau Kar Yung)   Actor
Chinese
Cantonese: Lau Ga Yung
Mandarin: Liu2 Jia1 Yong3
36 Crazy Fists, The (1977)
Black Wall, The (1990) +Dir
Challenge of the Masters (1976)

Crazy Couple
Deadly Mantis (1978)
Five Fingers of Death (1972) Action
Gold Hunter
Lantern (1994) Dir
Legendary Weapons of China (1982)
Master of Disaster (1982) +Dir
New Kids in Town Dir Prod
Shaolin Disciple, The

Lo Lieh   Actor   Chinese
Cantonese: Loh Lit
Mandarin: Luo2 Lie4
18 Swirling Riders
Assassins
Master Killer, The (1978)
Occupant, The (9/1984)
Oh! My God!
One Armed Against Nine Killers
One Armed Swordsmen, The
Queen of Temple Street (1990)
Sex and Zen (1989)
Slice of Death
Sword and the Lute
Temple of the Red Lotus
Tigers, The (1991)
To Be Number One (1991)
Trail of the Broken Blade
Truth - Final Episode, The
Twin Swords

Lo Meng   Actor   Chinese
Brave Archer 3 (1979)
Chinatown Kid (1977)
Crazy Shaolin Disciples
Crippled Avengers (1978)
Daredevils of Kung Fu
Destroyers
Five Deadly Venoms (1978)
House of Traps (1981)
Kid With the Golden Arm, The (1978)
Killer Army
Masked Avengers (1981)
Ninja's Deadly Trap
Ode to Gallantry

Black Magic II
Black Magic With Buddha (1983) Dir
Bullet for Hire (1991)
Chinese Boxer (1970)
Dirty Ho (1979)
Don't Play with Fire (1980)
Executioners From Shaolin (1977)
Fists of the White Lotus (1980) +Dir
Five Fingers of Death (1972)
Ghosts Galore
Girl With the Thunderbolt Kick, The
(1968)
Mad Monkey Kung Fu (1979)
Magnificent Trio
Manhunt Across the Border (1993)
Spearmen of Death (1980)
Super Ninjas (1982)
Ten Tigers of Kwangtung (1979)
Unbeatable Dragon
Weird Man

Lo Wei   Director   Chinese
Cantonese: Loh Wai
Mandarin: Luo2 Wei2
Big Boss, The (1971)
Comet Strikes, The
Dragon Fist (1978)
Fearless Hyena Part II, The (1980)
Fist of Fury (1972) +Writer
Forced Nightmare (1992) Prod
Killer Meteors (1977)
Magnificent Bodyguards (1978)
Man Called Tiger, A
Naughty! Naughty!
New Fist of Fury (1976) +Actor
News Attack
Shaolin Wooden Men (1976)
Snake and Crane Arts of Shaolin (1977)
Spiritual Kung Fu (1978)
To Kill with Intrigue (1977)

Lone, John   (1952 -)   Actor
      Chinese
1976   King Kong
1978   Kate Bliss and the Ticker Tape Kid

1984 Iceman
1985 Year of the Dragon
1987 Echoes of Paradise/Shadows of the Peacock
1987 The Last Emperor
1988 The Moderns
1990 Shadow of China
1991 Shanghai 1920
1993 M. Butterfly
1994 The Shadow
1995 The Hunted

Luke, Keye (1904 - 1991) Actor
Korean
1989 The Mighty Quinn
1990 Alice
1990 Gremlins 2: The New Batch

Mako (1933 -) Actor
Japanese
Popular Asian character actor appearing in dozens of American films. A handful of his best known films:
1966 The Sand Pebbles
1966 The Ugly Dachshund
1974 The Island at the Top of the World
1975 The Killer Elite
1979 The Bushido Blade
1980 The Big Brawl
1981 An Eye for an Eye
1981 Under the Rainbow
1982 Conan the Barbarian
1983 The Last Ninja
1984 Conan the Destroyer
1986 Kung Fu: The Movie
1988 Silent Assassins
1988 Tucker: The Man and His Dream
1990 Fatal Mission
1990 Hiroshima: Out of the Ashes
1990 Pacific Heights
1991 The Perfect Weapon
1993 Rising Sun
1993 Robocop 3
1993 Sidekicks
1994 Highlander 3

Has appeared in hundreds of American films and televisions shows from 1934-1990. This is a small handful of his films:
1934 The Painted Veil
1935 Charlie Chan in Paris
1935 Oil for the Lamps if China
1935 Shanghai
1937 The Good Earth
1940 The Green Hornet
1972 Kunf Fu
1984 Gremlins
1986 Kung Fu: The Movie
1988 Dead Heat

1995 A Dangerous Place

Mao Ying, Angela Actress
Chinese
Cantonese: Maau Ying
Mandarin: Mao2 Ying1
Angry River 1970
Back Alley Princess
Best of the Martial Arts Films, The (1990)
Broken Oath (1977)
Enter the Dragon (1973 USA)
Fate of Lee Khan, The
Hapkido 1970
Invincible Eight, The (1970)
Lady Whirlwind 1971
Stoner- the Shrine of Ultimate Bliss
Thunderbolt (1970)
When Taekwondo Strikes (1973)

Mifune Toshiro (4/1/1920 - 12/24/1997)
Actor Japanese
1947 Snow Trail
1948 Drunken Angel
1949 The Quiet Duel
1949 Stray Dog
1950 Rashomon
1950 Shuban
1951 The Idiot
1952 The Life of Oharu
1954 Miyamoto Musashi

1954 Seven Samurai
1955 Record of a Living Being
1957 The Lower Depths
1957 Throne of Blood
1958 The Hidden Fortress
1958 The Rickshaw Man
1960 The Bad Sleep Well
1961 The Important Man
1961 Yojimbo
1962 The Loyal 47 Ronin
1962 Daitozoku
1962 High and Low
1971 Zato-Ichi to Yojimbo
1972 Red Sun
1975 Paper Tiger
1976 Midway
1979 1941
1979 The Bushido Blade
1979 Oginsaga
1979 Winter Kills
1980 Shogun
1982 The Challenge
1982 Inchon
1983 Jinsei Gekijo
1984 Seiha
1984 Umi Isubame Joe no Kiseki
1987 Taketori Monogatari
1991 Journey of Honor
1991 Strawberry Road
1993 Shadow of the Wolf
1994 Picture Bride

Mo Shun-Kwun, Teresa
Actress　　　　**Chinese**
Cantonese: Mo Sun Gwan
Mandarin: Mao2 Shun4 Yun2
　　92 Legendary La Rose Noire (1992)
　　All's Well, Ends Well (1992)
　　All's Well, Ends Well Too (1993)
　　Daddy, Father and Papa (1991)
　　Don't Shoot Me, I'm Just a Violinist (1994)
　　Hard Boiled (4/1992)
　　His Fatal Ways
　　It's a Wonderful Life (1994)

1962 Sanjuro
1963 Legacy of the 500,000+producer, director
1964 The Lost World of Sinbad
1965 Red Beard
1966 Grand Prix
1967 Rebellion
1968 Admiral Yamamoto
1968 Hell in the Pacific
1969 Nihonkai Daikaisen
1970 Machi-Buse　+executive producer
1970 Shinsengumi +producer
　　Lady Super Cop (1993)
　　Lamb Killer
　　Laughter of the Water Margins (1993)
　　Legend of the Dragon (1990)
　　Magnificent Scoundrels (1991)
　　Mainland Dundee
　　Master Wong vs. Master Wong
　　My Americanize Wife
　　Now You See Love, Now You Don't (2/1992)
　　Once Upon a Time a Hero in China (1992)
　　Perfect Couples
　　Red Shield (1992)
　　Touch and Go (1991)
　　Tricky Brains (1991)
　　What Price Stardom

Mok Siu Chung, Max　　　**Actor**
　　　　　　　　　　Chinese
Cantonese: Mok Siu Chung
Mandarin: Mo4 Shao3 Cong1
　　Angel of the Road
　　Assassin, The (1993)
　　Blood Call
　　Blue Lantern (1994)
　　City Kids 1989 (1989)
　　Close Escape (1989)
　　Eye for an Eye, An (1993?)
　　Fait Accompli (1994)
　　Fire Dragon (1994)
　　Fortune Code (1989)
　　Gambling Baron (1994)

Heart of Killer (1995)
Hearts No Flowers (1989)
Hero of Tomorrow
Holy Flame of the Martial World
How Deep is Your Love (1994)
Lantern (1994)
Last Eunuch in China (1988)
Lucky Star
Lung Fung Restaurant
Mission Kill
Never Say Regret
Pedicab Driver (1989)
Secret Signs
Sister in Law
Slave of the Sword (1993)
Son on the Run (1991)
Summer Lovers (1992)
That's Money
Twilight of the Forbidden City
Usurpers of Emperor's Power
Whampoa Blues

Morita Noriyuki, Pat   (1930 -   )
Actor   Japanese

1967	Thoroughly Modern Millie
1968	The Shakiest Gun in the West
1972	Cancel My Reservation
1972	Every Little Crook and Nanny
1972	Where Does It Hurt?
1976	Farewell to Manzanar
1976	Midway
1980	For the Love of It
1980	When Time Ran Out/Earth's Final Fury
1981	Full Moon High
1982	Savannah Smiles
1983	Jimmy the Kid
1984	The Karate Kid
1984	Slapstick (Of Another Kind)
1984	The Vegas Strip Wars
1985	Amos
1985	Night Patrol
1986	Babes in Toyland
1986	The Karate Kid, Part II
1987	Captive Hearts+screenwriter

Night Life Hero
No Regret, No Return (1993)
No Way Back
Off Track (1990)
Once Upon a Time in China 2 (1991)
Once Upon a Time in China 3 (1992)
Once Upon a Time in China 4 (1993)
Once Upon a Time in China 5 (1994)
Outlaw Brothers (1988)
Path of Glory

1987	Collision Course
1989	The Karate Kid III
1990	Hiroshima: Out of the Ashes
1991	Auntie Lee's Meat Pies
1991	Do or Die
1991	Lena's Holiday
1991	Moon Over Paradise
1991	Strawberry Road
1992	Honeymoon in Vegas
1992	Miracle Beach
1993	American Ninja 5: Young Ninja Warrior
1994	Even Cowgirls Get the Blues
1994	The Next Karate Kid

Mui Yim-Fong, Anita
Actress   Chinese
Cantonese: Mooi Yim Fong
Mandarin: Mei2 Yan4 Fang1

100 Ways to Murder Your Wife (6/1986)
Au Revoir Mon Amour (1991)
Banquet, The (1991)
Better Tomorrow III: Love and Death in Saigon, A (10/1989)
Drunken Master II (1994)
Executioners (1993)
Fight Back to School III (1993)
Fortune Code (1989)
Greatest Lover, The (7/1988)
Happy Bigamist
Heroic Trio, The (1992)
Justice, My Foot (1992)
Kawashima Yoshiko (1990)
Lucky Diamond

Mad Mad 83
Mad Monk (1993) Cameo
Magic Crane, The (1993)
Miracles: The Canton Godfather (1989)
Moon Warriors (1992)
Mr. Boo 8: Inspector Chocolate
Musical Dancer (1985)
My Father is a Hero (1995)
One Husband Too Many
Young Cops

Ng Ka Lai, Carrie   Actress
        Chinese
Cantonese: Ng Ga Lai
Mandarin: Wu2 Jia1 Li4
Angel Hunter (1991)
Angel Terminators (1990)
Armed Policewoman, The (1995)
Au Revoir Mon Amour (1991)
Best of the Best (1992)
Big Brother
Black Panther Warriors, The (1993)
C'est la Vie, Mon Cherie (1993)
Candlelight's Woman (1995)
Changing Partner
Cheetah on Fire (1992)
City on Fire (2/1987)
Crystal Hunt (1991)
Days of Tomorrow (1993)
Dragon Fighter (198?)
Dragon from Russia (1990)
Family Day
First Time is the Last Time (1988)
Give and Take (1994)
Gun N' Rose (1992)
Gunmen (1988)
Hero Dream (1993)
Inside Track, The (1994)
Justice, My Foot (1992)
Ladies Killer
Lovers, The (8/1994)
Magic Umbrella
Mission of Justice (1992)
Misty
Modern Romance (1994)

Rouge (1987)
Rumble in the Bronx (1995)
Saviour of the Soul (1991)
Scared Stiff (3/1987)
Shanghai, Shanghai (1990)
Three Wishes
Top Bet
Trouble Couples (1987)
Why, Why, Tell Me Why?
Mountain Warriors (1990)
Naked Killer, The (1992)
One and a Half (1995)
Passion Unbounded (1995)
Police Confidential (1995)
Raped by an Angel (1993)
Rascal's Tale, A
Remains of a Woman (1993)
Right Here Waiting (1994)
Rock N' Roll Cop (1994)
Sentenced to Hang
Sex and Zen (1989)
Skinny Tiger and Fatty Dragon (1990)
Story of Pei-Li, The
Taking Manhattan
Thrilling Story
Twilight of the Forbidden City
Ultimate Vampire (1987)
Weakness of Man
Young Wisely II

Oh Soon Teck   Actor
        Korean
1971   One More Train to Rob
1974   The Man with the Golden Gun
1980   The Final Countdown
1982   The Letter
1983   Girls of the White Orchid
1985   Legend of the White Horse
1985   Missing in Action 2: The Beginning
1987   Collision Course
1987   DeadthWish 4: The Crackdown
1987   Steele Justice
1988   The Red Spider
1993   A Home of Our Own

Oshima Yukari (Cynthia Luster)
Actress   Japanese
Cantonese: Daai Do Yau Ga Lei
Mandarin: Da4 Dao3 You2 Jia1 Li4
  Angel (1986)
  Angel of Vengeance
  Angel Terminators 2 (1993)
  Angel's Mission (1989)
  Burning Ambition (1989)
  Cinema of Vengeance (1994 UK)
  Close Escape (1989) Cameo
  Deadly Target (1994)
  Devil Cat
  Direct Line, The
  Dreaming the Reality (1991)
  Fatal Chase (1992)
  Ghost's Love
 Godfather's Daughter Mafia Blues, The
(1992)
  Guardian Angel
  Hard to Kill
  Kick Boxer's Tears (1992)
  Kung Fu Wonder Child (1986 Taiwan)
  Lethal Panther 2 (1993)
  Love To Kill
  Lover's Tear (1991) Cameo
  Lucky Seven 2 (1989)
  Midnight Angel (1988)
  Mission of Justice (1992)
  Once a Cop (1993) Cameo
  Outlaw Brothers (1988)
  Power Connection (1995)
  Punch to Revenge, A (1990)
  Shanghai Express (1986)
  Story of Ricky (1991)
  Story of the Gun, The
  Ultracop 2000 (1992)
  Yes Madam '92: A Serious Shock (1992)

Ozu Yasujiro (1903 - 1963) Director
Japanese
Incredibly well respected and prolific
director who kept working until his early
death.   Sadly, Ozu's films are almost
unknown among mainstream American

  Angels, The
  Avenging Quartet (1992)
  Beauty Inspectors (1992)
  Big Deal, The
  Bloody Mary Killer
  Book of Heroes, A (1987)
  Brave Young Girls (1988)

audiences. This is a sample filmography:
1927 The Sword of Penitence/Zange no
Yaiba
1928 Body Beautiful/Nikutaibi
1928 A Ccouple on the Move/Hikkoshi
Fufu
1928 The Dreams of Youth/Wakodo no
Yume
1928 Pumpkin/Kabocha
1928 Wife Lost/Nyobo Funshitsu
1929 Fighting Friends Japanese Style
1930 Lost   Luck/Ashi   ni   Sawatta
Koun/Luck Touched My Legs
1931 Young Miss
1949 Late Spring   +screenwriter
1951 Eealy Summer
1953 Tokyo Story   +screenwriter
1956 Early Spring
1957 Tokyo Twilight
1959 Floating Weeds +creenwriter
1959 Good Morning
1960 Late Autumn   +creenwriter
1961 The End of Summer
1962 An   Autumn   Afternoon
      +creenwriter

Reis, Michelle (Lee Ka-Yan/Michelle Lee)
Actress   Chinese/Portuguese
Cantonese: Lei Ga Yan
Mandarin: Li3 Jia1 Xin1
Winner of Miss Hong Kong Pageant 1988.
  Black Morning Glory, The (1993)
  Casino Tycoon II (1992)
  Chinese Ghost Story Part II, A (1990)
  Dragon from Russia (1990)
  Drunken Master III (1994)
  Fallen Angels (1995)

Fong Sai Yuk (1993)
Fong Sai Yuk II (1993)
Kid from Tibet, A (1991)
No Risk, No Gain
Other Side of the Sea, The (1994)
Perfect Girls

Ryuichi Sakamoto   Composer/Music
Japanese
1983 Merry Christmas, Mr. Lawrence +performer
1985 Tokyo Melody, A Film about Ryuichi Sakamoto   performer
1987 Brand New Day   performer
1987 The Last Emperor   +performer
1987 Wings of Honneamise: Royal Space Force music director
1988 The Laserman   song
1989 Black Rain (Japan)   songs
1990 The Handmaid's Tale
1991 High Heels/Tacones Lejano
1992 Tokyo Decadence Topaz
1994 Jimmy Hollywood   song performer
1994 Little Buddha

Shigeta, James   Actor
Japanese
1959 The Crimson Kimono
1960 Walk Like a Dragon
1961 Brdige to the Sun
1961 Cry For Happy
1961 Flower Drum Song
1966 Paradise, Hawaiian Style
1968 Nobody's Perfect
1969 The Young Lawyers
1973 Lost Horizon
1975 Matt Helm
1975 The Yakuza/Brotherhood of the Yakuza
1976 The Killer Who Wouldn't Die
1976 Midway
1980 Enola Gay: The Men, The Mission, The Atomic Bomb
1982 Tomorrow's Cchild
1988 Die Hard

Royal Tramp II (1992)
Sword of Many Loves, The (1992)
Swordsman II (1991)
Wicked City, The (1992)
Zen of Sword (1992)

1989 Cage

Shimura Takashi   (1905 - 1982) Actor
Japanese
One of Japan's leading character actors, this is a selected handful of his best known films.
1941 The Last Days of Edo
1949 Stray Dog
1950 Rashomon
1950 Scandal
1951 The Idiot (Japan/USSR)
1952 Ikiru
1954 The Seven Samurai
1956 Godzilla, King of the Monsters
1957 Throne of Blood
1958 The Hidden Fortress
1959 The Mysterians
1959 Samurai Saga
1961 Yojombo/ The Bodyguard
1962 High and Low
1962 Sanjuro
1964 Hoichi the Earless
1964 Kwaidan
1965 Red Beard
1966 Frankenstein Conquers the World (Japan/US)
1973 Zatoichi's Conspiracy
1979 Oginsaga

Siao Fong-Fong, Josephine
Actress   Chinese
Cantonese: Siu Fong Fong
Mandarin: Xiao1 Fang1 Fang1
Always on My Mind (1993)
Fong Sai Yuk (1993)
Fong Sai Yuk II (1993)
Friend from Inner Space, A (1984)
Girl Friend

Hu-Du-Men (1996)
Jumping Ash (1976) + Dir Writer Prod
Lam Au Chun
My Sweet Lady
Plain Jane to the Rescue (1982)
Saviour of the Soul (1991)

Sun Chien   Actor   Chinese
Chinatown Kid (1977)
Crippled Avengers (1978)
Daredevils of Kung Fu
Destroyers
Five Deadly Venoms (1978)
House of Traps (1981)
Kid With the Golden Arm, The (1978)
Killer Army
Masked Avengers (1981)
Ode to Gallantry
Spearmen of Death (1980)
Ten Tigers of Kwangtung (1979)
Unbeatable Dragon

Takei, George   (1940 -   )   Actor
Japanese
1960   Ice Palace
1965   Red Line 7000
1965   The Saboteur, Code Name Morituri
1966   An American Dream
1966   Walk, Don't Run
1968   The Green Berets
1975   The Young Divorcees
1979   Star Trek: The Motion Picture
1981   American Dream
1982   Star Trek II: The Wrath of Khan
1984   Star Trek III: The Search for Spock
1986   Star Trek IV: The Voyage Home
1989   Return to the River Kwai
1989   Star Trek V: The Final Frontier
1990   Blood Oath
1991   Prisoners of the Sun
1991   Star Trek VI: The Undiscovered
Country
1993   Live by the Fist
1993   Oblivion
1994   Chongbal/Vanished
1995   Kissinger and Nixon

Spooky Bunch, The (1980) + Prod
Summer Snow (1995)
Too Happy for Words (1992)
True Story of a Rebellious Girl, The
(1969)
Wrong Couples, The (1987)

Takeshi   Kaneshiro   (Gum   Sing-Mo)
Actor   Japanese/Chinese
Cantonese: Gam Sing Mo
Mandarin: Jin1 Cheng2 Wu3
China Dragon (1995)
Chung King Express (1994)
Don't Give a Damn (1995)
Executioners (1993)
Fallen Angels (1995)
Mermaid Got Married (1994)
No Sir (1994 [Taiwan])
School Days (1995)
Scripture with No Words, The (1996)
Trouble Maker (1995)
Wrath of Silence (1994)
Young Policemen in Love (1995)

Ti Lung   Actor   Chinese
Cantonese: Dik Lung
Mandarin: Di2 Long2
7 Blows of the Dragon (1972)
7 Soldiers of Kung Fu (197?)
Bare-Footed Kid, The (1993)
Better Tomorrow, A (8/1986)
Better Tomorrow II, A (12/1987)
Black Magic II
Blade of Fury (1993)
Blood Brothers (1973)
Brave Archer 3 (1979)
Cinema of Vengeance (1994 UK)
City War (12/1988)
Deadly Duo (197?)
Death Chambers
Death Mask of the Ninja
Drunken Master II (1994)
Duel of Fists
Duel of Iron Fists
First Shot (1993)

Five Shaolin Masters (1975)
Friend from Inner Space, A (1984)
Heroic Ones (1970?)
Just Heroes (1987)
Moonlight Blade (197?)
New One-Armed Swordsman (1972)
Ninja Kung Fu
Ninja's Deadly Trap
One-Armed Swordsman Returns (1969)
People's Hero (1987)
Roving Swordsman
Run Don't Walk
Savage 5 (1979?)
Ten Tigers of Kwangtung (1979)
Tiger on Beat (3/1988) Cameo
True Colours (1986)
Vengeance (1970)
Warrior's Tragedy, A (1993)

Tsui Hark   (1951 -   )
Director   Chinese
Cantonese: Chui Hak
Mandarin: Xu2 Ke4
Aces Go Places (1982) Cameo
Aces Go Places 2 (1982) Cameo
Aces Go Places 3 (1983) + Cameo
All the Wrong Clues (1981)
All the Wrong Spies (1983) Actor +
Banquet, The (1991)
Better Tomorrow, A (8/1986) Prod
Better Tomorrow II, A (12/1987) Writer
Prod
Better Tomorrow III: Love and Death in
Saigon, A (10/1989)
Big Heat, The (1988) Prod
Blade, The (1995) + Writer
Burning Paradise (1994) Prod
Butterfly Murders, The (1979)
Chinese Feast, The (1995)
Chinese Ghost Story, A (1987) Prod
Chinese Ghost Story Part II, A (1990)
Prod
Chinese Ghost Story Part III, A (1991)
Prod
Close Encounters of the Spooky Kind

Killer's Blues, A
Kung Fu Emperor, The
Legend of Wu (1986)
Love Me Love My Dad
(1980)
Diary of a Big Man (7/1988) Prod
Don't Play with Fire (1980)
Final Victory Actor
Green Snake (1993) + Prod
Gunmen (1988) Prod
I Love Maria (1988) Actor Prod
Iron Monkey (1993) Prod
Just Heroes (1987) Prod
King of Chess (1988)
Laser Man (1986)
Love in the Time of Twilight (4/1995)
Lovers, The (8/1994) + Writer
Magic Crane, The (1993) Prod
Master, The (1989)
New Dragon Inn (1992) Prod
Once Upon a Time in China (1990)
Once Upon a Time in China 2 (1991) +
Prod
Once Upon a Time in China 3 (1992) +
Writer Prod
Once Upon a Time in China 4 (1993)
Prod
Once Upon a Time in China 5 (1994) +
Prod
Peking Opera Blues (1986) + Prod
Raid, The (1991) Actor Prod
Run Tiger Run (1985) Actor
Shanghai Blues (1984)
Spy Games (1988) Prod
Swordsman (1990) + Prod
Swordsman II (1991) Writer Prod
Swordsman 3: East is Red (1993) Prod
Terracotta Warrior, The (1989) Prod
Twin Dragons, The (1992) + Cameo
We Are Going to Eat You (1980)
Web of Deception (1989) Prod
Wicked City, The (1992) Prod
Working Class (1985) Actor Prod
Yes Madam! (1985) Actor
Zu: Warriors of the Magic Mountain

(1983)

Tsui Kam-Kong   Actor
     Chinese
1941 Hong Kong on Fire (1994)
All Men Are Brothers - Blood of the Leopard (1992)
Ancient Chinese Whorehouse (1994)
China Dragon (1995)
Chinese Torture Chamber Story (1994)
Deadful Melody (1994)
Eternal Evil of Asia, The (1995)
Fatal Obsession (1994)
Full Throttle (1995)
Girls Unbutton (1994)
Give and Take (1994)
God of Gamblers' Return (12/1994)
Great Conqueror's Concubine, The (1994)
Gunmen (1988)
Hail the Judge (1994)
It's a Drink, It's a Bomb (1985)
Kung Fu Cult Master, The (1993)
Law on the Brink (1994)
Long Arm of the Law II
Long Arm of the Law IV
Lord of East China Sea (1993)
Lord of East China Sea 2 (1993)
Lover's Tear (1991)
Lovers, The (8/1994)
Meaning of Life, The (1995)
Prison on Fire 2 (6/1991)
Royal Tramp (1992)
Sentenced to Hang
Sex and Zen (1989)
Sixty Million Dollar Man (1995)
Spike Drink Gang (1995)
Sword of Many Loves, The (1992)
Sword Stained With Royal Blood (1993)
Three Swordsmen, The (1994)
Tragic Hero (2/1987)
Underground Express
Wonder Seven (1994)

Wang Lung-Wei   Actor

Cantonese: Chui Gam Gong
Mandarin: Xu2 Jin3 Jiang1
01:00 A.M. (1995)

     Chinese
Cantonese: Wong Lung Wai
Mandarin: Wang2 Long2 Wei1
Chinatown Kid (1977)
City Warriors (1991) Dir
Death Chambers
Eight Diagram Pole Fighter (1983)
Escape from the Brothel (1992) Dir
Five Shaolin Masters (1975)
Martial Club (1981)
Master of Disaster (1982)
Master of the Flying Guillotine (1974)
My Young Auntie (1981)
New Legend of Shaolin, The (1994)
Run and Kill (1993)
Shanghai Express (1986)
Twin Dragons, The (1992)
Two Shaolin Kids in Hong Kong (1994)
Widow Warriors (1989) Dir

Wang, Wayne   (1949 -   )
     Director   Chinese
1975 Man, a Woman and a Killer
1982 Chan is Missing   +producer, editor, performer
1984 Dim Sum: A Little Bit of Heart +producer, story
1987 Slamdance
1988 Dim Sum Take-Outs +producer
1989 Eat a Bowl of Tea
1990 Life is Cheap, but Toilet Paper is Expensive   +executive producer, story
1993 The Joy Luck Club   +producer
1995 Blue   in   the   Face +co-screenwriter
1995 Smoke

Wang Yu, Jimmy   Actor
     Chinese
Cantonese: Wong Yue
Mandarin: Wang2 Yu3

Assasin, The
Assassin
Assassins
Cinema of Vengeance (1994 UK)
Fantasy Mission Force (1979)
Girl With the Thunderbolt Kick, The (1968)
Island of Fire (1990)
Killer Meteors (1977)
Magnificent Trio
Man Called Tiger, A
Man from Hong Kong, The (1975 U.S.A.) +Dir
Master Killer, The (1978)
Master of the Flying Guillotine (1974) +Dir
Once Upon a Time in China (1990)
One Armed Against Nine Killers +Action
One Armed Swordsmen, The +Dir
One-Armed Swordsman (1967)
One-Armed Swordsman Returns (1969)
Queen's Ransom, A
Royal Fist
Shogun & Little Kitchen (1992)
Sword and the Lute
Sword, The (1980)
Tattooed Dragon, The
Temple of the Red Lotus
Trail of the Broken Blade
Twin Swords

Wong Chou San, Anthony   Actor
       Chinese
Cantonese: Wong Chau Sang
Mandarin: Huang2 Qiu1 Sheng1
    Angel Hunter (1991)
    Awakening (1994)
    Big Score, The
    Bomb Disposal Officer: Baby Bomb (1994)
    Brother of Darkness (1994)
    Cop Image (1994)
    Daughter of Darkness (1993)
    Day That Doesn't Exist, The (1995)

Beheaded 1000 Dir
Boxers of Loyalty and Righteousness
Chinese Boxer (1970) +Dir Writer
Erotic Ghost Story 2
Executioners (1993)
Fight Back to School III (1993)
Full Contact (7/1992)
Gleam of Hope, A (1994)
Hard Boiled (4/1992)
Her Fatal Ways 3
Heroic Trio, The (1992)
Highway Man (1995)
Husbands & Wives (1995)
Lamb Killer
Legal Innocence (1993)
Love to Kill (1993)
Mad Monk (1993)
Madame City Hunter (1992)
Master Wong vs. Master Wong
Moment of Romance 2, A (1993)
New Tenant (1995) Actor Dir
News Attack
Now You See Love, Now You Don't (2/1992)
Now You See Me, Now You Don't (1994)
Organised Crime and Triad Bureau (1994)
Our Neighbor Detective (1995)
Retribution Sight Unseen (1993)
Rock N' Roll Cop (1994)
Taxi Hunter (1993)
Tiger's Legend of Canton, The
Twinkle Twinkle Lucky Stars (1985)
Underground Banker, The (1994)
Untold Story, The (1993)
What a Hero (1992)
When Fortune Smiles
World of Treasure (1995)
Wuniu
Yes Madam! (1985)

Wong Yiu-Ming, Anthony   Actor
       Chinese
Cantonese: Wong Yiu Ming

Mandarin: Huang2 Yao4 Ming2
01:00 A.M. (1995)
Golden Swallow (10/1988)
To Liv (1990?)

Wong Ka-Tat, Carter   Actor
Chinese
Cantonese: Wong Ga Daat
Mandarin: Huang2 Jia1 Da2
18 Bronzemen
Big Trouble in Little China (1986 USA)
Born Invincible
Legend of the Living Corps
Magnificent Fist
Shaolin Invincible
Shaolin Kung Fu Mystagogue (1976)
Time for Murder, A
Transmigration Romance (1991)
Way of the Lady Boxers (1992)
When Taekwondo Strikes (1973)

Wong Jing   (1956-)
Director   Chinese
Cantonese: Wong Jing
Mandarin: Wang2 Jing1
Big Score, The Actor
Born to Gamble
Boys Are Easy (1993) + Prod
Casino Raiders
Casino Tycoon (1992)
Casino Tycoon II (1992) + Prod
City Hunter (1992)
Crocodile Hunter
Dances with the Dragon
Fight Back to School (1991)
Fight Back to School III (1993)
Flying Dagger (1993) Prod
Fortune Code (1989) Writer
Frog Prince, The (1984)
Future Cops (1993)
Ghost Fever Actor
Ghost Lantern (1993) Prod
Ghost Snatchers Actor
God of Gamblers (12/1989)
God of Gamblers II (1989)

King of the Sea (1994)
Kiss Me Goodbye (1986)

God of Gamblers III: Back to Shanghai (1991) + Cameo
God of Gamblers' Return (12/1994) + Writer
Hail the Judge (1994) + Writer
High Risk (1995) + Writer Prod
Hitman Blues (1993) Prod
Holy Weapon (1993)
I'm Your Birthday Cake (1995) Prod
Kidnap of Wong Chak Fai, The (1993) Writer
Kung Fu Cult Master, The (1993)
Last Blood, The (1990)
Last Hero in China, The (1993)
Legend of the Liquid Sword (1993) + Prod
Lover of the Last Empress (1995) Prod
Magic Crystal (1987) Actor
Mean Street Story, The (1995) Prod
Millionaire Cop (1993) + Prod
Modern Romance (1994) + Prod
Money Maker Actor
Mr. Possessed Actor
Naked Killer, The (1992) Writer Prod
New Legend of Shaolin, The (1994) + Writer
Perfect Exchange, The (1993)
Perfect Girls
Raped by an Angel (1993) Writer Prod
Return to a Better Tomorrow (1994) + Writer
Romancing Star, The (6/1987)
Royal Tramp (1992)
Royal Tramp II (1992)
Saint of Gamblers, The (1995)
Seventh Curse, The (10/1986) Actor
Sixty Million Dollar Man (1995)
Sting 2, The
To Live and Die in Tsimshatsui (1994) + Prod
Tricky Brains (1991)
Tricky Business (1995) Prod

Trouble Couples (1987) Cameo
Twin Dragons, The (1992) Cameo
Wizard's Curse Writer Prod
You're My Destiny (1987) Writer Cameo
Young Policemen in Love (1995) Prod

Wong Ki Chang, Joey   (Joey Wang)
        Actor   Chinese
Cantonese: Wong Jo Yin
Mandarin: Wang2 Zu3 Xian2
100 Ways to Murder Your Wife (6/1986)
All Men Are Brothers - Blood of the Leopard (1992)
Banquet, The (1991)
Beheaded 1000
Big Heat, The (1988)
Big Score, The
Butterfly and Sword (1993)
Carry On Hotel (1988)
Casino Tycoon (1992)
Casino Tycoon II (1992)
Chez 'n Ham (1993)
Chinese Ghost Story, A (1987)
Chinese Ghost Story Part II, A (1990)
Chinese Ghost Story Part III, A (1991)
Chinese Legend, A (1991)
City Hunter (1992)
Cyprus Tigers, The
Demoness from Thousand Year
Diary of a Big Man (7/1988)
Eagle Shooting Heroes, The (1993)
Eternal Combat, An
Eye for an Eye, An (1993?)
Family Honor
Fantasy Romance (1993)
Flower Love
Foxy Spirits
Fractured Follies (7/1988)
Ghost Busters
Ghost Snatchers
Gift from Heaven
God of Gamblers (12/1989)
Green Snake (1993)
Hearty Response, A (10/1986)
Hong Kong Godfather (1991) Cameo

Whatever You Want (1994) + Writer

Killer's Romance (1990)
Kung Fu vs. Acrobatic (1991)
Lake Sprite (1991)
Law or Justice
Legend of Wu (1986)
Life After Dead
Ming Ghost
Missing Man
My Dream is Yours
My Heart Is That Eternal Rose (1987)
Painted Skin (1992)
Point of No Return (1991)
Portrait of a Nymph
Prince of Temple Street
Red and Black (1991)
Reincarnation of Golden Lotus, The (1989)
Spirit Love
Spy Games (1988)
Swordsman 3: East is Red (1993)
Tale from the East, A (1990)
To Err is Human
Web of Deception (1989)
Where's Officer Tuba (1988)
Working Class (1985)

Wong, Victor   Actor
        Chinese
1984   Dim Sum: A Little Bit of Heart
1984   Nightsongs
1985   Year of the Dragon
1986   Big Trouble in Little China
1986   The Golden Child
1986   The Mosquito Coast
1986   Shanghai Surprise
1987   The Last Emperor
1987   Prince of Darkness
1989   Eat a Bowl of Tea
1989   Solo
1990   Life is Cheap, but Toilet Paper is Expensive
1990   Tremors
1991   Mystery Date

1992　3 Ninjas
1992　The Ice Runner
1993　The Joy Luck Club
1994　3 Ninjas Kick Back
1995　3 Ninjas Knuckle Up

Woo, John (Ng Yu-Sum)　(1948 -　　)
Director　　Chinese
Cantonese: Ng Yue Sam
Mandarin: Wu2 Yu3 Sen1
　　Better Tomorrow, A (8/1986) +Actor Writer
　　Better Tomorrow II, A (12/1987) +Writer
　　Broken Arrow (1996)
　　Bullet in the Head (1990) +Cameo
　　Countdown in Kung Fu (1975) +Actor
　　Dragon Tamers, The (1974)
　　Face-Off (1997)
　　Follow the Star (1977) +Writer
　　rom Riches to Rags (1979) +Writer Cameo
　　Hard Boiled (4/1992) +Cameo
　　Hard Target (1993)
　　Heroes Shed No Tears (1985)
　　Just Heroes (1987)
　　Killer, The (7/1989) +Writer
　　Last Hurrah for Chivalry (1978)
　　Laughing Times (1981)
　　Mission Impossible 2 (2000)
　　Money Crazy (1977)
　　Once a Thief (2/1991)
　　Peace Hotel (4/1995) Prod
　　Plain Jane to the Rescue (1982) +Writer Cameo
　　Princess Chang Ping (1975)
　　Rebel from China Actor
　　Run Tiger Run (1985)
　　Somebody Up There Likes Me (1996) Prod
　　Starry is the Night (1988) Actor
　　Time You Need a Friend, The (1984)
　　To Hell with the Devil (1981)
　　Twin Dragons, The (1992) Cameo
　　Young Dragons, The (1973) +Writer Cameo

1992　Cageman

Wu Ma　　Actor　　Chinese
Cantonese: Ng Ma
Mandarin: Wu3 Ma3
　　All Men Are Brothers - Blood of the Leopard (1992)
　　Beware of Pickpocket +Dir
　　Big Circle Blues
　　Buddhist Spell, The
　　Burning Sensation +Dir
　　By Hook or by Crook
　　Chinese Ghost Story, A (1987)
　　Chinese Ghost Story Part II, A (1990)
　　Chinese Ghostbuster, The (1994) +Dir
　　Chinese Legend, A (1991)
　　Circus Kids (1994) +Dir
　　City On Fire
　　City on Fire (2/1987)
　　Close Encounters of the Spooky Kind (1980)
　　Close Encounters of the Spooky Kind 2 (1989)
　　Dead and the Deadly, The (1982) +Dir
　　Deadful Melody (1994)
　　Deaf and Mute Heroine, The +Dir
　　Don't Give a Damn (1995) Cameo
　　Drug Tiger (1993)
　　Fat Cat (1988)
　　First Mission, The (1982) +Prod
　　Foxy Spirits
　　Gambling Soul
　　Ghost in Me
　　Gold Hunter
　　Heroic Brothers
　　High Risk (1995)
　　His Way, Her Way, Their Ways
　　In the Blood (1987)
　　It's a Drink, It's a Bomb (1985) Cameo
　　Just Heroes (1987) +Dir
　　Kick Boxer (1992) +Dir
　　Kid from Tibet, A (1991) Cameo
　　Laughing Times (1981)
　　Legend of Fong Sai Yuk
　　Little Kids Beat the Boss

Lover's Tear (1991)
Magic Cop (1989)
Magnificent Scoundrels (1991)
Magnificent Warriors (1987)
Master of Zen (1994)
Miracles: The Canton Godfather (1989)
Mr. Vampire (1984)
Mr. Vampire 2 (1985)
Mr. Vampire 4 (1987)
My American Grandson (1991 China)
Off Track (1990)
Oh! My God!
Once Upon a Time in China (1990)
Painted Faces (1988)
Peking Opera Blues (1986)
Police Story Part 2 (1988) Cameo
Portrait of a Nymph
Raiders of Loosing Treasure
Red and Black (1991)
Return of the Demon
Revenge of Angel
Shanghai Express (1986)
Switch Over (1994)
Sword Stained With Royal Blood (1993)
Swordsman (1990)
Takes Two to Mingle
Tantana, the
Twilight Siren
Twin Dragons, The (1992) Cameo
Twinkle Twinkle Lucky Stars (1985) Cameo
Wheels on Meals (1984)
Yes Madam! (1985)

Xie Miao (Tze Miu) Child Actor
Chinese
Cantonese: Je Miu
Mandarin: Xie4 Miao2
God of Gamblers' Return (12/1994)
My Father is a Hero (1995)
New Legend of Shaolin, The (1994)
Teenager Master (1995)

Xiong Xin-Xin (Hung Yan-Yan)   Actor
Fatal Termination (1988)

Chinese
Cantonese: Hung Yan Yan
Mandarin: Xiong2 Xin1 Xin1
Blade, The (1995)
Chinese Feast, The (1995)
Forced Nightmare (1992)
Heroes Among Heroes (1993)
Little Drunken Masters, The (1995)
Musical Vampire, The
Once Upon a Time in China 3 (1992)
Once Upon a Time in China 4 (1993)
Once Upon a Time in China 5 (1994)
Other Side of the Sea, The (1994)
To Live and Die in Tsimshatsui (1994) [Cameo]
Wonder Seven (1994)

Yam Tat Hwa, Simon   (Simon Tam)
Actor   Chinese
Cantonese: Yam Daat Wa
Mandarin: Ren2 Da2 Hua2
Awakening (1994)
Because of Lies (1995)
Black Cat (1991)
Black Panther Warriors, The (1993)
Bullet for Hire (1991)
Bullet in the Head (1990)
Burning Ambition (1989)
Cash on Delivery
Chinese Cop-Out (1989)
Cinema of Vengeance (1994 UK)
Crossings (1994)
Crystal Fortune Run (1994)
Cyprus Tigers, The
Day Without Policemen, A (1994)
Deadly Deal
Devil's Box, The (1994)
Doctor Lamb (1992)
Don't Stop My Crazy Love for You (1993)
Dragon Killer (1995)
Drunken Master III (1994)
Farewell My Dearest (1995)
Final Judgement, The

Final Run
First Shot (1993)
Framed
Friday Gigolo
Full Contact (7/1992)
Future Cops (1993)
Ghostly Bus (1995)
Gigolo and Whore (1994)
Gigolo and Whore II
Goodbye Mama (1985)
Great Pretenders (1991)
Gun N' Rose (1992)
Guns & Roses
Hard to Kill
Holy Weapon (1993)
Hong Kong Gigolo
Incorruptable, The (1993)
Insanity (1993)
Killer's Love, The
Killer's Romance (1990)
Legendary Couple (1995)
Live Hard
Love Among the Triad (1993)
Love, Guns & Glass (1995)
Lucky Star
Man Wanted (1995)
Mission Kill
Mistaken Identity
Naked Killer, The (1992)
Night Rider, The (1992)
Once Upon a Time a Hero in China
(1992)   Operation Foxhunt
Osmanthus Alley
Passion 1995 (1995)
Police Confidential (1995)
Powerful Four (1991)
Prince of Portland Street (1993)
Queen of Gamble
Queen's High (1991)
Raped by an Angel (1993)
Return Engagement (1990)
Rose, Rose I Love You (1993)
She Starts the Fire (1992)
They Came to Rob Hong Kong
Tricky Brains (1991)

Run and Kill (1993)
Sea Wolves (1990)
Tiger Cage (1988)
Tragic Fantasy: Tiger of Wanchai (1994)
True Hero, The (1994)
Twist (1995)
Wild Ones, The

Yau Suk-Ching, Chingmy (Yau Su Jun)
Actress   Chinese
Cantonese: Yau Suk Jing
Mandarin: Qiu1 Shu2 Zhen1
1941 Hong Kong on Fire (1994)
Blind Romance (1996)
Boys Are Easy (1993)
Casino Tycoon (1992)
Casino Tycoon II (1992)
City Hunter (1992)
Deadly Dream Woman (1992)
Future Cops (1993)
Ghost Busting
Ghost Lantern (1993)
God of Gamblers' Return (12/1994)
High Risk (1995)
I'm Your Birthday Cake (1995)
Kung Fu Cult Master, The (1993)
Lee Rock I
Legend of the Liquid Sword (1993)
Legendary Couple (1995)
Lover of the Last Empress (1995)
Millionaire Cop (1993)
Modern Love, The (1994)
Modern Romance (1994)
Mr. Fortune
Naked Killer, The (1992)
New Legend of Shaolin, The (1994)
Psycho Killer (1993)
Raped by an Angel (1993)
Return to a Better Tomorrow (1994)
Royal Tramp (1992)
Royal Tramp II (1992)
Saint of Gamblers, The (1995)

Yen Ji Dan, Donnie (Donnie Yan)
Actor   Chinese

Cantonese: Yan Ji Daan
Mandarin: Zhen1 Zi3 Dan1
   Asian Cops - High Voltage (1995) +Action
   Butterfly and Sword (1993)
   Cheetah on Fire (1992)
   Cinema of Vengeance (1994 UK)
   Circus Kids (1994)
   Crystal Hunt (1991)
   Drunken Tai Chi (1984)
   Heroes Among Heroes (1993)
   Holy Virgin vs. the Evil Dead (1990)
   In the Line of Duty (1987)
   In the Line of Duty 4: Witness (1989)
   Iron Monkey (1993)
   Love Meets the Match
   Mismatched Couples
   New Dragon Inn (1992)
   Once Upon a Time in China 2 (1991)
   Saint of Gamblers, The (1995)
   Tiger Cage (1988)
   Tiger Cage 2 (1990) +Action
   Tiger Cage 3 (1991)
   Wing Chun (1994) +Action

Yeoh, Michelle   (Michelle Khan/Yeung Chi King)   Actress
      Chinese
Cantonese: Yeung Ji King
Mandarin: Yang2 Zi3 Qiong2
1985   Twinkle Twinkle Lucky Stars
1985   Yes Madam!
1987   Easy Money
1987   In the Line of Duty
1987   Magnificent Warriors
1992   Heroic Trio, The
1992   Police Story 3: Supercop
1993   Butterfly and Sword
1993   Executioners
1993   Holy Weapon
1993   Once a Cop
Yip Tong, Cecilia   Actress
      Chinese
Cantonese: Yip Tung
Mandarin: Ye4 Tong2

1993   Tai Chi Master
1994   Shaolin Popey 2: Messy Temple (Taiwan) Cameo
1994   Wing Chun
1994   Wonder Seven
1997   Tomorrow Never Dies (first USA film)
2000   Crouching Toger, Hidden Dragon

Yip Chi-Mei, Amy
Actress   Chinese
Cantonese: Yip Ji Mei
Mandarin: Ye4 Zi3 Mei2
   Blue Jean Monster, The
   China Dolls
   Easy Money 1991 (1991?)
   Erotic Ghost Story (1990)
   Erotic Ghost Story 2
   Faces of Death
   Ghostly Vixen
   Great Pretenders (1991)
   Inspectors Wear Skirts 2
   Jail House Eros
   Le Club
   Legend of the Dragon (1990)
   Lethal Contact Cameo
   Look Out, Officer!
   Magnificent Scoundrels (1991)
   Mortuary Blues (1990)
   My Neighbors are Phantoms
   Prostitute Cop
   Queen of the Underworld
   Raid on Royal Casino Marine (1990)
   Robotrix (1991)
   Sex and Zen (1989)
   Stooges in Hong Kong
   To Be Number One (1991)
   To Spy with Love
   Underground Judgement (1994)
   Vampire Strikes Back

   Amnesty Decree
   Beyond the Sunset
   Call Girl '92 (1992)
   Chaos by Design

Esprit D'Amour (1983)
Faithfully Yours 1995 (1995)
Final Judgement, The
Fumbling Cops
Hong Kong 1941 (11/1984)
King of the Sea (1994)
Legal Innocence (1993)
Lord of East China Sea (1993)
Lord of East China Sea 2 (1993)
Love, Guns & Glass (1995)
My Heavenly Lover
Nomad (1982)
Organised Crime and Triad Bureau (1994)
Peace Hotel (4/1995)
Rebel from China
Reincarnation
Right Here Waiting (1994)
Set Me Free (1989)
Strange Bedfellow
Swordsman (1990)
This Thing Called Love (1991)
To Be Number One (1991)
Weakness of Man
Wonder Women (1987)

Yip Fong-Wah, Francoise
      Actress   Chinese
Cantonese: Yip Fong Wa
Mandarin: Ye4 Fang1 Hua2
Infatuation (1995)
Rumble in the Bronx (1995)
Wild (1996)

Yip Tze Man, Sally (Sally Yeh)
      Actress   Chinese
Cantonese: Yip Sin Man
Mandarin: Ye4 Qian4 Wen2
Aces Go Places 4 (1986)
Banquet, The (1991)
Love Among the Triad (1993)
Mother of a Different Kind (1995)
Pretty Woman (1992)
Red Rose White Rose (1994)
Retribution Sight Unseen (1993)

Certain Romance, A (1984)
Cupid One (1985)
Diary of a Big Man (7/1988)
Funny Face (1984)
Golden Queen's Commando (1984)
I Love Maria (1988)
Just for Fun (1985)
Killer, The (7/1989)
Laser Man (1986)
Mariana (1982)
Mob Busters (1985)
Mr. Boo 1: The Private Eyes (1982)
Mr. Boo 6: Teppanyaki (1984)
Occupant, The (9/1984)
Peking Opera Blues (1986)
Pink Force Commando (1984)
Protector, The (1985 U.S.A.)
Shanghai Blues (1984)
Sisters of the World Unite (1991)
Spirit vs. Zombie
Vampire Strikes Back
Welcome (1985)

Yip Yuk-Hing, Veronica
      Actress   Chinese
Cantonese: Yip Yuk Hing
Mandarin: Ye4 Yu4 Qing1
01:00 A.M. (1995)
1941 Hong Kong on Fire (1994)
Bogus Cops
Call Girl '92 (1992)
Cash on Delivery
Eagle Shooting Heroes, The (1993)
Emotional Girl (1993)
Gigolo and Whore II
Hero from Beyond the End of Time (1993)
Hidden Desire (1990)
Law on the Brink (1994)

Roof With a View (1990)
Rose (1992)
Rose, Rose I Love You (1993)
Run (1994)
Summer Lovers (1992)

Take Me (1991)
Three Summers
Treasure Island (1994 Taiwan)

Yu Rong Guang   Actor
    Chinese
Cantonese: Yue Wing Gwong
Mandarin: Yu2 Rong2 Guang1
Combo Cop (1996)
Deadend of Besiegers (1992)
Fox Hunter (1995)
From Beijing with Love (1994) Cameo
Gleam of Hope, A (1994)
Green Hornet (1994)
Heart of Killer (1995)
Holy Robe of the Shaolin Temple
Iron Monkey (1993)
Lover of the Last Empress (1995)
Man Wanted (1995)
My Father is a Hero (1995)
Once a Cop (1993)
Red Fists
Red Zone (1995)
Rock N' Roll Cop (1994)
Shanghai Noon (1999)
Swordsman 3: East is Red (1993)
Taxi Hunter (1993)
Terracotta Warrior, The (1989)
Third Full Moon, The (1994)
Wind Beneath the Wings (1995)

Yu Yan Tai, Ronnie   Director
    Chinese
Cantonese: Yue Yan Taai
Mandarin: Yu2 Ren2 Tai4
Bride with White Hair, The (1993) +Prod
Bride with White Hair 2, The (1993)
+Prod
Chicken and Duck Talk (1988) Prod
Just Married (1995)
Last Hero in China, The (1993)
Legend of the Liquid Sword (1993)
Prince of Portland Street (1993)
Sword Stained With Royal Blood (1993)
Talk to Me Dicky (1992) Cameo

China White (1990)
Deadend of Besiegers (1992)
Extras, The (1978) Prod
Great Pretenders (1991)
Legacy of Rage (1986)
Master Wong vs. Master Wong Prod
Occupant, The (9/1984)
Once Upon a Time a Hero in China
(1992) Prod
Phantom Lover (1995)
Postman Strikes Back (6/1982)
Saviour, The (1980)
Servant, The (1979)
Shogun & Little Kitchen (1992)
Trail, The (1983)

Yuen Wing-Yee, Anita   (4/9/1971-
)   Actress   Chinese
Cantonese: Yuen Wing Yi
Mandarin: Yuan2 Yong3 Yi2
01:00 A.M. (1995)
Age of Miracle, The (1996)
C'est la Vie, Mon Cherie (1993)
Chinese Feast, The (1995)
Crossings (1994)
Crystal Fortune Run (1994)
Days of Being Dumb, The (1992)
From Beijing with Love (1994)
Golden Girls, The (1995)
Handsome Siblings (1992)
He Ain't Heavy, He's My Father (1993)
He and She (1994)
He is a Woman, She is a Man (1994)
Heaven Can't Wait (1995) Cameo
I Want to Go On Living (1995)
I Will Wait for You (1994)
I've Got You, Babe (1994)
Incorruptable, The (1993)
It's a Wonderful Life (1994)
Taste of Killing and Romance, A (1994)
Tears and Triumph (1994)
Thunderbolt (1995)
Tom, Dick, and Hairy (1993)
Tragic Commitment (1995)
Tricky Business (1995)

True Hero, The (1994)
Two of a Kind (1993)
Warrior's Tragedy, A (1993)
Whatever You Want (1994)
Wrath of Silence (1994)

Yuen Biao   Actor   Chinese
Cantonese: Yuen Biu
Mandarin: Yuan2 Biao1
Best of the Martial Arts Films, The
(1990)
Champions, The
Circus Kids (1994)
Countdown in Kung Fu (1975)
Deadful Melody (1994)
Don't Give a Damn (1995)
Dragon Lord (1982)
Dragon, the Odds, The (197?)
Dragons Forever (1987)
Dreadnought (1981)
Eastern Condors (1986)
Enter the Fat Dragon (197?)
From the Great Beyond
Iceman Cometh (1989)
Kick Boxer (1992)
Kid from Tibet, A (1991) Actor Dir Prod
Knockabout (1979?)
Licence to Steal (1990)
Miracles: The Canton Godfather (1989)
Cameo
Mr. Vampire 2 (1985)
My Lucky Stars (1985)
On the Run
Once Upon a Time in China (1990)
Peacock King (1987) Actor Dir
Portrait of a Nymph
Prodigal Son (1983)
Project A (1983)
Righting Wrongs (1986)
No Retreat, No Surrender II (1989)
Nocturnal Demon (1991) Actor
Raid, The (1991) Actor
Righting Wrongs (1986)
Righting Wrongs 2: Blonde Fury (1987)
Prod

Rosa
Saga of the Phoenix (1990)
Setting Sun (1993) Actor Action
Shanghai Express (1986)
Shanghai, Shanghai (1990)
Shogun & Little Kitchen (1992)
Snuff Bottle Connection (1977)
Sword Stained With Royal Blood (1993)
Tough Beauty and the Sloppy Slop
(1995)
Twinkle Twinkle Lucky Stars (1985)
Wheels on Meals (1984)
Winners and Sinners (1983)
Young Master, The (1980)
Zu: Warriors of the Magic Mountain
(1983)

Yuen Kwai, Corey
Director   Chinese
Cantonese: Yuen Fooi
Mandarin: Yuan2 Kui2
All for the Winner (1990) +Actor Writer
Prod
Bodyguard from Beijing, The (1994)
+Action
Bury Me High (1990) Actor
Dragons Forever (1987) Actor
Fong Sai Yuk (1993) Dir Action
Fong Sai Yuk II (1993) +Actor
High Risk (1995) Action
In the Blood (1987)
Legend of the Dragon (1990) Actor
Action
Lethal Lady (1990)
Magic Crystal (1987)
My Father is a Hero (1995) +Cameo
New Legend of Shaolin, The (1994)
Action

Saviour of the Soul (1991) +Actor
Saviour of the Soul II (1992)
Shanghai, Shanghai (1990) Prod
She Shoots Straight (1990)
Thunderbolt (1995) Actor
Top Bet   +Actor Prod

Women on the Run
Yes Madam! (1985)

Yuen Woo Ping
Director   Chinese
Cantonese: Yuen Woh Ping
Mandarin: Yuan2 Huo4 Pin2
Cinema of Vengeance (1994 UK) Actor
Crouching Tiger, Hidden Dragon (2000)
Action Director
Dreadnought (1981)
Drunken Master (1979) +Action
Drunken Tai Chi (1984)
Eastern Condors (1986) Actor
Exciting Dragon (1981)
Fire Dragon (1994)
Fist of Legend (1994) Action
Game Kids (1992) Actor
Heroes Among Heroes (1993) +Prod
In the Line of Duty 4: Witness (1989)
Iron Monkey (1993)
Kick Boxer (1992)
King of Beggars (1993) Actor
Last Hero in China, The (1993) Action
Legend of a Fighter (1982)
Madame City Hunter (1992) Prod
Matrix (1999) Action Director
Merry Christmas (1984) Cameo
Miracle Fighters (1982) +Actor
Mismatched Couples Actor
Snake in Eagle's Shadow (1978) +action
Tai Chi Master (1993)
Taoism Drunkard (1983?)
Tiger Cage (1988)
Tiger Cage 2 (1990) +Action
Tiger Cage 3 (1991)
Wicked City, The (1992) Actor

Wing Chun (1994) +Action Prod

Yune, Johnny   Actor/Comedian
Korean
1982   They Call Me Bruce?
1986   They Still Call Me Bruce

Zhang Yimou (1950-)   Director
Chinese
1987   Red   Sorghum/   Hong   Gaoliang
        +song composer
1989   Ju Dou
1990   The   Terra-cotta   Warrior
        performer, producer
1991   Raise the Red Lantern
1992   The Story of Qiu Ju
1993   Mary of Beijing   associate
producer
1994   The Great Conqueror's Concubine
        executive producer
1994   Hua Hun   supervising director
1994   To Live

Zhao   Wen   Zhou   (Chiu   Man-Cheuk)
Actor   Chinese
Cantonese: Jiu Man Cheuk
Mandarin: Zhao4 Wen2 Zhuo2
Blade, The (1995)
Chinese Feast, The (1995)
Fong Sai Yuk (1993)
Green Snake (1993)
Once Upon a Time in China 4 (1993)
Once Upon a Time in China 5 (1994)

Appendix V
Distributors & Retailers

Originally I had planned to list dozens of specialty retailers that carried Asian films, but as I wrote this book a wonderful thing happened. Asian films became incredibly popular, Jackie Chan, Jet Li, Japanime, and Hong Kong films popped up in theaters throughout the country. Then a number of Asian-related books and magazines appeared in stores, and many hard to find Asian videos landed for sale and rent in local chains and major retailers. Sadly, the small specialty sellers began to vanish under stronger copy protection laws, so I decided to avoid listing sources that possible condoned illegal, bootleg copies. So your best bet is to go to any major video store, and eight out of ten times, you'll find a Japanese animation section, a martial arts section, and plenty of goodies in the foreign section. Not all films will be found everywhere and you may still have to trek into an Asian community or major city, but a good percentage of films can now be found in big chains like Tower Records, Sam Goody, Suncoast Video, Coconuts, Blockbuster, West Coast Video, Palmer Video, online renters like Netflix, Amazon, Hulu, and other establishments that sell or rent video tapes. My apologies but many of the video retailers are not defunct or permanently closed due to competition from online sources.

If you still can't find that film, don't worry, I've listed some of the biggest distributors of Asian films in the United States. If they don't have it, most likely no one does, unless you know someone from Hong Kong. Also check the internet for numerous distributors/retailers in America that provide Asian films for sale.

In the world of Japanese Animation there is only one place that I would go to:
Central Park Media Corporation
250 West 57th Street
Suite 317
New York, NY 10107
800-833-7456 retailers
800-626-4277 consumers
www.centralparkmedia.com

There are other sources, but Central Park Media is the single-largest distributor of Japanese animation with hundreds of popular titles available. Formed in 1991, they carry almost every major anime release in the country and have strived to better represent the market with three in-house divisions. U.S. Manga Corps for mainstream, Anime 18 for adult, and a classic line. Their unique Manga Club offers plenty of bonuses and the copy features a detailed and attractive catalog of their products. Titles can also be found on laserdisc and DVD.

Some other major Anime distirbutors:
AnimEigo, Inc.
P.O. Box 989
Wilmington, NC
28402-0989
910-251-1850
800-242-6463 (orders)
www.animeigo.com

Pioneer Animation
P.O. Box 22782
2265 E. 220th Street
Long Beach, CA 90801
800-421-1621
www.pioneer-ent.com/

The Right Stuf International
P.O. Box 71309
Des Moines, IA 50325-1309
800-338-6827
www.centsys.com

Streamline Pictures
2908 Nebraska Avenue
Santa Monica, CA 90404
310-998-0070
www.streamlinepic.com

For Hong Kong films, the largest leading distributor in America is Tai Seng Video Marketing. Professionally organized, they carry hundreds of films on video, DVD, laserdisc, and video CD with a wide range of genre categories. You can contact them directly or through their user-friendly website. Tai Seng Video products are also available through retail/mail-order outlets and quality is top-notch.
Tai Seng Video Marketing
170 South Spruce Avenue, Suite 200
South San Francisco, CA 94080
1-800-888-3836

Far East Flix
59-13 68th Ave.
Ridgewood, NY 11385
718-381-6757
A great place to get those hard to find kung-fu/action films. Easy to order and very convenient with an extensive catalog of films. Give them a try if you must see a movie.

Voyager Criterion Collection
578 Broadway, Suite 406
New York, NY 10012
1800-446-2001
www.voyagerco.com
A great place for classic Asian films reproduced from the finest quality prints for DVD, laserdisc and video tape. They'll don't have the largest Asian selection, but they carry some of the best-known titles...Akira, The Killer, Hard-Boiled, The Hidden Fortress, Ikiru, Osaka Elegy, Rashomon, Samurai Trilogy, Sanjuro, Sansho the Baliff, Seven Samurai, Supercop, Throne of

Blood, Ugetsu, Yojimbo, and so on.

Appendix VI (Conventions & Internet Websites)

Due to the rapid changing nature of the web, certain listings below may no longer be valid.

Anime America
929 Delbert Way
San Jose, CA 95126
Email: anam@rahul.net

Anime Expo
530 Showers Dr. #7-287
Mountain View, CA 94040
Email: info@anime-expo.org
818-441-3653

Anime Weekend Atlanta
P.O. Box 13544
Atlanta, GA 30324-0544
Email: awainfo@mindspring.com
404-364-9773

Fanime Con
P.O. Box 8068
San Jose, CA 95155-8068
Email: fanime@fanime.com

Far East Expo
P.O. Box 10371
New Brunswick, NJ 08906-0371
Email: fareast@net-lynx.com
908-719-9770
(This is my home turf, so maybe I'll see you there.)

Icon XVII
P.O. Box 550
Stony Brook, NY 11790
Email: icon@sunysb.edu

Katsu Productions Ltd.

P.O. Box 11582
Blacksburg, VA 24062-1582
Email: katsucon@vtserf.cc.vt.edu

Otakon c/o Dave Asher
661 A Waupelani Drive
State College, PA 16801
Email: dcasher@delphi.com
814-867-3478

Project Akon
3352 Broadway, Suite 470
Garland, TX 75043
Email: phoenix@cyberramp.net

World Science Fiction Convention (WorldCon)
LoneStarCon
P.O. Box 27277
Austin, TX 78755-2277
512-453-7446

Japanese animation is very popular in the world of comics and science fiction conventions, almost every major convention will have some anime items for sale and offer an opportunity to meet fans of the genre. I've always been a participant of Creation Conventions which travel throughout the country. New York City also has plenty of conventions and Asian film festivals. Another great source to check for information is the internet.

Internet Websites

With each growing day, newer and bigger websites on Asian films have appeared over the years. As you can see from the list of distributors and conventions, practically everyone has a website. If you have a web search engine, the best way to access websites is to type in a word of interest (Godzilla, Hong Kong, Korea, samurai, ninja, kung-fu, etc.) and let the computer do the work for you. From there, find a link page and weave your way through thousands of websites on every subject imaginable. You'll be able to find written reviews, data, biographies, trivia, photos, video clips, sound/music clips, and clubs. It's the best way to look for information on Asian films (next to buying my book.)

The following list is only a small sample of the link pages available.

Please note: I do not take credit for creating the following link pages nor do I assume responsibility for what's written. They are simply a reprint of the link pages found on three major websites: Hong Kong Cinema, Barry's Temple of Godzilla, and Anime Website. These are three of my favorite websites, so I thank them for a great job and helping with my research.

HONG KONG FILMS

The Hong Kong Movies Homepage - Expansive, informative, and easy to use.

The Asian Movies Homepage - Another excellent site.

Contemporary Chinese Cinema - New films being developed.

Hong Kong Film Critics Society - Professional reviews by Hong Kong critics.

Mandrake's Hong Kong Movies Page alt.asian-movies - Discussion is primarily Hong Kong movies.

Archive - alt.asian.movies - Searchable archive of all articles
posted since October 1995.

Regional Information

Hong Kong Films in the Boston Area - Boston (USA) and
surrounding regions.

The Hong Kong Popstars Archive - A huge selection of popstar

Hong Kong Films in Denver - Theaters and video stores in Denver
(USA).

HK Star Internet - Now Showing - Films currently playing in Hong
Kong (requires Chinese BIG5 viewer).

The Web Connection: Entertainment - Movies - What's playing,
coming attractions, and video rental charts from Hong Kong.

Ryan's Movieplex - Full roundup with reviews of movies playing in
Hong Kong.

What Hong Kong Movies are Showing in LA - Greater Los Angeles
(USA) Area.

Neighborhood Film / Video Project - A great lineup of movies is
scheduled for January in Philadelphia (USA).

Hong Kong Movies Net - Now playing in New York City (USA).

Sydney Chinatown Cinema - Downtown Sydney (Australia).

Asian movies in the Toronto area - Complete Toronto (Canada)
coverage.

I-Channel Cantonese Movies - Saturday HK movie showings on the
cable channel network serving much of North America.

Pictures

bst - Don't miss the Christmas collection of pictures.

Datatron Gallery - Images of selected HK pop stars.

Hong Kong Galleries - See high-quality images of your favorite pop
stars.

The Hong Kong Movies Picture Library - Movies, film stars, and movie
posters.
pictures.

Jonah's New Picture Gallery - The title

says it all.

The Lam Palace - A huge gallery of pictures, nicely divided into
rooms.

Andrew Lee's Homepage - High quality scans of popstars.

Entertainment News

Hong Kong Entertainment News - Translated articles from the
entertainment industry (requires Netscape 2.0).

Ming Pao Daily Entertainment News - Good articles occasionally
accompanied by color pictures (requires Chinese BIG5 viewer).

Ming Pao Daily News Archive - Articles from the past month
(requires Chinese BIG5 viewer).

Next Magazine - Official site of the weekly Hong Kong magazine
(requires Chinese BIG5 viewer).

Sing Tao Entertainment News - Up-to-date, complete archive of
articles usually with color pictures (requires Chinese BIG5 viewer).

Sing Tao Journal Film Reviews - Daily film reviews of movies
currently showing in Hong Kong (requires Chinese BIG5 viewer).

Tyatt's Daily Entertainment News - Tidbits of news from the show
business scene.

World Journal Entertainment News - Entertainment articles presented
in Chinese (no Big5 viewer required).

Miscellaneous

Asia Channel Network - Movie clips, articles, and entertainment news.

Asian Pops Information - Complete Movies

Mandarin Films' WWW Web Page

NAKED KILLER THE HOMEPAGE

Rumble in The Bronx

coverage of the Asian music scene.

Girls on Film - A hilarious look at Hong Kong movies from a female
perspective. Two snaps up!

Hong Kong Bridge 96 - The four best HK entertainment sites have
combined to form the ultimate HK Web Wide Mag.

Hong Kong Albums Review - Reviews for all the latest CD and
LD releases.

Hong Kong Collection - The most comprehensive collection of
HK entertainment links on the internet.

Hong Kong Entertainment News - Translated articles from the
entertainment industry (requires Netscape 2.0).

Hong Kong Galleries - See high-quality images of your favorite
pop stars.

Made in Hong Kong - A mail order company dedicated to Hong Kong
movies.

Ray's World - An insider's look at the HK music scene.

Rock Records - The latest releases from the innovative record
company.

The Sino Gangstas Homepage - Links to Asian related topics.

son.ic control | 3 - Playground for HK pop and anime lovers.

Sword, Spirits and Romance; The Legends of China Page - The lives
and stories of Pu Sung-Lin and Jin Yong.

WWW Guide to Louis Cha/Jin Yong - Everything you wanted to
know about the greatest wuxia novelist of our time.

Somebody Up There Likes Me - Aaron Kwok and Carman Lee.

Temptress Moon Home Page - Official site for Chen Kaige's new movie starring Gong Li and Leslie Cheung.

Thunderbolt Home Page - Official site for Jackie Chan's car racing

movie.

The Umbrella Story - A look at the special effects in Clifton Ko's new

movie.

WONG FEI HONG -- THE TV SERIES - Tsui Hark's series continues

in a TV series with most of the original cast.

People
Kelly Chan Wai-Lam
  Kelly Chen's homepage
  Wai Lum's Corner!
Sammi Cheng Sau-Man
  Sammi Homepage
Jackie Cheung Hok-Yau
  The Official Unoffical Homepage of Jacky Cheung
Leslie Cheung Kwok-Wing
  Leslie Cheung Homepage
  Leslie Cheung Internet Fan Club
  Leslie Cheung's Home Page (at Rock Records)
Emil Chou Wah-Kin
  Emil's Home Page (at Rock Records)
Vivian Chow Wei-Mun
  Pictures of Vivian Chow
  Vivian Chow Collection
  Vivian Chow's Individual Homepage
  Vivian Chow's Profile
Athena Chu Yun
  Chu Yun's Profile
  Athena in Athens
Andy Hui Chi-On
  Andy Hui's Paradise
Gong Li
  Years
  The Legend of Bruce Lee
Carmen Lee Yeuk-Tung
  Carmen Lee's Home Page
  Carmen Lee Yeuk-Tung

Gong Li Home Page
Gong Li, the MOST famous actress in the world
Aaron Kwok Fu-Sing
  Aaron Kwok's Homepage
Gigi Lai Chi
  Gigi Lai's HomePage
Leon Lai Ming
  LEON LAI On The INTERNET
  Leon, The Man.
Vivian Lai Shui-Yan
  Homepage for Vivian Lai Internet Fan Club
  Sunny Chan's Vivian Lai Homepage
  Vivian Lai
  Vivian Lai Gallery
  Vivian Lai Homepage
  Vivian Lai Hong Kong Support Site
  Vivian Lai Internet Fan Club
  Vivian Lai WWW Homepage
  VLIFC Pages
Sandy Lam Yik-Lin
  Sandy Lam Home Page
  Sandy Lam Home-Page (HK)
  Sandy, The Woman.
  Love, Sandy (at Rock Records)
Carina Lau Ka-Ling
  Carina's Home Page (at Rock Records)
Winnie Lau Siu-Wai
  Winnie Lau Gallery
  Winnie Lau Home Page
Andy Lau Tak-Wah
  The World of Andy!
  Andy's World
Rene Lau Yeuk-Ying
  Rene's Home Page (at Rock Records)
Bruce Lee Siu-Lung
  Bruce Lee
  Grand Royal Magazine -- Bruce Lee -- Still Dope After All These
Jet Li Lian-Jie
  Jet Li Homepage
John Woo (Ng Yu-Sum)
  John Woo Central
Jacky Chan (Sing Lung)

Jackie Chan's Home Page (at Rock Records)
The Jackie Chan Trivia and Gossip Page
Paul's jackie chan home page
Project A: An Unofficial Jackie Chan Web Site
The Temple of Jackie Chan
Cynthia Rothrock
Unofficial Cynthia Rothrock Home Page
Alan Tam Wing-Lun
Alan Tam WWW HomePage
Alex To Tak-Wai
Alex's Home Page (at Rock Records)
Eilen Tung Oi-Ling
Tung Oi Ling's gallery
Faye Wong Ching-Man
Faye's Area
Faye Wong's Fayevorite Site
Faye's page in Japan
Faye Wong's personal profile
it's all faye...
Pictures of Faye Wong
Linda Wong Hing-Ping
Linda Wong Hing Ping WWW page
Linda Wong Homepage
Linda Wong's Home
Linda Wong's personal profile
Anthony Wong Yiu-Ming
Anthony Wong's Homepage
Wu Chien-Lien (Ng Sin-Lin)
Pictures of Ng Sin Lin
Nicky Wu (Ng Kei-Lung)
Nicky Wu & Little Tigers' World
Charlie Yeung Choi-Nei
Charlie Yeung Gallery
ChauManChun's Charlie HomePage
Pictures of Charlie Yeung Choi Nei
Sally Yeh (Yip Sin-Man)
Sally Yeh's Personal Profile
The Godzilla "Movie Monster" Newsgroup
The Godzilla Discussion Forum
Godzilla Obituary: USNews
The GODZILLA script
GODZILLA'S CHAOTIC GODZILLA

Cecelia Yip Tung
Info on Cecilia Yip Tung
Anita Yuen Wing-Yee
Anita Yuen Gallery
Anita Yuen's Unofficial Web Page
Anita Yuen's Picture Collection

Godzilla/Monster Links:
ArKa/D/ia! présente: Daikaiju !
Bill's Monster Island Godzilla Review Page
B's Tasty & Delectable Page of Godzilla
Bryan's Monster Island
Chuck's Monster Madness
Connie's Museum of Godzilla
Death Ghidorah's Godzilla Page
The Dinosaur Interplanetary Gazette Presents Godzilla!
Dr.Zauis Presents GODZILLA!!!!
SUBSCRIBE TO G-FAN! G-FAN the official fanzine of G-FORCE,
the Godzilla Society of North America. Published bimonthly and for serious fans.
Subscriptions rate: $20 U.S. and Canada, $30 overseas. For
more information, or to subscribe, write:
Daikaiju Enterprises
Box 3468
STEINBACH
Manitoba, Canada
R0A 2A0
G-FORCE AMERICA
Godzillalance: The Motion Picture
The Godzilla FAQ "Frequently Asked Questions"
Godzilla Care Sheet PAGE
Godzilla's Domain
Godzilla's Playground
The Godzilla vs. Mecca-Godzilla Page
GODZILLA vs XENA
Godzilla vs. the President!

Goji-World!
Gorosaurus's Home Page
Gorzilla's Kaigu Datapedia
The Hanna-Barbera Godzilla Cartoon Page
Mario's Godzilla Page
Masato Matsumoto's Godzilla Page
MarlocKs Picturepage
Mars Attacks The Kaiju!
The "official" Godzilla vs. the Smog Monster Page
The Official Top-10 Monster Page!
Ph0ng's Godzilla Repository: "The G-Site"
The Royal Godzilla Society
The Sons of Godzilla
Stomp Tokyo Movie Reviews
Tetsugyu's BIG Page of Godzilla
Alan's Kaiju Room
CHRIS NICKERSON'S MINI-GODZILLA PAGE
Domzilla's Godzilla Page Godzilla
Gen's Godzilla WebPage
Godzilla King of the Monsters
Godzilla's Gazebo
GODZILLA'S REALM
Grant's Godzilla Page a 7 year-old's perspective
Kevin's House of Godzilla
mAsSaCrE's Radioactive Godzilla web page!
novel-in-progress, "Godzilla v.s. The Annhiolator"
The Mini Mall of Godzilla
Nuclear Godzilla Page
Tyzilla's Destroyer Page

Miscellaneous:
Izzy's lil Web Page *adult*
sk80's Humble Anime Gallery
Anime Movie Archive
The Gathering
L.J. Newt's Anime Gallery
AnimeFan-Online
Anime Hasshin

The unofficial Temple of Godzilla Theme for Windows 95!
The OFFICIAL Temple of Godzilla Theme for Windows 95 Plus!
Animated Godzilla Cursors or Windows 95!

Japanime Links:
Usagi-chan's Anime Peeji - My sister's page!
Anime Web Turnpike
Anime and Manga Resources List - Updatable!
Tenchikun's Anime Collective
Michael Kim's Anime Home Page
Anime FAQs
Anime Web Guide
David Gaxiola's Anime Resources and Info
Manga Titles
Anime Otaku's Co.
Anime Net
Anime and Cartoon Movies
Gambit's Anime and Comic Playground
Capsule Corporation
Serpent's Anime Page
Geoff's Shoujo and General anime page
Masato's Anime-Manga-Launchbase
manga, anime, comics
Vuthy Ou's Homepage
ANIME TOKUSATSU and MANGA for OTAKU
Animanga: Anime and Manga Services
Anime Nation
Eurodata Anime Links (Spanish)
Kat's Anime Connection
Italian Kame House
Charles Kwong's Anime Support Centre
Mega Manga Archive
Ayisa's Page *adult*
Japan*Net
More Anime Than You Could Shake A Stick At
Ranma RPG Survey
Otaku! Anime Directory

The Swedish Manga & Anime Gallery
Anime Lair
Emiko's Genesis
Anime Grove
The Anime Inner Realm
AnSuomi's Anime Gallery
The Anime Cafe
Lord M's Anime Vault
Manga Palace
The Black Moon
Manga Page
Paranoia
BCASR Web Site Anime Review Page
AquaGirl's Anime Homepage
Studio Mercenary

Anime music sites
    Son Gohan's DBZ Songs
    Raistlin's CD Guide
    FTP Anime MIDI Archive
    Anime Karaoke Archive
    Ego's Domain
    Cyber Namida
    Serpent's Anime Songs
    Anime Sound and Music Archive
    Ranma Sound Shrine
    Armitage's Dimension
    Ming's Anime Jukebox
    Elmer's Anime Music Page
Japanese Language Pages
If anime has gotten you interested in the Japanese language, check out these pages.
    Shodouka Launchpad (view sites in Japanese)
    Learn Japanese with RealAudio
    Kana for Anime Fans
    Japanese Books and Translation Services

Japanese/English Dictionary Gateway
Reiko-chan's Japanese for anime lovers
Travel Languages

Anime FTP Sites
    venice.tcp.com: Images,   Manga, Synopses, Scripts
    anime.berkeley.edu: Images,   Manga, Sounds, Movies
    ftp.tcp.com: Images, Info, Scripts
    ftp.white.toronto.edu: Scripts,   Manga, Images

Anime Products Sites
    Anime & Manga Mall of North America and Japan
    Library of Comics
    Anime Frontier - Anime CDs and LDs
    Anime Videos
    Animaddict
    Chinese Online Comics
    Anime Hand-Made Toys

Southeast Michigan Anime Clubs
Animania
Manna Anime
UMD Sci-Fi Club
Kodocha Anime

Also look for links on: Korean Films, Samurai Films, Ninja Films, Akira Kurosawa

APPENDIX VII – Glossary

Impress all your friends with a knowledge of Asian terminology.
Aikido - Japanese style of martial arts, best known as the style with baggy pants. Steven Seagal is a practitioner and the style uses many joint locks, throws, and breaking techniques.
Akindo - the commercial class, lowest of the four major classes.
Anime - Japanese word for animation, normally used for all forms. In the U.S. refers only to

animation from Japan or with Japanese influences.

Bo - Japanese word for a long pole or staff used in traditional martial arts.

Boxer Rebellion - a critical event in Chinese history. With the rise of foreign powers in China, a group of martial artists rioted against Western Powers in the infamous Boxer Rebellion. Casualties were high and China suffered the most, having to pay for damages.

Broadsword - classic Chinese sword, single-edged, but much thicker than the Japanese samurai sword.

Brother/Sister - It is common practice for Asians to call male or female friends brother or sister. Also older men and women are called uncle/aunt or grandpa/grandma as a sign of friendly informality. This does not mean they are related in any matter, since translations can be very confusing especially when a man calls a woman his sister and starts making love with her.

Buddhism - an ancient religion of eastern and central Asia growing out of the teaching of Gautama Buddha that suffering is inherent in life and that one can be liberated from it by mental and moral self-purification.

Bushido - the warrior's code. A set of etiquette honored by samurai in Japan.

Butterfly knives - two large knives similar to a butcher's blade with a handle grip and metal prongs.

Cantonese - the main language spoken in Hong Kong, a dialect of Chinese.

Cantopop - lively, light dance type music popular in Hong Kong and sung in Cantonese. A number of young singers have jumped back and forth from the music charts to the box office screen. Similar to Madonna and Whitney Houston's endeavors in films.

Category I/II/III - Hong Kong ratings system Type I is for all ages, Type II falls in the PG category, while Type III is for adults only.

Cattie - Chinese unit of measurement used in older time periods.

Chanbara - Japanese action/gangster genre, often used for samurai movies with plenty of action and violence.

Char siu bao - roast pork buns.

Chi - "Ki" inner energy that flows through all living things. By controlling the flow or disrupting the flow, great harm or help can be done to the body.

Ching - Manchurian dynasty that came into power. Popular villains for kung-fu films. See Manchu.

Confucius - ancient Chinese philosopher, very influential and considered the greatest living philosopher in Asian culture. Ironically, there are not too many movies about the philosopher available to American audiences.

Confucianism - is the study of Confucius philosophies.

Currency - It can get confusing with foreign currency, especially since the exchange rate varies with time and place. Just remember: yen - Japanese, won - Korea, tael - old China, rupee - India.

Daimyo - a Japanese general or warlord of a province/region.

Daijyobu - "Are you okay?" (Japanese)

Dojang - Korean word for martial arts training hall.

Dojo - Japanese word for martial arts training hall.

Double hook swords - two fancy, long-bladed swords with a fish-hook shape at the end for grabbing and tearing an opponent apart. Colorful tassels are attached at the end of the handle.

Drunken Fist - style of martial arts often portrayed in martial arts films for its comic approach. The practitioner imitates drunkenness, attacking with speed, randomness, and impropriety.

Eunuch - members of the Imperial Court who were castrated to avoid impregnating royal lines. They gradually rose to prominence and are often depicted as cold, heartless villains.

Face - term of respect, to show someone face is to show them respect and not to embarrass them in front of peers and elders. To lose face can be a serious cause for argument or vendettas.

Feng shui - a Chinese art of practicing harmony by placement of objects and design.

Gwailo (Gaijin) - somewhat derogatory term for non-Asians used by Chinese-speaking people. The Japanese word is Gaijin (outside person) and also comments on a lack of knowledge and etiquette for the culture. "The Ugly American" stereotype, but don't take it too personally.

Halmoni - Korean word for grandmother, also used affectionately for elderly women.

Hapkido - Korean form of martial arts, similar to aikido but with the addition of kicking

Hongkie - reference to someone from Hong Kong, used in a negative way.

Jeet Kune Do - martial arts philosophy invented by Bruce Lee.

Karate - Japanese form of martial arts, means open hand.

Katana - single-edged, long sword used by samurais.

Kimono - Japanese traditional dress worn by woman. A long wrap around garment seen in traditional films tied with an obi (belt).

Kung-fu - Chinese form of martial arts, considered the origins of martial arts. Various styles exist, many based on animal imitations: eagle style, tiger style, crane, snake, dragon, leopard, praying mantis, etc.

Lion dancing - popular tradition in Chinese culture.

Mahjongg - Popular Chinese game involving pieces with symbols/pictures. Similar to the western concept of card games and gambling.

Manchu - Chinese people of Manchurian descent. The Manchus gained power and established the Ching dynasty in China and ruled for centuries until 1911 when the Nationalist Party declared a democracy.

Mandarin - official language of Mainland China, a dialect of China.

Manga - the Japanese word referring to printed comics.

Mecha - Mechanical vehicles or robots commonly found in Japanime.

Ming - The dynasty that preceded the Ching and the main rivals.

Ninja - ancient Japanese assassin known for their stealth, deadly skills, and professionalism. Nowadays, the ninjas have taken a legendary status in Japanese folklore. Trained from childhood within their family clans, ninjas knew little else except to spy, murder, and scout.

Nunchaku - The most famous weapon in martial arts, next to the sword and staff. An Okinawan weapon derived from farming implements, the weapon is simple in design, but deadly. Two rods are connected by a chain or rope. The rods are swung and used to strike an opponent with incredible speed. Screen legend Bruce Lee popularized the weapon on the big screen, which has since been banned in many countries and states. No other martial arts star has tempted to repeat Lee's nunchaku presence on screen.

OAV - Original Animated Video, a direct to video release which avoids the high cost budget of theatrical releases or the confines of television. A popular format to release a multi-volume animated series on video. Some of the best Japanime is available through OAV.

Otaku - term used to describe a fanatic viewer of anime or manga. The word has a slightly negative connotation, since the word refers to someone who is so obsessed with their field, they lack social graces and common sense (ie Trekkie Nerd). Some fans will take the term in tongue in check and proudly declare themselves as Otakus. If you're an Otaku, welcome to the club.

Oyabun - Japanese word for mob boss of high ranking, similar to Godfather.

PRC - People's Republic of China, mainland China.

RHKP - Royal Hong Kong Police, their organization fell under Great Britain, but in 1997, mainland China assumed authority.

Sai - Okinawan Karate weapon derived from farm implements. A long metal prong with a handle

Samurai - a feudal warrior from Japan who carried two swords and worked under a lord. They followed the code of Bushido and were known for their loyalty and fierce combat skills. The Asian version of the knight.

Sensei - Japanese word for teacher or elder, commonly referenced when speaking to a martial arts instructor of a Japanese style.

Seppuku - ritual suicide often performed by samurais to prevent dishonor/disgrace. A ceremonial short sword is plunged into the abdomen and drawn across while another samurai (if available) would strike the back of the neck.

Shaolin - the best known name in Asian folklore and history, the Shaolin Temple is a Buddhist place of worship and meditation that became famous for its world renowned expertise in martial arts. Popularized in hundreds of movies, books, and comics plus the American television program Kung-Fu starring David Carradine.

Shogun - Japanese warlord/military general who controlled Japan for centuries. Thought they lacked the divine royalties of the emperor, they held the true military control of Japan. The most famous is Tokugawa Ieyasu who unified Japan and establish the Tokugawa ere for two and a half centuries.

Sifu - Chinese word for teacher or elder, commonly referenced when speaking to a martial arts instructor of a Chinese style.

Swastika - Hitler's infamous symbol existed in Buddhism for over 8,000 years before gracing the halls of the Nazi Chancellory. The symbol will often appear in Chinese movies dealing with Shaolin Temple or Buddhism, but the symbol is actually reversed and has no reference to Nazi Germany

Tae Kwon Do - Korean martial arts with a strong emphasis on powerful kicks.

Tai Chi Chuan - Popular form of martial arts practiced by millions of Chinese citizens of al ages. The style is a soft meditative technique that is good for circulating the chi energy within the body.

Taoism - 1 : a Chinese mystical philosophy traditionally founded by Lao-tzu in the 6th century B.C. that teaches conformity to the Tao by unassertive action and simplicity 2 : a religion developed from Taoist philosophy and folk and Buddhist religion and concerned with obtaining long life and good fortune often by magical means

Thank you - kamsahamnida (Korean), syen syen ni (Chinese), domo arigatoo (Japanese).

Three-sectional staff - traditional Chinese weapon comprised of three wooden poles connected by chains. Similar in length to a six foot staff, the chain links offer extra mobility and speed to attack. Made popular in the film Master Killer

Triads - organized gangs of China, appearing in Hong Kong and throughout the world like Chinatown NYC.

Wing Chun - A popular form of martial arts practiced by Bruce Lee. Developed by a woman, the style utilizes blocking and counterattacking techniques.

Wirework - Term used when referring to martial arts or stunts that use wires to support an actor/actress. A popular method to create the illusion of flying and multiple tumbling stunts.

Wok - traditional Chinese cooking pan.

Wu Shu - the official term for Chinese kung-fu.

Wu Tang - another school of martial arts popular in traditional kung-fu films, often seen as rivals to Shaolin Temple Buddhist monks. Their disciples often use the double-edged sword and study Taoism.

Yakuza - Japanese crime organization, known for their ruthlessness, body tattoos, and century old involvement in gambling, prostitution, and crime.

"Yatta" - Popular Japanese word for accomplishment or victory, means "I did it".

Zen - Part of Buddhist philosophy of harmony and meditating.

APPENDIX VIII
- (I own them, I love to read them, and I thank all the authors for their outstanding work and dedication which helped inspire my own book.)

Bibliography

The Complete Anime Guide, by Trish Ledoux & Doug Ranney, Tiger Mountain Press: 1997.

Asian Cult Cinema, by Thomas Weisser, Berkley Publishing Group: 1997

The Films of Akira Kurosawa, Donald Richie, University of California Press:1996.

Godzilla: King of the Movie Monsters, Robert Marrero, Fantasma Books: 1996.

Hong Kong Action Cinema, by Bey Logan, The Overlook Press: 1996.

Kung Fu: Cinema of Vengeance, by Verina Glaessner, Bounty Books: 1974.

The Making of Enter the Dragon, by Robert Clouse, Unique Publications: 1987.

Martial Arts Movies: From Bruce Lee to the Ninjas, by Ric Meyers, Citadel Press: 1984.

The Samurai Film, by Alain Silver, The Overlook Press: 1983.

Sex and Zen & A Bullet in the Head, by Stefan Hammond & Mike Wilkins, Simon & Schuster: 1996.

To The Stars: The Autobiography of George Takei, Pocket Books: 1984.

CD-ROMs

Corel All-Movie Guide: Volume 2

Microsoft Cinemania '97

NAME INDEX –

(Asian names are properly pronounced with the family name first, followed by the surname. For your convenience, the names listed below are by family name. Alternative names and complete Asian names can be found in the filmography section - Appendix IV.)

Van Damme, Jean Claude
Wada Takuya
Wai Ka Fai
Wang Lung Wei
Wang Yu (Jimmy)
Wang Wayne
Wei Pai
Wong Anthony
Wong Carter
Wong Jing
Wong Joey
Wong Kar Wei
Wong Kirk
Wong Russell
Wong Taylor
Wong Victor
Woo John
Wu David
Wu Kuo Ren
Wu Ma
Wu Vivian
Xie Miao
yakuza
Yam Simon
Yamada Katsuhisa
Yau Chingmy
Yee Chik Ki
Yeh Sally
Yen Donnie
Yeoh Charlie
Yeung Kuen
Yip Amy
Yip Cecilia
Yip Veronica
Yu Rong Guang
Yu Ronnie
Yuen Anita
Yuen Biao
Yuen Bun
Yuen Corey
Yuen Woo Ping
Yeung Bolo
Yune Johnny
Zhang Yimou

INDEX: My apologies but due to digital conversion, this section will not be accurate.

THE END

Printed in Great Britain
by Amazon